"From the humblest beginnings in Austria, Conrad Kain created a life of adventure that most of us can only dream of: from the sun-drenched cliffs of Corsica to the gaping crevasses of New Zealand's highest peaks. But it was in the Canadian ranges where Kain's legacy assumed heroic proportions with his numerous futuristic first ascents. One by one they fell: Mt. Robson, Mt. Louis and Bugaboo Spire. *Where The Clouds Can Go*, the dramatic story of this uncommon man, is a mountaineering classic that shatters the boundaries of the genre."

—Bernadette McDonald, author of *Tomaz Humar*,
past vice-president of Mountain Culture at The Banff Centre
and former director of The Banff Mountain Film and Book Festivals

"In this American and Eurocentric mountain world, things Canadian get little
recc   fortunate oversight,
fo   ..iv vears or ine 20th centurv he was one of the greatest mountain
r   th   ....se of this new ed...... of his autobiography I
.il   ...   .   deserves."

—.... Scott, author of
Pushing the Limits: The Story of Canadian Mountaineering and
Deep Powder and Steep Rock: The Life of Mountain Guide Hans Gmoser

"Conrad Kain is one of the most remarkable characters in Canadian mountaineering history, and the story of his life, *Where the Clouds Can Go*, is a classic. It is appropriate that this wonderful book is back in print on the 100th anniversary of his arrival in Canada."

—Brian Patton, author and historian

"A marvelous treasure of anecdotes in which Kain reveals an extraordinary connection with his environment and an uncommon intimacy with clients."

—David P. Jones, author of the climbing guides *Selkirks South*
and *Selkirks North*

"A stunning masterpiece of mountaineering literature…. That a fourth and expanded edition of Conrad Kain's autobiography is being published to mark the 100th anniversary of his arrival in Canada is testament to the legacy of this extraordinary guide."

—Zac Robinson, Postdoctoral Fellow,
Department of History and Classics, University of Alberta

D1558896

WHERE THE CLOUDS CAN GO

BY CONRAD KAIN

ORIGINAL FOREWORDS BY J. MONROE THORINGTON & HANS GMOSER

NEW FOREWORD BY PAT MORROW

EDITED, WITH ADDITIONAL CHAPTERS BY J. MONROE THORINGTON

Rocky
Mountain Books

VANCOUVER • VICTORIA • CALGARY

Rocky Mountain Books   Rocky Mountain Books
#108 – 17665 66A Avenue   PO Box 468
Surrey, BC V3S 2A7   Custer, WA
www.rmbooks.com   98240-0468

Library and Archives Canada Cataloguing in Publication

Kain, Conrad, 1883-1934
Where the clouds can go / Conrad Kain ; introduction by J. Monroe Thorington, Hans Gmoser, Pat Morrow.

Includes bibliographical references and index.

ISBN 978-1-897522-45-5

1. Kain, Conrad, 1883-1934. 2. Mountaineers—Canada—Biography.
I. Title.

GV199.92.K35A3 2009   796.522092   C2008-907162-X

Library of Congress Control Number: 2009920175

Front cover photograph: Conrad Kain climbing Mount Resplendent, Smithsonian-ACC Robson expedition. 1911.
Byron Harmon photo V263/6036. Whyte Museum of the Canadian Rockies.
Frontispiece: Conrad Kain. 1910. Byron Harmon photo v58/408. Whyte Museum of the Canadian Rockies
Page 514 photographs by Pat Morrow

Printed in Canada.

This text has been produced on 100% post-consumer recycled paper,
processed chlorine free and printed with vegetable-based dyes

Mixed Sources
Cert no. SW-COC-001271
© 1996 FSC
FSC

Rocky Mountain Books acknowledges the financial support for its publishing program from the Government of Canada through the Book Publishing Industry Development Program (BPIDP), Canada Council for the Arts, and the province of British Columbia through the British Columbia Arts Council and the Book Publishing Tax Credit.

Canada Council   Conseil des Arts
for the Arts   du Canada

BRITISH COLUMBIA
ARTS COUNCIL

To
his mother
FRANZISKA KAIN
and three friends of his youth
AMELIA MALEK
ALBERT GERNGROSS
ERICH PISTOR

For
KONRADL

"Where the clouds can go men can go; but they must be hardy men."

- Andreas Maurer

"Mut und Tatendrang gehören auch zum Leben."

- Andreas Fischer

"De perdre un ami, c'est dur, mais de perdre un ami de montagne, c'est pire."

- Albert I

CONTENTS

BOOK ONE
The Alpine Years with A Corsican Interlude

BOOK TWO
The Canadian Years with A Siberian Interlude
and Three New Zealand Seasons

FOREWORD TO THE 2009 EDITION

▲

first crossed paths, so to speak, with Conrad Kain in 1968. A 16-year-old neophyte, I found myself leading the crux gendarme pitch on Bugaboo Spire, half a century after Kain and friends first summitted the then unnamed mountain. I had just read the first edition of *Where the Clouds Can Go*, and now that I could actually feel the texture of the granite that Kain's fingers had first gripped, the book's vivid account helped me understand the weight of his early accomplishment.

Some 40 years later, as I look back on all the wonderful adventures I've enjoyed in the mountains, I've no doubt that this early exposure to his uncomplicated philosophy and lighthearted approach to life has rubbed off on me. And now that I'm living in the hamlet of Wilmer, British Columbia, where Kain was based for the last 17 years of his life, I've been drawn back to this book once again.

In this book, Kain's client Albert MacCarthy describes the situation on Bugaboo Spire for generations of young climbers, who, like me, followed in Kain's footsteps:

> Our route was completely blocked by a most formidable gendarme, whose base completely spanned the width of the ridge … which immediately suggested to our minds the appropriateness of the name 'Bugaboo' for this spire.
> Half an hour we waited while Conrad's body disappeared and reappeared at the edge. The whole trouble, he explained, was due to the lack of any sort of hold or footing on the steep, smooth face for a distance of six feet to a crack beyond.

Kain's gear consisted only of a hemp rope, of dubious strength, supplemented by the trademark pipe clenched in his teeth. His well-worn mountaineering boots offered little purchase on the bare rock, and the party had no way of anchoring themselves to the rock (pitons weren't in common use in the mountains of Canada until the 1940s). A fall would have been disastrous, since his rope would have pulled the others off with him.

And if by some miracle they survived a fall, chances of a rescue were practically zero. Helicopters and satellite phones hadn't even been dreamed of in 1916, and the nearest climbers capable of mounting a rescue that required technical work on rock were Kain's rivals, the Canadian Pacific Railway's cadre of Swiss guides based in Golden, a gruelling three days one way by horse and the newly completed Columbia Valley railway.

Just how he finally got into the crack is a mystery to us, but after a dozen reappearances, he smiled and said: 'I make it,' and soon began to call for rope, until about 60 feet had run out and he called from the top of the ridge above the gendarme.

At this critical juncture on my own first attempt of the peak, I drove an iron piton into the crack just below the committing move. But even with the security of a piton at my waist, and with at least six inches more reach than Kain's compact five-foot-five frame allowed, I didn't have the guts to launch across the glacier-polished slab to grope for the jug hold that Kain eventually found on the other side.

Contemplating his bold lead, I reconsidered the wisdom of my own Bugaboo debut and used an approaching electrical storm as an excuse to lean back on my anchor and rely on my equally inexperienced partner to lower me off into the abyss.

It would be a couple of years before I acquired the skills and courage necessary to go back and finish the notorious gendarme pitch. After numerous ascents of Bugaboo Spire and some of Kain's other peaks, I am still amazed at the audacity of his party of 1916. At the time, the 20-metre gendarme section was perhaps the hardest single pitch on a Canadian peak, and remained so until its more difficult neighbour, Snowpatch Spire, was finally climbed in 1940.

Kain was on a roll that year, notching up over a dozen first ascents, many of them with MacCarthy. Just the month before, they had made the first ascent of the technically demanding Mt. Louis, near Banff. And as a sign of their prowess, they brought out their rope only a couple of times, and then only on the descent!

Historian Zac Robinson offers a verbal snapshot that illustrates why Kain would have been a fun person to hang out with in the mountains:

Accounts of Kain reveal a thoroughly personable and professional guide. He had a stocky build with broad shoulders; his moustache and pipe were constant features. In camp and on the trail, he could be charming, harmlessly flirtatious and an entertaining storyteller. An expert axe man and cook with a great capacity for carrying weight, he was patient with novices and discreet in his treatment of overzealous climbers disinclined to appreciate natural splendours.

In 1909, at the invitation of the fledgling Alpine Club of Canada (ACC), the 25-year-old Austrian guide left his village of Naßwald for Banff, Alberta. Kain immigrated to Canada in search of high adventure and economic opportunities he couldn't find within the rigid class system of the European Alps.

Over the next 20 years, Kain achieved renown as the outstanding mountaineer during the Golden Age of mountaineering in this country: "the prince of Canadian alpine guides," in the estimation of historian Esther Fraser. He made upwards of 69 first ascents or new routes on peaks in the Rocky Mountains and the Purcell Range, a record surpassed in volume, but not in difficulty, by Swiss guide Edward Feuz Jr.

Kain made a name for himself outside Canada, as well. Many of the great mountains of Austria, Switzerland, Italy, France and Corsica were ascended by him prior to emigrating. The guiding spirit took him as far as the Altai Mountains on the Siberian–Mongolian border, and he spent four seasons in the Southern Alps of New Zealand, where he scaled 59 mountains by his count, 29 being first ascents. His grand traverse of Mt. Cook, the highest peak in the range, while guiding 59-year-old Mrs. Jane Thomson, was described as a "marvellous feat unequalled for daring" in the history of those mountains. Foreign contemporaries credited him as one of the world's greatest living mountain guides.

The practical needs of life dictated that he supplement his income by working for surveying and hunting parties. He also tried his hand at farming and trapping in the vicinity of Wilmer, British Columbia, where he made his home with his wife, Henriquita "Hetta" Ferrara, whom he'd met at Albert MacCarthy's nearby Karmax Ranch.

Although raised in a household in British Guiana where servants did the heavy work, and educated in a convent in the West Indies, Hetta was able to fit into the life of a farm wife. Confident and capable, she was a serious person who happily cared for the farm and animals when Conrad was away on his many climbing and guiding trips. A sociable hostess, Hetta had high standards in her domestic chores yet maintained the ability to be playful. Ninety-one-year-old Vera Hurst Wikman, her niece, remembers showering under the sprinkler with her on warm summer days, Hetta wearing an old housedress.

Vera enjoyed visiting and staying with Hetta while Conrad was away. "I had chores that I liked to do – feeding the mink and pine marten (the Kains tried their hand at fur-farming) and weeding and deadheading the bed of pansies. ♦ The marten were quite tame and liked raisins." Vera made a game of feeding them this treat, placing one at a time at different spots in the cage. She believes Conrad and Hetta were perfectly matched and happy together.

The garrulous guide with peasant origins befriended a wide spectrum of society. It turns out that his most significant first ascents in Canada were made with Americans who either attended the ACC camps or were personal clients. Two stand out: Albert MacCarthy and J.M. Thorington. Kain completed 19 first ascents with MacCarthy (who would go on to lead the first ascent of Mt. Logan, Canada's highest mountain, without him) and covered a lot of virgin territory and peaks with Thorington.

If it weren't for Thorington, this book wouldn't exist, and Kain's name might have faded into obscurity. Although he was a living legend among his climbing contemporaries, it appears many locals were only vaguely aware of his esoteric occupation as mountain guide. In obituary notices published by the Cranbrook *Courier*, Kain was variously referred to as "the well-known Hungarian guide," and "the first of the Swiss guides brought to this country by the ACC." And even though one of the obituaries states that he ". . . expressly wished that his remains be buried beside that of this late life partner (Hetta)," who was interred in the Roman Catholic section of the Cranbrook graveyard, Kain somehow found his way to a final resting place over 100 meters away, in the "commoners" section. However, thanks to the loyalty of his old rope and saddle partner Thorington and a number of other friends, his epitaph was mounted on a headstone aptly made from his favourite climbing medium, a lovely block of granite.

One can imagine the "gathering of the clan" here in Wilmer in the 1920s when Kain's photographer friend Byron Harmon (who took most of the striking photos of Kain in this book with his heavy 5x7 Graphic View camera) arrived with his family on the dusty dirt road from Banff for a picnic at the Kains' cottage, or a visit with the MacCarthys at Karmax Ranch on the hilltop above before proceeding to their own summer home.

Harmon's daughter Aileen, now age 97, recalls a poignant moment when Kain took a few moments to explain to her the magic process of a spider spinning its web. "When I was a child, possibly 10 or 11, my brothers and I spent a couple of summers in a house with an old apple orchard near Wilmer. Conrad Kain had a small farm, but he was seldom there in summer, of course. His wife was from South America, a quiet, kindly woman. The last time I saw Conrad, shortly before he died, was when he came looking for Dad. I found him, as I was used to, sitting on our steps, quietly watching a spider tend its trap. He was always keenly aware of the world."

Ninety-nine-year-old Shelagh Dehart, granddaughter of Shuswap Chief Pierre Kinbasket, remembers him well:

> *I was a teenage girl when he came to visit my aunt Rosalie Kinbasket in Stoddard Creek (directly across the Rocky Mountain Trench from Wilmer). Rosalie broke many horses for him over the years. He had to have many horses, pack and saddle, that were sure-footed and gentle. He was always talking about horses, brands, horse thieves, medicine, mountains and stupid climbers, etc. He was a friend of my mother's and when lunchtime would come around well here comes Conrad, always at lunchtime!*

Shelagh also recalls:

> *His English was like a kid's. I was telling my mother that he said 'I was coming down the heel' instead of hill. When I was young I thought it was cute. He was always with his pipe smoking, with one leg over his knee. He was a man that seemed always alone but always happy. Very content. Conrad was a very nice man in every way.*

It seems appropriate that this classic book is being republished on the 100th anniversary of Kain's arrival in Canada so that yet another generation may appreciate the legacy of his extraordinary life. As Hans Gmoser pointed out in the prologue to the 1979 edition, the generous and honest manner in which Conrad Kain lived his life represented a code of conduct in the mountains that all of us would do well to emulate.

PAT MORROW

Wilmer, British Columbia, 2009
on behalf of the Conrad Kain Centennial Society
www.conradkain.com

PREFACE TO THE 1979 EDITION

▲

I n the 1935 Introduction to *Where the Clouds Can Go*, I wrote: "In Conrad Kain there was a splendid fire." It is most gratifying to know that the fire has been rekindled. Scores of mountaineers will be introduced to an extraordinary man, and many others will renew an old acquaintance. I wrote further: "In putting the fragments of his book together I have thought that 'They who one another keep alive ne'er parted be,' and have done my best to hold in memory one who was indeed *der besten Führer einer*, with whom I spent some of life's happiest hours." I am indeed proud that the memory has remained steadfast.

When I edited Conrad Kain's autobiography in 1934, the thought never occurred to me that there might be a subsequent edition of *Where the Clouds Can Go*. Thus it was a great surprise to me when I learned that a third edition of the book would be published. After all, so much has been done in mountaineering during the past forty-five years that an entirely new book could be written about those mountains Conrad Kain pioneered; but of course, it would not be Conrad's book.

The fact that so much has changed during the past two generations does not alter the history that Conrad Kain made. The splendid fire will always live.

J. MONROE THORINGTON

Philadelphia
September 1979

FOREWORD TO THE 1979 EDITION

A s we pause and look back, certain memorable events and features always stand out clearly as being those happenings in our lives which greatly influenced our direction. This is true whether we are on our way up a mountain, on a journey through the wilds, in our career or along the course of life in general.

Conrad Kain's *Where the Clouds Can Go* was definitely one of those events in my life. Already, I had been deeply moved by my first impressions of the Canadian Rockies; and now, in the winter of 1953, I was sitting in Lizzie Rummel's cabin at the base of Mt. Assiniboine reading Conrad's book. Naturally the fact that he was a fellow Austrian and a Mountain Guide had something to say, but here I read the words of a man who had been through the hard school of life. Yet he was never bitter; he was never afraid, even when, with torn shoes, infected feet, hungry and cold, he was tramping the roads of his native Austria, perhaps even unnoticed by other mortals. His straightforward philosophy of life, his respect for and tolerance of others no matter how they treated him, his gratitude for and loyalty to his friends all sank in deeply.

The next time I skied to Sunshine and passed by the little cabin at the foot of Citadel Pass, I could almost see Conrad sitting there, writing his letter to Mrs. Thomson. As I skied along the base of Nasswald Peak alone on many a quiet morning, my thoughts would go back to his early days trying to poach a chamois on the Rax above Naßwald; and as I swiftly slid along the Golden Valley and Valley of the Rocks, I wondered how Conrad would view this way of travelling through the mountains in winter.

His Canadian climbs are only a small part of his worthwhile mountaineering exploits. One is awed by the skill, drive and mental fortitude which powered the "Tour de Force" of Mt. Robson; yet Conrad never comes across as a bravado mountaineer. Rather, one gets the impression of a very humble man who loves life in the out-of-doors, especially in the mountains, but who has the strength and discipline to call on the physical reserves necessary to succeed on Mt. Robson or on a solo ascent of Whitehorn.

Here lies the appeal of this book. The great achievements are never dramatized – they are well-described. One can easily suffer through the winter on Smoky River, the dangerous night descent of the Whitehorn Glacier and the bivouac on Mt. Robson; but nowhere does one detect the iconoclastic superman who is impossible for the rest of us mortals to identify with.

Rather, Conrad Kain is always present as a human being with all the frailties and strengths. Beneath Conrad the man, the Mountain Guide, there is still Conrad the boy – approachable, curious and amused by the small and simple things in life.

One chuckles when Conrad turns to his companion after the first ascent of Mt. Louis with the words: "Ye gods, Mr. MacCarthy, just look at that; they never will believe we climbed it." Here is a man who is at the pinnacle of his career as a guide and climber, who is making history with his ability as a climber, but who still finds almost childlike pleasure in doing his thing at a level of seldom-attained perfection.

In his humble, thoughtful way of telling about his life, his climbs, his friends and companions, Conrad gives us a very wholesome philosophy of life: something which is sadly missing in much of the recent mountaineering literature of today.

Where the Clouds Can Go is not only an inspiration to follow some of the great routes of this master of the art of mountaineering – in its modest, unauthoritarian way, it is actually a code of behaviour in the mountains and among people.

HANS GMOSER

Banff, Alberta
September 1979

PREFACE TO THE 1935 EDITION

I was born at Naßwald on August 10, 1883. My father was a miner, my mother the daughter of a woodcutter. From my seventh to fourteenth year I attended the Protestant private school in Naßwald. We were there more than a hundred children and had but one teacher. But, for this very reason, I should have been able to learn more. It was my fault and not that of the teacher that I could scarcely write my name when I left school in the spring of 1897. My father died in 1892.

We were four children, I the eldest, nine years old, and had a miserable existence. When I was 14 I became a goatherd on the Rax. I was there almost a year. Then I went to Veitsch and worked for quite a while in a stone-quarry. When I received my first pay and could not figure out how much it made per day my eyebrows rose: I bought a writing pad and an account book and began to study by myself.

By my school companions at home I was regarded as peculiar, since I preferred to be by myself, most of the time in the forest. So far as I can remember I liked best the awakening of spring. I also recall that people in my home said: "The fellow will never amount to anything, he is quite different from his friends."

At 17 I began wandering and travelled as a journeyman to various places, for I wished to see much of the world. From 1903 until 1907 I worked as quarryman at Hirschwang. During this period a mountain guide evolved from a poacher. Life became more interesting, and so I began to write a diary. I have written it only for myself, and have never thought of publishing my recollections. Friends who thought well of me have encouraged it. To them I am indebted for the pictures these memories recall. I beg of the reader one indulgence. An unlettered fellow, a former breaker of stones, has written this book.

KONRAD KAIN

FOREWORD TO THE 1935 EDITION

▲

In Lower Austria, not far from Vienna, rises a little mountain called the Raxalpe. More than 400 years ago Emperor Maximilian hunted chamois on its slopes. The inn below the Preiner wall is known to this day as the *Kaiserhof*, and peasants still point out a spot on the cliff as the *König's Schuss*. Every corner of the district has its story.

The village of Naßwald, half hidden below the northern wall of the Rax, was founded in 1731 by Protestant woodcutters after their expulsion from the Gosau Valley by the Archbishop of Salzburg. Far from the beaten tracks it has remained a place of poverty, and its children more than once have gone hungry. There Conrad Kain was born on August 10th, 1883. The Alps and their legends (for he had little more) were his heritage. These and the constellation Leo (for drama and virility) determined his life. He would see far countries and magic sights, endowed with a gift of laughter and a sense that the world was quite mad. To have known him was to have seen Pan dancing in the woods, with birds, beasts and flowers bewitched into human speech and nodding to the music of his pipes.

He became a mountain guide, one who was every inch a man, with qualities of sympathy and patience that made him much loved. The dash of a pirate was in him, and few have been better able to make the commonplaces of life romantic. That he should have left an autobiography almost completed will come as a delight to his many friends in many lands. As might have been expected, it is a unique document, rich in human interest, exceeding in this respect almost anything ever written by an Alpine guide.

Guides have recorded their experiences before this – the books of Mattias Zurbriggen and Christian Klucker are well-known. All intended, when their technical adventures were described, to turn to the human relations of their sport. Andreas Fischer would assuredly have done so had he not perished on the Aletschhorn. Kain alone has succeeded.

That his life story should have been preserved is merest chance: some of it in German, some in English, written in broken diaries and on scraps of paper in a dozen countries of the world; part of it kept by Amelia Malek, of Reichenau, Austria, a friend of Conrad's youthful days in the Alps; other parts written for me. Some of it I wrote down myself, during days with the pack train in the Canadian Northwest, where we were together for six seasons; some of the story was found among his papers after his death.

One feels that he has left a book such as the reviewer of *From the Alps to the Andes* assumed would never be written: containing a candid opinion of the relative merits of guides and amateurs; displaying the real attitude of the guide toward his employment and his employers; revealing the subject of those discussions that rage whenever two or more guides are in conclave, and which cease uneasily on the approach of the complacent *Herr*.

There are faults in it, to be sure, for the talents of the fraternity are seldom of a literary character; but a real genius for description and sustained narrative are everywhere evident. It is a *Herrenbuch* as well as a *Führerbuch*, devoid of malice, to be read with understanding heart by those of us who are good-naturedly aware of our shortcomings. The pages brim with the refreshing vividness of youth, with the ecstasy of life poured forth without reserve. Think, then, how remarkable it is in one whose career in the Alps was over, and most of his writing done, before he was 26 years old.

Many peasants have been good enough as guides, willing to face the familiar perils of rock and snow, but few have eagerly accepted the hardships of foreign travel, of voyaging on strange seas. In Conrad Kain there was a splendid fire. To him a new country in itself was high adventure. Not only did he take his mountaineering art abroad, but taught it to others, inspiring them with his own deep delight in the things of Nature. He adapted himself to foreign life and customs, delving into natural history and learning the ways of the trapline and the pack train.

His reputation in the Alps was once considerable, and for years to come, in Canada and New Zealand, the cairns he built on virgin summits will be found. Great mountains and far trails hold the marks of his pioneering. Equally with Emile Rey he might have said, "J'ai toujours eu de la chance."

One remembers him best upon the peaks, lingering until the last lights caused the shadows to lengthen; looking upon the glory he would miss when death came near – the heritage he could no longer hold.

"Each generation," wrote Martin Conway, "makes of the world more or less the kind of place they dream it should be, and each when its day is done is often in a mood to regret the work of its own hands and to praise the conditions that obtained when it was young." For some of us the loss of our friend seems to mark the passing of our own youth.

Conrad Kain now belongs to

"The flood of things that come, and pass,
Beckon, and shine and fade away."

In putting the fragments of his book together I have thought that "They who one another keep alive ne'er parted be," and have done my best to hold in memory one who was indeed *der besten Führer einer*, with whom I spent some of life's happiest hours.

◆ ◆ ◆

For much of the material contained in Book One (The Alpine Years), as well as parts of the first Canadian season, I am indebted to Miss Amelia Malek, of Reichenau, Austria, who had the wit to preserve the scattered notes and letters which he continued to send her. Miss Malek and her sister were the young ladies he guided at Gstatterboden in the autumn of 1906. For the translation and editing of this portion of the book I am alone responsible, but I have tried to avoid some pitfalls of the translator by using simple words that I know Conrad would have employed, believing that by so doing I might carry over at least the spirit of the original.

In connection with the Canadian chapters I must thank A.H. MacCarthy, T.G. Longstaff, B. Harmon, G.B. Kinney, D. McCowan, J. Simpson and L.C. Wilson for their recollections. P.A.W. Wallace supplied data on the summer of 1913, when Mt. Robson was conquered. A.O. Wheeler tran-scribed valuable notes from his diaries; J.C. Dun Waters and R.W. Everett presented vivid descriptions of Conrad as hunter, while Prof. I.A. Richards, Dr. Oastler and C.F. Hogeboom added to the collection of stories.

For the New Zealand interlude, J.S. Shanks, Secretary of the NZAC, has been at considerable pains to list Kain's many ascents. H.O. Frind, Mrs. J. Thomson and H.N.P. Sloman have told of their association with this guide, while Prof. R.M. Algie and A.P. Harper have placed me in their debt for numerous courtesies.

H.S. Kingman and my wife each read the entire typescript and suggested improvements. The editors of the *Alpine Journal*, the *Canadian Alpine Journal* and the *Sierra Club Bulletin* have furnished illustrative material, as has also Miss Malek. Members of the American Alpine Club and others have contributed generously to make this publication possible. Indeed, my obligation to these and many others is so great that I can only accept their efforts as a tribute to the memory of Conrad Kain himself.

It should be added that Kain, after coming to America, changed the form of his first name from Konrad to Conrad.

J. MONROE THORINGTON

December 1934

Contributors to Publication Fund (1935)

CANFIELD BEATTIE, MD

EDWARD P. BECKWITH

COL. F.C. BELL, MD, CMG

O. EATON CROMWELL

LEWIS L. DELAFIELD

DYSON DUNCAN

RANDALL W. EVERETT

W.B. OSGOOD FIELD JR.

JOHN W. FORBES

ALLYN K. FORD

COL. W.W. FOSTER, DSO

LILLIAN GEST

LAWRENCE I. GRINNELL

MRS. LAWRENCE I. GRINNELL

WILLIAM R. HAINSWORTH

HENRY S. HALL JR.

CHARLES F. KEYES

HENRY S. KINGMAN

WILLIAM S. LADD, MD

ALBERT H. MACCARTHY

MRS. ALBERT H. MACCARTHY

WINIFRED S. MACLAREN

EDWARD MALLINCKRODT JR.

DEAN PEABODY JR.

MRS. DEAN PEABODY JR.

ALFRED E. ROOVERS

JUSTICE HARLAN F. STONE

KATHERINE STUART

J. MONROE THORINGTON, MD

DANIEL UNDERHILL

PAUL VAN ANDA

MRS. GEORGE E. VINCENT

FRANK N. WATERMAN

J.C. DUN WATERS

MRS. SYDNEY WEBBER

WILLIAM B. WILLCOX

BOOK ONE

THE ALPINE YEARS

with
A Corsican Interlude

CHAPTER I

(1902–03)

▲

THE OPEN ROAD

Like every man, I remember my boyhood, and many of the plans I laid down for the future, and of what I would do when I was a grown-up man.

My chief ambition was to travel; but, as far back as I remember, I did not think of travelling by train or boat because, as a matter of fact, I did not know that there were such things in existence.

I was born and raised in a mountain valley of Lower Austria, six hours' walk from the nearest railway. The first time I saw a train was when I was 13 years old, and even then it did not occur to me to travel by it as I came of poor people and had often heard my grandmother grumbling about the train fares. "It is too much for poor people to pay, one can't afford it," she would say; so there was nothing left for me to do but travel 'round the world on my own feet.

A high pass led from my home valley to another one. This highway had been used for at least a hundred years by all sorts of travellers, and was known to tourists and mountaineers for its grand Alpine scenery. In the summertime, once in a while, a stray tramp takes advantage of this pass as a shortcut to Salzburg. I never missed the opportunity of speaking to a tramp, first of all asking him if he were hungry. When he was, I used to take him up to our hut and ask mother to give him a drink of goat's milk and a bite of bread. If he were not hungry I would ask him if he knew the way over the pass, and tell him that I could show him a shortcut.

Every one of them accepted my offer to act as guide, making me feel very proud of myself. On the way I would ask a great many questions: where he came from, where he intended going, what the place was like where he stopped last, and so forth. I never forgot to tell him that I meant to be a tramp myself when I became a man. They all had a kind word of thanks for my guiding, and I felt lonely when I had to part from them. I envied them, and in the bottom of my heart I wished I were a man instead of a little boy, so that I too could go over the pass to Salzburg and see what the country and the people were like on the other side of the mountains.

It was always a great joy to repeat to my people what the stranger had told me, though at the same time it used to break up the peace in our family for a day or two. My grandmother was of a mean and selfish disposition and would not sympathize with anyone; my mother, however, was just the opposite, and to her it was a pleasure when I did a kind deed, such as calling in a hungry man for a cup of milk, or showing a stranger the shortcut up to the pass. Years passed by, and quite unexpectedly I found myself on the road as a tramp. I am sorry to say that this life did not turn out to be so delightful as I had imagined it would be in my boyhood.

Before I go on any further with my adventures I must describe the laws and regulations that a tramp in Austria has to obey. Austria, like all other countries in the world, has her trouble with the unemployed, which is indeed a very hard problem to settle. The authorities agreed on the following points, or, rather, they found themselves forced to accept them.

Suppose a man is living in a place and unable to find employment. Perhaps there may be suitable work for him in another province – how is he to get there without money? He must have something to eat, but begging is prohibited by law, the first offence meaning four to six weeks imprisonment. The government, therefore, has established stations where the man out of work may obtain a meal and lodging for the night. These stations serve at the same time as employment bureaus where, if a man of a certain trade is wanted, the tramp of that trade must take the work or lose the right of using this station, and probably ends by getting into jail. The government controls these stations and provides the tramp with a document which he must carry with him, presenting it at each station so that he may obtain food and shelter. Every meal and night's lodging is entered in these papers, with date and stamp. They also contain the printed rules and regulations the tramp must follow.

The tramp may not obtain more than one meal and one night's rest at the same station within the space of three months. If he does not succeed in obtaining work within three months he will be sent back to his own community. The cost of supporting this system of dealing with the unemployed problem is borne by three different bodies: first, the community the tramp belongs to; second, the province in which that community is situated; and third, the general government.

These stations are run on military principles and are kept neat and clean. The tramp may not leave before carrying out his duties, such as making his bed and scrubbing the floor. The food is just good enough to keep a man alive and give him strength to reach the next station. Each station keeper is allowed so much per meal, and it is well-known that they all get rich in the long run.

Quite unexpectedly I became acquainted with these stations in 1902. I had been working in a tunnel at Göstling, Lower Austria, in connection with the great water pipeline for Vienna. I was one of a gang of 12 men. The foreman was of a brutal, overbearing disposition, who dismissed one of our comrades without any reason. The rest of us struck and demanded the reinstatement of our friend. The consequence of this dispute was that we were all dismissed, and I found myself on the road with very little money in my pocket, looking for work.

This happened in November, when many out-of-door works close down for the winter. So long as the money lasted all went well. One of my friends went in the same direction as I did and we travelled together over a high pass leading to Palfau. The weather was pleasant and cool, the country in its autumn dress, and some trees had already shed their leaves, making it a most fascinating journey through the mountainous country. We met people on the road and talked to them on different subjects, and I felt quite happy and at home. After a few days on the road we inquired for work, but found that none was to be had in these places in the autumn. We were told that the only place where work could be obtained was at the tunnel on the new railway to Eisenerz.

To get to Hieflau we had to travel to Gesäuse, a high and romantic valley shut in by lofty mountains through which the river Enns finds its way out to the flatter country, and on to join the Blue Danube. We met some very kind, good-hearted people, and I remarked to my friend: "You can't beat the people in the mountains, they have kinder feelings than the people who live on the flat land and in the cities." He was quite a philosopher and replied: "They can't help being kind. They are born here in the mountains; they live here all their lives close to the heart of Nature, which is kind and true. These pure surroundings gradually affect them so they can't help being kind."

4

I did not tell him that I too came from just such a mountainous country, nor did I allow him to see the joy he made me feel by giving me his reasons for the kindness of the people in the mountains.

We arrived in Hieflau on a very cold day and stopped at a simple inn, and inquired from one of our roommates about the work at the tunnel. He did not give us a very enticing account of it, and told us besides that we would not stand any chance of getting work there at this time of the year. This did not cheer us much. The night was so cold that next morning we found ourselves half frozen in the bed. Our money did not allow us to have a good breakfast, but only a cup of hot milk, costing ten hellers. Then we went to the engineer's office and asked for work. On the way we met a few working men who told us that we could save ourselves the trouble of going up to the tunnel, but we wished to find out for ourselves and went on.

We found the engineer in charge in a very bad temper, and we, of course, did not get work. The tunnel was being constructed by means of electric power, and the work was stopped on account of the cold weather, all the streams supplying the power house being frozen. My friend met an old chum of his who had some money and who paid his train fare to Amstetten, where he expected to find work. He also asked me to go to a restaurant with him, where we had a good lunch together. After they left I went on my way, feeling a sensation I had never felt before – here I was on the road, with only two hellers in my pocket and the cold almost unbearable.

I travelled in the direction of Liezen, and after an hour on the road met a gendarme who asked me who I was, where I was going, and other questions. He looked through my papers and found them all right. As he handed them back to me he asked me whether I had any money. I answered, "Yes." He wanted to see it, so I felt in my pockets and produced the only two-heller piece I was in possession of. With an inquiring look he asked me if that was all. "Yes, that's all I have in the world," I replied. He said: "That's bad luck! You tried to bluff me!" "Oh, no," I said, "I did not tell you any lies; that is money is it not?" "Yes, it is," said the constable, "but it is not enough according to law."

I knew that myself, and the end of it was that he arrested me in the name of the Emperor. The constable was one of the finest officials of his class that I have met. He did not put the handcuffs on me as it was so cold, and allowed me to walk beside him. On the road we spoke of different things, and when we passed through a village I went ten yards in front of him. As we came to an inn he said: "Come in here and let us warm ourselves a bit."

I was also much surprised when he treated me to a glass of whisky. Before putting me in the hands of the jail warden in Liezen he advised me how to get a certificate for the station – saying to the warden: "I picked up this fellow on the road in my patrol town, but he has no money and no papers for the station; will you kindly bring him before the judge as soon as possible?"

The warden did not speak much to me, but put me in a cell which he did not lock, and in which I had to stay for some hours. The cell did not leave a good impression on me. I thought it would be a very lonely place for a solitary man. The warden then brought me before the judge, who cross-examined me for some minutes and looked over my papers. He told me to sit down and wait. I did so, and ten minutes later a clerk brought in a paper which the judge handed to me, asking me to read it aloud. Then I was told that I could go and felt very pleased to hear it.

The paper procured me admittance to the first station, which was only one block away from the courthouse. It was just lunch time when I arrived, and only one tramp was there, a professional as I found out a few hours later. On leaving, we walked over the Pyhrn Pass to Windischgarsten. He turned to me and said: "You go ahead, and a mile out you will see a big farmhouse on your left; go in there and get some bread. I know a butcher, who will give me a sausage, as usual." He then left me, and for a while I did not know what to do. I couldn't help wishing I had not met this fellow. I had never in my life asked anyone for bread without having money to pay for it. Still, the spirit of adventure ran high, though at the same time I was trembling all over, being ashamed to beg as I was young and strong looking.

With a beating heart I opened the gate to the farmhouse. I stopped before the doorway until an elderly lady appeared. I wished her "good day." She gave me a sharp, inquiring look as if to say: 'A beggar again.' In a low voice I told her that I was very hungry and would be much obliged if she would give me a piece of bread. She looked at me, and I could read anger in her face. In a second or two her anger broke out, and this is what she said to me in one breath. "You beggars make me tired. Day after day you come with always the same old story: 'I am hungry.' In summer, when one needs help to bring in the hay and grain, nobody turns up, but when we don't want anybody, then you turn up by dozens. I know you fellows don't want our help in summer, that's your fine time, sleeping by day and travelling by night and stealing fruit. One should really not take pity on you beggars!"

I wanted to explain my position to her, but she ran away and brought back a hard crust of bread. I thanked her and began to eat it at once. Then I told her that this was my first attempt at begging, and that, if I had not been so hungry, I certainly would not have come in.

My second attempt at begging turned out worse than the first. As I approached a farmhouse a large dog reported my arrival. I was so much afraid of this savage-looking animal that I did not open the gate, but shouted toward the house. A little boy came out and called the dog back. He came to the gate and I inquired whether his mother was at home, but he replied: "No, only father. He is somewhere in the back of the barn."

I told the little fellow that I was very hungry and would like a piece of bread, but that I had no money with which to pay for it. "That's all right," said the boy, and he disappeared into the house, returning with a big loaf and a knife. I was in the first act with the loaf and the knife, when a deep voice sounded from the barn and the boy's father came out in a rage. He looked as if he could have eaten me up – with the loaf of bread and his own son on top for dessert!

He took the bread away from me, called me all the bad names he could think of, kicked his son and told me that if I did not disappear that very moment he would put the dog at my heels. That was enough for me. I did not listen any longer, but ran away.

I travelled with a shoemaker and a carpenter. The carpenter said: "The people here know nothing but hard work all their lives, and I am certain that they are more healthy, contented and happy than their lazy sisters in the cities. I mean those high society women who have nothing to do but spend their husbands' money and take care of little lapdogs." "Which, in many cases, represent the children they should have had," broke in the shoemaker.

"That's quite true," continued the carpenter, "it reminds me of a case I saw myself. I was working in Linz, helping to build an addition to a fine villa, the owner of which was one of the richest men in the country. They had no family, but only a dog, whose name was 'Darling.' Perhaps you boys will not believe me, but it is true that that dog had a nurse and I saw her many times cleaning the little dog's teeth. One day I had the opportunity of speaking to the girl, and asked her how she liked being nurse for a lapdog. 'Don't remind me of it,' she said, 'it is sickening; you have no idea of what I have to go through with this dog. I would rather look after three young children. When the little fellow takes one spoonful less of milk than usual, they send straight away for the doctor who, of course, makes a great fuss – and the more fuss he makes the more the mistress thinks of him. But what can I do? I must just stick to it until I can get another situation.'"

"Well," said the shoemaker, "I think it is only right that an animal should be looked after when it is kept shut up in the house, but to feed a dog with a spoon and to treat it better than a child is going a little too far. But what can you do? Such people don't need to worry as to where their bread comes from, and they must have something to occupy their brains, otherwise the government could not build enough asylums to hold them. But just wait, boys. The time will come when these things – I mean the extreme differences between rich and poor – will disappear."

"That is what I would call progress," remarked the carpenter. "Yes," replied the shoemaker, "but progress goes on too slowly. What we want is a revolution to change the laws at once." The carpenter could not agree with the idea of revolution, and explained: "Before you revolt against the government you must have the people educated up to the point of knowing what the revolt is for. Otherwise, the revolution will be a failure." "No," said the other, "it takes too long to teach the people, and then you have to wake them up before you can teach them. To awaken all those sleeping and dozing fellows would take you 50 years, and then you would find it just as hard to teach many of them the ABC as it would be to teach an elephant to climb a greasy pole."

2

MY FIRST THEFT

Quite a number of days went by without great excitement. The weather grew colder and it certainly was hard on us tramps. Most tramps look for rest in hospitals and prisons. My friend the shoemaker broke a shop window on purpose, so that he would be sent to prison for a few weeks. The carpenter insulted a gendarme, and also got shelter.

One day I travelled all alone. I was cold, hungry and lonely, which made me downhearted. I asked for work at a farm, and got a lecture, as usual, for being a lazy tramp. I was ordered off the place. This gave me food for deep thought – one who has never been in similar circumstances cannot imagine how a person so situated looks at life. It appears to be all chaos; the earth with its great beauty seems to lose its attraction. It seems worthless; yes, worthless! The world looked very cold and hard to me then. I was broke, homeless and alone on the road. I had a great longing for companionship, but even that was denied me. I found out that hunger is more keenly felt when alone. I also discovered that the brain is apt to be more active when the stomach is empty. Under such circumstances I solved many a problem, which would have been impossible if I had had a life of ease and comfort.

Confronted by such difficulties I still kept travelling on, until I came in sight of a farmhouse, from whose chimney clouds of smoke rolled out. I thought that where there is smoke there is sure to be a fire – the sight of smoke sent a thrill of joy through my half-frozen body. I could not resist the temptation of going up to the door and rapping. In a few seconds the door opened and I had a pleasant-looking woman standing before me. "Come in," said she, "it is terribly cold." "Could I warm myself before your fire?" I asked. "Yes, certainly," she answered, "I suppose you are hungry." "Oh, yes," I said, "I am, but I have no money and I do not like to beg."

The good woman went out and brought a loaf of bread. She cut a big piece off and gave it to me. I thanked her and she went out once more, returning with a big jug of apple wine, putting it before me with the words "Here, take it with your bread. The bread alone is too dry. I hope you won't get drunk." She left the room, smiling.

I still remember the taste of that good black bread, and can feel the apple wine going down my throat. It was a sensation one remembers for a whole lifetime. It did not take me long to eat that tasty homemade bread. The loaf and knife were still on the table and, my hunger being still great, I did not like to help myself, but waited for the woman's return. I thought probably she might give me another piece of bread. At last, she came back and inquired how I felt. I replied that I was feeling much better, but that my feet were yet very cold. She advised me to take off my boots and dry my socks. I took her good advice while she, meanwhile, put the loaf away in a drawer and left the room. My feet soon got warmed and my appetite for that good bread grew bigger every second.

It was impossible to stand the temptation any longer. I got up, went to the table, opened the drawer and helped myself. I ate the bread in a hurry as I was afraid of being caught. I put my boots on and, while doing so, thought of the remainder of the loaf in the drawer and of the poor food awaiting me at the station. A great longing came over me to possess that nice bread. I looked at the drawer and listened as I laced my boots. When I finished I examined my sack and saw there was plenty of room for the rest of the bread.

With trembling hands I cut the loaf in two, placed it in my pack and hastened out of the house. Out in the yard I met the good woman. I thanked her, and bade her goodbye with the old tramp phrase: "God protect and bless you for your kindness."

When I was at a safe distance from the farm, I opened my sack and started to eat the stolen bread. It was hard work for me to swallow it. The thought of being a thief weighed heavily on my conscience, but my starved stomach did not care whether it was stolen or bought, so it was satisfied. I never felt so nervous in my life. At every corner I would stop and look around. I felt as if somebody would grab me by the shoulder. I could hear the words: "Halt, there!"

After much uneasiness I came to the conclusion that it was only my guilty conscience that kept bothering me. In the meantime I had reached a frozen creek. I stopped there and broke the ice, washing down the last piece of stolen bread with some icy water. After doing this I felt easier because, if I had been searched, they would not have found the bread on me. To make sure, I turned my sack inside out so that not even a crumb was left.

Between six and seven o'clock I arrived at the station, at Münster. With fear I entered. I had a presentiment that I was going to be arrested. I don't remember ever spending such a miserable evening – whenever the door opened my nerves throbbed with fear. I thought it was a gendarme coming in to arrest me. I was glad indeed to get out of that town.

The following evening I had company, two tramps having joined me during the day. Nothing happened until I reached Ybbs. My boots were worn out and my feet were all blistered. Through this, I was late in arriving at the station and missed my supper. Instead of something to eat I got a lecture from the station-keeper. I told him of my misfortune and showed him my feet, but to no avail. He was a heartless man and did not pity my condition. "That's only an excuse," he said, "you have been begging all along the road and should be put in jail."

One of the old tramps felt sorry for me and said: "Let me see your feet, young fellow." First he looked at my boots, then shaking his head remarked: "They are in pretty bad shape." As he looked at my feet a very sad expression came over his face. He told me that I could not go on with such sore feet. "You poor boy, you must go to the hospital. Do you know where it is?" "No, I was never in this town before." "Well, don't worry," he replied, "I will take you there tomorrow morning." He washed my feet and another good-natured tramp gave me all the vaseline he had.

Next morning I was so stiff that I could hardly stand up. The old tramp did as he had promised. He took me to the hospital, wished me good luck and went away. I waited over an hour in the waiting room before my turn came. I was taken to the superintendent by a Sister of Charity, who looked very tired. Naturally, the superintendent could see that I was a tramp, and without asking any questions said: "We are crowded just now and have no room for you. Go to Neustadt; they have two hospitals there."

I asked if I could see the doctor. "Yes," he said, "what is the matter with you?" I answered that I was suffering with very sore feet. "Oh," he remarked, "if that is all, the Sister will examine you." The Sister took me to a bathroom, where I washed my feet. All she did was to open a few blisters and put some plaster on. When she had finished she told me that I would be all right at St. Pölten. This town was only 38 kilometres away. Not a hard day's work for sound feet, but mine were far from that.

I walked on and kept a lookout for a doctor's sign. At last I saw one. With beating heart I went up the stairs. A nice young lady came to the door and asked me whether I wanted the doctor. I said: "Yes, madam." She told me that I would have to wait a little. After a while the doctor made his appearance and asked what he could do for me. I told him my troubles and he took me into his room. Before he looked at my feet I told him that I had no money and that I had been refused at the hospitals. The doctor asked how long I had suffered. "Three days, sir." "How is it that you have sand in your wounds?" I then showed him my boots and that explained everything. He said: "Did they not take you in at the hospital?" "No, doctor, I tried the hospital at Ybbs and both hospitals here and they all tell me that they have no room."

He took the sand out of my wounds and dressed my feet. In the meantime he asked me several questions. "Are you from the Tyrol?" "Yes, sir." "From what part?" I answered that I lived near Bozen. He said: "I thought so. Do you know a family by the name of Humber, living in Blumau?" "Yes, I do." "Do you know them well?" "I know George and the old man." "How many daughters have they?" I replied that I believed there were only two daughters. "Do you know their names?" "Yes, one is called Bertha and the other Ella."

The doctor said: "That is quite correct. You said that you did not know the girls." "No, only by sight." The doctor then informed me that Bertha was his wife, saying: "I am sorry that she is away on a visit. I am sure she would be glad to see you and talk to you in dialect. Where are you going now?" "Wherever I can obtain work." "It is very hard to find work at present and you can't go very far in those shoes," said the doctor. "Let me see if I can find you an old pair of mine."

He brought two pairs and they were two sizes too large for me. However, I decided to take a pair as they were better than mine. He also gave me a pair of stockings. I thanked him for his kindness, he wished me luck and we parted. This was certainly a piece of good luck. I felt fine for the first 10 kilometres – then the boots got soaked through and became softer and softer. The pain came on again.

I stopped at a house and asked if they could give me some old clothes to put in my boots. Anything would do, and I explained the whole matter to the good folks. There was a rather large family in this house. I saw children of all ages. The mother had an infant in her arms, which she gave to one of the older children to nurse whilst she pulled a woolen shawl out of the baby's crib. She gave it to me, saying: "This is soft and warm." I thanked her and told her that I could not take it as I might be robbing the baby of its warm clothing. "Oh, no," she said, "I have plenty more of this kind – take it, you are very welcome to it. I know what it is to be out of work and penniless. My husband was out of employment last winter. I know from experience what it means to tramp the frozen roads with sore feet. If we working people don't help each other, no one else will."

I could not find words to describe my feelings as I left that house. Eleven days later I arrived at home. The first thing I did was to try and get a job, but work was scarce and there was no prospect of getting any in a hurry. I was at home only a couple of days when a heavy snowfall came on and blocked all the roads in the village. I got a job then to work on the road.

Two weeks later the community got the doctor's bill for attending to my feet, also bills from the government stations for board and lodging. It did not take long until the whole village knew that I had been a tramp. Oh, how dreadful! It was certainly something terrible, that had never happened in that village before. My poor mother had to listen to all the nasty things the villagers said of me. One fellow thought that my mother should have drowned me in the river when I was born.

The burgomaster also made a few remarks: "I pity Fanny (my mother). That boy will surely make trouble for her. No doubt he will run away again and most likely get mixed up with the Socialists and end on the gallows."

The burgomaster was right on one point, for I did run away again, and, naturally, I have taken democratic views through hard experience. I have travelled since then in almost every part of the globe; my adventures have been various and I have seen many things, but I have not seen a gallows yet – I am positively sure that the burgomaster's prophecy was a false one.

CHAPTER II

(1904)

1

THE POACHER ON THE RAX

My mother writes that she does not know how to begin to pay our living expenses. Everything is lacking. I have always too little money. I am a worker in a quarry and must support my five brothers and sisters, mother and grandmother. Since the death of my father my mother receives a little pension of eight hellers daily, and grandmother six kronen each month from the poor fund. So any reasonable man can understand that this is scanty.

The new year has begun badly, with only a few kronen, and I am burdened with care. On New Year's day I rose early, and while I cooked my pancake[1] and black coffee for breakfast, I considered how I might lessen our worries. But my thoughts were not on the right track. I packed up the cooking apparatus, coffee and a big piece of bread in my rucksack. Meanwhile day had broken. I took my alpenstock and left the house. After only a few steps I met an old woman. She greeted me kindly and asked: "Well, what is Konrad doing today with an alpenstock?" My answer was: "I am going a little way into the Höllenthal." She hesitated a little and then said in an earnest tone: "But on such a day..." and went off shaking her head. But I thought to myself: 'My dear woman, if you only comprehended that I have no money at all you would say I was doing the right thing.' And in going along I thought how fortunate I was in not being superstitious. Another might be much annoyed at meeting an old woman as the first person on the New Year's morning. That might bring trouble for the whole day, perhaps for the entire year!

I continued on my way until I came into the great Höllenthal; here I left the road and went into the cirque to the foot of the Loswand. I traversed over the boulders and looked carefully in every corner for fallen chamois. But I did not find a single one. The gamekeepers are always there before one!

When I came to the Teufelsbadstube I climbed the first ladder. Everything was covered with ice! I went on rapidly to the second ladder, but after that conditions became worse. If I wished to keep on I must cross a large cornice. It was too dangerous and I gave it up.

As water dropped from the rocks here and was easy to collect, I emptied out my rucksack, set up the cooking apparatus, warmed up my barley-water and ate bread with it. Now that my simple meal was over, I took out my harmonica and played a dance tune until the harmonica became disconsolate and refused further service! Then I prepared to climb down.

In a short time I was again amongst the boulders. All at once I heard a loud cry on the Kloben wall. There were ravens! 'Stop, it must be a fallen chamois! That's what that means,' I said softly to myself, and climbed up on a huge rock to observe the birds. They flew up and down. I went to the place, wading in snow to my chest. When I came within a hundred paces, I saw the beast lying there and my heart beat for joy. But the delight was short. On my arrival I saw that it was an old doe! Scornfully I turned about, complaining that my trouble had been in vain. Hungry and thirsty I took the homeward way.

During that year there was again work at the quarry. In the beginning it was very cold and during the whole week an icy wind kept up which one could scarcely endure. With unfriendly faces we went to work in the spring. Only occasionally did Saturday improve the situation. In the first place the work was not so long; secondly, Saturday was payday; thirdly, one made plans on Saturday as to how Sunday was to be spent.

One fellow would go home to his family and be happy with his wife when he handed over his wages; another would think all week of that Saturday night on which he could sneak off to his sweetheart. The elders were glad to rest, and my plan was to go off hunting on Sunday. I could not do anything else, for again no money remained. I received 14 kronen pay, of which I sent my mother eight; the rest I needed for purchases. If I killed a fine chamois buck, I could get 100 to 120 kronen for the beard, as at this time it had great value. Of course, I knew that if I was caught poaching by a keeper it would not improve my existence, but if no one discovered me and I brought down a fine buck I would be rid of my financial distress! I said to myself: 'If you have no courage, stay at home. A poacher dare not fear.' With these words I took my rifle out of the mattress where I kept it hidden and started out.

I was comparatively safe from keepers, for one does not go so easily through the snow of winter. I went into the Höllenthal. Very quietly I stole along the road, taking the rifle on my shoulders and letting a part hang down each side. I hung my big weather-cape over it. On the road I met several people, who noticed nothing as it was still pitch-black night. As I came to the Teufelsbadstube day broke. Softly I went farther on the climb, for I was still wary. Above the first ladder I took off my rucksack and rested a little. There I heard a chamois whistle. I took the rifle, loaded it and climbed farther. I crept always in the direction from which the whistling came and arrived above the second ladder. Here was the big cornice, and as I reached up my head I saw the buck standing 60 paces in front of me. I dropped back, raised the hammer and had the animal on the sights. He stood before me, such a beautiful target, and when I pressed there was no discharge – only the hammer snapped. The buck sprang into flight and I hurried after him. When I came into the Kanitz gulch[2] he stopped ahead of me. I pressed the trigger and again it failed. The buck climbed on. I remained sitting, took out the powder and probed the firing chamber with a pin; then I reloaded and followed. When I came to the last corner, where the great cirque is, the buck went on the other side. I looked and gauged the distance – it was quite far. I thought to myself that if I shot he would go still farther. So I sighted on the buck, pulled – and the noise was as if a cannon had been discharged. The buck fell, rolled a little, stood up and ran like the devil! I had shot him in the thigh from behind as he stood edgewise to me. I hurried to the spot and saw that he was lagging. I put up the gun and went in search.

But I did not get far for there was much snow lying and the chamois sprang down over a rock, while I must remain behind. I looked to see whether I might approach from another direction, but it was impossible and I had to leave the beautiful buck lying there. I went back to my rifle, wrapped it up and hid it. If a gamekeeper found me now he could do nothing for I was now on a marked path. I went as far as the Grünschacher Hütte where the keepers usually are. But there was no one about, and not even an old track to be seen. Very unhappily I went homeward over the Lahmgraben.

The week simply would not pass. It is terrible when on Monday one will have it Sunday! But, no, that was not exactly the case – only if one is happily awaiting Sunday, time stands still. I do not know whether I am alone in feeling this way, or whether it occurs to others? My people in Naßwald were in great need. That was always a sad thought to me. I would like so much to help my mother and cannot, for I have no more than I earn and she has everything above my barest living expenses. I considered constantly what to do to help them. But nothing occurred to me. A workman has only what he earns and that is soon spent. It is almost to despair when one thinks that often a person who does no work lives better than he who day after day must slave and drudge. And if one thinks of old age. What will one do then? When one is no longer capable of working he is wiped out. Who will trouble himself about a greyhead? No one. If one can no longer work it would please the overlords if one were no longer in the world. Such thoughts came to me frequently during the weekdays. But I found that one should not become too introspective or one loses all desire to work. Sunday came and I wanted to try once more to get a chamois!

In the night I was on the alert, stood up to make a light and broke the lamp chimney. I had no watch and did not know how late it was. I cooked some dumplings to take along, and to do this lit a pine-torch so that I could see. The moon shone and I thought it would soon be day. I started out and wandered into the great Höllenthal. I came to the ascent. Below the Teufelsbadstube I rested and thought to wait for daybreak. But I did not wait, and went on farther. Soon I was above the second ladder. Here I must go over the moat. A few days before, an avalanche had come down and since then it had been cold and all was icy. I proceeded carefully, but just the same I slipped and rolled down about 40 metres. If a large stone had not been in the middle of the ravine there would have been no stopping place for me. The stone was my good fortune.

Quite terrified by the fall I crept a little way on all fours and came to the place where my rifle was hidden. All was in good shape. I slung it on and went step by step with greatest care. At last I reached the climbing place and the chief danger was over. On the ridge I loaded the gun. Day had not yet come as I waited in the woods. Not until I reached the roped place did it dawn. I sneaked slowly to the snow ravine, but could not see and thought that I must cross to the Kloben, for there I would be safest. Then the mist came in so that I could scarcely see a hundred paces. Now there would be no passersby so I went quickly to the marked way and walked on. At the blue marks I branched off and went in the direction of the Hofhalt Hütte.

I met two white hares, but did not get a shot for they were quicker than I. I rested in the hut and ate something. All at once the fog lifted. Quickly I packed up and made off in the direction of the Gaisloch. When I came to the hump that divides the cliff I stopped, listened and heard chamois clattering on the stones and whistling close at hand. But mist covered everything; there was no view and I went on to the Kloben. At the walled hut I stuck up a roof shingle, for I wished to test my rifle carefully. I made five shots and noted that they went quite high. After I had loaded once more I went on. Now I saw the sign with the inscription "Forbidden Way."

About 200 paces from the sign I wanted to take one more shot – I bored it through. 'A fine thing to remember!' I said to myself, 'for the sign will be there a long time.' I slipped over slowly to the Kloben wall – almost at once I found a fresh track. That was indeed a consolation! I came to the upward route through the Kloben precipice – the hunting-path, where it forms a little saddle. I heard a noise and stood still with rifle raised. After several minutes three chamois came up; I kneeled and covered the finest with my sights. It was a joy how it resounded and the chamois fell in the smoke. I remained standing in order to reload, but it was unnecessary for he had such a wound that he would not rise again. A great happiness was in my heart: it was a magnificent animal!

I took my knife and opened the chamois, skinned it and laid it beside me. Well, now I could rest properly; and with such an opportunity ate up my provisions. Then I thought about the shortest way down to the road, and that was over the Rudolfssteig, with which I was not acquainted. I took the chamois on my back and went along the wall. Now I came to a woods which stretches toward the Höllenthal. I thought that the way led down here. Presently I came to an abyss. This could not be the way. Meanwhile the mist had lifted and I saw where I was. I was directly opposite the Teufelsbadstube, high on the Kloben wall and must climb up again. That was a drudgery! The snow came up to my middle and it was difficult to go on. At last I reached the plateau once more. My feet were quite finished. I thought it best to go on a long way in order not to descend too soon, and I continued to the pointed wall which one sees from the Höllenthal road. Once again I was uncertain where to go. I took a direction to the left and thought that I could climb right down into the little Höllenthal. I descended the cliff.

Now my eyes went up again, for I saw a precipice over which it was impossible to continue. I looked about, but all in vain and must reascend the wall. Snow above snow! I must have used up an hour and a half on this one piece of the way. When I again reached the divide it was dark. After another 200 metres I came upon an old path. Now I could not lose my way any longer! Quite luckily I came down into the forest, and there heard people below on the road. Now I took off my outer clothing (blue knickers and blouse); under this I had my ordinary clothes. After I had packed everything in the rucksack and was ready to go on, it had become pitch dark. That didn't matter! I could not go wrong now for I was certain that I had looked over the rest of the way accurately.

I took the chamois on my back, grasped rifle and pole, and with these felt out the path that I could no longer see. And now I grasped the branches of a tree – 'Stop!' I thought, 'you must take a step downward.' As I took the step, I tumbled over a wall. First I fell on a pine tree and then onto a rock. I was wordless with terror. When I came to my senses I felt for the chamois but it could not be found. I tried to stand upright but could not, and discovered that one hand was sprained. Now there was no choice but to slide down in sitting position, leaving everything behind. Again I went head over heels, and when I began to roll I thought for certain: 'Now it's finished.' Then I struck a tree and stopped. I considered what to do; I could not remain lying there. Then I saw people with lanterns passing below me on the road.

By their light I could see that there was no more danger. It occurred to me that I still had the ramrod hanging on me, and laid it and the powder, which I had in a wooden box, between stones at the foot of a tree, for if anyone caught me on the road I must have nothing of the sort with me. Very cautiously and with much pain I crept down to the fodder piles, from there on all fours to the street. Once there I held myself up by the fence and hopped a little, then crept farther and came in this way to Weichtal. There the tavern was full of people from Hirschwang; I dared not go in, and with great difficulty went by behind the house. I knocked on the kitchen window and called to Kathi, who thought I must be there for another purpose and dared not come to the window, especially as the landlady sat behind the stove.

I did not stop knocking until the old lady also heard it. Now they were quick enough to open up! My shoes were taken off at once. The foot was already much swollen. They made cold compresses and brought me soup. Then the landlord carried me up into a room. Next morning the pain was not so bad, and I could hop down the steps by myself. The landlord wished to take me to the doctor and have it harnessed up. I sat on the bench, the servant brought out the wagon and said to me: "Perhaps you have poppy seed in the rucksack?" "Yes," I laughed, "I had a cake along with me." If the servant had not noticed it I would have kept the rucksack on my back and others would soon have seen that it was not poppy seed, but powder!

When we came to Hirschwang I took out a certificate of sickness at the bureau, and the landlord drove me to the doctor at Reichenau. I told him that I had gone out at night from Naßwald and had tripped on the street. The whole story was entered as "Accident."

2

GUIDING

When I was sound once more and could resume work, I was like another person. I thought to myself: 'On weekdays I am in danger from hard work at stone-breaking, and on Sundays I also risk my life. I must consider the situation.' And I came to the proper conclusion: *I sold my gun.*

At first I was regretful. Still I could not forgo my wanderings in the woods and rocks. Always I went to the mountains, and more and more began to give myself up to Alpine sport. In winter it was with skis. As long as snow lay I ran every Sunday in the Kesselgraben; at first with unnumbered falls. At Easter I guided a party for the first time: the first day over the Loswand of the Rax; on the next day over the Stadlwand pitch of the Schneeberg.[3] I earned 26 kronen. That was joyful! By this money my mother and I were much helped. This Easter was for me an unforgettable holiday: I had money and after long waiting could again buy some meat. The tourists that I met all encouraged me to "guide," so I went every free day into the Höllenthal in order to learn all the climbing routes.

At first it went badly; it was on the Quartette climb. I led a man, known to me from work, up the Katzenkopf climb and down the Akademik route. As it was still very early and both climbs were solved, I said to my companion: "I will now do the Quartette climb and come down the Preinthaler route." For about 30 metres in a chimney it went well enough; this gave me an idea. I took off my shoes and scrambled up to the last five metres. But here is a cleft, where the rucksack must be roped up. When I began preparations my sack came off and fell into the depths. I saw my shoes bounce down in a huge curve to the screes. In going back I had not courage enough and descended the chimney with great trouble.

Then the difficulty was over, and if I had only had my shoes it would have been well enough. But I must go downward step by step very slowly; after a few metres over the gravel the skin of my left foot was in ribbons. At the second chimney of the Preinthaler climb two gentlemen and two ladies met me; they saw that blood ran from my foot and asked what the trouble was. I told them the story. The people were very kind-hearted, and one lady wanted to give me her shoes, but they were too little. Then one of the men gave me old stockings, and after that it went much better.

When I reached the place where the shoes lay (luckily I found them right away) my stockings were torn to rags. The rucksack was stuck in the rocks at the base of a tree; I could get that another day. For the time being I was only concerned with the shoes; the sack was not worth much. Without telling anyone of this little adventure I went to Hirschwang, happy that nothing worse had happened to me.

On the following Sunday I brought my rucksack down from the Quartette route. It was hard work for me and almost not worth the trouble; besides, the frequent stone fall from the Preinthaler route was rather unpleasant. Once the rucksack, which hung on a fallen dead tree, was in my hands I went down quickly in order to be out of reach of the dangerous falling stones. Then I climbed up over the Gaisloch and through behind the Lechner wall to look for dead chamois. Today it was not in vain: I found a buck with a halfway decent beard! I took the descent of the keepers' path between Wolfsthal and Staudengraben. Here I found a fine roebuck. Today's walk had brought me as much as I would earn in a week; for more I had no need.

Beautiful May came gliding in with lovely spring weather. It was really so delightful that I remembered many a song of the month of May that once I had sung on the school bench. But again an unlucky star followed me and my contentment was shattered with one blow. One fine day the parish agent came with summons for military registration.

In the mountain districts the order is a pleasant one for the young fellows, since they can then carouse to their hearts content. For a couple of months previously one heard of nothing else but with whom they would travel, and whether perhaps they should not also take one or two musicians with them to make things lively. I was obliged to be present on the 11th of May in Gutenstein. On the day before, I still worked in the quarry; my friends had been celebrating the entire week. About two o'clock in the morning I left Hirschwang.

It was a beautiful May morning; the birds sang the gayest songs and through the Kloster Valley it became ever more lovely. If it were only another day except the one on which I must depart. In the tavern zum Stiegelthaler were my other friends from Naßwald. Should I too go in? But there was such a racket that I thought it over and went quietly on my way. When they saw me in Gutenstein they reviled me for not going with the others. I said that I had no money for such things.

But it was not long until the comedy was over. The day seemed to me like that of a cattle market, nothing else: a lowing, an alarm and there they were, some of them much more stupid than cattle. I was one of the first. "Fitness without Infirmity" was the slogan, just as I thought. Now it would be quieter as one marched in after the other. There everyone came to his senses as if after intoxication! When it was time to take the oath there were silly faces, and when the business of shooting was read aloud to us a gulping here and there was evident.

But now the correct thing had to be done! Now the hat must be dressed up as if for a carnival clown! I did not want to surrender mine, but could not finally avoid it. I thought the decoration of the hat a great foolishness. It would be much more sensible if one could take the money that the decoration cost for use on the march.

When it was time to leave Gutenstein, I would have liked to steal away by myself, but many eyes were upon me and it was impossible. In Naßwald we were already awaited with curiosity. But it may as well be admitted that my mother was not pleased that I must go marching. Great tears rolled down her cheeks.

With a little headache I awoke next morning. It was Ascension Day. I went over the Kaiser path to the Zikafahnler Alm. That was a different, much more beautiful day than the one before! Alone with the splendour of Nature! In the hollows there were still great expanses of snow, where the Schildhahn [black cock] plays. Blackbirds sang the sweetest songs, and the cuckoo, wishing to have his art heard as well, began to call right bravely in the Nass basin. And there stood the gay little flowers, awakened from long winter sleep – as I saw so much beauty about me the song came into my mind:

> Ein schön'res Leben kann's nimmer geben,
>   Als bei uns im Hochgebirg!
> Ich tausch' mit keiner Gräfin nicht,
>   Samt all ihr' Pracht und Zier!
> Und wann i' aufsteh' in der Fruah,
>   Schau i' den Himmel und die Natur,
> Dann sing i mir eins auf almerisch g'schwind
>   Dass in den Mauern klingt.

> [A happier life there can never be
>   than here with us in the mountains.
> I would not trade with a countess,
>   for all her pomp and circumstance.
> And when I arise at dawn,
>   I gaze upon Heaven and Nature,
> and quickly sing a song of the alm
>   till the walls resound.]

Never, with such heavy heart, have I descended from the alm to the valley.

On May 15th I led a man and a woman up over the Innthaler[4] ledge and down the Karl Berger route, descending to Prein. Both were in good humour, but the weather was unfavourable. For the most part fog veiled the splendid view from the Innthaler ledge. What a shame when one has no view from these bare walls! In good weather this climb is one of the finest on the Rax.

Pentecost week began with rain and mist, so that there was a bad outlook for holiday weather. But just at the right moment it changed. I was engaged by a gentleman for both days. About eight in the evening Dr. P.[5] came to Kaiserbrunn. His first request was for a room. But unluckily it was in vain. We now went into the Weich Valley; there even the hayloft was taken. What was there to do? We must again return to Kaiserbrunn and at last secured a little room under a corner of the roof at the forester's. Naturally, if a gentleman gets a place with so much difficulty, what is to be done with a guide? For me it was: "In the hay – if there is any room!"

It is an old story that one goes to the hayloft for pleasure; there is no question of rest. With a good friend I found another camping place. Without asking we took a blanket and looked for a spot to sleep in the Wolf Valley. My friend B., however, was not in a good humour. He had no comrade for the morrow with whom to make a spectacular climb. B. was a very wise fellow, a good climber, but undertook no serious ascent by himself. He was so downcast that I felt sorry and at last gave him good advice. I spoke to him as follows: "I and the Doctor are making the lower and the upper Zimmer climbs. Go up *ahead* of us to the beginning of the climb, and when we arrive you start and knock down stones so that I can ask you to let us precede you. You go behind then and the rest will take care of itself. But you must try not to give yourself away, and must do it all as if we did not know anything about it." And so it was arranged.

About three o'clock in the morning the Doctor and I left Kaiserbrunn and tramped comfortably through the Höllenthal to the climb. I was very curious to see how the adventure would turn out. Before reaching the ascent we saw a man (it was B.) going ahead of us and I said to Dr. P.: "Today we have a nuisance! See, there's someone before us! He will throw all the stones down on our heads!" The Doctor was quite aroused by this for he had already been struck by a stone on a previous occasion. He thought we should wait until the fellow was above the climb. My answer was: "Perhaps the man will be pleasant and permit us to go ahead."

Correct. When we came up to him I made my request, which was granted without question. To the difficult ledge, where the dangerous traverse is, we went quickly enough. Here the rucksacks must be roped up. In order that I might offer the rope to my friend B. across this difficult place, I asked him to kindly tie the sacks on. His own as well. The youth agreed. When the rucksacks came up to us, I said to Dr. P.: "That's a fine fellow." "Yes," he replied, "to thank him I will throw the rope down for him!"

I asked B.: "May I offer you the rope? The place is not easy!" And he answered: " If I am not holding you back and your gentleman has no objection, then I would be glad to have it." In a few minutes friend B. stood beside us. We had still a difficult bit ahead of us: the well-known Ausstiegswandel. That it is not so simple is shown by the fact that it had already cost three men their lives. Quietly and slowly I went to work; here one must test every grip and step with care or it is useless. To Dr. P., a huge strong man, it was not so hard. "But it's nothing to make light of," said he, panting.

Friend B. is again kind and ties on the rucksacks; I give him the rope once more and he follows. Seldom have I seen a youth so happy in the mountains! We took a long rest after unroping. Friend B. thanked Dr. P. many times for his kindness in allowing him to use our rope. To me he said: "To the guide I should certainly give something for his trouble, but I am to my sorrow a poor devil and cannot. But I will never forget you." And at the same time he shook hands. (All this time Dr. P. was unaware that we knew each other so well.) Up to the chimney of exit from the upper Zimmer route there was no further difficulty. Here another short halt was made, for the spot is too lovely to leave it immediately. From the green meadows of Höllenthal one is observed by many eyes, and by most of the audience declared a complete fool; naturally, however, only by those who do not understand that there is an entirely different kind of pleasure to be gained in looking down from above than up from below!

So we ascended the crack and the tunnel-like gorge and stood at the end of the upper Zimmer climb. Now the nailed shoes were resumed, and meanwhile an acquaintance, Mr. R., puts in an appearance. A council of war is held as to how the descent shall be made. Mr. R. suggested the Akademik route and this was accepted. The descent is quite abrupt. The "little window" interested Dr. P. very much and it is the best bit of the climb. Just as we got out of the danger zone a stone avalanche came from above. Mr. R. was ahead and had a difficult piece of the wall behind him. Dr. P. and I had no protection; Dr. P. was still on the most difficult portion. Luckily, nothing serious occurred. I received a stone on my rucksack which smashed a bottle. But this was no loss since it was empty. Dr. P. had his ice axe struck by a stone. We could really talk about luck. With complaining stomachs we hurried down into the Weich Valley.

About a quarter before four we started again, for the Katzenkopf route was still in Dr. P.'s mind. Our companion of the morning (R.) lay on the Höllenthal meadow, well content. In an hour we were at the climb. We had not much time for it was five o'clock. Soon we arrived at the 30-metre wall. Here it was uncomfortable for Dr. P., for I made quite a spectacular figure going over the plaque in my nailed boots.

He called to me: "Konradl, don't you think it would be better if you took off your shoes? You may slip." I replied: "Don't be concerned, I won't fall off the Katzenkopf!" Soon I had a firm position and shouted: "Now, you can follow." And Dr. P. inquired: "Are you firm?" "Like iron!" I answered.

Now the traverse and the projecting block must be overcome and after that the hard part is over. In a little while we were on the beautiful resting place, from which one crosses over to the Preinthaler route. Here the provisions were finished up, with a bottle of Krondorfer and a cigar. Then we went down the Preinthaler way. The program was completed, day was at an end and we had had quite enough.

I remained overnight at Weichtal. There were people who had come by automobile, and on the morrow I must go with the group into the big Höllenthal in order to show them the climbs. There was a woman along who could not keep her eyes off me. She would have liked to make an excursion with me, but a gentleman was against it. He had spoken with me in a superior manner, and it was just as if he were in the highest degree of jealousy!

At noon it began to rain, and as there was no chance of improvement we went back into the Weich Valley. I was invited to the table with the company. Everyone (except the one gentleman) was very friendly toward me. After the meal we went a little way into the Weich ravine; then I was asked to accompany them to Hirschwang in the auto. Riding in a motor interested me so much that they let me go with them to Payerbach. When I climbed out the lady gave me ten kronen and one of the gentlemen six kronen. So, together, that made 16 kronen. I would have had to work more than a week in the quarry to make that much! Right contentedly I went homeward, and as I had made 16 kronen so easily, I took out a bankbook a few days later.

3

A SPRING DAY ON THE SCHNEEALPE

On Sunday, May 29, there was nothing in the guiding line. The holidays were over, and besides it was the end of the month, a time when most of the money has been spent. The old Viennese song came into remembrance: "Children, he who has no money remains at home!"

On Saturday I went to Naßwald. What should I do next morning? Stay at home? That would not be easy for me if it were not necessary. So I made plans to visit the Schneealpe. About four o'clock in the morning I started off and chose the Peter path for ascending. How lovely it was to walk over the forested crests, so quiet and lonely! Only here and there one saw a little bird, searching diligently after nourishment for its young.

After three quarters of an hour one reaches the rocks, where one looks down into the Strohtenn basin. There, if one is quiet, one may see 10 or 15 chamois. When one looks upon these graceful, brave animals and considers how many people there are (and I was one of them until lately) who would kill them just for their horns and beards, it can only be classed as an enormous lust for slaughter!

Proceeding, one comes to the path. Slowly and quietly I went forward, for the deer like to stop here. I came within 150 yards of one. On the Karl Alm the luscious spring vegetation was coming up, and the pleasant sunlight brought its first rays. The heart can desire no more! If such beauties of plant life do not bring a man to contemplation he has no feeling for the beautiful – the splendour of Nature.

So I wandered over the floral carpet on the so-called "little ledge of the alm" to the ravine. Here on the edge of the flat it was finest of all, for here were more alpine flowers than at the Karl Alm. Dwarf azaleas, common and flesh-coloured heather, various gentians, cowslips, anemones, double-flowered saxifrage, amaranth, alpine tragacanth, cotton grass, soldanella, spring sassafras; in a word, all the alpine plants of spring are to be seen here. I am only sad that I have not the ability to write down all the loveliness as it was before my eyes.

Spellbound in wonder I continued on the way to the Ameisbühel Hütte. There I took a long rest and was happy with the thought that not everyone could see such beautiful things even though they wished to.

Again the sweet and thoughtful song rises up:

> "Ein schön'res Leben kann's nimmer geben,
> Als bei uns im Hochgebirg…"

Peasants who kept watch in the huts started me out of my meditation, and for more than an hour we chatted together, mostly about housekeeping affairs.

In order to complete my program I took leave of them and wandered over to the Schneealpe. Here the vegetation had somewhat lessened, but the widespread view of the Windberg is a sufficient substitute. To the right is the Oetscher with its outliers, to the left the Hochschwab, Veitsch and Ennsthaler mountains. The sun was already sinking in the west and I must descend into the valley. With fond farewell I left the alpine flowers behind.

The Schneealpe district exceeds all its neighbours as regards the vegetation. This is easy to explain as it is not so much visited as, for example, Rax and Schneeberg. He who wishes to see the alpine flora at its best should make an excursion in the time between May 20 and June 15 from the Nass ravine to the Schnee Alm. "But do not tear out a single flower by the roots!" This request I would like to make of everyone.

In the following week several letters arrived from acquaintances in Vienna, who wished to reserve me for Sunday. I was much gratified at the opportunity, for now the mountain guiding was becoming profitable, and I counted up how much I would again be able to put in the savings bank. There was perfect weather for the whole week, but on Saturday it began to rain, without chance of improvement. But in Vienna it was all clear and the gentleman with whom I was to make a tour arrived that evening in the Weichtal. "Perhaps tomorrow will be clear," we said mutually, but I knew for certain that it would be raining in the morning. Yet I could not bear to disturb the good humour of the gentleman.

The night on the straw mattresses was again a restless one. About one and two in the morning wet and tired tourists arrived, and it was daybreak about half past two, again with disturbance. To be sure, there was nothing to do but leave this time, for it rained even harder than on the day before. But now reason went out of the window. One cursed about the weather and said, if he had known that it would be so miserable, he would certainly have remained in Vienna, where one can at least be in a coffee house. Another complained about the expense and would much rather, next Sunday, go to the Gesäuse peaks. Far back in the sleeping-room someone muttered in a sleepy voice: "If you please, if it is raining, at least be quiet so that one can sleep!" "I haven't heard that yet," laughed someone else.

Finally it seemed as if it might come to fighting. In the guest room there was scarcely room to stand, and as there seemed no chance of improvement, most of the tourists departed for the railway at Payerbach. I joined a group and reached Hirschwang, cooked myself a good midday repast and used up this failure of a Sunday in patching my torn working clothes. That's the way it is: one should not sell the skin of a bear before one has it.

Monday I received a pleasant letter from Dr. P., which read:

Dear Konradl! I propose to use these two holidays in the Gesäuse and will gladly take you along so that you may learn something about the Enns Valley. The question is, whether you can get away from quarrying. As you do not know the excursions which we wish to make you must go there a few days earlier and look up the routes. Travel and mainte-nance will naturally be at my expense. We wish to do the north wall of the Planspitze, and to go over the Totenköpfl on the Reichenstein. Please answer at once. With greetings and Bergheil, Dr. E.P.

That was luck for me! I could scarcely wait until the superintendent came. With beating heart I went to him and asked permission. At first he would not hear of it, but as he was really a friend of Nature he could not deny me, and said: "Yes, you may stay off four days, but no longer. You will fall anyway, sooner or later, you are such a fool about your climbing!"

4

IN THE ENNSTHALER MOUNTAINS

I could not wait until Saturday! On Friday I received a special-delivery let-ter stating that the tour would be postponed for a few days. But I was so eager that I departed in spite of this, hoping that possibly I might secure some guiding at Gstatterboden. I spent the night at St. Michael and arrived in Gstatterboden at nine o'clock next morning. But all the tourists had already left. As there was no other train arriving and I did not care to stay in the valley all day, I wandered alone over the Petern path to the Hochthor. At the begin-ning of this climb I met two gentlemen and a lady. They were astonished that a mere native should be interested in alpine sport. Naturally I did not at once tell them the story of my life or why I had come to the Gesäuse.

As the sun was too good in its intentions, the gentlemen and the lady were very uncomfortable, for carrying rucksacks was not easy for them, as I noticed at once. I said to the lady: "If you wish, I can carry your rucksack for you!" She did not consider long, but threw the sack at my feet with a friendly gesture. Now it went much more easily!

When we came to the wall where the "Ennsthaler Step" is, the men brought out a rope. When I saw that they did not manage it properly, I took hold and distributed it. They were struck by the fact that I could get around with a rope, so I told them that I was an expert mountain guide. With that they let me go ahead. At the Petern notch a little rest was taken, after which we wandered over the Dachl ridge of the Hochthor. We had a splendid view and climbed down over the Gugel ridge to Heß-hütte, and on to Johnsbach, where the gentlemen and the tired lady remained.

They asked me what they owed. I said: "If the gentlemen wish to give me something I will take it readily, but I do not demand anything." Then one of the men handed me 20 kronen. I think that was the first day that I earned 20 kronen, and was very happy about it.

Then I took leave and went to Gstatterboden in order to do the Planspitze on the following day. On the way I met Messrs. Jahn and Kauba, who described the Planspitze minutely to me. When we came to the Hotel Gesäuse we heard of a tourist who had fallen. I went to the guide Zettelmaier, who told me that the tourist had fallen either in the Haindl or the Ross cirque, and there was nothing to do except to go early to Heß-hütte. About half past two I was awakened by the servant. I had been obliged to sleep in the stable, for which I would not forgive the landlord, and must go out without a warm breakfast. My goal was the Planspitze.[6] Without much searching I arrived in two hours at the beginning of the climb, where there is a cairn. As I looked over the mighty wall I began to wonder where I should go up. The climb is not marked as on the Rax! And the fallen tourist was also on my mind. But the lust for climbing overcame all this, and ambition had something to do with it as well. I said aloud that I was proud that Dr. P. had placed such trust in me with a mountain about which I knew nothing.

When I was 30 or 40 metres up the wall I saw a piece of red paper, and another bit a little farther along, and so the way was easy for me to find. There were also many nail scratches, which caught my eye at once. The ascent of the north wall did not seem difficult to me, and I was quite astonished when I reached the peak. From the start to the top I took two and a quarter hours.

Now I rested, ate a little lunch and looked over to the Hochthor to see whether I could discover anyone on the search for the unlucky tourist. But there was nothing to be seen or heard. Despite this the thought of the poor fellow gave me no peace; I started off once more and went over the Petern divide to the Rosskuppe and from there over the "Dachl" to the Hochthor. When I came to the high scree slope I noticed a black object; I thought it must be the unfortunate man, but it was only a dark bit of rock.

But I was on the right track, for a few steps farther along I found a hat, a few yards frther a certificate of guarantee for a watch, and a tourist card of the "Naturfreunden" with the name of Franz Hahn, whom I well knew from my excursions on the Rax. A little way along I saw still another paper, and I laid myself on my stomach to reach it. As I supported myself on my hands I saw to my right blood mixed with marrow and hair on a pointed stone. It was only by chance that I had not grasped it! I thought that probably the accident had occurred to that Mr. Hahn.

At heart I was so afraid! I remained scarcely five minutes on the peak of the Hochthor and hurried down to the hut in order to give news of the affair. When I arrived at the hut some people were assembled, and in their midst lay the dead tourist on a litter. It was Franz Hahn!

The people were glad that I had come, for there were not enough bearers there to transport the body. I fortified myself at the hut, and then we departed with the poor tourist, for whom I was very sorry. The rest were, to be sure, not much disturbed by it, for they had not known him in life and could not understand anyway what one wanted to be on the mountains for. Often enough one heard the natives talking about such accidents: "Such idiots ought to all fall!" "I would like to know what they have lost up there," and other similar remarks.

We brought the body down to the vault at Johnsbach, and I wandered thence to Gstatterboden in order to make another trip in the morning. By chance I met two doctors from Vienna. One of them I had already guided on the Rax. They asked me what I was doing in the Enns Valley and I briefly told them about my affairs. Then they asked whether I would like to go with them. After a short consideration I said: "Yes, I will accompany you, but I do not know many routes in the Enns Valley." And I outlined what guiding I could do. To one this tour was not suitable, and to the other that route was not agreeable, and finally they chose the north wall of the Ödstein. I informed them that I was ignorant of this excursion. The answer came: "That doesn't matter; we have a good guidebook along. We will certainly find the beginning of the climb and then you must show your skill!" The matter was settled. We went for a little walk and then sat down to supper. (I must not omit to say that the landlord today was of much more friendly disposition, since I had come with two gentlemen; and I secured a little room for the night.)

Next day we set out about four o'clock; the morning looked promising. But I was not quite sure that the expedition would turn out well, for I put no great trust in the ability of the gentlemen to find the way. If I am *alone* it is different; then I have only to look out for myself. It happened just as I thought. In the Gesäuse "guide" it states: "four hours to the beginning of the ascent." But that is if one has an idea of the route. We turned off too soon in the Haindl cirque and searched around until we came to a long groove, and lived in hopes that this was the crack that led direct to the start. But it was not, and as there were some difficult places we took four hours to the top of the crack.

Then we saw that our way was not the right one; at the same time we were confident that we could not be mistaken much longer. We made the first halt of half an hour. It was quarter to nine in the morning. We crept forward through timber, over slides and snow patches, and at last reached the beginning of the ascent. It was eleven o'clock.

The gentlemen now counted up the time required for the rest of the tour. They thought to be on the peak of the Ödstein about five o'clock and in Johnsbach three hours later. According to their reckoning it would go nicely and we could still reach the valley before dark. (Our party on the Ödstein was the first of this summer; in any case it is not done often as it is considered a "drudgery tour.") Now the climbing began. At first one cuts up over a large snowfield. These were the *first steps* that I chopped in ice. Every beginning is difficult. It was that way with me. More than an hour passed until we were above, and then we asked one another: "Where now, right or left?"

The Pfannl route was selected. It went up a very nasty ice couloir. Possibly it is better to do this bit late in the season. Now one of the men began to curse: "Stop that ice-chopping! If a piece strikes me in the face and breaks my goggles I am finished and can't take another step!" That went right to my heart. The other asked whether I could see the peak, and so on. At last the way became better, but it did not last long. To the left an overhanging rock barred the route and we must go directly upward. It was difficult enough for me and more so for the already tired men. I was obliged to use my entire strength in order to get them up.

Again a halt was made to rest them. For afterward, according to the description, the worst would come: an overhanging rib. Calmly and securely I went to work and in a few minutes it was all behind me. The best thing about it is that one has a firm position and a good projection of rock for belaying. Now I called down to the men: "Well, Dr. B., come along!" He had gone very well over the traverse, and so I thought that this would not give him much trouble. But one should not praise the day before evening! When he came to the rib I heard a little gasp, and – Dr. B. was hanging in the rope, almost in the air. I had to let him down at once to his comrade. There I heard them talking about me and expressing doubt as to whether I could hold them if one fell.

The rest lengthened into a quarter of an hour, until I demanded they proceed, and said to Dr. B.: "When you come to the rib, press closely to the rock and come up as quickly as possible so that you do not lose your strength." My good advice was insufficient. Dr. B. again fell from the rocks and I must again let him down. This time he struck his head, and quite a time passed until it was tied up. Then they talked of turning back. But I reminded the gentlemen of the ice gully: "If only that were not there" – for *that* both men had respect.

Now Dr. W. tried to come over the rib. He did the business better, in that he did not fall. "That is certainly hard!" were his first words when he stood beside me. I was convinced that his colleague would not make it. Dr. W. called to him: "Oh, come up! It is not as bad as it looks." But poor Dr. B. even this time came no farther than before, only with this difference that he now began to cry out as if he had been impaled. There was nothing to do but pull him up over the rocks. Both of us heaved with all our might until we had him lying exhausted beside us.

Now he began to curse: "Crazy business, to make such a climb!" And so on. I thought to myself: 'If we were only on top. A second time I would not go with you again.' The watch showed it to be five o'clock. About this time the men thought they would be on the summit. With many more such stops the way of progress would be barred, until night came with its attendant discomforts. It was almost nine o'clock when we arrived in the notch between the Teufelszacken and the Ödstein. A very little overhang would be our roof for the night, and stones could be carried to make a small protecting wall.

But we could not finish our "dwelling" quite according to plan, because it became dark in the interval. If we had only had something to eat and warmer clothing a bivouac on this fine night would not have been so bad. But to go to sleep without a bite of supper, which one had well earned this day, that was indeed bad! We saw the light of the convent cellar at Admont and thought longingly of a glass of wine. It would have been consoling to us there in the quiet loneliness.

Now an attempt was made to go to sleep. The rucksacks were emptied, the shoes placed beneath our heads, and "good night!" But the rest did not last long. One man became chilled, the other was poked by a stone. I had such unspeakable cramps that I was forced several times in the night to take a few little climbing exercises. We had omitted so much in the construction of our home that we begged each other's pardon, as it was the first time we had undertaken any building.

Dr. W. was overcome with fatigue and slept several hours beside us, although Dr. B. and I talked loudly. Dr. B. told me a great many things, but on the whole it had not much point. Finally he seemed to have talked himself out, but all at once he began in the following manner: "Dear Konrad, what would happen if we were to die here?" "Oh," I said, "I surely believe they would search for us and carry us down to the valley." "Well enough," he replied, "but *how* would they do it?" And he asked still other really stupid questions, to which I made no answer. At last he said: "It seems to me you cannot explain that." "Yes, indeed," I told him, "I have already had something to do with that kind of transportation. One will be tied up in a sack, roped and pulled down into the woods. Then one is laid on brushwood and carried to the road." And Dr. B. exclaimed: "But doesn't that hurt, to be dragged down over stones?" "Dr. B., you should really understand that you would be *dead*." "Ah, yes," he moaned, "I know it well enough, but it hurts just the same."

From his talk I could not believe he was in possession of his five senses, and in order to get away from him, I left. But as I stayed away too long he began an awful shouting. It really sounded as if a wild animal was in the neighbourhood. His slumbering friend was awakened out of deep sleep, and did not know what had happened or where he was. When I came back to them I heard them talking strangely. Then Dr. W. called loudly: "Konrad, come, Dr. B. has gone insane." I walked over: "What's the matter. So much noise!" And Dr. B. screamed: "Imagine, he said I was crazy. Such a dirty trick." Then they talked angrily. The strife lasted until nearly daybreak.

I could no longer contain myself and said: "Sirs, why do you fight up here? Straighten things out in the valley. Instead of ending up happily a completed tour, we are quarrelling." I saw that it was not quite agreeable to the gentlemen to have to listen to a lecture from a youth, but at last they were silent. About half past two it was light enough for climbing, and I climbed ahead on the wall, which did not look too inviting. There hung the old rope which the renowned Hans Robert Schmitt had used in the '8os. Although it was not far to the summit, we took another hour. We wrote in the book, probably the oldest in the Ennsthaler mountains. Then we proceeded, indeed more than slowly, so that everything was vexatious.

The descent is a bad one, on top of a night in the open without anything to eat or drink. To make matters worse we got into the underbrush of the forest and about eleven o'clock reached the Donner Inn half dead. For 31 hours we had been separated from mankind and had had nothing warm in our stomachs. But now that organ should have whatever it wanted. First a hot soup. But it seemed as if, after such long hungering, the stomach had become a stranger to nourishment. After the soup I really had no desire for any other food.

About half past twelve the mourners of the unfortunate tourist Hahn arrived. There were only six: his brother, four friends and the tourist who had been with him at the time of the accident. His mother could not give him her last attendance, for she was a poor laundress and could not secure the money for the journey. It was indeed a sad case. Poor Hahn was carried from the vault to the church and then to his last resting place. Representing the "Naturfreunde," a gentleman from Vienna made a moving address at the grave. It was quite noticeable how it went to their hearts. I stood behind a gravestone and my tears ran down on the ground. I could not control myself. After the preceding day the speech at the grave was doubly impressive. I cannot describe its true meaning to me. Hahn's brother said, among other things "that rest may be granted to him in this beautifully situated cemetery, as he was through and through a friend of Nature and now had found his death in Nature."

Of such men one can really say he is a "Friend of Nature." He who exchanges his hard-earned money for journeys into the lovely mountain world, that one glimpses the splendour of the world with entirely different, much more grateful eyes than the person to whom the money for a mountain excursion is of no importance. I know many tourists, worn-out fellows in the manner of speaking, whom nothing more in the city interests. Theatre, play, women; they have had their fling with all of them and are satiated by everything. When they become older and obtain insight that it cannot go on much further without their body and health suffering too much, they are apt at last to turn to sport. It is the best cure for that kind – if it is not already too late. But even if they are equally eager for mountain sport I do not regard them as actual friends of Nature. Only those, who like poor Hahn, whom they have buried today, laying out his hard earned kronen in *youth* for Nature, and finding his joy in the mountains; only such, in the true sense of the words, can be called friends of Nature.

That evening Dr. P. and his party (a gentleman and a lady) arrived at Gstatterboden. But the guide Zettelmaier could go with them and so everything was all right. Next morning at five o'clock we left the hotel with Zettelmaier, who led us by another route to the north wall climb of the Planspitze, a much finer one than I had taken three days before. There were already several parties in front of us, which was not so nice. Zettelmaier went ahead with a man, I with my group behind them. It was a lovely day. The gentlemen and the lady were in high spirits, as one should be on a mountain tour. We advanced rapidly. Assistance of the rope was scarcely needed, for they went well and safely, the lady even better than the men. Compared with the last party I had guided this was a real pleasure!

At the last ledges we caught up with a Club group, led by Mr. Krempl. I noticed that he ascended too soon and remarked to him about it. Mr. Krempl asked me whether I knew the route. "Indeed I do, sir, I did it for the first time several days ago." "And I have done it six times," he called, "so I should certainly know best where the way lies!" I said quietly, "If you think so," and went on. When the man saw that I was right he climbed down again with the words: "That is very stupid of me."

But the best of all was when both our gentlemen began on the summit to discuss the incident; in some parts they were not in agreement, for there are some little affairs that have two sides, an easy and a difficult one. As it gave me pleasure I took the difficult one, while guide Zettelmaier, who was much older, took the easy one. When I am old I will do the same thing.

After a long rest on the summit we went to Heß-hütte and had a good feed. As Dr. P. wished to do the Totenköpfl on the Reichenstein he took Lechner from Heß-hütte along so that for each climber there was a guide. An accompanying storm blew over us during our descent to the valley, so that we arrived in a thoroughly wet condition at the Donner Inn. We spent the night there and left next morning at five o'clock. That was a little late for such a trip. Because of the rain of the day before there was an unpleasant haze, and on the upper part of the way the sun burned frightfully. A big viper was on the path and we killed it. I had to laugh heartily at the Zillerthal man, Lechner, when he said: "Die, you devilish reptile!" ["Bischt a hiaz hin, du teiflisch Viech!"]

Zettelmaier lagged farther and farther behind with his man; I believe that neither wanted to work very hard. Before beginning the climb we rested. From there the ridge looks dreadful. I went to the start of the climb, and when I returned Dr. P. told me that we would take the ordinary way as the two who remained behind would not accompany us. They lay down in the grass and looked at the Reichenstein from below, awaiting our return.

I believe that we were on the summit in an hour. We paid a call on the *Sennerin* of the Treffner Alm and wandered happily and contentedly into the valley. We had lunch at the Donner Inn, then went to the station where we took leave of one another. The party set out for Vienna, while I went home by way of Leoben. I felt that I had been fortunate, and told everyone with joy that I had been for some days in the Enns Valley.

5

MY TRAVELS BEGIN

One evening I met some people in Naßwald who asked me whether I would like to go to Tyrol. I said that naturally I would accept if someone would take me. But I did not think at all that the question was put in earnest.

Wednesday I received a telegram at Hirschwang: "Will you come with us for three weeks in Tyrol? If yes, reply at once. You must be in Vienna at ten o'clock tomorrow morning. H." I went at once to the superintendent for permission, and he granted it. That night I could not sleep for pure joy, and next morning, in impatience, I came to the station so early that I had to wait more than an hour for the train.

In Vienna I was met by a servant of Mr. H. As soon as I was brought to the gentleman I was first informed about the journey, and then Mr. H. gave me 40 kronen so that I could buy an ice axe and other necessary things. I made my purchases at Mizzi Langer's,[7] and naturally told her with pleasure that I was going to Tyrol. When I returned to Mr. H. he gave me 80 kronen more. Never had I had so much money! I thought to myself: 'My, he must be a good fellow!' This belief made me very happy. Only one thing was un-comfortable: I was afraid I would lose the money. So I would grab it every five minutes or so to see whether I really still had it.

At eight o'clock in the evening we left the West Station. The train was filled to overflowing, and it was hot in the car, without any room to stretch out. The night was long, fearfully long. Changing at Tarvis, we left the express and went on a few minutes later by the local to Ratschach–Weissenfels. There I had to do some little thing for Mr. H. I probably stayed away too long, for he said to me rather harshly: "Why were you away so long? Take notice that if you are sent somewhere you must go quickly!" Then it came over me that the gentleman was not quite as nice as he had seemed in the beginning.

As we went on he said nothing to me as to where we would go today, or what the names of the mountains were. He didn't speak to me. After half an hour we came to the world-renowned Weissenfels Lakes. It was the first time I had seen such a beautiful sight. The loveliness of both lakes so raised my spirits that I quite forgot my ill-humoured patron. He turned no kindly face upon the splendid scene, although his wife was quite enthusiastic. The view of the charming lake at the foot of the mighty precipices of the Mangart is indeed in a class by itself. Now I knew that the Mangart was our goal.

We climbed up over the Lahnscharte. On a green meadow there grew many little wild roses, and we saw a herd of goats which accompanied us part of the way. On the Lahnscharte we left our superfluous baggage, as we would pass by in returning. The partly guarded climb on the Mangart is without difficulty. The view was perfect, although on account of the late hour of the afternoon haze prevented a distant panorama. The lofty Tauern, the Dolomites and the sea were invisible; but there was a wonderful glimpse of Wischberg, Canin, Montasio and Triglav. (Of the latter mountain I had already heard as a schoolchild – of Zlatorog and the red Triglav rose.)

We then went to the Mangart Hütte. As I was not an official guide I would have been obliged to pay two kronen for my night's lodging, but the good landlady took pity on me and offered me an inexpensive place. She had noticed at once that I was not treated in the best manner.

Next morning I left the hut a few minutes after my people, while the lady of the hut told me her opinion of them. We wandered down over the Mangart Alm to the Predil road and across to Fort Predil and the pleasant Raibl Lake. There we awaited a gentleman, and upon his arrival I was obliged to go ahead in order to reserve beds at the Ricovero di Nevea.

As I passed the Austrian prison fort and saw the poor soldiers it came sadly into my mind that within a few weeks I would also be put into such clothes. But the variation of the lovely valley soon repressed this thought. The Ricovero di Nevea, which belongs to the Società Alpina Friulana, looks like a woodcutter's hut. There is no-iron stove. I made the woman, who spoke not a word of German, understand that three people were coming. There were chickens here, of which two must later give up their lives and be roasted on the spit. To be sure, I didn't get any of it; for myself and the Italian guide, stationed at the hut, polenta was cooked. We also had milk, which I tried once and never again. Near the hut is a huge alm with about a hundred head of cattle. I saw how the work was being done, and my appetite for milk was gone!

We next looked over the route for the next day's ascent of Monte Canin. The only sleeping place was in the hay. About one o'clock the alarm went off and at two we started out with lanterns. Going on as far as we had followed the way on the day before, we waited for daylight and then climbed over the Fontana Sot di Bareit and the glacier to the summit of Monte Canin.

The view was superb. For the *first time* I saw the *sea*. But I thought we must be on the wrong peak, for there was no book and no cards to be found. We took a rest, and then I looked for a route of descent. I found one which was not entirely simple. Below was a large crevasse. On the descent I was leading, then came Mrs. H. and the two other men. Mr. B. was the last. Suddenly he missed his footing and we were all pulled down with him. Immediately we all began to shout: "Dig in the axes, dig!" As the slope of the snowfield lessened we held. It was time, for blood was flowing from my hands.

First we asked one another whether anyone was injured, then we went on quickly, as a storm was brewing. A few minutes later the lightning flashed and our axes began to sing, so that we were obliged to throw them away. We fled to the Casera Canin but unfortunately it was closed up. However, we succeeded in forcing our way in and made a fire. Thus we waited until the worst of the storm was over. Then I brought in the axes and we wandered down to the Ricovero Nevea. The weather became fine again, and it was very pleasant to lie in the sun in front of the hut.

On the following morning we climbed over the Fischbach Alm to the Wischberg. The view was exceptional: Tauern, Dolomites (Monte Cristallo) and the Karawankas. Especially fine were the nearby Montasio and the Julian Alps. My patron became daily more perverse. My money had come to an end, and when I told the gentleman about it he became pale as death. He could not understand how I could have used up the money so soon, so I presented him with the bill.

Now the cat was out of the bag and I saw him in his true light. "Konrad," he said, "things must be arranged. From now I will pay you four kronen daily (!) and you must take care of yourself." "My dear sir, that is too little," I replied. "What do you mean, too little?" he blustered. "You can live for two kronen and you can't earn more than that at home." What more was there for me to do in a strange place than to agree. Without money I could not go home. Wherever our further journeying would take us I did not know, as he had said not a word about it.

We went to Meran. There I witnessed an incident that one really did not expect of a millionaire (as my gentleman was). We went for a walk and Mr. H. bought peaches from a poor old fruit woman. When he inquired how much they cost, the woman said: "Eight for ten kronen." "My, so expensive," complained Mr. H., "why, they cost that in Vienna." And he haggled so long that the old woman gave him ten for the money. Then he went to his wife and said: "Here, look how cheap fruit is here!" I was ashamed of him. Even a humble workman would not let such things be told about himself.

We continued next morning with an Italian coachman through the beautiful Vintschgau to Gomagoi. There again occurred a scene with the driver, to whom Mr. H. did not want to pay the full amount. Of course, there was no question of a tip.

From Gomagoi we went on foot to Sulden, where we saw a splendid sunset. I spent the night in the "Alpenrose" for 1.20 kronen, Mr. and Mrs. H. living in the Hotel Sulden. Next day we went to the Hallesche Hütte. Guide Friedrich

Pinggera accompanied us. The hut was completely full. Fourteen guides were present. In the evening, prayers were said, and as I could not pray with them one of the old guides reproached me. I listened quietly to his lesson and thought: 'If you only knew that I was a Lutheran, perhaps you would be even more afraid for me!' Then adventures were related, and everyone tried to exceed his fellows.

About three in the morning we left and climbed all three summits of the Cevedale. (All above 3700 metres.) It was not necessary for us to have started so early. But the guide was insistent, in order that he might be back early in the valley and bring up another party. He would go back on the same day to the Hallesche or to another hut.

We stopped in the hut, as we wished to ascend the Königsspitze. Next day we started out with lanterns; the moon appeared only occasionally through the clouds, which did not promise much for the day. The climb over the Schrötterhorn and Kreilspitze was not entirely without danger; just before the Königsjoch the gentleman slipped – I could not hold him and had to go along. Only a thought: 'Now we are lost!' We dug in our axes but could not stop, on account of the great jerk I was obliged to let go. Fortunately the snowfield became softer and at last we were able to halt. Mrs. H. and Pinggera were much frightened when they heard our shouts. My unhealed finger bled again. Pinggera came to assist us. We looked for our lanterns and axes and after we had found them the man began to curse me for not holding him. But Pinggera told him the real truth and then he became silent.

I thought to myself: 'It's pretty bad to endanger one's life so much for *four kronen per day* and then be cursed out on top of it!'

Now we all roped together, and since several parties had been on the Königsspitze the day before it went easily enough. One should start early on this tour because of the danger of falling stones. The view was nothing remarkable for the mists hid the distances. Here and there, if the fog parted, one could look down to Sulden. We descended by the same route.

Next day was a day of rest. I had my shoes resoled and took a little walk alone, for Ortler guides, as is well known, are rough to strangers. At evening Mr. H. had invited several guides to the table and drank a couple of bottles of good wine with them; but he did not think of me. He engaged yet another guide for the next day, to make the tour of the Ortler by the Hinter Grat. But on the same evening he twisted his foot, so that the party came to nothing. But on the following day I joined a group for the Ortler.

As Mr. H.'s foot did not improve there was nothing to do but leave Sulden. He called me into his room to settle up. Instead of receiving money I owed him 30 kronen! Within a couple of hours the wagon stopped in front of the hotel, and all the servants assembled, but without a friendly face to be seen, for they had fewer traces of my patron's riches than even I.

As we missed the Post, we had to spend the night in Schlanders, leaving early next day. About five o'clock the first wagon departed. I took my place on the bench with the driver. He was a very kindly fellow and told me the names of the mountains and the ruins that we passed. Upon our arrival in Meran there was a peasant wedding, most pleasing to see. Although I had not much money left, and must use it so that it would last me home, I gave the coachman a krone for a tip. The transportation, which I had to pay myself, cost me five kronen. Mr. H. gave only 60 hellers as tip for himself and his wife, and the coachman began such a racket that quite a crowd collected. He shouted: "It has never happened to me before that the guide gave me more than his people!" And he called out the amount of the tip he had received. Mr. H. stood beside him, listened quietly to it all and was unashamed. He said: "Who can compel me to give *more*?"

The coachman was so pleased that I had given him a bigger tip than the gentleman that he invited me to a good lunch. Mr. H. gave me two kronen at the station for the wagon journey (which cost five). But I said: "If you cannot pay the *entire* cost, please keep the two kronen." Then he threw the money on the ground, and just as the train started I picked it up.

In a discontented frame of mind I went home, richer by many an experience. Mr. H. is one of the wealthiest in all Vienna, but one of the shabbiest. When I was by myself my anger rose, and I looked sadly at the beautiful surroundings. At Bozen, guide Mühlsteiger, an acquaintance of mine, who was also going home, got in the train. He sat beside me and counted his money. I could not see exactly how much he had, but there were some banknotes. I was almost ready to cry, and I thought: 'He at least has the money that he has earned.' Naturally I told him not a word about my "remarkable" reward!

On arriving in the Enns Valley I made the plan of going with my remaining kronen to Gstatterboden, hoping that I might get a couple of parties to guide. I also wrote to Dr. P. that I would stop for a while in the Enns Valley.

6

TAME AND WILD TOURS IN THE ENNS VALLEY

In Gstatterboden I was received kindly, for guide Zettelmaier had gone away with a man and the time had come when many were in need of a guide. I was happy and thought that I might make up here for what I had lost in Tyrol. But it was as if the desire for a guide had suddenly been cut off, and I waited two days in vain, thereby using up my last money so that I was not even able to go home. I was sad at heart, for I did not dare to tell the landlord that I had no money. I do not know whether he read the hunger in my face, but he said: "Say, what's the matter with you? You really look like nine days of rain. Haven't you any money?" When I gave him the sad news he said: "Why didn't you say anything? You can surely ask for a little." I made the request that he would be so good as to let me sign for my keep.

Next morning I met the first train, but no one came who needed a guide. About nine o'clock I went up the north wall of the Planspitze alone in order to become acquainted with the Innthaler Chimney. When I arrived at the beginning of the climb black clouds were sweeping above the Buchstein. For a long time I waited for the storm behind an overhanging rock, but it did not come and so I went quickly ahead. Up to the boulder I went with ease, but from there on it became most difficult for it was wet in the chimney and my climbing shoes were of no service. Just before the famous difficult point of emergence I sat myself in the cavern, brought out my sewing materials and mended my shoes. After some minutes it became dark and the storm broke with lightning and thunder. Who has not experienced such a storm in the mountains can scarcely imagine it.

In a short time a stream of water was flowing down right where I must ascend. If I had had enough rope to rope down I would not have gone up but descended! But there was nothing else to do. It was a hard task and my most difficult hour up until now. Meanwhile the weather had broken and bright daylight was on the peak. Despite my bad financial position I was again one of the happiest!

Then I climbed down to Heß-hütte. But in my mind I was uncomfortable: no money and hunger for two! With "Grüß dich Gott" I was welcomed by the sweet maiden from the Zillerthal. I informed her at once that I had hunger but no money. Naturally there was nothing more to say. In a little while there was an abundance on the table and my famine was soon quieted. I went down the waterfall path to the valley, and a splendid sunset ended the day. The thought came to me of how much danger good luck had again placed behind me. Then I remembered the kindly people from the Zillerthal. How good they had been to take me in without money! Even in the valley I received food without paying. Only a true child of Nature, who knows what it means to fight for very existence, can have such memories of good fortune and of friendly people in a strange land.

In the Hotel Gesäuse they were already expecting me. I was to take a man over the Petern path. I went to bed happy. About four o'clock I arose and woke the gentleman. It was not very pleasant when he said he could not start that day, as he had scarcely slept. On my advice he promised to get up just the same, but then he wanted to go by the waterfall way. (The Petern path would have been better for me as it cost about six kronen more!) But I thought to myself: 'Today is already taken care of,' and so we went up quite comfortably to Heß-hütte.

As the man was not fatigued he went on to the Hochthor. Flames of joy flared in me for now I had earned six kronen more and could cover my debts. From the hut to the summit we took almost three hours. On the peak I sent a couple of loud yodels down into the Enns Valley. In response to my enthusiasm the man said: "Well, you seem to like it. You are to be envied!" I let him finish his speech, and then told him of my "fortunate" circumstances, but not with the thought that he would pay me more, although I did emphasize that. For a long time he looked at me without missing a word, and then inquired: "Just why did you tell me that?" "Well, my dear sir," I replied, "one can't tell everything all at once until one knows with whom one has to deal." "Quite right," said he, kindly.

At Heß-hütte we had another little rest, and then separated. The man went to Johnsbach and I to Gstatterboden. The first thing I did was to pay my debts. I had two kronen left. That, of course, was not much, but just the same it is a good thing if a fellow has a few kronen in his pocket. Then along came a letter, by which I was engaged on Sunday for the Innthaler Chimney. Next day I had a party for the Tamischbach Tower. A very pleasant tour: I had only a little camera and a jacket to carry, and the man and the girl were in addition quite pleasant. At the Ennsthaler Hütte they paid for my lunch, which was a very rare thing. The sun meant well, and one loses quite a few drops of sweat in going from the hut to the summit about midday.

The view was wonderful, and I had another peak to exhibit. We rested for a long time and chatted quite comfortably about the mountains, for, as I realized, the man was an old tourist since he talked of some first ascents. I happened to mention that I was a pupil of the guide Innthaler, which interested the man very much as he had often been out with him.

In Gstatterboden I was given my supper in addition and 12 kronen, which is very good pay for this half day's tour. With renewed courage I went to bed, so happy that I could not go to sleep until early morning. As there was no party in sight for this day I quickly made plans to undertake a new tour and selected the north wall of the Hochthor, which is supposed to be one of the most difficult in the Eastern Alps. I packed bread, sausage and a bottle of water in my sack and went quickly through the Haindl basin. Here I examined for some minutes this really frightful wall, and it came over me that it was rather a gamble to undertake such a dangerous route alone. Then I thought: 'Oh, it can't be so bad. If others do it, I can too.' With this I started for the wall. I required two hours to the beginning of the climb, which I recognized by a little cairn. Here I took out my climbing shoes, had a drink of water and went at it.

In the beginning there were nail scratches which soon ceased as things became increasingly worse. The route became more and more complicated, and I often had to stop climbing for a while in order to set myself right. Then I saw a *Mauerhaken* (peg)! The place was known to me by description, and so the route became easier for me, as I knew I was on the right track. But in reality it became always more difficult, and some parts are really on the limits of human possibility, as there are little overhangs with holds nicked usually on the downward side, so that one must have gigantic strength in the fingers.

On the worst places I roped up my rucksack, in order to make it easier for myself. I came to a spot where there were several *Mauerhaken*. It was the so-called "Flying Ledge," of which I had already heard. But that did not seem so difficult to me. Through the cleft up to the peak of the Hochthor there are some very troublesome places.

From Gstatterboden to the summit I took almost six hours. One can only do it this quickly if one is alone. With one or two persons in addition there can be no fast going. I now took a brief rest, ate up my provisions and wandered over the Dachl ridge to the Peternsattel and down the path. From below I looked over the wall carefully again and was quite content with my day's performance.

I made use of the following day in writing notes and in walking through the forest. About ten o'clock that evening Dr. P. arrived, in order to do the Innthaler Chimney next day. But we almost had no luck, for in the morning a gamekeeper stood at the branch in the road and informed us that we could not go there that day, as the owner of the hunting rights was coming this week. We tried to impress him with the idea that we would be very quiet, but he would not permit it. Dr. P. was somewhat downcast, but finally he said that we must take a different excursion, and we left the keeper with hunters' greeting.

Dr. P., of course, thought it was all over, but I said to him: "Oh, we can do it in spite of that! The best of it is that the keeper is stationed down in the valley and not up on the climb!" So we went along the road a bit and then climbed straight up. It was a detour of about half an hour, and Dr. P. was afraid that someone would discover us. I had, of course, asserted that this was impossible, for one of the keepers stood at the fork, while the other was in the Haindl basin, and "there aren't any more" as I told my man.

Wet through with perspiration we came to the start of the climb, known to me by my recent tour. A little rest and we climbed on, chatting with one another. The Innthaler Chimney pleased Dr. P. very much, and he was not undeceived by the difficulties. I had torn my breeches so badly that I had lost almost half of them and could only tie them up with a string. We were alone on the Planspitze, and it is very pleasant to contemplate the beauties of Nature without being disturbed by anyone.

I almost didn't dare to go into the hut with my torn trousers, and was received with laughter. But the people had only a short time for mirth, for Hans brought me another pair at once. In the hut were several well-known men. They praised my performance and some almost overdid it. But that did not affect me much, and I thought to myself that I would not be very much better off if people put me on a pedestal.

We went to Johnsbach. The men all went home and I climbed out to Gstatterboden. Next day I would spend in comfort. A comfortable day of rest! I went up to the Scheiben Alm, that is an alm of the Gstatterboden peasants. At the hut of pretty Liesl[8] I met the gamekeeper, who, it seemed to me, was staying there quite a while. Liesl was really a fine *Sennerin*, but I have heard much *more* said about her good looks. We all talked together for a while and then I went with the keeper to his hut, where he offered me a drink. Then we lay down in the grass and told each other our experiences. It is an old story that all hunters like to tell tales that are untrue, and this one tried it also. But he did not succeed very well, for I could tell wilder things than he!

In the afternoon I went with him on a stalk. It was nothing new to me, but it carried my thoughts back to so many splendid and dangerous hours at home. The keeper had no luck. Beside chamois there was nothing to be seen, so I went back to Gstatterboden and stayed lying on the meadow until sunset. I did not wait in vain. It came as beautifully as one could have wished for. I made plans for the coming day. If there was no party to guide I wanted to make another *new* tour.

So in the morning I strolled along the road to Johnsbach as far as the long gravel-fan, for today I wanted to do the north wall of the Reichenstein. It was indeed my biggest "drudgery tour," taking three hours over the rubble before one comes to firm rock! When I was up about 200 metres I saw that I could not be on the best and proper way, for there was a much finer climb coming from the Hofergraben, and I was annoyed that I had not recognized the approach. As far as difficulties are concerned it is one of the easiest northern walls in the Gesäuse mountains, but the tour is not entirely free of danger for there are apt to be falls of stone, according to weather conditions, as I could see by the polished chutes.

On the summit I took quite a long rest. The distant view embraced the Glockner and the Dachstein. To both of these mountains I would have liked to pay a visit. If only money were not so hard to get! Thirst drove me to descend, otherwise I would have feasted my eyes still longer on the lovely prospect.

From Gstatterboden to the summit I had taken six and a half hours; for the descent to the Treffner Alm not quite one. Before one reaches the alp there is a large pond that one might almost call a little alpine lake. To the right and left it is surrounded by fir trees, with the Reichenstein, Sparafeld and Kalbling in the background – an artistic picture. Add to that the sound of the cattle bells and the deep peace of it all. It occurred to me that after all I was a *rich* man, even if I had no *money*.

From the *Sennerin* I got some sour milk in a dish, but as it was almost evening and she was busy, she said: "Don't be hard on me, I haven't any time today!"["Derfst net harb sei, i hon koa Zeit heit!"] So I went slowly down into the valley.

At the Huber Alm I also looked in, for there was a very pretty *Sennerin* there, who liked to hear her good housekeeping and her good looks praised. Then one got milk without much trouble!

I was sorry to leave, but it was almost dark. Since in Johnsbach at the "Donner" there was at that time an insolent innkeeper, I did not go in but kept on my way to Gstatterboden. People had arrived (three ladies and a gentleman) who were quite excited because no guide was there and they wished to make an excursion to the Große Buchstein. But as I had not as yet been on this mountain I went that evening to the head keeper, Auer, and asked for information. He told me that I could not go wrong, and so I was quite comforted.

In the morning I overslept; the people were waiting for me and complaining. We went in the pleasant morning air through the woods for a short distance along the left bank of the Enns. At the Pichelmayr Alm, where I again inquired about the route, we had breakfast. The sun had risen fairly high by the time we had trudged up through the clearing in the forest – the so-called Krautgartl. The two elder women asked continually: "Well, does this go on forever? How far is it to the peak?" I replied noncommitally for a while, not knowing myself, as I had never been up there. The young lady and the man were far ahead. As I later discovered, it had little to do with young feet, as the two women thought, for they kept saying: "Those two can run so easily with their young feet!"

Above the Krautgartl we wanted to take a rest, and I went ahead to look for a good place. But when I looked through a kind of small saddle I saw the two who had hurried ahead sitting joyfully hand in hand and mouth to mouth. Of course I didn't let them see me, but coughed and then came on with noisy steps, acting as if I had not discovered them.

Then the two women arrived. The halt lasted almost an hour and when they had recovered I went on. As the slope is steep and covered with stones I requested the two lovers not to go too far ahead on account of falling stones. This was not very agreeable to either; I took pity on them, for I knew well enough that the kiss that one gives in the freedom of Nature has a double effect, especially to those who do not have much opportunity and are deeply in love. When we came to the wall where one traverses to the north side I said to both of them: "There, now you can go on ahead!" "You must look out carefully for the lady," I said to the man.

On arriving at the plateau they asked me which of the two rises was the summit, and as I did not know I took a chance on the first one. In much doubt I continued, hoping that I had answered correctly, otherwise they would realize at last that I had never been up there before. To my delight I discovered the summit book.

After a long rest we began the descent. In Gstatterboden the mother of the young lady awaited us. The daughter greeted her mother pleasantly and said: "Mother, that was the loveliest trip I have ever taken!" I thought to myself: 'I can well believe it!'

Two days later I went as porter with two men and two women to Heß-hütte. They had a dog along and we started in the afternoon. It was damnably sultry. By the time we reached the waterfall I was bathed in sweat. One of the men inquired about my military service, and tried to praise me up, for he said: "Konrad will make a flashy soldier!" Then they asked me whether I was glad about enrolling, and when I replied: "How can one be happy if one's freedom is taken away?" they tried to frighten me, because one of the men was a captain.

He said that I would be in his regiment and he would then show me what it meant to be a *soldier*! But I only laughed for I did not yet know the real truth. I was soon an enemy of the dog, because I had to carry him up the ladders and he would not hold still. At the hut we were properly taken care of. Hans played the guitar well and sang. When we went to bed we overheard the two women, as I and the servant slept beside the ladies' room. It was most amusing to hear them both. The women did not know that one could hear every word through the thin wall. The servant interrupted it finally with his loud laugh.

Next day the men went up the Hochthor. I guided the women back to Johnsbach, where we waited for the men and then all went by coach to Gstatterboden. Two more days of wonderful experience amid the beauties of Nature!

But for some days following there was nothing to do, as both men and one of the women had gone, and I had to take little walks with the other lady. The favourite stroll was along the left bank of the Enns; there is a charming point there, especially in the moonlight. With longing I awaited the 13th of August when I should start for Tyrol with Dr. P. On the evening before that I took leave of the lady, who was a grand-opera singer. We had a last walk and drank a bottle of wine together before her departure, wishing each other the best of luck. It almost made a scene in the dining room, as I did not fit in very well with my dirty trousers at table with such an attractive woman!

When I went to bed the journey to the Zillerthal took such hold of me that all night long I saw the train coming like a ghost! But in the morning I had to wait a long time for it, as there was a considerable delay. At last the signal at Hieflau was set. It was the excursion train for Innsbruck, overflowing with tourists. 'Can it be that my people are not in it?' – as I thought of such a possibility I heard my name called. Dr. P. and his bride, an Englishwoman, were in the last carriage. There was no place for me to sit. When I got on the train I greeted the other tourists with whom I was acquainted.

7

IN THE ZILLERTHAL

In Jenbach I met Dr. Spannagl. It was pleasant to leave the main line and climb into the Zillerthal train. Happily and curiously I looked out of the window, talking meanwhile about the tours that we would make. Dr. P. also taught me a little about reading maps, of which as yet I had not an inkling.

At Zell am Ziller there was a road festival. The peasants' costume pleased me very much. A loden jacket and a black hat with long white cock's feather. In the afternoon we came to the terminal station of Mayrhofen and entered the "Old Post." I had several greetings from Lechner, the keeper of Heß-hütte, to deliver, but I did not succeed very well as I was almost unable to understand the people. Dr. P. and his bride spoke only English to each other, and it looked as if I would have to content myself with my own company!

But in the guest room it was quite pleasant, for many people, including the parson, were there. They asked me where I had come from, as they could not tell from my accent. And I told them that I had been in the Enns Valley, where Lechner was at one of the huts. "So thou comest from there. Thou art a Styrian boy!" As I spoke to everyone in the polite form of "You," the parson said: "And if thou art at home in Lower Austria thou needst not be uppish about it. Know then that among ourselves one says 'Thou!'" And so I accustomed myself to it. The parson still remonstrated with me for some time on account of the "You"; I could scarcely trust myself about it, as it sounded so strange to my ear. I thought to myself that such an opportunity of my saying "Thou" to one of the clergy would not come often.

In speaking of the beauty of this place, one must really say that it is ideal: dear little houses of wood, with gay flowers on every balcony, and even the people make a good impression for they are pure unadulterated Tyrolese.

From Mayrhofen we went to Ginzling and remained overnight. I visited the children of Lechner at Dornauberg, a quarter of an hour distant from Ginzling. Lechner has a very attractive house on the edge of the forest, beautifully constructed. The pretty children with their rosy cheeks pleased me very much. One knows at once when an exemplary family life is being led. At evening we remained seated before the house and entertained ourselves well with the native people. There was present an old guide named David Fankhauser, who had much to tell about the mountains. But little Nannie [Nannerl] interested me a great deal more, and in order to be near her I helped to clean the eating utensils. Till that hour no one had ever pleased me as much as she. Beautifully formed, with keen healthy glance and a face that might have been painted by an artist. She was so gentle in her speech that one could easily fall in love with her. Later I discovered that she was much liked by the tourists. Whoever saw her simply had to go in whether he needed anything or not. But she was not proud on account of her beauty, and it was just this simple naturalness that appealed to me so much.

I got a good bed and slept until eight o'clock next morning, went to church, and afterward stretched myself in the grass in front of the hotel and had a breakfast that kindly Nannie brought me. In the afternoon we started off as we wished to reach the Greizer Hütte, situated on the Floiten Glacier. A splendid path leads there past the chalets. It was a shame that not a single *Sennerin* was in sight! There were only men in the huts. An hour before the Greizer Hütte we overtook a guide who was also going there. Schneeberger was his name. A giant, strong, robust man, a proper model for a painter.

The Greizer Hütte has only *one* room; everything together: cattle, guest room and guide room! The hut was so well patronized that one could scarcely rest. The landlady was a little old woman, and to help her she had a 12-year-old girl, and since there are actually nasty tourists who think that because they are in a managed hut everything must be just as they wish, it was too much for the woman and she began to curse the young girl. The girl began to cry and the woman did the same. Then we took a hand! One went for water; another peeled potatoes, and I cleaned up the eating utensils.

It was not much use trying to sleep, for everything was damp. About three o'clock came the call to get up. The poor landlady had not even lain down, and the girl was sobbing in the hay. All in a line we went to the glacier, the Floitenkees, for today the Schwarzenstein was the objective. As we had to return to the hut we left there all our extra baggage. The glacier was quite crevassed, so that the greatest care was required. There is a hut on the summit of the Schwarzenstein, built by the guides, where wine may be had, which is very pleasant if one is a friend of wine. But I dared not drink any, for Dr. P. is an *enemy* of it.

The sun shone warmly, so that it was a pleasure to lie on the granite slabs and look out upon the beautiful glacier world. The distant view of various mountain groups (Olperer, Rieserferner, Venediger, Ötztal etc.) was superb. A Dutchman arrived with his wife, and interested me very much on account of his unnailed shoes and leather leggings.

Dr. P. had changed his original plan, and instead of returning to the Greizer Hütte in order to climb the Großer Löffler, he now wished to descend to the Berliner Hütte and ascend the Feldkopf–Zsigmondyspitze in the morning. He joined up with a group and I had to go back to the Greizer Hütte and get the baggage. But as it was dangerous to return alone I went to the Schwarzenstein Hütte in hopes of meeting someone there. But no one was to be found and I had to go alone. The tracks had almost the best of me, for the preceding day had been very warm and the steps had melted away. But just the same I arrived safely at the hut.

There were not as many people there as yesterday, so that it was just that much more comfortable. A young married couple approached me as to whether I would take them along to the Berliner Hütte. "Oh, certainly," I said, "but I must tell you honestly that I don't know the way, and about nine or ten o'clock I have to be at the climbing place for the Zsigmondyspitze."

Before going to bed a guide showed me the route for the morning. We started off about four o'clock. One must descend a little below the hut and then traverse the moraines in a northeasterly direction below the Mörchner and Ochsner. An indescribable route! No firm footing and up and down in addition. I had to hurry continually. The lady was already far behind me, but the man was even slower. There was also a chance of falling stones. When at last we reached the snow we at once gave a sigh of joy: "God be praised!"

When we came to the Mörchnerscharte I heard Dr. P. singing happily at the start of the climb. I made a sign that I was coming and was answered joyously. Then I took leave of the married couple. The man gave me ten kronen and wrote me a testimonial. I departed with a "Bergheil!" and was more than content at having earned ten kronen so easily. In a little while I was at the climb. A party with guide Schneeberger was already ahead of us; baggage was left below and we ascended merrily, being quite curious about the famous "Floiten Step." But all at once we were on the summit and had not even noticed the Step. From the start to the top had taken 32 minutes. (We were three: Dr. P., his bride and I.)

So we took a real comfortable rest as we were not pressed for time. During the descent we looked carefully again for the "Floiten Step," but still would not have found it if guide Schneeberger had not pointed it out. On the occasion of the first ascent of Zsigmondyspitze they had been obliged to spend a night out, while today one made it in half an hour. To be sure, there were no huts in those days.

At the Schwarzensee, on the way to the Berliner Hütte, we sat down and gazed upon the wonders of Nature: the lake is deep blue in colour and is surrounded by blocks of granite. On one side are glaciers, and from the lake downward the little flowers begin. And the different stones to be found there – it is indeed a pleasure to look upon so much beauty!

We went into the Berliner Hütte for refreshment. The hut is the second largest of the German–Austrian Alpine Club and occupies a fine position. But the hut did not please me. It is built almost like a big hotel, and I did not like the way the visitors went about in good shoes, white shirts and finery. In addition the showy people were presumptuous, for which the simpler tourists were obliged to suffer. Many people go to the huts who have not the least feeling for the loveliness of Nature; they come only because of the "good air."

Ten minutes farther on we spent the night in the private Alpenrose Hütte. There one is well put up, and it's much more homelike. A zither was played in the evening and songs were sung, and I lapped up almost a quarter of a litre too much Tyrolese wine along with it!

The 16th of August was a day of rest. I had my shoes repaired, for there are even cobblers and tailors at the Berliner Hütte. During the morning I went up to the Waxeck, and in the afternoon lay down in the grass. After that I helped Rosi the chambermaid hang out the washing. In reward she gave me a kiss. But it didn't come from the heart, for a kiss [Bussel] isn't of much consequence to a Zillerthal girl.

On the 17th of August guide Schneeberger arrived with his man, in readiness to take us down for the Großer Greiner. Just as we reached the glacier the sunlight broke through and gave promise of a fine day. For the first time I saw and picked edelraute and was delighted by the pleasant odour. We took a rest at the first rock-band and put on the rope. I had to laugh when I heard Schneeberger say to his gentleman: "How would you like a drink of Schnaps?" The man was an officer from Magdeburg. Both went ahead and we followed. The ridge is splendid to climb. Slabs, lying one over the other, look as if they would fall into the depths at any moment, but they hold like iron. Some parties, coming from the Furtschagel Hütte were on the summit; while we rested I glanced through the book and found the names of many acquaintances inscribed. The view was just as fine as we had had from Schwarzenstein and Feldkopf, except that one sees the Olperer and Hochfeiler, the loftiest uplift of the Zillerthal mountains, from a much nearer point of view.

We remained overnight in the Furtschagel Hütte; it was kept by the guide Alphons Hörhager, a real good fellow. In this hut as well there was music and song. I saw a magnificent sunset. The ice wall of the Hochfeiler made a deep impression upon me. Not far from the hut there was edelweiss with long stalks, and I picked some for remembrance.

On August 18th we visited the Mösele. As the other parties were leaving later we had to go alone, but Hörhager had kindly described the way to me exactly. About five o'clock we started out; one can see the greater part of the route right from the hut. First it leads up over the moraines, and I thought we would be easily across in half an hour. But I deceived myself, as it took more than an hour. At the end of the moraine we put on crampons; one of mine broke and I left it lying there. Then we put on the rope and started off.

In the beginning the glacier was much broken up; I went carefully ahead, testing every bridge. It was better beyond and we rested there. As no more tracks were to be seen we considered how we should proceed. The doctor thought to the left and I to the right. I was correct. Partly over rock and partly over ice we came to a little plateau. There were the tracks again. Soon we reached the ridge; one more crevasse had to be passed with care and then one goes easily to the summit. As we had luck with weather we could take a long, well-earned rest on the summit of the Mösele, the best reward of all for the fatigue of an ascent! Parties from the Wiener Hütte came up, so that again a large group was together on the peak, and it wasn't very pleasant to have so many people disturb one's contemplation.

Slowly and carefully we descended. The route demands even greater care in going down, for the snow had softened. We had lunch in the Fürtschagel Hütte and then went down the valley to the Dominikushütte. On the way a storm broke, with lightning and thunder. One crash after another, as if the peaks would fall. Dr. P. and his bride were a bit ahead. Cascades poured down the mountainsides and we were afraid that all the bridges would be torn away. A couple of telegraph poles were split through the middle and our ice axes began to sing. All at once I saw two axes lying in the path, and a packbasket, and a few metres farther on Dr. P., his bride and a porter were lying behind a huge boulder. Shuddering, they looked out. There was no room for me so I ran along. Other people were running behind me, among them a woman who kept shrieking: "Wait, oh, wait!" But no one listened to her, for in such a panic everyone looks after himself.

Before we reached the hut the storm lessened somewhat. I looked about, saw that my people were following, and kept on. When I reached the Dominikushütte I had had enough of running and so had the others. In spite of capes, everyone was wet to the skin. We changed our clothing and soon everything was all right again. Then a little "Kaiserfest" was arranged. The 18th of August is the birthday of our dear emperor, and many a full glass is drunk to Franzl (as the Tyrolese call him).

As no tour had been planned for the next day it became very jolly in the hut. The Germans present joined in, for it's an old story that if there is a chance to drink they don't neglect it! Finally we kept it up in the guides' room until four in the morning. But that was only allowed as long as we did not disturb anyone's sleep, and because the weather was bad and everybody could rest on the following day.

One gentleman remained with us guides; he also tucked away many a litre. But he only did that on account of Anna. She was an attractive girl. The nicest part was when she played the guitar and sang:

> Grün ist's halt überall,
> D'rum g'fallst mir gar so wohl,
> Mein Tyrol!

> [Now it's green everywhere once more;
> that's why my Tyrol makes me so happy.]

I, too, fell in love, but at the same time I noticed that Toni, who could play the zither so well, already had little Anna [Annerl] at his side. On this account the man from the city ordered one litre after another of "the best." But he didn't get anything out of it and was thoroughly laughed at, the boys saying to the girl: "If you could have fooled him once more he would have paid for one more litre!" ["Hatt'st ihn *no* mehr zum Narren halten sollen! Der hätt *no* an Liter zahlt!"]

It was snowing on August 19th and no chance of making an excursion. In the afternoon I went down to Breitlahner, known throughout the Zillerthal. I met a tourist from Neunkirchen, whom I had known at Hirschwang. He went back with me to the Dominikushütte. The caretakers there understand how to get on with tourists and are in high favour on that account.

During the evening it again became jolly in the guides' room, but sleep would not let me sit around and my eyes would close. I slept my "Katzenjammer" quite away and on the next day was myself again, quite ready to make a climb. But it looked hopeless. Through the window one saw snow and driving mist, and it began to be monotonous in the hut. Dr. P. occupied himself with official business and the day passed slowly. Most of the men and their guides departed, and since there seemed no chance for improvement in the weather Dr. P. and his bride also left the hut next morning. I waited for the mail; then I went also.

8

MY FIRST CLIMBS IN THE DOLOMITES

In the beginning my legs were quite stiff, but gradually I developed a more flexible tempo. It was quite necessary, for I must make the train in Sterzing about which Dr. P. had written. At noon I was on the Pfitscherjoch. After a short rest I descended by way of St. Jakob, Kematen and Wiesen to Sterzing. Between St. Jakob and Sterzing I made use of the post wagon. I will never forget that journey; to stand *that*, one must come of sturdy parents!

In Sterzing I had to wait an hour for the train. Across the Pfitscherjoch the weather was already much better. I should have gotten out at Waidbruck; I overlooked it and got off at the next station, asking the watchman when the next train went to Waidbruck. Tomorrow at five o'clock! So there was nothing to do but go on foot. It was pitch dark. After I had gone a little way I reached a large peasant house and did not know how to proceed. I called out but no one heard me except the dog. I did not trust myself any further, and went back to the station. There I lay down on a bench, set up the rucksack as a pillow, and my axe in my hand as a weapon in case anyone should attack me. Sleep did not last long, for I was awakened by a freight train and was so cold that I could rest no longer.

When the watchman saw how my whole body shook he took pity and gave me a cloak made out of sheepskin. After that I slept quite well, and when the first train came in the morning the watchman had to wake me up. About five o'clock I reached Waidbruck and met Dr. P. and his bride at the inn "zur Sonne." In the afternoon we went up on the meadow called the Vogelweide. At the sight of the splendid Dolomites my legs began to twitch for very joy of climbing.

Next morning we wandered through the Gröden Valley. At the beginning of the valley there is a customs office, where Dr. P. demanded three "cattle tickets." The official looked at him with staring eyes, and Dr. P. said: "Well, you can look all you want; that's all you'll get out of us!"

By way of St. Ulrich and St. Christina we arrived in rain at Wolkenstein, spending the night in the inn "zum Hirschen." At first the people did not seem to me to be very sympathetic. Some guides were standing by themselves and did not look quite friendly. It was easy to understand. Such bad weather, and now along comes a strange guide!

Naturally, I was questioned on all sides: Where I came from, what tours I had accomplished, why my party took no local guides etc. I told them that my gentleman did not wish to take a local guide and that both members of my party were quite expert. "Sure," they replied, "we believe that they climb well enough, for both have the proper build for it. But do you really think that *you* will find your way up without help?" Then I let out a sharp answer, in which I said: "Well, there won't be anyone else along to do it!"

With that the roof was on fire: "You are only a youngster, and don't understand. In the Dolomites it's not so easy as in the Zillerthal. In our mountains there are not so many tracks to be seen," and so on. I retreated, for I saw that I could not do much against so many. But the innkeeper was very kind to me, and at evening, when I started to bed, he said to the chambermaid: "Give the stranger a room to himself"; whereupon she took me to a nice little room up under the roof. I could not go right to sleep, for I was aroused against the guides. Compared with the Zillerthal people they were mean rogues.

When I awakened in the morning I saw to my dismay that there was snow down in the valley. For three or four days no excursion could be made. So Dr. P. and his bride wanted to go to Bozen and I was to remain here. "If the weather improves, telegraph us, Konrad! Then we'll come and do the Gross Fermeda Tower. Go up ahead and look over the way." Then he gave me some money and instructions to secure everything at the post office. I was much pleased by the trust. Finally, Dr. P. gave me the good advice not to drink too much and not to fight with anyone! The post wagon was filled with departing guests, and the innkeeper, the guides and those concerned with tourists looked sad as they started off.

• I took a walk to the Sellajoch and smoked my pipe, filled with fine English tobacco. I also gave some of it to the other guides, and one after another stuffed his pipe tightly with it, for the tobacco tasted good to everyone. But they were not more friendly toward me on this account, although I had hoped for it. With mending and sleeping the day passed. At evening a little group of singers got together. It was a joy to listen. It seemed remarkable to me that everything was sung in "high German," although the people at other times spoke nothing but the Gröden dialect.

It was the old story of weather: at evening it was clear, as on the day preceding, and bad again on the next morning. Next day I let everything be done for me and played the *gentleman*! I had coffee and the paper brought to my room, a cigar in addition and I stayed in bed until noon. In the afternoon I went to the Regensburger Hütte in order to get my bearings a little, and I was so pleased with it that I remained at the hut. It wouldn't take long, the woman told me, and I could help the servant with the wood; she promised me a supper for it. So I went in.

That evening it was very pleasant in the guides' room. Next morning I went to St. Christina to get the bread. I did not care much about doing it, but I could not say no. The natives all looked curiously at the strange porter. From St. Christina I took the opportunity of going on to Wolkenstein to ask for letters at the post office. I was not heavily laden, so the packing was not difficult. By noon I was back in the Regensburger Hütte.

I had scarcely eaten when the woman found a new job for me. I was to carry water. I went once for water but not a second time, for I did not know how to manage the Italian carrying machine, a yoke that fits over the shoulders, with a tub in front and behind. I brought in almost no water, having spilled most of it. She said quietly: "You will have to go twice more." But I told her that I had to look over the route to the Fermeda, and disappeared!

I looked for the start of the climb, finding it easily, but did not go far up, as it was wet, but instead walked to the Jochscharte and arrived late at the hut. There was almost no one there. On Saturday everyone goes down to the valley in order to attend church on Sunday, with the exception of guideless parties.

About four o'clock in the morning the woman awoke the servant. A little later she came to me: "Get up! It will soon be five o'clock. It's high time to go to church." To her astonishment I said that I didn't want to go to church. How she cursed me out! "Well, what a youngster! And he won't go to church. I would be ashamed." And she made such a disturbance that I had to get up. She said that she had orders from the Section not to allow a guide to loaf in the hut of a Sunday morning. I replied that religion was a private affair and no Section could do anything about it. But I could not prevail upon this point, and so I added that I did not know how it happened that I was obliged to spend a day of rest in going to church, one hour down and three hours back. "That is really too much for a day of rest, and it is just as well or perhaps better if I say my prayers in contemplation of God's out-of-doors!"

But she continued to fuss. At last she said, "Well, the matter is clear to me. Your home is not far from Vienna and there are the 'Soci.'" (She wanted to say "socialists," but could not pronounce it.) I laughed, left the hut and thought to myself: 'If she knew that I was a Lutheran, she would not have slept all night for terror!' In religious tolerance the Tyrolese, one can assert with confidence, are about 50 years behind.

At Wolkenstein I was pleased to receive news that my people would arrive that evening. I awaited them with joy. But as it was still not good enough, we did not go up to the hut until afternoon. Because of the unfavourable weather the hut was overflowing with tourists, and we had to look up a nearby hay hut, where everything was jolly because the natives were there who work in the hay. On the last day, when their work is done, they get wine and schnaps from the farmer, and the "hay dance" is held, for which we arrived just at the right moment There are songs, play and dances, and when it is over all crawl into the hay, men and women together. They sleep off their tipsiness, and next day say with their still-sleepy faces: "Well, now *yesterday* it was merry enough!"

Of course, it wasn't very pleasant for us that the people in their excitement would not go to sleep, but yet we dared not complain for we were lucky to be under a roof at all. That evening a fight occurred between myself and a guide from Taufers. He said to me: "What, *you* are going all alone with both those people on the Grosse Fermeda? Even the best local guides don't do such a thing. And you, you who don't understand the matter at all, you undertake it. It would really be for the best if someone knocked you down a couple of times."

Anger boiled in me and I began to shout: "Watch out that I don't give you something that will make you dream of the Devil! You aren't a local guide yourself and so the affair is no concern of yours. You are only trying to get in with the people here by such talk." Then everyone crowded me and threatened me with blows. In spite of it I could not be quieted for a while, and the quarrel lasted for some time.

Next morning we left the hut at seven o'clock. It takes one hour to the climb. As some parties were ahead, rucksacks, nailed boots and ice axes were already stowed in the cavern where we put ours as well. At first one mounts through a gorge. Some overhangs are not very easy; then one climbs out of the gorge and upward to the right on easier ground. Then it goes over levels to the well-known placque, which looked bad to me. It is to be sure exposed, but the holds are splendid: almost holes, they go in so far. At this point we were obliged to wait, for a party was descending. Then I accomplished it quickly, as the other guides were watching and would have been delighted if I had gotten stuck somewhere and could not proceed!

After the plaque there is a little gully, where some snow lay but could easily be avoided. At the notch on the ridge two young men were coming up; complaining of stonefall and snow. On the ridge, we walked upright and side by side, and I said: "Just hold firmly. There is no trouble about it!" And the others, who were on the summit, looked in wonder. I heard them speaking of "idiocy." In looking back, they were right, for it is really a ridge not without danger. If one loses his balance he will pull the others down into the depths.

On the peak I met two well-known men from Neunkirchen: H. and R. We talked about the Rax, and I said (to be sure, against the other guides) that one had just as good climbing on the Rax. But they would not believe that. Still, it is the old story: every merchant praises his own wares.

During the descent we were all together. But down the plaque, where the others roped off, I went without assistance, having let the others go ahead because we wanted to take some pictures. We caught up with them at the end of the climb and went together to the hut. The woman there was not yet willing to speak kindly to me, because I had not gone to church. That didn't matter to me, for I knew that I would not be in this hut again that summer, and I left them to their black looks.

Then I had to go to St. Christina, to inquire after letters. Dr. P. and his bride went to Wolkenstein, where I met them that evening. Next morning, we went over the Confinboden to the Seiser Alp. We took a rest in the hut at noon. Then I went ahead over the Molignon Pass to Grasleitenhütte to reserve beds. But I had no luck, for there is no reserving, but "he who comes first does the grinding." Fortunately there was room enough. In the hut there were some right jolly guides and a merry girl in charge. Next day we did the Grasleiten Tower by way of the Mühlsteiger Chimney. One man turned back because it was wet. (He was a well-known tourist, but I have forgotten his name. Once, in Switzerland he had been in a crevasse for 36 hours and was not frozen. Twelve guides pulled him out and received an enormous sum for doing it.)

Ahead of me climbed guide Schroffenegger, of Tiers. On the difficult places he offered me the rope, which I declined with thanks. There are some places which are just not easy, but for a climber who has strength in his arms it is nothing. The last bit below the summit is unpleasant, as it is brittle and looks quite bad and unsafe. There is not much room on the peak, but for this very reason there is a splendid view down to the Bärenloch and into the Grasleiten Valley. Mist had covered the rest.

During the descent we were all together and exercised like monkeys down through the chimneys. We just made out with the weather, for when we reached Grasleitenhütte the storm broke and a regular waterfall streamed through the chimneys which we had vacated a few minutes before! Now a glass of wine went to the spot. As is always the case, one heard here nothing but complaints about the weather. But soon there was a different humour among the guides. One took the guitar, another a harmonica, and a third shouted: "Waitress!" – and the party began. About five o'clock the weather improved and we decided to go on to Vajolethütte. After a quarter of an hour I noticed that I had forgotten the rope and had to go back. Then a guide went along, but I didn't catch up again with Dr. P.

It was pitch dark when we arrived at the hut. Dr. and Mrs. P. were not there and no post wagon had departed. What should I do? It was dark and I was here for the first time. But the landlady advised me to remain and the people would surely arrive in the morning. I thought too that they would take a day of rest, and so I stayed at the hut. But I could not sleep, being troubled by thought as to where my man could be. Next morning the sun was smiling and excursions were being arranged and rucksacks packed. What should I do?

Guide Schroffenegger was taking a gentleman up the Delago Tower, and as the man was strong and not a remarkable climber, he said to me: "Come along. You will learn the route and I will give you 30 kronen." I was happy about that, not on account of the money but because he showed his confidence in me, a stranger, to make this unknown tour with him. When we were about 300 to 400 metres from the hut I heard a familiar voice. It was Dr. P.!

He had come up from Perra, and I must go back. I did not like it much. Now it would be argued, how it happened that we did not meet yesterday. I blamed him, and he declared it my fault, and at last I was given a lecture which depressed me. Then Dr. P. and his bride conversed in English as to which of them should go with me on the Delago Tower, and the decision fell upon the lady. In a few minutes we hurried after Schroffenegger and his man. They waited for us at the climbing place. The climbing shoes were put on, the rope arranged, and a few minutes later friend Schroffenegger puffed ahead. Then his man went, whom he had almost pulled through the air. I climbed right behind, and then came the English lady. It was a pleasure to see how well and rapidly she climbed. Soon we stood below the most difficult chimney. A *stemmen* chimney, only to be done with back and feet, without a single handhold. In spite of this the chimney is really not so dangerous, for if one loses his strength, one falls into the crack and bumps one's head at the very worst.

I said to the guide: "You can let me go ahead. I want to do a bit now!" but he would not stop, but went up gasping. Up above one has a good position. Now I followed and was glad to take hold of the rope. Of course, I did not pull, but it required my whole strength to keep from being a dead weight. Then we took a little drink on the quiet and caught our wind. After that he let the gentleman come up and heaved mightily on the rope. The guide said: "Don't pull right away. He ought to hang for a little bit, like a thief on the gallows unable to help himself until Messieurs les Guides take a hand!" Thus we began the "mealsack technique." In a short time he lay at our feet, panting like a hunting dog. I went down a couple of steps to say a few words to the lady, because one can't handle a woman like a man, and she requested not to be dragged up. Up until the last two metres she worked very well. But finally her strength failed and I heard for the first time: "Konradl, hold now; hold now!" The worst was over, and a good rest was taken on the ledge.

But not for long did we sit so quietly, as a sighing wind arose with un-pleasant sound. Some minutes later lightning and thunder followed, so that one would have believed that the mountains might fall. Great hailstones pelted down. We pressed against the wall. Schroffenegger smoked his little pipe with great attention, his man was silent and pressed his face against the rocks, but the English lady looked about composedly. I was the first to feel the cold, for I had on only thin clothing and every raindrop went through to the skin. We saw lightning strike the Rosengarten, the summit book and the iron rod, we heard stones fall as the lightning flashed some hundreds of metres down in the depths – then came a clap of thunder that went through our marrow and bones. I began to have gooseflesh! One can hardly describe what a feeling that is.

For three hours the storm bound us in the same spot. As soon as it stopped we took council as to what we should do. I did not know the tour and must accept Schroffenegger's judgment when he advised retreat. Everything was slippery, and the rope had become stiff from being wet. Still we reached the stoneheap without misadventure, where it was indeed a pleasure to put on nailed boots. When we arrived at the "Gartl" we looked about and saw how beautiful and blue the sky was once more. In a few minutes it had become a fine day. But they didn't want to repeat the climb, for everything was wet through, and it was just as well that we didn't go back. For, upon our arrival in the hut, it rained again with a vengeance.

Formerly, when I heard about anyone who had been up the Delago Tower, I held him in respect. But now I knew what the affair was. It is a tour on the border of human possibilities, but good wishes are only required for the person who goes first, whether he be guide or tourist; the second person always gets up if the first has strength enough to pull him up like a stick of wood (as has often been the case).

Once I read in the paper: "Mealsack technique on the Delago Tower." A man described how he had been handled in this fashion. He was an honest fellow to tell everything truly which most the Delago climbers hide.

Next day we wanted to try the expedition again, but to our sorrow we saw the majestic King of the Rocks in winter costume, and as the vacation time was up, we must take leave of the charming Vajolethütte and go to Perra. There Dr. P. took a carriage and returned to Bozen. I had to go to Campitello to get some letters, and then went afoot to Bozen by way of the Karersee. As I could not do it in a single day, I spent the night in Welschnofen and went on next morning.

It was the 6th of September and the General Assembly of the German–Austrian Alpine Club. I heard a few of the speeches and met many friends, even some from Reichenau. At noon we boarded the train, which would take us home. At Franzensfeste I took leave of Dr. and Mrs. P.

It nearly broke my heart, for when one has been with the same people for three weeks and knows that they have trusted their lives with him, it isn't very easy to separate one from the other.

9

THE MOUNTAIN GUIDE AS SOLDIER

I was obliged to spend the night in Villach and next day reached Naßwald, where I was joyfully awaited by my mother and brothers and sisters. September 8th was a holiday and I went to Hirschwang in great expectation. To be sure I had had but three weeks' leave and had been absent for eight. Would I again be allowed to work? I had, of course, thought up an excuse, and had written a letter of regret from Gstatterboden in which I stated that I had an injured foot and was detained on account of it. But I was not sure that they believed me.

In Weichtal I met the superintendent and asked whether I might go to work again. "Certainly," he said, "and how's your foot?" I told him that it was almost well. A few days later we met at work and when he said "You were all right all the time," I begged his pardon and told him it had been a lie of necessity. If my master had not been a great friend of Nature (and therefore lenient with me), I wouldn't have been able to count on working anymore.

During the last week of September, to my surprise, there came the military summons for eight weeks. As it had been so long in arriving, I really believed that perhaps it might not be forthcoming. On October 2nd I went once again to the Pfannl Chimney, this time with Dr. B., and it was a good lesson. If by chance there had not been two young fellows at hand, I would not have been able to get him up by myself. But, for the two youngsters, it was highly amusing to pull and to make fun of half-simple Dr. B. Just the same I made 24 kronen.

On October 3rd, at seven in the morning, I must be in the Prater barracks, so I had to travel to Vienna on October 2nd. I had already taken leave of my people on October 1st, and so did not go back after the tour, but marched in just as I came from the Rax. In Vienna I bought a trunk, for I had only my rucksack, linen and a brush with me; nothing else. Somewhat troubled, I went across the Prater to the barracks. There we had to wait in the court and had a medical examination. Then there were evasions! This hurt one fellow and that another, but only a couple had enough luck to be able to go home.

At last it came down to equipping. All the clothing was torn and dirty, for the very worst is given out to the reserves. No one knew what to do with the straps. The old servants had a good day, since they made tips. They helped everyone and everybody who could gave them something. But I paid up properly, for when I had dressed and packed my knapsack, I found there was not a cent left in my civilian clothes. Nothing else was possible but that someone had stolen it from me! I announced this at once, but nothing made an appearance. Now I was without a krone in money and had not a single acquaintance who could help me. From the very beginning I had had no pleasure in military things and now this had happened.

A corporal who knew me came up and asked me how it was on the Rax. I told him a few things and also of my misfortune. He took me into his company and I thought to myself that now I had an ally. And he really was one.

By cattle train we were taken to Bruck an der Leitha. It was dark and the fallen leaves made such a noise under our feet that, as we marched into camp, no one could understand a single word. Next day everything was divided up. I stayed as "boots" to my corporal, as I had no cleaning things of my own. To be sure they could be bought, but I had no money. The corporal gave me enough for a postage stamp and I wrote to my friend Leopold K. at Hirschwang to send me six kronen.

Before and after meals my comrades ran to the cantine to quiet their hunger. It was lucky for me that they did not eat the commissary bread (in the beginning, while their money lasted) and gave it to me. It was hardest for me when the man with little sausages arrived on the field so that one could buy some during rest periods. Everyone was hungry after the unaccustomed exertions. One fellow bought himself three pairs of sausages at a time; another, two jugs of beer and two buns, and when he was through was still hungry. I could not buy anything and had to wait for the regular mealtime. Then I would search all corners of the camp for bread.

For three or four days I had quite a passion for all that had to do with knowledge. But when I heard the usual expressions of the officers, like dogs' food, cannon-fodder and all possible names from the animal world, the pleasure and the zeal were finished. I said to myself: 'A defender of the Fatherland is a man of honour all the same, but he is treated like cattle and called all sorts of names except human ones! How could one have any joy, if in case of war he must risk his life for his country, under such treatment?' And from that day on I really was one of the beasts. Unthinking and stolid, I stood in rank and file.

The corporal was rather a good chap. When he was angry he said to me: "I can't understand it! How can anyone act so stupidly? Look after it a little or the lieutenant will be down on me again." *That* officer was really an inhuman creature! He had a starved look, and the poor soldiers suffer when such a one doesn't thrive. Later on I was put into another company and was no longer near my friendly corporal. Then for the first time my troubles really began. My only luck had been that I was "boots" to the corporal, so that in barracks I was at least safe from mistreatment. Of those things that had to be endured one can't even begin to write, for there was no end of them. Only one incident need be related, concerning the time when I wanted to kill a lance corporal.

Once the worst of the company were taken out and turned over to the inhuman lance corporal with the words: "Get after this mob and don't leave the dogs their skins." And he was a past master at punishing people. We had to follow him into a thicket where nothing could be seen, for the first lieutenant or the major would not have dared to let it be observed.

We were placed at attention and had to repeat after him the following: "Honoured lance corporal, we dutifully request you to punish the life out of us!" We had to repeat that at least 50 times. Then he said: "I assure you that I will do so to the best of my ability, and if anyone makes complaint he will see what happens to him."

First we had to make knee bends until everyone fell to the ground from fatigue. Then there was a rest of five minutes, during which he sarcastically inquired whether the dear recruits were enjoying it, and one had to say "Yes," because one is of course a defender of the Fatherland!

Then came the attack exercises, two or three hundred times, until sweat ran down the face as if one came from a bath. After a short rest the worst came. We had to go "up" and "down" on a dirt pile. The commands were given: "Up!" "Down!" "Up!" "Down!" and everyone must throw himself down forcefully so that it could be *heard* distinctly, and there was no escape.

First it was done on the dirt, and then on the stones. During this drill nearly everyone began to cry, all except three of us. Anger did not allow me to. But as we three did not shed tears, the others were all allowed to cease while we had to keep on playing the game, with the extra pleasantry that the officer went behind and gave each a push with a rifle so that one fell down. And at "Up" he struck us on the heads with his boot. Anger rose in me so terribly that I thought to myself in this torment: 'As soon as he lets us up I'll run him through with the bayonet and make my escape, so that we shall all be rid of him.' I made a movement and he shouted: "At rest!"

Then the thought went through my head that it would last only another month and I could stick it out that long. But if I had had three years to serve, I probably would have done the deed; naturally I would then have made away with myself.

I will write no longer of things that are over, for they were too unmanly. I think that not even animals that are trained for circus exhibitions receive such beastly treatment. At last my money affairs improved, for I received some from several places. But I did not look at it often, as I was apt to throw the whole company out of step. Once I hid behind a manure pile, and they thought I was in disgrace. That didn't matter to me. I took out my pipe and lay down in the grass. I thought how fine it would be to lie below the rocks once more instead of, as now, beside the dunghill.

Naturally, when I came back, there was plenty of laughter, and I was received with the words: "Aren't you ashamed? No one is allowed back of the manure pile. You are the first. You ought to be ashamed." "He wants to be a Man of Nature," called out a stupid corporal. I thought to myself: 'That's true, but not as a soldier.'

That evening a great crowd of soldiers came into our room to see "the most stupid fellow in camp," and everyone asked me what I did and where I came from. Someone remarked: "He really don't look so dumb. He's doing it on purpose." Another suggested: "He'll soon get over that if he has to stay here after the rest of us go home." One of the soldiers was from Edlach. I often cleaned up for him and he had bought beer for me. I sometimes got on the good side of him by saying: "Well, you are a soldier! If I could only march as well as you." I always said that, when I was thirsty. It didn't fail often, and most of the time it meant a jug of beer for me. But when I had to go to the manure pile it was all over; he was bothered and angry about me. He said that he would tell the girls in Naßwald what kind of a soldier I was. That was all the same to me.

At last the day of release arrived. It was November 25, 1904. I will not forget that joyful day! We spent the night in Schwadorf. We were stuck into a shed and had to lie in the straw without covering. Everyone was so cold that our teeth chattered, and so we left our camp about eleven o'clock at night and fled to an inn, and from there to a bakery where it was nice and warm. On November 26th, my name day, we arrived in Vienna at noon. That was a racket and a noise! Even I took part in it.

A comrade owed me two kronen and promised me that his uncle was awaiting him and that he would give me the money at once. But there was no uncle and I had not a bit of money and must get home. It came to my mind that I should look up Dr. Sch. and borrow some. I looked around a long time before finding his house. I rang and the Bohemian maid answered. "Is the doctor at home?" "No, only his wife; what do you want?" "Tell her I have been mustered out today and have not enough money to get home. My name is Konrad Kain, mountain guide of the Rax." The maid returned with none too cheerful news: "The gracious lady can't get at the cash because the doctor took the key with him and won't be back until ten o'clock. But you wait because the lady wants to speak to you."

In a little while I went in. She came toward me kindly and asked what she could do for me. But after what the maid had said to me I could not mention again my need of money. The lady offered me tea and ham, and filled my pockets with good cigars. With an uncomfortable feeling I departed.

Then I went to the Weyringergasse. A man lived there who had once given me a knife when he could not pay all the expenses of a trip. When I got there he was not at home but his mother was. I told her the story and she asked me how much money I needed. "One krone." She gave it to me and I went cheerfully to the South Station. When I tried to buy my ticket I had about six hellers too little and didn't get it. I went to a man who stood beside the booth and asked him to buy my cigars as I had not enough money for the journey. He took two cigars and gave me ten hellers. I was saved!

About eleven o'clock I reached Payerbach and went to Hirschwang. Two work companions were still up. They cooked tea and meat for me, and I told them my experiences. Next morning I went to the office and presented myself to the new superintendent. To my astonishment he gave me my papers and said: "I haven't any work for you." I protested violently: "What, two years I have worked here in the quarry, and now when I come from the army and need work so badly I am thrown out?"

But cursing didn't help. I went on, almost in tears. On the way it occurred to me that once upon a time a famous doctor told me that if I needed anything of Baron H., the owner of the quarry, I should turn to him. I wrote to the doctor, and a few days later the news came that I might resume my work at the quarry, but the guiding had to stop. I made the promise, but of course could not keep it. The following Monday I had to guide a man over the Teufelsbadstube, and when I returned to Hirschwang I was dismissed, and the baron said: "I really can't use such people who have more friends in Vienna than I."

On Sylvester Day I packed my things and went to Eichgraben, where I hoped to find work at the second aqueduct. Wearily I carried my burden to Hohenberg, on the railway. My money had been counted with care. The journey cost 2.30 kronen and a few kronen were left. In St. Pölten, by mistake, I got into an express train that did not stop at Eichgraben. There was a great discussion. I would have to pay for it. But when they saw that I emptied all my pockets and had nothing more they took pity on me, and one of the people took up a collection for me. I was in Second Class and received almost four kronen.

In Hütteldorf the conductor took me to the station master and asked him to let me ride back, as I was a poor boy. At midnight I reached Eichgraben; it was quite dark. I rang time after time at inns, but there was no place for me to spend the night. I put up quite an argument with one of the people, so he gave me a place – in a stable! I spent New Year's Eve of 1905 in an ox stall. Happy New Year!

CHAPTER III

(1905)

▲

1

GOOD AND BAD TIMES

On January 2nd I began work on one of the galleries. My companion was an Italian and we got on well together. The following weeks I was put with Slovaks, and next with Germans, among whom I actually found friends. Then quarrels began. The pay was quite good for eight hours of work, although it is dangerous business under the earth. For me, always accustomed to the fresh air, it was an imprisonment!

On Sundays skiers came frequently to Eichgraben. Once I followed some of them and asked them pleasantly whether I might accompany them for a little way. I showed them how I could go on the "boards." From this day on I became homesick and the work in the pit pleased me no longer. Besides, my co-workers were always fighting and drunk most of the time. I quit and went to Buchenstuben for the new road work.

When I arrived there it had snowed so hard that all work had to be suspended. More than a hundred men were out of employment. Three of us went by way of Annaberg and Wienerbruck to Mariazell. As my money was at an end, I took to shovelling snow, which was better than nothing. An innkeeper let us have a room. Keep 1.20 kronen; bed 20 hellers. My pay was two kronen. I stayed four days in Mariazell, then went home by way of Kernhof and Hohenberg.

On the way I met a man with a nine-year-old boy, whom I joined. The man had been at work in Frankenfels, but had been dismissed because of the great snowfall. A sad case! We spent the night with a farmer in Kernhof, and the poor fellow had to explain why he was wandering around with his boy, seeking work. I went outside, for I could not stand the noise and did not want to see the man with tears running down his face.

66

From Kernhof I crossed the Ochsensattel to Schwarzau. To go one kilometre, which one usually does in ten minutes, I took almost an hour in the deep snow. At last I came to a stretch which had been shovelled out. I took a rest in a hut with the workmen, who were at their noon meal. I gazed sadly upon the people, who seized their food so eagerly. Well, I was hungry too and couldn't satisfy it. Proceeding farther, I met two relatives of mine who were working with wood on the road. They told me to go into their house and cook myself something. With great joy I did so, made a fine pancake and coffee, and stayed overnight. Next morning I continued homeward.

On account of the deep snow on the road I found work at once in Naßwald. But I didn't tell anyone what I had been doing in the days just passed. On the next Sunday I took my skis and went off early, to climb over the Nass ravine and the Ameisbühel to the Schneealpe. More on account of chamois, however, than with the pleasure of a tourist. When I went out in the morning it did not occur to me that it would be a fateful day. The weather was beautiful and clear, but very cold. I went along the Mitterberg–Schneid, and when I heard chamois whistling I went too far out on the cornice. A little crack and the cornice broke, and I went down head over heels – fortunately always *behind* the avalanche. I went over a rock, a ski broke in half and the other flew into the depths. The rucksack was left behind. 'Now I am lost!' said I to myself and tumbled over the avalanche. Then the thing stopped in a hole. I looked in vain for my rucksack, and my heart fluttered: my provisions and my guiding-book, in which I had such good recommendations – all were gone. What should I do?

There I sat without skis, without snowshoes in a wooded valley. I looked over the ground but it was impossible, for I broke in wherever I stepped. So I tried rolling and made some progress. But I was too tired. The idea came to me of tying on brush and branches so that I would not break through so much. Luckily I had a string in my pocket. For three hours I slid along in this manner. At the Ochsenhalter Hütte I took a rest; it was half past ten. From this point it was not very far home, but I could not wade uphill through the snow and had to go down through the valley. I could scarcely take 20 steps without resting for several minutes.

About six o'clock I reached the last house of Steinalpl – it is called "beim Edelbacher." From there on I had old tracks as far as the Goldgrubhöhe. My best fortune was that the moon shone a little. Every step was slower than the last. I began to eat snow and became so feeble that I really wondered whether I should have strength enough to reach the Ameis meadow. At midnight I arrived, quite exhausted. I aroused myself, however, with the confident thought I could reach home from there.

Because of my great fatigue I needed four hours more to do it. From worrying about me my poor mother had not been able to sleep; she thought that the keepers had caught me and taken me away. Next morning I was not in condition to get up. I had frightful nausea, which certainly came from eating snow. I did not regret the broken ski, but only the loss of my tour book. I related my misfortunes to my friends in Naßwald, but was only laughed at and told that I was a fool.

I occupied myself in the following week with snow shovelling in fearsomely cold weather. Sunday I could do no more than stay at home and fix up my other pair of skis. Just the same it was fine to rest properly for a day, but the entire week that followed was depressing. I worked as assistant to the foresters until lovely spring came once more. Then there was climbing for me again.

Sunday, April 2nd, I did the Stadlwand ridge with a gentleman. Weather and view were splendid. The man could not get over the ordinary alpine jackdaws, which take bits of food from one's hand. Later in the spring I went to the "re-forestation" at Kaiserbrunn, where things were quite gay. Old school-friends! Our exuberance often went beyond proper limits. On one of the Sundays I was reserved by two men, whom I awaited in Kaiserbrunn. As an easy climb we first took the Akademik route. When we were above the so-called "Schinder," I heard happy shouting on the lower Zimmer route, and when we arrived I called up: "How is it? Are the rocks wet?" The answer came down in a tipsy dialect: "Sure they are! We've been here two hours already and can't get up." They were just at the "Buch," where the most difficult place is. I saw how each in turn tried to go up the wall but always had to go back, and at last I shouted: "It isn't right to endanger my men! Hold still. I will go up the Akademik route and down the upper Zimmer climb and will throw the rope to you." And so I went on climbing with my two gentlemen.

Halfway, one of my men shouted over to ask them how it was going. "Pretty good, but we haven't a match, and a cigarette right now wouldn't be so bad." I saw at once that they were a thankless lot, and my opinion was later confirmed. In an hour and a half we had finished the Akademik, and in another hour were at the start of the Preinthaler route. After a little rest we went down rapidly, traversing to the outlet of the lower Zimmer climb. I roped my men down, left them in a safe place, went to the two tourists and threw them the rope. One fastened himself on and I helped him up. When he stood beside me he said curtly: "Thank you," and then pulled up his companion. I took both of them to my party. Sitting opposite, the youths told of how cold they had been etc., but there was no mention of gratitude. They went with us into the Weich Valley. On the way I said to my men: "You will see that they will not acknowledge that they owe us any thanks."

In the Weichtal we had plenty of refreshments and when the coach came along they all got in and, with a brief goodbye, were off. I wrote to one of my gentlemen and asked him whether the youngsters had thanked him and his friend. "No," came the answer, and "Konrad, you certainly know men!" There was no question of payment, and I wouldn't have taken anything for I saw that they were poor devils; but they might have expressed their hearty thanks.

On that day I had seen a dead chamois lying above the Preinthaler route. I could not go after it, as I had the two tourists to care for. Now I was sorry. Since they were so thankless they might just as well have waited an extra hour.

Early on Monday morning I went once more with my fellow workers to Kaiserbrunn. At the beginning of work the head forester came and asked: "Where was Kain yesterday?" I told him briefly. "Didn't you find anything?" Then I told him of the chamois. "Do you think he still has a beard?" he asked. "I'm pretty sure of it," I replied. That gave the forester no peace, so he said: "Go up this afternoon, look for it and bring me the hairs." My heart leaped for joy, and after lunch I went up the Staudengraben and down the Preinthaler climb as far as the "Buch." When I reached the chamois I saw that the head was missing, and my happiness departed. I wanted to go away, but I was disturbed and looked for the beard. There it was! So I tied up my nose and mouth and went to work.

The hairs were coal black and the frost was pure white. I did not care much to bring the hairs to the forester; 'What's to be done?' I sat down at some distance from the chamois and tried to think of an excuse. A real good idea came to me. I took out my knife, cut the hairs of five-centimetre length, pulled them out, wrapped them up in paper and took them to the forester, who was awaiting me with expectation.

"Well, what's this?" I showed him the hairs I had pulled out, and began at once to blame the tourists. The forester cursed roundly; I laughed till I shook, thinking that tourists were, after all, rather useful. I hid the beard under a stone beside the hut, so that none of my friends would discover it. Next day we wandered with sacks and packs to the Knofel plateau. The forester was not pleased about the beard, and I had almost given myself away with my heedless laughter. A friend noticed it and remarked: "I'm not sure this will be the end of the 'tourist.'"

We stayed in the game keeper's hut on the Knofel plateau. It was an unforgettable day. Not much work, fine weather, and spring besides, with every tree and bush, down to the tiniest flower, rejoicing to look about in the sunlight after the long sleep of winter. Then the happy birds, and the white hares that came every night on the meadow in front of the hut, although they were frightened by the wicked fellows and their lives put in danger. I was one of those bad boys!

Twice we went through the lovely forest, along the almost level path to Lakaboden, one of the finest and most silent woods in the entire region. When we had to go back to the valley, none of us was lighthearted, although the others were not such great friends of Nature as I. But everyone who experiences such splendid days on the heights must take pleasure in Nature.

On Sunday I did the lower Zimmer climb with Dr. and Mrs. Sch., and afterward the upper route. At the crack tears were almost shed, for the woman was too heavy and only got up with great strain and difficulty. To the annoyance of the lady, two young men were there watching, and one remarked: "Today I would certainly like to be Konradl." (That was my nickname.) But in Otto-Schutzhaus, where the couple met friends, the woman forgot all unpleasantness, and when someone inquired how the trip had gone, she replied: "Oh, fine! Only the crack is a little narrow," and lifted her eyes to me as if to say: "Isn't it?"

In the afternoon I took three men over the Karl Berger route, and then went by way of the Scheib forest and the Habsburg-Haus to Naßwald. During the following week we were busy with our work in the Stadlwand cirque; it was the last week and everything was very jolly. Once I scared my friends by climbing up the "chamois pinnacle," where during the hunts it was often said that wounded chamois fled, so that no one could follow. I got up the place all right, but there were no chamois heads to be seen. During the descent I had to take off my shoes, but my friends did not think I could get down without them. They thought every minute that I would fall, but that was because all difficulties look worse from below.

Two days were spent at work on the roped place of the Wachthüttel ridge, and we finished the last bit on Saturday. It was May 14th. On May 15th I guided Dr. P. over the Wiener Neustadt climb. He had not yet tried such a difficult trip on the Rax. For the Pentecost holidays I was engaged by two men for the Enns Valley. Dr. P. invited himself along. I was able to arrange it so that he could accompany us. As always I was happy to be going to the Enns Valley. On the Saturday of Pentecost I went at an early hour over the Nass ridge to Kapellen and on by train. The weather was not of the best, and when I reached St. Michael it rained as hard as it could. Although Gstatterboden is quite a stormy corner the heavens were blue by the time of my arrival. I waited longingly for the train. It came, and it was just as if I were at home in the Höllenthal: full of friends! My three men were there as well. Dr. P. introduced himself to the other two and thanked them for allowing him to join them.

About four in the morning we left for the north wall of the Planspitze. It was sultry and misty as we went up through the forest. Everyone said it would rain. I took the opposite side. Naturally! It was for my own good. Because of the holiday train there was a formidable crowd of people. At the foot of the north wall there were six young fellows of whom I inquired which route they were doing. "Pichl route." I told my men to be careful and stay right behind me as there was danger of stonefall above, and farther on the route is easy to miss. We roped up. Dr. B. behind me, then Dr. P., whom I at once christened "guide-aspirant," although I was not an authorized guide myself. Dr. W. came last. We climbed up rapidly, for I only had to look after one man with such an expert assistant along.

It began to rain at the Plattenschuss, and we had to wait for the youngsters, who didn't come for quite a while. Again I made the request that they join us. First we had to give them a hand at the plaque and again at the traverse. Then, as it went more easily, we did not have to look after them so much. We came to a corner and waited for them. They did not arrive. One of the gentlemen said: "There was nothing else to do, they had to turn back." I went out and called. Then J. heard that the young men had lost the track. I climbed down to them and put them on the proper way. At two other difficult places we waited and gave them the rope. At the last of these I said: "Look, one must go up through this gully. Then it's all over and nothing more can happen. We are going right ahead, otherwise we will be chilled." As a matter of fact we were cold from the long waiting.

About half past two we reached Heß-hütte, which of course was filled with drenched tourists. When the conversation turned on the six young men it came out that they were quite inexperienced. Two of them had been a couple of times on the Rax, the others only on the climbing school of Peilstein. Five, six, seven – eight o'clock came and the six fellows did not arrive. I considered the possibility of their death, and thought that we should still wait a little while. At last they arrived about half past eight. The keeper of Heß-hütte heard the following story when their friends, who had so anxiously waited, inquired where they had been so long: "Well, listen," said one, "there was a guided party ahead that held us up, otherwise we would have been here by noon!" The keeper (my friend Lechner) did not know what to do. He did not dare to tell me or there would have been an argument and a scandal, and that would not be pleasant for him as keeper of the hut. (He did not inform me of the affair for several days.)

As for sleeping during such festive days one can well imagine! On the second day we wanted to do the ridge from the Hochthor to the Ödstein, but new snow spoiled our plans and there was nothing to do but to go by way of Johnsbach to the station. During this trip Dr. P. promised to take me with him to Switzerland! That was indeed a day of happiness for me.

On Tuesday, Lechner and I went with Dr. and Mrs. L. over the Petern route on the Planspitze. It was a very pleasant and agreeable party, for snow lay where otherwise it is very toilsome. Next day I made the same tour with Miss B. This time it was not so nice. In the first place I had a heavy rucksack to carry, and then the girl got sick, so much so that she had to take some medicine at the beginning of the ascent. On the crest things improved, so that we could go on to the Planspitze. We met five men, of whom two were quite exhausted. During the descent we overtook another and were much entertained by him in Heß-hütte.

There was a very vain fellow there who even wanted a shave in the hut. As no one else was about I had to be the master of ceremonies, but I dare not call myself "master" for I gave him two real good cuts!

2

THROUGH THE HOLE ON THE TRISSELWAND

Next day I was to go with Miss B. to Altaussee. For several years she had planned a first ascent of the Trisselwand by way of the Tauben-Ofen but had never found anyone in Aussee who would go with her.

I got out at the Kitzerhof Inn and inquired whether anybody had been up to the Tauben-Ofen. Someone said: "Yes, poachers!" Others looked at me – I don't know just exactly how to describe it – and replied: "No human being can go up there; it's impossible." When I heard that, I answered: "Well, just the same I'm going to try it." (For I could easily see from the valley that it was not so very difficult.)

Then I went for information to an authorized guide, and did it properly. I asked him to please tell me some things, and listened patiently while he told me he was the best of mountain climbers, and God knows what else. Then I began to talk and told him that I wanted to do the Trisselwand by way of the Hole. He got angry. He looked me over from head to foot, and pushed himself forward with voice rising: "None of us here have climbed up there, and you arrive for the first time, understand nothing about it and want to go up? You will roll right down into the pebbles." (Then I knew at once with what sort of fellow I had to do.) "I'll try all the same," I said, "and now we'll talk of something else." But he continually renewed the argument, and others backed him up. Finally, all tourists were called fools!

Next day I went for the young lady. But as she was sick in bed she could not go with me. So I walked alone along the edge of the lovely blue lake as far as Seewiese, and from there directly up through the woods to the "chamois place" [Gamsstell] as the natives call it. Then along the Trisselwand to the right to a huge fan of rubbish that one can plainly see from Altaussee, and over turf-covered walls to a ledge. From this point up a little cliff, several metres high, to a level ground at the Hole (which peasants call the "Tauben-Ofen" – the pigeons' stove).

People assert that the hole must go in deep because it looks black, but such is not the case. One can climb down through a tunnel for five or seven metres and emerge at the left side. Of course, one can't see that from below. Then the route will go over a ledge to the ridge. This is the hardest spot. Farther on it goes rather easily to the split, and then up the heights of the Trisselwand.

The view was splendid: a lake in every direction, and lovely vegetation besides. I must confess that it pleased me greatly to be alone once more in mountains that were new to me! During the descent I used the Ochsen route as far as the saddle and then down to the lake. I described the trip exactly to the lady, and she begged me to do it with no one until she had been up. I promised and went home.

Next evening I went to Kaiserbrunn, where my "aspirant," Dr. P., awaited me. Nothing difficult was accomplished on the following day, only the Vienna Alpine Club route. We chatted pleasantly up to the beginning of the ascent. The doctor and his bride put on *Kletterschuhe*, as the rest of the way required care. The climb is not hard, but a little later we would have lost our lives if Dr. P. had not secured the rope on a tree. I went across a grassy ledge, about four metres in length; while I was in the middle, it broke under my feet and I was hanging on the rope. For the first time! It was not for lack of care; it was an accident of Nature. I soon recovered myself and the excursion was continued.

At the end of it we took a good rest, and then selected, since it was very warm, the shady Staudengraben for our descent. Again a lovely day in the mountains was over.

Next morning we did the Wiener Neustadt climb. The bride came along. I was astonished how she ascended the second chimney without assistance, a place where most men require help. It was the Sunday on which the third announcement of the wedding had been made. Quite a lot was said about the wedding tour and what excursions would be made. On parting Dr. P. said to me: "Konrad, get things ready. We start next week! For Tyrol and Switzerland!"

3

THE WEDDING TRIP OF DR. AND MRS. P.

On June 22nd I left Naßwald and went over the Nass ridge with a thousand joyous thoughts. We were to meet in Tiers.[9] It was a terribly long ride in the excursion train to Villach. A woman with three children, who sat in my compartment, began to cry. I asked her about her distress and she told me briefly that she was being sent from the parish of Gottschee to Germany to fetch the children and bring them to Gottschee, where they lived. Their mother was dead and their father had disappeared. Now they had no money with which to reach Gottschee. Some good-hearted people collected a few kronen for the poor woman.

In Villach a long stop was made and I bought her and the children their supper. Then I had to get a ticket to Blumau (near Bozen). I discovered that I had been too generous and had only 40 hellers left.

At eight o'clock in the morning I arrived at Blumau. I left a message with the doorkeeper to tell the gentleman, who would arrive with his wife, that the "guide" had gone on ahead. I gave him 20 hellers, which still left me 20 for breakfast. In my pocket I found a couple more hellers. That made things easier. I walked into the nearest inn. For the first time in my life I asked how much the coffee cost. The waitress looked at me in astonishment and said: "Twenty-four hellers." She must have told the innkeeper, for he came up to me and inquired in a friendly manner where I was going. We talked for a while, and he asked me whether I was a guide. I told him the circumstances, and informed him of my need of money. "But what will you do if your man doesn't arrive?" "That doesn't matter," I replied. "I know Schroffenegger at Tiers, who will lend me some money."

Then a stranger got up and called pleasantly to me: "If you know Schroffenegger I will give you some money. Will you go to Tiers without drinking it up?" I thanked him and told him that I could hold out four or five hours, and went on my way.

The Corpus Christi procession was taking place in Tiers and a shooting contest was being held along with the religious celebration. It was quite jolly. I went into the inn "zur Rose." Without saying much, I ordered a good meal. Then I inquired for my friend Schroffenegger and heard that he was at the inn next door, playing in the band. I went over; he recognized me at once and came out when the dance was finished. After greeting one another we began to talk of climbing. Then I asked him to lend me a little money in case my gentleman did not show up. "Certainly," came the answer.

Then I met guide Wenter, who had quite a reputation as a Dolomite climber. Dr. and Mrs. P. arrived in the afternoon and I was at once free of financial difficulty. Dr. P. informed me that he was going to Weisslahnbad and that I could stay a while here with my friends. I bought some climbing shoes, and when I left Tiers it was so late that no one heard me at the hotel in Weisslahnbad. I lay down on a bench in front of the house.

Early in the morning someone opened a window. It was Dr. P. In a tone of displeasure he told me that he and his wife had waited for me a long time on the preceding evening. The complaint was deserved. We wandered to Grasleitenhütte, and after a brief rest looked for the route on the south wall of the Grasleitenspitze, finding it immediately and climbing it without difficulty, since it is marked with little piles of stones. (The prolonged rest we took on the ridge was, as I shall later relate, fateful for us.)

We then climbed farther along the ridge in the direction of the Junischarte. It isn't very easy. Once my handhold broke, and I cried out, but I recovered myself; still, my feet trembled, as Dr. P. noticed, and on that account we proceeded somewhat more slowly. I always called Mrs. P. "Fräulein," and Dr. P. said with a smile: "I thought that there were three of us on this wedding trip! But there are four: I, my wife, this 'Fräulein' and yourself."

One couldn't make a mistake along the ridge, but when it ended we were somewhat uncertain because we had not found the way down to the Junischarte. Twice we roped down. As usual the rope stuck. So I was obliged to go up again and put a bit of cloth underneath so that the rope would not catch. At last, when we reached the Mühlsteiger Chimney, we thought every difficulty was over. But it happened otherwise. The day should have been about 15 minutes longer. Roping down in pitch-dark night is indescribable. It was difficult for Mrs. P. and the rope often tangled.

Fortunately I had two packages of matches along, but they were not enough. I think that, because of the darkness, we took two hours to the first chimney. First I roped down Dr. P., then his wife, next the rucksacks, and at last I swarmed down the rope through the air until Dr. P. grabbed my feet and pulled me toward him. Again the coiling of the rope, and almost no space or step visible. For a few metres things went more easily. It was lucky that the doctor and I had made this tour earlier in the year and had a precise idea of the worst places. Several hours elapsed at the second chimney. Now it would soon have to be finished. I lowered the man down 30 metres and he was at the end of the climb. Then his wife followed. It was the rucksack that made the trouble; it always stuck so that I had to jerk 15 or 20 times to bring it farther. For myself I attached the rope strongly to a ring and climbed down with greatest care. God be praised, it was over!

Now we had only the short distance over rough slopes to the hut. To our joy the moon peeped out a little. It was two o'clock in the morning. For the little stretch to the hut that usually takes five minutes, we needed a quarter of an hour. We stood before Grasleitenhütte, knocked on the door and no one answered. We went around the hut, banging on every window until we came to the right one. An old bearded guide opened up for us. As we were the first guests of the season the caretaker was kindly disposed. She fixed us up some hot wine at once. Dr. P. slipped a banknote into my hand, with the words: "You did that very well, Konrad."

About four o'clock we went to bed, just as the hut people were getting up. I was awake at seven and looked out. Snow had fallen, and my good rope hung on the ring in the wet chimney. I was sorry for that and could sleep no more, so I breakfasted and brought down the rope. In consequence of the snowfall the ascent of the Vajolet Towers was not possible, so we went by way of Tiers to Bozen.

Wandering about the town I came by chance upon the well-known Batzenhäusl. I had to have a look at it. That meant a big drink, of course, and I ordered a quarter of a litre of wine for 40 hellers. I tasted it. It was excellent – nothing like that at home in Naßwald! By the time I had drunk half of it the inscriptions and paintings were all double. I tried to see whether I could stand up – it didn't work very well. The waiter noticed it and asked me how the wine tasted. "Well, see for yourself. An eighth has finished me!" "You don't come from a wine district," laughed the waiter. Then he advised me to drink soda water. Things improved, but not so that I would have dared let Dr. P. see me, for he would not have believed that I had not taken more than a quarter of a litre.

I remained seated on a bench until eleven o'clock and then, going to the hotel, slept soundly, in fact so long that Dr. P. complained of my lateness. At noon we left by the express for Milan. The journey along Lake Garda was extremely beautiful. As we had an hour in Verona, Dr. P. took a coach so that we could see the city and the old Roman buildings.

In Milan we got out at the Hotel Terminus. I went to a small inn where German was spoken. On the same day we climbed up in the cathedral and looked over the sights of the city. That evening I went to a concert, but to my sorrow could not understand the fine songs. Next morning we had to buy climbing irons. After considerable search we discovered a place, but the things did not fit and cost 18 lira. This made us miss the train and we had to go later on a local. Dr. P. called it the "climbing-iron train."

4

ON MONT BLANC

We reached Aosta about eleven o'clock at night, and next forenoon took a carriage which brought us, after a journey of several hours, to Courmayeur, our first headquarters. The road is kept in good condition, and there are also remains of the old route built by the Romans, by which Napoleon I crossed the Great St. Bernard from France. For a few minutes the "King of Mountains," Mont Blanc, was in sight.

Soon after the deviation of the St. Bernard road one reaches Courmayeur. A small, poor village! Not a wooden roof to be seen; everything of stone. The houses press one against the other and the lanes are often so narrow that one has to go back if a wagon is encountered. We got out at the Hotel du Montblanc. The people were friendly toward me, although we could not talk to each other. But I had no need either to talk or inquire, for at meal-time the bell rang and my room was shown to me.

First of all I had a dinner of six or seven courses. I was sorry that I was not more hungry! Next morning brought us an unpleasant surprise with mist and rain. Such a day is occasionally to be expected. Although it was the middle of July we were told that the Rifugio Torino was not open, and that we must take the caretaker with us. We looked him up, and found to our satisfaction that he could go. He showed up promptly in the morning, but with sour expression for it was still raining. We had to wait three days until there was a possible chance of attacking the Aiguille du Géant, which looked down upon us so splendid and proud.

The hutkeeper looked after provisions, and we took leave of our good inn-keeper. He looked just like a Lower Austrian farmer, as he had no moustache. A good path leads first through two little hamlets, then through a lovely larch forest and many alpine roses to a place of refreshment, the Pavillon du Mont Fréty. The vegetation reaches right up to this house. Beyond this the way grows constantly worse, and there are a few places to be climbed. Our companion had a good deal to carry, and besides it was his first trip of the season, on which the climbing is always hard work. So we went ahead.

To the Rifugio Torino (built by the Italian Alpine Club) we took three hours; it is the most loftily situated hut of the club. Before reaching it there was a fine snow-ridge. Our fingers were stiff, and first of all we had to shovel off the place as everything was still covered with winter snow. In half an hour we were through and could enter the hut. It was very comfortable inside, only the old story that every stove smokes when it has not been heated for a long time. First we had tea, then minestra, then cutlets and trimmings. Then came conversation. The hutkeeper spoke three languages, including a little German, which was pleasant for me. We looked up our sleeping places; the rooms were very small but had good beds. It was the first time I had slept at such an elevation, and I noticed it very much, waking in the night with so much difficulty in getting my breath that I had to sit up and breathe deeply for quite a while.

The day did not look so bad and we hoped the expedition would turn out well. On account of cold rocks we did not need to leave before eight or nine o'clock. The good hutkeeper went with us as far as the Col du Géant in order to show us the way. I deceived myself, for I thought that we could be there in an hour. It looked so close. In reality it took three hours. We were the first party of the year, and of course there was no sign of old steps which are usually an indication of the route. We looked up through cracks and couloirs and soon saw a fixed rope. What, go up there? It didn't look so nice. At the beginning of the climb we took a rest and stamped our feet, for the new snow was cold. The famous guide Emile Rey was said to have fallen near the first rope.

Little misty clouds floated over Mont Blanc, not a good sign, and we considered whether Mrs. P. should go along or whether the ascent would take too much time with three. But the good lady did not want to deprive us of the peak, and remained below. From the very start there were some places that were not altogether easy, because the rope was frozen. When we reached the first stopping place we glanced at one another: the mist had become thicker and it began to snow. Before us rose the steep plaques, which look far worse than they really are. First comes a 40-metre crack through a smooth wall, which is probably not so hard when free of snow. Then a little cliff. From there the rope hung down, but unfortunately we could not reach it. I carefully cut some steps, while Dr. P. secured me. Now came a smooth place that was so snowed-in that the rope could not be dug out. Finally we reached the traverse we had seen from below; it is not as dangerous as it appears from that viewpoint, but under conditions of snow and cold one is glad to have it over with. Later there are some precipitous cracks.

The first conquerors, who had to overcome these difficulties without rope, are truly to be congratulated!

The weather became steadily worse, and we decided to turn back. As our hands were suffering from the cold, thick fixed rope, I belayed with my own as well, and it frequently stuck. I pulled and jerked for a long time, until Dr. P. said: "You'll have to climb up again." Quite involuntarily I replied: "If I am still able…" My answer hurt Dr. P., as he told me later during descent, and I saw for myself that it was not the proper one.

Going down took much more time than ascending. The mists parted just as we reached the second platform. There was a wonderful view of the little lakes on the glacier below our feet. For a moment we thought of renewing the attack, but five minutes later we were again of another opinion. Soon we were going down, where Mrs. P. was waiting for us. While we were crossing the glacier, Dr. P. remarked: "You should have encouraged me to go on to the summit." But at once he saw the impossibility of such a thing, for the fog became more and more dense. We did not get to the col for a long time, and doubts arose within me as to whether we should reach the hut. There was nothing to be seen of our tracks. Finally we found it, and our much worried companion, who quickly made us some tea. He advised us to await better weather, which he did not think would come at once, and so we went down to Courmayeur.

Although we had not attained the summit of the Aiguille du Géant, Dr. P. gave me full tariff. Dr. P. spoke to the guide Petigax,[10] well-known in Courmayeur, who had been on the North Pole expedition with the Duke of Savoy. Petigax was to go with us up Mont Blanc by way of the Dôme Hutte, but he declared that there was still too much fresh snow. But Dr. P. didn't want to wait any longer, gave up the idea and, to save 17 francs per head, decided to cross the western passes to Chamonix, a 20-hour route.

He sent me to the house of Petigax to tell him that we were leaving. "Partir" was the French word I had to say. As I came into the simple courtyard of the house a barking dog put himself in my way. I was so frightened that it was quite a while before I could say "partir." Petigax was very kind to me, invited me to enter, showed the skins of ice bears that he had shot at the North Pole, and offered me a glass of wine.

On the morning of the following day we started off. My rucksack was quite heavy. At first our route took us through a fragrant forest, but it didn't last long and the way became worse and worse. The trees came to an end, and we were out in the broiling sun. We reached a beautiful lake, the Lac de Combal. Its colour is deep blue. Hanging glaciers (Glacier de Miage) are to the right, reflected in the lake. The fearfully long Péteret ridge is in view, with the Aiguille Blanche, the Aiguille Noire and all the rest. Here there are still some virgin peaks to climb.

Before reaching the first pass (Col de la Seigne) we met the Italian boundary guards, who lay on sheepskins beside their hut. We had not taken much in the way of provisions, as Dr. P. thought that we would soon find an inn, so the cheese and bread were divided and eaten. The guards accompanied us to the boundary and told us that only rarely was an official visit made up there. Dr. P. inquired about their term of service. The poor devils had to stick it out five years! And eight weeks had already been too much for me.

At the pass we shook hands pleasantly with the guards – a step farther and we were in France. The vegetation on this side was striking. Not far from the Col de la Seigne we came to rich green meadows and saw the alm huts. Cattle stood in rank and file. They were tied, and so it looked as if they were being drilled. As we proceeded farther we had to battle with swollen brooks, which must be crossed. It couldn't be done without getting wet. At one of the alms we had some coffee. It wasn't very clean there, and quite expensive. Dr. P. had to pay five francs for each person. But the woman was willing to bargain.

Now we had two more passes before Chamonix. We wandered down grassy slopes where there was almost no path. Again I noticed my heavy rucksack. Then we came to a saddle. It didn't agree with the description. We debated, but nothing was certain. Dr. P. ran ahead, his wife and I remaining behind. We reached some old huts; we called out without result. At last, some direction poles, really hard to find, showed us the way to the second pass (Col des Fours). Now it agreed with the guidebook. We even saw the way we still had to take, but the valley seemed to grow longer and longer, and the chalet where we were to spend the night seemed an eternal distance.

It was quite dark when we at last got there. We were hungry and thirsty, but had to wait patiently until the dinner bell rang. The people were astonished at seeing me and came with all sorts of questions, which I did not understand and consequently could not answer. Next morning quite a few legs were stiff. Dr. P. took a carriage to Bionnay and then we went after the third pass, the Col de Voza. The sun and the huge gadflies were very annoying. Our necks and faces were badly bitten. Mrs. P. and I nearly shed tears. The view from the Col de Voza to Chamonix was splendid. We could see a railway train going along, and in a little while we ourselves were in the valley. In Chamonix we had to find a place to stop, and then rested.

During the wanderings about Chamonix we were always gazing at the "King of the Mountains," and the painful thought crept through our hearts: 'Shall we succeed from this side? How will the snow conditions be?' The alarm clock did its duty at four o'clock next morning. Our porter was already outside the hotel. He looked at me from head to foot somewhat mistrustfully. I thought that no one would have taken my young and beardless face for that of a "Mont Blanc guide." We started off. A lovely day! We went slowly along through the splendid larch forest and past masses of alpine roses. Numerous goats relieved the solitude. The mighty Glacier des Bossons formed the background of the landscape.

We took a long rest at the edge of the glacier. A huge crowd of people came across who had been making observations for 14 days on Mont Blanc. The Chamonix guide Garny[11] was present, whose appearance made such a great impression upon Dr. P. that he at once engaged him for the Aiguille du Grépon, which we wanted to climb next. Then we went slowly over the glacier, where there was a well-trodden track. I was very curious about the crevasses with the ladders, which one sees so frequently on postcards. But, as it was the beginning of summer, they were not so dangerous.

Three hours later we arrived at the Grands Mulets, the "Robbers' Hut" as it is known throughout the tourist world. And the caretaker isn't even pleasant along with these high prices! We went to bed early, for morning would come very soon for us.

About two o'clock the man came and woke me. Sleep had done me good despite the fact that the porter had inconsiderately snored like a sawmill all night long. I lit the light and made a sign to the porter that he could stay in bed, for we intended to go to the summit of Mont Blanc *without* him. He looked at me with an unpleasant expression, murmured something and then came to breakfast. Dr. P. told him in French that he had only engaged him as far as the Grands Mulets. Then what faces the porter, the hutkeeper and his wife made. Just like cats when there is thunder and lightning!

We left. Those who remained didn't have much that was nice to call after me! Slowly and carefully we followed the track, leading in long slants to the Grand Plateau. Always one more rise beyond. Soon we were in mist. I know of nothing more monotonous than traversing a glacier under such conditions. As we approached the "four-thousand" level doubts arose, but when we saw the Cabane Vallot on the ridge things improved, although the distance to the hut was still considerable. Then the storm came on and we fled to the hut.

Fingers were rubbed and we stamped around like cattle in a stable. Food and drink disappeared, for now we must gather our strength to face the wind, or rather storm, and fight it courageously. At first it went very well, but when we reached the Bosses du Dromadaire – the humps of the camel – it looked much worse. It was impossible to talk. One jerk on the rope meant "stop"; two, "proceed." The storm was so violent that we often had to lie prone. My nose began to bleed, and the doctor was almost finished, but his wife uttered not a word of complaint.

About 200 metres from the summit the doctor wanted to turn back, but as his wife said nothing I was against it, and I made the assertion that we would not turn back "even if all three of us die!" (For I was thinking of the attempt on the Aiguille du Géant, when Dr. P. had insinuated that I should have encouraged him to go to the top in spite of everything.) Almost exhausted we gasped up the narrow snow ridge to the summit of Mont Blanc.

What was the reward of our labour and endurance? That we had to turn right around, for the icy storm would not allow one to stand, much less stop on the summit – that finest thing in mountain climbing. But we were happy and proud of our success, for under such unfavourable conditions many a Mont Blanc climber would have turned back.

The descent was much easier. There was a wonderful play of the elements, with intermittent rain. The lightning was indescribably beautiful. At the Grands Mulets they did not believe that we had reached the summit, as no French guide had been along. But during the descent we were able to show the porter that we knew a thing or two, going as fast as if we had stolen something on Mont Blanc! We sprang over crevasses, where the porter could not follow.

How good it felt in Chamonix to wash the whole body and change the clothing! Then I went to see Dr. P. in the hotel. Instead of the customary cannon-shooting and a drink from a fine glass, he put a shining gold piece into my hand. Well, I preferred the money to the spectacle of cannon-shooting and champagne-drinking! My delight in having ascended Mont Blanc was considerable. As a matter of fact I had seldom been amongst the higher mountains, and now I could say that I had come from the little Rax direct to the highest peak of Europe, without a guide's badge, and two people had entrusted their lives to me.

The following day was naturally one of rest. We took a little walk to the Glacier des Bossons and to the grotto, and talked of next day's trip, Aiguille de Blaitière.

At three o'clock in the morning we set out. Through bushes and high, wet underbrush the almost trackless way goes from behind the station to a hut where we had breakfast. The man there showed us the path ahead. We had to struggle over huge piles of rock until the glacier came in sight. We rested and took council. Our impressions differed. Dr. P. had the description, I the orientation. Against my own conviction I allowed him to be right.

First of all we crossed a steep snow slope on which, for the first time, we put on our Milanese climbing irons. But not for long. I got angry and threw them down the glacier. If irons do not fit well it is better not to use them. The climb, which followed, to the glacier was quite interesting over plaques and rock towers. The glacier was most complicated. There was a crevasse to be crossed, presenting a formidable obstacle and waiting for us with its yawning mouth.

Just before we reached the col we found the track, leading up this side, where, according to my reckoning, I wished to go. But on the col we rested and decided to return as we had been so slow. We descended to the Montanvert, where the guide Garny waited for us. He approached us pleasantly. At the Montanvert there were Swiss guides, with whom I could converse: the famous Pollingers (father and son) and the brothers Lochmatter.

In the hotel there is a large guides' hall, possibly the biggest in the Alps. Dr. P. came in with us, to talk to the guides. They told fearsome tales of the Aiguille du Grépon, but Dr. P. laughed heartily and called it a "Cat's Back." That pleased the guides: they laughed with him and said: "You will see soon enough. You will get to know something about the Grépon – that cat's back."

5

THE AIGUILLE DU GRÉPON

I t was July 10th, a day I marked well. I was awakened about one o'clock in the morning. One seldom finds such a breakfast table as at the Montanvert. Coffee, milk, cold meat, cheese, onions, vinegar, oil, wine. Guide Garny accompanied us. A monotonous serpentine trail leads up to the glacier. Then the rope is put on and soon we reach the well-known spot where a rest for breakfast is usually taken. Master Garny spoke: "Here we rest a bit and leave everything extra." There was a brief exchange of words between man and guide. Garny emptied his pockets, down to the cognac.

It all goes easily as far as the 'schrund, after which one mounts rapidly by the rocks to the ice gully, which can be very bad. Here I said to Dr. P.: "You can tell the guide that I too can cut steps." Garny replied to Dr. P.: "If your guide is good on the rocks he can go ahead, then!" Then both kept on talking to one another.

I asked Mrs. P. what they wanted and she told me that the guide Garny thought we should let the Grépon alone today and do the Charmoz, since other people were going on the Grépon tomorrow, which would make it easier. With this idea we did not agree. There on the col, where the routes for Grépon and Charmoz diverge, Garny halted and gave his opinion. But we were set on the Grépon and so he was obliged to go along. In a little while we were at the world-renowned Mummery Crack. We put on our *Kletterschuhe*, and I put the three pairs of nailed boots in my rucksack. Then the difficult work began.

I climbed ahead. The entrance into the crack is not so hard, and one can rest again some two metres higher. "How is it going, Konrad?" called the doctor. And I: "It isn't so bad, doctor; I've seen worse!" "Are you up already?" "Bravo." Soon afterward Mrs. P. was beside me, and her husband a few minutes later. All three of us had expected the crack to be quite different and much more difficult. Finally, up came Garny and the rucksacks. He had nailed boots, for the Chamonix guides do not understand *Kletterschuhe* and are not willing to try them.

He kept calling: "Hold tight! Hold tight!" I pulled, just as he requested. After the crack there comes a hole, where Garny went ahead, and then a block over which he went very well. Then there is a fissure by which one emerges on the south wall; and then in front of us an oblique crack that isn't easy. Mrs. P. and I were a little behind. All at once the doctor called: "Konrad, come quickly!" Garny was demanding that the doctor should enter the crack so that he (Garny) could climb up on his head. The new spikes (which the Swiss guides have instead of climbing irons) in Garny's boots wouldn't have done anything except injure the doctor. I had to support him in this decision, otherwise he might have come to harm.

Ridge climbing follows this crack as far as the "Great Gendarme," the well-known roping-off place. Naturally, Garny as the local guide had to descend first. He and I had a slight argument about the placing of the rope. His ideas on roping down were a little bit crazy. He shouted: "All three of you hold tight!" (And he had the reserve rope to hang onto in addition.) We (the doctor, his wife and I) needed no one to secure us.

As Garny had already finished off his schnaps, he wanted some of our tea. But we had not enough for ourselves. Then he began to grumble. After the gendarme come a ledge, then the "Step in the Blue," and after a trifle more we were on the ridge, Garny pointing out that the route went down where an old rope and a wooden ladder were visible. This was work in earnest! The rope was always catching and I must climb up for it. On the last bit I grew angry. I climbed up again, threw the rope down and descended without its assistance. Now come the C.P. [Charlet et Payot] rocks and then we are on the summit of the Grépon.[12]

After a short rest Garny became restless and thought that a storm was approaching. During the descent he remarked: "A good bottle would certainly be a help!" He went to the Montanvert, to celebrate his conquest in the big guides' room. One is a guide of importance if one leads on the Grépon.

We went to Chamonix and had two days of rest. When I was going into a coffeehouse for lunch, Garny turned up and said that I should follow him. A gentleman was standing in a crowd of babbling guides, and the porter, who spoke German, said I should inform the gentleman that Garny had been with us on the Grépon. The man, hearing that I spoke German, asked me: "Are you German," "Yes, sir, from the Rax in Lower Austria." "Were you contented with the local guide?" I replied: "If you want to know anything about him – my gentleman lives here." And I took him to Dr. P.

After the men had seated themselves opposite one another, Dr. P. said: "I can only tell you that without Konrad we would not have gotten up." The stranger then asked me whether I would accompany him, if my patron permitted, and Dr. P. replied: "Certainly, you may use my guide, but only if you pay him well!" And so it was arranged. Dr. P. lent the man his *Kletterschuhe*, and his wife furnished an axe, and in an hour I had departed from Chamonix with the man. We talked quite a bit about Tyrol, which he knew very well, and he was pleased at making such a difficult tour as the Grépon with an Austrian.

We sat together at the Montanvert, and when my man wanted to order provisions I told him that I had already taken some with me from Chamonix. Then I received complaint from the proprietor, who had the Swiss guides tell me that if everyone did that sort of thing he would have to go out begging!

Next morning I did the Grépon with the man, exactly as I had made it several days before with Dr. P. It was much easier for me this time, for I was not carrying so much and did not have to argue with Garny. On this particular day the elder Pollinger was up with his son, and I witnessed the "transportation" of an old Englishman. One heard nothing but "Pull! Pull!" "Slacken," and again, "Pull." In 12 hours we were back again, and I must remark that this time we had been on the true summit, to which Garny had not led us. I received 130 kronen from the man – and a good pair of trousers. That was really the best reward!

Now comes the story of the Chamonix guides, who were raging because I had made the tour of the Grépon with a stranger instead of turning him over to a local guide. On reaching the Montanvert I received a telegram with the following contents: "Konrad, come right back to Chamonix today. The guides are after you. Dr. P." I went into the dining room, and at that very moment a Chamonix guide threatened me. But the Swiss guides protected me and told me to watch out that evening, for even Zermatt guides had received blows in Chamonix. I thanked them and went down.

When I reached my inn that evening the cook said to me: "Well, my dear Mr. German, you are going to get beaten up tonight!" It was lucky that she spoke German and could warn me. She told me that the French guides had come repeatedly during the day and inquired for me. She advised me to go directly into the dining room, as nothing could happen to me there. After I had been there a short time, two fellows came and cursed at me. I demanded quiet and the landlord insisted on the same thing. Now affairs became bitter. To reach my room I had to go outside, and the guides were waiting there to give me a beating! The cook took pity on me and hid me in her room, which had an entrance from the kitchen. With thumping heart I lay there until midnight, when the cook arrived and I must go. I wanted to express my thanks and give her some money, but she replied: "It's a German pleasure, and so I take my thanks in words!" Then I climbed through the window into the court, and by this means reached my own room.

But Messieurs les Guides were still at their post, lying in wait for me. I ran up the stairs so fast that they could not catch me, and quickly barred the door. At the same moment some stones came flying through the window, but I was uninjured. Then a shouting began, until at last the police came and restored order. I could not sleep during the whole night.

Next morning I went to Dr. P. and told him everything. We took another walk through the place, and saw all the "gentlemen" of the preceding night, even Garny, who stood beside a mule and was just on the point of starting on an excursion. One can readily imagine that he had no friendly glance for us!

6

MATTERHORN AND MONTE ROSA

About ten o'clock we took leave of Chamonix and went by carriage to Martigny, in order to go thence by train to Zermatt. The German whom I had taken up the Grépon accompanied us. The carriage journey, the many splendid views and the widespread panorama lasted eight or nine hours. At Martigny both men did business on my account, for the German wanted to climb the Matterhorn as well, and finally Dr. P. agreed to let me make the tour with this man on the day after next.

On the express, which runs only once a week, we went to Visp. For the first time in my life I had the opportunity of riding in such an elegant train, and I was sorry that it didn't last longer. I was very curious to see the splendid, world-renowned Matterhorn. We could not stop long in Zermatt, as we had to be in Matterhornhütte on the same day. At the first sight of the mountain I was indeed surprised, for the Matterhorn was much more beautiful than I had expected.

My man took a mule to the Schwarzsee Hotel, three hours distant from Zermatt. When one leaves Zermatt, the view of the Matterhorn in changing scenery becomes finer and finer. But at the Schwarzsee one has the entire glacial world directly in front: the mighty Monte Rosa with its numerous peaks, Allalinhorn, Fluchthorn, Täschhorn, Rimpfischhorn, Lyskamm, Zwilliuge, Breithorn, the Gabelhorns, Wellenkuppe, Trifthorn, Zinal Rothhorn, Weisshorn etc.

At the Schwarzsee there is a chapel where formerly everyone who was going "on the Horn" (as the Swiss say) attended mass. Today that is all over. There has been no reading of mass there for many a day. After a little rest we started off; we had taken a porter, who carried wood for us to Matterhornhütte, which we reached in two hours. I have heard this hut much criticized, and I myself found it pretty dirty. "Six men are on the Horn, and it is doubtful whether they will get back to the hut this evening," said the porter.

The sunset was not very fine, for wind and cloud arose. The wind increased to a storm, and it was questionable whether we would be able to make our expedition in the morning. We went early to bed, and at one o'clock crept out from the covers. Tea was soon ready, and we stood in front of the hut with our lanterns. We must halt repeatedly to relight them. How wild will the wind be higher up?

When we met the six people they advised us to give up the tour, being of the opinion that the storm would prevent us from getting higher than the "Shoulder" at the very most. So we turned back. We found a little fire still in the hut, and I put water on for some tea for the half-frozen tourists, who had been on the Matterhorn for 25 hours. They were guideless. A clergyman was their leader, which interested me very much. At daylight we looked to see how much of a nuisance the wind was making. The gentleman decided to wait over a day, and I went down with the other six to Schwarzsee to get provisions and to secure another guide, Hans Peter Perren.[13]

Lying on the grass in front of the hotel I was waiting for the guide, when all at once I heard a familiar voice: the doctor and his wife. A hello when he saw me: "Are you back already?" Then I told him all about it. "Tomorrow I can't let you go again," he said, "and if the man wants two guides, we'll have to take him up another one!" And so another guide was engaged, and we all went up to the hut together. Mrs. P. remained at the Schwarzsee Hotel.

This day was far finer and promised better for the morrow. We started out about one o'clock in the morning. Both guides were kind to me and said they would go ahead, for at night the route of ascent is not easy to find. When dawn broke I went ahead with Dr. P. We rested beside the old hut, and went on when the others arrived. We did not have to search much, for there were tracks here and there. The wind was not blowing strongly at the Shoulder. Still it took my hat for a plaything!

About half past seven we stood on the summit of the Matterhorn. To my sorrow we could not stop long, for the wind was too annoying. We met the other party just as we were descending the Shoulder. On the last part of the descent I missed the way and went too far to the right. It came to a little, but not serious, exchange of words. We had to cross a steep ice couloir, where I slipped. But Dr. P. had secured the rope and said: "This is one time when

I caught *you*." If Dr. P. had not been such an expert and careful climber the matter would have taken a worse turn.

About half past three we were in the hut once more. Mrs. P. awaited us at the Schwarzsee Hotel, and that evening we were in Zermatt. It was very jolly in the beer hall. The music was playing and the people walked up and down in the narrow street. He who has a fine tour behind him is doubly happy over gay music!

Next day we went to Monte Rosa. We wandered in leisure up the Gornergrat, meeting on the way a Dutchman who was very entertaining. It is too bad that so many people use this trodden path that it disturbs the real purpose of the glacial landscape. At the Cabane Bétemps we met a German with two guides, who also wanted to climb Monte Rosa. The Cabane Bétemps is provisioned and well cared for in the Swiss manner.

Next morning the old Swiss guide stuck his head out of the window and said through his nose: "Nothing doing today." I looked out also and the weather did not look good to me. "It may do," he said in a grumbling tone. It was time to get up in the hut, but as the German and his two guides did not go, we remained in the hut as well. About seven o'clock the weather turned bad, but it didn't last long. The morning went by with all sorts of storytelling. After lunch I looked up a bed of straw and stretched myself out. Just as I was sound asleep Dr. P. woke me up and told me I was to go to the Riffel Alm and fetch champagne and glasses. The German wouldn't look at me. I was surprised at this request, and wracked my brains to discover what was going on.

Dr. P. gave me some money and I started down over the big boulders. I went quickly over the Gorner Glacier and in an hour and a half was at the Riffel Alm. I had to deposit 20 francs for the borrowed glasses. I went slowly back to the Cabane Bétemps, trying to think what the champagne was for. Dr. P. met me with an old tin box for a "cooler." I asked no questions, but Dr. P. told me of his own accord. The German had been married just four weeks and was also celebrating his birthday; and because he was a good fellow, Dr. P. was doing the honours and giving a little party. The rest of the day passed in festive spirit.

Two guideless Swiss arrived, who were very pleasant. The German gentleman gave me ten marks in gold for my trip to the Riffel Alm. That was good pay for a day of rest!

At two o'clock in the morning there was a racket in the hut. Today will be fine! Everything was carefully packed up for the trip. The guideless party was the first to leave. (I discovered later that these two guideless Swiss were killed eight days later on the Jungfrau.[14] I was very sorry for them.) By the light of lanterns we went slowly over the boulders. First there is a steep snowfield; then the grade lessens. But the snow was bad; we broke in so that we were almost wading. Soon we overtook the guideless men, which pleased them to have us go ahead for a little while. But one of them was soon played out, so that I had to do the advance work alone. I had boots that were too small, and my feet became chilly. I had also caught a cold, which held me back from rapid progress. I was almost at the point of tears. It went more and more slowly – the Swiss guides would soon be catching up.

As soon as we were in the sunlight we stopped and waited for them. As they came along we called out: "Lucky for us that you are here. Now you can stamp out a bit of the track!" "Right," came the answer, and now we could have something to eat. On account of the cold we could not delay any longer, and there was nothing to do but "bite the sour apple." But, being cross, things went better.

On the ridge everything was filled with snow, and the wind is almost always blowing at such an elevation. We stopped in a protected spot. I had no appetite, although Dr. P. offered me everything imaginable. I thanked him and only took something to drink. We had reached the summit of Monte Rosa without the Swiss guides.

Going down was naturally easier, and by the time we reached the Cabane Bétemps the worst of our annoyance at the snow-tramping was over. Monte Rosa was the last peak of the four weeks' wedding trip in the mountains, and we went happily down into the valley. Monte Rosa is a "drudgery," second only to Mont Blanc!

Next day we went to Visp and crossed the lovely Gemmi Pass, which, on account of the artistic location of the road and the lakes, may be called the finest pass in Switzerland. We reached Kandersteg and proceeded to Interlaken. There I saw an unforgettable sunset. For five minutes the Jungfrau was a glowing ball. I was with Dr. P. and his wife for the last day. He gave me my pay and a picture of the Matterhorn, with the inscription: "In memory of your first foreign tour and the wedding journey with Dr. P. and his wife."

When I put out my hand to take leave of the couple I was sad at heart, for I could not believe that we must separate. It was very hard for me when I thought over the trip in my little room, and recalled how kind Dr. and Mrs. P. had been to me. Dr. P. had taught me so much, and shown me so many beautiful things, and besides we had experienced many hours of peril together! Unforgettable days!

7

AS TOURIST ON THE BACHL ALM

Next morning at eight o'clock my train went by way of Bern and Zürich to Buchs, and on once more to the mountains of my home. Gstatterboden was my destination. I climbed out with such a bad toothache that I had to have the thing extracted at once. The operation was performed by one of the workers at the station!

Rather knocked apart and tired from my journey, I was lying about in the little inn when two well-known, keen scramblers from the Rax appeared. After considerable talk I told them that I was going home on the next train. But they overruled that. "Go with us to the Dachstein peaks. You haven't been there yet!" The landlord said: "You have plenty of time to think about going home. The train won't be here for a long time." At that very moment it pulled into the station. I was too late. And so I agreed to go with them.

As I had to be in the Gröden Valley on August 1st, it was scarcely worthwhile to go home first. So the three of us went to Mandling. From there, half an hour along the brook to the first bridge; then on the other bank and through the woods, where many bilberries grow, then into the lovely Bach Valley at the foot of the Dachstein.

Roth had already been in this locality and told me much about the beautiful Bachl Alm, where our headquarters were to be. On the way we met a young tourist, who introduced himself as Paul St., of Gmunden. He too was going to the Bachl Alm. It seemed very jolly to me to be going there with the three young fellows.

On our arrival at the alm, Resi was busy at work. She dried her hands on her apron and greeted us kindly. "Go right in." It made a good impression: clean, roomy and in a lovely location. We were given excellent milk and butter; then we looked over the route on the southern wall of the Dachstein with the aid of our spyglass and guidebook. "It doesn't look so good," I said. "Can it be that you are afraid, Kain?" "Afraid? Why should I be?" And with much interest I looked through the glass at the route.

Then we laid ourselves flat on the ground and held a council of war. Meanwhile Mirzl came along. She too greeted us pleasantly. Then I went to see Resi in the stable and talked to her about cattle. "But you aren't from Vienna" ["Sie san oba koa Weana"], she said. So I told her how I happened to be there. In the evening we chatted by the hearth and then went to sleep in the fragrant hay.

Everyone slept bravely; only W. snored. Soon it was day on the alm once more. By half past three Resi and Mirzl were already in the stable. So it wasn't possible to sleep any longer. "Tourists, do you want coffee or milk for breakfast?" "Milk," we all shouted at once. I was the first to rise. A lovely morning! It is really good fun, that tramping around. During the forenoon we chased the goats and scuffled with one another with the simple enthusiasm of children.

In the afternoon we went to Austria-Hütte, the better to study the route on the southern wall. We remained quite a while with the women at the Neustadt Alm; at the hut I inquired whether any guide had yet done the south wall. "Oh, no; no one has been there," they told me. In the evening I strained my knee in wrestling, so that I could not make the tour on the following day. The time passed in eating, drinking and lying around.

Next morning the alarm went off about two o'clock. "Konradl (as they called me in fun), how is your foot? Can we go?" "I think so." In a few minutes we were ready. Resi had set out our breakfast by the window. We left the house quietly. On the preceding evening Resi had given her blessing for the success of our tour. We had marked with little piles of stone the path that we must now follow in darkness. We were sorry that W. could not go with us. He had to go down to the post office in the valley to get some provisions, and the man from Gmunden must wait for a friend. So R. and I went alone. We did not have to use the lantern very long; dawn came soon.

There was a shepherd on the rocky slope, who came with us to the beginning of the climb. There we took a rest and put on our *Kletterschuhe*. The 'schrund was in good shape, so we crossed it with ease. At first R. went ahead. The ledge and the first two chimneys gave us no trouble. We were already at the snow basin. That was fast going! We had taken scarcely 20 minutes. We went side by side along the ridge. At the ledges I went ahead. We reached high elevation without much search for the way. We saw tracks here and there. But we couldn't find the difficult chimney, and thought that it must be still higher. One place was quite troublesome: an overhanging block. R. secured me well, and when I climbed onto the rickety boulder I said to R.: "Look out! – if I get there it will be all right." I gave myself a swing and was up. But my friend R. didn't trust the block and went farther to the right. It was more difficult there, but more secure.

Then we reached the narrow ledges. "Where are the chimneys, of which it says that the right is the better one?" Now came a very steep chimney in which water dripped. It looked like very hard work. I attacked it slowly.

92

"There is a good hold. And there a step," called R. I was already up. Now we would soon be off the wall. "Fine slabs," I said. Then, for a short distance, we moved together on the rope; a short and not easy little cliff and we were out. Including halts it had taken three and a half hours.

Nailed boots were put on once more and we proceeded over the made path to the summit of the Dachstein. A guided party was descending, and asked us where we came from. "Up the south wall." A strong guide was present, who looked down scornfully, but said no word, not even a greeting.

We stretched out comfortably on the summit, pleased with our success. Descent was made by way of the Huhnerscharte. We looked down right sadly from the Schönbühl to Austria-Hütte; our throats were dry and a couple of bottles of beer would not have lessened the pleasure of our conquest. But for that amount of money one could live at the Bachl Alm for two days! At the first spring we lay down and drank to our hearts' content. Just one more, and then another. Well, the water was fine, and more healthy than that expensive beer at Austria-Hütte.

The four of us met at the Bachl Alm once more. St. had been up the Eiskarlspitze, coming from Schladming with his package and the things purchased for Resi. We had chipped in and bought her a linen apron and a kerchief.[15] In a word, there was contentment in the hut. We three with our climbing, W. with his sweets, Resi with her apron and her kerchief, and Mirzl telling us with joy that the calf that had been lost yesterday was found again.

Contentedly we took ourselves to rest. But we were disturbed by other tourists, who often come to the Bachl Alm. One went to the hayloft. "Is Hans there?" "No." It was Mr. Zimmer[16] (I knew his voice) who had made the first ascent by the south wall. We were most curious to know who the others were, and it was time to get up. Mr. Z. recognized me: "Well, Konradl is here also. It seems to me you are everywhere," he remarked.

Resi was going to church at Filzmoos today, and so was early at work. We had a day of rest. What should we do? Resi not here, W. on the Eiskarlspitze, and St. again looking for his friends. Still, friend R. had a solution. "We'll go to the Moser Alm. I'm known there, and you'll see some pretty girls," he said. They really were more handsome than Resi, but there was not such good order and cleanliness as at the Bachl Alm. Nor were they as pleasant as Resi. Because it was Sunday we bought a regular dinner at Hofpürglhütte, and took a nap at the Mandling spring. Then we went home to the Bachl Alm once more.

That evening we had visitors. Many tourists arrived, Mr. Blattmann among them. Resi had to put the big pans at the hearthside. We sat at table like one big family, and it is well-known in tourist groups that everyone who comes to a hut cuts his name on the table. Perhaps some day it will be very valuable and find a place in an alpine museum.

Everyone left in the morning. We went for the south wall of the Thorstein. At the foot of the slope we examined the wall. Would it be possible to find a way through? I and Mr. P., the friend of St. (who arrived yesterday), made a quick decision. We worked up through difficult chimneys to a ledge which led us to the right onto the wall. This was the key. Our friends followed us with their eyes. Next a long chimney, which I ascended rapidly to the overhang. Then I had Mr. P. follow and secure me as well as possible. The feet must be spread as far apart as possible, and there was a good hold for the left hand. But when I tried it I got cramps in my leg, and had to go back. I tried it again after a long rest, but with the same result. Then Mr. P. climbed up. "That's hard," he panted. He worked for a long while. The minutes seemed endless to me. Between his legs I could see nothing but sky, and a bit of rope hung shaking in the chimney. All at once he took his right foot from the wall and pulled himself up. The place was easier for me as I was on the rope. When our friends saw that we were by this place, they followed. But they got stuck there, and we had to go back and help them.

We let the rope down; R. tied himself on and came up. The others followed in the same manner. The further climbing did not go so fast, so that we thought it might come to a bivouac for the night. But I had to leave for Waidbruck in the morning and said to my companions: "You may stay here for the night, but I cannot and so must give up the climb." And so all of us turned around. We looked for another route of descent, but it was not easy to find. I was constantly ahead. With some trouble we discovered a hole, and after twice roping down reached the easier slope.

Next morning I took leave of the Bachl Alm with a hearty German "Bergheil!"

8

AS GUIDE IN THE DOLOMITES

I went to Waidbruck, and on the following day to the Gröden Valley. At Lardschneider's inn at St. Ulrich, "zum weissen Rössel," I met my tourist, Dr. B. In the afternoon we went to the Sella Pass in order to do the Fünffingerspitze on August 2nd. Dr. B. wanted to ascend the Schmittkamin, but I was unwilling. As there was no room in the German hut we went down to the Italian.

One doesn't have to start early in the Dolomites. We went out about noon. Over the Daumenscharte. We put on our *Kletterschuhe*. There are a few steps to climb on snow. Right at the beginning there is a little overhang. I climbed up. "Come along, doctor," I called. "My dear Konrad, I can't. My shoes are all wet." "Just come, doctor, it goes better here." "What does that matter to me if I can't come up? Pull, Konrad." I was accustomed to doing that for the doctor. 'What more will happen today?' I wondered.

I think nearly an hour passed and we had not put more than 50 metres of elevation behind us. "Doctor, we must be getting along," I said. "I know, I know, I am sick. My stomach is bad. Turn back." So Dr. B. went back, and I went on alone. At the Daumenscharte I met Mr. D. Elbogen, of Vienna, with guide Kostner.[17] "Where is your man?" he inquired. "Oh, he's sick today," I replied. In a little while I was up and down again. I did not take more than an hour, and overtook Dr. B. just below the pass. "It was very easy, doctor; it will have to be done tomorrow," I said to encourage him.

On August 3rd we went out again, and it went off like nothing. Two Swiss guides were with an Englishman in the Schmittkamin. We met on the Fünffingerspitze. While we talked together, Dr. B. asked one of the guides, while showing him my rope: "What do you think? Will it hold? Can one trust oneself on it?" The guide looked at me questioningly and answered: "Oh, I think so. The rope is almost new." It annoyed me very much that Dr. B. should ask the guide such questions. How often he had already *hung* on that rope!

The Englishman went down very badly, so that we continually overtook him. Once down I asked Dr. B.: "Have you no trust in me that you ask a strange guide whether my rope will hold? What will he think of me?" "My dear Konrad, if I had known that I would not have said a word. You are too quickly aroused." "Not often, except in such cases, my dear doctor." Then everything was all right once more and we went to Campitello. Dr. B. had torn his trousers so badly that the tailor had a big job. I went ahead alone to Vajolethütte, where I met a few guides that I knew. Dr. B. arrived that evening.

For next morning we made an attempt on the Winkler Tower. Dr. B. went very slowly, I perhaps 60 metres ahead. "Konrad, don't be angry, I must tell you something." "Well, what is it?" "Don't you know that a guide should not be farther than 20 metres ahead or behind his man? A guide has to be just like a dog." "Then you won't get far with me, doctor, we'll be through right away." I didn't listen to him any further, and during the climb we made up our difficulties. "Do you think we shall succeed?" he asked. "Why not, doctor?"

Everything went well as far as the famous ledge, but there it was too exposed for him. I was already over the worst of it, and he still stood there where the ledge was almost a metre wide. "Come along, doctor," I called. "Does it get much worse?" "Certainly, it isn't bad where you are standing." "Don't talk so stupidly, Konrad." I went back to him.

"Tell me honestly, will it be much worse than here?" "Of course it will!" I said. "Oh, if it only went *up*," he lamented, "that would be easier, but I cannot *go across*. Can't you pull me?" "No, doctor, I can't pull you." And so it went on with a dozen similar questions. At last he said: "We'll go back." "I don't like to do that, doctor; you know how people talk, and instead of getting a reputation one is written down as a bad guide, and declared a weakling – which is not the case with me. If it's all the same to you, let us climb the Stabeler Tower." "Yes, Konrad, let's do that."

One can go right over to the Stabeler Tower from the ledge on the Winkler Tower. At the "pillar, or leaning block," as it is called in the guidebook, I climbed up. But Dr. B. could not do this either, although it was not exposed. "I can't go any farther," he mumbled. "I am not well." Again I had to turn back with him. "Doctor, you must realize that I am not to blame for turning back. And if another guide asks you for the reason you must tell him the truth." "Am I compelled to do that?" "Yes, if you are a man, it is naturally your duty. Otherwise I will be unjustly discredited." "But, Konrad, if you had not yielded, I would surely have gone on!" "Well, doctor I have nothing more to say. I can't carry you over, and you can't get over by your own strength. You must see that for yourself." "Yes, you are right, Konrad. If anyone asks me I will tell him that it was my own fault."

When we reached the "Gartl" I showed him, in pleasant manner, the route on the Delago Tower. "Do you think I could make it?" "Yes, if pulling on the rope doesn't matter to you, doctor. But I can't get you over there by myself; if another party were doing the Delago Tower it would be easy." "Konrad, perhaps you'll hear in the hut of a party ascending the Delago. I would be so pleased if I could climb it. It is really the most difficult of the three towers – even if I do have to be pulled up."

He returned with me to the hut in good humour. There I found Johann Schroffenegger. I told him about the matter. He said: "The same thing has happened to me. My man wants to do the Schmittkamin, but will not take along a second guide." "Well, that's fine," I said. "We will go together on the

Delago Tower and then up the Schmittkamin." I told the doctor of my conversation with Schroffenegger; he introduced himself to the other gentleman and affairs were arranged.

On August 5th we started out at nine o'clock. We chatted pleasantly and I said to Schroffenegger: "You will see a merry chase today." Schroffenegger climbed ahead. The first chimney is not so hard. I climbed behind him. Above the chimney there is a firm position. We had the men follow. We held the rope tightly and Schroffenegger's man came up breathless. Then Dr. B. After that it grew worse. We had to pull diligently on the rope. Just as always, so today he had excuses. "My hold has broken out," he gasped. Then I wanted to go ahead, but Schroffenegger intimated that there were several difficult places to follow, on which he wished to lead. In a masterly fashion he ascended the difficult chimney. No holds, only back- and footwork. There was a good place above.

Now the men followed. Both were pulled up through the chimney. Then the customary rest was taken. The place reminded me of the time in the preceding summer when we had spent three hours there in violent rain and hail. At the next chimney I went ahead. It didn't trouble me much, for I was accustomed to such cracks. A *Stemmkamin* seemed always harder. The best thing about climbing on the Delago Tower is that one always has solid footing above the bad places. After the crack there is a sort of gully, then the traverse.

The doctor had to cross – halfway it went all right, but it was unpleasant for him to stop, as it is very much exposed. "Shall I stand up, Konrad?" he called in fear. "Sit down, doctor." "One can't sit here." "Oh, certainly." "Konrad, ask Schroffenegger." So I called: "Schroffenegger, the gentleman is asking whether one can sit down there." Sch.: "Sure, tell him so." I: "You tell him." Sch.: "What's the trouble, my dear doctor?" "Tell me, Schroffenegger, whether one can sit here?" "Surely, just like in a chair! Kain has told you that already. I have nothing more to say. Come along." Dr. B. hesitated: "I can't see anything. My glasses are smeared up. Hold tight."

The other man was highly pleased at seeing that he went much better than Dr. B. After several similar incidents we soon reached the traverse of the airy Delago spire. We secured the gentleman and took a rest on the summit. After eating, Dr. B. took out his cigar case and gave each of us a cigar to make things right again. The descent was easy. One lets the men down the length of the rope to a good place, and in a short time the worst is over. In the afternoon we went to the Sella Pass, to climb the Schmittkamin on the next day.

We arrived in Perra, took a carriage to Canazei and from there were on the Sella Pass in an hour. That evening we had a good time with two Italian girls. Next morning we left the hut at nine o'clock. Because of the cold rocks it is best not to go earlier. During the ascent Dr. B., despite the sunshine, got cold fingers (in preparation for another alibi) and put on gloves, while Schroffenegger and his man laughed at him. One easily reaches the climb in an hour, and changes shoes, leaving the nailed boots lying there. Before the difficulties began we had a drink of tea mixed with wine which I had brought with me, for yesterday the mixture tasted so good to my man that he requested me to take it along in the future. Dr. B. took a deep pull: "Well, what's this," he began, "tea with wine? You know, Konrad, that I do not allow any wine on a trip." "But, doctor, you demanded it yesterday. The others are witnesses!" Dr. B.: "Is that so?" "Yes, doctor, that is what you told your guide." I: "If you are not feeling well, doctor, you do not have to go. I will have the chance to climb the Schmittkamin."

Schroffenegger went ahead, and I followed. When we were alone and the gentlemen could not hear us, Schroffenegger said: "Don't say another word about turning back. There is nothing the matter with your fellow. He is only fixing things so we shan't blame him for his bad climbing." Now we were at the so-called "Kirch!" Schroffenegger said: "Go ahead. Then he'll have to come, for one can't go back from here with less than a hundred metres of rope and we haven't that much!"

Trembling and shouting the doctor came up on the rope. "Now the company must permit me to catch my breath. But I am happy to be here," he added. I continued slowly above the difficult block. One pushes up with back and feet for some 12 metres to the overhang, which is very dangerous for the leader. Then come the rucksacks, which are sure to catch on the rock. I jerked the rope about for quite a while. Dr. B. began to grumble. "What's the matter? We can't stop here." "Certainly not," I promised. Schroffenegger arrived and said to me: "Well I wouldn't like to travel with that fellow." "I am not any too pleased myself," I answered, "but when one is not known as a guide, one takes anything." Dr. B. came over the block almost crosswise.

Short but not difficult places follow. The Toni Dimai route diverges here. Schroffenegger and I followed the Schmitt route out on the wall and back again into the chimney. Meanwhile, the gentlemen began to quarrel. Dr. B. was sarcastically calling the other an "expert." Up above on the wall we were laughing, our hands full. It was like theatre to us. I roped myself into the chimney, threw the rope down, Mr. K. tying himself on while we secured him. Schroffenegger was above me and helped pull. We let Dr. B. wait a little longer as punishment. To get him over the cliff we had to lift him almost two metres through the air!

As we were now on the bluff we went as two parties, Schroffenegger and his man ahead. It was now too slow for the doctor. "Konrad, go faster, I can't stand this!" "Doctor, if anyone can go faster I would like to see him." "Well you are a good enough climber, Konrad, but you should take in the rope more quickly. Watch the Swiss guides just once. You are a slowpoke in comparison." These words angered me to the utmost. "Listen, you, don't be so impertinent or I'll cut the rope and throw you on your head. Get yourself a Swiss guide if you like!" (And if such a thing ever happens to me again I will go back to breaking stones rather than risk my life for such a man.)

We all shook hands on the summit of the Fünffingerspitze, but Dr. B. received no grasp from me. A little later he offered me a cigar. "Keep your cigars and smoke them yourself." He: "But, my dear friend Konrad, I beg your pardon. Really I didn't mean it. You know how nervous I am. Even Mr. K. has forgiven me." Without further words we descended by way of the Daumenscharte. At the end of the climb he asked my pardon once more. "No, doctor. We have often quarrelled and made up, but not this time."

At the Sella Pass he fell on his knees and with upraised hands requested my forgiveness. He wept bitterly at the same time, so that I took pity on his crazy actions. "Stand up and don't do such stupid things in front of me. It would be different if we were alone. But Mr. K. and Schroffenegger have heard the whole thing. What will they think of me if I quietly put up with all your abuse? And how will I look if Schroffenegger tells all the other guides and I want to come back to this district?" "Dear friend, forgive me, I owe you my life. I will buy silence from Schroffenegger." "Get away from me, doctor," I thundered. "How much should I pay him? Ten kronen?" "I have no idea."

A few minutes later we reached the Sella Hut. Once Dr. B. was among the tourists he talked quite differently. After his story was told they thought the best of him and looked upon him as a "King." That evening Dr. B. gave Schroffenegger 20 kronen, with the request to say nothing more about the incident. Schroffenegger wanted to give me half, but I would not take it. We went together over to the German hut and celebrated our parting with a bottle of Magdalena. It was paid for with the hush money!

Schroffenegger had to depart early next day, as he had to be in Bozen by nightfall. Right at the best season he had to leave for military service. Dr. B.

and I went our leisurely way to St. Ulrich. There I met all the guides who had been at the Regensburger Hütte in the previous year. In their dialect they shouted: "Well, here is Kain. You have done the Schmittkamin, and the Delago and the Winkler towers. Bravo! Come, drink a glass of wine with us. A health to our colleague!"

9

THE END OF THE SEASON

I was engaged for the Dachstein's south wall on September 20th. I arrived at Mandling on the day before, and went to the Bachl Alm. There I awaited my man. About half past two in the morning we were standing beside Resi in the kitchen, waiting for our coffee, and then left the hut by lantern light. It was quite mysterious to go through the autumnal mist. Today the climb on the south wall would not be so easy.

Mr. St. had informed me that the guide Sterner told him it was impossible to do the south wall so late in the autumn. The snow had receded about 25 metres. Instead of the fine snow bridge we had a smooth wall in front of us. I had to search for a long time until I spied the right place, and then I climbed up Mr. St.'s back, shoulder and head, and succeeded after a stiff battle in reaching the ledge. It was necessary for me to pull Mr. St. through the air a little, for he had no "climbing tree." But after that we ascended comfortably. The man climbed very well, but much time was lost in taking pictures. Otherwise we would have done the south wall in the very shortest time.

A lovely autumn day! A sea of cloud had been before us throughout, with the pointed Tauern peaks emerging from it. On the last part of the way a cold fog met us, so that our fingers became stiff. From the Bachl Alm to the top of the wall we had taken ten hours. On account of wasted time we could not continue to the summit of the Dachstein, but went direct to the Simonyhütte, where considerable argument arose between the guides who were there and myself. They wished to make light of it, but soon found they were in the wrong. The Hallstatt guides are not my match in dispute or experience. I will say no more, except that they are not in good repute on this account and probably deserve it. The guides of Ramsau and Schladming are better and more sought after.

Next day we took the monotonous descent over the Reitweg to Hallstatt, where we had lunch. Then I went home. There I made a few more tours on the Rax, with and without companions. On St. Christopher's Day I took two men up the Stadlwand ridge. The weather was splendid, but we bemoaned our cold fingers. Then we descended through the cirque to Weichtal, continuing to the "Binderin" in the Reiss Valley and doing the Red Gully on the following day. The weather was good, but there were huge masses of snow, and icy rocks. The plateau was full of people. A tourist on every pinnacle. We returned to the Reiss Valley and climbed the Wilde Gamseck next day. During the descent we met a party that had turned back. It was the proper thing, for the tourists were badly fitted out, the women in ordinary shoes.

I was in Otto-Schutzhaus on Sylvester's Day. We had come up the Preinthaler route. The last day of the year was spent in comfort and gaiety. I really must say that the year 1905 was a much better one than the preceding, and it ended in human habitation with happy people, not, as in 1904, in a stable.

CHAPTER IV

·*(1906)*

▲

IN THE MOUNTAINS OF MY HOME

There was no lack of work. I was busy all through January with the building of water conduits on the "Heufuss" at Naßwald. I also had work during the entire month of February. During Easter week the climbing began again. On Good Friday I took two men over the Maler route; or rather, I let myself be guided, first by Dr. W. and then by Dr. B. It gave both men much pleasure to pull me once in a while! Our descent was made by way of the "wilden Rauchfänge" and the little Gries saddle, and then down over the snow. The night was spent at the cooper's in the Reiss Valley.

On Saturday we went in lovely spring weather over the Wilde Gamseck. The sun shone so brightly that we took the first sunbath of the season. On Easter Sunday I did the Akademik climb with two men from Brünn, but there were too many people out and the pleasant quiet was continually being disturbed by "He-oh!" On account of the sun's warmth the snow of the plateau had become so soft that it was really toilsome to reach Otto-Schutzhaus. After lunch we continued across the plateau to Habsburg-Haus. A great time was being had there with fiddle and zither playing, and frequently the lovely song "The Old Splendour of Youth."

On Easter Monday we descended the Red Gully. A dangerous business. There was scarcely a hold or a footing in the frozen snow, and I thought to myself: 'If I were only at Gries.' Cautiously I put the men ahead. It was worst for me as the last. There was only room in the steps for one row of nails. I imagine that the men were in fear when they saw how I descended the icy slabs. One would have perished without hope if a single step had given way. Later on, where there was more snow than ice, things went better. At the Binder Inn we had a little breakfast and then went by way of the Nass cirque to the Wilde Gamseck. The men climbed so well that I had no work at all. I went with them to Karl-Ludwig-Haus and then down to Naßwald. One of the gentlemen told me that possibly he would take me to Switzerland that summer. It was very pleasant for me to think about it.

On April 20th I took Miss B. over the Katzenkopf and the upper Zimmer climb, which pleased her very much. Only the narrow crack gave her a little trouble. I consoled her by saying that it gave many people a lot of work. We sauntered slowly along to Otto-Schutzhaus. After a long rest we started for the Preiner wall, with the intention of descending by the Karl Berger route. Dark clouds appeared, notifying us that we should be wet today. Quickly as we completed the climb, the storm was quicker and we were thoroughly soaked on reaching Edlach, where the lady lived.

Next day I did the lower Zimmer climb with Dr. W. We were out early in order to be safe from the stones. We came slowly to the plateau, for Dr. W. was very tired from the exertion. Then he descended from Otto-Schutzhaus by way of the Thörl path. I stayed for a while in the hut, and three young men came along who inquired whether I would take them on the Karl Berger climb. I accompanied them, and they were pretty good goers. We separated at the Preiner slide and I climbed over the Trinksteinsattel to Habsburg-Haus. There was a fine sunset, from which I could not tear myself away. So I remained overnight. Next day it seemed very difficult to go down into the valley. That is the way it often is.

On April 26th, in fine weather, I took Miss B. over the Maler climb, then across the plateau and down the Blechmauern route. There was a wonderful view down into the Höllenthal. The beech trees had their soft decoration of green leaves, and a few bird-calls grew in volume, bringing the song to mind:

> Wann's kan Schnee mehr aba schneit
> und der Kirschbam Blüten treibt, ,
> Und's Tauberl g'schami wird
> und der Tauher Herzweh g'spürt:
> Das ist die wahre Freud,
> die Frühlingszeit.

[When the snow no longer falls,
and the cherry blooms unfold,
and the doves are making love,
Spring's the time for joy.]

Next day we climbed the grand Stadlwand ridge. In a short time we were at the start. Black clouds gathered, and we were in doubt whether to proceed. The lust for climbing conquered. But when we were at the halfway mark, the wind, then lightning and thunder, came suddenly. The young lady was afraid of lightning, but I laughed to cheer her up. At the top of the route we were met by a furious hail, and sought shelter under a big tree. But the storm passed quickly, leaving the air spicy and clear, and the green of spring so beautiful once more! I conducted the young lady by way of the Wasserofen (over the "Schiache" it is called) to Kaiserbrunn, a route that is not yet known by tourists.

On May 18th I received a telegram: "Come to Vienna; Kaiserstrasse 15. A long trip. Kauba." On Saturday, May 19th, I went to Vienna and walked into Mizzi Langer's. "Grüss Gott, Mr. Kauba. What is going on?" "Do you know Mr. G.?" "No." "He wants to make a trip to Corsica. Would you like to go with him?" "Certainly, with pleasure." "But there are bandits and wild boars there." "That doesn't matter to me!" I laughed.

At noon I went with Mr. and Mrs. Kauba to an inn, where Mr. G. came as well and to whom I was introduced. We then went to the sporting-goods house of Mizzi Langer, where everything necessary for the journey was purchased. I received a rucksack and an ice axe from Mr. G.

Monday night was set for our departure. I was engaged for the Stadlwand ridge on Sunday. About a quarter before one in the morning I arrived in Payerbach by the night train from Vienna. There I left my baggage for Corsica and went on to Kaiserbrunn, where I had to sleep in a cart. We started out early. A company of five persons: three men, who went together, and two ladies, whom I guided. It was a pleasure to see how well both of them climbed. At the Stadlwand Hut (a hunting lodge) we rested at noon. Then we went down over the Hochlauf, where I lost the route slightly, which annoyed me very much. It was really excusable, for I already had too many thoughts of travel in my head!

That evening I went to Naßwald and told my mother in great joy that I was going away for several weeks. When she heard that I would journey on the sea she was much afraid. On Monday at midnight I took leave of Naßwald, and about one o'clock was sitting in the train.

2

MY JOURNEY TO CORSICA

The ride to Pontafel was endless. There was the Customs and money-changing. When this was finished an officer came into the compartment and asked me: "Where are you going?" "To Italy." "Where?" "Livorno." "Have you a passport?" "No, but here is my round-trip ticket and provisional guide's book."

There was a police clerk in the corridor, reading out of his notebook the following description of my person: "Middle height, face oval, eyes brown, eyebrows black, hair black, often in jail." "Come out!" he commanded. I said: "I tell you, sirs, I have never been sentenced for a single hour!" "Have you no documents with you?" asked the commissioner. Then I recalled that I had a certificate of my place of residence and showed it to them. I had to sign my name on a slip – and was free. (The men had been in doubt as to the accuracy of my personal description.) The train left a moment later.

At one of the larger stations an attractively picturesque Italian girl got on. I helped her lift up her basket and she thanked me politely. A little later she spoke to me in Italian (probably asking me where I was going) and as I could not reply, she asked: "Parla lei italiano?" "Si, un poco." I knew only a few Italian phrases, and the thing was too troublesome for me. "Parla il tedesco?" she inquired. "Un poco!" she said also. And so we worked it, half in German, half in Italian. Then she unpacked her basket and invited me to join her. It tastes better when there are two! I did not hesitate long and dived in. To be sure the fish and bread were not so tasty, but just that much the better were the wine and fruit. She asked about my business. I could not make it clear for a long time; she did not understand until it occurred to me to say "Guida delle Monte." She told me that she liked the mountains, and we chatted and entertained ourselves until we reached Mestre.

We had to change cars there. She was going to Milan, and, like myself, had to wait two hours for the train. I enjoyed her company until the train left. We went together to the restaurant and had supper. Then she wanted to show me the city, but it was so foggy that we could see nothing. When she had gone I gave a guard half a franc to let me go into a second class compartment. He brought me a pillow and I slept well until three o'clock. For safety I tied both my rucksacks to my feet. But the travel fever, in a foreign country, let me sleep no longer. At noon, in Bologna, there was a stop of two hours. I got out and went into the city. All at once someone called: "Where are you going, fellow countryman? Tyrolese? Well, I'm one too, from the

Zillerthal." I asked him where I could eat well and cheaply, and he showed me an inn. Then I inquired about the sights of the city. He thought that the finest thing was the church.

I ordered my lunch in Italian, according to the Grammar that I had with me and the people understood quite well. Then I had a look at the church. Several hundred people were inside. But I didn't stay long for I could not bear the smoke of the incense. At two o'clock the train continued to Florence, where I was to meet Mr. G.[18] The journey was very beautiful and reminded me somewhat of the surroundings of Semmering. My fellow travellers were astonished by my woolen stockings and wondered that they were not too hot.

"Firenze, Firenze!" shouted the conductor. Quick as lightning my eyes swept over the many heads. I could not see Mr. G., but I was easy to recognize with my two packed rucksacks and two axes. Mr. G. was standing at the exit, and we greeted one another with a cheery "Grüss Gott!" "You got here all right?" he inquired. "We haven't much time left; the train leaves for Livorno [Leghorn] at eight o'clock." We quickly climbed into a carriage; he bought me my supper in a fine trattoria and then left.

After the long rail journey my hands were begrimed with soot, and a man who sat with a lady at an adjacent table asked me: "Did you come by automobile?" Then he inquired further, where I came from and where I was going. They were Viennese, and it was easy to see that they were on their honeymoon. They were much amazed that a Rax guide had been around so much. While I was paying my bill Mr. G. came in – it was high time to leave.

At Livorno we entered an elegant hotel; the bed was so good that I hardly dared to get in. Next morning I was up early to see a little of the city. There were also a few purchases to be made. We left about eight o'clock. Beside our little steamer there was a much larger one in the harbour on which there was much merrymaking. Music played and there was laughter and shouting. I had thought a ship would be quite different.

The vessel went slowly out. It was a windless day, and the sea spread its wonderful blue before us. My first voyage! We talked much of our coming mountain tours in Corsica. About six o'clock that evening we reached Bastia. Hundreds of people were standing at the landing. Mr. G. took several pictures; a crowd of women and children followed us. Our tourist costumes attracted them. We took up our quarters in a hotel beside the station; we saw the city, and that evening climbed to the top of a nearby hill. Till then it was my most splendid hour; for the first time I saw the sun descend into the sea! I could not tear myself away from the sight, and I was sorry when night came and we had to return to the city.

Bastia is thickly populated. Officers and sailors go walking with lovely ladies and girls. I noticed that when women went together it was always in parties of three, and always an older one along. On May 25th we went by train to Corte. The journey was wonderful, through fields of flowers. We made our headquarters in Corte. Someone spoke to us in the station who was connected with both the postal coach and the guidance of strangers. He took us to a hotel and then showed us the birthplace of the great Napoleon, which is quite shot to pieces, with cannonballs sticking in the walls.

Corte, like Bastia, is a very uncleanly spot. At noon the guide ate with us and told us of his journeys. The meal was excellent. Seven plates stood one upon another. That meant seven courses! Then there was good Croatian wine, which we had already enjoyed in Bastia. Our next goal was Calacuccia. A 10- or 12-year-old boy ran alongside of our post carriage and beat the mules in a senseless fashion. At Ponte Castirla we had a long stop. The people were astonished by us. Then we went on to Calacuccia by way of the lovely Golo Valley and the deep ravine of Santa Regina.

Fig trees and cork wood were everywhere. On stony ground every spot is used, and one often sees a vineyard surrounded by stones. The rocks were also interesting: granite slabs, often of remarkable form, frequently resembling the heads of animals. At Calacuccia we went into the tourist hotel. There the natives crowded around us. One offered himself as porter and was engaged. We were alone in the hotel, but another man arrived later. A pretty little girl served us, and the landlady was also quite attractive. She was neatly dressed but her hair was too much smeared with oil.

Each of us had a room, Mr. G. and I. Price: one franc. The beds were very good, so good that we didn't get up until five o'clock in the morning! Today we were to climb Monte Cinto (2710 metres), the highest peak of the island. We left about half past six and wandered over hillocks toward the mountain. With Monte Cinto once before us we rested and looked to see where the best route lay. It was nowhere bad, so each of us selected his own way, mainly over stony slides and snow. When the snow walking became too stupid for us we left the usual route and went up a ridge to the right where there were some quite good and not very easy climbing places. The sun was bright and blazed down upon us. The summit of Monte Cinto was all covered with snow. The view was splendid: to the north and west was the shimmering sea. To the northeast extended the fine ridge from Capa al Ciuntrone, Punta Sellola to Capo al Berdata, which almost attracted us but the time was too short.

With the true curiosity of a climber I looked down the north wall of Monte Cinto! To the northwest avalanches thundered down from Capo al Barba. How fine it looked! As there was still much snow in the hollows of Monte Cinto we had a good slide during the descent. I think we must have come down 1500 metres in that fashion. So we quickly reached the Lago di Cinto, lying in the midst of snow and ice. During the descent to Calacuccia a peasant called to us from a stone hut and offered us a drink of wine, but since it was not far home we did not go in. Are those the bandit manners of which Mr. Henter writes?

No one in the hotel would believe we had been to the top of Monte Cinto, for Corsicans are very wary of snow. If one were dependent upon these people, one would never reach a mountaintop under such conditions. Next day, the porter appeared with a mule and packed up our things. We started off. He went by a different way and we were to meet him in Calassima. Mr. G. and I went in a two-wheeled cart to Albertacce and from there continued to Calassima (1100 metres), the loftiest village of Corsica. The path to Calassima grew ever worse. Before reaching the Bergerie de Ballone (1450 metres) we got out beside a huge block of granite. The tent was set up on the ground. The porter made us some good soup, while Mr. G. and I examined the ridge descending from the Punta Castelluccia. We were to climb that in the morning!

Lovely was the evening in the pleasant solitude beside the rushing Viro. I spent my first night in a sleeping bag. A big stone was set across the entrance of our rocky roof lest the wild boars (which are not there!) come into our dwelling. There was a huge forest of pines on the opposite bank of the Viro.

The alarm went off about three o'clock in the morning. "Did you sleep well?" "No, the ground was too hard." We made cocoa for breakfast and started off. A large, half-rotted tree was our bridge across the boiling Viro. We sauntered through the lovely forest toward the southeastern ridge of the Punta Castelluccia. It was easy at first, then came slabs which increased the difficulties. Now there is a snow-filled gully, overhanging at the top. It is better for us to try the crack on the right. The *Kletterschuhe* are put on and the rope made ready. After ascending some very difficult slabs we stand at an overhang and a rickety bridge of stones.

I said: "It will be best to put on the rope," and after this was done I tried the overhang. It didn't go. So we had to pass over the bridge. "Can you hold firmly, Mr. G?" I climbed carefully across and had a good position. Mr. G. followed. On account of the snow we had to put on the nailed shoes once more. To the left is a gully, just like a staircase. Shall we go down there? Mr. G. thought it would be better to stay on the ridge. Again we changed our shoes. Now comes a little wall where I have scarcely no hold. I must jump to catch the crack. While I fumbled about I felt something cool and soft. I was surprised and jumped back. What was that? I had squashed a lizard, so that its flesh stuck to my fingers. That was a moment such as I never before experienced! Trembling, I tried the place once more. Then came an easier slab. One must lie prone in passing it. Now there were ledges, and then a crack. I climbed out the length of the rope. The crack was very strenuous for one could only get the left foot and hand in it.

Mr. G. came on to this place, the only spot where one could rest. I climbed up another 20 metres. Then, through a niche, I saw the head of an animal with huge shining eyes. I went by as quickly as possible, without saying anything to Mr. G. But he had also noticed it and asked me whether I had seen the animal. What was it? A gigantic owl.

During the further climbing there was one more difficult and much-exposed shelf. Then it was finished. The nailed boots were resumed. One slipped from Mr. G.'s hands, luckily sticking in the snow one or two metres below us, where I could get it without trouble. In a few minutes we were on the summit of Punta Castelluccia. The view spread over the splendid forest to the right; to the left was the Paglia Orba with the Capo Tafonato, the most beautiful mountain of Corsica, and a virgin peak, behind. There, tomorrow, we should try our luck!

On the other side the mountain is a grass slope. After four hours' rest we descended through a snowy couloir. A glorious glissade, but a bit dangerous. Down at our hole in the rocks there was a good supper. We had fish, which the porter had caught in the Viro during our absence. But before eating we had a bath in the brook. That evening we had a visit: the herdsmen came and Mr. G. offered them English tobacco. I was very sorry that I could not talk to them. The night was perfect; the moon sailed out of the clouds and bathed the landscape in silvery light.

We left our cave about four o'clock in the morning. This time we slept much better than before. It was not so easy to cross the brook as yesterday. I had to throw a tree across to the other bank, and it always slipped off the stone on which I wanted to put it. By setting it between two stones the bridge building succeeded at last. But the bridge itself was dangerous and a fall into the racing Viro would have had a bad outcome.

It was wonderful in the forest to go through the tall ferns. In a short time we were standing on the pass, the Bocca Fuggi Gallo, then sharply to the right and we saw the lovely Capo Tafonato before us. The mountain is renowned in legend: the Devil, in anger at St. Martinus, struck a blow at the mountain and a gigantic door of rock appeared, 30 metres wide and eight to 12 metres high.

Mr. G. took pictures and then looked for a route up the south wall. I went to the west ridge. In a short time Mr. G. followed me. "Will it go?" "Here, certainly," I said, "if there is not some cutting to be done higher up." We put on our *Kletterschuhe* and for about 18 metres there was no trouble. Then came a little wall, not easy for the holds were quite small. There was a good position above. Mr. G. followed rapidly. Then the route turned behind an overhang in brittle rock on to the north side; thence upward over slabs, again of brittle stone. We did not consider a serious hindrance any further, but it came. Before reaching the summit we waged a hot battle with the last teeth of the ridge, and the place is really exposed in an annoying way. Not a hold to be reached. I tried throwing the rope at least 50 times. When it caught at last and I pulled, it slipped down again.

As nothing could be done with the rope, it went better with a "climbing tree." I stood on Mr. G.'s shoulders, lifted myself to a hold – which broke! The second one likewise. Then I stood on Mr. G.'s head and reached a good grip for the right hand. Then left, over a shelf and it was won. There is the peak. The virgin peak! A few steps and we were the conquerors. No stone man and no human trace. My first peak that I trod as the very first!

Mr. G. took pictures, while I built a huge cairn in which we deposited an empty preserve tin with a book, in which we wrote our names and the date of the first ascent. Our joy was great. One must be very careful on the summit, for stones lie about quite loose. This is also an indication that no human being had ever been there.

During the descent we had to rope down once. We went once again to the rocky door and looked down into the Valle Rosso and the Tondo hollow. Then we climbed over the northwestern side through several couloirs on the Paglia Orba (2523 metres), making the first ascent of the northwest wall. This mountain is probably much visited in summer, for there were numerous visiting cards in the cairn. The view from here into the Viro Valley is one of the best.

Our stone man on the adjacent Capo Tafonato stood up boldly. Now, when tourists come to the Paglia Orba they will see that their neighbour, the mighty rock peak of Tafonato, has fallen. After a long rest on the summit we descended over the southwest side, which Mr. Cube has described in the Yearbook of the German–Austrian Alpine Club for 1901. Paglia Orba was ascended for the first time by survey officers in 1820. It is the queen of the Corsican mountains because of its beautiful, pleasing form. It drops precipitously to the Viro Valley. Between the Paglia Orba and the Capo Tafonato there is a great gorge into which drop smooth perpendicular walls 600 to 700 metres high.

During the day our porter had again been fishing diligently. For hors d'oeuvres we had Corsican ham, sardines and butter; then there was soup, fish and even a drink of wine. What more could the heart desire, here in the midst of Corsica's wild mountain world? But at night it was loveliest of all. The moon shone, the "Queen" looked down and threw a huge shadow on the fir forest. The faint sounds of the herds and the rushing of the Viro. That was something to remember.

On May 29th we climbed the Capo Uccello. Going along the Viro we continued across snow and loose granite slabs to the southwestern ridge, where we found a rope sling that perhaps had been used by Mr. Cube and his companion, or perhaps even earlier. It was quite cold. As there was the threat of sliding snow and ice we rounded the southern side, on slabs not altogether easy, to the ridge between Capo Tighietto and Capo Uccello. There we rested. A large snowfield mantles the eastern side of the Uccello. "I will cross and see how it goes." I traversed the snowfield with care and saw a couloir with slabs. That would do. I went back to Mr. G.

"How it is, Konrad?" he called over to me. "I think it will be all right, Mr. G." At the rocks we put on our *Kletterschuhe* and left our rucksacks behind. But the ascent cost us a hard battle with those cursedly smooth slabs. The whole eastern wall is not more than 100 metres high. On the summit was the fine stone man of the conquerors, Cube and Kleintjes.[19]

By roping down we descended the eastern wall; the boots were put on once more and we continued. As Mr. G. did not like to use the rope, I put it in my rucksack. I went ahead and curved toward our track. Mr. G. wanted to do the same thing, but got onto hard snow, his feet slipped and away he went. I shouted as loudly as I could: "Stick in your axe! Stick it in!" and went after him across the steep snowfield – with much uncertainty. Mr. G. succeeded in stopping himself, but 200 metres more and he would have been lost. He was glad to take the rope after that.[20]

We rounded the Capo Tighietto on the south side and paid a visit to the Punta Minuta (2547 metres). A very easy mountain, on which we loafed for a long time. The view was rewarding. Monte Cinto was in front of us, the little Cinto lake below; behind us was the beautiful Paglia Orba with its outliers. The descent was again accompanied by a little glissading. Down in the valley we found huge fallen trees. We measured one three and a half metres in circumference. Again we had a bath in the Viro, and dried ourselves in the sunlight. The sun shone so brightly, as if it didn't want evening to come. During the night a wind arose and awoke us. It knocked on the stones and threw our cooking utensils about.

Today, May 30th, is a day of rest. After our midday nap the shepherds came. Mr. G. made playful remarks and told them I was a young physician, and I had to feel the head, heart and pulse of one of them who felt sick.[21] It was only with difficulty that I kept from laughing. Then I showed the herdsmen how to climb on the big granite block (our house), put in a *Mauerhaken* and rope down. They had never seen anything like that! Then I tried fishing, but my effort was in vain. Not a single bite.

In the morning we were to make our last climb from this camp: the Cinque Frati from the north. We were at the foot of the climb in an hour. We entered the ravine between the first and second towers and climbed up for about 100 metres. Then, to the right, there was quite a difficult little wall, and ledges afterward, leading to a much-exposed overhang. Now comes a chimney almost 100 metres high with some difficult places, all without rope for Mr. G. is a good rock climber. An exit was found on the third tower. We crossed the fourth and finally the fifth, and rested for four hours on the summit.

On the southeastern side the mountain is rugged, so that sheep can come almost to the top. We climbed one more nearby tooth. Then we roped down and returned to our camp. The last evening on the lovely Viro!

At noon of the following day we wandered to Calassima. The afternoon service was just being held in the little church. We entered and looked at the interior. The parson came and invited us to his home. It was very poorly furnished; round stove, table, bench, an old chest and a bed, such as in my home are to be found in woodcutters' huts. Beside the bed, on a shelf, was an alarm clock without hands, and beside it comb and brush and things for cleaning shoes. Some curious people from the village had sneaked along and stood with us in the parson's house. Everyone gnawed tobacco and spat on the floor.

The parson put a bottle of wine on the table, and all at once we had strange visitors. Black swine came into the room. Then there was a chase, and one pig got under the bed and wouldn't come out. Never in my life have I laughed so much! After the hunt Mr. G. showed the parson his camera. He had never seen one like it. Mr. G. presented him with a thermometer, and as the parson did not understand it we had the porter explain the gradations of heat and cold. Then the parson showed us his cows, the open hearth and the sooty pans. How miserable it was! And what pay did he receive? Our clergy in Austria are millionaires in comparison.

From Calassima we went down to Albertacce, the parson with a fishnet accompanying us part of the way. In Albertacce Mr. G. inquired whether one could purchase any antiques. We found a dealer, but he lived in La Pietra and we had to go with him for a good quarter of an hour up the mountain. The people thought us fools when we entered this man's house. First he showed us how to roast chestnuts, and then took us into his room and brought out Italian woodcarvings such as we have for sale in Austria. Then he brought us an old staff of a spinning wheel. I said to Mr. G,: "I could send you just such a piece of a spinning wheel from Naßwald and you wouldn't have to carry it so far." Then he showed us his two funnels, which pleased me better than the piece of the spinning wheel.

On our way back to Albertacce two priests called after us and invited us into their dwelling. After some talk we went in and drank a bottle of wine with them. They then accompanied us for a great part of the way. It was not so pleasant at our hotel in Calacuccia as on our first stop. Many strangers had arrived during the interval, even our rooms had been given away and the dark young landlady had no time to chat with us. Twenty people were at the table, even a gentleman from Munich among them. At least a few with whom I could talk!

Mr. G. ordered some bottles of wine to celebrate our successful ascents; then an old man conducted us to a private dwelling where we could spend the night. The room was spacious, and the bed so large that one could lie across it. Mr. G. inquired about a toilet, but I cannot write down the reply he received.

Next morning we took leave of Calacuccia, went by the postal coach to Corte and after several hours' stop continued by train to Vizzavone, a lovely spot at the foot of the Monte d'Oro (2392 metres). After lunch Mr. G. called in the proprietor and asked him whether many people had recently been up Monte d'Oro. "Oh, no. Too much snow. And, besides, no one has ever climbed it from here." At a nearby table two men and two women were seated, who took us for anarchists and thought we were only disguised as tourists. A waiter from Salzburg served us, and inquired whether we understood what they were saying at the other table. Mr. G. laughed heartily about it.

It was about half past one when we left the hotel. Without danger or exertion the way went easily upward. We were on the summit by about six o'clock. The view was splendid. To the northwest we saw the peaks we had visited some days previously. To our sorrow, on account of lost time, we could not halt on top. Down we went happily. About half past seven we were back in the hotel. This surprised the people very much. And for us it had been only a stroll.

The hotel at Vizzavone was much better than the one at Calacuccia. The surroundings are magnificent. A splendid beech forest all around, with deep shadows. Next morning we went to Ajaccio, the largest city on the Island. I saw palm trees for the first time! We entered a fine hotel belonging to a Swiss who had once been servant to a man of importance in Vienna. Just as we were occupied with the best of the eatables it came time to run for the train. If we missed it we would have to wait two days in Bastia. We climbed aboard and the train started off. The journey from Ajaccio to Bastia is lovely, frequently reminding me of the stretch of road between Visp and Zermatt.

The steamer left at ten o'clock at night, and at eight the next day we landed in Livorno. We went at once to the station and went to Genoa by way of Pisa. There I took leave of Mr. G. The journey to Corsica had been my most interesting experience. I saw so much that was new and beautiful. My patron had divided everything with me, and I never felt that I was just a guide. As long as I live I will always remember with pleasure that journey with Mr. G.

3

A LITTLE ADVENTURE

Before my train left for Milan I had time to look about in the famous cemetery and the harbour of Genoa. In the carriage where I sat, Italian was at first the only thing spoken; after a while a young couple beside me began to quarrel in old-fashioned Viennese. I took up a book, in order to hide my face behind it, so they would not notice that I understood.

They went at it for quite a while, and the woman always had the last word. The whole fight had to do with the past life of the lady. In Novi we stopped for some time. The man climbed out, and in order to get into conversation with the woman I acted as if I were looking for something, and said a few words in excuse. "Please, please, nothing is the matter," she said, and then inquired: "Are you an Austrian?" "Yes, from the Rax district." "We are from Vienna." "Gracious lady, are you on your wedding trip?" "Yes, I am sorry to say. You will think it a fine affair after all you have heard. We have been eight days on the journey, and I will regret it as long as I have hairs on my head."

"Well, why did you get married, then?" She: "He has a good business." "Is that the only reason you got married? Don't you care for him?" "Oh, yes, but look for yourself and see what sort of an insipid fellow he is." "Didn't you know that before?" "Naturally not, or I would have given him the whistle, the idiot!"

'That's a fine title for a young husband,' I thought to myself, and began to talk of something else. The man returned; I took a book in my hand and the quarrel proceeded. Finally I could not stand it any longer. There are not many honeymooners like that! We got out at Milan. The gentleman was engaged with the baggage, and as soon as he had gone the wife ran after me and inquired: "Are you acquainted with Milan?" "Yes." "Where are you going to stop?" "Right there in the German inn on the corner." "Adieu," she said. "Perhaps I'll pay you a visit." "Good day and good luck, madam."

I engaged a room, changed my clothes and went into the dining room. I had scarcely finished eating when I heard the woman ask the waiter whether a young man, an Austrian, had come in. The waiter came with the message that someone wanted to speak to me, and I went out. She greeted me in friendly manner and asked me to accompany her to the Exposition. What could the woman really want of me?

Once we were on the street I asked her where her husband was. "I have left him, telling him that I would wait for him at the Exposition." The affair didn't please me very much, and instinctively I hid my pocketbook in a safer place. One never knows. I told her that her husband would be alarmed, but she assured me that she would meet him that evening at the Exposition. So we boarded a tram and went to the Exposition.

On the way she told me her tale of woe, and if it was the truth she had plenty to regret. It was a forced marriage, and she had had to leave her "beloved Rudolf." "He was just like you," she said. "And you appear upright and honest, so I tell you everything."

We had a glass together in a beer hall. Viennese waltzes were playing, and my companion was gay and light of heart. Soon it was time to go, and the chance befell that we did meet her husband at the Exposition. He spoke sharply to me: "You have seduced my wife!" "Sir, don't get aroused; let your wife tell the story." But she began to weep bitterly and could not speak a single word.

Then I told the man that I had met his wife, who declared that she had awaited him in vain at the Exposition, and at last had sought me out in the hotel to guide her. There was nothing else to say to the man, for I could not put the blame on the lady. The outraged husband begged my pardon and we separated.

Next morning a knock came at my door. "Sir, there is someone here who wishes to speak to you." "In a moment." I dressed and opened the door. Who was it? – the lady! She asked me if she might come in. "Get away from me," I said quietly. I was angry that she was there again. The woman walked in, put her arms about my neck and kissed me, then fell on her knees and begged me to forgive yesterday's unpleasant scene with her husband. How was I to get away from this half-crazy woman?

She began to call me her "dear Rudolf," and wanted to know what the journey back to Vienna cost, for she wanted to leave then and there. I advised her to return to Vienna with her husband, and then to bring her complaints and assertions before her parents. The lady asked me whether she could meet me at the hotel that afternoon. To get rid of her I said yes, and goodbye. God be praised, I was free! I told the waiter to tell the woman, if she came again, that I had gone.

Next day I went home by way of Brescia, Verona and Trient. I had to be at Altaussee on June 30th to climb the Trisselwand by way of the Trisselberg Pass with Miss B. I was making this tour for observation purposes, as the people there did not believe that the Trisselwand could be ascended from that side.

I was engaged by Dr. B. to do the south wall of the Dachstein on July 5th. A young man came with him, whom he introduced as a good climber to be taken along on the south wall. Mr. A. Baum, director of Section Austria, met us at Ramsau. He warned me not to take two tourists on the south wall. He knew the young fellow and said he was not capable enough for this route. Next morning I could not go with Dr. B., who had slept very poorly. So I went with the young man up the Kleine Dirndl and saw that he was not fit to do the south wall. The man descended to Simonyhütte, and I returned to Austria-Hütte.

As the "great" guide Seethaler arrived, there was another sharp exchange of words. But that didn't matter to me, and I gave him my opinion although the head of the Committee on Guides was present.

At three o'clock in the morning I started off with Dr. B. to ascend the south wall. As this was the first time I had approached it from Austria-Hütte, I went somewhat too high and therefore over slabs that were not very easy, especially as they were covered with snow. We had to traverse several large snow patches, and while crossing one of them I told Dr. B. to secure himself well. For I noted that it would not hold for very long. I went over easily and quickly, placed myself as firmly as possible on the other side and had Dr. B. follow.

A few metres farther and he would have been alongside, but he did not quite get there. There was a little crack and the avalanche toppled over the wall with a thunderous noise. Dr. B. lay on his stomach, and did not recover from fright for quite a time, since it carried him down the length of the rope. Then he began to curse.

We rested at the foot of the actual ascent and then climbed on to the basin, where snow was lying. Then it began to rain and our trip was finished. As there was danger of falling stones I proposed to climb out by way of a ledge (which seemed to me to be easier; but there was again an argument, as there had been on the Winkler Tower and in the Schmittkamin). Once we were up, things improved and Dr. B. decided to descend to Gosau. Repeatedly I had to advise him not to take so much cognac. Frequently he fell down as if dead from exhaustion. It came to the point when I had to take the cognac away from him.

The descent went somewhat better, and we parted once more. He even praised me for the lesson I had given him on the subject of schnaps drinking. And so we reached Gosausee, of which I had heard so much. The sun was just setting – a magnificent spectacle! Dr. B. was very tired, and after many halts we reached the "Gosau Smith" at ten o'clock that night. We had a good supper and slept in the same room, for I was his "good friend" once more. Next day we met the young man and went together to Hallstatt. There we took a boat and went across to the other shore for a bath.

A storm came up during the return journey. Both men took off their shoes so that they might swim the more easily in case of accident. For the first time in my life I experienced a deathly fear. As I could not swim I had to trust myself to fate. I was heartily glad when we reached shore once again.

4

A JOURNEY TO SWITZERLAND

I began a Swiss tour with Advokat Otto Liebling, of Brünn, on July 23rd. We went by way of Buchs, Zürich and Bern to Interlaken, and from there Grindelwald, whence new snow compelled our return. Then on to Visp and Stalden. From the latter point we went on a quite narrow path, but the valley broadened and one waterfall after another delighted our eyes. At Saas Grund we waited for a friend, Finanzrat Franz Popischil, of Brünn, who had a Zillerthal guide, Schneeberger, with him. Then up to lofty Saas Fee, in its lovely situation.

The foreground was made of fine fields, joining to larch forests, with the magnificent glaciated peaks to the right: Alphubel, Dom, Südlenzspitze, Nadelhorn etc. To the left were Weissmies and Portiengrat. Of all places in Switzerland I had seen, Saas Fee pleased me most.

On the afternoon of the following day we went out to climb the Weissmies. We reached the Hotel Weissmies (really only a hut, 2400 metres) on the Trift Alp. There we had a new experience. We were asked whether we had any provisions. If so, one has to pay five francs extra for a bed. In the hotel there were three other Austrians present. Drs. März and Ronchetti of Bozen, and Dr. Renner of Hausdorf, in Moravia. Things were not in good shape in the guides' room. The proprietor of the hotel was drunk and allowed some bottles to disappear.

Next morning we were first out, and started with lanterns. A visible path led over the moraines. We waited for daylight at the first crevasses, as it was not advisable to cross them in the dark. We went in two parties. This was not wise, but I left it to the older guide. Dr. L. and I went ahead and were about 30 metres in advance. All at once we heard a low call. We looked around – Schneeberger was up to his neck in a crevasse.

Dr. L. secured me, I rolled on my stomach, anchored my axe and pulled with all my strength on Schneeberger's rope. His man also tugged away and Schneeberger was soon in the daylight once more. Nothing had happened to him, but he was pale with fright. Then we went up to the right, where there were no more crevasses. But it was slow work to the summit. The first 4000er of the season! Mr. P., with Schneeberger, was somewhat ill. We went ahead, spent a half hour on the summit of the Weissmies and then descended the south side, for we wanted to do the Portiengrat as well.

We left the rucksacks behind in the notch between the peaks in order to make better time. We climbed one tower after another; some of them not easy. Finally we came upon loose slabs; whether we were on the very highest point I do not know. I was of the opinion that it was a frontier peak. We descended the same (north) ridge, but traversed the towers along the eastern side. One has to climb down grass slopes (not pleasant!) for a long time to an alm hut, where there are beds for tourists who climb the Weissmies from that side. Then there is a comfortable path down to Saas Fee.

We arrived too late at our table d'hôte, and freshly prepared dishes were very expensive (for example, cutlet cost five francs). Next day was one of rest, and there I made the acquaintance of the famous guide Zurbriggen,[22] who had been clear around the world and had written two books. He made a good impression upon me.

Most pleasing to me were the native women, who smoked pipes while they worked. Two days later we went to the Mischabelhütte; it was built by the Swiss Alpine Club and is one of the best in Switzerland. It is clean and neat, with wood at hand, two stoves, mattresses and good beds. There were a lot of people there, most of them were intending to do the Nadelhorn.

We went up the Südlenzspitze. Behind us came an Englishman with two guides.[23] Dr. L. and I climbed ahead. The tour is not easy, but there is no chance of losing the way for one is almost always on the arête. The most difficult place is the descent from the great tower. Once that was behind us we rested, and it was fine to see how the two guides roped the Englishman down. The tower seems to overhang so far that one would think it almost impossible to climb. One of the guides was amazed that Schneeberger and I, as strangers, could find the route so well.

We remained for an hour and a half on the summit, then followed the Englishman over the ridge to the Nadelhorn. We descended to the Dom Glacier and got into a fall of stone. "One ought never to stay so long on that summit," remarked Schneeberger, and he was right. We had to search for quite a while in order to get over the 'schrund. I had myself well secured and jumped down. Then the others followed. We were often obliged to wade through snow up to our waists on the Dom Glacier, and there were dangerous ice bridges to cross. We rested in the Festi Hut, and took off the rope, which had become burdensome. The descent to Randa in the Nicolai Valley is very monotonous.

We stopped in the Hotel Weisshorn. A good hotel, but usually filled up, so that one frequently spends a bad night. It was the first of August, the day of Swiss Independence. Everywhere there was celebration, the railway station and the hotel entrances being decorated with leaves and branches. Songs of freedom were sung, and bands played in every corner.

On August 2nd we went to the Weisshorn-Hütte (four hours). There we found six guideless Swiss and it was very pleasant. A lovely evening! The cooking was done in front of the hut. At two o'clock the alarm went off. Tea, cocoa, some eggs, and breakfast was finished. As the Swiss gentlemen already knew the way across the glacier we let them go ahead. Just before the rock ridge we rested, and then I took the lead. Schneeberger had told me earlier that he was not feeling quite well.

When we were on the ridge, and came to snow, the three had mountain sickness. Schneeberger wanted to turn back right away with his man, and Dr. L. was this time "all in" and had to stop frequently. The Swiss followed us no farther. The Weisshorn is a splendid peak, but the route goes on and on. I had to do quite a lot of cutting on the last bit. A long halt was made on the summit and those who were mountain sick recovered. The distant view was perfect. Descent went quite easily.

We spent the night at Randa, and next day proceeded to Zermatt. (Rest day.) There were many Vienna tourists there, about 20–25, and some Austrian guides: Oberhollenger, Wenter,[24] Karlinger, Kührer, Kostner. The Swiss guides did not like that very much, nor did my colleague Schneeberger, for he wanted a local guide for the traverse of the Zinal Rothhorn. My man asked me whether I also wanted a local guide, and I said: "No, I don't need one! And if Schneeberger has no faith we'll go alone, doctor." But at these words, Schneeberger and his gentleman accompanied us.

On August 5th we went to the Trift Hotel, where we met some men from Bozen and two from Graz. There were right nice people in charge, not to mention a dark-eyed maiden who made up an extra good bed for me! Next morning we all went away together. The gentlemen from Graz went for the Obergabelhorn. A fine path had been trodden out for us to the Zinal Rothhorn; only the well-known plaque was not so good. We met a party coming from Zinal. The view of the nearby Weisshorn was splendid, while to our right was the Dom group, Monte Rosa, and the Matterhorn, on which some people could be seen.

The descent to the Constantia Hut is grand: first somewhat difficult climbing, then a steep snow ridge, which was unpleasant for me as I dropped my axe into the depths below. Because of stonefalls it was too dangerous to look for it. It was not very agreeable at the Constantia Hut. Not a word of German and no room. A 70-year-old guide was there, who intended to climb the formidable Dent Blanche on the day following. As I had lost my ice axe and could not get another in the hut, we had to give up the

Obergabelhorn. But perhaps we wouldn't have gone anyhow, for we spent a night of misery pressed in like herrings (without covering!).

In order to accomplish something we traversed the Trifthorn. On the Zinal side it is an easy snow stroll, but on the Trift side there is excellent climbing which is quite unknown. That is because it is not a 4000er! (The Trifthorn is 3737 metres high.) We returned to the Trift Hotel. I told the brunette maiden right away that I had slept badly in the Constantia Hut. She thought I had better stop here again because of it. That was the first Swiss girl who made me remember the lovely hours at the huts in Tyrol. That evening the Munich beer tasted good, and everything was jolly with music playing.

On the following afternoon we proceeded to the Cabane Bétemps, in order to do the Lyskamm. In the morning (August 9th) we looked at the weather. It did not seem to be of the best, we thought that a few parties might be out. The group for Monte Rosa started off. The weather improved. The Matterhorn looked as if it had been powdered with gold! But about half past seven a very tiny cloud rose above Mont Blanc – a bad sign – so that we took council and gave up the expedition, just below the Lysjoch.

We continued toward the Capanna Margherita, thinking we would be there in an hour. But we had gone scarcely ten minutes when a strong wind came up with snow and fog, which became ever thicker until we could no longer see a trace of the way. And so we lost the direction. Dr. L. and I were several metres ahead. The other man was already tired, and Schneeberger had no storm cap. Luckily Dr. L. had two and could supply him. The snow and mist became more and more dense and we decided to return.

There was a block of ice. We could stop in its protection and rest. But there was no desire for eating or drinking. What should we do next? When four people are together there are always differences of opinion. I, as youngest, could not say much, for there was an old, well-tried guide with us. First we roped. I go ahead. We wander around. After an hour and a half we are back at the ice block. We shout. Naturally, in vain. And the fog will not lift!

The seriousness of our situation was becoming more and more evident. Mr. P. could not speak any more. Schneeberger began to weep and complain: "What will my poor wife do with three children? We shall perish miserably!" Dr. L. thought that if his affairs at home were all in order the idea of death would be easier.

What good did all this complaining do? I decided to burrow into the snow, to protect us from the cold. That was not agreed upon. Dr. L. said the best thing was to go right on. I was against this, and said: "You would prefer to fall than to freeze slowly here? Or do you care one heller for our lives?" Now I began to be afraid. In my illusion I saw my mother, who was dependent on me and whom I must support. I saw the clamour in the little house when they learned of my death.

We walked slowly onward. That I felt remorse or any other sensation of fear I cannot say. But every step I took seemed to me as if it would be my last, that everything would give way beneath me, ice and snow breaking and everything rolling into the depths. Schneeberger would often shout "Keep to the right," or "Keep to the left," for he could observe how I turned.

All at once – like a miracle – the mist lifted, only for a second, and we saw that we were on the Grenz Glacier. And it had always been my idea that we were on the Italian side. This was at an elevation of 4400 metres, and if we had gone 200 metres farther we would have been corpses on the Grenz Glacier. In this single glimpse, which oriented us, our courage was renewed, and as the fog was no longer so dense we could hold a definite direction.

At 3500 metres the weather was fair again and we saw the truth of the statement that to be wrapped up in a storm is the greatest danger of the Swiss mountains. On the finest of days the weather can change so rapidly that the happy mountaineer, caught without aid or advice in ice and snow can become a corpse in a few minutes.

Tomorrow, the 10th of August, is my 23rd birthday. I almost did not live to enjoy it! In the Cabane Bétemps I said to the two local Swiss guides, who had also turned back with their party in the fog: "Well, if you can't do it, how can we foreign guides find our direction in the mist?" And they replied: "In such weather it is the same for everyone, whoever he may be. The local guide is no better than another." At evening we were joyous, almost too joyous, but it really takes a few bottles to celebrate such a day!

5

FROM COURMAYEUR TO CHAMONIX

The weather had gone to pieces. Dr. L. and I went to Courmayeur to make some expeditions in the Mont Blanc group. I was pleasantly received in the Hôtel Mont Blanc, but I saw at once that something had changed: the old innkeeper had died.

Next day we went to the Rifugio Torino, to do the Aiguille du Géant, starting out on the following morning at eight o'clock. Three hours to the climb; one hour to the top. Conditions were much better than a year ago with

Dr. P. We lay about for a long time on the exposed summit. During descent we met three gentlemen who spoke German. A voice I recognized was that of guide Wenter, from Tiers, with the two Germans. The hut was overflowing. We had engaged a local guide, as we wanted to traverse Mont Blanc, but everyone had to leave the hut without accomplishing anything, for the weather became bad and promised no immediate improvement.

We went across the Mer de Glace to Chamonix, and on another day, in weather not much more favourable, to the hut of the Plan des Aiguilles to ascend the Grépon. On our arrival at the hut, black clouds soared across Mont Blanc, so we had to return to Chamonix, arriving wet through. There I was engaged by another man. Dr. L. had lost patience with the weather and left for Tyrol the following day. I looked for my Dr. B. and found out he was stopping at Bossons, the station below Chamonix. Naturally he did not make a pleasant face when he saw me in such bad weather! There was nothing to do but stay in the valley.

I stayed in the house where Dr. B. was living. They were almost all Germans there, a Viennese family, and a Russian woman who spoke German. I entertained myself well with all of them, with the exception of my gentleman. He was not well-liked, at least by the Viennese family. But the people were very kind to me and often invited me to go for walks, although they did not include Dr. B., to his annoyance.

We remained at Bossons for eight days, and when the weather improved we went for the Grépon. But it didn't come to anything, for I saw that my man was not up to it. So we climbed the Aiguille Charmoz, and I had plenty of work with him on account of new snow. In addition, through his own carelessness, he fell into a crevasse, from which I pulled him with difficulty. Dr. B. was very anxious to ascend the Aiguille du Géant, but as I did not want to go as a party of two on account of danger from crevasses and he wouldn't take a porter, we said goodbye to Mont Blanc and went to Tyrol.

6

IN THE DACHSTEIN AND GESÄUSE MOUNTAINS

On August 25th we went from Kufstein through the Kaiser Valley to Hinterbärenbad. A lovely spot! In the afternoon we did the Totensessel, a half day's tour of no difficulty. Then we went to the Stripsenjoch. On August 27th we climbed the Predigtstuhl through the Botzong Chimney. Once again some words were said. (This tour is as difficult as the Schmittkamin on the Fünffingerspitze.)

Everything went well enough as far as the overhanging portion of the chimney. Even for me the chimney was very hard, as it was still wet with rain. Dr. B., whom I secured on the rope, fell into the air at the overhang. I had the feeling that my last hour had come. When I shouted to him that he should do something to help himself and get up again, I received the answer: "Just keep on pulling. What have I got you for, anyhow?" And I pulled with all my might. It was really my greatest exertion, and I realized that one's strength is three times as great if one has Death to face. And so we went back.

As the bad weather continued we left Tyrol and went to Schladming, in the Enns Valley. On the way to the Bachl Alm such a quarrel arose and I became so vehement that Dr. B. was going to report me. We had supper with guide Steiner at Ramsau, and then went in lovely moonlight to the Bachl Alm. Resi was awakened to get us a glass of milk, and I told her to give us some hot milk at half past two in the morning.

At two o'clock I awoke Dr. B., who got up unwillingly. After breakfast we went out with lanterns, without saying a word, to the Windleger Pass (a toilsome business!). All at once Dr. B. stopped and said: "Konrad, I wish to have a few words with you." I replied: "Sir, it would be best if you say nothing, otherwise you will only arouse yourself." "Konrad, I will give you some good advice. Before we part give me a written apology for yesterday's quarrel." "I can't do that, doctor, for you might show it all over Vienna." "Then I'll have to report you." "Very well, sir, do that." And without saying another word we went on to the ascent.

I roped him and we went along. Up the Thorstein. I had to cut a few steps across a large snowfield. Then Dr. B. began to use flattery: "Konrad, you learned in Switzerland to cut steps very well." I said pleasantly: "Yes, naturally, doctor." And when he saw that I replied affably he returned again to the matter of "settlement." I said: "Doctor, we are now making a dangerous tour, so we must think of something else." It was quite icy, so that some steps were rather risky. In spite of this we advanced rapidly and took not longer than three and three-quarter hours to the Thorstein. (By the Windleger, or west ridge. In the "Hochtourist" the route is described as requiring nine hours, but this must be a mistake.)

On the summit Dr. B. began again: "Konrad, recall what you said to me yesterday. You will realize that as a physician and an officer, I am displeased. I will have to report you to the German–Austrian Alpine Club." "Sir, what has the Club to do with me? I am not even an authorized guide." He: "If the Club will not act in this matter, then it is the duty of all its officers to resign." I: "On your account, doctor?" Then he went on in another track. "Look, Konrad, I have known you six years and was your first tourist, and the affair turns out this way. Give me your hand and apologize." I hesitated a little and then put out my hand: "Well, I suppose that I was too hasty with you, but you are to blame, doctor, that the matter went so far." So we were good friends once more.

He slipped while descending to the Gosau Glacier and I held solidly. Then he said: "I owe my life to you." I replied: "Oh, sir, I have seen your gratitude already. You were willing to ruin the future and very existence of a man who protects you and has saved your life!" And at that he began to weep like a child, so that I again took pity on him. Dr. B. went over the Steinerscharte to Simonyhütte, and I to Hofpürglhütte, as I was not on the best of terms with the guides at the former place.

Once across the glacier I took a rest. I saw two men approaching. All at once one of them disappeared. I hurried to the spot, just as he emerged with a bloody head. He was a native, and the well-known guide Karl Fischer was with him. We bandaged up the wounds and went together to Hofpürglhütte. There I was well entertained until the next forenoon. I spent half a day at the Bachl Alm with Resi. My gentleman had also chanced upon her. "'He isn't all there," she said, taking her head in her hands. Dr. B. came back from Simonyhütte that evening. In the morning we were going up the south wall! At three o'clock we left the hut, followed by Resi's blessing that nothing should happen to us.

It was a misty morning and dawn came slowly. When we reached the slopes behind the south wall a rabbit hopped up on a stone. The doctor was very much frightened, became deathly pale, and said with difficulty: "That means bad luck. Shall we not turn back?" I answered: "Sir, surely you, a learned man, do not believe in such superstition? That is all over with." He: "Are you certain nothing can happen?" "Oh, yes, we may yet be corpses today, but the rabbit will not have anything to do with it!"

On the way to the foot of the climb words began again, but I cut it short with the remark: "Doctor, this is our last difficult excursion together, and so we had better not fight right at the start." He did not go as badly as I expected. Six hours, including halts. But at the end his temper broke out anew: "You are to blame that we were not faster today. You went ahead too slowly and I had to wait a long time." I need not mention that he received a proper reply from me. It was too late to go down to the valley, so we spent another night at the Bachl Alm. On the following morning we went to Schladming by way of Ramsau and parted there.

I went to Gstatterboden and rested there on September 3rd. On the next day I tried to make a first ascent on the north wall of the Planspitze – a "Kain" route, but I was very cautious and returned, for going alone over such smooth walls is too dangerous and I had no *Mauerhaken*. In the evening the head waiter in the Hotel Gesäuse told me that there was a party of two ladies requiring guidance in the morning. I introduced myself. I was to be ready about four o'clock.

On leaving the table where both young ladies were seated with their mamma, it occurred to me that I could not have made a good impression upon them with my patched stockings, blue shirt and broad-brimmed hat. We left the hotel about four o'clock in the morning and climbed up the waterfall route, to Heß-hütte and the Hochthor. I discovered at once that the girls had seldom been on a mountain excursion, and they were very happy at the Emesruhe, exclaiming about the view.

One of the women was an excellent botanist. She collected flowers which I had never seen or noticed. We went down to Johnsbach, and back in a carriage to Gstatterboden. Both girls were highly contented with the excursion, and I as well. For it was the first time in three weeks that I had been on a mountain with good people.

On September 8th I took two men up the Pichl route on the north wall of the Planspitze. A splendid day! Everything was taken at Heß-hütte, down to the very last place. My quarters for the night were on a table, with guide Zettelmaier underneath, and guide Innthaler by the foot rail in the kitchen. It was a pleasant chance that brought us three mountain guides together.

On the 9th I took my two men over the Hochthor–Ödstein ridge. Everything went very well. But we got into a fearful storm while descending from the Ödstein over the Kirchl ridge. This ridge is the most toilsome business in all the Enns Valley. Next day I went home.

On October 10th the mountain guide's book was presented to me in the parish of Schwarzau, for which I had applied in the years 1904–5. I had hoped, as authorized guide, to secure a better clientele. But in 1906, when I made journeys and expeditions in Corsica and Switzerland, I had a different attitude with respect to my authorization, for I was certain that even without it I would succeed and maintain the trust of my patrons. Some weeks after the arrival of the book I also received the guide's insignia of the German–Austrian Alpine Club, and the badge of the Touring Club, both of which I held in respect. But I usually left them at home, for I did not like to show that I was a guide.

7

AUTUMN DAYS IN THE MOUNTAINS

I received a telegram from Miss B. on October 30th, engaging me for the Enns Valley. It was pouring in torrents at Gstatterboden. There was thick autumn fog in the valley on November 2nd, and in order to do something I told the lady that we could climb the Große Buchstein. It was really mysterious to go along through the dense fog. But, on arriving at the Bruck Sattel, we had a marvellous view. The sea of cloud was over the valley, with the snow-powdered rocks rising through it, and the bluest of skies above us. There was so much snow on the "Krautgartl" that we were obliged to take the usual route.

Next day we did the Pichl route on the north wall of the Planspitze. The rocks were quite cold, and snow already lay on the difficult traverse, making some of the little walls far from easy. But it was warm as summer on the summit, the view much finer. Dachstein and Großglockner were visible, even the Julian Alps with the Triglav plainly recognizable. We went down the waterfall path to the valley.

On the fourth of November we went to Altaussee, and from there to Mandling, taking a porter to Hofpürglhütte, which we reached at eleven o'clock that night. The porter was sent back. I boiled some tea and prepared a resting place. The young lady took the living room for the night and I stayed in the kitchen. As we were not planning a great expedition for the coming day, we were under no necessity of getting up early. About ten o'clock we went up the Bischofsmütze.

There was so much snow in the ravine that one could not use *Kletterschuhe*. A long rest was taken on the summit. During descent a little mischance took place. In the saddle there is a little wall that is not easy even in summer. Today it was all snowy, and the lady slipped. I was not quite prepared for such a thing and held the rope with one hand only, and the ice axe in the other, which I dared not let go of or it would have fallen on her head. I held the rope so tightly with one hand that it burned my palm. For this reason we had to give up the ascent of the Kleine Bischofsmütze. The descent concluded with a fine glissade.

The rest of the afternoon was spent in the sunshine in front of the hut. That evening there was such a sunset that my heart fluttered. It was the most gorgeous I had seen in Austria! For almost an hour we gazed at this miracle of Nature without speaking a word.

Next morning also gave promise of a lovely day. In the forenoon we left the hut and went by way of the Sulzenhals and the Bachl Alm to Austria-

Hütte. It was not as nice there as at Hofpürglhütte, and Scanty Hans [Schmalhans] was head cook! Next day was also beautiful, and we climbed the Kleine Dirndl by way of the Huhnerscharte. Splendid view! Fine glissade in descending. Hunger and thirst we had when we got back to the hut, but the provisions were finished. There was only a little tea, without sugar and lemon!

On the way down to Schladming we got into a storm. The lady spent the night in the Hotel Seebacher. I went home and undertook some work at roadbuilding in the Reiss Valley. And so the year ended, without any remarkable happenings.

CHAPTER V

(1907)

▲

1

A RAINY SPRING

During the winter months of January, February and March I guided a few ski parties, and to my joy was several times at the Schnee Alm, Rax and Sonnleitstein. Spring was very bad, and there was no guiding until Pentecost, and it rained even then. On Pentecost Monday I had to attend military exercises. That was difficult, for I had only ten kronen. At Korneuburg I was in the rail and telegraph regiment. That was not as bad as at Bruck a/L. Better food and not so much discipline. I worked diligently there at various things and saved up 34 kronen. At noon of Saturday, June 16th, we were dismissed.

I was engaged to guide on Sunday. At ten o'clock that night I reached Payerbach, and went on without stopping. At Hirschnwang a carriage going to Naßwald overtook me, and I asked the driver to take my trunk along. At Kaiserbrunn the men let me go along with them, and in this manner I quickly reached home. Early on Sunday we went (Innthaler, Binder, I and a porter) with an American motion picture company to the Gamseck. Climbing pictures were taken. Binder and the porter went with an American over the easy Gamseck, while Innthaler and I took two men over the Zsigmondy Gamseck, then over the plateau through the Gaisloch to Kaiserbrunn. As there was bad weather next day, the people departed.

On June 23rd I took three gentlemen over the Wiener Neustadt route, with descent over the Blechmauern route. I waited in the Weich Valley for the two young ladies with whom I had climbed the Hochthor in the autumn. We went into the Reiss Valley. Both ladies called on my mother, which so surprised and pleased her that tears came to her eyes. We had coffee at the Binder Inn, and then ascended the Wildfährte. But during the first hour on the way, fog came down, obscuring the view. I was very sorry, for both girls were true friends of Nature. While we sat in Karl-Ludwig-Haus it hailed violently, and next day snowed and stormed as if it were mid-winter. At noon we went to Prein, and I took leave of the pleasant ladies.

On June 26th I left home, this time for long, for I was engaged for almost the whole summer.

2

OVER THE TOTENSESSEL TO THE TOTENKIRCHL

On the journey to Gstatterboden I had an interesting experience. A lady got on at Leoben. We both sat beside the window. We said nothing to each other until we reached St. Michael. All at once she asked me whether I knew the district. Possibly she thought from my clothing and outfit that I was a climber. I replied that I did not know these mountains very well, but farther along, in the Enns Valley, I could name every peak. So we began to talk and she asked me where I made most of my excursions.

"On the Rax." "Well," she said, "do you happen to know Kain?" "Certainly, I am well acquainted with him," I replied. Then she told me my whole life's story, without having the least idea that I was actually Kain! We had to wait four hours in Selzthal for a connection, and after eating we took a little walk to a small elevation nearby. I showed her the mountains and explained to her how they were ascended.

She sighed deeply and said: "If I only had more money I would like to make many mountain tours. I would get a guide, but if it was a long excursion then I should like to have Kain." And again she began to talk of Kain, informing me that he had been in Corsica, in Switzerland and Tyrol, and I was amazed how truthfully she told it all. But I must contain myself carefully while listening, lest I should give myself away and destroy the little adventure.

As we continued through the Gesäuse I pointed out the various routes, in which she took great interest. Just before reaching Gstatterboden I prepared to get out, and made her a little speech of farewell. Then she said: "If you are ever on the Rax again, take greetings to Kain from his Unknown Friend." At these words, I answered: "My dear lady, you will forgive me for introducing myself. I am Kain, about whom you have told me so much." And in proof I showed her my guide's book. (One can imagine the lady's astonishment.)

At the same moment the train stopped and I must descend. I looked back and saw that there were large tears in her eyes. I waved a friendly greeting. If I had been wearing my badge in the prescribed manner this lovely little episode would never have come to pass.

On the 28th I went to Johnsbach to see all my friends. The first was the old parson who, as always, greeted me heartily. I wandered over to Hinter Johnsbach. It is finest there at this time of year on account of the flowering meadows. The whole valley is a tapestry of bloom. In the evening I went back to Gstatterboden and there met guide Innthaler. Both of us were waiting for a tourist train. It arrived, and in a twinkling the station was full of people. Dr. P. and Dr. L. called to me from a carriage: "Climb in! Climb in! We are going to the Reichenstein."

At five o'clock in the morning we set out from Johnsbach. The way to the climb is toilsome. With much conversation we overlooked the shortcut and had to go by way of the Treffner Alm. But at last we came to the beginning of it and changed our shoes. Both men cast questioning glances at the east ridge of the Totenköpfl, for the route looks impossible. But in a short time we were above the ridge. Both gentlemen are experienced, safe climbers. From the summit of the Totenköpfl I pointed out the east wall of the Reichenstein, which looks equally bad. But soon we had overcome it as well. After a long rest, combined with a sunbath, we left the peak and at evening were back in Gstatterboden.

It was just as if I were at home in the Höllenthal: friends everywhere. On June 30th I did the Innthaler Chimney (Planspitze – north wall) with Dr. L. This time the chimney was very wet and it required my entire strength to get up. One proof that the chimney was very bad to ascend was that, right on the plaque, Dr. L. hung on the rope, something that had never happened to him before on difficult tours.

We had too few provisions with us: only a bit of bread, which we divided in brotherly fashion. On this account we had all the better appetite at Heß-hütte. Descent over the waterfall path to Gstatterboden. Dr. P. had already gone on to the Dachstein district and was expecting me at Austria-Hütte. At six o'clock on the morning of the 30th I went to Schladming, and was at the hut by evening. The landlady said to me immediately: "Well, Kain, now you have a real lively gentleman. He is much more genteel than the one last year."

On July 1st we did the Dachstein by the south wall. We left the hut about half past two, and were at the start of the climb at quarter before six. As Dr. P.

is a good climber we were on the summit by half past ten. As there was still time, we took in the Kleine Dirndl for something extra. Then came storm and rain, but it did not spoil the good humour of this beautiful excursion.

On July 2nd we went to Kufstein, in an extra train from Wörgl on. We got into a train which was quite empty and which took the cars only to the German border. We spent the night in Kufstein at the Hotel Post and wandered comfortably the following day through the Kaiser Valley to Hinterbärenbad. (Noon.) Then we climbed the Totensessel, arriving on the summit in a short time. That evening we reached the Stripsenjoch (1605 metres), where I met a guide whom I had known before and with whom I immediately talked over business conditions.

On the forenoon of July 4th we climbed the Predigtstuhl through the Botzong Chimney. This time it was a pleasure, for I did not have to argue and pull, as I had with Dr. B. in August of 1906. Dr. P. remarked: "How you single-handedly got up there with Dr. B. I can't imagine!" In good time we were back at the Stripsenjoch and, as we wished to spend another night there, the waitress asked me how long we were likely to stay. Just for fun I said: "Eight days!" and so this was another evening to talk with her. I saw that the young girl would be easy to persuade, but the better thought came into my mind: 'What good would it do me? Day after tomorrow I would be leaving, and she would have a turned head!'

The following day was one of rest. As a lady was climbing the Totenkirchl with the guide Kaindl, I went along. I would have liked to remain still longer by myself on the summit, but Kaindl and the lady asked me to accompany them over the southeast ridge. So I went right along. Then a young student arrived, who also accompanied us. The southeast ridge is a dangerous one for descent, and more than one man has lost his life on it. The student, as solo climber, went ahead; I assisted the guide in roping down. There is one place of six metres where one swings in the air. (The last rope-off place in the Winklerscharte.) Kaindl and the woman then went on to the Fleischbankspitze. The student and I descended through the "Snow Hole."

The 'schrund gave us some work. Not so much for me as for the student, for he was wearing *Kletterschuhe* on the snow. We reached the Stripsenjoch, and at the hut it was decided to take the student with us to the Vajolet Towers, as he was very anxious to climb them.

On July 6th Dr. P. and I did the Totenkirchl up and down over the usual route. One should have the greatest respect for the Totenkirchl, especially when it is foggy, and not without reason has the peak such an awful name.

3

IN THE DOLOMITES AND THE SILVRETTA GROUP

We went by way of Kufstein to Blumau and thence to Tiers. We entered the "Weißen Rose" thoroughly wet. Next day we made our way to Grasleitenhütte, where we met the student who had been with us on the Totenkirchl. After a little rest we continued to Vajolethütte. It was not inviting there; the proud towers were covered with snow, and we were almost alone in the hut.

The morning of July 10th promised much. About eleven o'clock we left the hut. As far as the difficult ledge on the Winkler Tower snow forced us to keep on our nailed boots. As we thought it would be better higher up we took a chance on the crack, the student ahead. There I saw some climbing! With rope slung over his shoulder he forced himself upward. Water dripped down. Dr. P. talked of turning back, but I advised him to continue, for, from the crack upward, there are not many difficulties so great. When we reached the peak the student was stretched out there, waiting for us. After a little rest we traversed the Stabeler Tower as well. So much snow lay on the north side that one could really not avoid it. There was no longer any firm footing. Despite this we did the Delago Tower over the Pichlriss in addition. I must say in all truth that if the student had not climbed ahead of me and let down the rope, I do not know whether I could have got up.

This was the first time I had done the Riss. On the summit of the Delago Tower I thanked the young man and congratulated him on his masterful climbing. The descent from the Delago Tower is nothing remarkable. We then had to climb up a little bit on the Winkler Tower in order to fetch the nailed boots which had been left behind on the ledge. We were hardly in Vajolethütte before a storm broke. Formidable waterfalls streamed down the east wall of the Rosengarten, which we wanted to climb in the morning. It was impossible to wait for favourable conditions on the east wall. So we went down to Perra, took a carriage and continued to Canazei. From there we went to the Sella Pass. It was fine to wander over the Alpine meadows amid the profusion of roses and edelweiss. I thought again of the many poor city-dwellers who seldom or never see such beauties of Nature, and I felt that I was rich and fortunate.

Dr. P. had sent a telegram to his wife, that she should come to the Sella Pass. I went as far as Plan to meet her. As she arrived late, we were obliged to spend the night there, and next morning I went back with her to the

Sella Pass. In the afternoon we were anxious to do the Fünffingerspitze, but had to turn back at the Daumenscharte on account of the fresh snow. That evening we met two Vienna climbers: Plaichinger and Teufel.

On July 13th I took Mrs. P. up the third Sella Tower. We almost got into trouble, for the rock is very brittle. I was standing about 15 metres above her and had anchored well. All at once a shriek and then silence. I called: "Has something happened?" "A stone has given way." The rock had fallen first in her face and then onto her knee. When she was beside me I noticed that on one hand and one cheek there were blue spots. She complained of pain in the feet. We rested and then went on. Right at the end of the ascent there is a crack, which she was unwilling to risk because of her painful foot. So I climbed the few metres to the summit of the tower alone. Then we turned back.

I saw how bravely the lady endured the pain, bearing it patiently. We walked to Plan, and from there by private carriage to St. Ulrich where we met Dr. P. My time with the doctor was up, and I took leave of both of them. Those were again beautiful and pleasant days that I had experienced with them, and I had once more learned many things.

Then I went to Innsbruck. Just at that time the general assembly of the German–Austrian Alpine Club was being held, and there were no quarters to be had. I went to the Club's office, and a straw mattress in the Speckbacherhof was offered to me without charge. Next morning I had to be at the station at eight o'clock. I overslept. I had to tell Mr. K. the truth, as he had waited for me a long time. But we did not miss anything, since it was pouring in torrents. About ten o'clock we left for Landeck.

There the second guide, Hohenegger of Langtaufers, met us with Dr. L. and Mr. K. We continued with them to Pians, and from there by the postal coach to Galtür, situated in a lovely valley. It must be very dangerous there in winter on account of avalanches, of which one could still see the remains. Mr. K. and I sat in the front of the coach. A young lady got in and secured a place between us, while her sweetheart had to stand behind on the running board and see how pleasantly we smiled into the face of the pretty girl. Soon he began to be annoyed, and at the next post station she had to leave her place beside us.

We spent the night in Galtür. I had my shoes resoled, and looked into the church. I was much pleased to see the 60–70 skulls lying together in a pile. I inquired what it meant. The people looked at me with opened eyes and said that I would know in due time. But I never discovered the answer. The dialect of this district is for the most part difficult to understand.

On July 16th we went to Jamtalhütte of Section Schwabia; it was kept by old Lorenz,[25] one of the first guides in Austria. I observed in this hut that prayers among these people are only a custom. Sincerity and contemplation were lacking, for old Lorenz had almost completed the Lord's Prayer by the time the others began to pray, and there was laughter here and there. I could not pray with them, and they looked at me with suspicion. But no one dared to ask me why I did not join them in prayer.

The alarm clock went off at three o'clock and we were out at four. July 16th was given over to the Fluchthorn. The Fluchthorn is supposed to be difficult, but it was easy for us. There was still much fresh snow, and we were the first party of the year. We wanted to traverse, but the snow conditions compelled us to return by the same route.

We left the hut at four o'clock on the morning of July 17th to ascend the Piz Buin. It was a beautiful day. Several parties, coming from the Wiesbadener Hütte met us at the so-called "Gratl." The Buin is a mountain well-known because of the view and presents no difficulty. With the exception of a little chimney one can walk upright throughout. The view is excellent, especially of the Engadine and the Bernina. We went down the Silvretta Glacier to the hut of the Swiss Alpine Club and spent the night there. Mr. K. and Hohenegger took a day of rest. Dr. L. and I went up the Groß Litzner, the most difficult peak of the western Silvretta group.

I was quite respectful when I saw a picture postal of this peak: a real tower! We started at an early hour. It is real toil as far as the beginning of the ascent, five hours distant. We passed little lakes, deep blue in colour. On reaching the climb matters changed at once, and we were on the summit in 20 minutes. We had not found the dangerous slabs of which so much is spoken, so very difficult, and we were sorry to have left our things below; otherwise we could have done the Seehörner in addition. But we had another fine glissade, and afterward a vexatious path through stone slides.

Then we came to a huge cheese-making alm, where we had ordered a carriage, and went through the beautiful valley to Klosters (Switzerland). Two guides there asked me whether the aiguilles of the Mont Blanc group were more difficult than the Groß Litzner. For the moment I did not know what to say, for these mountains are not to be compared with each other.

4

FROM CHAMONIX TO ZERMATT

We journeyed to Geneva by way of Lausanne. There we spent the night in the Hôtel de la Poste. The gentlemen and I had a bath in the Rhône, but Hohenegger did not join us. I took him around the city, and we began to talk about heresy. But that got Hohenegger "up in the air." I had to laugh to myself. That evening we continued the conversation in our room. Several times I took the opposite side of his views and, being much surprised at his often childish ideas, said to him: "But one can't really believe that. One tells such things to children, not to grown people!" He was very sorry for me, that one so young had already started on the downward path. Naturally, he did not know that I was a Lutheran.

Next day we travelled to Chamonix, in order to reach the hut on the Plan des Aiguilles the same evening, and then ascend the Grépon. Hohenegger was afraid of the aiguille, for he had never done such climbing, although he was an excellent guide on ice. There was a lady with two guides at the hut, a local man and a Swiss named Hasler, who was said to be a millionaire and taking up the profession of guide for pleasure. (There are quite a few tourists in Switzerland who have the guide's diploma.)

As I had made the tour of the Grépon several times already (see 1905), we were able to start early. But the lady and her two guides were ahead of us. It was Sunday. We caught up with the first party at the breakfast place. In the saddle between Charmoz and Grépon I remarked to one of the gentlemen that we ought to go first on the Aiguille des Charmoz, so that we would not have to wait so long on the parties that were ahead of us.

From that viewpoint the Grépon looks fearsome. We had a beautiful sight of the other parties at their climbing. Back again from the Charmoz to the col and then on to the Grépon. The *Kletterschuhe* were put on below the difficult crack. When Hohenegger heard me panting, he thought: "Well, I won't be able to get up there!" Then Dr. L. followed. He was soon above the difficulty, Hohenegger after him. He asked continually: "Kain, is it all secure?" "Oh yes, just come." Although I was sorry he was so troubled, I still had to laugh. I let him rest and got the rucksacks and Mr. K.

Then we climbed on again in line. We took a rest behind the "window." At the Grand Gendarme the other parties waited for us, as they could not loosen the rope they were using for roping down. I threw it to them, and the "millionaire" thanked me politely. When roping down I had Hohenegger go first. He had never done anything of the kind before, and it was "Spanish" to him to swing all at once through the air. Soon we reached the highest point.

Just as we were making ourselves comfortable for a rest on the summit, one of the other party shouted to us: "Come! Come!" "No, we are taking a rest," we called back. "You must come!" they shouted anew. So I first lowered Mr. K. quickly and then Dr. L. Mr. K. was soon beside the other group. A critical moment: the "millionaire" had been taken with cramp in one hand and, as last man, could not help himself. Mr. K. roped to him. On the same spot I broke out in profanity, for the rucksacks swung me out on the wall.

On reaching the glacier, Hohenegger said: "I will never go up the Grépon again," and thanked me pleasantly. During the descent to Chamonix he added: "Kain, you can say what you like, but if a person makes a mountain tour on Sunday, without going to mass, it will always go worse with him than on any other day." I allowed him to be correct in order to silence him. (One can see right there what imagination does.)

The 22nd was a day of rest. There is really not much going on at Chamonix for one who has been there several times and knows it all. One goes to the station to look at strangers arriving, to the German beer hall and, in the evening, to the casino.

On July 23rd we went up Mont Blanc. We had lunch in the "Robbers' Hut" (Grands Mulets) and continued to the Cabane Vallot. Just before reaching the hut I froze my hands and could not help myself when we arrived. The front room was so full of snow that one was obliged to creep in. Even in the sleeping room things were not much better arranged. There was only one advantage: one didn't have to go out to get snow for cooking – there was plenty in the bedroom!

Dr. L. was most active. He was diligently making tea. There was plenty of covering and we soon went to our rest. The boots were taken off in bed and used as pillows, so that they would not freeze. The wind (or his bride) whistled the loveliest tunes. If the hut had not stood there so long, with-standing the wind and storm, I really believe that one would have found us down on the Grand Plateau. By daybreak the storm had diminished, but not so much that we could go to the summit of Mont Blanc in the usual one and a half hours.

Mr. K. and Hohenegger did not want to proceed. I advised Dr. L. to wait until noon, for I thought the weather would become more favourable. But no one believed me, so we went down. I was angry about it. When we stood on the Grand Plateau the sun was shining on the summit of Mont Blanc.

Then my temper rose, because we had taken the return route so quickly and without waiting longer!

From Chamonix we went to Zermatt. There I met a number of tourists and guides with whom I was acquainted. We were obliged to wait over a day on account of new snow, and went to the Cabane Bétemps on July 24th. On the way we ascended the Riffelhorn over the north slope. Mr. K. was no longer with us, so we made a party of three: a gentleman and two guides. At the Cabane Bétemps there was a Vienna tourist (alone), whom I had known on the Rax. We let him come with us.

We started off about half past two to do the Lyskamm. At sunrise it was a lovely morning. We reached the Lysjoch in five hours, where we left all superfluous things. In another hour and a half we were on the summit of the Lyskamm, where we came into cloud which did not lift and forced us to return at once to the Lysjoch. We met with good snow conditions, but on other occasions the Lyskamm is one of the most dangerous mountains in Switzerland, and one is quite right in calling it a "man-eater" on account of its cornices.

At the Lysjoch there was a slight misunderstanding between the two gentlemen and myself, because it was foggy and they wished to go by compass instead of following me. But as I had the conditions of the terrain very well in my head after 1906, I did not agree and matters soon showed that I was right. We went up the Signalkuppe and spent the night in the Rifugio Capanna Regina Margherita. It is the highest managed and provisioned hut in Europe. Next day we descended on the Italian side, doing the Parrotspitze, Ludwigshöhe and Balmenhorn.

During descent we entered a beautiful valley where the Italian king spends the summer. I have forgotten its name. The Viennese tourist had to go back to Zermatt. We reached Riva Valdobbia on the same evening and on the following morning journeyed to Milan. Dr. L. travelled from there to Lake Garda, and I waited for him at Mori.

5

THE GUGLIA DI BRENTA

We went to Mezzolombardo and then to Molveno, where we spent the night. On the way to Molveno we saw for the first time the famous Guglia di Brenta. Early next day we passed Lago di Molveno. I think it is the most beautiful lake in South Tyrol. It is a long way to the Rifugio Cima

Tosa. On the same afternoon we ascended the Cima Brenta Alta to get a better look at the Guglia.

Early on August 2nd we started for the Guglia di Brenta. In an hour and a half we had reached the foot of the climb. There we left behind everything except something to drink, and made ready for the ascent. Soon we were at the "Red Spot." One cannot go wrong from here, for there is only one possibility, only one exit. Who is unable to join up this bit must relinquish the Guglia. I thought it over carefully afterward, and the final wall is really worse. But now I put my climbing technique above all doubts and thoughts.

Further up the southern wall the route was marked by strips of paper, and without more trouble it continues to the northwest flank. There I saw two iron spikes and a new rope-off ring. Without doubting that I was on the proper route I stormed upward to the overhang. That stopped me! I tried it three times. Impossible! Dr. L. became impatient for he was getting cold. I told him to rope down, and I anchored myself. It came into my mind: 'This may be your last day!'

Dr. L. thought it unlikely that the correct route should have such difficulties that I could not overcome them. So I climbed back to the "Hole" to look at the guidebook. As I turned around I saw a little cairn. My heart grew lighter. I roped down and followed the correct route – a short traverse on the north wall – very much exposed. (To this day I have never done another bit so exposed.)

And now the finishing wall. Although I was completely out of breath [ausgepumpt] it gave me no trouble. We were the 42nd party to visit the Guglia, and I the seventh guide to ascend it. Descent everywhere required great caution – for a guide, even greater care and good rope technique. At the bottom we put on our nailed boots once more. Joyously we returned to the hut.

On August 3rd we did the Torre di Brenta, a peak not often visited. We went close by the Guglia and saw for the first time what a magnificent tower it is. Naturally, both of us felt proud and happy. The Torre di Brenta is poorly described in "Hochtourist," and we looked for a long time until we discovered some nail scratches, which we did not let out of our sight thereafter. There are two chimneys to overcome, neither of them easy. Then we descended to Molveno, where we remained overnight.

On August 4th we went on foot almost to Mezzolombardo and then took a carriage. Soon we almost had a mishap in the valley itself: the horses shied at a passing train. In the evening we reached Bozen and stopped at the "Kaiserkrone." On August 5th we travelled by the postal coach to Welschnofen, thence by way of Kölner Hütte and the Tschagerjoch to Vajolethütte. August 6th: traverse of the towers from Winkler to Delago. This time it was a pleasure in comparison with the last tour. Everything was dry! In three and a half hours we had finished all of it, and wanted to do the east wall of the Rosengarten. But a shower ended our plans.

On August 7th we took a carriage over the new Dolomite road, and again there was a terrible storm. I met some Vienna acquaintances on the way. We spent the night at Buchenstein. I sent a telegram to the district judge [Bezirksrichter] at Mödling. The clerk read it "Gesichtsrichter," and became angry when I laughed, although I had made no mistake in laughing.

From Buchenstein our way led to the Passo Falzarego and thence up the Sasso di Stria over the Witzenmann route. (A stretched cable makes the route possible; otherwise it could not be done.) Then back again to the Falzarego Pass. As we did not obtain at the hospice the key to the Rifugio Tofana, we had to go to the Albergo Pocol, and then, after a short rest, to the Rifugio Tofana, which is not managed. We left the hut at five o'clock on the following morning, in order to ascend the south wall of the Tofana di Mezzo, the "Via Inglese" – quite a difficult tour.

I had the misfortune to knock down a stone onto Dr. L.'s head, the rope being the actual cause. He bled profusely and I received a complaint. Also an earned one! We descended by the usual route to the Rifugio Tofana and walked to Cortina. On August 10th we went over the Tre Croci to Pfalzgauhütte. From there we wanted to do the Sorapis. There I had only myself to blame! I attacked the mountain from exactly the wrong angle. And to make it worse, three gentlemen joined us. We had to give up the ascent. But, as a local guide who was on the right route had to turn back also because of falling stones, the affair was a little bit easier for me. But I was very sorry to lose this summit!

We wandered on to Misurina. A lovely moonlit night! Next day we went to the Cadin peaks and climbed the Wundtspitze. A very short tour, but the tariff is 50 kronen. (We had many such climbs on the Raxalpe, but no one pays 50 kronen.) On the same day we went on to Dreizinnenhütte. There I became acquainted with the renowned guide Sepp Innerkofler;[26] a friendly, pleasant man. I asked him about the route up the east wall of the western Zinne, one of the most difficult expeditions.

We left the hut at eight o'clock on the morning of August 13th, and, as Innerkofler had showed me the route exactly, we reached the start of the climb without search. The overhangs are indeed very difficult, and one can utilize all one's skill at pulling up and other gymnastics. On arriving at our goal, a hearty "Bergheil!" came from the Große Zinne, where they had been watching us. The descent by the usual route made fools of us: we could not find it for a long time.

When we reached Dreizinnenhütte the guides there had more respect for me. On the day before they had looked at me questioningly when they heard that I was from Lower Austria, from the Rax district, and wanted to go up the Kleine Zinne! That evening we went on to Zsigmondy-Hütte, to do the Einser. We left at six o'clock in the morning and were at the climb in an hour. It was our farewell tour, and today I was the "Herr Tourist" and Dr. L. the guide.

I said to him: "Doctor, we have now been together for a month, and why should I always be the leader?" Dr. L. took me at my word, roped me up and went ahead. The handling of the rope did not suit him very well, and so he asked in a little while: "Well, do we need the rope?" And so we took it off. In a short time we were on the summit of the Einser and back again in the hut.

After an hour on the way I discovered that I had left my pocketbook and the guidebook at the foot of the climb, and had to go back for them. We had lunch at Innerkofler's Dolomite Hotel Fischeleinboden (I became acquainted with the guide Nagler of Gröden), and then took a carriage to Sexten and Innichen. Here I bade farewell to Dr. L. and went on foot to Toblach.

The place was filled with soldiers and no bed was to be had. At an inn I asked the waitress whether I might spend the night. She stood in front of me, looked me over and said it was not for one so dusty and dirty. For her lack of manners I cursed her – with military variations – down to the last button on her shoes, went on my way and found a bed at a private house.

6

IN DAUPHINÉ

About eight o'clock on the morning of the following day I boarded the train for a 25-hour railway journey to Grenoble, in France. On the train I met some friends, and was in their company as far as Bozen. The stop there was long enough so that I could go to the post office and get my things. The journey then continued by way of Verona, Milan and Chivasso to Turin, where the train arrived at midnight.

At Turin I had to get additional tickets, and when I returned the train was empty, everything dark, and my rucksack and ice axe gone! No one could understand my bad Italian, so I went to a guard, who conducted me to a storeroom where the things I had left in the train were lying. Naturally, I had to give him a tip, and as is the usual custom in Italy the man said to me all the while; "Poco, poco, ancora, ancora!" – "too little, too little, more, more!" But it was high time for the train; I jumped in and off it went. At Modane, at the frontier, a gentleman and a lady were arrested, and when I asked what the matter was, I was informed: "They are murderers!"

From Modane on I had to keep my ticket in my hand, for one must get out shortly afterward. I could not pronounce the names of the stations (it was Chambéry), and so had to compare the spelling at every stop until the right one came along! I had breakfast in Chambéry, then continued and reached Grenoble at eight o'clock. I entered the Hôtel Nord and asked for Dr. K. He had not yet arrived. With signs and pointing I made the people understand that they should give me a room. But talking was out of the question for me. I had to point at everything, just like a dummy.

After an hour Dr. K. arrived. The first thing he said when he saw me in my clothes, ragged from Dolomite climbing, was: "Why, Konrad, you can't go to Dauphiné looking like that!" So we went into a store and bought everything necessary. Shoes I was not able to get, which disturbed Dr. K. very much. In the afternoon we got into the interesting streetcar which runs between Grenoble and Bourg d'Oisans. We passed Uriage, a town of lovely parks and bathhouses. The biggest place is called Vizille, with a castle of the same name. Now the beautiful, though poverty-stricken, mountain landscape begins and, a few stations farther on, we arrived in Bourg d'Oisans, the point of exit for tourists.

Then, as the car went off the track (as happens almost daily), we were delayed for four hours. We took a room in the finest hotel and then went to the proper shop where I got some boots (20 francs). The village looked very poor, with narrow lanes. The houses are roofed with flat stones. It is a shame that one also finds here the filthy streets, as in the old French and Italian mountain villages.

On August 16th we went in the postal coach to La Freney. Here we left the fine highway that leads to La Grave. A narrow road, over deep ravines and past waterfalls, led up to the Lac de Lauvitel. We took pity on the mules and, therefore, descended to continue on foot. The lake is finely situated in the narrow valley and offers a lovely introduction to tourists who come for the first time into these mountains. Beyond the lake the road is artistically built on the rocks. In a short time one reaches the village of St. Christophe.

This village is known by name to most Austrian climbers, for one of the best mountaineers has there found in Nature his last resting place. We at once visited the grave of Dr. Emil Zsigmondy, who fell on the Meije on August 6, 1885, and now sleeps eternally in this lofty little mountain village. We laid a few flowers on the beautiful stone. I saw beside this grave two new ones, of Italian climbers[27] – two more sacrifices to the mountains – who had met their end on the Meije in July; and the sad thought came into my head, which I repeated to myself: 'That may also be *your* fate.'

I must relate that the native guides were very friendly toward me. With my few words of Italian I could not come to an understanding with one of them. But he took me into his house, showed me the pictures of his family and gave me a drinking cup for remembrance.

The road comes to an end at St. Christophe. Our baggage was put on mules, and we followed them along the narrow path to La Bérarde. We were both curious about this lonely mountain village which we had chosen as headquarters for our excursions.

It was more beautiful than I had expected. Half an hour from St. Christophe one already sees the snow-covered peaks of the Barre des Écrins, Ailefroide etc. We were pleasantly received in the simple hotel. But as we had to make best use of our time, we could remain there only an hour, then packed our rucksacks and went on.

During almost the entire way to the Refuge du Carrelet we had the southern side of the Meije before our eyes, and the words of L. Purtscheller came into our minds: "He who has not seen the Meije has seen nothing." And E. Pichl adds: "But he who has not seen the Meije from the south side has not seen the Meije."

We reached the Halterhütte in an hour from La Bérarde, where four sheep dogs gave us an unwelcome reception. As I was afraid of dogs above all things, I trembled with fright. Dr. K. laughed at me. We went on for a bit farther. The Refuge du Carrelet must be somewhere near. After looking around a little I saw the smoke of the hut, which one can not see as it is behind a huge rock.

There was an Englishman with two guides in the smoke-laden hut. To my regret I could not talk to the people, but as far as I noticed they were very pleasant to guests. Late that evening we found our sleeping places in the hay. The alarm went off about three o'clock; breakfast was quickly prepared and we left the hut by the light of lanterns. At first the way goes steeply upward over broken rock. We did not have to use the lanterns very long, and soon we had taken leave of the Englishman and his guides. They were going for Ailefroide.

The old guide showed us the way to the foot of the climb. For an hour we had hard work over the moraines before reaching the glacier. In a short time we came to the col between Barre des Écrins and Pic Coolidge. Here good advice is not cheap in finding the route from the English guidebook. I have already found many a route from the guidebook, but I could not find this one according to description, and yet we wanted to reach the peak from this side. So we went at the rocks, hit or miss.

This agreed with the description, and in addition we found an empty bottle. I asserted that this was the proper route, but the doctor would not believe it. I know very well that it was not the correct one, but saw that it would do and so added the cunning of a guide to it. A couloir about 50 metres high gave us hard work; then it became easier, and so I quickly made a stone marker and showed it to the doctor with these words: "Here is an old marker, so this must be the right way?"

From this point we went out on to the southwestern side. Fine, happy climbing brought us quickly upward to a very sharp, much-exposed ridge. The doctor asked me in a mocking tone: "Konrad, do you see any nail scratches or a cairn?" "No, doctor, but it will go, we will soon be on top!" He indeed complained a little about the sharp rocks, but followed me well and easily. "Where do we go from here?" "Well, up there, I think." It was a little, very difficult bit of cliff. From this buttress we climbed somewhat toward the southeast. Here it was quite easy. Loose stone. There we had an almost incredible experience. We were roped together, and the rope caught in the stones lying about. I said: "Doctor, loosen the rope, it is stuck." I tried to pull in the rope and, to my astonishment, it was cut through as if by a knife. We looked at each other without saying a word.

But with all our searching the sharp stone could not be found. Strange! And the rope was quite new, one that I had bought only a couple of weeks before. (A superstitions person would say that it was a warning!)

Now we had the choice of two routes: one to the right, which looked to be dangerous from falling stones; the other, to the left, a steep, sharp ridge. So we took the ridge. I went up about 20 metres, then had the doctor follow, calling his attention to the loose stones. Where now? The much exposed overhang seemed almost impossible. "I will try it. Stand where you are, doctor."

It was not easy and, besides, a large handhold broke away. But I held myself up by the other hand. The stone hit Dr. K.'s ice axe, which he had placed to one side, and it followed the stone several hundred metres into the depths. It is lost! Some 20 metres farther on I reached a good position. Despite the difficulties Dr. K. came up in short order. Now it seemed to be easier, and in a few minutes we attained the western peak. A splendid view of valleys and distances was our reward.

After a short rest we went with ease to the highest point. Thus we had gained the loftiest summit of Dauphiné, the Barre des Écrins, over a new route from the southwest. The view was fine. We remained lying for a long time in the afternoon sunlight, almost too long, but at the same time we had much to think about. Where would we spend the night? We had no wood and only a few provisions. Somewhere on this glacier the Cabane Ernest Caron was supposed to be, but we could not discover it with the naked eye. So we went down by the usual route on the Glacier Blanc.

But it went slowly, for Dr. K. had no ice axe. Luckily we found old tracks visible, guiding us to the hut, which we reached in gathering darkness. We were glad to find people there: two native guides with an Italian from Turin who spoke a little German. They allowed us to do our cooking with theirs. A meal in common; two different kinds of soup in one pot. We told them of our tour, and the guides said that they had never heard of anyone ascending from the southwest side, so I suppose we were the first.

We were rather tired and, despite the plain quarters, slept well until the other party started off. Then we went to sleep again and did not wake up until the sun was high in the sky and the party had almost reached the summit. I looked for wood with which to cook something warm, but in vain. Wood has to be carried up for three hours' distance, and no one takes more than is needed. We left the hut without breakfast. We had to cross the Glacier Blanc, found a good way and could soon see the summer chalet, where we breakfasted. We lay about for quite a while in front of the chalet, for it is one of the loveliest spots in Dauphiné.

To the left the black glacier, with the white to the right and Mont Pelvoux straight ahead, the Barre des Écrins and the Pré de Madame Carle. The little hut stands among some larches, surrounded by green meadows. The sound of the cowbells, the rushing of the glacial brook and, a little farther on, a waterfall, all combine to make the picture even more beautiful. In the late afternoon we went down to the Chalet Ailefroide. There were the valley wanderers; even a rich Frenchman with a large family.

We had a day of rest on August 19th. We took a walk to Vallouise, where Dr. K. bought an ice axe and had to pay 20 francs for it. The valley of Vallouise is fine, but it is to be noted that 80 per cent of the people are idiots, as is stated in Baedeker. Most of them have not all their senses, and it is especially to be recognized in the shapes of their heads. Some say that the foggy district is to blame; others think it due to inbreeding. That is probably the correct reason. On the whole the people of this region are very poor.

On the afternoon of the 20th we left the Chalet Ailefroide to climb Mont Pelvoux. We followed the brook almost to the Sélé Glacier. There we met a herdsman who showed us the way to the hut. First one comes to the old bivouac-place at the edge of the woods. There were still some old blankets to be seen. Several years ago the French Alpine Club built the new hut, the Refuge Lemercier. That was the one we wanted to find. I gathered a lot of wood, since not many tourists visit Mont Pelvoux. One had to look out and not lose the way to the hut. There is really no path, only a few nail scratches to be seen.

Dr. K. and I were in good humour and talked a lot, thereby involuntarily following a little path used by shepherds. The way was lost, and we saw from the map that we must go to the left. We came out a little too high and had to descend a bit to the hut. It consists of a front room and a well-constructed sleeping room. There were plenty of cooking utensils, blankets and straw sacks there. But most of the French huts have the mistake of containing no stoves. One has to make a gypsy fire in front of the hut, and in good weather that's all well enough. But how does it look on a stormy day?

The hut was built on the best spot. A little plateau, with a deep gorge to the right and a fine view. It was quite late when we reached the hut. I made a fire and looked after the evening meal. The doctor aired the hut and the blankets. The moon shone brilliantly, everything was silent, except that in the ravine one heard the water, always on the same note. For a long time we lay in front of the hut, for it was too fine to go in. It was almost midnight when we went to bed. From my mattress I could see the frontal peak of Mont Pelvoux through the window.

It was quite cold when we left the hut at five o'clock next morning. We went along a crest of moraine to the glacier. From there two routes diverge: one through the snow-filled ravine, where stonefall threatens, the other over the rock to the left. We chose the rocky way, which was not difficult; only one or two places can be called hard and they are short. So we were soon on the glacier and had a magnificent morning view. Finest of all was the sight of Monte Viso, king of the Maritime Alps.

From the glacier onward the way crosses a snowy plateau to the summit of Mont Pelvoux, third elevation of Dauphiné. Almost within reach was the Barre des Écrins, and we were amazed at the ridge we had followed a few days before. After a rest of about two hours on top we made our descent by way of a not-very-steep couloir leading to the glacier. But soon it became risky. We glissaded the first part, but soon came to the ice where I had to cut steps. Suddenly we heard a stone fall. Dr. K. wanted to run, but I shouted: "Stop where you are! Stop!" For it was bare ice, where one could not go without steps, and a few metres below, the bergschrund was waiting for us with yawning mouth. Luckily the stones caught in the soft snow; that is, the snow cut their speed. One hit Dr. K. on the knee, but he was able to go on. We crossed the bergschrund with care, but after that it was easier and we could glissade again.

Once we were on safer ground and could consider the dangerous situation we had been in, the doctor remarked: "It is just as well that in mountain climbing the pleasant hours outnumber the dangerous ones, and that the happy moments in comparison with the bad experiences are in the majority." Soon we came to the Refuge Lemercier. There I had a little wood reserved and cooked some soup and canned things. We were hungry! Then I put everything in order and we bade farewell to the hut. In what mood one leaves a place where one has spent such lovely hours, I cannot describe. For it is a matter that one can only discuss properly with a like-minded friend of Nature. And even then I am not sure that one can pour out everything in words as it exists in the mind.

Meanwhile, the doctor and I strolled down good-humouredly to the valley. That evening we again reached the Chalet Ailefroide, where a bottle of good wine was not lacking. It was the sequel to a splendid day.

On August 22nd we left the homelike chalet to cross the Col du Sélé to La Bérarde. During the leave-taking I had a new experience. As we started off the German girl put a message in my hand, which I wanted to read at once. But she said: "Put it in your pocket, please." I did so. When the chalet was no longer in sight I took out the slip with curiosity. On it was written: "Dear countryman! I would like to hear from you very often. Please write to me." On the other side was her winter address. I was surprised that she had not said all this, and I asked Dr. K. about it. He laughed and said: "That's woman's weakness."

We knew the first part of the way to the Glacier du Sélé from our former tour on the Pelvoux. We went along the shale beside the cool glacial torrent, until a cliff with a waterfall shut off the valley. As the wall did not look easy, we put on the rope. There were large, long-stemmed edelweiss on this wall. We took a few along for remembrance. Soon we reached the actual glacier, the beginning of which is stone-covered. A little later we were on the Col du Sélé, the shortest crossing from Vallouise to La Bérarde, where we rested at noon and enjoyed the splendid view.

The descent to the Glacier de la Pilatte was not so simple. First over brittle rock, and then down a very steep slope, the last part much crevassed. On this glacier a very peculiar arch is to be seen, high, wide and deep. We looked for a good place to cross the brook, but at last waded through. Day ended with a splendid sunset. Although I had seen so many on my tours and travels, yet these colours were quite new to me. Each peak had a different colour. Most pleasing were the deep greens and blues.

An author who has written much about Dauphiné has this to say of the colouring: "On the whole the Alps of Dauphiné excel the Swiss mountains in one respect, namely that of light. Sometimes the light of the heavens gives to the Dauphiné peaks the melancholy majesty of northern lands, and sometimes again the southern provençal lustre, reminding one of the clearness of African skies. Especially in the group of the Meije one wonders at the play of colours in the glaciers and the clouds, a realm of colour tone not to be found on the Jungfrau or the Aletschhorn." I have never been in Africa, and so I do not know how this clarity appears. But I must admit that, in the Swiss mountains, I have never seen such a range of colouring.

7

THE TRAVERSE OF THE MEIJE

That evening it was gay in the little Hôtel la Bérarde, with even a jolly time in the guides' room. In the morning a whole company of tourists and guides were going up the Meije. Dr. K. engaged a local guide for the traverse (see also the later traverse in 1908) because every man takes two guides. I did not request it, and it would have given me great pleasure if Dr. K. had gone with me alone.

After lunch on August 23rd we left La Bérarde, 17 people all told. It was quite a warm afternoon as we wandered through the Vallée des Étançons. This is the valley for pictures, and Dr. K. took plenty. The Meije, with its ferocious south wall, is ever before the eye, with two men again sacrificed to it only a little while before. At the old hut, the Refuge du Carrelet, we rested.

The guides took a bundle of brush for firewood. We reached the Refuge du Promontoire at six o'clock. So many people had not gathered together there for a long time!

The hut is well-built, with a stove as well. The cooking was done in two groups. As the Swiss and French guides like wine more than the Austrians, there was plenty of it. Although I could talk with no one except the doctor, I found out just the same that every one was well-meaning. I looked through the hut book and found many noted names. Two Austrian guides had also been to the hut: Kerer of Kals, and Wenter of Tiers. It is probable that I was the third Austrian guide to visit this hut.

The hut stands on a rock in a dizzy place. The alarm went off about one. As always, on awakening one looks at the weather. A fine, moonlit night. About two o'clock the parties were ready. One will find no other hut except this where the rope is put on inside. And when the last one closes the door the leader already has two difficult walls below him. We were the last party, and I was last of all, for our local guide went ahead. The feeling was one of seriousness. All quiet save for the scratching of nails and the drawing up of axes. As I had never been the last before, it was unpleasant for me. Also, I was afraid of stones.

In the moonlight we reached the foot of the Grand Mur. There we halted and waited for dawn. It was the place where the two Italian tourists had fallen several weeks before. I had already been on many places where I knew that accidents had occurred, but none ever made such an uncanny impression upon me as this one. I must admit that a little shudder went over me. But the deep silence and the ghostly light was the cause of it. And if one is not acquainted with an expedition it seems much worse than it really is. Especially on such a mountain, about which so much has been written, as the Meije.

At last the column set itself in motion once more. Then I was deceived again. It was not so difficult by far as I had been given to understand. But soon, on the Grand Mur, a stone almost hit me, loosened by one of the first parties. It missed me by only half a yard. In spite of the large size of our company we made rapid progress. Dr. K. said to me: "Now comes the *pas de chat*," the "cat-step," of which so much is made. But as with all of these steps and strides, this one too was not as hard as it was supposed to be. It is indeed exposed, but the holds are good.

After four hours we reached the Glacier Carré, the four-cornered glacier. A rest was taken. Then comes the Cheval Rouge, the Red Horse. There the wind played its game. Everybody complained of cold fingers, and there was no place where one could stop for long. Crossing the ridge the guides changed places at step cutting, so things went quickly. In a little while we reached the Grand Pic. From there the ice wall has to be crossed to the Brèche Zsigmondy, and then the dangerous part is over. The guides asked Dr. K. whether I could go as last. I told them they should have no fear, that I could do so. I was even last at the roping-off places.

Slowly we went across the ice wall, but as there were good steps it was no trick for me. The French guides told Dr. K. to tell me that I had done it very well. It ended in a race across the glacier. About three o'clock we were in La Grave (13 hours from the Refuge du Promontoire). The whole trip had been a chase, and we had not enjoyed much of the view.

There was a woman in La Grave who spoke good German and translated what the guides said – they were all glad that the stone had not hit me, and wished to drink a glass of wine with me. I had the woman interpret to them that Dauphiné pleased me greatly and that I was delighted to find the guides of the region so kind to strangers.

The 25th of August was a day of rest. I met three Austrians: Mr. Bock of Brünn, Dr. Wessely[28] of Linz and Mr. Mayer of Innsbruck. In La Grave it is noteworthy that the highway goes through two tunnels, just behind the village, one 600 the other 400 metres long. They are lighted day and night.

In the afternoon we went to the Refuge de l'Alpe. There we met two guides who had been with us on the Meije. The region is poor in wood, and cow dung is used for fuel. Something new again for me! In this hut there was a great time with dancing and song. There are cattle huts in the vicinity and the herdsman came at evening to the hut, which is provisioned. The two guides, like ourselves, were going with their man next morning up the Grande Ruine. Lucky for me, I wouldn't have to search for the route!

We left the hut at three o'clock on the morning of August 26th. Fair weather was promised. The way went slowly over the loose stones, and for two hours we followed the valley of the Romanche, then upward to the right over scree until we came to the glacier. I think it is named for the mountain. As the snow was rather soft, we changed places in making a track. The summit of the Grande Ruine was soon reached. A long halt was made and a sunbath taken. Proudly and contentedly we gazed upon the sharp Meije, which from here had quite a different appearance; we cast friendly glances across to the Barre des Écrins and the Pelvoux. The linen summit book interested me very much, inscribed by the Viennese tourists, Otto and Emil Zsigmondy, and L. Purtscheller. Since the beginning of the year 80 people had already been up here.

We descended by way of the southwest ridge and then had to cross a dangerous glacier. Stonefalls and ice avalanches were to be watched for. Scarcely had we reached the moraine when a little avalanche came down. We were soon in the valley, and while the other party went direct to La Bérarde, we lay in the grass and looked at the mountains once more. It was our last excursion in Dauphiné. The Grande Ruine is really an easy peak; only our descent had been dangerous.

On August 27th we took leave of La Bérarde. Happy and contented we descended the trail to St. Christophe. Again it was an indescribable feeling for me to leave a mountain group in which so much had met with success, where everything one had on the program had been carried out in favourable weather. We had lunch in St. Christophe. Once again I went to the cemetery and laid a few flowers on the grave of Zsigmondy. A sad thought came into my head: the stone on the Grand Mur! If it had struck me I would have been the second Austrian sleeping there. Naturally one thinks of the word "if," which plays such a part in human life.

From St. Christophe a carriage took us to Le Bourg d'Oisans, and we were still able to make the evening train for Grenoble. On the way the engine and two cars ran off the track, luckily against the slope. Unfortunately, a man was killed. There were curses in all languages and everything in fearful confusion. Only one couple remained calm; I guess they were on their wedding trip. They kept on making love and kissing. Everybody was looking at them!

After three hours another train came along, bringing us to Grenoble at midnight. We took a room at the Hotel du Nord, and next day went to Chamonix, arriving in fine weather that evening. It was the second time for me that year. We stopped in the Hôtel des Alpes. On August 29th we took an easy day. In the morning I met some friends, among them two men from Wiener Neustadt. In the afternoon we went up to the Chalet Plan des Aiguilles. But it began to cloud over and we were afraid we should not be able to do the Grépon.

At two o'clock in the morning the innkeeper came and woke us. The weather was unpromising, but we wanted to try it anyway, and started off by lantern light. The day was in doubt and we did not know what to do: proceed or turn back? I decided to continue, for if we could not ascend the Grépon, the Charmoz might at least be done. It began to snow by the time we reached the rock walls. One party was already returning, having gone up at an early hour. Hope of climbing the Grépon was abandoned, so I left the second rope behind in the col.

As Dr. K. was a good climber, we attained the summit of the Charmoz in short order. It began to snow harder, and it was lucky that no wind came up. Soon we were back in the chalet. All the peaks were hidden. That was my last tour with Dr. K.

At the Hôtel des Alpes, in Chamonix, there was a telegram for me from Miss B. I was to come to Altaussee as soon as possible. As the weather was hopeless, Dr. K. and I travelled to Munich on August 31st. There we separated, I going by way of Salzburg to Aussee. The journey with Dr. K. had shown me many new and beautiful things, and I knew one more good and kindly man. Dr. K. was not only a good tourist, he belonged to those who are not ashamed to be pleasant with a guide and to recognize his abilities. The whole expedition will remain a happy memory.

8

THE ENNS VALLEY ONCE MORE

On the afternoon of September 1st I arrived in Aussee. It was Kermesse Day in Altaussee, with animated life in the streets – everyone, even the summer vacationists, in Styrian costume. And there was no lack of dancing. In Styria these festival days are celebrated according to old custom much more than with us in Lower Austria.

I went with Miss B. to Gstatterboden on September 2nd. Prospects bad! Everything in mist, with snow on the mountaintops. On entering the dining room of the Hotel Gesäuse I saw three women sitting at a table. I knew them. At the same moment one of them said: "Why, there's Mr. Kain." "Yes, here I am," and so we greeted one another. They were the ladies with whom I had been up the Hochthor in the preceding year. But I noticed at once that it was not agreeable to Miss B. to have the two girls and their mother on such friendly terms with me.

I would liked to have talked longer with my friends, but Miss B. had the horses harnessed and we went to Johnsbach, where we intended to climb the Totenköpfl. The lady was in as sour a mood as the weather. When we reached the bridge it began to rain harder, and I said: "Possibly it would have been better if we had stayed in Gstatterboden, it is more pleasant there in bad weather than in Johnsbach." With that I received a scolding. "Yes, for you," said Miss B. I replied: "Not as much for me as for yourself,

Miss. You will admit that there is more to do in Gstatterboden than in Johnsbach?" And she: "Who are those women you were talking to?" "Oh, those are two nice girls that I took up the Hochthor." "Yes, there are girls like that who spoil guides," she remarked earnestly, "and you are pleased when someone calls you 'Mr. Kain,' and at last you will think that every-one should address you as 'Mister.'" And in this way it went on until we reached the Donner Inn.

The people who had leased the inn were from the Zillerthal; I was heart-ily welcomed by them and, as everyone in Johnsbach knew me, and un-derstood that I had just returned from a long journey, I had to tell them everything that had happened. The weather was so cold that the innkeeper was obliged to light up the stove, and so, that evening, it was very pleasant in the guest room. That night, as on all other evenings, the old parson was present, again telling his life story which I had often heard before. Other tourists sat around the room: an old man from Pöchlarn with his daughter and some other young Viennese. The old parson had already drunk enough beer, and asked for water, which I quickly brought him. Then I lit his pipe for him about a dozen times. One puff and it would be out. Then he said: "Well, Daniel is a good boy, I like him very much." (I was always called "Daniel" there because the people thought that I was the son of the guide Daniel Innthaler.) Thereupon the daughter of the old gentleman remarked to Miss B.: "Your guide is really a nice boy." Miss B. answered quickly: "Please don't say such a thing so that he can hear it. He is much too proud and spoiled already."

The weather was even worse on the following day, with snow almost down in the valley. I told Miss B. that nothing could be done. Later the old man and his daughter asked me how the woman and I got on together. "I am a guide, nothing more, and I have known her for several years." The girl laughed, and hinted: "But something very amusing happened yesterday." I inquired: "What was that?" "Well, you say you are nothing but her guide – and she is jealous of you just the same. Why else would your lady have told me not to say that you were a nice fellow? I meant nothing by it, only that you looked after the old parson so carefully." I smiled and said: "Miss, I can explain it all very briefly. It is this way: I know the lady quite well, and as she speaks almost the same dialect as I, we talk easily with one another. She is all right. I know that she has already assisted many poor mountain people. But she has her own views about tourist affairs. She does not like it very much if one speaks pleasantly to her guide, or calls him 'Mister.' She thinks that this spoils a guide, and that, as guides, they'll think themselves God only knows what! She looks upon a guide as just another servant."

"Well, but with a guide to whom one trusts one's life, with whom one takes trips, as, for example, you with this woman – how can one compare that with servant's work?" When the old man had finished this speech, I replied: "My dear sir, you are quite right, but there are many people like that, who have exactly such an unjust viewpoint." And with that we sat down to breakfast together, and I had to tell them of my recent journey.

The weather had somewhat improved, and the old gentleman and his daughter decided to go to Heß-hütte. Miss B. and I accompanied them as far as the Wolfbauern waterfall. But when the weather turned bad again in the afternoon, Miss B. and I went home. If the weather should turn fine there would be a telegram for me. So I went to Gstatterboden, as there was no climbing to be done.

On September 7th I had a message from Altaussee to meet the lady that evening at Johnsbach in order to do the Totenköpfl on the Reichenstein that Sunday. At five o'clock in the morning we left Johnsbach in much better weather. The air through the forest and up to the Treffner Alm was rather sultry. Some tourists were ahead of us. By the time one reaches the start of the climb one is tired, for the route is drudgery. So we rested. Then the climbing began, and soon we were on top of the Totenköpfl. The ascent is not long but it is strenuous and much exposed. From the summit we descended into the saddle, thence over the east wall to the top of the Reichenstein. The view was fine! I met some friends there.

There were many tourists at the Donner Inn when we returned. Even the ladies from Gstatterboden. On September 9th I took one of the girls up the Planspitze by the Petern route. About four o'clock her alarm went off, and as my room was above hers it woke me too. It was a cool autumn morning and still rather dark when we left the hotel. The mists swung midway through the narrow Gesäuse Valley. All was quiet: only the Enns rushing at its old rate and the fallen leaves on the road gave the proper tone to a splendid feeling of autumn.

I was much concerned that morning about what had happened to the girl, but could see no reason for it. Soon we reached the Haindl ravine. It was easy to see now that we would have a fine, clear day. We chatted cheerfully as we mounted the basin. We sat down on a rock, a little above the forest, where one crosses the Wildbach for the second time. The sun was casting its first beams into the ravine, and the varied colours of the foliage were wonderful.

At the start of the Petern route we had breakfast, and I took the opportunity of pointing out to the girl the different routes on the northern walls. Then I took out my rope and tied it to the girl, now making her first real ascent. We climbed slowly as far as the second terrace, with its splendid view of the Haindl ravine and of the Enns. Then comes the "Ennsthaler Step," which is called to the attention of every tourist making it for the first time. But if one says nothing, they cross it without knowing that it is the worst place. The girl went over without any trouble. A few rope-lengths more and the climbing is over.

Again a little rest while I put the rope away. The view as far as the saddle was very good; we went on to the Planspitze, reaching it shortly. The girl was quite delighted with the panorama and the view into the depths below. I could read the pleasure in her face, and so I asked: "Are you happy?" She sighed deeply and answered in the affirmative. After a long rest we descended to the Seekar and Heß-hütte. Scarcely had we arrived when a heavy storm broke, such as one would not have thought of an hour before. But it did not last, and in the late afternoon we said adieu to the hut and its good people.

We descended to the valley along the waterfall path. It was very pleasant there, as the air after the storm was soft and clear. We halted at the Emesruhe, one of the finest spots in the Enns mountains. In a little while we were down by the rushing river, and in the Hotel Gesäuse just as darkness was approaching.

On September 12th I left Gstatterboden by the same train on which the three ladies travelled, for Weyer, where I said goodbye to the family, or rather, my new friends. From Weyer I went to Groß Hollenstein; the way was known to me, for I had been there five years before as an apprentice, out of a job, and many sad hours came into my remembrance. From Hollenstein I went by train to Göstling, where I visited my sick friend E.K., and stayed overnight.

On September 14th I returned to Gstatterboden. Everything was changed, the hotel empty, stormy weather, while snow on the mountains indicated the end of the climbing season. So I went to Kapellen by way of St. Michael and Mürzzuschlag, and wandered on foot to Naßwald. On the way the weather improved, and by the time I stood on the Nass ridge and looked down into the Reiss Valley and to the Binder Inn I had a pleasant feeling of being back again, well and healthy in the valley of my home.

Some days later I had a telegram from Miss B., to come to Altaussee as quickly as possible. So I left my mother, who as usual gave me good advice.

I had been so often across the Nass ridge that I knew every root and high step. I needed no light. When I got to the Styrian side the fog was so dense that I was afraid little could be done in the Enns mountains.

But it was only dry fog, what the people in Altenberg call "Krautnebel," and it is interesting how it keeps to its own boundaries, never extending over onto the Lower Austrian side. On this account the Altenberg Valley is always much colder on an autumn morning than the Nass Valley. I reached Kapellen so early that I had time for a second breakfast at the Schnabel Inn.

I arrived at Aussee in the afternoon and went on foot to Altaussee. All the lanes were empty, only a few people to be seen. I have already explained that Altaussee is finely situated on a blue lake. Now I have also seen this valley in autumn, and as there is much foliage this season, too, has a certain charm. The first thing to do was to look up Miss B. at her villa, where she told me that she wanted to do the Dachstein by the south wall, but did not have enough courage. I described the trip to her and told her to have no fear of it.

I spent the night at an inn, and at evening an old man approached me in the guest room and said: "Surely you are from Naßwald. I know it by your accent!" Then he told me that his brother had once been a forester in Naßwald and that he himself liked the people there very much, as being upright and jolly. He asked whether I had known the forester. "No, I was still quite small at that time, but I have heard much about him!" But when the old man learned from my talk that the Naßwald people spoke well of him, he said: "I myself was that forester, and not my brother."

He took great delight in meeting a man from Naßwald once more, sent for his fiddle and played the Naßwald woodcutters' march for me. I was astonished how the old man had mastered his instrument. It was hard to get away from the old hunter, for he had so much to say and ask that it became late.

Next morning I went to Miss B.'s and had breakfast there. Then I helped her pack her rucksack, telling her that she was taking too many unnecessary things along. But I could not make it any lighter, for she kept saying: "But I need that – and that." Ready at last! So we took a carriage to Aussee and train to Schladming. It was a lovely autumn day.

We crossed the Ramsau to Austria-Hütte. I had never seen it before in autumn. Before reaching the hut we had for a short time a splendid view of the Tauern chain, lighted a bright red in the sunset. The hut was quite empty and, as it was Kermesse time at the Kolm Inn, there were no guides present. That evening four jolly fellows came up, but their noise lasted so long that we almost had an argument about the night's rest. But Cilli, the landlady, restored order.

About half past two I heard the alarm going off, and in a little while the fire was roaring in the stove. It was not easy for me to leave my good bed, and it must have been the same way with the lady, as it was after four when we left the hut. The morning had an earnest, quiet mood, and without much talking we came to Schönbichl. That is the place where one usually turns off to the Huhner saddle. In a little while the snow was reached, where we put on the rope, as the snow was frozen hard. I had to cut steps at several places. Before getting to the rocks we saw two men, who had come from the Bachl Alm and were also going up the south wall, not very agreeable to us.

Shortly before the start of the ascent we came up with them, and just as we said good morning, the Dachstein did a bit of greeting. Not very kindly, but with an avalanche of stone, which for a short time placed us in utmost danger. I put Miss B. in a little crack where she was protected. With what wonderful good fortune it all went by! Despite the many stones none of us was hit. The two men were in even greater danger than we, for they were almost in the line of the fall. One of the men was Mr. König, the leader in the first ascent of the Triglav by the north wall.

We rested while the lady changed her shoes. Both men went ahead and found the route up to a certain point without asking me. As soon as we were above the first difficult chimneys the men went ahead at a faster pace, but we caught up with them later on. The day was wonderful, with a splendid view of the Tauern, and as the lady was going rather well we soon came to the difficult crossing.

Just before reaching it a hold broke away and I rolled down a short distance. But I stopped myself at once and was not in the least disturbed by it. Miss B. blamed the nailed boots, but that was not the reason. The stone had been lying loose, a thing that I could not see from below, as I had to swing up in order to use it as a hold.

We rested at the cave, and I changed my shoes. Both men were on the most difficult place, and it was not pleasant for the lady to wait in the face of the thought: 'The worst is yet to come!' I explained the matter and told her that I was sure she would make use of the rope. (I have described the difficulty of this place in my notes for 1905 and 1906.) I was soon across, roped up the rucksacks and had the lady follow. I was in a good place, but could not see her, but I knew all the same that she was staying too long in one spot, so I called: "Don't wait too long, Miss! You lose too much strength if you do. Trust the rope; it will hold."

Naturally she wanted to make it without its aid, but this could not be done for at last she was too tired (people will not believe a guide about this!). So she swung out nearly a metre and a half, and lost her hat. When she came up to me she said, disconsolately: "No, I could not climb the south wall!" I comforted her by replying: "Well, Miss, there have been many before you who hung in the rope, and many will follow – and will require the help of a guide." (The last sentence I said only to myself.)

I changed my shoes again and put on nailed boots, as we were coming to small, exposed ledges where a heavy rucksack is a hindrance and, indeed, may be the cause of a catastrophe. A guide should really never carry two pairs of nailed boots on such an ascent, and it should not be required of him. Of course money plays an important role in the matter! One can take a porter to the start of the ascent, who then takes the boots around by an easy way to the summit. (That will cost possibly 20 kronen.)

Slowly and carefully we went across the ledges, and when we emerged the fog was down. Part of our baggage had been left in Austria-Hütte, with word that if a guide or a porter came he should bring it to the summit, and so guide Steiner was correct in waiting for us with the things. Soon we were on the summit of the Dachstein, where we could not remain long. So we said farewell to the two men and to Franz Steiner, who were going to Austria-Hütte. Miss B. and I descended over the Gosau Glacier.

This side of the Dachstein gives one an entirely different impression, just as if one were in another country. One is now on the north side of the mountain, very different in condition from the south side. Instead of ex-posed ledges and small holds, one has hewn steps and a good hempen rope to hold on to. Because of the steepness of the rocks, the glacier seems much flatter than it really is. In a short time we were at Adamekhütte, cared for this summer by the guide Gamsjäger. We were the last guests, as it would be closed up on the following day. Two guides from Gosau were also there, wondering that even women undertook such breakneck expeditions. I must mention, however, that most of the Gosau guides are only woodcutters who, in the old days, guided only on Sundays and went up only from the easier sides. But most of them could tell marvellous stories of wild animals and of fog on the snowfields. I spent a most interesting evening with them.

On the following morning (September 23rd) we went from Adamekhütte over the newly constructed Linzer path to Hofpürglhütte. There we were well-received, the only guests. Liesl was concerned about my torn stockings and mended them as well as possible. Frau Vierthaler, Liesl and another girl entertained themselves with Miss B., while colleague Vierthaler, the manservant and I enjoyed a couple of glasses of good Salzburg beer.

Next day we went up the Kleine Bischofsmütze. It was as fine and warm as in summer. The view was unusual: we could see the Großglockner distinctly, and the Hochkönig so clearly that the hut was visible to the naked eye. By noon we were again in Hofpürglhütte. Then we went by way of Filzmoos to Mandling and by carriage to Schladming. There, as in Tyrol, the people called me the "Vienna Guide." As the lady was quite tired, she spent the night at Seebacher's. I stopped there also, going by the express on the following morning by way of St. Michael and Leoben to Mürzzuschlag. Next day across the Rax and home. I saw the landslide on the Wetterkogel route and descended over the Bärenloch. While I was going through the little chimney a chamois sprang over my head! Never before had I been so close to a live chamois.

On the following Sunday I went into the big Höllenthal with Dr. F. He wanted me to try with him a new ascent of the Kloben wall. Dr. F. had fractured his foot while trying it in the preceding year, and 14 days later a young fellow by the name of Seltner had fallen to his death. Dr. F. took me to the beginning of the ascent, and in a short time we were at the spot where he had formerly turned back, injuring himself during the descent. We climbed a little higher, finding a rope hanging which remained from Seltner's accident. The rope was still quite good. I considered how the misfortune could have happened. There was an overhanging rib, followed by a flat chimney. Mayer,[29] who was leading, must have been at the top of the chimney, and Seltner fell from the rib. The rope was cut in two by a sharp stone, so that the poor boy fell 70–80 metres.

I ascended the flat chimney and had Dr. F. follow. The rib was brittle and gave no hold for the *Kletterschuhe*, being full of earth and much slippery grass. I was not in the proper mood for a first ascent; also, I was afraid that if a stone went down it would fall right on the doctor's head. So I gave it up, descended and told Dr. F. that the thing seemed too dangerous.

I let Dr. F. down with the rope, roped myself down and then traversed to the Südbahner route, which is not much better and also goes up through the woods. There we looked down into the Kloben gulch. I glanced at the doctor and saw that his eyes were filled with tears. I was sorry for it. Without saying anything more about it, we went on. It was the first time I had been over the Südbahner route. While we were resting at the top, Dr. F. wanted to give me ten kronen, but I would not take it. So he thanked me for my company and gave me his Vienna address, telling me to look him up there some day.

Then I crossed the plateau to the Scheib forest and lay in the sun all afternoon. That evening I went to Habsburg-Haus to spend the night. Next morning a boy came from Karl-Ludwig-Haus, bringing me a telegram. It was from Miss B.'s sister, and read: "Can you meet me on October 2nd, two o'clock, at Steinach-Irdning? South wall! B." I sent an answer: "Yes. Coming. Kain." Then I quickly went home, packed my things, went to Kapellen on the following day and was in Steinach-Irdning at eleven o'clock, waiting for the lady. She arrived at one.

I was not a little astonished to see her enormous rucksack, and another pack in her hand! I took her things, and so could judge the weight. There were certainly 18 kilos, if not more. Then my own pack in addition: rope, lantern, first-aid kit, shirt, *Kletterschuhe*. I did not say much at the time, but when we got out at Schladming I remarked: "What have you in your sack that weighs so much?" "Besides my own things some provisions, since the huts are closed," was the reply.

I had to repack the rucksack in order to get everything in, and what did I find: four pairs of boots! I took out a pair of the nailed boots and asked: "What do you want with these, Miss?" "Those are my ordinary boots! These I have on are not nailed, but I will take them as far as the hut, as the path is good and they are not so heavy as the others!" (I nodded my head with an Aha!) Then came two pairs of *Kletterschuhe*. Again I looked at her questioningly. " If one pair gets wet I have a dry pair in reserve!" (A good idea, Miss!) "But who is going to carry all this?" Then came a pair of light slippers, and many other things she did not need for the trip.

The heavy rucksack had spoiled my good humour; the woman noticed it and said: "I have never seen you in such a mood, Konrad!" "Yes, Miss, and I have never seen you with such a heavy rucksack!" And then followed an exchange of words. Then she wanted to get a porter, but there was not much time to look around for one. So I said: "I'll carry it all as far as the Kolm Inn, where it will be easier to get a porter than here!" I sweated considerably, and to my surprise, when we got there, found no guide or porter. We were told that guide Steiner was higher up at a hay hut. So I took the rucksack patiently. It was quite dark when we reached the hut, very close to Austria-Hütte. We went in and asked for Steiner. But the peasant girl said he was not there. We left a message for him to carry our baggage up next morning to the top of the south wall.

I was of the opinion that Steiner really was in the hut, but had hidden himself when he heard us coming, not knowing who we were. I think he was afraid of the farmer, the girl's father!

We went to Austria-Hütte. I started the stove, cooked supper, after which we went to bed. I woke the lady about four o'clock, made breakfast and left the hut by moonlight at five. In two hours we were on the snow, where I told her we would put on the rope, which seemed not quite right to her. But I said: "I am the guide, and know my duty!" I was not in a good humour. Scornfully she took the rope, and went ahead to show that it was not needed. But it turned out otherwise. She went perhaps a hundred yards, missed her footing and was a rope's length below me, and would have kept on going without it!

Then I made a great mistake, for I laughed at her and inquired what she thought of the snow and of the rope. I went ahead, and had to cut steps at the top of the snow. Then an argument started, which kept up all day. It is an old story that, when the leader cuts steps, those behind get bits of ice in the face, naturally unpleasant. But she thought I did it on purpose and said: "In all my life I have never met such a malicious man as you are! I am sure that if I had Innerkofler or as good a guide here, such things would never happen." Thereupon, I replied: "I don't have to go with you, Miss; we can turn around and you can try it with another guide, who will cut steps with one hand and catch the ice-splinters with the other! Of course, I can't do that."

When we reached the rocks the worst was over. She was a very good climber, only self-centred and of different character from her sister, and I told her to what group she belonged. The lady made the difficult traverse very easily, and I must admit that she never put her whole weight on the rope.

The day was pleasant until the end of the climb, when a wet fog blew in and made the rocks uncomfortably cold. Of Steiner, who was to bring up the baggage, there was nothing to be seen, so I told the lady we must descend to Austria-Hütte. That annoyed her anew, for she thought that I preferred to go down to Schladming rather than to Hallstatt. But on the Huhner saddle we found Steiner with our things. A young gentleman, whom I had known on the Rax, came with him. I took over the load and we went to Simonyhütte, spending the night there. That is, we had to because of bad weather.

I went home from Hallstatt, and found numerous letters awaiting me. A man from Oedenburg, Prof. G., had me go up to the Binder Inn and, next day, I took him up the Rax by the Innthaler ledge. The man was a sincere friend of Nature and took great pleasure in the trip. I went home by way of Habsburg-Haus. It was a fine evening, so I stayed up until twilight, but I had to get home, for the weather was good and I did not wish to lose engagements. I found a telegram: "Expect you October 7th in Gstatterboden. P."

I was there at noon. Mr. P., with whom I had been out once before, arrived at one o'clock. "What shall we do, Mr. P.? The weather is fine and will continue so!" "The Totenköpfl on the Reichenstein." After a brief stop in the Hotel Gesäuse we went to Johnsbach. I have already attempted to describe the autumn beauty of the Enns Valley, but I can never find the proper words. I will only add that the peace and quiet was more profound than in September. Our conversation dwelt on the loveliness of autumn until we reached the Donner Inn. It all seemed so strange, to find the inn empty. The people from the Zillerthal who leased it had departed for the winter, so the natives were looking after it.

For a time we sat in front of the house but, as no one came, I went in and called – no reply. I entered the kitchen and walked around on the first floor: not a soul in the house, and every door open! Then I looked around outside and, at last found Johanna, the daughter of the landlord, in the garden. As always, I was greeted as young Innthaler. Since the people expected no visitors during the week at this season, it was quite a while before we got coffee. Then we inquired about the Treffner Alm, whether the hut was open and whether there was hay to be had, but Johanna could not give us much information. She presented us with fuel for our cooking apparatus and dried our little tent, remarking that it was a useful thing (which we, to be sure, did not find it that evening!).

We took a bottle of wine along to lighten the loneliness of the alm. Slowly we ascended the steep path to the Huber Alm. It was four o'clock when we started off. The air was so soft and transparent that it could not possibly be better, and soon we came to the clearing, a half hour from the Treffner Alm. It was full of blackberries and cranberries, and we could not pass by without tasting them. But often, while picking berries, we stopped and marvelled at the splendid form of the Ödstein, lighted by the sun with countless colours. Still, the Ödstein looks best from the Treffner Alm, and no mountain of the Enns Valley can compare with its appearance from that side.

Before getting to the alm we met a wandering calf, which followed us to the hut like a faithful dog. The alpine glow hung in the west, indescribably beautiful; eastward it was already quite dark. We watched it for a while, wondering at the splendid spectacle offered by Nature. It is impossible to see such a play of colour from the valley, and for most of those who have witnessed it there are no adequate words of description.

Then we had to look up our quarters for the night. I went into the stable and examined the hayloft. To my surprise there was not a blade to be seen; I entered a second one – only the bare boards, not much for beds! And the hut was locked. Most of the time, however, the people do not keep the key very far from the door, but I could not find it. I tried to open it with a piece of wood, using it like the latch usually to be found at the alm huts. But that did not succeed. After brief discussion we decided to force an entrance, promising to make good the damage. I looked for a pole with which to get up on the roof; a bit of an old ladder assisted me.

To break into such a simple alm hut is no great trick; one does not need to be a professional! But with the first shingle I tore off I discovered that I was not an expert. It was my first forcible entry, and I must admit that an anxious feeling went over me, although I knew that in our position it was not a great liberty. It was dark already and there was no other way.

I removed only a few shingles and let myself down, and just as I opened the door from within, Mr. P. discovered on the outer side a bolt wound with wire, actually the key. In daylight it would have been easy to find. We lit a candle and looked about in the hut. It was not entirely abandoned. Pans and other cooking utensils stood by the hearth, while meat, flour and a sack of salt hung from a cord. I went up above and saw that a bed was made. But there was no one in the hut! We emptied our rucksacks and began our cooking – which was very simple. Only the cooker was no good for the new fuel. (Or perhaps it was the other way around.)

After supper my pipe was filled with Mr. P.'s tobacco. He told me that he was always well-supplied with tobacco on trips, taking enough for the guide. Then came a couple of glasses of wine. We made a better fire, for there was enough wood in the hut, and each of us told jolly stories. The calf, which had not left the hut, made little noises, and it was just as if some person were going about. It was late when we retired.

Mr. P. lay down on the bed, which, to be sure, did not look very inviting. I put more wood on the fire and lay down beside it. My sleep was not of the best, and at four o'clock Mr. P.'s pocket alarm went off. Breakfast was simple: tea with eggs and ham. We made some tea to take along, and Mr. P. had even brought a Thermos bottle, which we tried.

The day was clear and cold, and when we reached the edge of the woods the sun rose behind the Hochschwab mountains and promised fine weather. This morning the air was again transparent and the sunrise had quite a different colouring from that of summer days. A herd of sheep was on the grassy slopes ahead, adding to the autumn picture. And the deepest silence that one can imagine.

We were above 1800 metres, a level at which, in autumn, there is often an unpleasant gale. Mr. P. took some pictures. We rested at the start of the Totenköpfl ascent. Like everyone else who stands in front of it for the first time, Mr. P. threw a questioning glance at the ridge. But the only difficulty is right at the beginning, a slab, which I crossed in nailed boots, at which the man wondered, and said: "I cannot understand how you do it!" I explained that there were, to be sure, not many footholds and one had to trust to the hands – as he discovered a few minutes later. Without further trouble or loss of time we reached the summit.

The first thing to do was to examine the Thermos bottle, to see whether it lived up to its claims. They were right: the tea was so boiling hot that one could not hold the cup with bare hands. We left the top after a long rest, descended to the saddle and from there went over the east wall of the Reichenstein. The combination of the splendid view, the friendly gentleman and the good, hot tea, made this time spent on top the best in my experience. We went down the usual way and, as we had left some of our things at the Treffner Alm, we went back to the hut. We found it open, and saw the herd boy to whom we explained the forcible entry. I repaired the roof, and Mr. P. left a krone for the accommodations. When Mr. P. told the boy it was for him, he wanted to kiss Mr. P.'s hand from pure joy.

We took leave of the happy youngster and went to Johnsbach. We had spent a fine night and day in this region, so that we, as friends of Nature, had the right to feel fortunate. Then, too, the young mountaineer would not forget it either, for one could see by his expression that it was the very first time he had had a whole krone for his own. Later on, the kronen would teach him another side of life, when he would sigh and say "Where has Time flown?" And so it will be with us as well, when we are old and can no longer see the peaks from on high, and we shall ask ourselves: "Where has the time gone?"

A brief stop at the Donner Inn and then we went on to Gstatterboden, planning an ascent of the Planspitze by its north wall for the next morning. It was all quiet at the hotel, and the fire in the stove was very agreeable. We left at six o'clock. On this day the air was not so soft; we were almost too warm as we went through the woods. The valley was filled with mist, and it was for this reason that the day was so sultry.

The rocks were rather cold, and there was snow at many places in the upper part of the wall where the sun did not reach. But Mr. P. was an expert climber and it did not take as much time as usual. We were on the summit in a little while, where I looked through the book and discovered that, in the last month since I had been on the Planspitze, there had been but two other parties. The sun shone warmly, inviting us to a prolonged stop. But the wind was too strong. So we descended to the Kölbl Alm, and down the waterfall path to Gstatterboden, arriving at four o'clock. Mr. P. left for Vienna.

During these excursions I came to know Mr. P., with whom I had been out but once before. I count him among the best of those who go with guides. In the mountains one finds out more about a stranger in a single day than in the city during months or years, and a friendship originating in the mountains is not so easy to dissolve.

I remained in Trieben overnight and arrived home on October 11th. There were many letters to be answered, and next day I had to go to the station at Payerbach to meet a party. They were new people to me. Mr. T., Mrs. Z. and Miss E. We went by carriage to the Höllenthal, did the upper and lower Zimmer climbs to Otto-Schutzhaus and from there to Habsburg-Haus, really too much for one afternoon. At Otto-Schutzhaus I took a lantern, which I had to light at the Trinksteinsattel. With the fog came wind, and I had to look sharply as I went from one marked rock to another. Just before reaching Habsburg-Haus such a storm arose that it was almost impossible to remain standing.

We heard the dog barking, and though I had surely gone this way 50 times before, on this night it was quite unknown to me. It was a critical moment – at last we reached the hut. Some tourists were there already, and we had a very pleasant evening.

Next day, in fine weather, we went to the Kölbl cliffs, descended the Wilde Gamseck and back over the Zsigmondy Gamseck; then to Habsburg-Haus and over the Maler climb to Prein. Both women, as well as the man, were excellent climbers such as I had seldom met on the Rax. (I had been recommended to these people by Hans Schroffenegger, guide from Tiers, Tyrol.)

I climbed up again over the Preiner slide to Habsburg-Haus, and on October 15th took three men over the Wilde Gamseck. They were from

Vienna, and all three very pleasant fellows. I cannot recall their names. One said, as he climbed along: "What a shame it is that my wife can't see me!" "Why?" asked one of the others. "I am sure that my wife would like it so much that she would never let me go alone again after seeing what a daring expert I am!" Thereupon the other two shouted "Hurrah!" In this manner we entertained ourselves all the way.

On October 19th I met Mr. B.G. in the Nass basin, and we did the Wilde Gamseck in finest weather. A splendid view from the Heukuppe. In the afternoon we met Dr. and Mrs. D. and another man. We crossed the Trinksteinsattel, leaving Dr. D. to descend the Preiner wall. We then went to Otto-Schutzhaus, descending after a short rest into the Höllenthal. It was a lovely evening. Thoroughly as I knew this region, if one of my companions rejoiced in these splendid views it made it ever new for me.

It grew dark as we were descending the last bit of the Wachthüttel route, and it was not pleasant to try and find the steps and the rises. I was annoyed with myself for again neglecting my duty as guide in having no lantern, which would have saved us so many uncomfortable minutes.

Next morning we went up the Akademik route to Otto-Schutzhaus. In the afternoon over the Blechmauern route, down to Weichtal, where we spent the night. The following day we did the Stadlwand ridge, descending over the Hochlauf. Mrs. D., on leaving, said that possibly she would meet me again the next Sunday.

On one of the days that followed I took a Frenchman up the Wiener Neustadt route, which interested him greatly, and he was amazed that one could have such good climbing so near Vienna. On November 1st I did the Stadlwand ridge with Mr. Sp. and Mr. B., descending through the Stadlwand cirque. On the last part of it we met Dr. and Mrs. D., who had been on the Schneeberg. That evening I introduced Mr. Sp. to Mrs. D. and told him that the ladies would like to accompany us in the morning if he did not mind. I was glad he agreed. We did the Katzenkopf and the upper Zimmer climbs. The day was perfect. We stopped at noon in Otto-Schutzhaus and took leave of Mrs. D. Mr. Sp. went with me down the Maler route to Prein. During this excursion I had become acquainted with one more kindly man.

During this autumn I had begun to think more seriously of my future, and made plans to learn a foreign language, of course selecting English. I told all my hopes and aspirations to my good mountain comrade, Dr. P. I wanted to spend the winter in England, but Dr. P. was unable to find anything suitable. Still, he was interested in my idea, and took pains to do what he could for me. He wrote letters to Mr. G. and Mr. B., asking them to contribute money in my behalf. Favourable replies from both men. So he wrote to me and, in a long letter, the following was of importance: "Come to Vienna. My wife will give you free lessons in English and we will furnish the books. Mr. B., father of the young woman whom you have so often guided, will furnish 20 kronen monthly, and Mr. G. will do the rest. Consider it well, and let me know."

Thereupon I went to Vienna on December 8th for several days, visited the men and thanked each one for his kindness. I saw other friends, including Dr. F. He offered me a room without charge. So everything went well, although it gave me no pleasant sensation to be kept by friends and acquaintances. But my few kronen were insufficient for a stay and the many expenses in a city. My thoughts were always the same: how could I earn more money in a short time? Working for 2.40 or three kronen a day does not allow one to save much. What could be done? I asked myself that often enough. And though I decided to go through with it only by honourable means, at this time, with my tormenting thoughts of how to make money quickly, dishonesty gained the victory.

I decided to go poaching once more. I laid aside my resolutions, borrowed a rifle and tried my luck in the forest. But it was no use, for I didn't get a big buck with a fine beard. Nothing, nothing at all.

CHAPTER VI

(1908)

▲

AS STUDENT IN VIENNA

In the first week of January 1908 I went to Vienna to begin my studies. It was the first time in my life that I had stopped so long in a city, and I can truly say I had more experiences than I expected. I had many adventures, good and bad. I think I shall do better to keep most of them to myself, for they are unbelievable, and so I will not have much to say of my doings between the beginning of January and May 10th. Just a little.

Dr. F. had placed a nice room at my service, and I felt quite at home. I even had breakfast with the doctor. I got the same books and pictures that a six-year-old English boy receives at the start of school. The first lesson was: the pencil, the book, the paper etc. Questions and answers according to the pictures. I did my tasks well and thought that I should soon have it all in my head. Even my teacher, Mrs. P., was, it seemed to me, quite contented. So it went on for several weeks. But then! Everything seemed difficult to me. The words were harder and longer, words that I could not pronounce well and some that I could not say at all (like perceive, amphibion, quadruped, respiration, pleasure). Most difficult of all was the English article "the."

In addition there were other difficulties. My money was all gone, and I was obliged to depend upon the kindness of friends. That hurt! First I went to Mr. G., who had promised Dr. P. to do something for me. I cannot describe my feelings in words. I had little more than a krone in my pocket, and went next day to —— Street to see Mr. G. Well, there I was in front of the house; should I go in? Begging! I went up and down in front of the house four or five times, my heart beating strongly. I did not go in.

I went back to my dwelling, took my books and went at the English. I bought my lunch in a small restaurant. Next morning I went off to the address once more. This time it would have to be! Much troubled I entered the house, asking for Mr. G., who did not keep me waiting long but asked me kindly how much I needed. "What you will give me, if you please." And he gave me 20 kronen, saying that I should come back again when it was gone. That was a load off my heart. But how long does 20 kronen last if one eats in a restaurant?

I did not approach Mr. E.B. at first, always lacking courage to go to his house on the Ring. Thereafter I always ate at the public kitchens; the money would last longer. But when at last it was gone, and I must again visit Mr. G., it was the old affair. So I pawned my watch and put off the bitter task a few days longer. Then I redeemed my watch once more and pawned it again. I never felt just right in Vienna! If I went along the streets and saw all the people, I seemed poor and helpless. I said to myself: 'How many mountain guides have succeeded without knowing English?'

I was overcome with homesickness and wanted to get away. I should have gone, except that one single person prevented it. Not with words. There was nothing bad about it, nothing but good. This girl had power over me such as no man had ever had. I had trusted my fate to her so often, and always, after her kindly words, my courage was revived to endure the unhappy days in Vienna.

I do not know whether I shall ever have so much respect for anyone on earth – man or woman – as for this girl. And I know that she was not only kind to me but to everyone. She made a good impression everywhere, and was much loved in the places where she spent her summer vacations. I cannot thank her in words for all the good she did me. But I will hold her memory all my life. Thus I made the discovery what a woman can do for a man if she be kindhearted and upright.

During my stay in Vienna I found out how men alter in the city. First, in the matter of clothes, then in character, and I soon knew which of them who had called me a "good friend" in the mountains really meant it. I understand quite well that he who has his occupation in the city often has many cares, must use every minute, and not always has time to stop and talk to a friend on the street. To be sure, when one is with them in the mountains one is asked, "Do you often come to Vienna?" "Not often." Then comes the offer: "Visit me next time you are there. I will show you the city and we will spend a couple of pleasant hours together." And then the mountaineer is happy and thinks the best of his gentleman.

Well then, one arrives in the city and looks up the other. It is often different from what one expects. The following may happen: one knocks at the door. The maid comes and opens it. One inquires whether Mr. So-and-so is at home. She doesn't say yes or no but asks your name and what you want. As soon as you open your mouth they can tell where you come from.

She goes in, announces that a youth or a man is there, and adds without being asked: "He must be from the country!" In a little while she comes back to the visitor and says what she has been told within: "The man is not at home." "When will he be at home?" "Oh, he'll be here late this evening, about ten or eleven o'clock."

Very often that is nothing but a bare-faced lie. The man is at home, but possibly a friend is calling and the visitor from the country doesn't fit in. Why not? Because he is to a certain extent embarrassed to be in company with such a person, and his friend will not understand if he talks in mountain dialect!

I was very careful about going to see people that I did not know well. But I had a great surprise. My sister came to Vienna, looking for a position. But when I saw that neither of us had any money for the employment bureau, I decided not to tell her, otherwise she would write to mother about it and make her anxious. I wanted to borrow a few kronen and chose Dr. B., who had often said he would gladly do anything he could for me. So I was quite prepared to accept his assistance, and accordingly went to his home and made my request!

As soon as he heard the word "money" he became much agitated, argued with me for an hour and at last would not give me the ten kronen I had asked for. "Here," he said, "take these five kronen. I can't give you more under any conditions, but I will give you some good advice. Go to Dr. W., with whom you have been as often in the mountains as with me, and he will give you the other half." I didn't want to accept the five kronen, but I was compelled to, for I needed the money and thought that I must see the business through even if it hurt.

Once outside, with all his words running through my head, I could not keep from weeping. Next morning I had a postal from him. "Dear Konrad! I am in and out of the house, busily engaged with work. This intensive labour will last probably all year. I beg you therefore to refrain from calling until a later time. Should I have more freedom I will write to you, although it is doubtful whether such will be the case this year. It is even questionable whether I shall be able to leave Vienna during the Easter or Pentecost holidays. With the best of greetings, Dr. B."

This message disturbed me very much, for I knew exactly why he had written it in that manner, and I was downcast by his unkindness and my own bitter disillusionment. Mrs. P. noticed that something was altogether wrong, and asked me about it. I told her of the foregoing matter; she listened, went into her room and brought back an envelope and five kronen, saying: "Send these five kronen back to Dr. B. and don't have anything more to do with him." I think there are not many people so mean as that man. With that exception, all who had been in the mountains with me were good and kind.

On February 28th I received an invitation to take part in the course for guides held at Villach. The night before my departure (March 1st) I went to a gathering of the Alpine Club and met many of my friends. It was the first time I had been in the Sofien Hall, and the first time I had seen about a thousand people at a ball!

About half past five I was at the West Station. I slept as far as St. Pölten, but after that the train was crowded from one station to another, as it was Sunday. From Klein-Reifling onward there was a fine winter landscape to be seen. It was the first time I had passed through the beautiful Gesäuse in winter. The mountains seemed as splendid and lovely as ever in their winter dress, and I counted the days to the Pentecost holidays, the time when, for some years, I had always come as guide to the Enns Valley.

In Villach I found all the guides at breakfast. Of the 12, I knew but one: Josef Stocker of Sexten, whom I had met during the preceding summer at Dreizinnenhütte. We were quartered in the Hotel Lamm, with good fare and service. In a little while we all felt at home. Always at evening the mountain songs were sung, and on this account we were invited to other inns. In addition to our food each of us received a litre and a half of beer each day. I had only one krone and 30 hellers in my pockets when I reached Villach, and made it last a whole week.

We had classes every day from nine until twelve and from one until four o'clock. The following things were taught: map-reading, natural history, first aid and the technique of mountaineering. Mr. Aichinger, a most experienced climber, instructed us in map-reading and technique. During the second week we made an excursion to Tarvis under his leadership, and from there to Raibl and the Predil Pass to practise map-reading. At evening we were in Villach once more.

On March 8th there were ski races and jumping on the Dobratsch. Examinations were held on March 15th. Several members of Section Villach were present, as well as some of the officers. The central committee of the German–Austrian Alpine Club was represented by Mr. Müller of Munich.

My examination questions were as follows: "Can you tell us from what place one makes the Katzenkopf climb? To what river system do the streams of the Rax belong?" Then I had to tell something about the origin of limestone, and something about atmospheric pressure. The examining physician presented the question as to what I should do with a person dug out of an avalanche shortly after the accident? How does one give artificial respiration? Knee bandages? Head bandages? How one could make a litter from articles of clothing, rope and ice axes? The following questions concerning foreign districts were given: "How high is Mont Blanc? From whence does one ascend the Matterhorn?" None of these questions was difficult for me. I passed the examination in the First Group.

That evening we had supper and a dance with Section Villach. There were some speeches made, and I presented our thanks to the Alpine Club. A guide from Heiligenblut thanked the sponsors of the course for their kindness and trouble. On the same evening we said farewell to our new friends in Villach and all of us went home on March 16th. I was the last to leave and was alone on my return to Vienna. I would very gladly have interrupted the journey at Gstatterboden; I had time enough, but unfortunately no money.

Although I had studied no English during these two weeks, the lessons went well enough. When next I went to see Mr. G. a misunderstanding was cleared up. He said: "You are looking well, Konrad." "Oh, yes, I had a good time and was well fed in Villach." Mr. G. looked surprised: "But certainly you can't complain of your living in Vienna, when Dr. P. looks after you?" But this was not the case, for I was patronizing the public kitchens. So there had been a misunderstanding from Dr. P.'s letter, and Mr. G. did not know that I had to feed myself.

Before the Easter holidays I visited several men and inquired about their plans. But I did not hear what I should have liked, and gave up hopes of a party. Then I would have to stay in Vienna. Shortly before the holidays I was with some good friends. I received the travel money as an Easter present, without having to tell of my need for cash, and so it was possible for me to go.

Before leaving Vienna I met Mr. B. and we made a date for an excursion on the Rax on Tuesday. I felt well again when I saw the old Rax once more! On Good Friday I went to church, in the afternoon into the Große Gries, and on Saturday to Habsburg-Haus. My mother wanted to give me a couple of kronen, but I would not allow it, for she had not much herself. As always, I was well-received at Habsburg-Haus. The keeper asked me whether I wanted to help him out over the holidays; I could have my keep free. I agreed. Sunday morning I went on skis to the heights of the Scheib forest. To my sorrow it was a cloudy day without view. My thoughtful mother had put cakes and eggs into my rucksack, and I had my alcohol cooker; so I had lunch in the hut and a good run down to Habsburg-Haus.

The tourists arrived in the afternoon, and by evening there were nearly a hundred people there. It was a gay time, with dancing until two in the morning. In the main room there was space for 40 people, some on mattresses, some on the bare floor. By noon of Monday they had all departed. That evening, I descended the Kleine Gries and stayed for some time in the Binder Inn.

Thursday morning I went to see a relative to whom I had loaned a hundred kronen two years before, and asked whether part of what was owing could be paid. But it was impossible to get money, so I did not leave Naßwald in the best humour. About noon I reached the Weich Valley, where I was expecting Dr. P. Instead, a telegram came. He was prevented by business and could not come. That was bad for me, for I had no money with which to return to Vienna. The thought came into my mind: I will never go back to the city. But then I changed my mind, and saw that it would be better to finish my course.

I was more eager than ever for English, for now I could speak a little, and my good teacher had often told me recently: "Only a month more, and you will be far enough along to make yourself understood and will then be able to continue by yourself." The innkeeper in the Weich Valley lent me ten kronen, and I was able to go back to Vienna.

But there I had to look up a place to stay, for I could live no longer with Dr. P., and found a room with a workman's family on the Schönbrunnerstrasse. Once more I went to Mr. G., then borrowed 40 kronen from Dr. L. Dr. P., as always was very kind to me and said that if I needed anything I should go only to him, as I once did at a later time.

At the end of April a lady engaged me for a Rax trip, and when she had to give it up sent me ten kronen. These ten kronen were too much for me. I could not hold back, I had to make an excursion, and as an excursion train was just going to Puchberg, I rode to Grünbach and went up the Hohe Wand. It was a rainy morning. After breakfast at Grünbach I went a little way up the usual route on the Hohe Wand, and when the weather improved a little later, traversed below the cliffs to the Kanzel ridge. While ascending I met two young tourists who were climbing up. I asked them whether that was the Kanzel ridge. (I knew it was, as I had made this trip before.) "Yes," came the reply. "Do you want to do the ridge?" asked one. "Yes, I do," I replied. Probably I did not look like much of a climber, much less a guide. So both of them asked me whether I had ever done such a climb before. "Yes, the Akademik and the Preinthaler routes!" "But the Kanzel ridge is ever so much harder, especially this morning when the rocks are wet. It would be better for you," they said, "to use the rope while crossing the Testament cliff." I could not refuse their kind offer and said: "That's very nice of you; very well, I'll take the rope when we get to the cliff." Above the cliff, where it is quite easy, we took off the rope and I thanked them both very much.

As we went on I heard one say to the other: "Say, you, I think that was Kain!" "Oh, do you think so?" said the other. "*He* wouldn't have needed the rope." I kept talking about climbing and all sorts of things, so they would not discover who I was before we got to the hut. On arriving there several tourists greeted me, and it came out that one of the young fellows was right. On their asking why I had not told them I was Kain, I replied that I much preferred to be tourist rather than guide!

In the afternoon I took a walk to the plateau, picked some spring flowers, snow-drops among them. During this hour I was happy again and forgot all my troubles. I could not pull myself away from the hut, and spent the night there, for I knew they would not charge me much, and I had no English lesson with Mrs. P. until noon of the following Monday.

We were all good friends in Wilhelm-Eichert-Hütte: Hanni from Karl-Ludwig-Haus; Cilli from Otto-Schutzhaus and Rudolf from Habsburg-Haus. Monday morning at five o'clock I said goodbye to Wilhelm-Eichert-Hütte and went down to Grünbach. I almost missed the train; it was a matter of minutes. After an hour of English I made some calls and divided the flowers among my friends.

On May 1st I saw the workmen's procession, the largest gathering of people I had ever seen. On May 11th I turned my back on the metropolis and went home for good. On the day before, I visited everyone who had made my stay in Vienna possible and gave them my best thanks, and to the Alpine societies as well.

During my stay in Vienna I was sometimes given theatre tickets, often going with Mr. P. to the Kaiser Panorama, and visiting the museums several times. Once I went with Mr. P. to the art gallery, where the pictures interested me very much. I was always happy to go to the Galizynberg, to the Schönbrunn and City Parks, but most of all I wanted to go back to the mountains.

2

AT HOME AGAIN

I was as if born anew when I got out at Payerbach! The fruit trees were at the height of their blossoming, the birds sang their sweetest songs and I rejoiced in the fresh green as never before. Everything seemed so beautiful. I put my baggage in the postal coach and went home on foot. I think that I had never been in a lighter frame of mind before while going through the Schwarza Valley.

I was making plans as to what I should do in the future. My deepest desire was to cross the ocean, so that I might see much of the world and at last improve my situation. I was home on May 13th and took a walk to the Zikafahnler Alm during the fine weather. Two days later I went up to the Knofel plateau and through the lovely woods to the Lakaboden Hut. This excursion I often made for my own pleasure and I must add that this forest is one of the finest things I know near my home.

On May 24th I did the Maler climb with Dr. D.'s wife. As she wanted to learn something about technical climbing, I allowed her to lead as she wished. Naturally we were roped. Once or twice she asked: "Where now?" I replied with a smile: "I don't know. You are now the guide and must find the way. Today it is my pleasure to go as tourist." It went very well, except that at the worst place, the overhang, I took care to go ahead. Then I let the lady lead once more. In a short time we reached the plateau. Of course I thanked her for her careful guidance!

At Otto-Schutzhaus the lady told with joy that she had led over the Maler route. Her husband asked me about her ability as guide and I gave her the best of references. In the afternoon I went with her to Habsburg-Haus, where we spent the night. On the following morning we wanted to do the Red Gully and descend into the Große Gries cirque. But on reaching the precipice, Mrs. D. became dizzy when she looked down into the Große Gries. We discussed what route to take down and, as we had the whole day, I advised the main Uebel Valley. This climb is made by few tourists, and its start is not easy to find. There is wild rock scenery there such as is hardly to be found elsewhere on the Rax and its vicinity.

We went down to the Zikafahnler Alm, which I have often described in my journal. It was a lovely May day. Here and there the snow was still on the meadows of the alm, with new-born grass and many beautiful spring flowers at the edge of the snow. The songs of blackbirds, of thrushes and even cuckoos were to be heard. And very lovely was the view into the depths of the Nass Valley. If I am ever rich enough to spare perhaps a thousand kronen, then I'll build myself a hut on the Zikafahnler Alm. For that is a place where I could spend a year.

During the descent to the Uebel Valley we rested a little, and then climbed slowly down into the cirque. The lady did not require the rope on this trip. After my recent experience with loose stones I showed her how to go on shale. Always upright and rather quickly. Never sit down! If a stone rolls out under one's foot, one should not try to stop the stone. One can remain upright amid the moving stones, if the field is not too steep and coarse. I have often noticed that most tourists, who have not grown up in the mountains, are all more or less unsteady during descent, and often nervous.

About two o'clock we came to the Naßwald road and followed it into the Höllenthal. I got out in Weichtal and took leave of Mrs. D. I was expecting Dr. P. that very evening.

On the 26th we did the Wiener Neustadt route. It was a fine morning and Dr. P. was happy about the good light for photography. But when everything was ready for an exposure, the camera fell down for a distance of more than 50 metres. We looked for a short time, without saying a word; then I climbed rapidly down to the camera, which had caught in a windfall. I looked to see whether the lens had been damaged, and called to Dr. P. that nothing had happened. Then I climbed up again. He was glad that the camera was not as badly smashed as we had expected. So we went slowly along. In the middle ravine we did the "Kain Step."

On this day Speckbacher-Hütte was opened – that is, provisioned – and we were the first guests. Then we went on to Otto-Schutzhaus, taking a long rest before going down the Maler route to Edlach. There I said goodbye to Dr. P. A week later we were to meet in the Enns Valley, and so we shouted a cheery "Auf Wiedersehen!"

I went back to Naßwald and climbed the Wilde Gamseck with a man. On the 15th, at three in the morning I crossed the Nass ridge to Kapellen in order to start on my summer's journey. The weather was splendid and it was always a happy feeling to be returning to the Enns Valley with its friendly inhabitants. In the afternoon I reached Gstatterboden, finding everything as of old. There were several letters as well, from dear friends.

On the next day I went to Selzthal, where I met Dr. P. We were in Schladming about two o'clock. Without stopping we crossed the ridge to Ramsau. There I met my friend G. Steiner, and Mr. B. of Section Austria. When he heard that we intended to ascend the Dachstein by its south wall, he made an earnest face and remarked that it was much too early for this tour. It seemed to me as if he would like to have said "Reckless Kain."

I must say a little more about the variegated colour of the lovely meadows and fields of Ramsau. Mr. P. and I were quite delighted by the beauties of spring. It is a gift of God if one enjoys Nature, and indescribably delightful if one passes through such fabulous loveliness with a friend who has similar feelings. It seems to me as if each one could read the other's thoughts.

There were only a few guests in Austria-Hütte. I met Mr. Müller, who had examined me at the guides' course. We went early to bed, and left the hut on the morning of June 17th at three o'clock. We gave up the idea of the south wall. Without saying much, we went along in the mysterious silence of waking Nature. The sunrise did not promise much of a day. Soon we were on the Huhner saddle, and after a short rest wandered across the icefield to the Dirndl climb. First up the little one. The snow was good and we were soon on the summit. Mr. P. took several pictures and then we climbed down to the ice gully, which is often a problem. For one who has already done more, it is nothing special. As we had time enough, we climbed the Große Dirndl in addition. Scarcely half an hour was required to the top, and we remained only a short time, for we wished to cross the Dachstein.

As we needed no rope for this excursion, we were soon up. The view was fine, and I thought of the days that I had spent as "tourist" at the Bachl Alm. We descended across the Gosau Glacier to Adamekhütte, putting the rope on as a precaution. In the hut we were pleasantly received, for I was acquainted with all these people from the Zillerthal.

On June 18th we went up the Thorstein by the usual route. A fine day and a wonderful view! We stayed on the summit for a long time, photographing, smoking, telling each other our experiences and feeling happy on this lonely height. We descended over the saddle between the Thorstein and the Mitterspitze, ascending the latter, which was new to me. An easy viewpoint. At four o'clock we were back again at the hut. The sun was shining and we lay down on the warm rocks.

That evening there was a brilliant sunset, one of those that doubles the joy of a successful excursion. On the following morning at six we left the hut, following the Linzer path for a short distance, then circling toward the Windleger saddle, as we wanted to ascend the Eiskarlspitze. On the way one is apt to find beautiful fossils – fish and shells – which must be very interesting to a person who understands them. In an hour and a half we came to the Eiskarlspitze. A tricky tower! We left our nailed boots behind at the start. I think this climb is the best in the Dachstein mountains. It closely resembles the Stadlwand ridge on the Schneeberg, but is more exposed. We took a long rest on top, with an especially fine view of the jagged Bischofsmützen, standing up like Dolomites, with the Gosau Lake below.

We descended by the same route and went on to Hofpürglhütte. During the evening it clouded over, and there was little hope for the next day. But, to our joy, we looked out next morning at a clear, blue sky, and left the hut at five o'clock to climb the Bischofsmützen. Rapidly we ascended the big one, then the little one, not stopping for long, as we wanted to make the train. In three and a half hours we were back at the hut, descending after breakfast to the artistic village of Filzmoos. It was noon, and at two o'clock we reached Mandling, hoping to find a carriage there so we could make the express at Schladming. But it was in vain.

We would gladly have paid double fare for a vehicle, but there was no chance. The peasants were all working with the hay. There was nothing to do but go on if we were going to catch the express. Tired and thirsty we entered the station at Schladming. Three minutes later the express came through. There was a long stop at Selzthal, so we had time for some nourishment, and at seven o'clock we were at Gstatterboden, where I left the train and shouted "Auf Wiedersehen" to Mr. P.

Something unexpected happened as I was walking up the steps from the station to the hotel. Everybody there came rushing out at me, proprietor Arlhofer at their head, all in great excitement. He held a telegram in his hand, and said, excitedly: "Kain, Kain, what has happened? Here, read!" He gave me the telegram: "Kindly inform me whether Konrad Kain is dead or not. Franziska Kain." My mother! The second wire was from Schladming: "Konrad Kain was seen leaving Austria-Hütte several days ago to ascend the south wall of the Dachstein. Bad weather. Possibly an accident. Hotelier Seebacher."

First of all they congratulated me that the news was not true, and ten minutes later all of Gstatterboden was assembled in the hotel. Then the whole story came out. The first telegram was from Naßwald. When I first left Gstatterboden they knew only that I was going to the Dachstein mountains, so inquiry was made in Schladming. Thereupon Seebacher sent his wire to Gstatterboden. So then they wired Naßwald: "Kain departed Monday. No further information. Arlhofer."

Naturally, at first they thought in Naßwald that an accident had taken place and, as I was told later, all sorts of rumours arose. It was even said in

Kaiserbrunn that early on Thursday morning Kain's body had been brought in. Some said that a man had pulled me down during a first ascent; others said, "Well I thought a long time ago that the fool would fall sooner or later." I could not discover how the news of an accident originated. Although I knew that it started in Höllenthal, I could not get on the track of it.

I wired to my mother at once: "Information about what? I am all right." And sent a telegram to the *Deutsche Volkszeitung* to refute what had been written of my mishap. Thereupon I received so many letters of congratulation that I needed almost two days to answer them all. Section Reichenau and the Austrian Touring Club also sent friendly notes. Never before in my life had I received so many letters. But what annoyed me was that many people, even good friends, were skeptical and would not believe that the whole matter had come out of the air. Whoever had started the falsehood was either a malicious or a thoughtless person, for in such cases it is easy for a guide to lose his good reputation. There are many people who would rather believe evil than good.

At six o'clock on the evening of June 28th, Dr. L., K. and L.B. arrived. We departed at once for Heß-hütte, reaching it about ten. We were expected, as beds had been reserved. We left the hut early to make the tour over the Rossschweif on the Hochthor. Dr. L. had made this trip several times, and undertook the guidance of Mr. K. I went with Mr. L.B. All three were good climbers, so we went fast and almost together, reaching the summit in a short while. We unroped, rested and went without the rope along the ridge until past the Festkogel. During descent we roped again. There are two routes: one on the south side, the other on the north, which is the one I advised, as it is harder and more interesting.

The views into the depths from the north wall are marvellous! But the rock is very brittle, and a little later we almost fell off the ridge in a bunch. Mr. L.B. took hold of a big block and everything loosened. I shouted "Forward! Go ahead quickly!" and pulled in the rope. Two minutes later we saw an enormous avalanche of stones go down. Dr. L. and Mr. K. were still behind us, and had to go around this place. The occurrence did not leave a feeling of comfort; we said nothing, but I am sure each of us had the same thought: our lives were in danger!

Soon we reached the Teufelszacken, where I took over the guidance of the other men, and an hour later we were in the col between Teufelszacken and Ödstein, Here there is the well-known Schmittplatte, which many fear, but in modern climbing circles is not considered as much. There were already some tourists on the Ödstein, who had come up from Johnsbach over the Kirchl ridge, our route of descent. Toilsome as ever, and stones knocked down in the long couloir by tourists.

At noon in Johnsbach we met many friends. The men continued to Admont, and I to Gstatterboden, where I was expected. I had undertaken an excursion for the following day, and took a gentleman by way of Heß-hütte to Johnsbach. Then I went from the Donner Inn to Kölbl, meeting guide Zettelmaier and Martin from Heß-hütte, who told me we had to go up the Teufelszacken on July 1st and make things safer. The rope and the spikes were already at the Koder Alm. There the hard work began.

The rope weighed 20–25 kilograms. We went as far as the Rinnerstein, alternating with the packing. But when we came to the rocks, I had to carry it all by myself, for Zettelmaier had rheumatism in his shoulder and Martin's balance was unsafe. Zettelmaier took me on the rope, but at that it was not easy climbing. I had to rest every ten minutes, and we pulled up our burden at many places. We reached the Teufelszacken about noon, fixing the rope after some two hours of hard work. Then we went along the ridge to the Hochthor. On the way, I learned a new variant: one goes from the Festkogel saddle right across the walls and reaches the Josefinen route just below the Hochthor summit. It was almost dark and we were half dead with weariness when we reached Heß-hütte.

My feet were quite stiff next day; I remained at the hut and went down to Gstatterboden in the evening. On July 4th I was expecting Miss B. from Altaussee. She arrived at four o'clock and we went back that same evening to Heß-hütte. On the following morning we were off early and did the Rossschweif on the Hochthor–Ödstein ridge. The weather was perfect. This tour is long, almost too long for a woman, especially when it is hot. I was astonished at the endurance of the lady.

Next day was one of rest, which I spent with my friend Auer at the Scheiben Alm. On July 7th I went with two ladies and a gentleman up the waterfall route to Heß-hütte, and back to Gstatterboden. On July 10th with a man from Graz up the Große Buchstein. But we had to turn back on account of fog and rain.

On July 11th I travelled by way of Selzthal and Leoben to Payerbach. Everyone who saw and greeted me said: "Here is one arisen from the dead," and of course I had to tell them all about it. I met many friends and tourists in Payerbach. About seven o'clock my men arrived and I went with them to Kaiserbrunn. On Sunday we did the Wiener Neustadt climb.

That evening I went to Naßwald to see my dear mother. She wept for joy, rejoicing that I was well and unhurt.

On July 14th I went to Kaiserbrunn and up the hunter's path to the Knofel plateau and Lakaboden. I have already mentioned this excursion in connection with the beauty of the forest. I went down to Reichenau, visiting good friends with whom I had been promised a tour. I expected Miss M. at Hirschwang, and we went into the Weich Valley next day to do the Stadlwand ridge. It became windy when we reached the "Gassel," so much so that I was afraid we should have to give up the trip.

At the start of the climb we put on our *Kletterschuhe* and rested. In an hour and a half we were at Stadlwand Hut. We sat in the sunshine and then went over the southern Grafen path and down the Hochlauf wall. The lady was met in the Weich Valley by her mother and her sister, the latter remaining to make the same trip on the following day.

The wind was now not so strong and the weather remained fine. The girl had been in doubt whether the climb would not perhaps be too much for her. But on seeing it she thought quite otherwise. We took a long rest at the hut, then went down over the Hochlauf into the Weich Valley, where I took leave of the lady.

I said goodbye to my weeping mother at three o'clock on the morning of July 18th. It was for a month. It was not with a great feeling of security that I left my home this time; it affected me, for my mother had never cried before when I went on my travels.

3
TO ITALY

It was a cloudy morning. When I stood on the Nass divide, I looked back into the Reiss Valley, then wandered through the mist-filled Altenberger Valley to Kapellen. At six o'clock the train arrived from Nauberg. I went to Mürzzuschlag and by way of St. Michael to Villach. There I spent the night in the Hotel Lamm, where I had been quartered during the guides' course.

Dr. L. and Mr. P.[30] arrived next day by train, and we started off at once for Bruneck, as we wanted to go into the Taufers Valley and make some climbs there. But it poured in torrents and we had to give it up. We spent the night in the Hotel Post, travelling next day by way of Franzensfeste, Bozen, Ala, Verona and Milan to Turin, spending the night in the Hotel Florian and making some purchases (ice axes).

On the 23rd we went by rail by way of Cuneo to Borgo Dalmazzo, a real Italian mountain town, with ancient ruins and narrow streets. Next day we took a carriage through a wonderful forest to Entraque, inquiring at the inn for the guide who had the key to the Rifugio Genova. The guide was busy in the field, making hay. He came after a while, a very friendly fellow. There are only a few guides there, for there is little tourist activity in the Maritime Alps.

About half past five we left the pleasant village with our guide. The path to the refuge, which passes an unusually lovely blue-green lake, is in fairly good condition because the Italian king has his hunting preserve there. We reached the hut at dusk; it is built of wood and supplied with cooking utensils, stove, good blankets and straw, even wood, which is carried up. (One bundle costs a franc.) We were the first tourists of the season.

We left the hut at four o'clock in the morning to ascend the Punta de l'Argentera, highest peak of the group. These mountains are easy to climb, although the rock is brittle. We went up over grass slopes and scree. Mr. P. who was not in training, became very tired, had an attack of mountain sickness and had to give up. I stayed with him, while Dr. L. and the Italian guide continued. After half an hour, during which Mr. P. almost recovered, I followed and overtook them on the south peak. There is a little glacier on the last part, as well as a bit of climbing. The panorama was magnificent. We could see the Mediterranean, and many little lakes of all colours. The green alm meadows afforded an unforgettable sight with their lovely surroundings of rock and snow. There was a splendid view of Monte Viso, which we hoped to climb in a few days.

After a short rest we descended to Mr. P., thence traversing over the Gias del Bans to Terme di Valdieri, a bathing place in the midst of lovely foliage. To our sorrow it began to rain, so we had coffee and then went by carriage to Cuneo, and on the following day by train to Turin and Barge. On July 26th we proceeded to Crissolo, walking the long but good path to the Capanna Quintino Sella. This district in winter would make a good skiing ground. I went ahead on the last part of the way and met the women splitting wood. They called to me pleasantly, but I knew too little Italian to converse with them, despite which they kept on without interruption.

We found there an excellent cook and were well-treated. Next day we started out with lanterns at three o'clock to ascend Monte Viso. First we had to go down to the lake, frozen throughout most of the year, thence traversing over scree and snow to a col. We looked in the guidebook and found out that we could now see the old hut, which had not been visible before. None of us had been in these mountains previously.

Monte Viso was now in front of us, but we did not go far enough to the right to get onto the usual route, but climbed straight up steep snow slopes. In order to reach the arête we had to go up through a narrow couloir, which cost us some hard work, not entirely free of danger. Once on the ridge we immediately saw that this could not be the customary way, for too many difficulties presented, overhangs of ice, and cornices such as I had never met on the usual routes on Swiss peaks. In addition, we suffered from wind and cold.

The last part to the summit was an easy ridge of snow. Soon we were standing by the iron cross. No doubt now: we were on Monte Viso, and had reached it over the Viso Vallante and the redoubtable west ridge! (The fourth ascent.) The view from the top is really splendid.

We took the usual route for descent, and after a rest in the Capanna went down that same day to the valley to Piano del Re, an ancient and not very clean hut near the French frontier. Next morning we started off early to cross the Col de la Traversette to Adries. A tunnel leads through the top of the col. We met some guards but were not searched. This crossing is very much worthwhile but is seldom made, the Cottian Alps being but little visited by tourists. I was delighted by the beautiful meadows and the lovely larch trees!

From Adries we went by carriage to Mont Dauphin Guillestre, and on by train to Argentière la Bessée, where we took a carriage that brought us at a late hour to Vallouise. On July 29th we looked up a guide to accompany us on the Barre des Écrins. After some questioning we found one at last, but he had a fearful Katzenjammer and wanted to postpone the expedition, which we could not do. He was quite truthful, telling us that he had gotten drunk the day before at a christening party. At last he allowed himself to be persuaded to come with us.

We wandered along to the Chalet Ailefroide, where I had been for several days the preceding year. After we had had some coffee, we went on through the Pré de Madame Carle, taking another little rest at the last inn. I was against taking the guide any farther, but the doctor thought there would be no harm in letting him go as far as the Cabane Ernest Caron, where he might be of assistance in carrying up the wood that we gathered at the edge of the trees.

The glacier was in good condition, so we did not put on the rope; it was farther than I recollected, and darkness came on before we reached the rocky rib on which the hut is situated. There was no stove, and we did our cooking in the open. A cold wind carried the flames away from the kettle, but at last our simple supper was ready. My colleague was so tired that a few minutes after arrival he threw himself down on the straw and ate not even a piece of bread. We slept well also, but with filled stomachs!

Early next day I heard the doctor get up and look at the weather. It was one o'clock. "It will be a fine day, Konrad," he said. So I got up, but I would have liked to stay three or four hours more in my straw bed. I made tea and cooked some canned things. The guide was sick and could not go with us. About half past two we left the hut, just at daybreak. I had already ascended the Barre des Écrins in 1907. Dr. L. thought it would be too strenuous for me as the only guide, but I told him with certainty that I did not need a second one.

We crossed the icy rocks to the Glacier Blanc, and as snow conditions were good we soon approached the steep slope. This loftiest summit of Dauphiné was first ascended on June 25, 1864, by Whymper, Moore and Walker with a guide, and for a long time had the reputation of being an expedition of the first order. Even today it is considered strenuous.

As an ascent had been made several days before, we had things easier than we expected, for in some places we could even use the old steps, thus saving much time. Still, the icy rocks just below the summit required great care. We took a long rest and enjoyed the splendid view about us. During the descent we met our local guide on the Col des Écrins, who congratulated us on having made the trip in such fast time.

After a brief stop we roped together and descended across the col. This way is seldom taken, and we found out why. One traverses icy rocks toward the right and then down into a steep and narrow couloir about 200 metres in length. I went as last man. It took a long time, as there was work in cutting steps. The last minutes were very risky, possibly my most dangerous moments in the mountains. The situation was as follows: the local guide and Dr. L. were already around a rocky corner, Mr. P. and I still in the narrow ice gully. Suddenly a fall of stone – take shelter, such as there was!

But there was no protection at all for the last two. I took an extra turn of the rope around my anchored axe, and lifted my rucksack higher against my head. At that very moment the stone avalanche arrived. One stone struck me on the shoulder, ten seconds later (which seemed a year) another hit me on the head, giving me a severe wound. Blood streamed; I could hold myself no longer, fell and slipped down for the length of the rope. I was unconscious for several minutes, and they carried me beneath a rock and bound up my injuries.

When I looked at Mr. P., blood was pouring from his face. A stone had cut his cheek. A wonder that it had not broken his cheek-bone. Much time was consumed by this mishap. Our local guide lost his head, his nerves failed and he could not act as last man during the descent of the remaining 400 metres of steep snow. So I had to do it! We remained roped until the moraine was reached. Then I washed off the blood as best I could. I did not show my pain. The wound on my head didn't matter, but my shoulder became quite lame and hurt at every movement.

Late that evening we reached La Bérarde; many tourists there were curious about the marks of blood on our clothing. I went right to bed, and had to stay there all next day. Everyone cared for me most kindly, but I revealed my pain to no one. I got up in the afternoon and went for a walk by myself. I exercised my arm, which hurt terribly, but brought the stiff muscles back to life.

At evening some tourists came in, among them two gentlemen from Dresden and a guide arrived from the Refuge Promontoire, bringing me the following message: "Should the foreign guide be Konrad Kain, we send him best greetings from the Meije. Vineta and Alfred Mayer." These two were well-known Vienna tourists.

Dr. L. said to me next day: "If you do not feel well enough, we will remain here." But the weather looked good, and I did not want to hold the men back on a fine day, so I said that I was all right. So we got ready for the Meije. When the Dresden men heard this, they left La Bérarde several hours ahead of us, as they also wanted to do the Meije, to show their independence.

It was a lovely, clear day, and we wandered comfortably through the Vallée des Étançons. As I knew the region, I showed the men the routes and passes. At timberline we took some firewood, each of us carrying a little bundle. About seven o'clock we reached the Refuge du Promontoire, where we again met the Dresden men. They were just about to melt snow, as they had not found water. I fetched some, we did our cooking, filled our pipes, and then conversation began – about nothing but trips. (The Dresden fellows declared themselves to be quite independent Hochtouristen, but they had not yet done the Meije, and that peak has a lesson in store for even the most experienced.) We talked for quite a while, and went to bed at ten o'clock. It was a clear, cold evening. As I have written so often about the play of colours in a sunset, I would like to say more about moonlight in Dauphiné. But it is impossible for me to describe that wondrous quiet of Nature and the splendour of such a night.

I got up about two o'clock, made a fire, cooked breakfast and put the hut in order, according to directions, leaving with full knowledge that we had a hard day's work ahead. The two men from Dresden went ahead. But, as it is difficult to find with lanterns a path that one is unfamiliar with, we soon overtook them. Then I went ahead, since I knew the way. Both men lagged behind. We waited for them at the Grand Mur. And there it was evident that the Meije had something in store for them! Although we started up the wall at the same time, the Dresdeners got behind and kept shouting for directions. I told them pleasantly how and where.

But they doubted my knowledge and talked against it. That made me angry: "Do you think you know better than I who have already done it? Go your own way and don't ask so much!" And we went on. Dr. L. was somewhat annoyed at my plain words. It was not long before we heard them call again. We waited. Dr. L. told me to go back and offer them the rope, which they accepted willingly and without objection. Five persons on one rope! That makes the going slow!

From the Glacier Carré to the Cheval Rouge the two men again went alone. Then I gave them the rope once more and continued in this arrangement *across the entire Meije*! We rested on the Grand Pic and then descended to the Brèche Zsigmondy. It was very icy and the roping-off went slowly. I was cold already and the men simply would not go ahead. Finally, the last one was in the saddle. I threw down the rope, and climbed down without it. Dr. L. said I was reckless. He was right.

The most dangerous part of the work begins at the Brèche Zsigmondy. There was much ice and fresh snow. One place seemed to me so difficult that I thought: 'If one of them slips, we are all lost.' It was perhaps the most hazardous expedition of my life, for it was the first time I had been quite alone with my two men on such a tour, and besides this I had (only from considerations of humanity!) two entirely strange climbers on the rope or "thread of life."

We reached the Pic Central without accident. From that point the descent was slow, especially across the ice wall. The bergschrund was bad, and the snow on the glacier quite soft. Even while descending the ice wall I knew that we would not reach La Grave that day. It was still daylight during our passage of the Glacier de la Meije, but the last portion took much time before the first stones were reached. It grew dark and clouds gathered. It was almost impossible to proceed. Mr. P. became so ill that we had to stop where we were. We made a bivouac on the moraine.

It was a cold, foggy night. One could hear the clock striking in the church at La Grave. We remained in our camping place until two o'clock, when the cold drove us out. We descended farther to a little meadow; things were better there and we slept until half past five. Then down to the hotel, where everything was yet quiet. We had been out more than 30 hours, almost 20 on the rope!

The men from Dresden did not go to our hotel, but I met them during the course of the morning. They conducted themselves exactly as if I owed them my thanks, instead of the other way around. I gave them my opinion just the same. We needed quite a few hours on our day of rest to make up for lost sleep. Then everything was all right. It was as if we had slept away the dangers. But my memories remain forever

4

SLY METHODS ON THE AIGUILLE D'ARVE MÉRIDIONALE

Next morning (August 4th) we wandered over to the formidable Aiguille d'Arve méridionale. The night was spent in a shepherd's hut below the Col Lombard. We met two Italians who were going up the aiguille with two guides. The panorama there was splendid but the hut was almost too small. One may well quote the proverb: "Patient sheep have plenty of room in a little stable."

We left at an early hour to ascend the much-discussed aiguille on which many a climber has lost his life. It is not a long distance from the hut and one is almost at the beginning of the climbing. One ascends to the right through the ice gully, which takes three or four hours under bad conditions. But we found it in a favourable state and reached the saddle in an hour and a half, where the real difficulties begin. I had thought that this expedition would be much more difficult.

We put on our *Kletterschuhe* at the saddle, leaving everything but the provisions behind. The two guides went ahead with the Italian. Here we learned a bit of guides' cunning, which really is not an injustice. This aiguille is recognized as one of the most exposed climbs in the Alps, and rightly so because of the fearsome overhang, the *mauvais pas*, which requires a human ladder to overcome it. This kind of a tour, with such a risky place, does not really pay from a guide's viewpoint. For if one is with a tourist who, for example, has not strength to take part in the human ladder, the ascent cannot be carried out.

So the Dauphiné guides once got together and considered how the business could be made easier and more reasonable. Despite this, however, this aiguille remains the most difficult tour in Dauphiné. They decided to bore a hole at a certain place and put in a wooden peg, which could be removed during the descent, hidden and kept at a spot that all the guides knew. But whoever does not know about the peg, and has to ascend the Aiguille d'Arve without it, finds the climb most dangerous.

After the *mauvais pas* there are a few stretches of good ridge climbing, but it is otherwise easy to the summit. One finds there the visiting cards of well-known tourists, even of Viennese. Descent by roping down is not hard, although the ledge in the saddle is a little troublesome. About three in the afternoon we were again in La Grave, and left next day by the postal coach for Bourg d'Oisans. My attention was drawn by a priest who over and over again kissed the sides of his prayer book, and one could see that he had kissed and chewed right through some of the leaves.

From Bourg d'Oisans we went to Grenoble, bidding adieu to the lovely peaks of Dauphiné. In Grenoble we said goodbye to Mr. P.

5

SOUTH WALL OF THE MARMOLATA

Dr. L. and I went by way of Chambéry, Modane and Ala to Bozen, spending the night in the Hotel zur Sonne and going on the following day by the postal coach to Welschnofen. Then we climbed the well-marked path to Kölner Hütte and crossed the Kölnerjoch to Vajolethütte, arriving rather late.

On the following day we did the traverse of the three southern Vajolet Towers. Up the Delago, down the Winkler. I have made this tour often. Ever anew I have been in raptures at the view of the three southern towers, especially the Delago. It seems almost incredible that one can do the Pichlriss! In the afternoon we climbed the three northern towers[31] for "something extra." The guides marvelled.

Next day was set aside for the east wall of the Rosengarten. But we were invited by guide Piaz[32] and his gentleman to accompany them up the south wall of the Marmolata. The plan was accepted, and we took fond leave of Vajolethütte and went to Pera, then by carriage to Canazai and on foot to

Rifugio Contrin, where Piaz caught up with us in the evening. A porter was engaged to carry our boots from the foot of the south wall across the west ridge to the summit.

We left for our difficult trip about six o'clock in the morning. There is a good path, over which one goes easily to the start of the climbing. There we gave the porter our boots. Good luck! – on with the climb. Piaz went ahead with his man, we behind him. Soon the overhanging block is reached, which is really not easy. There, I went as second, behind Piaz. Then we separated our ropes again and went in two parties. Above the overhang there is some strenuous wall climbing, then the two traverses. In four and a half hours we were on the summit.

We had climbed too quickly. It gave me no pleasure. In addition, it was the most arduous tour I had made. Even Dr. Leuchs, of Munich, says it is one of the hardest if not the most difficult ascents in the Alps. Ours was the 19th party. I can recommend this expedition to those who have already done the most strenuous things in the Dolomites.

We descended the west ridge, which is artificially secured. We were in Rifugio Contrin by noon, going thence on foot to Vigo, where we spent the night, bidding farewell to our friends, and travelled next day to Neumarkt. I parted from Dr. L., who wrote some pleasant lines in my Führerbuch and went on the following morning by way of Ala and Verona to Milan.

6

A BIT OF CARELESSNESS

Next day I travelled past the beautiful Lake Maggiore to Visp and was in Zermatt by evening. On the way I met two English ladies, with whom I conversed in my broken attempt at their language. In Zermatt I met many well-known tourists and stopped at Seiler's Hotel Monte Rosa.

In the morning Mr. P. arrived with fine weather. On the following day we set out at noon, wandering across the Riffel Alm, Riffelberg and the Gorner Glacier to the Cabane Bétemps. The view was splendid and the good weather seemed likely to last for several days.

We were awakened next morning at two. The weather was not quite up to our expectations, but we wanted to make a try for Monte Rosa and accordingly left the hut at half past three. Mr. P. took a number of pictures, so progress was not rapid. The snow became worse and worse, and Mr. P. felt the rarity of the air and had to rest frequently. While we were on the arête a strong wind arose, so that we could not remain long on the summit. We went from the Dufourspitze to the Grenzgipfel, descending to the pass, thence up the Zumsteinspitze and the Signalkuppe.

We spent the night in the Capanna Margherita. The old, friendly Italian was there, and as much smoke as ever. Mr. P.'s eyes and mine hurt during the night, for which we blamed the smoke. The following morning was fine but windy; we left the hut at eight o'clock and ascended the Parrotspitze. Snow conditions were excellent but our eyes became worse and worse. That cursed smoke! Or – cursed carelessness! Yesterday we had not put on snow glasses! Yes, that was it: carelessness.

We descended to the Ludwigshöhe and across the Lys Pass to the Grenz Glacier. Our eyes did not improve; frequently everything looked double and red. It was really dangerous. About three o'clock we reached the Cabane Bétemps once more. There there was not so much fresh snow – the better for our eyes. Next morning we were once more in Zermatt, remaining all day in a darkened room. That evening we sat in Seiler's hotel, with pleasant music and good Munich beer.

We remained in Zermatt for several days, and when the pains in our eyes had disappeared we wished, despite the not very favourable weather (there was snow on the Matterhorn, our next goal), to try our luck, and so went up to the Schwarzsee Hotel. On the way we met two English ladies, to whom I gave information in their own language, and was proud of being able to say and understand so much. At the hotel we had coffee, bought some provisions and went on to the old Matterhorn Hut, known to travellers for its filthy condition.

7

HOCHTOURISTS WITH A VENGEANCE

At first we were alone. Later a man arrived with torn clothes and down cast expression. He had a little cut on his face. He told us he had gone up the Matterhorn with two other gentlemen, and turned back below the Shoulder when his strength failed. While returning alone, he fell several metres. His friends had gone on.

We bandaged up the almost exhausted man, and made him tea and soup. Toward evening we saw his friends, off the right track, shouting and calling. I pointed out the route, but they were too far off to understand me. They got onto snow and had no ice axes; I called to them to keep to the rocks. But it seemed they wanted to cut across the snow. Being without axes on the steep slope they went into an involuntary glissade, which might have turned out badly. We watched them and I thought it improbable they would come out with their lives. Both men were buried in snow and for a long time were invisible.

I took rope and axe and hurried to the spot. Before I got there, one called out and the other also worked himself free of the snow. They said no damage had been done, and I remarked that it was more by good luck than good management. "Why?" they asked. "Well, don't you see the bergschrund and this steepness?" "Oh, that's nothing," said one, "I have often glissaded on snow." This sort of talk continued, and I realized that they were unskilled and unreasonable people. I offered them the rope, which they refused. That made me very angry; they were really behaving ungratefully. So I naturally troubled myself no more about them and went back to the hut.

Mr. P. inquired what had happened. I told him of the encounter and declared that the men were boorish and thankless. The patient in the hut heard this and tried to excuse the others. I remained aloof. Then the two doubtful Hochtourists came into the hut. They had nothing to eat and had brought no wood. I gave some soup and tea to the injured one, but not even hot water to the others. That was not kind of me, but I wanted to punish them.

As night fell, and all three were so tired they could not stir, they had to remain at the hut. So our pleasant mood was much disturbed. The weather became worse. Next morning there was fresh snow in front of the hut, and an ascent of the Matterhorn was out of the question. I prepared breakfast and gave some tea to the sick man. As there was no chance of improvement, we went down to the Schwarzsee Hotel. After a few minutes on the way, I discovered I had left my watch in the hut and went back to get it. When I saw how the poor fellows had brushed together every little piece and splinter of wood and still could make no fire, it would have broken my heart to leave them so. I built a fire and gave them some of my leftover wood. Thereupon they thanked me heartily, and one begged my pardon for not acting properly on the preceding day. So I explained to them the relations between guides and guideless climbers, and left the hut.

We stopped for several hours in the Schwarzsee Hotel. I proposed to Mr. P. to go up the Breithorn. It is the easiest 4000er in the Zermatt mountains, being nothing but a long wandering over snow. On summer days the

Breithorn is frequently visited by a hundred or more tourists. Mr. P. agreed to my suggestion, and we went over to Gandegghütte.

As it was Saturday evening, and the Zermatt guides held fast to their custom of going to mass every Sunday, we were the only guests at the hut. Later on, our three Matterhorn friends arrived, but we had little to say to them. I must remark that we discovered excellent beds in Gandegghütte. At five o'clock in the morning we started off, following the route toward the Théodule Pass as far as the point of deviation for the Breithorn.

It was a lovely day, promising a continuance of fair weather. We walked on snow all day and roped as a precaution, for the fresh snow was rather deep, making many of the crevasses invisible. In four and a half hours we were on the summit, so rich in its views. On the way back we again met our Matterhorn friends. One carried a sash cord around his waist, to serve as a rope, but never used it. Another had a child's ice axe, while the third had an ordinary cane! They were badly fitted out with shoes. When one meets such "mountaineers" as these, one really wonders that more accidents do not occur. I showed them that it was dangerous to go unroped on fresh snow, and that their cord was not much better than no rope at all.

We ascended to the Théodule Pass and entered the hut at noon. It has little rooms, is not very clean and was kept by four women. The fattest I ever saw! During descent we stopped again in Gandegghütte. The weather turned bad. Everything covered with cloud. We went on down to Zermatt.

8

SIEGE OF THE MATTERHORN

We heard so much said next day about the numerous parties going up the Matterhorn that we were afraid of not getting a place in the hut, and so went up to the Schwarzsee Hotel about two o'clock in the afternoon. We stopped there for a little while and looked after some provisions. The weather was more than doubtful, despite which we continued on our way to the old Matterhornhütte.

Around two o'clock in the morning I looked out: "Miserable as a dog; nothing to be done. Stay in your bed, Mr. P." But when morning came Mr. P. became impatient. Should we again spend a whole day in the cold, damp hut? Not much pleasure in that. So we returned to the Schwarzsee Hotel. The Matterhorn was covered with fresh snow, and one could see how the wind was playing a game with it on the Shoulder and the summit. I went down to Zermatt to get mail.

As the weather improved on the following day, we wished to try our luck a third time. We arrived at Matterhornhütte; by nine o'clock the last bit of space was occupied. Two women, several men and even a Tyrolese guide. The Tyrolese guide was not getting along with the Swiss guides. As I have already mentioned in my notes, there are always some guides who are unfriendly to strangers, no matter from what district they come.

About two o'clock in the morning there were signs of life in the hut. There was a quarrel about the cooking – the stove was a little too small for 27 people! To avoid the strife I waited until last to do my cooking, and so we were also the last to leave the hut. We went with lanterns as far as the first couloir. There we already overtook some of the parties, and progress was slow, for the danger of falling stones demands great caution.

Again it went slowly, for there was much fresh snow and it grew colder. A Frenchman developed mountain sickness. Mr. P. gave him some kola pastilles and a drink of very hot tea from a Thermos bottle. We overtook most of the parties. In consequence of the bad snow conditions we took nine hours from the hut to the summit and seven hours for the return. There were 29 people on the Matterhorn, 27 from the Swiss side and two from the Italian.

Many regained the hut by lantern light, but some had to bivouac. Luckily the night was calm. We descended by the same route to Zermatt. Next day we rested. I met the guide Karlinger, from the Oetz Valley, and we visited with him the Alpine Museum, which recalls sad hours to many a mountaineer. As we had the same program as Karlinger and his gentleman, the men introduced themselves and decided to make the ascent of Mont Blanc together.

9

THE KING OF THE ALPS FROM THE TÊTE ROUSSE

We went together by the new rail route to Chamonix. The journey itself is highly rewarding. The weather was beautiful and clear, and I pointed out all the aiguilles and summits to my friends, who were in these mountains for the first time.

We went into the Hôtel des Alpes; unfortunately there was no room there for Karlinger and myself, and after some search we found one at the Hôtel du Dôme. After a walk through Chamonix we went into the German beer hall, where many German tourists meet and where one hears all the gossip. There I found the guide Garny who, after last year, was very kind to me.

On the following morning we ascended through the lovely forest to the Pavilion on the Col de Voza, where we stopped for lunch. Then on to the Inn Tête Rousse on the Aiguille du Goûter, which is provisioned. But we took some food along in addition, and as we started the sky became cloudy, with no very good prospects. The approach to the Inn Tête Rousse is not entirely free of danger, and there have been several accidents from avalanche. Progress was slow and it was becoming dark. We were still several hundred metres from the hut and I advised haste, for I knew from experience that it often takes much time to find the snowed-in door and requires considerable work to clear it.

At last we arrived. It was very cold in the hut, but the window had to be opened for the stovepipe. There was enough straw and blankets there. The cooking was soon finished and we went to bed with no great hopes for Mont Blanc in the morning. A storm arose, becoming stronger during the night, and when we looked out there was a half metre of fresh snow. Karlinger, the Tyrolese, was heard to say: "Well, nothing doing today. Damn weather!"

We had to stay in the cabin the whole day. Fortunately it was permissible to take boards for fuel from the old hut nearby; otherwise it would not have been possible for us to remain so long. At evening the weather cleared slightly, but by night the storm sprang up again. There was not much chance of sleeping, as we had had no exercise all day. About three o'clock Karlinger looked out: "Nothing again. Devil take it!" With these words he awoke us. Everybody made a long face and lay back again in the straw.

We discussed the matter, for we had brought provisions for two days only. The weather improved, so we decided to stop for one night more. At noon Karlinger and I went down to the lower Cabane Tête Rousse for more provisions. Avalanches made it dangerous, but luckily we were back unhurt by evening. I will always remember how we tried to make ourselves understood to the two French women who kept the hut! Karlinger with his bad Italian, I with my little English. But without success. At last we went into the pantry, showed them what we wanted and obtained the desired things: bread, sausages, two bottles of wine, tobacco etc. There would be something doing in the morning: it seemed to be clearing!

About three o'clock in the morning we opened the window and stuck out the stovepipe. In a little while the tea was ready, with some left over for the Thermos bottle. We started off about four. Within an hour all of us were complaining of our cold feet. And the snow plodding was not as bad as we had expected. But the cold! And a penetrating wind in addition. We alternated in breaking track and reached the Dôme du Goûter in good time, all things considered. From there on, the snow was better, although the wind became stronger. We rested in Cabane Vallot, whence we had old steps, rather snowed under but which brought us rapidly to l'Observatoire Janssen on the summit of the King of the Alps.

Now a hot drink from the good Thermos flask. A clasp of the hand. *Bergheil!*

Mr. P. took some pictures, but after ten minutes of standing around all four of us had almost no sensation in our feet. So, forward and down again to Cabane Vallot, where we rested once more. Then down the usual route. Karlinger's man was very tired. The snow was quite deep on this side, and so it was slow business, especially across the Grand Plateau to the Grands Mulets. There we had a glass of rum.

It was much better farther down. Several parties were at the hut, and the track was well-trodden. It grew dark shortly after the glacier was behind us. We stopped a short time in the Pierre Pointue, and when we entered Chamonix there were crowds on the streets as on every evening.

This time Karlinger and I had a room at the Hôtel des Alpes. After a good supper we went to bed. How good it was to sleep in fine white sheets! On the day following we were more tired than on the evening before.

10

THE CLEVERNESS OF MEN

Karlinger and I took leave of the gentlemen and went to Geneva that afternoon. In the evening I took him to an Automat buffet, which seemed to him an extraordinary marvel. First he tried different kinds of beer, and laughed heartily. Then he discovered the compartments with sausages and warm dishes, which was more than he could understand. He laughed uproariously, wondering at the cleverness of people. The other guests began to make fun of the Tyrolese, with all sorts of remarks.

I felt sorry for him and went over to the adjacent table, asking the Swiss gentleman in friendly fashion not to let it continue, or otherwise something would come of it. But they ridiculed him the more. I thought that if Karlinger were alongside of me, for he had the figure of a giant, they would soon be quiet. But such was not the case. One gave me a box on the ear, and in two seconds he had as good a one from me. And so it began! But I found the right words and talked so sharply that no one touched me after that.

My friend Karlinger had paid not the slightest attention to all this, still marvelling at human inventiveness and standing there with his hot sausage. Naturally I accused him of not supporting me in the argument. "Well, I didn't hear anything about it," said he, calmly.

About one o'clock in the morning our train left Geneva, and by daybreak we reached Zürich. A woman got in, who looked at our rucksacks. "You are mountain guides, aren't you? Where are you from? What was your last peak?" she inquired. "Mont Blanc!" replied Karlinger proudly. "Oh, Mont Blanc. I have never been there. But I have been up the Rigi. Have you?" "No, madam." "Ah, then you have really never seen the beauty of Switzerland!" was her reply.

I asked the lady whether she had gone up by rail. "Oh, no, on foot," she answered enthusiastically, "and down again on foot." "Well, I congratulate you," I said pleasantly. Friend Karlinger laughed scornfully, took out his flask and remarked: "Have a drink, lady, and tell us a bigger one!" We entertained ourselves highly with our lady mountaineer.

When she got out and we were alone, Karlinger said: "Well, she thinks she's done everything with her Rigi!" I explained to him that the woman was just as willing to talk about her effort as we, for example, about our ascent of Mont Blanc, and that it was proper in any case to agree with the ladies and to praise them, the more so when one sees what joy they have in their climbing.

I bade farewell to Karlinger at station Ötztal, and went on by way of Innsbruck to Gstatterboden. There I took part in hunting and made some excursions for my own pleasure.

11

THE WITNESS ON THE TRISSELWAND

On September 21st I went with Miss B. to Altaussee to climb the Trisselwand. I was already known there and, as the native guides were aware of the lady's project, they came to me and said that we were both fools, that it was impossible to surmount such a rock wall. I told them that it had already been done by engineer Reinl. "It has not," they shouted together.

Then one said that if it was really to be done, and I knew it, then he could do it too. So I invited him to accompany us, remarking only that I would not take him on my rope. He did not accept.

About six in the morning I looked up Miss B. at the Villa. We had engaged a boy to take our boots from the foot of the climb by the usual route to the summit. About eight o'clock we were at the starting point, the boy took the boots and we were off. First over grass slopes, then up brittle rock. Here we found some paper markers. (Mizzi Langer.) We came to a chimney. There lay an almost new rope – a sign that a party had been there a few days before. I did not want to carry the rope along, rolled it up and threw it down, so that I could get it while returning.

The climbing went slowly on account of the broken rock. Before coming to the big slab, there was a rough chimney, much exposed and requiring great care. In three hours we were at the point of exit, where our porter awaited us. In addition, a girl from Altaussee had climbed up, curious to see whether a woman could really ascend the Trisselwand! (I think she was sent up as witness and proof!)

We took a rest and descended to Sattelbauer. There the lady, who was well-known to the peasants as an artist, was spoken to and made much of. But if we had not had the boy at the start and the girl at the finish of the climb as witnesses, no one in Altaussee would have believed that we had done it.

That evening several friends of the lady arrived, and I knew that there was a reporter among them! On the following day I said goodbye, and went home by way of Gstatterboden.

12

A NIGHT ON THE NORTH WALL OF THE FESTKOGEL

On the following Sunday I awaited Mr. W. at Weichtal, intending to do the Wiener Neustadt climb. That morning a young lady came to me saying the Dolomite guide Piaz had recommended her to me. She wanted to make a trip at once, telling me of her ascents in the Dolomites and being quite delighted that I could take her along on the Neustadt route.

I introduced her to Mr. W. and we went into the Höllenthal. At the start of the climb the lady refused the rope, which greatly excited Mr. W. She wanted to give me a written statement that she went unroped at her own risk, and I allowed her to ascend the first chimney, which she did very well. But at the second chimney I would permit her to go no farther without the rope, and she put it on with the request that I should not pull. She did require a little help at this chimney.

The young lady was really an excellent climber, her whole manner sympathetic, and so one more link in the chain of mountain friendship was forged.

I was to meet her at Gstatterboden on September 26th. I went ahead a day in advance and awaited her at seven o'clock in the morning. It was a beautiful autumn day and we were quite alone in the Gesäuse. We went along talking through the Haindl basin to the Jahn–Zimmer route on the north wall of the Hochthor. During the early part of the ascent we kept on our nailed boots, as it is rough and dirty, but put on our *Klettcrschuhe* at the slabs and went without many halts to the dangerous ledge.

The lady was not pleased with herself; she had thought these places would give her less trouble. But nothing further occurred and we reached the summit of the Hochthor. The distant view was clear and we took a long rest, then descended to Heß-hütte. Next morning we ascended the Hochthor by way of the Tellersack and went down the Rossschweif. We were the last guests of the season at Heß-hütte. The young woman went down the waterfall path, while I conducted the Lechner family from the hut to Johnsbach, where we held a pleasant farewell party in the Kölbl Inn.

I spent a few splendid autumn days at Gstatterboden, made excursions for my own enjoyment, and took Mr. W. up the Hochthor by the Jahn–Zimmer route in the fine weather of October 11th.

During the forenoon of October 13th I made an attempt to ascend the north wall of the Festkogel through the gully. It presented more difficulties than I expected; I made traverses and climbed overhangs, using up much time. I saw an ice axe lying in a chimney and tried to get it but could not. I think it was the axe of Mr. Galler, who fell on the Pichl route. In one chimney I was stuck for more than two hours.

It became dark before the climb was over, and I was compelled to bivouac. I stopped on a ledge a metre wide and five or six long, where I could make myself comfortable. An unforgettable night! The moon shone in all its splendour; the stillness was uncanny. I could only hear the rushing of the Enns and the puffing of the locomotives. The little lights of the cars shone pleasantly at me. I have already described my feelings in a similar situation.

Every time in such a bivouac, one thinks: This was the longest night of all! There was no question of sleep; it was too cold. But even the quiet of such a night of wakefulness has its beauty, and the sensation, when one sees the sun again, is indescribable! I greeted it from the summit of the Festkogel and descended over the Rinnerstein.

In Johnsbach I met the old parson once more, to whom I of course told my adventures. He replied in these words: "Daniel, you really ought to be wiser, and crawl around on the mountains only when you have to!"

13

MY LAST CLIMBS IN THE GESÄUSE

In the afternoon I was engaged at Gstatterboden by Mr. P. We took provisions to Heß-hütte, going up by the waterfall path. Two strangers were already ahead of us, taking the key of the hut with them. It was a perfect day and we reached the hut just as darkness was coming on. We spent a pleasant evening and early the following morning crossed the Seekar to the Peternsattel, going up the Hochthor by way of the Dachl ridge.

One of the two men, a clergyman from Rottenmann, had joined us. While resting on the Dachl, remarks were made about the stillness. Mr. P. said: "Such quiet is only to be found in Nature. It never exists in a church. These are the moments for reconciling oneself with God!"

We took leave of the parson on the summit of the Hochthor. He descended to Heß-hütte, while we crossed the arête to the Ödstein and mounted the Kirchl ridge. It was very hot and dusty on the broken rock. Much thirst and no water! We required six hours for this tour from the Hochthor to Johnsbach. Happy and contented we walked along the lovely brook to Gstatterboden.

The Hotel Gesäuse was being closed; we were the last guests and received the last bit of meat and the last bottle of Rathauskeller wine. Mr. P. went to Vienna that evening, and I home the next morning. But I went to Gstatterboden again on October 20th, meeting Miss B. there. We went to Großreifling, thence by carriage to St. Gallen, and started off next morning to do the northeast ridge of the Große Buchstein.

It was a cold, foggy morning, and the lady was not feeling very well. Rather uncertainly we ascended the steep, wooded slope to the beginning of the climb. It was already noon, and the lady was no better. So we turned back and went to Großreifling, thence by train to Gstatterboden. She seemed to improve, and became interested in a tour of the northern walls. She chose the north wall of the Hochthor (Jahn–Zimmer route).

Next day we started off early. I could see by the woman's expression that she felt bad, and told her that the trip was a very hard one and that one should be quite well for such an undertaking. At the start of the ascent we

199

spoke of the matter again. The lady would not give up her plan of making the climb. She wanted to do it because at this time of year mountaineering is almost over and this would be a fine ending. So we went on, in nailed boots as far as the slabs, where we made a change.

Then, of a sudden, she wanted to turn back. That was bad, for one needs almost as much time for the descent as for the ascent. So we continued. At the dangerous traverse I fastened the lady to the *Mauerhaken*, and it was an uncomfortable feeling for me, just as I was on the worst place, to hear the woman say: "Everything is getting blue and black before my eyes." "Only a minute more, then it is all over," I called to her. Once across the traverse I spoke to her encouragingly. In view of the fact that she felt so ill she got over better than I expected.

We proceeded very slowly; I never urged her, although I knew we would be late in reaching the valley, if at all. I was very sorry for her. We had the key of Heß-hütte and enough provisions, and so decided to spend the night there. It was already dark by the time we descended the Josefinen route. When we tried to open the hut, the key would not fit. We had brought the wrong one. Fortunately the moon was shining clear as day and we could go on to Johnsbach without further trouble.

About half past nine we reached the Kölbl Inn, got a carriage and went through the valley of Johnsbach to the Bachbrücke Inn, where we stayed overnight. Next morning I took leave of Miss B. and went home.

On Sundays I made various ascents of the Rax, working during the week for the commune of Vienna on the reservoir at Naßwald. More than two months. I even had to work on Christmas Day and Sylvester Eve.

Now the year 1908 is over. What is the result? The summer season was not much, the earning even less. In my private life I had had some heavy blows of fate which, however, have nothing to do with my profession of mountain guide. On my travels and expeditions in this year I had collected additional experience, and I was just the same as in the year preceding – healthy, even contented, but with nothing in my pockets! What would the year 1909 bring forth?

CHAPTER VII

(1909)

▲

1 Plans and Troubles

On New Year's Day I went through the Reiss Valley to the Binder Inn. The path was quiet and lonely, and I thought of all the New Year's Days that I could recall. I was more serious than usual.

On the fine winter days I made ski tours on the Rax, but most of the time I was at home, absorbed in the English language, repeating everything I had learned, and wrote English letters to good friends with the request that they should send them back to me corrected. I looked at my opportunity and thought of my future. What is life? It is splendid. But one cannot live long from hand to mouth, and there would be many things lacking if I remained here.

What I earned, or rather what I saved, in summer had to be set aside for winter, because during the cold season there was nothing in the guiding line, and the labour to which I was accustomed was not profitable. Guiding itself is only a side issue, not a real profession. One should and must think of his old age.

The result of my earnest consideration was that I wrote to Dr. P. about a journey to America, concerning which he had often spoken to me. In my behalf he wrote to the Canadian Pacific Railway for a position as guide, giving me the highest recommendation in his letter. I could scarcely await the reply, and when it came it was a disillusionment. The representative of the railway wrote that it was too late for this year, that the old Swiss guides had already been engaged and that there was no place vacant. Still it was possible that the Alpine Club of Canada might need a guide.

Dr. P. then wrote to the president of this club. The answer was rather favourable, and after a brief interchange of letters my reception as guide was a certain affair. For the summer months I was guaranteed two dollars per day, two dollars for each mountain excursion, board and lodging free. Travelling expenses were promised.

Then came the difficult point: the money for the journey. Who would advance me the money? Then I made a bitter discovery. I asked a gentleman, who I knew could well afford it, promising to repay the money with interest by autumn. He was a good friend of mine. Just the same, money breaks friendships. Despite this he meant well by me, writing out a petition to which he signed as the first to lend me 40 kronen. This list I was to send to all my friends, and he believed that no one of them would put up less than 40 kronen.

His words, which he wrote as an introduction to the collection, sounded well enough, but I considered the matter carefully and came to the conclusion that it would never do. That is beggary! I do not have to do that! If one with whom I have risked my life on the rope during difficult climbs has not the faith that I would pay back his money, then I do not require his counsel and advice! "So there is nothing doing about any journey to America this summer," I said to my mother, and thanked the gentleman for his proposal, with the remark that I could not accept it, as it would leave me with no character at all.

After this discovery I had no desire to ask any other friend or acquaintance, for I thought it would be just the same with the second as with the first. But this left me no peace. I want to go out in the wide world! The chance is there, but no money for the journey! Day and night I pondered over it, who would lend me money for the voyage. I thought of my grandfather, who had the money, and went to him one day. I told him of my requirements. He didn't say yes, or no, but was only amazed that I wanted to go so far away, saying that it was not really necessary for me to go to America, as I had already seen half the world! But of how large the world was the old man had really no idea. In his whole life he had never been farther than Wiener Neustadt, and at that only for registration. That was all, except of woodcutting, that he knew of the world.

Well, if my grandfather would not give or trust me with the money, of whom should I next ask it? 'I need it of no one,' I said to myself. 'I will be frugal this summer and go to America in the autumn!' In this frame of mind I wrote to Dr. P. and worked in the following weeks as a day labourer until the end of April.

2 Joy and Sorrow

About this time I made a ski tour on the Rax. The lessee of Otto-Schutzhaus, Mr. Kronich, asked me whether I had time to clear out the trail over the Brandschneide. I took on the work. On the day I began I met Mr. A.G. in Kaiserbrunn, and he inquired about my American journey. When he heard that I lacked the money for travel he said: "If there is no other way, then I can help you. Why didn't you come to me when you knew that I was a good friend?"

I was quite aroused by this pleasant and friendly encounter and at once wrote to Dr. P. that a good friend had advanced me the necessary funds. Then I went right home and told my mother the joyful news. My next business was at Kaiserbrunn, where I finished up my work. On May 11th I received my pay at Otto-Schutzhaus and climbed down to the valley through the Wachthüttel ravine. It was really a strange feeling to say goodbye to the mountains of my home.

Next day I went into the Reiss Valley, taking some flowers from my native valley as remembrance and took leave of the Binder family. During my return I stopped more than once and looked back. I could scarcely drag myself away from the lovely precipitous walls! That evening I went to my grandfather. He was not pleased at my going and remarked: "A sea voyage is really most unsafe! If a strong wind comes up and throws the vessel topsy-turvy, then it's all over! And you can't swim a bit – no, my boy, there's nothing to it!" It was hard for me, to see how the good old man was really concerned about me and wept when I took leave.

The last evening at home: I packed up my things, the younger children gathered about me, my mother serious and contemplative. These were sad hours. Next morning (May 13th) I gave my weeping mother a kiss of farewell, comforting her with the words that I would certainly come home again, perhaps in just a couple of years. Once more I gazed back at the limestone walls, then went on.

A feeling of depression and insecurity was in my heart. I stopped at the entrance to the great Höllenthal. How many happy and serious hours and days had I spent on the Loswand in the course of a year, and with what hard work. Sad thoughts rushed through my head.... I arrived in Vienna, stopped at the Hotel Sauer and went directly to Dr. P., who introduced me to the representative of the CPR. Then I was sent to Dr. Berl, with whom I was to travel to Quebec.

He told me that we should leave on May 25th. I used the time in studying English diligently with Mrs. P. The day of departure was changed to May

29th. During the last days in Vienna a travel fever came over me; it was not easy to part from my many good friends in the mountains. To those who were dearest to me I went last of all. With some I had to hold back tightly lest I reveal my emotion. At nine o'clock on the evening of Pentecost Saturday the train left the Northwest Station. With my travel fever I was already there at eight o'clock.

My baggage consisted of a large travelling bag, a chest, rucksack and two ice axes. A man spoke to me: "Where are you going, Kain?" "To North America." "And where are you heading for, Mr. Beer?" "To South Africa!" Just before the time of departure Dr. Berl and his family arrived. There were only a few minutes during which we could look back at the beautifully il-luminated city of Vienna, but they were unforgettable, for one had only the thought in mind: I am going now on a long journey; who knows when I shall return?

My friend Beer nodded a last farewell toward his lovely native city; the tears in his eyes were a sign of his affection for Vienna. I comforted him as well as I could, speaking of our future in foreign parts of the world. I took leave of him in Dresden and of Dr. K. in Leipzig. At Hanover I discovered that my chest had been left behind, and sent a telegram to Tetschen. At [the name is omitted] we boarded the steamer. There I could try out my knowledge of English in talking to the ship's personnel.

3 A Naßwalder in London

The crossing was stormy. On a boisterous day we reached Harwich. After a two-hour journey by train we were in the Victoria station of London. Dr. Berl's maids and I took a cab to the Hotel Cecil, the largest in London. In a few minutes we were lodged, on the fifth floor. Now it is time to think of London, to see London! But I didn't see much from my window: only walls and smoke. Later I took a walk on the Strand in the vicinity of the Hotel, made some small purchases, chiefly for the opportunity of improving my English. I knew words enough, but my ear was not accustomed to the English of London, and comprehension was not as easy as I had expected.

On the second day I took a walk to the Houses of Parliament. I noted the direction in which I went and found my way back to the hotel all right. About eleven o'clock that morning I went out with Dr. Berl's maids. We had breakfast in a kind of out-door kitchen. It was my first experience as inter-preter. The fare was not to the taste of the Viennese, and when a bystander noticed that we were not contented he recommended a better restaurant in the neighbourhood. Well, that looked nicer with its finely covered tables.

I ordered the lunch, the girls chattering in German all the while, one asking for beer, the other for wine. But here, drinking at the table is not understood, and the drinks have to be fetched from the bar; and as this was not quick enough for the thirsty ladies from Vienna they both began to make adverse remarks about this famous London: "The food is tasteless, the beer is no good etc."

While eating, the cook said: "Well, now I know why the English are so thin! The food is miserable, and they drink nothing but tea, that stretches one, and that's why they are all thin as a lath. Just look at those fellows there, built like fiddle bows!"

4 Something to Laugh About

In the afternoon I went to Charing Cross and saw there many people coming up out of the Underground railway, of which I had heard so much. So I went to the window and asked for a ticket. "Please give me a ticket." "Where do you want to go?" asked the cashier. Well, where? I didn't know that. What station should I name? I began to stammer. He named some stations and on a chance I said "yes," and rode off for a long time blindly. Then a conductor came along and my ticket was far overrun. The man was annoyed, and so we came to no agreement. He threw me out at the next station!

To this day I do not know where I was, but I think in Norwood. By this time I was afraid of the Underground and so climbed up on the roof of a bus.

Again a conductor inquired: "How far?" I could name no destination. He did not talk long, but gave me what was probably a ticket to the end of the line. Again I rode for a long time. All at once it was over. I climbed out and asked a policeman the direction of Charing Cross. He pointed with his hand to the right, and as a tram had just come along, I got aboard. That also reached its terminus. So, I had tried going in three ways and had not gotten back to the hotel. The most stupid part of it was that I had forgotten the name of the hotel where I was stopping.

I told a policeman that I had lost my way, but that I was lodging in a very big hotel. He took out his book and read the names of hotels aloud. "Yes?" "No." "Yes?" "No." He became angry and sent me off. I considered what to do. At last I hit upon a very good idea. I didn't know the hotel names, so I would mention the big monument that was nearby. Of the next policeman I asked somewhat as follows: "Please excuse me. I want to go to my hotel. I don't know the name of it. Not far from it is a big stone; on top a man is standing, and animals are lying on the ground." He laughed heartily, went along a little, showed me the direction and told me to ask the next officer.

And so I repeated the business 12 or 15 times, and every one showed me the direction. I was already very tired and weary. At last I inquired of an old gentleman. He laughed for about five minutes. Then he asked me whether I was French. "No, an Austrian." We got along very well together, and the kindly man took me to the Hotel Cecil. "You must be very tired. Come with me for a bit of refreshment." And with these pleasant words he led me to a table.

Next day I was so tired that I could scarcely stir. After that I never went further from the hotel than within seeing distance of the "Big Stone" with the man on top. The Strand, on which I went up and down, is one of the most lively streets. The mass of traffic there must interest everyone. Rightly one can compare London with Vienna as one would compare Vienna with Wiener Neustadt. It is fine to have seen London, but for a mountain man it would be difficult or impossible to remain there.

5 Farewell, Sweet Home

The fever of travel was burning in me. On the third of June, in the afternoon, we left the Hotel Cecil and went by train to Liverpool. The landscape is ancient in aspect, especially with the garden walls that figure in so many romantic stories. At Liverpool we spent the night in the Station Hotel, and had enough time to look about in the old commercial and maritime city.

As I had a third-class ticket, I had to be aboard next morning (June 4th) about nine o'clock. First and second class did not need to arrive until two or three in the afternoon. I took a carriage to the harbour and, as I thought the coachman overcharged me, I went straight to a police officer, but it didn't help. I had to pay the price demanded.

At last I was at the port and on board the "Empress of Britain." It didn't look very nice in the rooms of the third class; it was so dark, the people busy with carrying baggage and similar tasks. I saw in the first half hour, as I paced the moving deck, that I did not have to do with high-class company. As there were no more cabins to be had, I was taken down to the bottom of the ship. That didn't please me very much; but, to be sure, it would only be for eight days.

To observe a company of travellers is always worthwhile. These different voices! Some sing, others laugh and rejoice. Here and there one sees a tragic or a thoughtful face. And now the departure! They wave and cry: "Farewell, sweet home!" The voyagers are all on deck, many of them climbing up ladders and ropes. As long as sound would carry they shout and call. Then many a one returns to his cabin with tears in his eyes. I remained on deck. I was really not sad at heart, for I realized that I did not know a single one of the thousands of people standing around the harbour.

Just at dusk the last bit of land was still to be seen, and so I said with the English people: "Farewell, sweet home – if I have good fortune I shall see you once more!"

BOOK TWO

THE CANADIAN YEARS

with
A Siberian Interlude
and
Three New Zealand Seasons

CHAPTER VIII

(1909)

▲

1

BY CANADIAN PACIFIC FROM QUEBEC TO CALGARY

The crossing was favourable, only one day of storm on which no one could go on deck. Most of the people were seasick. Under such conditions the third class looks like a pigsty. On June 11th we landed in Quebec, Canada's oldest port. It was a right comfortable feeling to be on firm ground once more, although I had not been seasick.

Our "Empress of Britain" was awaited by many people, and much time was consumed before the immigration officer came through and everything was in order. Mr. Wheeler, president of the Alpine Club, had sent a letter to the dock officials with the request that they assist me. He really thought that I knew no English at all.

About eight o'clock the train started off for the Wild West. The trains go perceptibly faster than in Europe. The noise is terrific. More bells than whistles, and I have noticed as well as often heard that, in the beginning, it makes one very nervous. There are special cars for immigrants, practically furnished, as they must be on account of the long distances that one travels.

There are seats for groups of four persons, with a demountable table in the middle. Then there is a bed, a shelf to be pulled down and used as a bed for two people, and for the other two the seat is used. Good drinking water is at hand and, in the larger stations, ice is put in. There is a good stove in every car, on which one can cook little things. The employees of the Canadian Pacific are very kindly, and it does not at all agree with what I have heard of foreigners being handled like cattle. But it is true all right that, in Austria, outsiders are treated like animals!

On the first few days en route from Quebec to Winnipeg one doesn't see much of fertile Canada. Nothing but bushes and rocks. For half a day at a time there is not a house or human habitation. Before reaching Winnipeg it becomes more interesting, especially if one goes to Lake Winnipeg. Winnipeg is a large city and, for a long time, was the point of departure for the West. It is said that 18 languages are spoken there. We had three hours' stop in this city. I met several Germans.

The prairie begins at Winnipeg. As far as the eye can see there are nothing but fields, all the way through Manitoba. It is said to be the best province for wheat growing. The region was too flat for me and the broad plain hurt my eyes.

Farther along, in the province of Saskatchewan, I noticed that nearly everyone had a piece of brushwood in his hand and was beating about with it. I soon discovered why. Here begin those awful, annoying mosquitoes, of which naturally no land agent in Europe informs a person!

On the afternoon of June 16th I arrived in Calgary, where the Canadian Alpine Club has its headquarters. I gave my sack into the charge of the checkroom and went into the town. First to a barber, who was also a German. He told me where to go. But I didn't find the avenue, and went into the post office, where the Club was located. A gentleman of friendly countenance advanced toward me. "You are Conrad Kain!" he said. "Yes, and you are Mr. Wheeler!" "No, the secretary." The president was not at home. Mr. Mitchell conducted me to the Queen's Hotel, where he introduced me and told them, on account of my poor English, to look after me.

Calgary is a sprouting city in western Alberta. All nationalities are to be found there, and Germans are well represented. I saw a Chinaman for the first time. Near the city there are even Indians – Stoneys. "Calgary" is an Indian word meaning "slow flowing water." The city is situated in the foothills, outliers of the Rockies. I looked at the snow-covered peaks with longing!

2

FIRST CANADIAN SEASON. LAKE O'HARA

Conrad never kept up his journal after the first year in Canada. He often promised to do so, but life had become too strenuous and our knowledge of his activities comes from isolated articles written by him and through information supplied by various friends. From this point onward it is therefore necessary to bridge numerous gaps and, before continuing with his own narrative, to present the background of his first Canadian summer.

Mr. A.O. Wheeler, director of the Alpine Club of Canada, writes: "Conrad was but one of the many employed upon my Boundary Surveys and for the Club Camps.... My closer relationship is in my memory and recalls a charming personality, a most amusing raconteur and a very competent guide."

Wheeler continues with quotations from his diaries:

> 1909 ◆ *Conrad came to the Alpine Clubhouse at Banff in June. He was recommended to me by Mr. Pistor, of the Board of Trade of Vienna, who wrote asking me to get him work with the* CPR. *This could not be done, as all their guides were from Interlaken.*
>
> *Mr. Pistor stated: 'He is a fine fellow. With ladies he is as gentle as a lamb, but with men he is like a lion.' I took him on with the* ACC *and he helped me settle into the new Clubhouse just completed at Banff. He was working there throughout June and part July on tent houses, grounds etc. He put in the trails that are in use there today, with some few additions. He was with the 1909 camp at Lake O'Hara meadows as* ACC *Climbing Guide.*[33]

Conrad Kain, a guide – his first Canadian season. Surely no more inspiring place for his introduction to western mountains could have been found than Lake O'Hara. With its blue water, sparkling falls and towering, snowy peaks it had been the inspiration of artists. Conrad, encamped in the fragrant pine forest, watching the celebrities arrive.

It was a notable company of guests that year. H.B. Dixon, Mumm, Amery, Tempest Anderson and others in the British contingent; and last of all, Whymper, now in his old age, conqueror of the Matterhorn and of the Andes. Whymper, he of that strange, frustrating campaign in the Rockies in 1901, of which Christian Klucker,[34] at long last, revealed the truth. There were still faint echoes of wild orgies held in the hotel at Field.

Whymper, a sad and lonely man; yet his speech by the campfire rose to a semblance of old inspiration, which Conrad could easily grasp:

> *Ladies and gentlemen, live, live, while you can. We're born to live, but born to die. Unite prudence with courage. Take heed to your steps lest you fall. Whatever you set your hands to do, do it with all your might. Act well your part, there all the honour lies. This, ladies and gentlemen, is the first, and it will be the last occasion on which I shall have the honour to speak to you. I came out from Europe expressly for this meeting, and*

tomorrow I start back. But, if unable to be with you in body, I shall, so long as I live, be with you in spirit, and wish you success and prosperity.

Did Conrad that night, sitting at the base of a gnarled tree, smoking his pipe, see in the evening sky a shadowy vision of a Zermatt peak, and four men falling?

AUG. 4TH ◆ *Ten parties went out to graduate on Mt. Huber. Soon after the start it began to snow and snowed off and on all day. All parties except that of Conrad returned early. He alone graduated his party and they carried him in on their shoulders amidst cheers as soon as he came in sight of camp.*

Conrad, a youth from the faraway Raxalpe, ending his 26th year.

AUG. 10TH ◆ *With me (Wheeler) on the six-day trip of our English AC guests around Yoho Valley, for the first three days, above timberline. He climbed Mt. Stephen at the end of the trip (Aug. 17th) with R.H.N. Cook.*

On Friday, the 13th of August, Conrad led Bartlett, Pilkington and Harmon to the summit of Mt. Habel, and thence to Mt. McArthur.[35]

Conrad, however, thought he detected a sporting rock climb to the left, which if feasible would lead more directly to the summit. He was let out to the full length of the rope, which was just long enough to enable him to cross a smooth slab of rock with almost imperceptible holds, and reach a place of secure anchorage. Pilkington and I followed in our turn, and were glad to know there was one above in whom we could put our trust.

Mr. L.C. Wilson, of Calgary, who took part in this trip, recalls his first climb with Conrad, up the north ridge of The President, then across to The Vice-President and down to Summit Lake.

The first Canadian summer was passing. Wheeler notes, in closing:

SEPT. 11TH ◆ *Helped me to set out new row of plates for observations of Illecillewaet Glacier. During balance of September and October with*

*me on Govt. Surveys on Shuswap and Adams lakes, BC, where I was
examining lands for settlement purposes.*

Conrad's account of his first Canadian season now follows.

3

EARLY EXPERIENCES IN THE NEW HOME

At last, on Saturday, I could continue on to Banff, and was to meet Mr.
Wheeler there. The train left about nine o'clock in the evening and arrived
at Banff about 12:30 a.m. Pitch dark! I went by bus to the Hotel King Edward.
I shared my room with another man. He asked me in English how much the
room would cost. "I don't know," I replied quite involuntarily in German.
"Well, I don't know either," said the man in German. A German again!

Next morning first thing I went to the window. It was raining, but I
could see a beautiful mountain, Cascade, almost 10,000 feet high. After
breakfast I went to the Sanatorium Hotel to look for Mr. Wheeler. "He has
already left." And then to the CPR Hotel. "Not here." Back to the Sanatorium
Hotel. "Mr. Wheeler is at the Grand View Villa." I went up. "just gone!" It
was becoming uncomfortable. What should I do if I did not meet him?

I went back to the Sanatorium Hotel and there found him at last. Mr.
Wheeler approached me pleasantly. He took me to the clubhouse, then being built, and showed me the work. Then he took me to a boarding house
near the sulphur spring, where I was to have my meals. Then back to Banff.
The lovely surroundings of the village made a good impression upon me.

Next day, with bag and baggage, I went to work. A carpenter showed me
the tools, and I started in. I cleared the woods around the clubhouse and
made paths to the sleeping-tents. The clubhouse has a fine situation. Thirty
years before there had been an enormous forest fire; thick undergrowth had
sprung up and it was hard work to clear it.

At noon I went to the boarding house. Many nationalities were there. The
first night in a tent! My camp was hard as a stone! Next day I made it softer
with brush. At evening I was invited by the carpenter and his friendly wife
to have a cup of cocoa. They asked me how I liked the mosquitoes. I didn't
understand. "Well, the little flies!" "Oh, they don't bite me!" But by next day
I was so swollen from their stings that I could scarcely lift my hands.

I spent my first Sunday with a Swiss, long resident in Canada. He told
me many things about the United States, and that it was better to live

214

there than under the "pious" English in Canada. He asserted in the following words: "If all these holy fellows get to Heaven, then I prefer to be in Hell shovelling coal!"

On July 19th I became homesick for the first time in my life. I went to Lake Minnewanka, two hours distant from Banff. A lake, 16 miles long, one or two miles wide, in a wonderful location surrounded by rock peaks. Lovely flowers on its banks, especially red and yellow lilies. And over all this beauty a profound silence. If only I had had someone along with me to break the stillness, the homesickness would probably never have come. I have often heard that to be homesick is a stupidity and evidences weakness.

The days passed with hard work. Mr. Wheeler arrived one day and was contented with my progress. Then Mrs. Wheeler came to the clubhouse, as well as Secretary Mitchell, and a servant girl who spoke good German. They brought along a kind of cook, a Chinaman, with whom I was no longer friends after the hour when I saw him stir the soup with his finger to see whether it was too hot to bring to the table. It pleased me very much to see that no distinction was made between servant and employer. That was also true in hotels. It was all the same whatever kind of clothes a person wore or who he was, as long as one behaved properly. That makes a good impression upon every poor Austrian in America. Especially upon one like myself, to whom it had already happened in his own home that he was put out of a hotel for having too little in the way of "fine raiment."

On another occasion, in the Stephanskeller in Vienna, I went in dressed very respectably and was shown to the horse trough. The same thing happened to me in the Hopfner Restaurant. Oh, how pitiable is our class distinction! But in America one recognizes no difference either at table or at work. Every man is out for himself, and so even the labourers work much harder than in Europe.

One day, when we were busy moving heavy cases in the cellar of the clubhouse I saw that Mr. Wheeler also entered into this work, and remarked that he should let it alone and I would finish it. Then I heard the following: "Conrad, I am not a European! I do my own share of the work. Everyone works here in America and no one is ashamed! Everyone takes an axe and fells a tree if it is in his way." Mr. Wheeler is in government employ; his son is an engineer and was home on leave; and as we had much work to do he undertook woodcutting also, and worked just as hard and as long as I.

At the beginning of my stay in Canada I took my hat off on greeting, and one day Mr. Wheeler said to me: "You do not need to take your hat off to me, for if you do it I shall have to also, and I am not accustomed to any such thing. You can look upon me as just an ordinary man!"

On the last Sunday but one of July we went up Sulphur Mountain, where there is an observatory. An easy mountain with a splendid view. We saw the peaks, among which we would pitch our camp in a few days. In the last week of July some tourists came to the clubhouse. It was very pleasant to be in the company of Mr. Fynn, an Englishman, who preferred to speak German, having studied at Zürich. Fynn is a renowned and much-travelled mountaineer.

4

THE ALPINE CLUB OF CANADA

B efore going further I must say something about activities in the Rocky Mountains. In the year 1906 several friends of Nature from the various Canadian provinces assembled at Winnipeg and founded the Alpine Club of Canada. The purposes of the club are: 1. The furtherance of scientific study and increasing the knowledge of the Canadian Alps and of glacial motion. 2. The encouragement of art in relation to mountain scenery. 3. The education of Canadians to the value of their country. 4. The preservation of natural beauty and the protection of fauna and flora. 5. Literary exchange with other alpine and geographical organizations.

The members are divided into five classes: honorary, active, supporting, graduating and subscribing. The club has, as previously mentioned, a house in Banff which is open for members during the summer. It has a large meeting room, a hall, a dining room, a smoking and reading room, two little bedrooms, two large fireplaces, an office and a kitchen. Everyone is obliged to sleep outside in tents, which are arranged in three groups: for men, for women and for families. Then there is a tent for the maid and one for the guides. According to present conditions the club will never develop, as for example our German Austrian Club. Few huts are being built and the tent is used largely. Still, the foundation is being laid. Tourism is still at an early stage in Canada; on which account the people have not made such strides in alpine technique as in Europe. One climbs the mountain from the easy side.

First ascents in the Rocky Mountains create no such sensation as in the Dolomites or Switzerland, because only a small part of the Canadian mountains have been climbed at all, and one takes it for granted that on a peak 20 miles from the railway, one is the first or at least the second to ascend. Every climber, male or female, carries for himself. It is one of the best qualities they have! In Canada the guide is never looked upon as a beast of burden, as one so commonly sees him in the Austrian mountains and especially where the North Germans have huts.

With food the Canadians are easy to please. Things do not taste so good for the first few days of camp life, but if there is nothing else to be had, one soon gets accustomed to the simplest fare, for hunger is painful!

5

INTRODUCTION TO THE ROCKY MOUNTAINS

On July 20th we left Banff, to put up the big summer camp. Mr. Fynn, I and a workman, who was very kind to me and explained many English words. We went westward for an hour by train to Hector (the first station in British Columbia). There young Wheeler awaited us with the horses.[36] There is no hotel at Hector, so two tents were put up and lunch prepared. Then the horses were packed and we started off. Our packer was [Clausen] Otto,[37] a woodsman through and through. Hector lies in the midst of the mountains. In the background mighty,, glaciated peaks with rock needles group themselves.

Full of expectation we entered the Rocky Mountains. It went on through swamp, over stones and windfalls, tiresome for man and beast. For me the long, dry, often charred tree trunks, left by fearsome forest fires, formed a novel picture. At evening we reached Lake O'Hara. Really a magnificent lake. Surrounded by fir trees and mossy ground, the lovely mountains surrounding it are all from 10,000 to 11,000 feet high, the colour of the lake being from clearest green to deepest blue. It reminded me of the Weissenfels Lakes at the foot of the Mangart, except that Lake O'Hara is much larger.

We went a little further to a small alpine meadow, and there made camp. We unloaded the horses and put up the cook tent for the Chinese, who was along as cook, and then a tent for the three of us: Fynn, Wheeler and myself. Tired, we lay down to rest.

Next day was vacation, which we wished to devote to an ascent of Mt. Odaray. I was the first to awaken, and when I opened the tent saw to my astonishment – snow! We had breakfast, smoked a pipe and things got better. So we started off and after 20 minutes reached the edge of the woods, continuing to the glacier.

Here we took precaution to use the rope, and let Wheeler junior go ahead. A steep little snow slope leads to the ridge. It was easy, except that the last part was somewhat brittle. We took a long rest on the summit. The view was superb, especially of Lake O'Hara and the Kicking Horse Pass, the great water-parting between the Atlantic and Pacific Oceans. Soon we were back in camp again, had a good lunch and went to Lake O'Hara, where we met the Swiss guide Edward Feuz, with a party. They had also been on Mt. Odaray, but only on the south peak. The man had had his head hurt by a falling stone and was obliged to give up the trip. The Swiss was very reserved toward me; he spoke only a few words and those in English. I had my own thoughts about it!

6

OUR SUMMER CAMP AT LAKE O'HARA

Throughout an entire week we were busy at putting up 50–60 tents, a difficult task. It was necessary to collect poles for doing this, and to fit them up with brush for beds and prepare everything for the arrival of club members and guests. We had assistance during the last few days (six young club members), and with hard work things were ready by August 1st. Every evening we were almost dead from fatigue, and suffered martyrdom from mosquitoes. We were cursing in five or six different languages! Our necks swollen, we ourselves somewhat feverish – there was nothing to do but get out. Mr. Fynn fled several times to timberline, since when one ascends and emerges from the woods the mosquitoes cease.

Sunday was a day of rest. I proposed to ascend Mt. Victoria. Past Lake O'Hara and the lovely waterfalls, I followed the little brook coming from Lake Oesa; it is renowned as being a frozen lake, open during only four to six weeks of the year. From it there is a magnificent outlook: two glaciers go directly into the lake, in which blocks of ice float. I took a short rest. Suddenly the thunder of avalanche! An avalanche fell right into the lake. That was something to see! I continued over scree to Abbot Pass, between Mts. Lefroy and Victoria.

This pass is well known in Canadian climbing circles; there, on August 3rd, 1896, occurred the first accident in the Rockies: a Mr. Abbot fell on the slopes of Mt. Lefroy and was killed. I ascended Mt. Victoria in a short time, as I discovered old tracks. It is one of the finest tours in the Rockies and may be compared with Swiss climbs. The view of the famous Lake Louise and the Chalet is exceptionally beautiful.

During descent I met on the pass the Swiss guide Aemmer with another man, who also was in the mountains for the first time. They descended the "Death Trap," so called on account of avalanche danger. I returned to camp by my same route and went on to the two little lakes near Lake O'Hara that I had seen from Victoria's summit. Oh, that was a lovely picture, unforgettable and indescribable! A bit of forest separates the two lakes. One is deep blue, the other light green, hemmed in by candlestick firs. Countless moss flowers grew on the bank. I thought at the moment of my old mountain friends at home, those who love flowers so much. It was like a dream, and I am not yet sure but that I dreamed it all.

That evening the first guests arrived, about 50 people, and we had our first big campfire! On the following day we made the first tour on Mt. Huber (named for a Swiss, one of the first explorers of the Rocky Mountains); Mr. Fynn, three men from Calgary and I. Where the climbing begins we fixed a rope for the parties following, for Mt. Huber is selected as the "climbing mountain" for graduating members who wish to become "active."

First we attempted to reached the summit from the right, but the bergschrund forced us back. So we went to the left, over a rather steep ice slope, cut big steps, after which it went easily to the top. About six o'clock in the evening we were back in camp and were received with congratulations. The place was full of tourists (mostly women). There were also three Swiss guides there, which the CPR had loaned for several weeks to make excursions in the vicinity of the camp.

Next day quite a number went on Mt. Huber, led by the Swiss and some amateur guides of the club. I went with 20 people to Lake McArthur, a fine lake in which a glacier terminates, so that little icebergs float about, most interesting to see. In the background is Mt. Biddle, with Mt. Schäffer to the left, named for a lady well known in the Rockies who has carried out many explorations. On the way back we saw numerous mountain goats.

That evening all the registered guests were present; more than 200 people! Not in vain have so many pleasant stories been written about the campfires in the Rockies! It makes a unique picture to see so many people grouped about such a huge fire, lying, sitting, standing. There are songs, laughing and joking. Recitations are given; in short, everything in the best humour.

When I went into the tent I saw a familiar face sticking out of a sleeping bag – I could not recall whose it was. Next morning, at table, I recognized him: it was Moritz Inderbinen, whom I had met on the Südlenzspitze in Switzerland.[38] A gentleman as guide! He had already travelled for 23 summers with his employer and had been to all parts of the earth.

Again I had a party for Mt. Huber and by evening was very tired, so I sneaked off to the two beautiful lakes in the forest and stayed there until dusk. I fell asleep, for the mosquitoes were not so bad. Later that evening, by the campfire, I became acquainted with the famous trapper Jim Simpson.

7

HIP-HIP-HURRAH!

Again a group for Mt. Huber. Fifty-five people all told. It was a frosty morning, and when we, climbing through a gully from Lake O'Hara, reached the pass between Wiwaxy Peaks and Mt. Huber, it began to storm and to snow. Everyone turned back. Only Mr. Fynn, who also led a party, and I with three women and a man, waited in the shelter of the rocks for better weather.

I promised sunshine, and told amusing little stories of climbing and from experiences as guide, so that the people would not lose their courage and desire for the ascent. We waited in the cold, and at last, at last, a blue patch appeared in the sky! For a few minutes the sun even appeared through the fog. Right above the pass some easy climbing begins. But the rocks were very cold and progress was slow. Mr. Fynn had to turn back with his party, as one of the ladies had almost frozen her fingers. I would have had to do the same thing if I had not fortunately brought several extra pairs of gloves for my women. Now we came to the glacier, which we ascended diagonally, then over a short ice ridge to a wall of rock, a step which interrupts the glacier. Then over the glacier again to the col between Mt. Victoria and our peak.

The weather changed in the meantime, but as the ladies knew we were the only ones out of 55 people who had not given up the tour they were full of joy and desire to reach the summit, despite the obstacle presented by the unfavourable weather. I promised to bring them safely back to camp, and told them they should not be dismayed by the fog, and that if only a wind did not arise we would attain the peak without trouble. In this fashion I kept up their confidence and courage.

The man had nothing much to say (as is usual when ladies are in the majority) and without difficulty we reached the ice slope, now covered with fresh snow, where there are the only really dangerous places of the whole excursion. I was obliged to improve the old steps which Mr. Fynn and I had made several days before, as they had melted out considerably, but without especial incident we reached the summit of Mt. Huber. For the few minutes of our halt we had a good view down to camp.

While descending the risky spots on the ice slope a wind sprang up, and away went our good steps in the snow. That was not pleasant for me, for, as guide, I could not go first in descending and my tourists were all beginners. I put the strongest woman in front. Slowly and with great care we went down step by step. A single misstep would have been fatal, for I could not anchor myself. I breathed easier when the last woman descended over the little bergschrund.

As we approached camp I announced our approach by a loud yell. Everyone came toward us, more than a hundred people with the club president at their head. Mr. Wheeler offered me his hand and said: "I thank you, Conrad. Now you have your witnesses, and I see that it is just as Dr. P. wrote to me about you, that Conrad never stops until he has completed his task." As he finished his speech, the young men lifted me on their shoulders and carried me to the campfire, with a fearsome shouting of "Hip-hip-hurrah!" and singing "He is a jolly good fellow!" Naturally the ladies were also given a thunderous hurrah.

The Swiss guides present in camp did not join in the felicitations. When I entered the sleeping-tent, one said to me rather scornfully in his dialect: "Well, they thought quite a lot of you today!" ["No, heit ham's Di aber verehrt!"] and began to grumble that such a trip was a stupidity and that in his home no one went out in such weather. I replied: "If I had not met with even bigger storms in Switzerland I would not be able to say very much about the dangers of the mountains!" He: "O, what do you know about Switzerland?" And I: "I know Switzerland, your home, better than you do, and certainly have made more ascents there than you!"

And when he still looked unconvinced I became angry, hunted up my guide's book and threw it to him. He read it and discovered the truth of my assertions. He approached me pleasantly: "Don't be angry! You look much too young, and one can hardly believe that you have travelled so much." We shook hands and were friends.

8

ANOTHER PLEASURE?

For the next day I had a party of 17 for the southern (easy) summit of Mt. Odaray. Good glissading in the snow. On one of the following days there was another excursion up Mt. Huber (an elderly lady and two young men). While descending I met Inderbinen; he was leading a very fat woman, whom he had to pull over the glacier. He looked quite exhausted and said: "Meet me with a lantern, for I need another two hours to the peak and have to pull already." So we met them with lanterns. That was transportation!

A year previously this woman had written an article entitled "Mountaineering for Women." "If only I hadn't done that," she complained. But as soon as she was in camp and heard the hurrah that was made over her success, her fatigue was as if blown away by the wind. But not that of Moritz Inderbinen! "There's nothing in that for me," he gasped. Sunday was a day of rest, general assembly and services. We had plenty of parsons in camp.

The Swiss guide Ernest Feuz and I had still another party to take up Mt. Huber next day. E. had a lady and a gentleman, who wore low shoes, and I an old, deaf gentleman from Montreal. He was a collector of butterflies and flowers. During the ascent I saw a fine butterfly and a big spider and called his attention to them. He had more pleasure from these little beasts than from all the rest of the tour.

We had a splendid view and I wrote down for the deaf man the names of the highest peaks that we could see. He was in bad humour during the descent and grumbled to himself. But in camp he made everything right: a five-dollar tip and flattering words. The camp was almost empty. Most of the people had gone home, and the others were on the six days' trip – we were to overtake them that evening at Sherbrooke Lake.

Feuz went ahead with his party to Hector. I waited for Mr. Fynn, who made the first ascent of Mt. Ringrose with another man and came back late. Then we went on hurriedly to reach Hector before dark. On the way a fearsome storm overtook us, with vicious lightning and thunder. Wet through, we reached the Hector camp. Should we still go on to Sherbrooke Lake? We deliberated and remained in camp.

9

ACROSS THE BALFOUR ICEFIELD

We left early next morning. There is no trail to Sherbrooke Lake; we followed the horses' tracks through the burned forest. Repeatedly we lost the tracks. Here I saw for the first time what horses mean for the Rockies. With their burdens they sprang over windfalls a metre high!

At last we were at the lake, which is a mile long, with lovely situation and colour. We went along the right bank through bushes and over stones and met Jim Simpson at the end, using Wild West language on his horses. Another hour to camp! I yodelled and heard a reply. So we knew in what direction to go. We found the group in the woods, busy with packing, and were not received in the pleasant manner customary in camp. Everyone looked tired and exhausted. The president, Mr. Wheeler, had the dourest expression of all. I knew right away that something was wrong.

Jim, as I heard later, had given him his opinion of the expedition which, from the standpoint of the mountaineer, was really no pleasure at all, as the reader will discover for himself.

After 50 minutes' rest we started off. Thirty men (three guides among them) and three women. Everyone, with the exception of the ladies and old gentlemen, had a big and heavy pack to carry. We were transporting the entire cooking outfit, provisions and two tents along, as well as blankets and axes – in short, so much baggage that we could not carry it all at once to Niles Pass. We had to return in order to haul up a second load.

A few parties went up Mt. Daly. We then crossed the Balfour Icefield. The climbing from the timberline to the glacier was easy enough, although not so simple for those who had to carry the heavy burdens. We made camp at the edge of the woods. There was a tent for the ladies and one for the elderly men. Just as those were put up, a violent storm broke. Lightning struck twice on the rocks above us. Our numerous ice axes were put off at a distance. The storm passed and we began with the cooking. There was bacon, potatoes, beans, tea, bread and jam. It was interesting to see how everybody wanted to help and everyone understood the matter better than his fellow. During the meal I fell asleep from weariness.

Our campfire was not big, for there was insufficient wood; everyone was tired and looked up resting places under overhanging rocks or trees. I climbed rather high up and made myself a bed under a tree, in a half-sitting position. I do not remember how I slept. During the night I felt rather wet, rolled closer to the tree and went to sleep again. About eight o'clock one of the Swiss guides woke me up. The sun was high in the heaven. I had certainly overslept! When I went to put on my shoes, I found that one was eaten through – a hole, through which one could put a finger! Both laces were bitten through. I had used the boots as a pillow, but despite this I heard nothing of the night visitor and saw no traces of him. It was a porcupine.

About nine o'clock we started off. Two parties went for Mt. Balfour. The rest of us, heavily laden, traversed scree and snow across the slope of the mountain. The view was reward enough, but such a load (I had easily 50 kilos) takes the pleasure away from even the finest scenery. Then we climbed over slippery ground and bushes to the Yoho Glacier; but we had to get to the other side of it, and as it was unthinkable to wade through the glacial brook, we were obliged to go up the ice and descend on the far side. Everybody was all in.

I was already across the glacier when I saw a man on the other side who had just fallen down. I went to him and took his pack; it was so heavy and so badly packed that I could hardly stand up with the load. First of all I congratulated the man on being in good enough condition to carry the sack so far. Then I called him a fool. "Yes, a damn fool you are!" He admitted that I was quite right.

In the woods we met Otto, who brought us provisions from Field. At evening the two parties arrived from Mt. Balfour. Here, in the depths of the forest, we had a much better camp, for there was sufficient wood and brush, as well as protection under the trees. We made a good bed for the women, then looked up resting places for ourselves. We slept well that night under the giant cedar trees. Next day we had an easy excursion. We went along the trail to Twin Falls through the lovely, wooded Yoho Valley.

10

RECOGNITION OF NATURAL BEAUTY

"Yoho" is an Indian word which means, translated, the "beautiful valley." So one can see that even the wild (wild in that time) Indians were already appreciative of Nature. Many valleys and mountains of Canada were christened with appropriate names by the old Indians, an indication that even these savages had an understanding of the beauty and characteristics of their mountains – valleys and lakes.

In my home I often heard tourists say: "The mountain folk do not appreciate the beauties of Nature for, in respect to culture and schooling, they are far behind us city people. I myself think, however, that man who looks upon Nature intelligently is not in much need of school to assist him in recognizing beauty.

The mountain dwellers have just as absurd an outlook on the learning of the city man. They think he knows *everything*. But my experience is quite to the contrary. Certainly the man of the city has studied and prepared himself for his calling. But the simplest things that happen in Nature are strange to him, and in this respect he is far behind the ignorant mountain people.

Naturally there are exceptions to every personal experience and opinion. But it is certain that the city-dweller who comes to the mountains for the first time, and is not gifted with keen perception, asks the mountaineer many more stupid questions that would be the case were their positions reversed.

11

CAMP IN YOHO VALLEY

A quarter of a mile from the interesting Twin Falls is a little light-green lake in the woods. There we placed our camp. This evening was much more pleasant. Stories were told and joyful songs sung.

Next day there was a climbing party on Mt. Habel. (It is named for a German explorer, the first to visit the Yoho Valley.) There were 19 people. Our route went past the waterfalls, then through the forest to the moraines and Habel Glacier, which, although quite large, is flat and almost without danger. The last bit to the summit is a fine ridge. The panorama from Mt. Habel is splendid. One sees almost nothing but glaciers: Habel, Bow and Mummery. One estimates them to cover 25 square miles; more than half the glacial expanses of Monte Rosa in Switzerland.

After a long rest we descended over the southwest shoulder. With my two men I made a little tricky variant and had a fine glissade to the glacier between Mt. Habel and Mt. McArthur. There we overtook the other parties. One man of the company said to me in German: "On rocks the Canadians go like snails, on ice and snow like horses!"

With my two gentlemen I carried out a nice, difficult ridge traverse on Mt. McArthur. The others turned back and avoided the difficulties. We were the first on the summit and descended into the Little Yoho, where we met the rest of the people and were received with shouts. Supper was prepared; but it took a long time to find a proper name for the special dish. After some

225

discussion it was unanimously called "Yoho-kohu." What "kohu" meant no one knew exactly. Probably it was an Indian word for "mixture," of which our meal consisted. Beans, rice, peas, onions, potatoes etc. "Hunger is the best sauce!" It tasted fine.

Camp was in a beautiful situation, right at the edge of the woods, surrounded by alpine meadows, a little waterfall nearby and a rushing glacial brook. The whole picture in a frame of snowy peaks. Everyone settled down in good humour by the campfire, and about ten o'clock each one looked up his little resting place. The Englishmen and I slept under a great cedar. It was a lovely night!

About five o'clock in the morning the president called: "Roll out!" After breakfast we started out (17 people) to ascend The President and The Vice-President. The rest of the party went to Summit Lake, where another camp was being put up. I went with three men over a broken rock ridge to The President, then down into the pass and to the top of The Vice-President. We descended after a short rest and had a fine glissade over the snow to Summit Lake. This lake is one of the most beautiful spots in the Yoho Valley, right in the midst of the woods and with a wonderful blue colour.

12

END OF THE CANADIAN ALPINE CLUB EXPEDITION

This was the last camp of the season and the place of farewell. A clear evening! There were toasts to the guests, to the officers and us guides, and it was late when we went to our rest. During the night, a porcupine came and chewed the shoes of a man who had not been careful enough to put them under his head.

The porcupine is hated by the packers, for this animal does great damage to saddles and bridles. The Indians love its flesh, which they consider a delicacy, although white people do not commonly eat it. But this beast all the same has saved many an explorer in the Rockies from starvation, and therefore many are opposed to killing such a harmless animal. One can knock them down anywhere, for the porcupine is very stupid and slow in motion. The Indians do beautiful work with the quills, as for example on hats and belts.

One party went up Mt. Burgess next day, while the rest of us marched by way of Emerald Lake to Field. On the trail from Emerald Lake to Summit Lake one sees some fine waterfalls: one of them is noteworthy, as it does not fall perpendicularly over the steep wall, but slants. At the end of the lake there is a chalet belonging to the CPR. A pleasant, quiet little place, seven miles distant from Field station. Every visitor to the Rockies should make the excursion from Field to Emerald Lake Chalet. The road through the splendid, dense forest, with its loneliness and indescribable peace, I can heartily recommend to those on their wedding trip. I am certain that one is likely to hear the angels of love singing there much more beautifully than in a town on the Italian Lakes.

We had lunch at the chalet, then went in a carriage through the woods to Field, the first village in British Columbia. There, there is a huge hotel of the CPR (100 rooms), where we stayed overnight. That was the end of the Alpine Club Tour. At the finish I saw that the Canadian tourists have the same attitude as so many European climbers: in the valley the guide is soon forgotten. In the mountains and in camp he is "dear friend!" None of the 30 people thought of me.

A Swiss guide was stationed at the hotel, who took me into his room. Gottfried [Feuz] said to me: "They won't trouble themselves any more about you. I know the Alpine Clubists, all right; in the valley or the dining room they would rather be guideless!" He took me into the room where the staff ate. One was not served and must bring everything from the kitchen himself. It took my appetite away to see the unbelievably messy Chinese cook. Still the Chinese meant well by us. He took a big bowl of beef, stirred with both hands (which one could never call clean!) until he found a large piece of meat, and laid it on my plate. The Swiss told me that during the early part of his stay he could get scarcely anything to eat for a week. At last the proverb "Eat birds or die" became a reality. In the dining room, where everything is nicely covered with white, one does not see much dirt. To be sure, our people were well supplied with beer and wine, and when everything was finished even we were on the veranda!

Next day Gottfried and I made a trip up Mt. Stephen. About 5:30 we started off. A good path leads to timberline. Gottfried had a lady and a gentleman. I went ahead with my man. Mt. Stephen is an easy peak; it is named for an engineer who was concerned with the CPR survey. In six hours we were on top, the others arriving a little later. It was cool, but quite clear and we had a splendid distant view.

Mt. Stephen is famous for its fossils, which one finds by the wayside, mostly fossilized plants which are plainly seen. On reaching Field the gentleman found a telegram, calling him home at once. So the tour was given up. I went by train to Hector that evening; there I still found Mr. Richardson (the camp overseer) and the cook, Jim. It was a fine evening, but the flies were fearfully bad. Next morning early I went off to the main camp at Lake O'Hara, where I discovered Mr. Wheeler and Secretary Mitchell. In the evening all the brush and unusable remains of the camp were burned. I stayed on alone at Lake O'Hara, as I was reserved by a party coming on the following day with the brothers Otto: 13 people from Chicago, who all spoke good German, so it was right pleasant company.

We went to Lake McArthur and made camp on a little meadow. On the following days we went up Mt. Huber and Mt. Odaray, over Opabin Pass into Prospectors Valley and up to the pass between Mts. Hungabee and Deltaform. Then came a day of rain and the people gave up the rest of their program.

13
EASY COME, EASY GO

The people had brought a good Italian cook along. I must tell of his experiences in America, in order to show how quickly a man makes something of himself in this country and how quickly he can lose it all again.

He related the following story to me. He had come from Livorno to America as a gardener 30 years before, making himself independent after five years, with a thriving business. But during one spring things were so badly damaged by frost that he lost all desire to work any more. He sold the business and went back home. "But Italy is fine enough if one has money; no good if one is poor! Money gone, I go back to America," he said in his broken German, continuing to tell me how he became cook in a big hotel, earned a good deal and saved most of it.

He became acquainted with a beautiful Englishwoman, married her, went to the country, bought a horse ranch and became rich. But he greatly spoiled his lovely wife. "She comes to me and says: 'Giovanni, I must have a new carriage for driving to the city.' I, good husband, buy a new one for my pretty wife," said the cook. His wife liked the city. He sold his ranch and livery stable and returned to town. His wife took sick and the doctor cost so much that the man was almost down and out. His wife died. He went on the land again and soon had 300 horses on the ranch.

Then along came a contagious disease; he lost all his horses and was a poor devil once more. Then he started in as a ditchdigger, took little contracts and made a lot of money. Once he took a big contract, all the money was lost and he was given a month's imprisonment besides.

"And now I am cook in the mountains," continued the Italian. "Well, that's life in America! But I give you this good advice: never marry a beautiful Englishwoman!"

14
AMERICAN PACKERS

The packers play an important part in travel through the mountains, and it is well known that the American packers are thoroughly unique characters; most of them hard workers and very reliable. It is no small thing to run a pack train, especially so that everything goes well and smoothly. The horses, which often work extraordinarily hard, must be well taken care of. Horse and axe are the best friends of the mountain wanderer in the Rockies.

Conflicts often arise between packers and tourists who think they understand the business better. But the Canadian does not give up his rights. I well remember many of the stories that I happened to hear, and knew personally the heroes of the three little episodes that follow: Tom Wilson and Fred Stephens, two very active Canadian packers, known far and wide. But the packers have no sense of inferiority, fear or respect for a person of higher or even highest position.

I will tell you some things about them. At the time when the railway was being built through the Rocky Mountains, and was finished as far as Calgary, a rich English lord arrived to make an exploring journey in the mountains. He engaged two packers and eight horses. On the very same day they made a long trip to Kananaskis, stopping there for the night. The first packer got supper ready, the second fixed up the sleeping-tent for the lord as well as possible. When the meal was ready, the packer called the lord to eat: "Supper is ready; don't wait, it gets cold." The lord came out of the tent and saw, to his great astonishment, that the two had already started in. So he shouted in his London dialect: "By Jove, don't you know, I am not used to eating with my servants." "Goddamn," said the packer, "if you are not, then just wait!"

It went even worse with a Spanish prince who was on a bear hunt in the Rockies. The party had had a strenuous day in pouring rain through bush and windfalls and, as the packers were very tired, the cook made what is called a "quick lunch," consisting of tea, bacon, green peas, bread and butter. The prince's servant brought the food into the tent, but came right back with the news that His Royal Highness did not care for the lunch and that His Royal Highness wanted scrambled eggs. "So," said the first packer, "he wants scrambled eggs does he? Get along and tell that fellow if he doesn't eat the lunch he doesn't get anything! If it's good enough for us after all our hard work, it's going to be good enough for His Royal Highness!"

When the trip was over, a few days later, the prince said to the first packer, Tom Wilson: "I have gotten more game than I expected; I have also learned in this time what 'hard work' means. I will never again have anything to say against a simple meal. If ever I come back to the Rockies, I shall go out only with you, Tom Wilson!"

It went pretty roughly with a German officer during a trip with the packers. One morning, after breakfast, the officer took a map and an ice axe, stood on a rock and gave orders for the day. The free Canadians naturally know no discipline and thought that the man had gone crazy during the night. When the preaching and commanding came to an end and the people realized that they were not dealing with a lunatic, the packer, Fred Stephens, interrupted with the words: "Are you all through, you goddamned silly fool? If not, I'm going to knock you clear off the place you're standing on! Do you think you have soldiers or slaves in front of you? We know what to do and how to bring you quick and safe to the place you're going to. But don't give us any more of your German sauerkraut stories, you damned fool!"

15

IN THE SELKIRK MOUNTAINS

When the men from Chicago had left camp, I went to Banff by way of Hector. I met no other tourists in the clubhouse and saw, to my astonishment, that the season was over. Mr. Wheeler asked me whether I was contented. "Yes, so far," I said, "but if there is nothing else to do from now on, it isn't really worth the trouble to come as guide for such a few weeks in Canada." Mr. Wheeler promised me that I should accompany him during the survey, on which I could earn just as much as at the summer camp of the club. I was to wait for him at Glacier in the following week.

So I went to Glacier in the Selkirk Mountains of British Columbia. The hotel, Glacier House, is a centre for mountain excursions and during the summer there are always two Swiss guides there. The Selkirks really belong to the chain of the Rockies, but they are quite different in character. The Selkirks consist of primitive rock; they have larger glaciers, greater forests, thicker trees, so that the tours in the Selkirks are combined with many more difficulties than in the main range of the Rockies.

I stayed at Glacier House for eight days, going up Mt. Avalanche to pass the time. The path leads at first through a very lovely forest of Douglas firs and beautiful cedars, where I also met with the attractive looking devil's club, which, however, is cursed by every explorer or hunter on account of its almost invisible little thorns which pierce the skin at once and often come out in another place. Horses suffer very much from this, and it sometimes happens that the beasts bite at their feet until they are bloody. The best thing to do for these little thorns is, after a trip, to wash at once with hot water. The same thing for the horses. When one is out of the woods, one comes to a little lake, then over meadows and scree, where hundreds of marmots live, up to the glacier. At last, over very easy rocks to the summit. The view is exceedingly grand.

The mountains of the Selkirk chain afford greater contrast in the range of colour than do the mountains in the vicinity of Banff. The blue glaciers everywhere descend almost to the green forest. The alpine flora is also better displayed. There are some flowers resembling our alpine blooms, but it is remarkable that most of them are without odour, whereas in our European Alps every flower has more or less perfume. Mt. Avalanche has its name on account of avalanche danger. Every year huge avalanches go down, covering the railway at Rogers Pass, six miles from Glacier.

In the archives of the Alpine Club of Canada Mt. Avalanche is of sad memory, for in the year 1908, one of its members, a lady, became a sacrifice to the mountains.

My next excursion was with two gentlemen up Mt. Abbott, also a very easy peak. A riding trail leads up to lovely Marion Lake, at timberline. The little lake is surrounded by huge mossy trees, wonderfully reflected. Mt. Abbott is the best view-mountain; one calls it the Canadian "Gornergrat." But I think that those who have seen both would not compare the two.

The men were Americans and spoke good German; the younger one was enthusiastic about Bavaria and Tyrol and told me that he too went around there "window gazing" with the young fellows. He thought, with a sigh, that the people in the Austrian and German mountain regions were much more genial than those of the English race.

On the following day I guided a 70-year-old professor on the Great Glacier. We spoke nothing but German together. On discovering that he was a professor of geology I asked him about the fossil plants, as many things were not clear to me. He explained much, and so we went pleasantly across the glacier, which interested him greatly, as far as the Bone Pass[39] on the right side of Mt. Sir Donald, where we rested.

Then I descended quite slowly with the old professor down into the valley once more. His wife was waiting for us at the foot of the glacier; she wanted to help him over the last ice steps, and in so doing he stepped on her foot with his climbing-irons. She bore the pain like a hero and kissed him lovingly. Happily he told her everything, from A to Z, and that he had been on a glacier once more. Never in my life have I seen such mutual tenderness between such elderly people! They seemed to me like young newlyweds! The professor thanked me for my guiding with flattering words: "Yes, you are a real son of the mountains. I never met a guide who knew as much about glacial formations as you."

Glacier House was overflowing with tourists and travellers. As there were no parties to guide during the next days, I climbed Sir Donald, considered to be the most difficult peak of the Selkirks. The guides had told me much about it. But I found no difficulties at all, although naturally it is different if one is guiding people. The view from the summit is magnificent. Unnumbered peaks and glaciers lie spread before the eye. With a good glass one could easily count more than a thousand peaks. Northward of Mt. Sir Donald is a high mountain, Mt. Sir Sandford, often attempted but as yet without success, as progress through the dense forest is bound up with many difficulties. One party in a whole day of 14 hours' hard work could put no more than two miles behind them.

16

WITH THE SURVEY PARTY

M r. Wheeler arrived next day. We made measurements of the Illecillewaet Glacier, and observations of the motion of the ice. The glacier is receding 35 feet annually. When the work was over we went from Glacier by way of Revelstoke to Kamloops.

The stretches of rail to Revelstoke are very interesting, reminding me of the picturesque setting of Semmering. Fertile ground begins at Revelstoke. Here fruit and vegetables are grown. The district is also rich in luxuriant forest. From Revelstoke thousands and thousands of feet of all kinds of lumber are shipped each year. At this place is located one of the large CPR hotels, in an excellent situation.

Salmon come up to Revelstoke. It sounds unbelievable to one who has never seen so many fish, to hear that one actually cannot see the bottom of the brook because of their numbers! One sees hundreds of fishermen on the shores, mostly Indians. The fish are caught in all possible ways and manners, and then smoked, also canned and shipped to all countries. The salmon there is the chief food of the Indians. Fish morning, noon and night. Many things are told about the salmon. It is said that they are only in the mountain waters during summer and that they return to the sea in autumn. Another version is that the salmon ascends to the mountain brooks in the spring and never returns alive to the ocean. I am no great fisherman and so do not know much about it, but it is certain that salmon become sick in mountain streams and that it is an infection. The fish develop white spots and must, as it seems, die of this sickness; for one sees hundreds of these fish lying on the lakeshores and riverbanks, excellent food for bears, wolves, foxes, wolverines, wild-cats, American otters etc.

Between Revelstoke and Kamloops is the Sicamous Lake and its Salmon Arm. Beautiful scenery! Here is also the entrance to the Okanagan Valley, the most fertile part of British Columbia, often called the "California of Canada." Here, too, there are many other little lakes filled with fish.

We got out at Kamloops, took a carriage and drove 18 miles northward. There the surveyors were at work under Wheeler's direction. The road there was hot and dusty, as Kamloops and its vicinity is dry and can only be made fruitful by irrigation. We went to the end of the road, could not find the party and had to turn back. We spent the night with a farmer who kindly took us in. Two boys cared for the horses, the daughter set the table, the wife had things ready in a little while, and then we began to talk about the settlement of the Thompson Valley. The farmer's family came from eastern Canada. The daughter interested me most. She was a beauty, the first pretty girl I had seen in Canada. The house was quite clean, and the family appeared to be living in happiness. There was not much room to spend the night. Mr. Wheeler and I had to sleep together in the same bed.

He left the house at four o'clock next morning to meet the party in camp; I went back later with the horse, and had gone some miles when I was stopped by a boy, the packer of the party, Charles Logan, who had already spent three years with Mr. Wheeler. He took me to the camp on the shore of Thompson River, and upon arrival I was introduced to the survey party.

In the afternoon we packed up and went to the beautiful Kamloops Lake. We camped on the sandy shore. Mr. Wheeler and Charles departed; I stayed in camp and began to cook. To my sorrow I could not find the necessary things, so supper was not ready when the two came back. Never shall I forget that day!

17

WITH OARS AND SAIL

Late that evening Mr. Humme, of the survey party, arrived from Kamloops. Next morning we rowed across the lake; Charles went to the village, while Mr. Wheeler and I went further along the lake. My first rowing! Oh, how hard it was, for I put the oars too deep in the water. Then, when a good strong breeze came along, we put up the sail and then it went fast, uncomfortably fast for me.

We landed at Cherry Creek, a stopping place of the railway, and carried the boat up to the line. After lunch Mr. Wheeler took the next train to Revelstoke.

We waited in a baggage car for a train that was to bring us and the boat back to the Little Shuswap Lake. A freight came along, and others after it, but none for us. We made camp for the night in the boat, but I could not sleep at all, as I was afraid a train would come through and collide with our car. I was quite stiff next morning!

We waited through the whole of the following day, and the next night, and no train took us along. The worst of it was that all of our tobacco gave out. Finally we smoked tea leaves! After eating I tried to fish, but without any luck; still it was very nice to walk along the sunny shore. Workmen were collecting wood on the lake. It was very interesting to see how they went about on the tree trunks, as safely as on firm ground. At last, toward evening, a train gathered us up.

There was a long stop in Kamloops, and there I found my lost chest that had remained behind in Hanover during my journey to London. It was half open, but not a thing was missing. About midnight we reached Little Shuswap Lake, where the locomotive shoved us onto a siding. We made a fire, cooked our soup and slept in the open. During the night it began to rain. I woke up, heard a rustling and thought that a stranger was in the car. I jumped up and shouted: "You certainly haven't lost anything. Get out of there!" No answer. I took a stick, sprang up into the car – there I saw Humme, stretched out in the boat. He had not understood me as, in my almost dreamy condition, I had spoken German. But just the same I had shown him that I was no coward!

Next morning we took down the boat and made camp. At noon Mr. Wheeler arrived. We went to the newly laid-out village of Shuswap to make some purchases, and picked up a young fellow, a wandering cowboy. Then the train took us some miles further on to the lake. In a few minutes we had the boat loaded and crossed to the far shore, where we made camp for the night in a lovely woods. On the following day we rowed to the end of the lake, remaining there two days while the survey began.

I remained with the tent to act as cook and keep watch, as there were many Indians there. On Shuswap Lake I came in contact with Indians for the first time. They paid me a visit. I could not understand them very well, but this much I found out: that they wanted something from me. They begged me for flour and offered me fish in exchange. The Shuswap Indians have good land, but they do not cultivate it, as they are no friends of hard work. The women are to be pitied. They are slaves, and count no more in the home than do servants of a mighty master who has nothing to do with them. The women leave the huts when a White enters (why, I have not yet discovered), and it takes a long time before an Indian woman will make friends with a White.

The first thing about the Indian women that pleased me was the way they carried their children. They had the little ones on their backs, tied to a trough. The trough is finely carved and ornamented with strips of leather. It is interesting to go into an Indian hut. The first thing is to exchange greetings with the old man who is present, after which he takes a lighted pipe from his mouth and offers it to the visitor, who must smoke it. That is the sign of friendship, and a sign that the White thinks himself no better than the Red.

From Shuswap Lake a goodly stream of water leads to Adams Lake, six miles distant. Our two boats were taken there. At the outlet of Adams Lake is a large Indian encampment. During the summer, two steamers ply the lake, belonging to a company having extensive lumber interests in the mountains. Material is taken in for the winter and the wood brought out, which is cut only during winter. Such a little steamer brings 100 to 150 trunks at a time. They are all tied together and towed. From the outlet of the lake the wood is floated farther to Shuswap Lake; there there is a colossal steam sawmill, in operation day and night and cutting hundreds of trunks every day.

Adams Lake is 40 miles long and one to one and a half miles wide, in fine situation and very rich in fish. We rowed about a mile and a half farther, landed and made camp. Next morning we started off early, hoping we might sail, but the wind came against us and we had to row the entire day. Only at noon did we rest for an hour. We passed along through delightful scenery. Ten miles from the main camp there is a bay, and a settler there who supplies the company with potatoes.

It was already dark. Mr. Wheeler was alone in his boat and far behind, and we awaited him at the mouth of a little brook. After we had made a fire I went down to the water of the nearby brook. There were so many dead and half-dead salmon there that one could really believe it impossible to see the bottom. I took some fish out to see how heavy they were. The heaviest was certainly eight or nine kilos.

The night was fine, and so we slept in the open, really delightful and certainly not unhealthy if one does not lie on damp ground. Next morning we rowed farther for several hours, made camp on the shore and after lunch began to work. First of all we put up two fixation signals, then cut down all the trees and brush hanging into the lake so that Mr. Wheeler could use the instruments. In the evening we had trout, and Mr. Wheeler showed me how to bake bread with baking powder. We had two reflectors, used as bake ovens, but the bread was not a success! One says: "A noodle board and an alibi are in every house." We had no noodle board in camp, but plenty of alibi.

On Adams Lake I had my first experience as a sailor. One day I rowed alone to the Dam Camp to get mail. The distance is 20 miles. On the way there was no wind, but all the more on the return. I pushed the boat off from the shore and put up the sail. I wanted to stay in the middle of the lake, but could not arrange the sail properly and ran into a projection of the land. I studied for a time how to hold the sail in order to go in a straight line, then put the sail down and rowed to the middle of the lake. Then I put the sail up again and, to my anger, went back to land again. And that was repeated four times.

Then I rowed around a point of land and raised sail once more. At last with success! I stayed in the middle of the lake and had a grand time. The wind was so strong that I made more than 12 miles in an hour. I thought, now the thing won't make a fool of me again! But when I wished to land

and could not steer the boat ashore, there was nothing for me to do but take down the sail and row in. I was glad that nobody saw me; otherwise my experience in the sport of sailing would only have caused laughter.

18
LEAVE OF ABSENCE

We spent six weeks surveying at Adams Lake, which was done to measure the free land for settlement purposes. To be sure, it would be a long time before the land was occupied, but I think that, in years to come, there will be hotels and summer homes there. The climate is very mild; there was no frost during all of October. Opportunity for fishing and hunting, for sport on the water, for sunbathing and swimming is right at hand. The region is rich in beautiful walks, and there are still many protected spots for free life in camp!

There is also a possibility for a workman to enjoy his vacation there. What would a 14 days' holiday on Adams Lake cost? The lake is ten miles distant from the CPR line; the shipping of a boat costs five dollars. A spot for a camp is free for everyone. The wood costs nothing, and everybody can fish and hunt to his heart's content. One can secure the greater part of one's food there. I think that with 30 dollars one could have a fine two weeks' vacation, such as would be almost out of the question for us in Austria or elsewhere in the Alps. Yes, one can enjoy a cheap vacation there as, for example, at the Bachl Alm at the foot of the Dachstein, but not in such comfort as at a camp in Canada.

I might say yet another word about vacation conditions. If one of us in the Old Country takes a holiday it is only to be free of one's work and, like a lazy fellow, one tries to do it as comfortably as possible. To be sure, there are a few exceptions. The tourist who goes to the mountains, wandering from hut to hut and stopping where and when he pleases, cannot be called idle. He uses his time in healthful, manly pursuits.

But take a look at the real summer resorter one finds at such places as Aussee or Ischl. What do these people do with their time? I have often watched them. One hears innumerable times in a day: "Oh, how lovely it is here! This delicious mountain air! It really does wonders for me!" Yes, it does one good if one understands how to use it properly and breathe it rightly. But, without much concern, the "good air" is used by the lazy centrist in about the following way: At ten o'clock in the morning the maid or servant knocks. "Bring me my breakfast." Then a walk of half an hour is taken. "Oh, how nice the air is!" Then back to the house, for now the letters are arriving from relatives and friends left behind in the city. Lunch about one or two o'clock. Naturally, the stomach gets more than it has earned or can tolerate. Then a good rest after eating, especially in a hammock in the nice cool shadows of a tree, "Oh, the fine air makes me so sleepy." Next a call – a long, long gossip. One hears all sorts of complaints and troubles about poor health, but a glass of coffee and two or three buttered rolls won't do any harm.

So as not to have lost the entire day, one takes a walk. "Oh, how lovely the air is!" During this excursion the doctor, the professor or in some cases the judge, the lawyer, the chief inspector or the manufacturer, of such and such names, come into the conversation. All of this, naturally, on account of children eager to be married.

In the evening the "air sampling" takes another turn; one goes to the concert in the Kurhaus, then for dinner in a salon where the good mountain air is complicated by the smoke of cigars and cigarettes and the awful, nauseating perfumes.

Next morning, the doctor arrives and orders complete rest, so that even this little indisposition, often imaginary, lasts a few days more and additional "visits" go on the bill. Every physician must look after his sack, for earning money belongs even to his calling! So life goes on, day by day, until the vacation is over. Fat as butter the summer tourists return to the city. Oh, that good mountain air!

But it is much more pathetic to examine the vacation of a more or less skilled workman. To be sure he has but one holiday, and that without pay, for why should an employer pay him when he is not working? He is, indeed, only a common day labourer, a workman and not an important government or state official, who is so mentally strained that he really cannot work an entire year through. Such a man has to have a vacation, probably three months long! This distinction is unjust. Why does not one see in the worker a man who has need of recuperation?

In Vienna there are Savings Societies, and through their assistance excursions or even long journeys are made. There, as everywhere, the whole pleasure is concerned with alcohol. It is even so in the mountain districts. There the woodcutter or the farmer's boy takes his holiday on a day of festival; that is to say he "paints things red," saves his money for months just to enjoy himself at the festivities: "That was the time we cut up and raised the roof!"

and afterwards he says: "A great party! We were drunk as lords! Weren't we, Sepp?" ["Da wer me aufhau'n und saufen! Lusti' is g'wen! G'soffen hab'n ma wia die Bürstenbinder! gelt Sepp?"] To be sure in this class as well as in others there are exceptions, but as a rule in both town and country the vacation, sad to say, is usually spent in this fashion.

It is quite different with the Canadians. No one takes a whole month's vacation, for one is not paid for doing nothing, whether he be in a government or some other position. So on this point rich and poor are on equal terms.

When a rich Canadian goes to the mountains, it is a pleasure to him to look after and care for everything himself. He loves the camp life.

19

THE WHITE ROBBERS

From Adams Lake we once made a little excursion into one of the side valleys; we had to carry our things on our backs (tea, bread, bacon, sugar, salted fish, teakettle, a little pan, bowls and spoons). After a day of travel through the bush on an old Indian trail we reached a meadow, where many horses were pastured; at the same time we saw smoke, went to it and found a large Indian family about the campfire. A young Indian could speak some English. With the rest, as far as was necessary for understanding, Mr. Humme made out with them in their own language. They were really undisturbed Indians! The children had never seen a white man, and the dwellings as well as the clothing were pitiful to see. All in buckskin, but the people were not poor. They had some cows and more than a hundred horses – what one calls an Indian cow ranch. Besides, they made money in winter with furs, exchanging them in the nearest village for articles of clothing. The Indians bring no money back. In this respect he is really not a man but like a little child.

He has to have everything he sees, and one or more bottles of whisky are never lacking. The Old Timers made thousands of dollars by exchanging wares with the Indians. They gave a simple blanket for three large bear hides, half a sack of flour for three or four fox or marten skins, in a word only a tenth of their value, so that one can see that the whites were much greater robbers than the wild Indians.

But the poor Redmen were contented with the fraud, and if one had given them money they would have spent it for useless things and have destroyed their health with rum.

239

Next morning an Indian took us up a mountain where we had an excellent view. Mr. Humme made sketches for a map, as, from this summit, one could see hundreds of miles round about. Nothing but forests and valleys, here and there a lake, no city, no village, no settlement. One grasps from such a panorama the fact that the province of British Columbia, although it has as great a plain as Austria and Germany, has only something over a million inhabitants! And then one says in Europe: "Oh, how foolish to go to America! There's nothing more to be had there – everything taken up!" He who travels makes other discoveries. I recall that once I read in the paper a notice, or rather a warning, in which everybody was warned against going to Brazil, Argentine and North America. To be sure, everyone cannot stand the hot climate of South America, but in my opinion that was insufficient ground for advising them to stay out of a country where opportunity is still at hand; where every worker is sure of possessing a fine bit of ground such as could not be had in Austria or any other part of Europe.

20

BY BOAT FROM ADAMS LAKE TO THE CANADIAN PACIFIC

We left Adams Lake at the end of October, the boats being taken back to Little Shuswap Lake, from which we rowed through the river joining Little and Big Shuswap lakes. We saw there two little Indian children in a large canoe. The older child may have been seven or eight and steered the canoe with ease and skill, for which I envied him!

On the shore we saw a black bear. That evening it rained, and we had a bad camp: stony hard and everything wet. There was a homestead nearby and we paid a visit to the settler. He had his father, from Scotland, as his guest. Talk turned chiefly on land and settlement. It was the first time that I had a good look at a homestead. The cabins were built of boards and very small. Around the cabins everything was just as might be expected when there is no woman in the home. The old Scot comforted his son on this point and thought that a good girl could be found for him in Scotland. But I said to myself: 'Poor fellow, you'll have to take whatever pleases the old man!'

Next day we rowed from morning until night to the Sicamous Narrows, joining Shuswap Lake and Salmon Arm. It was dark when we made camp. There was another camper there, looking for land, who supplied us with fish. It was a lovely moonlit evening, and we sat with the man by the fire until late. On the following day we had another long excursion on the lake to reach Sicamous station on the CPR line. This was a splendid day! A fine scene of picturesque landscape. We camped at a farm opposite the station, where the farmer had much to tell us about fruit growing. He lived happily with quite a big family.

Next day was a day of rest, that is, given up to washing and mending. Here we could again buy bread, which tasted good, as our own baking was nothing wonderful. We made an excursion by boat to Notch Hill and stayed there several days.

21

A DISTRACTED HUNTER AND A RESTLESS COOK

We gave the boat away at Sicamous, and the trip was over. Mr. Wheeler went to Calgary, Mr. Humme and I to Kamloops. Then Mr. Humme took me to Savona, where Mr. McCaw waited for us, an engineer working under Mr. Wheeler. Humme went back to Revelstoke while I continued with McCaw into a valley which runs off from the Kamloops Lake. There, in the main camp, I found some acquaintances: Brinkman, Charles and Jim.

The surroundings were hilly, and there were deer, bear, prairiewolves, foxes and mountain lions. We had put out a fly-camp, where I had to stay for a day and bake bread. When my work was finished I took the rifle and went on a stalk. There was already snow on the hills. My thoughts were far far away, at home, on the cliffs of the Loswand. In a dreamy state I followed several tracks in the snow and came to a little meadow in the forest. A great black bear stood before me. He waited for me on his hind legs. I did not remember that I was hunting and had a rifle on my shoulder. Only when the bear went down on all fours and ran off did it occur to me how easily I could have knocked him over. I was angered by my thoughtlessness, but it happens to many a hunter and no one likes to talk about it. Late in the afternoon I shot an eight-point stag and returned half dead to camp.

A few days later we had an amusing experience with Brinkman, an Englishman who had not been long in the Wild West. We were laying out a line that we wished to complete, when engineer McCaw sent him to get supper ready while we finished the job. Brinkman knew less than nothing about cooking, and asked the engineer what he should cook. He said to him: "Cook bacon and fry some beans."

Late that evening we reached camp and found our friend nervous and agitated by the fire. One could read in his expression that something unusual had happened. He did not wait to be questioned, but began angrily: "You have made a fool of me with this bean-frying! It can't be done." "Why?" inquired the engineer. "Why? They all jump out, and if I hadn't put the cover on there wouldn't have been a single one in the pan." McCaw took the cover off and broke into loud laughter. "Well, you've been roasting raw beans. I'll bet they jump out when they get too hot!" We laughed at the Englishman, much to his annoyance.

22

TRIED AND TRUE

Our next moving of camp was to Deadman River. We went across a little mountain ridge, through dense underbrush. Hard work for the horses. Everything was covered with snow and we lost the trail in the bush. Luckily we met an Indian woman, who was packing a newly killed deer on a horse. Her husband was too lazy to bring his game home himself and his wife was obliged to look after it. The Indian woman put us on the right track.

We had to descend a thousand feet into Deadman Valley, arriving at nine o'clock at night and stopping in a ranch house. The rancher, who was living with a Chinaman, was a very rich man, we were told, but a miser who scarcely allowed himself enough to eat and dressed himself poorly. He had a wife in Vancouver, bought her the most expensive clothes and allowed her every luxury.

Next day we put up our camp on Deadman Lake, which was already frozen over. The nights were fearsomely cold (–30°F), and our Chinaman was almost frozen. I had almost nothing to do at this camp and took riding lessons from Charles until Mr. Wheeler came and went with us to the Red Lakes. These lakes are situated at an elevation of a thousand metres above the sea. It was a cold and stormy day, as of mid-winter. There was six feet of snow at the Red Lakes and no chance of pleasant life in tents. We shovelled the snow away and made camp.

A settler, who had taken an Indian wife, a pretty 18-year-old girl, was there. We visited the settler in his cabin; it was newly built and the furniture

242

consisted of a large bed, a table, two chairs and a stove. The Indian woman spoke English quite well and showed us her handwork, of which she was very proud. Her manner was childish. We argued in camp how such an attractive girl could live on good terms in the wilderness with an old greyhead. Some days later we discovered to our astonishment that she was really contented and happy with her lot. But it was our packer, Charles, who made the discovery that she was a virtuous wife, a quality not usually regarded highly by Indian women.

One evening the greyhead came to camp to play cards; Charles took the opportunity of visiting the Indian lady. He wanted to declare his love, but instead of listening to him the woman picked up a rifle and threatened to shoot if he did not leave at once. I was watering the horses, close to the cabin, and heard how she bawled out the redhead in English: "Oh, you think me Indian girl no good! Me just as good as white girl! Me married, stay with husband. You damn——!" I laughed heartily, and Charles sneaked back to camp like a whipped dog.

During the whole of the following day he had a sour expression and was afraid of the settler's coming back to camp that evening. The old fellow arrived to play cards. For a long time he said nothing, but then began with smiling face: "Now, Charles, don't you want to go over again?" Then he laughed in a pleased manner, and said: "I had to tell you that she is a brave wife!" and went on to add that the Indian women make good wives as soon as they become accustomed to civilized life – though, to be sure, that takes some time. It was lucky that the settler was of such a peaceful nature; otherwise Charles might have come to a bad end.

23
PAYOFF

The work in this area was difficult: we cut a trail through the snowy forest, suffering in the cold and wet. On one day we saw a mountain lion close at hand. It was a female and she watched us for a long time. We had nothing but axes with us, and probably would not have been able to do much with them. I must say in all truth that we were afraid, although we did not show it. Cougar is the Indian name for mountain lion; they are the most dangerous animals of prey and are much feared by the Redmen. It is a certainty that a cougar can attack and kill any other animal, for it lurks in the trees like a tiger.

It was the end of November. The weather became worse and work had to be stopped, for which we waited with impatience. We went back to the odd character in Deadman Valley and on the same day continued in a wagon to station Savona. The others spent the night in Kamloops, while I went on alone to Banff. The journey by moonlight through the Rocky Mountains was magnificent. There was already a foot of snow at Revelstoke and three feet lay at Glacier House. I arrived at Banff on December 1st, went up to the clubhouse and visited a friend. Banff was quite changed. No one on the streets. The train, by which I continued to Calgary, was eight hours late, as often happens in winter.

Next day was payday for the Alpine Club and the survey, and I received a large sum of money. I counted up the dollars in kronen: 2,000 kronen! 'Herrgott, that is something to spend. I must be getting rich!' said I to myself, and went to the hotel, closing the door and counting the money several times more. I played with the money by the hour. It occurred to me that if I were back in Naßwald I would feel just like Rothschild!

I stuck the money under my pillow and could not sleep for joy. I built huge castles in the air and asked myself questions as to what I should do with the money. Well then: so and so much I owed my good friend G. in Vienna, who had advanced me the money for the journey in such a kindly manner. Then came my dear mother: I would send her $100 – that makes 490 kronen. I pictured for myself what a surprise it would be for her when the letter carrier would bring her a money order for 490 kronen. My mother had not seen so much in all her life! In imagination I followed her going home from the post office with the money, and how she would count it again and again by the lamp in the little room. I saw how she would put it carefully in a box and hide it in the drawer of a chest, where so often, or rather, most of the time, there was not even a heller remaining – and now 490 kronen all at once! I saw her sitting on the bed in the faint light of the lamp. I heard her voice: "My Konrad! My son!"

I think it no shame to say that, after these thoughts, my heart was broken and my eyes dissolved in tears, for I knew that my mother loved me and that I was the only one upon whom she could depend, for the other children were still too young.

During the payment Mr. Wheeler thanked me in the name of the Alpine Club of Canada for my services and assured me that he would be pleased if I returned another year.

24

IN THE COMPANY OF TRAPPERS

My plan for the winter was to visit Dr. Berl at Fort Saskatchewan. I travelled from Calgary to Edmonton, the chief city of Alberta. In this city more than 30,000 Germans live, and there are even German newspapers. Besides this there are many Swedes and Norwegians in Edmonton. It is customary to hear six or seven languages on the streets and in the hotels.

The cold was so intense that there was nothing to do but sit in the hotel. On the third day of my stop I left by train at nine o'clock in the morning for Fort Saskatchewan. To my sorrow I did not find Dr. B. and learned that he had sold his farm and left for Vancouver. I stayed at the Mainson House.

Fort Saskatchewan is a rather large town, with two hotels and several businesses. Eastward, in the Beaver Hills, there are only German farmers and, to the north, only French ones. In the hotels German, French and English are spoken. I would have been able to get work on a farm at once, but decided to travel with one of three trappers I met in the hotel.

I left my trunk in the hotel and took only the most necessary things with me. The trappers told me that their shelter huts were all ready and provisioned. We followed the frozen Saskatchewan River and later a small side stream. We pulled our things along on sleds. It was fearsomely cold. When it grew dark we made camp. Lying on the frozen ground I could not sleep the whole night because of cold and so was very tired next day. Late in the evening we reached the trappers' quarters, after a second day's march. To my sorrow I saw only a cave and no cabin. Again a long sleepless night!

To comfort me I was told that conditions would be improved. On the following day a hunt was made for fresh meat. We had a little drive hunt with good success: one killed a big grizzly bear (really good luck at this time of year), another a moose, I a marten. That evening we had a jolly time. The bear steak tasted fine (like pork), but the night was once more too long for me.

I stayed in camp next day and decided to turn back. Luckily we met another party of whom one, an Indian, was also returning. He had frozen both hands while setting beaver traps. So we started off next morning. The Indian knew the shortest way; still, progress was slow and we could not reach the last homestead on the same day. We spent the night in the open; it was troublesome work to make a fire. It became terribly cold during the night, and we ran around the fire to keep warm. The poor Indian began to have severe pains, as I could see by his expression. I was so sorry that I could not understand him, for he knew only a little English. The night was the longest and blackest I have ever known. During it I also froze parts of myself.

Even before it was daylight we hurried on and after about three hours arrived at the homestead, where we were politely received. First we were given a good breakfast. When the young farmer discovered that I was a countryman of his, an Austrian, he told his wife that he would guide us to town (which he would not hear of, at first). He harnessed up the rather dilapidated sledge, but it did us good service and brought us almost frozen to Fort Saskatchewan at nine o'clock that night.

We went at once to a doctor, who immediately sent the Indian to hospital at Edmonton. He promised to have me cured in a short time. Next morning I went to the station with the poor Indian and got him his ticket for Edmonton. I learned later that he had to lose one hand and some fingers of the other.

The doctor gave me a good talking to and said that I should not do any such foolish thing again. He told me that many came to him with frostbite, and remarked that I was a "new bird" in the country.

25

AS CARPENTER IN FORT SASKATCHEWAN

The warm room where I rested in the hotel was very comfortable. One day a man came along and asked whether I wanted work, on a building job, and whether I could use axe and saw. "Yes, I work in the Old Country as a carpenter," I replied. Actually I had never been anything of the sort at home except a simple woodcutter.

The man looked me over a little, then said: "Well, if I'm contented with your carpentry I'll pay you full value." So I went into a hardware store and bought the necessary tools. With a conscience that was not quite clean and quiet I started in on the job next morning as carpenter. It went off all right. In America the lumber for building is already prepared at the sawmill. Every lath, every board has a planed side as well as a groove etc. Really a very practical arrangement.

I worked until the building was completed and was paid in full, that is, 35 cents an hour. During the construction I improved my English a good deal, often, to be sure, with misunderstandings.

One Sunday I practised with skis; I built a take-off on a little hill and had quite an audience. Soon I knew everybody in town. I was often invited to tea. In the hotel where I lived German was spoken. During my stay two girls arrived from Germany, who understood not a word of English. I often acted as interpreter and, at their request, gave them English lessons.

I spent the Christmas and New Year holidays at Fort Saskatchewan. The temperature was about −40°F. at that time. Dinner was free, but otherwise no special notice was taken of a holiday. On the day before Christmas I was asked whether I wanted to work on the next day. I was much astonished and replied in the negative. "Oh, we work on Christmas," said the boss. The people ended work with a rush for the bar. The entire hotel was filled with drunks. I spoke about it to a lady. She said: "Oh, at such a time one must forgive them!"

The farmers came into the barroom in their everyday clothing. However bigoted the people were they made no distinction between Christmas and a workday. Christmas week is the best week in the calendar for the barkeeper, just as are the festival days in the mountains of Austria and Bavaria. On Sylvester Eve I was also in a good frame of mind: I was so plagued by homesickness that I turned to alcohol. But what a Katzenjammer! The Canadian beer is twice as strong as the lager beer at home.

26
HOMESICKNESS

To explain homesickness to one who was never homesick is indeed a difficult affair. Just as it is to describe toothache to one who has never experienced this pain. There are people who say that only stupid folk become homesick. If so, then I was one of them! One has to say that, for it would not be quite fair to count oneself among the intelligent.

I am not inclined to call the homesick one foolish. It is not the same to every one and originates in various causes; one has a longing for his relatives, another for his sweetheart, a third for his native land, for cities or mountains. One calls all of these things homesickness. I have come to know what longing is, and so I feel for every one and am ready to comfort those who suffer from it. I blame my homesickness on the fact that never before had I lived for so long a time on a plain. I had a desire for snowy forests and peaks, for my good friends whom I would otherwise meet on festive occasions or with whom I exchanged letters. These things were interrupted by the very distance.

I felt as if no one in the world cared about me. And, in this way, home-sickness crept in. I had money enough to go back to the mountains, to the snow-filled woods that I had loved as a child, but I wanted to fight out the battle, to have experience of the prairies and their people. It is good for everyone to fight this acute homesickness, but not everyone is victorious, for it is a desperate fight.

CHAPTER IX

(1910)

▲

1

LIFE ON A FARM

The building was finished by the middle of January. I took a week of rest and wrote up my diary. There was also a pile of letters to answer. To get further insight and new experiences of a farmer's life I went, on January 22nd, to farmer Peter, a countryman of mine whose farm was in the Beaver Hills.

A land deal between two farmers had just been closed, and there was good humour all around the bar. About us were grouped the German farmers from Galicia. In great expectation I sat beside Peter on the sled.

The Beaver Hills are but ten miles distant from Fort Saskatchewan, yet, in the darkness of the winter evening, the journey seemed long to me. At last the farm was reached. I entered the house. Kitchen and dining room in one. At table I counted no fewer than eight children. The farmer's wife set the table and asked me whether I was so accustomed to the hotel in Fort Saskatchewan that their simple fare would not taste good to me? I reassured her by saying that I knew life from several sides, and the table as well. In the "room for all" a camp bed was set up for me. And it was all quite different from what I had expected.

It was a wooden house; the whole family used the upper part as a sleeping room, separated from the rest by only a board wall, extending as far as the middle. The roof was covered with sod and dung. The stable stood beside the house, poorly and badly built; then a shed, of which Peter was very proud, and some smaller huts besides, serving for pigs and chickens. A large haystack, a big manure heap – and we are through with the farm!

The landscape, the entire surrounding, is almost all flat and in winter very dreary. It was Sunday, and so the whole family went three miles to church.

Here there was even a Sunday School, held before the service. About the little wooden church 30–35 sleds were standing. The thoroughly German farmers were collected in groups, and business was being done until the church bell tolled. After church there was another little gathering, this time of the women.

In the Beaver Hills the people are almost all Austrian (German Galicia), who were very poor at home and have worked themselves up here on the land grant received from the government. So they are now better Canadians than Austrians. The church service was held in the German tongue. I had not been in a church for a long time, and it reminded me of when I was a very young child. Of the time when, as a child, I ran to my old grandmother during a storm and she told me that the heavenly Father was angry with me for not being brave.

The people here cling to their faith; the children must say their prayers six or seven times a day, a thing that was quite new to me among Protestants. On Sunday afternoons visits are made from one farm to another; I was glad to join in this in order to acquaint myself with the people and their customs. It would be too monotonous to write down everything, but it concerned itself mostly with housekeeping, interesting news of marriage and other gossip.

There was not much work on Peter's farm. He had an injured hand and I had to help him fetch building wood for a new stable. The trees were 12 miles from the farm. On the first day Peter wanted to explain and show me how to cut a tree! I had to laugh at that and told him kindly that he didn't have to bother, as I had certainly cut down more trees than he. It seemed rather unintelligent to me to go into the woods with a little axe and long saws, but one must fit oneself to conditions.

Besides the work in the woods, there were horses and pigs to feed at home, and besides that I learned to milk the cow. It is quite pitiful to see the cattle standing in the cold and snow beside stacks of straw which more or less serve in this section for fodder. Only the milk-cows were stabled for the night, the others being driven into a kind of pen only in times of severe storm.

During 25 degrees of frost we stayed indoors. The farmer's wife was very superstitious. I often saw her buried in the ancient dream-book of her grandmother. She often inquired about my dreams, but she was not in agreement with my observations on the subject. She also wanted me to learn some prayers, which were a half hour in length, but I told her that I knew enough of them. The poor woman put little trust in my fear of God! It distressed her that young people, who went about so much, for the most part leave the narrow path of righteousness and wander on the wide and wicked road. She said that it would give her no pleasure if her child wandered so far away from her. But I gave her to understand that travel is a second school.

Farmer Peter was an expert shoemaker; his character was just what one might expect of such a poor Galician. He was a good man, but his education was slight. When angry he used coarse and rough words toward wife and children. And she was just the same. It sometimes got on my nerves in the morning when one or another of the children was not ready for prayers and was punished with blows. And more than once I would hear: "Now get down on your knees for prayer, you jackass, you blockhead" etc. A fine Christian upbringing. A perfect understanding of religion! And that was the state of the elders themselves.

The children were of a different cut than the parents; the two older daughters were ashamed when the coarse words fell. Among themselves they preferred to speak English. Once the eldest daughter wept during an exchange of words between her parents, and said: "Father, you should be ashamed before a stranger!" But Peter did not regard me as such, for I was his countryman. So I was ashamed for him.

The family life of the neighbours was almost like this. But most of them were in possession of more land than Peter; some had modern and well-built farmhouses. But, strangely enough, no wc!

I was glad to visit the neighbours, who all invited me. Young and old liked to listen to stories of robbers and ghosts; they themselves interested me more than my experiences of travel and observations of Nature.

2

A UNION

During this visit a chance was offered to me, and they would soon have had me married – that is, matched! I must write down this experience completely, from beginning to end, for it gives a broad survey of the people and their customs.

I often visited neighbour Phillips, also a Galician. One could only talk with him about land. So he asked me what I thought about it and how Canada pleased me. He thought that the best thing for me to do was to take a homestead of 160 acres. But I was not of this opinion, for 160 acres is not enough on which to make a fortune in Alberta or Saskatchewan. It depends upon what part of the country one gets the land. I told him also that I did not like the loneliness of half the year. Phillips admitted that it was a lonely life, adding in a laughing way: "It is not right for a man to be alone! Least of all on a homestead. But that is easy to fix. You only have to take a wife and the housekeeping goes ahead quite differently!"

• I thought: 'Wait a minute, Peter, now I'm through with you and your homestead life.' "Yes," I said to him, "a wife. But how to find one?" And he, with a flattering smile: "A sturdy fellow like you, good-looking, young and healthy, need have no fear of not finding a wife." "I thank you for the compliment, Phillips. I have been but a short time in Canada and have made so few acquaintances. Besides, my English does not progress as well as it should." He grew angry at that and roared: "Are you getting the idea in your head of marrying an Englishwoman? They're no good to a farmer! They want nothing but to run around in fine clothes, and that is all."

We were both silent for a little while. Then a secret smile crept over his round face. He lit his pipe and said: "I know a real solid girl for you – yes, a German, a strong girl who can do things." His wife entered and interrupted his talk. She told him with joy that she had found in the haymow a hen's nest with more than 30 eggs in it.

On my way home I considered the homestead life, and the assertions of the farmer about the English. I said to myself: 'Oh, you poor German wives on the farms!' No doubt that the German women are more industrious than the English ones. But I think that if I were married I would treat my wife according to English rather than German customs. I mean, as a farmer.

One Sunday Phillips came to see us on his sledge. I sat in the room, busy with my diary. I was to go with him to his friend's. It was not very agreeable to me, but I did not want to deny him. "Clean yourself up a little, Conrad!" he called. As I got dressed I thought: 'What can that mean – fix yourself up?'

Bundled up warmly in the skins we sat on the sledge. The trip was a cold one, over dreary country. "How far are we going?" I asked. "Only ten miles, we are soon there. The horses are going well." I asked no more about his friends, and he, too, said nothing. Far across the bare, snowy fields a little house became visible. That was our destination. Soon the dogs began to bark, and at last we stopped directly in front of the house. In the doorway stood an old, not very tall man with grey hair. "Halloh! Phillips! I am glad

that you have come." Meanwhile an old but still vigorous woman came up
and said, in a clear, fine voice: "Oh! Uncle Phillips! Good morning! And
who is the young man?" "That will be your son-in-law if it is God's will!"
shouted Phillips, laughing loudly.

I do not know what colour my face turned when I heard that. My heart
stood still for several seconds, then beat strong and fast. I was angry with
myself for coming. "Oh, that's the young man, Conrad, isn't it, uncle?" 'Stop,
she knows my name already! The trap is set for me,' I thought. 'What will
the bait be?'

3

BAIT FOR THE TRAP

I do not remember how I got out of the sleigh. I felt the hands of the old
woman in mine. "Greetings," said she. Then the old man shook hands. "A
countryman of ours, aren't you?" "Yes."

Phillips and the old man unharnessed the horses while the old lady took
me inside. She brought me some slippers and then called: "Marie, come
here. Your uncle has arrived and the young man from Peter's!" "I'll be right
there," replied a voice above the stairs. The woman takes me into a room
and then goes out. Then I hear Marie going up the steps, and the voice of
the old one: "He is a neat young man; he has a fine face!" I was ashamed.
How had it happened? The impertinence of Phillips! Never in my life had
I been in such a predicament. Now was the time to watch out. Nothing
would happen to me if I did not go into the trap! So went my thoughts. In
a few minutes the embarrassment passed off. 'Ah, that's an adventure, an
experience that doesn't happen every day. You won't catch me.'

The door opens. There is Marie with her mother. She had some glasses in
her hands. She threw a glance at me; I looked her boldly in the eyes. "This
is our daughter, Marie," said the old woman. I held out my hand to the
girl, smiled pleasantly, spoke in a soft tone (High German, naturally) and
inquired how she was and said that I was happy to meet her. 'Here is the
bait for the trap,' I said silently to myself. Marie stood before me, somewhat
uncertain. I looked about and remarked: "You have a fine home." "Oh yes,
the house is almost new," the old woman replied quickly. Then the old man
and Phillips came in. Marie filled the glasses. "Scotch whisky isn't bad when
it's cold!" Phillips asked Marie what she thought about it. "Very nice," was
the reply. A few glasses more and conversation began.

The old farmer and Phillips sat by the stove, the two women with me at the table. I had to answer many questions, asked by the old lady. How long I had been in the country, whether my parents were alive, how many brothers and sisters, whether I liked a farmer's life etc. The girl sat in silence. She listened carefully, played with a glass in her hand and threw deep glances at me, as if she wanted to ask me something. Afterward she busied herself with setting the table; the old woman went to the kitchen – well, now I am alone with Marie. The two by the stove are listening. What shall I say to her?

Marie was a strong girl, well developed, her figure rather heavy as in the case of most farm women. That comes from hard work. Her eyes were brown; one saw shyness in her glance. Yes, a real solid girl, just as uncle Phillips had said. As far as I am concerned, a good bait! Now we sit down at table. The farmer's wife brings in very good, homemade roasted sausages and real German sauerkraut. I praised the food, thereby getting into her good graces.

After it was over, the farmer, his wife and Phillips went to the stable to look at a young colt. I wanted to go along, but Phillips sent me back with the words: "You wouldn't understand much about horses. Stay there and entertain yourself with Marie." I went back into the room. Marie followed and offered me another glass of Scotch: "You must drink a glass with me to our good friendship." "All right." I drank half and she the rest. "Well," said she, "we surely don't have to talk to each other in the formal way." "No," She embraced me and gave me a kiss, which I returned. But the kiss left me cold.

After the kiss of friendship and the drink, Marie was like another person. She began to ask all sorts of things, her looks were much more friendly and no longer shy. She began: "I am very glad that Uncle Phillips brought you here, and that Peter praises you so highly. He says that you are a good work-man and can adapt yourself to everything." She was silent for a moment. I looked her squarely in the eyes. They were fiery, her face red with shame. It seemed to me as if I could hear her heart beat. She sat down beside me with a deep sigh. I saw that she wanted to say and ask something. A feeling of pity came over me.

I was almost on the point of embracing her and asking what was the matter. 'Stop,' I thought, 'here one must be a man and not a fool. It is indeed a trap, not to be trifled with.' Very quietly I asked whether I could help her clear the table? "Oh, no. Oh, no." At last her mouth overflowed. I might compare it with a cloudburst. I was none the less astonished at the flood of words. She began: "And what do you think of me? Do I please you? Do you love me?" "Yes, certainly you please me. You are surely a very pretty girl." That quieted Marie. "I know very well that you could get someone more beautiful than I. But what good is a fine dish if there is nothing in it?" She said this, smiling. I agreed that she was right. How it brought back my courage I cannot describe. I said to myself: 'That is certainly an adventure!'

I was glad when her parents and Phillips returned. They had surely been talking more about me than of the young colt in the stable. The old lady was especially friendly with me on discovering that Marie and I were on terms of "thou."

Now it was time to depart. They tried to persuade me to spend the night there. I wouldn't hear of it. The old man harnessed the horses, while we stood at the door, and to my astonishment Marie pulled me back and gave me a noisy kiss. The farmer's wife acted just as if she had no ears, but I saw that she laughed in a pleased manner. Blushing with shame I took my place on the sledge. "Be sure and come next Sunday," Marie called out as the horses started off – a lucky moment for me!

4

FACING A GREAT TRIAL

I wanted to give Phillips a piece of my mind for bringing me into such a predicament, but the word "adventure" throbbed in my brain. We were only a few hundred yards from the house when Phillips began: "How do you like Marie?" "She is all right." "You bet she's all right. A very fine girl, who can work. Last spring her father was sick and she cultivated the whole field. No man can go wrong with Marie. And then you have to consider, Conrad, that there is no debt on the house, which is worth a good deal to a farm. Will you go out again on Sunday?" I replied uncertainly and with evasion.

Next day we went into the bush to get wood. At evening I was thinking over my strange experience. There was much to consider: a well-built farm, without debt. I a poor devil. Tomorrow I could be the owner and lead a peaceful existence by marrying Marie. Without doubt she is an industrious girl. But do I love her? But surely love will come if I find she is kind and upright. Those were the thoughts that urged me into the trap.

On the table leaves of my diary lie about me – I read some of them over. I recall that it was about a sunset and the play of colour in Dauphiné. Would I ever experience such magnificent hours if I became a farmer in Alberta on the dreary plain of the Beaver Hills? No! My mountains that I had loved from childhood would have to be given up. And what else would I have to forsake? To divert myself I picked up some letters. Letters from people I love, of whom I ask advice when I am in trouble. One such I read through, a long letter containing so much: questions, answers, comfort, encouragement. The best friend I had in the world had written it. The truest heart I knew, that meant everything to me. Would not this marriage with Marie make a difference? Yes, it would.

In future I would have to trust everything to Marie, to look upon her as my first and best friend. As my wife! But I really didn't know her at all. I hear that she is a fine, courageous girl. She works diligently. But is that everything one expects of the woman one marries? These thoughts raced through my tired brain all night. This adventure was not so simple. It was an experiment, a trial for me.

Again, next evening, I occupied myself with similar thoughts. Would I live happily on the farm with Marie? Had she all the good qualities I wanted in the woman with whom I might spend the rest of my life? All these different thoughts diverted me from the idea that the affair was a trap for me and that Marie was the lure.

A few days afterward I received a letter from Marie. It was written in very bad German and without important content. What could I ask of her? She would know no more and be able to speak of nothing else than what she heard from her parents and neighbours. And with that a part of the experiment was finished for me. If I joined my life with another it would have to be a different one. I was not anxious to talk of housekeeping with my wife. I was more desirous of discussing all the things that interested me, of Nature and its beauties, and I hoped that she would have as fine a feeling for it as I myself.

5

THE GAME OF ADVENTURE

I did not visit Marie on the following Sunday, but went to Fort Saskatchewan. On my return I heard that Marie had come in a sleigh. A few days later I went to Phillips. He was not at home, but his wife was. If I were to write down all the things that were dangled in front of me in regard to Marie, it would make a book as thick as the Old Testament!

Everything that she told me seemed like gold in the sun: only good things about Marie and her parents. But that left me cold as ice.

Next day I had another letter from Marie. She told me that her heart was broken because I had not come and she had not found me at Peter's farm. I was to come to church on Sunday without fail and go home with her. As I now looked upon the affair more as an adventure than anything else, and wanted to see it through, I went to her church on the following Sunday, eight miles from Peter's farm. It was too cold to stand in front of the church, so I went in and sat down on a bench.

I saw Marie and noticed how she looked at me every five minutes or so. It would have been very interesting to read her thoughts. The service was over; I hurried out and met some farmers I had known in Fort Saskatchewan. While I was talking to them, Marie pushed forward, greeting me loudly and pleasantly. The farmer who conversed with me said: "Oh, you know this gentleman?" "He is my good friend, and possibly more in a little while," answered Marie in a happy voice. "Well then, I congratulate you," said the farmer, shaking hands with me. "Oh, no, not so quickly," I replied. Marie made me known to other of her friends, introducing me with: "That's my boy."

Many people were standing in front of the church, and all eyes were upon me. "A stranger," I heard remarked. I was on pins and needles. Marie dragged out her horse with the sleigh; we climbed in and she drove off. All eyes followed us. What would not all the farmers be saying about Marie and her "boy"? Happy and contented she drove into the farmyard. Her parents greeted me kindly, the table was set and a good meal awaited me. After eating a prayer was said, the women cleared the table and we smoked our pipes.

The old man told me the condition of his affairs. "I am in poor health and cannot do my work any more. You are welcome to me as a son-in-law any day." He remarked in addition that it was not so easy for a girl to find a good husband in the wilds. "There are plenty of Englishmen, but I don't want one of them on my place, and Marie wants nothing but a German. And I must tell you that she is wildly in love with you! You will succeed. Even my age is not an obstacle, and you don't have to be afraid of your mother-in-law!"

I thought to myself: 'That's quite a lot.' But, because he was so pressing, I looked at the trap from another angle and imagined that there must really be something extra wrong with Marie. I would have to be hard as iron in this house, and must, as far as possible, fight against the urge of Nature.

The farmer's wife came in and said with a smile: "My husband and I are accustomed to take a little nap after eating. Go out to Marie in the kitchen." Of course, I did not want to disturb their sleep and so I went out. Marie had put things in order, and sat down beside me as close as she could. I did not offer her the kiss she expected. She told me how much she loved me, how well she would treat me etc. I gave her a little lecture, saying: "Look here, Marie, what do you want me for? I am a poor young fellow and should have at least four or five hundred dollars. I don't know anything about farm life, and you would have to teach me everything."

"No, no," she interrupted, "I wouldn't have to teach you much. Peter says you are very clever. Don't say such senseless things. When do you think, Conrad, that you will come to me? Oh, I do wish you would stay right here. I love you, Conrad!" And with these words she fell on my neck and covered my face with kisses. What would Marie have thought if I had given her no kiss in return for so many?

Certainly every man enjoys a kiss more or less, and I also. But Marie's kisses did not please me with the same delight that the lips of a girl against one's own should give. There is a pretty song: "Oh, a kiss is a funny thing, one eats it not, one drinks it not, but all the same it is so good it rules all blood." I couldn't say that about Marie's kisses! What an indescribable, unpleasant, horrible feeling it is to be kissed when one doesn't want it, by a person one doesn't love!

After this outburst Marie took me outdoors, showed me the boundaries of the farm, the fields, then the new English sawing machine, the ploughs etc. "Our fields are easy to work. I think they will suffice us; what do you think, Conrad?" she asked. "Oh, quite likely," I replied absent-mindedly. And I thought: 'Poor bit of a girl. She really thinks she has caught me!' Then Marie took me into the shed, showed me the new windmill and the grain, about which I understood as much as she of mountain guiding!

Then she exhibited the horses and cows, and last of all the pigsty, in which an old pregnant sow was lying. When Marie saw that, she pressed slowly against me. "She will soon have young." "So it seems," I replied. "What do you think; how many can she have inside?" "Oh, that's hard to guess. I might say, eight or nine." "Yes, that's just what father and I think too. I see that you have a good eye for animals, Conrad."

I could scarcely keep from laughing, thinking on the quiet: 'Conrad Kain – Farmer! With a good eye for cattle!'

6

THE EXPERIMENT

The afternoon passed, evening came and I wanted to go home after so much evasion. But to no avail; I had to stay. Now it is time to go to bed. The farmer's wife took me upstairs, stopped and said: "Well, Con, here's your little room. Marie sleeps there." And, with that, she pointed to the next door, as if to say: "Well, everything is understood now! My husband and I sleep downstairs. Good night!"

My room was well furnished, everything clean and neat. I went to bed. Soon I began to consider the situation I was in. A *trap*! It would be that for Marie too, or else her mother would not have said: "She sleeps there." I was in doubt as to whether I could remain firm. I saw that it was a great trial. Night added to it. During the day temptation can easily be fought. Hundreds of ideas went through my head. Finally, I said: 'No, I am a man and must be master over myself. Let the temptation be what it will.'

That was my final decision when I heard the heavy steps of Marie on the stairs. She went to her room, but must have left the door open as I could plainly hear her cough. I thought to myself: 'Whisper, whisper. It may be a signal for me, but I'm not coming.'

Not long afterward there came a knock on the door, and Marie was standing beside my bed, red and excited, indeed she was trembling. "Oho, Marie, what's the matter?" She: "I have to see whether you have a towel. Have you enough covers?" I: "Yes, thanks, this is a good bed." She: "Do you want some hot water in the morning to wash with?" I: "Very kind of you, Marie, good night." An old trick, known to every chambermaid.

Five minutes later she came again with a blanket. "Conrad, I think it will get colder during the night. You had better have the extra covering." And I: "That is really too good of you. Have you enough for yourself if you give me all these?" Marie: "Oh, yes. My room is much warmer. I think you have no idea how much I love you, Conrad!" "Yes, Marie, I can see that. I

259

have eyes, and feelings as well," I replied kindly. "Oh, that makes me very glad," she cried, throwing herself on the bed and weeping. "Marie, your parents will hear us if we talk so loud." "Oh, they won't hear us. Give me a kiss and then I'll go. Good night!" And she went to her room. It was a puzzle to me. Perhaps on her side it was real love, and not a dangerous trap at all?

Still, I am a greedy fellow! It would cost me nothing if I whispered a few words of love to her, if I kissed her and pressed her to my heart. I knew that I could approach her in a finer way than she was accustomed to. She would feel as if in Heaven if I treated her as my beloved. All these weak thoughts almost got the upper hand, and I was sorry that I had undertaken an adventure that would bring such deception upon the poor girl.

Then I said to myself once more: 'It is a trap just the same. Otherwise her mother would not have said: "That's where Marie sleeps." Otherwise Marie would not have entered my room.'

'If the night were only over. I would never enter the house again. Such adventures are not for me. My heart is too compassionate and my flesh too weak.' Thus I chatted with myself. Marie began to cough again. Well, the coughing disturbed the poor thing. She would surely be back. What would she have to say and ask this time? What would she want to know?

She came and stood in front of my bed, with tear-stained eyes, much aroused: "Conrad, did you hear a noise? Do you think someone is outside?" "I am surprised that the dogs don't bark," said I, thinking: 'Marie, Marie, I understand the noise. No one hears but you yourself. It is within you! The trap. Too dangerous for a fox who has once known the iron.'

"Conrad, I don't know what is the matter, I can't sleep," she whispered softly in my ear. "If you can't sleep, then stay where you are and tell me something," I answered. Marie hesitated: "Oh, that wouldn't be wise, my parents would hear us." ('Oh, the trickery of woman,' I thought, 'now the parents can hear us and a little while ago they couldn't.') "Come with me to my room, it is warmer there." But I thought it might be too warm for me, and replied: "Marie, I could not sleep in your room. We are not married yet." "There is another bed. Take the blanket and come. Carefully, the floor creaks."

Marie had the light in one hand, the pillow in the other. I stood up and took the blankets. Without a sound we went into her room.

CONRAD KAIN, BANFF, CA. 1911.

CONRAD KAIN, T.G. LONGSTAFF, "BERT" BARROW AND CHARLES LAWRENCE,
LONGSTAFF-WHEELER BUGABOO EXPEDITION, 1910.

JAMES SHAND-HARVEY, GEORGE KINNEY, CONRAD KAIN,
DONALD "CURLY" PHILLIPS, CHARLES WALCOTT JR., HARRY H. BLAGDEN,
NED HOLLISTER, J.H. RILEY AND A.O. WHEELER AROUND CAMPFIRE,
SMITHSONIAN-ACC ROBSON EXPEDITION, 1911.

CONRAD KAIN CLIMBING ROCK FACE DURING
SMITHSONIAN-ACC ROBSON EXPEDITION, 1911.

CONRAD KAIN ON SUMMIT OF MOUNT RESPLENDENT,
SMITHSONIAN-ACC ROBSON EXPEDITION, 1911.

BYRON HARMON ON SUMMIT OF MOUNT RESPLENDENT,
SMITHSONIAN-ACC ROBSON EXPEDITION, 1911.

GEORGE KINNEY, CONRAD KAIN AND DONALD "CURLY" PHILLIPS ON THE
SUNWAPTA RIVER ON RETURN FROM MALIGNE LAKE TO LAKE LOUISE,
SMITHSONIAN-ACC ROBSON EXPEDITION, 1911.

CONRAD KAIN AND DONALD "CURLY" PHILLIPS CROSS SUNWAPTA RIVER
ON HORSEBACK, SMITHSONIAN–ACC ROBSON EXPEDITION, 1911.

CONRAD KAIN DESCENDING SUMMIT RIDGE OF MOUNT RESPLENDENT,
SMITHSONIAN-ACC ROBSON EXPEDITION, 1911.

CONRAD KAIN, ALBERT H. MACCARTHY AND BASIL S. DARLING,
ROBSON ACC CAMP, 1913.

CONRAD KAIN, W.W. FOSTER AND ALBERT H. MACCARTHY
AFTER ASCENT OF MOUNT ROBSON, ROBSON ACC CAMP, 1913.

A.H. MACCARTHY, BESS MACCARTHY, CAROLINE HINMAN, CONRAD KAIN
AND UNIDENTIFIED BOY ON MOUNT RESPLENDENT, ROBSON ACC CAMP, 1913.

CONRAD KAIN (TOP) WITH TWO CLIMBERS ON THE GENDARME
OF MOUNT RESPLENDENT, ROBSON ACC CAMP, 1913.

CONRAD KAIN (TOP) WITH TWO CLIMBERS ON THE GENDARME
OF MOUNT RESPLENDENT, ROBSON ACC CAMP, 1913.

CONRAD KAIN ON GENDARME OF MOUNT RESPLENDENT,
ROBSON ACC CAMP, 1913.

BASIL S. DARLING, ALBERT H. MACCARTHY AND CONRAD KAIN,
ROBSON ACC CAMP, 1913.

BASIL S. DARLING, ALBERT H. MACCARTHY AND CONRAD KAIN,
ROBSON ACC CAMP, 1913.

MOUNT DE LA BÊCHE AND MINARETS, TASMAN GLACIER
AND SPUR ON MALTE BRUN RANGE, NEW ZEALAND, 1914.

CONRAD KAIN AND PETER GRAHAM, MOUNT SEFTON AND MOUNT COOK
FROM MAUNGA MA, (?) NEW ZEALAND, FEBRUARY 11, 1914.

CONRAD KAIN ON NORTHEAST ARÊTE OF MOUNT DARBY,
NEW ZEALAND, FEBRUARY 17, 1914.

CONRAD KAIN AND HERBERT OTTO FRIND, MIDDLE AND LOW PEAKS
OF MOUNT COOK, NEW ZEALAND, FEBRUARY 22, 1914. (?)

CONRAD KAIN ON CLASSEN SADDLE AND WATAROA PASS,
NEW ZEALAND, MARCH 7, 1914.

CONRAD KAIN BUILDING A CAIRN ON MOUNT CONRAD,
NEW ZEALAND, MARCH 9, 1914.

CONRAD KAIN AND ROBERT YOUNG ON SUMMIT
OF MOUNT SEFTON, NEW ZEALAND, MARCH 22, 1914.

MOUNT CONRAD FROM THE GODLEY RIVER, NEW ZEALAND, 1916.

CONRAD KAIN AND JANE THOMSON LEAVING FOR BALL HUT,
NEW ZEALAND, 1916.

CONRAD KAIN ON SUMMIT OF MOUNT COOK, NEW ZEALAND, 1916.

CONRAD KAIN ON TASMAN GLACIER, NEW ZEALAND, 1916.

CONRAD KAIN BESIDE CAIRN ON MOUNT DARBY, NEW ZEALAND, 1916.

CONRAD KAIN AT COOK BIVOUAC (8400 FEET) AND ST. DAVID'S DOME,
NEW ZEALAND, 1916.

JANE THOMSON ON SUMMIT OF MOUNT COOK, NEW ZEALAND, 1916.

ALBERT MACCARTHY AND CONRAD KAIN SURVEY THE SOUTH SPIRE
OF THE HOWSER GROUP, MACCARTHY–KAIN BUGABOO TRIP, 1916.

CONRAD KAIN ON THE GENDARME PITCH OF
BUGABOO SPIRE, PURCELL RANGE, 1916.

BESS MACCARTHY BEING LOWERED FROM THE GENDARME ON THE
DESCENT OF BUGABOO SPIRE, MACCARTHY–KAIN BUGABOO TRIP, 1916.

CONRAD KAIN, CATARACT CREEK ACC CAMP, 1917.

DR. CORA BEST, AUDREY SHIPPAM AND CONRAD KAIN AT MOUTH OF ICE
CAVE ON STARBIRD (HORSETHIEF) GLACIER, PURCELL RANGE, 1922.

DR. CORA BEST, AUDREY SHIPPAM AND CONRAD KAIN ON THE STARBIRD
(HORSETHIEF) GLACIER, PURCELL RANGE, 1922.

CONRAD KAIN IN HUT WITH MEMBERS OF
CORA BEST–AUDREY SHIPPAM PARTY, 1922?

CONRAD KAIN WITH MEMBERS OF CORA BEST–AUDREY SHIPPAM PARTY,
MOUNT ASSINIBOINE, 1922?

CONRAD KAIN AND WIFE HETTA IN FRONT OF THEIR HOME
IN WILMER, BC, CA. 1923.

HETTA KAIN IN WHEAT FIELD AT KAIN'S FARM
IN WILMER, BC, CA. 1923.

HETTA KAIN IN WHEAT FIELD AT KAIN'S FARM
IN WILMER, BC, CA. 1923.

CONRAD KAIN, J. MONROE THORINGTON AND JIMMY SIMPSON (LEFT TO
RIGHT SEATED, OTHER CLIMBER UNKNOWN) ON THE SUMMIT OF
MOUNT COLUMBIA, COLUMBIA ICEFIELD EXPEDITION, 1923.

CONRAD KAIN ON ICE WALL OF MOUNT ROBSON, ROBSON ACC CAMP, 1924.

CONRAD KAIN AND ANNETTE BUCK AT ROBSON ACC CAMP, 1924.

ALBERT AND BESS MACCARTHY, ROBSON ACC CAMP, 1924.

CONRAD KAIN PACKING SUPPLIES AT TIMBER LINE CAMP
ON MOUNT ROBSON, ROBSON ACC CAMP, JULY 1924.

CONRAD KAIN LEADS THE FIRST PARTY DEPARTING FOR MOUNT ROBSON
FROM TIMBER LINE CAMP DURING THE ROBSON ACC CAMP, 1924.

J. MONROE THORINGTON AND CONRAD KAIN (CENTRE) WITH COMPANIONS
AT "OLD CABIN" CAMP, DUTCH CREEK, SOUTHERN PURCELLS, JULY 24, 1930.

THORINGTON AND KAIN'S "MOSQUITO CAMP" AT THE HEAD OF
DUTCH CREEK, PURCELL RANGE, JULY 25, 1930.

CONRAD KAIN (LEFT) WITH J. MONROE THORINGTON (TOP) AND ANOTHER
CLIMBER, ATOP FINDLAY PEAK, SOUTHERN PURCELLS. JULY 30, 1930

CONRAD KAIN AT HIS HOME, WILMER, BC, *CA.* 1930.

HENRIQUITA "HETTA" KAIN AT HOME, WILMER, BC, CA. 1930.

CONRAD KAIN AND J. MONROE THORINGTON AT SUMMIT
OF TRAPPER PEAK, WAPTA ICEFIELD, JULY 1933.

CONRAD LETS LOOSE WITH ONE OF HIS JOYFUL TRADEMARK YODELS.

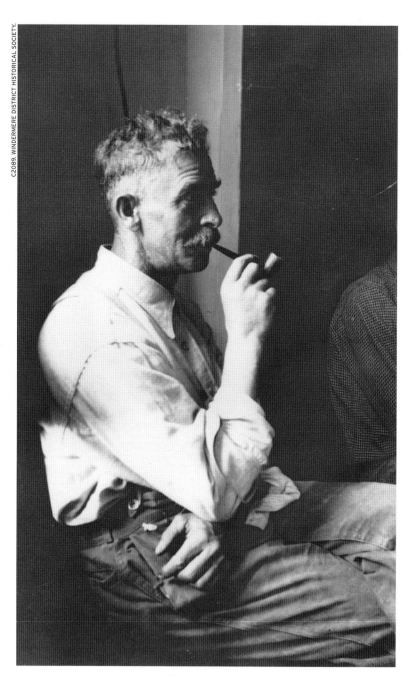

CONRAD KAIN, 1933.

7

BATTLE AGAINST DESIRE

Marie closed the door. I wrapped the blankets around me and she came back. "Well, Conrad, now we can talk loudly and openly. No one will hear us." She hugged me around the neck like a bear, and kissed me, saying: "Oh, how lovely it will be when we are married! I love you above all men. When shall we have our wedding? Don't keep me waiting too long, I can't bear it. You must marry me as soon as possible." In the meantime Marie had made up my bed. In order not to appear ungrateful I gave her a kiss, then put out the light and went to bed. Marie, too, returned to her bed.

In a little while she lit the candle again, and began to talk some more about the wedding. I sat up in bed and started on a stern lecture: "Now you listen to me, Marie! Marriage doesn't go so fast. First of all, my papers are in Austria; secondly, I must have the permission of my mother, whom I love very much. Without her knowledge I don't want to marry you or anyone else."

She was greatly disturbed and replied: "In Canada one doesn't need papers. What one says is what counts. And why must you first ask your mother? I will write to her first thing in the morning, and she will have nothing against it when she hears how much I love you." With these words she began to weep bitterly. I felt for her, but recalled that I had often heard the same thing before. Women can even shed false tears.

Marie sobbed: "God in Heaven, he doesn't love me. He does not see how I depend upon him." And I, to myself in the intervals: 'Herrgott, if this night were only over! I don't want any more adventures like this. Rather a mishap in the mountains, danger from wild beasts, than any more weak women. This affair is getting on my nerves!'

There was nothing else to do. I had to get up and quiet her. I stood beside her, took her hand and spoke to her kindly, asking her to be calm. I told her that I had made a great mistake in spending the night there at the farm, and that she should not have entered my room; then all these scenes would have been avoided. The girl came to herself and was quiet. I went back to bed. My words must have made a hypnotic impression upon her. She followed me and sat down on the bed, and began to speak once more: "Conrad, forgive me. I see that you are a good man. You love your mother, you are upright. But I am weak, and so much in love with you. I can't help myself."

These words softened me. Poor girl! I took her in my arms and spoke words of wisdom to her: "Later in your life, Marie, you will find that I have not treated you badly. Of a hundred men there are perhaps not more than ten who would talk so honestly to a woman as weak as you are." I held her hand and added many more kindly words, so that she and I did no experimenting.

At last she fell asleep. I remained awake, lying quietly, with Marie's head against me. At last the alarm clock went off. Marie awoke, and I went with a light heart back to my room.

I slept until the sun shone in my face: ten o'clock in the morning. What an unpleasant feeling: I have overslept in a strange house. At breakfast I encountered the farmer's wife and begged her pardon for rising so late. "Oh, that's quite natural," said the old woman, with a smile. "When winter comes it's time to sleep." Then she came closer and whispered: "Marie went in your room, I heard it." And, in serious tone, she asked: "Were you with her?" "No!" "Why not? It wouldn't have made any difference." Then, in a sorrowful voice: "Now I see why Marie cried. Oh, my poor Marie. It must be just as she told me; that you don't love her as she loves you. If you do love her, don't hold back. She is a strong, healthy girl, and it would be quite natural ... For a young Austrian you act very strangely! It doesn't matter if you go to Marie; certainly you would learn to know each other better!"

I know that I am not, and have never been, an angel. I have gone "window-gazing" in many parts of Austria, but my tongue never gave me away. Often from a window I heard: "You should have been a parson!" I have talked about love and its meaning with many girls and women, but never in my life had I heard a mother utter such words about her child.

8
"FENSTERLN"

A s I am on the subject of "Fensterln" [window-visiting], and these lines will possibly be read by some who do not know the mountains but may have heard what immoral life and manners exist there, I will explain clearly my observations of "Fensterln." I know the distinction between city and country life, so it is possible for me to look upon the matter from two sides.

"Fensterln" goes on chiefly in the mountain regions where the houses are separated and lonely and the young people are unable to meet as they do in cities. The young mountaineer has just as tender feelings toward the feminine sex as the young fellow in town. But how should one have opportunity of getting into a girl's company if perhaps one is working all week in the forest? And in the mountains there is not a dance or a concert every

Sunday, and the young mountaineer cannot invite his sweetheart for a walk or an excursion as the city man does, for the times and the customs of the country do not permit it.

But the young people want to get together. What else is there to do but to go to the window of one's beloved and chat for an hour or so? It is certainly unfair to think that every young girl who comes to the window when her good friend knocks is a light, weak thing. I often heard inexperienced people say: "Oh, let the peasant girls alone. They have no moral feelings. They are wantons. They'll open the window any time."

If one will consider the matter openly and broadly, I ask: "What can happen at the window, when the boy stands on a ladder? And even if an open window allows him to enter?" More than that can happen when one of the city fellows goes strolling with his sweetheart through the park. Or if two embrace on a bench or in a hidden corner. I see no difference. Whether in town or country it depends entirely upon mutual respect between the two people. How much respect the young man of the town has for his girl, and how much the peasant for his maiden. And turn about.

More than this, however, I regard the "Fensterln" for the mountain dweller as a special pleasure, almost as a sport. At the window he can show whether he is wise or stupid, cowardly or courageous. It would be narrow-minded to ask: "Oh, what need does a peasant, a woodcutter or a quarryman have for sport? He has sufficient exercise and fresh air." But "Fensterln" gives work to the mind as well. One can't understand that, who has never tried it.

Everyone who is well-acquainted with life in the mountains knows that there are often numerous obstacles: 1) The dog. 2) The position of the window, and how to reach it. 3) Where the old folks sleep. 4) What kind of ladder is needed, where to get it and many other things.

Going to the window is sometimes risky, so the affair has its own charm; for to overcome difficulties is what makes life and love sweet. Often it is a dog, or a stick, or the farmer's whip, or a bucket of water from above. It is especially dangerous if one starts this sort of thing in another village.

I am quite certain that many a girl has come to a bad end through sitting at a window. But is that worse than for a town girl to be seduced after too many glasses of champagne? And it is very sad that drugs are often used to put the helpless woman at the mercy of the fine gentleman. Certainly such a one is no gentleman. He who uses such methods to capture love is only a coward – a weakling.

9

THE EMBRYO FARMER TAKES LEAVE OF THE PRAIRIE

Now we must go back to Marie and her mother. I was anxious to go home. Naturally there were hearty farewells and an invitation for next Sunday, which I refused.

When I reached Peter's farm it was just as if I had been freed after arrest. I was sure that a long imprisonment could not be worse than that night on the farm. I am free, I am free. I felt myself *actually free*. I wanted to leave Peter and his farm so that I should hear and see no more of this adventure. But things did not happen as quickly as I wished. A horse was sick and we could not go for wood. And Peter needed more lumber. He begged me not to leave him; he would get another horse, and I should at least stay until Easter. When he secured the horse, the sick one died and the healthy one became ill. So there was great distress on the farm.

I had several more letters from Marie, which I did not answer, and avoided Phillips as much as possible, so that I would hear no more of Marie and her people. Several neighbours came in to see Peter on account of the sick horses. Some advice was given at this time to me, as a beginning farmer.

Spring arrived slowly. Here and there green patches gleamed in the endless meadows, chiefly in the moist places. It was always a joy to me to see the first signs of spring, but never before had they so depressed me. I had a longing for the mountains and for the forest. The dreary plain had made me tired out and melancholy. Only a few days more and then I would go back to the mountains.

On Ember Saturday I went to Fort Saskatchewan, for I was afraid that Marie would come to Peter's farm. But I could not escape my fate. On Easter Sunday I met her in the town. She had come after me and, after an unpleasant scene in the wagon, I was obliged to accompany her home again. On the way I made my viewpoint clear, declaring that I could never live with her on a farm. "I was born and grew up in the mountains, and have never been so long on the prairie as here. I know that I could not stand it, and would be sick at heart. Now you will easily see why I did not come any more."

But Marie did not understand it and, with many tears, tried to persuade me to alter my decision and remain. At the farm I took leave of Marie and her parents. All three wept. Finally, I would have been glad to weep with them – for very joy!

I think that, in this case, it will not be thought conceit when I say I was proud of having been a man, of having been master over myself. During a battle with a great experiment I had won the victory over myself.

10

A HORSE AS MATCHMAKER

I went on foot to Peter's farm and took leave of all my friends. Last of all I went to Uncle Phillips. In a very good humour he was sitting by the table with his pipe. "Halloh, Conrad!" he called. "Halloh, Phillips! I have come to say goodbye to you. I am leaving in the morning."

He was startled: "Well, aren't you going to marry Marie?" "No, I am not of a mind to." "Ach Gott, Conrad, you are trampling your future under your own feet. You are going away! How many would be happy if they could get Marie!" His wife came in from the stable. "Ella, just listen to this. Conrad is going away." Much surprised, she asked me: "Aren't you going to marry Marie?" "No, Mrs. Phillips." Then she broke down, weeping and moaning. "Ach, lieber Gott, and now we won't get our 'Charlie.' What shall we do? Conrad isn't going to marry Marie, and the black mare would have gone so well with our 'Prince' – they would have made a fine team. Now, with spring just around the corner, we have only one horse for the plough!"

When the lady began lamenting so, I could not understand what was really the matter. A little son of Phillips asked his older brother why his mother cried. "Oh, Mr. Kain isn't going to marry aunt Marie, and so we won't get the black mare from uncle." Then it all became clear to me. I was to have traded my liberty for a horse. It was to have been a marriage deal, with a reward for the accommodation. I wanted to give Phillips my view of the matter in real plain German. But when I saw that he was punished enough in not getting 'Charlie,' I remained silent, and left the matchmaker and his family behind me.

During my last walk to Peter's farm I wondered whether, if I had been a great statesman, with influence over the people, I would have proposed to Parliament that all such matchmakers and marriage merchants be punished with the same penalties served out to white slavers. For it is nothing else but an indirect traffic in girls. If such a law came into being, about 90 per cent of the upper 10,000 would be in cells.

The adventure was a good lesson for me. In the future I would avoid such. I need no help or advice on love and marriage. I think each man and woman should have independence and free choice in this matter. But I would have to go too deeply into the matter if I wrote anything more.

11

THE PRAIRIE AND ITS INHABITANTS

During the time I spent on the plains, I made numerous observations of the people. I am only sorry that I am not better educated, in order to put everything on paper that I should like to. But I shall try it anyway.

I believe that one can take it for granted that Nature makes a great impression upon the spiritual life, the thought and action of man. (By Nature I mean here the environment in which a person is.)

My observation, my conviction is that the dweller on the prairie is far less awake and alert than the inhabitant of the mountains and highlands. I found that the people of both sexes on the prairie were more stupid, dull and narrow-minded. Often they appeared tired of life. During my visits I noticed that it did not matter to them if one did not speak for half an hour, even if one was in their company on the road. The men are as uninteresting as the prairie itself.

The one really magnificent thing afforded the eye in all that dreary waste is the sunset. Without those splendid sunsets, life there would have been quite unbearable for me. In summer it may possibly be different and more pleasant, when one has the green of fields and meadows for miles before one's eyes. But if one wishes to describe the prairie in its winter dress the matter is soon finished: an endless white expanse, here and there a farm, a little house, haystacks on a snowy field, a few horses and cows scattered about. All quiet as the dead! Only the wind springs up and plays its game, sighing and whistling, while far away, at night, the prairie wolves are howling.

[Conrad Kain in his 27th year. Thus ends his journal.]

CALGARY, MAY 4TH, 1910 ◆ *On March 20th I left the farm and went to Edmonton. It was too early in the season to get work, so there was nothing for me to do but go north where there was railway construction, 200 miles northwest of Edmonton. We could go 100 miles by train and then had to travel four days on foot. Never in my life will I forget it! Mostly through bush, but twice we had to ford the river. Snow water! At last we reached camp. That was a pleasure, but not for long. On the first night I discovered that everyone was lousy. When one is away from the civilized world it is hard to describe what one must undergo.*

Each person has but one set of clothing. On Sundays most of them clean up as well as possible. Not a woman to be seen. I was there scarcely a week when a severe accident occurred in which I was almost involved. Three workmen were killed by a slide: a Swede and two Galicians. All nationalities are to be found on this work.

Now imagine the burial: 200 miles from church and cemetery. It is almost impossible to transport dead bodies so far, and no use either. There was a delay of four days until the police arrived. Burial on the fifth day. That was unpleasant – without a priest. More than 300 workmen were present. A last resting place was found in a corner of the valley. There were no coffins, the dead being shrouded in sacks and all three placed in a single grave.

Services were held in four languages: German, Swedish, English and Polish. I was the one to present the German version. I could not get out of it. I had two days to prepare. The two Galicians were married and had families in the Old Country. But the matter affected me deeply and I did not want to make any more grave speeches. Many Germans thanked me afterwards, one even suggesting that I preach a sermon on the following Sunday. The religious faith of the two Galicians could not be discovered. The Swede was a Lutheran.

On April 29th I went back to Edmonton. Yesterday, May 2nd, I continued to Calgary.

12

ACROSS THE PURCELL RANGE

The prairie adventure is finished forever. No more of the flat country with its scheming women for Conrad Kain. Married? A farmer? Perish the thought! Anything like that must be put far away in the future. The train carries him to Edmonton, and along the frontal range to Calgary. There are the beloved mountains once again, a shining wall mantled in the snows of spring!

Wheeler's diary continues:

1910 MAY 12TH ◆ *Conrad went with me to Banff – working on tent houses, etc.*

JUNE ◆ *Working at clubhouse.*

JULY 4TH ♦ *Conrad and Oliver (my son) went to Field.*

JULY 5TH ♦ *With pack train up Yoho Valley for ACC camp (subsidiary camp) there.*

JULY 9TH ♦ *At Consolation Valley Camp – construction and operation.*

JULY 30TH ♦ *Conrad ascended Mt. Fay with W.S. Ladd and S.H. Mitchell.*[40]

BANFF. SEPTEMBER 22–25, 1910 ♦ *The weather was not of the best. Camp was close to a really lovely lake (Consolation Lake). The peaks were easy to reach. On the very first day we had some difficulty. I was guiding two women and a man. The man and one of the women had never been on a big climb, so it went slowly. We were out 18 hours. One of the Swiss guides was on the mountain the same day. On the following day we were out 16 hours and never reached the top.*

Twenty people in all. On Mt. Fay one day and on Mt. Bident the next. After that we put up a higher camp, from which climbs could be made very easily.

Then we camped in Larch Valley, from which I climbed Mt. Temple, the highest peak of the district. Camp was situated between two little lakes amidst many flowers. I ascended Mt. Temple a second time, and also Mt. Eiffel. On the latter I had a poor party: a heavy woman, a man who was almost blind, and two young boys. One would scarcely believe that they could be gotten up, but I did my best and was congratulated.

There was a day of rest afterward, and in the evening I had to tell a story at the campfire. I did not want to, but the people said that I spoke English well enough. So I told them of my experiences in the Enns Valley during an adventurous ascent of the Ödstein. My next tour was up Mt. Fay with a gentleman. It was a magnificent day. On the same day Dr. Longstaff broke a finger during a climb. When we sympathized, he said: 'Oh, there has to be an accident once in a while.'

On August 1st Conrad left the railway with the Bow River Expedition,[41] in which Dr. and Miss Longstaff, Miss Vaux, Harmon, Fred Bell and others took part.

A transcontinental train was at the station as we filed past and our cortège seemed to afford its passengers as much astonishment and spec-

ulation as did the arrival of Tartarin in the lobby of the Rigi-Kulm.... The Doctor, with his arm in a sling fashioned from an enormous scarlet bandanna and mounted on a wild-eyed cayuse, was easily the most conspicuous figure in the cavalcade.... Charlie Logan and an earnest flow of most unparliamentary language brought up the rear.

From Bow Lake the party crossed the Waputik snowfield through Vulture Col to Yoho Glacier, Conrad's letter continuing the story:

On July 31st we started on the six-day trip to Bow Lake. When it was over some of the people stayed with me in Yoho Valley. We ascended some peaks, one of them new. On my 27th birthday I climbed Mt. Habel. A fine morning with splendid view. During the afternoon the weather changed and we got into an electrical storm, so fierce that I thought it would probably be my last birthday. My hair stood up straight in the air. We were on rock, but when we reached snow things improved. The ice axes hummed like grass in the wind.

There were two English ladies in camp, with whom I climbed six peaks. They had been in Tyrol, Salzburg and Styria but spoke no German. We went over a pass to Emerald Lake and then back to camp at Summit Lake. A long day! On August 23rd I crossed The President in much new snow with a young married couple to Emerald Lake and Field.

Wheeler notes:

AUGUST 26TH ♦ *Working at clubhouse.*
AUGUST 30TH ♦ *Left for Bugaboo trip[42] with self, Longstaff and Harmon. With Capt. Armstrong on the Klahowya, via Columbia River.*
SEPTEMBER 4TH ♦ *Dr. Longstaff shot three grizzlies. C. helped skin them. Assisting me with photo survey of Bugaboo–Howser Pass and vicinity.*

The Purcell Range rises between the Rockies and the Selkirks, south of the Canadian Pacific Railway, and the plan was to cross its divide from the Columbia to the Duncan Valley and travel north, so that the survey could be connected with old stations on the Prairie Hills, returning to the Columbia by another pass. But the country was really unknown, and the actual difficulties turned out to be too great for the time at the party's disposal.

However, one of the earliest and most important explorations in the Purcells was the result, bringing mountaineers for the first time into close contact with the group of magnificent spires, on which notable ascents would be made in years to come. Here were pinnacles and towers like the needles of Chamonix shooting toward the sky, their roots in a splendid glacier. This would be a battle ground; not only muscles, but all the tricks and art of climbing would be required.

Conrad was thrilled, regretting only that time did not permit him to remain and attack them at once.

SEPT. 22ND ◆ *Longstaff and Harmon with trapper travelled down Howser Creek to return home via Howser City and Lake. Conrad and I took back trail with pack train and occupied photo stations.*
OCT. 1ST ◆ *Back at Spillimacheen.*
OCT. 4TH ◆ *Conrad went back to Banff to work at clubhouse. Worked until Oct. 29th.*

This is the letter Kain sent home to Austria:

BANFF. SEPTEMBER 22–25 ◆ *Now I know what it is to be the first one through a new and unmarked valley. For the first days it was not so bad for there was a trapper's trail, but there were many laborious hours when this came to an end and we had to make our own way.*

On September 4th I went with rifle to get meat and succeeded in shooting a mountain goat. I took the skin and the four feet and so had a heavy load. I must descend a steep cliff very carefully, and then had a wide Alpine meadow before me. There I saw a brown bear and followed him without success. I fired twice, but was too far away. But I ran so that my heart and lungs nearly gave out. I had to lie down for a while. It grew dark. I didn't think that I would have to spend the night under a tree, but it had to be, as progress through the bush and windfalls was so slow. I rolled my burden down for quite a bit, and much time went by before I found the rifle. I had no lantern and was so tired that at last could go no farther.

I had a load of 30–35 kilos; it began to rain. I lay under a tree and tried to make a fire. What a nuisance! Matches and wood both wet. With a heavy sigh I struck the last match: it flickered and went out. So I covered myself with the goat skin, which protected me from the rain.

But it grew so cold that I had to get up. Pitch dark and not a star to be seen. Finally, at five o'clock, I left and reached camp in an hour.

Everything was quiet, everyone asleep. I got breakfast, changed my clothing and discovered to my astonishment that Dr. Longstaff had shot three grizzly bears. It snowed hard. Impossible to take the instruments up a mountain; one could see nothing. So I went with Dr. Longstaff and a packer to get the skins. Then I made goat soup, with rice, potatoes and flour stirred in. Dr. L. said it saved his life!

To improve our humour we held an Indian dance. Dr. L. and the two packers put on the bear hides and I the goat skin. Mr. Harmon, the photographer, was the band. His instruments the pans. So we danced about the fire, making a terrific din.

Next day we ascended a small peak and made a station. We spent five hours on top. My work was to make a cairn when the measurements were completed. The view was unique. A fine glacier, and aiguilles that will probably not be easy to climb.

On September 9th the horses had hard work in going over a pass. Mr. Harmon and Dr. Longstaff, as well as the two packers, in one place had to rope up the horses just as if they had been tourists! Until one sees it, it is impossible to believe what the horses must do. Dr. L. remained on the pass, making camp.

We had another peak to climb, but there was a foot of new snow next morning. We had provisions for only one more day. So I went into the valley on the other side to shoot something. I glissaded back to camp, seeing the fresh track of a huge bear. I returned to the pass and shot two grouse with my pistol. That evening we had a mulligan for supper. We sat by the fire until eleven o'clock and Dr. L. told me about his travels in the Caucasus.

Two days later camp was moved as far as the trail had been cut, and as we had no meat left I went goat hunting. The sun sank behind the mountains and I had shot nothing. I went over one more ridge. There I saw an old billy, far below me. I fired, and at the second shot the poor animal fell down over the wall. Next morning there was liver ragout for breakfast.

Then up a peak with the instruments. Dr. L. went out to shoot a grizzly. It was 'washday' for Mr. Harmon. In descending we came close to a bear cub, but Mr. W. had only a revolver and we could not kill him.

After five days of sawing trees and wading streams we came to a good trail. Halloh! All over! But the joy did not last. I went ahead and met a man. I called to him and he was much surprised, inquiring, 'Where do you come from?' 'From the Bugaboo Valley.' 'How many of you are there?' 'Six men and ten horses.' 'Well, you can't get the horses any farther.' I: 'What's the name of this stream?' 'Howser Creek.' We thought it was Reno Creek. He sat down and the man told us about the lay of the land. He was a trapper.

At last the horses came along. Mr. W. could not believe we were on the wrong trail. We looked over the situation and saw that there was nothing to do but turn back. Dr. L. and Mr. H. had to take the nearest way to civilization, so the trapper guided them to Howser Creek. So four of us were left.

At the pass I left Mr. W. and went out with the rifle. I had Dr. Longstaff's 'Mannlicher' and thought I would soon get something, as there were fresh tracks. I saw a goat but did not want to climb up to it in the new snow. So I went expectantly across the meadow. I followed a grizzly track but it went into a thicket. I continued up the slope, hoping to see a deer, and luckily got one close to camp. It was almost dark, but the bullet went through its head, killing the animal on the spot.

Things were different in camp that night. A few minutes after my arrival the meat was sizzling in the pan and there was a 'double portion' for everyone. The packers were glad the horses had come back across the pass and were on a trail once more.

On our last day in we made 15 miles. It was pleasant to see a covered table once more and a good bed with sheets. But I could not sleep – it was too soft and comfortable! The others said the same. The place is called Spillimacheen, 40 miles from Golden on the railway.

Finally the little steamer came and took us to Golden, where I had a hot bath and slept for 14 hours. Next evening I was in Banff.

CHAPTER X

(1911)

1

CANADIAN SPRING

BANFF. MARCH 8TH, 1911 ◆ *Now I am back in Banff from the survey. While in camp I often wanted to write, but it was too cold and often I was too tired.*

On December 20th I left Banff with the outfit and on the 22nd we made the first camp, five miles distant. During the day we had hard work. We had to cut trails through the bush, and that naturally brought down snow from the trees. It wouldn't have mattered much except that the cold snow would fall in one's face and down one's neck.

We were in Banff for the Christmas celebration. In the second week of January a fearful storm came, with great cold. For three days no train got through. The coldest day was –52°. It may have been a little warmer in the tent, but not much, for we had a bad stove. It would not burn well, except on one evening – and then the tent caught fire. Luckily we could save most of the things, but my blankets are badly burned. I was damaged the most, for I was not in camp that evening. I had gone with the dogs to Banff to get provisions, and reached camp at one o'clock in the morning, half-frozen. We always wore snowshoes. The snow was 4–5 feet deep. One always sleeps clothed. One gets hardened to it.

Minus 20° does not seem so cold, but when it goes below –30° then all comfort ceases, and during such weather one's thought often turns toward home or to a warmer climate. One fellow froze his hands and ears, and others left the work. The engineer in charge wanted to take me with him for two years to Hudson Bay, but I told him that I did not want to go so far from the mountains. He gave me a good recommendation in Banff. I have often used the instruments without making serious mistakes. To be sure, there is no great skill required, but no workman in Austria would ever be allowed to do such a thing.

Now I am cutting ice at $2.50 per day. I have not spoken German for so long that I am almost afraid I shall forget it.

Several weeks ago I founded a ski club in Banff. The people seem to take to this sport. We practise every Sunday, jumping as well, and many people assemble. My longest jump is 50 feet, about 12 feet beyond the last record.

I remember watching the skating when I was in Vienna. How poor I was then – could not skate and could not join in. But it will be otherwise when I am there again. Now I can skate and have the money. I am continually thinking of home, of my mother and my good friends. But I have no desire to remain there, for it is certain that Canada is better for a workman; he has a freer course and more opportunity.

MARCH 25TH ◆ At our winter sport festival we had more than 400 onlookers. It lasted all night. We had more than 100 lamps. A tent was put up and refreshments sold. We collected 55 dollars. I think I have made a good beginning. Yesterday a lady, sent by the railway, came to me for information as to the possibilities here for ski and toboggan. I talked to her about sport for nearly two hours.

Spring is on the way, and Nature will again put on her green mantle. All fresh and new once more. Is it not the same with men? Winter makes us sleepy with thought, and spring awakes us. The past comes to mind. I recall that three years ago today we made our lovely excursion in the Wienerwald.

APRIL 23RD ◆ I had a fine trip at Easter. I left Banff in company of a friend who was new to such things. In the afternoon we went by train to Field and on to Emerald Lake. The snow was good and I did not put on snowshoes. We made eight miles in three and a half hours. The lake was frozen.

On such occasions one does not carry blankets. One sits up most of the night or makes two fires, lying between them. Everything so quiet and still. My friend, who was tired, slept well for several hours. I stayed awake and kept up the fire, smoking my pipe while the happiest thoughts ran through my head. Of how the trees looked at home and how the birds sang.

At five o'clock I began to prepare breakfast. It was simple enough: coffee, bread and some bits of bacon, cooked over the open fire. All meat that has been put on a spit and held in the fire tastes good. At six o'clock we left our camping place and went on to Summit Lake, to go into Yoho Valley. By ten o'clock the sun shone so warmly that we lay down on a rock and went to sleep.

We reached Summit Lake about one o'clock. The snow was 10–12 feet deep. We stopped for lunch. There were splendid winter landscapes to see, altogether different from those of summer. Then we wanted to take the upper trail into the Little Yoho, but the snow was too soft. So we altered our plan and went through the forest to Takakkaw Fall, making our second camp there on Easter Sunday.

There was plenty of fuel, and we made a good bed with branches on the snow. The fire was also on the snow and by morning it had sunk through to the earth eight feet below. The night was not so pleasant. A heavy snowstorm arose and there was no question of sleeping. We got up about four o'clock and started for Field. There was six inches of new snow, but this did not hinder us.

At daybreak it was indescribably beautiful. On the way to Field we met Dr. Longstaff, who had discovered we were on this trail. We stopped, made tea and then went on. We reached Field about one. My dead-tired friend fell into bed and went to sleep. I went for a walk with Dr. Longstaff.

My friend left for home, and on Tuesday I accompanied Dr. Longstaff to Hector. Thence we went to Sherbrooke Lake, where the Club Camp had recently been. On the same evening, I returned to Banff.

Today, Sunday the 23rd of April, I have been with a friend on a canoe trip on Bow River, six miles from Banff. On the way back we met some acquaintances and had afternoon tea in the bush.

Now I am going to British Columbia. All alone, as I have not found a companion. It will be hard work, for I must carry my pack for 20 miles, and not everyone can stand that! I will make a few first ascents. This excursion will cost me some money, but I think it will be a great adventure.

ON THE WAY TO THE BEAR HUNT, NINE MILES FROM SPILLIMACHEEN, IN THE FOREST UNDER AN OLD TREE BESIDE A GOOD WARM CAMPFIRE. EVENING. MAY 3RD, 1911 ◆ *This morning at eight I crossed the Columbia and Spillimacheen rivers by ferry, and soon was in the green forest I had been longing for all winter. There were scarcely any flowers to be seen, only the tiny March violets. The soft grass was but a few days old. The mountains were still covered with winter snow, which their southern situation had not led me to expect. It is quite possible that the snow will halt my program. I am tired and sleep well. My bed is beneath a huge tree, four metres from the fire.*

MAY 4TH ◆ *I spent a good night. The moon shone clearly for a little while; this morning, a little rain. For breakfast I made a Naßwald Schmarrn and coffee. I left camp about six and followed the brook. The path became worse: windfalls and snow. Rain in addition. About ten o'clock I saw an avalanche go down the opposite side of the valley, the wind almost throwing me to the ground. I thought of the avalanche on the Rax.*

I stopped for lunch from twelve until one: bread and butter, cocoa, bacon, onions. Then onward for half an hour through the green forest, where I plainly saw an old bear track. Then into burned timber once more. It rained harder and the snow was deeper. I stopped at six and made camp under two dry trees beside the brook, trying to make a tent with the cloth I had brought for the purpose. But it didn't work out, so I made an Indian shelter of branches, some of which I had to carry 100 yards. In the evening I made the necessary snowshoes. I lay down at ten o'clock, rather tired. My roof was not watertight. A storm arose shortly after midnight and I found myself in water.

MAY 5TH ◆ *I arose about half past three and cooked my breakfast: pancake and cocoa. I was wet and rather cold. I took the teakettle and axe and something to eat and left camp at 4:30, following the brook for several hundred yards, then felling a tree as a bridge. I reached a plateau where I had been surveying with Mr. Wheeler in the autumn. Then onward toward the southeast to a pass, from whence I could see the mountain I wanted to climb.*

I took 20 minutes for rest, made tea and left everything except ice axe and snowshoes. The peak is very monotonous. Constantly I thought I was near the top, and always something intervened. Finally I reached it at half past two. It was snow covered with huge cornices, on which account Mr. Wheeler had called it 'Mt. Cornice.'[43] I could not build a cairn, for no stones were available. The view was poor, all in fog with flurries of snow.

About 1,000 feet below the summit I built a cairn and left a cocoa tin with my name in it. It is likely that I was the first person there. The mountain may be above 10,000 feet. During the descent I had fine glissades. The snow in the woods was six or eight feet deep. At nine o'clock I arrived in camp, having seen six goats on the way. I shot one of them so as to have fresh meat. I saw no bear tracks, but think it still too early and too cold.

MAY 6TH ✦ *Today the weather is very bad, with rain and a cold wind. I slept until ten o'clock and was rather stiff after yesterday's tour. I had liver and dumplings, roasted goat meat, rice and tea. Now it is six o'clock in the evening and it is clearing a little. I am lying before my Indian shelter, writing down the day's events – which have not been much besides eating!*

I have fixed up my camp somewhat, but injured my leg with the axe, not seriously. Before going to bed I shall go out once more with the rifle, and also hang a fishline in the water.

The surroundings of my camp are beautiful: burned timber in the foreground, with green trees behind, and, still farther back, the snowy peaks and two large glaciers. The valley is narrow, the rock reddish like that of the Dolomites. The stream is in flood and makes a great rushing noise. I like to hear it.

SUNDAY, MAY 7TH ✦ *Last night I slept well in my improved bed. I woke about half past six. It was a lovely morning. Before lighting fire for breakfast I went out with my rifle to an elevation and looked things over. But there was nothing to see but two marmots.*

Today I have been thinking of myself as a lucky fellow, well treated by Nature. I keep Sunday according to ancient law and have nothing to do. I am really alone in the wilderness. In one direction the nearest person is 15 miles away, while on the other side I know not how far.

Alone in the wilderness! What do you think? Is that to be envied? Not everyone would give me the same answer to this question. Many would say it was foolish, but I think it splendid. Not everyone can have the joy of spending some time in the wilds. Many have not the strength to endure it; others lack the physique to carry all their necessities on their backs. Many would not know what to take so that the burden would not be too great. Many do not know how to cook. Some who have the strength, fear the loneliness. They wouldn't spend a single hour alone in a forest where there are all sorts of wild creatures. But I have always had a taste for it. Now I must cook lunch. I am lucky – I caught a fish.

The meal is over. Dumplings, rice, fish, roasted goat, coffee and now a pipe! There can't be a finer life. But it won't last long. A few weeks from now I must go to work. But still I enjoyed my vacation.

WEDNESDAY, MAY 10TH ✦ *Monday the weather grew worse again. New snow on the ground, and I considered what to do. I would so much like to kill a big grizzly, but it is too early in the season. Spring arrives later. A mile from my camp the snow is still two or three feet deep. So I decided to go where there was less of it, and left camp at ten o'clock.*

On emerging from the burned timber I met a black bear in the bush. I fired and wounded him. He made an awful noise and quickly disappeared. I followed his tracks but could not find him. It is a dangerous thing to follow a wounded bear in the thickets. I did it with great care. When I came out again I had almost no trousers, and most of my shirt was missing. All torn to ribbons. I wondered how I should get back to Banff. Perhaps someone will lend me trousers until I can buy some.

After this adventure I went on for three miles to the vicinity of my first camp. Oh, how quickly Nature changes in springtime. Between May 3rd and 8th the grass had grown perceptibly, and some marigolds were out. One could scarcely believe it had happened so quickly.

By evening I was quite tired, but the beauty of it all refreshed me. The birds were singing sweetly once again. I slept in an old bear trap: a deadfall, of course not set! The moon shone down.

On Tuesday I got up early to mend my clothes. Then I went back to the place where I had shot the bear. After long search I found blood on a patch of snow. I think I hit his paw. With much hard work I made two deadfalls. A warm rain was falling as I returned to camp. I made a hut out of the old trap and slept well.

Today, Wednesday, it has been raining hard. There is new snow on the mountains. About eight o'clock it began to clear into a beautiful day.

In the forenoon I pottered around camp, then went along the brook to the remains of a bridge where there is an old mine. The stream goes through a gorge, and I followed the far bank for two miles. Then back again, and I lay down in the warm sunlight while many thoughts and plans ran through my head.

I could not tear myself away from the spot. Had I ever seen such fresh green grass before? I cannot remember. Then the gorge, with the foaming water, the snow on the peaks, the songs of the birds. What a shame that there are no cuckoos in this country.

On the way back I passed a beaver dam. They are the most intelligent of all animals. A human being could not build a better dam. Then I shot a grouse. I was sorry, but what could one do? In the wilderness one must live off the land, for it is impossible to carry everything one needs. This evening I had a mulligan: beans, rice, grouse, onions and a cup of cocoa.

Now it is after eight o'clock. The sun has gone behind the mountains. I think there will be a full moon, but there are so many clouds that it may not break through.

THURSDAY, MAY 11TH ◆ *Today I left camp at six and went for a long distance through the dense forest. Hard work! I was close to a cougar, a mountain lion. What a shame I could not kill him! But I saw him for only a moment in the thick bush, and it was impossible to follow.*

I rested from one until two o'clock, finding an easier route for return. I slept for a little while beside the brook. I shot two grouse on my way back to camp: one for my supper and one for noon tomorrow. Now I am baking bread. It looks as if it would turn out well. Yesterday it was not so good: too little heat or something.

Tomorrow I must look at the bear traps.

FRIDAY, MAY 12TH ◆ *Rain all day without ceasing. New snow far down in the valley. Tomorrow I shall go out to the Columbia Valley. If I am lucky I won't have to wait long for the boat. I must go ten hours on the water and another eight by train. What a shame that the weather was not better for hunting. But on that account I had the more opportunity for observing the advance of spring.*

If I had time and money I would make a similar trip in the fall, but I want to go home in 1912 and so must save my dollars.

SATURDAY, MAY 13TH ◆ *Today I went down the valley in pouring rain. Wet to the skin! Fortunately I caught the boat for Golden, and we shall be there at ten o'clock tomorrow morning and at Banff that evening.*

THE CLUBHOUSE, BANFF. MAY 14TH ◆ *All the hotels are opening. The CPR Hotel has been enlarged during the winter to 120 rooms. There are a few strangers here, a sign that spring is coming although there is not much of it to be seen. The seasons go directly from winter into summer. In southern British Columbia everything was lovely and green, the flowers growing, birds singing and women busy in the gardens. Here the frost has not even gone out of the ground.*

2

EXPEDITION TO YELLOWHEAD PASS

Conrad's favourite book in the library of the clubhouse at Banff was "The Animals' Alpine Club," a picture book with plates in colour of all the animals of the world in mountaineering attire and in climbing attitudes.

Dr. T.G. Longstaff, of Himalayan and Arctic fame, writes appreciatively of Kain:

> *In April 1911, I made with him some day snowshoe trips – over Tunnel Mtn., over Lake Louise, over Sherbrooke Lake, Emerald Lake etc. And I met him on other occasions.*
>
> *He was a real companion – interested in hunting and natural history as well as in climbing, with a love of fine scenery not common in guides. Happy and generating cheerfulness in his company. Very enterprising. With all the charm of an Austrian together with the competence of a Teuton. I remember him with affection, as I respect his manly qualities and envy him his power of inspiring confidence on a climb.*

The Expedition to Yellowhead Pass,[44] sponsored by the Alpine Club of Canada in this year, proved an important event for Conrad. As one of its members he met Donald (Curly) Phillips, of Jasper, well-known as a trapper and outfitter, and the naturalist Ned Hollister, of the US National Museum, both of whom would influence his life. Kain and Rev. G.B. Kinney left Banff for Edmonton on June 29, 1911.

Leaving Edmonton for the west on July 1st by way of the Grand Trunk Pacific train, they began survey work at Brulé Lake. A stop was made at Swift's ranch, Swift himself being an old prospector and miner who had settled there years before. Conrad and Kinney ascended Pyramid Mountain, building a cairn that could be seen from Swift's with the aid of a glass. This was the beginning of the first topographical survey of what are now Jasper Park and Mt. Robson Park.

IN THE PRIMEVAL FOREST, TEN MILES BEYOND YELLOWHEAD PASS. 8 P.M., JULY 10TH ◆ *I am now about 350 miles north of Banff. I am sitting under a big tree, surrounded by flowers. I shall send you some of them, but they will of course lose their beauty before arriving in Reichenau.*

At the railway construction camp of "Moose City," Conrad had his clothes stolen, almost off his back, and the cook's stove was abstracted while he was practically sitting on it. The West was still Wild in those days.

MOOSE LAKE. JULY 23RD ◆ *Not incorrectly is this called the 'Wild West.' No houses, no roads; only old Indian trails. The valleys are wet and boggy, and one often sinks in to the knees. We have already ascended some mountains. They are not difficult, but the getting there! On our first excursion we were almost buried by an avalanche, and Mr. Harmon had to photograph it at the very worst moment!*

This afternoon I shot a goat and Harmon took my picture as a hunter. I cannot describe the vast extent of these mountains. As far as the eye can see there are peaks, snowfields, glaciers and valleys. But the little flies bite so that one has little pleasure in the aspects of Nature. Luckily they do not go above timber.

Kinney contributes the following recollections:

Conrad was a choice spirit at a mountain camp or on the trail or on a climb, and our campfire gatherings and little parties rocked with mirth at the tales and capers of this lover of Nature.

We were locating for the first time hundreds of miles of the interprovincial boundary line between Alberta and British Columbia, and Wheeler got out the first official map of that region because of our work that season.

Once, as we were on a peak to the east of Mt. Robson, a train whistled far to the south of us. There was a good-sized peak [now Mt. Bridgland] in that region, and Mr. Wheeler said: "We will name that peak 'Mt. Toot-toot.'" Frequently, from that time on, Conrad would give a toot or two to emphasize some occasion.

We were never given our promised chance at Mt. Robson on that trip, and soon left the region.

On July 16th, during the circuit of Mt. Robson, a survey station was made at the extremity of the eastern arête of Lynx Mountain.

This also is on the line of the watershed and commands a splendid view of the peaks encircling Resplendent Valley. One in particular commanded attention. It rises from the centre of a snow massif, like a huge rock finger pointing heavenward. On seeing it Conrad exclaimed: 'Ach! That is my peak.' So the snow-covered mass was recorded as Mt. Kain and the great rock finger thereafter referred to as the 'Finger of Kain.'

ON A LITTLE PEAK OF THE WATERSHED, 8500 FT. JULY 30TH ♦ *As we spend 4–5 hours on every summit surveying, with which I have nothing to do, I use the time to write. We have been almost a month in the mountains and have seen many beautiful things and done much hard work.*

I am seated on a sharp rocky ridge, with nothing about me but peaks. To the right the wall falls several hundred yards to a glacier. On the left there is shale, also ending on glacier. To the southwest Mt. Robson, 'King of the Rockies,' stands out clear and distinct. Not far away is Mt. Kain and the 'Finger of Kain,' of which I am very proud. The finger is an elegant rock needle, reminding me of the Aiguille du Géant.

This is the eighth ascent we have made. Our camp is situated on a meadow at timberline. The grass is fresh and green, with many flowers in it. Yesterday was Sunday, the first time we had all been together. Twelve persons. Services were held in camp.

It is interesting to see how specimens are collected for the museum. Every method is used. Traps are even put high in the trees. One of the professors said to me: 'One could go about in the mountains for a hundred years and still find little animals that are unknown.'

Now Mr. Wheeler is finished and my job is to build a cairn. Then back to camp.

ON A PEAK NOT FAR FROM THE OTHER. NOON. AUGUST 12TH ♦ *When I had built the cairn we went down scree and snow to the right-hand glacier. At six o'clock we were in camp. Four caribou were shot. A better night than last, as it was quite cold. When the nights are warm there is not much sleeping, the mosquitoes are so bad. Much worse than at Banff.*

This morning we went over alpland for an hour to the glacier. A fine view of Mt. Robson. Two hours more up the glacier and then up a broken ridge of rock, very troublesome for Mr. Wheeler and Mr. Kinney.

Now I am sitting on the summit, a little apart from the others, watching the clouds travel from one peak to another. It is quite warm and I am in my shirt sleeves. We have been two months on our expedition and my beard has grown rather long in that time. We have still much work ahead.

On the way to Reef Glacier Station an ice slope covered by snow was crossed. Conrad was leading, with Wheeler following. Wheeler describes the incident:

Suddenly my feet flew from under me and I shot downward.... I saw Conrad come leaping down the slope with reckless bounds, a look of horror in his eyes. The worst that can befall a professional guide is to lose his man. He grabbed me by the shoulder and gasped, 'I've got you' – and then he began to slide himself. My axe held, and we were soon on our feet.

Conrad and Harmon shot two goats, a welcome addition to the larder. A little later Conrad was detailed to build a raft for crossing Moose River. Hunting was more in his line, and this was his first raft; as a result, instead of holding three, according to specifications, it would carry only one at a time. Phillips, a skilled river man, took it across, but Conrad got a ducking.

The station on Ptarmigan Mountain was a splendid viewpoint. Conrad picked out what he considered a feasible line of ascent on Mt. Robson, making the prediction that the day would come when the ascent would be made in eight hours from a camp at Robson Pass.

In cloudy weather, but much to their satisfaction, Conrad and Harmon made the first ascent of Mt. Resplendent. They returned late to camp, Harmon rushing in gasping, "A bear! a bear!" Conrad had been left to herd it while Harmon came on for the hunters. Rifles cracked in the dusk, but the wounded animal escaped.

Wet and cloudy weather continued. Overcome by ennui, Conrad went off one afternoon and did not come back at night. The rain poured in torrents. A good blaze was kept up, and rifles were fired at intervals, but no Conrad. He returned next morning, saying he had made the first ascent of Mt. Whitehorn.

This was his account of it:

3

THE FIRST ASCENT OF MT. WHITEHORN[45]

On the 12th of August I got off in good time, and went to the fly camp, where I found Mr. Wheeler and Mr. Kinney at timberline, half an hour from the main camp. We waited there till ten o'clock and had to return on account of fog. I could stand it no longer, being among beautiful mountains without climbing one. I left camp at half past to climb Mt. Whitehorn. I went so fast that it would not have been possible to take anyone with me. I crossed the glacier to a moraine and followed the rocks, which led me directly to the pass. From there, I had to descend 300 feet. After a very dangerous threading of the numerous crevasses, I reached the southwest ridge. Rain and thunder! I thought of turning back, but decided to go on, for I knew that it was my only opportunity to climb the mountain. I followed the ridge right to the summit without much difficulty. The climb reminded me very strongly of the scramble on Mt. Stephen. It was impossible for me to build a stone man on the highest point; the peak is snow covered. At the first rocks I made a little stone man, and wrote a few words on a paper: "Conrad Kain, Führer von Wien. Bei Sturm, 11–8–1911" – and afterwards I found that it was the 10th of August, my 28th birthday.

I folded the paper and put it in my match holder, which I received as a present from Mr. Hollister. On one side of the match holder it reads: "With compliments from the Continental Oil Co. for 1903"; on the other side, scratched in with a penknife: "N. Hollister."

I wrapped this in a handkerchief and put it in the stone man. For greater precaution I laid a few stones together underneath an overhanging rock that protected this second stone man from avalanches; because I knew that people would not believe that I had reached the summit.

The route of return was the same, but more dangerous. Before I came to the pass, the sun sank behind the mountains. I should have liked to see the sun two hours longer.

I thought I could get across the glacier by daylight. To my astonishment, I found that the snow bridge, which had brought me on the rocks, was broken. I had hard work to get on the glacier. I was quite helpless in the rain. I wanted to stay on the glacier overnight; but I could not stand it longer than ten minutes, and the cold warned me that I must go on, whatever happened. My one bit of good fortune was the lightning, which showed me the way. Step by step, I had to feel with the axe to find whether I were on the edge of a crevasse. Very often the axe fell right through and, more than once, I thought: "This is the last step." I tried again to stay overnight on the glacier, but in five minutes I would have been frozen stiff from head to foot. I felt indescribably glad when I found rocks underfoot; I yodelled with delight.

The way from the rocks was already familiar to me, and no longer dangerous, but still very uncomfortable through the windfalls. At daybreak I came into camp, in pouring rain. I found my supper by the fire, and ate it for breakfast. I laid aside all my wet clothing and, without a sound, went into the tent and to bed without disturbing anyone. I slept for a short time. Mr. Kinney felt in my bed to see if I was there. Without saying a word, he clapped me on the shoulder and I pointed in the direction of Whitehorn.

I had absolutely no pleasure in that climb. The time was too short and the dangers were too great. Two days later I went over the glacier and saw my tracks, and I think there was only one chance in a hundred of anyone coming through safe. I was appalled when I saw the dangerous crevasses. It was one of the craziest and most foolhardy undertakings that I ever made in the mountains, and all my life I shall remember the ascent of Whitehorn. As I found no stone man or any other sign of man, I believe that it was the first ascent.[46]

Harmon recalls an amusing story. The cook was burning the porridge every morning. Mr. Wheeler, who saw nothing wrong with the pot, decided to act as chef. Next day, in the tent before breakfast, Conrad began loudly to relate a gory, ghostly dream, concocted on the spot. Wheeler, outside, must perforce listen, with the result that the porridge was scorched once more!

Conrad once told us of a conversation between Kinney and himself, which may have been touched up a little for the occasion. It seems that the reverend gentleman was worried about the future salvation of our guide's soul, and tried to bring him back to the fold. "Conrad, when you have been in a tight place in the mountains, has the Angel of the Lord never stood by you and told you to be unafraid?"

Our open-minded philosopher replied that no such visitation had ever occurred, but that he was ever hoping for such a miracle. Kinney said: "I am sure there are mountains in the afterworld. I have always desired to make the ascent of the Matterhorn, a feat which my financial condition has prevented. The afterworld is, therefore, made up for different degrees of attainment. If I live my life righteously, I shall perhaps find my Matterhorn in the world to come. You, remaining unbeliever, will surely pass eternity on a prairie."

The doom sounded harsh to Con. A few days later, on the trail a straying horse snagged a pack and fell bodily into the creek. Much to his surprise Conrad heard profanity, seldom associated with the clergy. Con rode back. "Shake hands, parson," he called. "I don't know how far down in dot afterworld *you* come, but chust be yourself und maybe yet we climb dot Matterhorn together!"

Camp was moved from Berg Lake to near Kinney Lake on August 16th, and there Conrad nearly lost his life in the glacial torrent of the Grand Fork [Robson River] while returning across a thin, swaying tree, with his arms full of brush for beds:

> *An agonizing yell was our first appraisal of the catastrophe. One grabbed an axe, another a climbing rope, all leaped to the spot to behold poor Conrad clinging frantically to the branches of the dripping tree with just his head above water and the surging current, stretching his legs down stream like ribbons. The rope was flung and, with guide's instinct, he immediately secured it to his body, thus ensuring his recovery, dead or alive ... It is indicative of the man that through it all he held firmly to a small hand axe which he had borrowed.*

YELLOWHEAD PASS, BC. AUGUST 30TH ◆ *What an indescribable pleasure, after long time in the wilderness, to receive letters from friends once more! We reached Moose Lake on August 26th, climbed a mountain and then went back to Yellowhead Pass.*

I am well and healthy. We have made a journey around Mt. Robson. To my sorrow I could not attempt this beautiful peak. No time. But I have made the first ascents of the second and third elevations. Up to the present time we have made 20 ascents, all new, with the surveying instruments.

We were lucky with weather, but since August 3rd, when we left Moose Pass it had been continuous hard work. We carried all our things over a pass where horses could not go. There was enough to eat, and always fresh meat: goat, caribou, bear. I shot a big grizzly.

Mr. Wheeler's diary:

SEPT. 5TH ◆ *With me on my Topographical Surveys at Fitzhugh (now Jasper). Conrad assisted Capt. J.P. Farrar to pitch his tent at crossing of the Athabaska River. [Captain Farrar, of the Alpine Club, had arrived by train with his son and a manservant. He was on his way to visit Mt. Robson, and intended returning by the Big Smoky and Stony rivers.]*
SEPT. 7TH ◆ *With me on my photo surveys around Maligne Lake.*[47]

In his report on the work at Maligne Lake, Wheeler writes of mountain sheep:

While working at my transit on the crest, a wild shout from Conrad, who was sitting some 50 feet away, caused me to look up; as I did so, a bighorn passed between us within 25 feet of where I stood. Conrad declared it had jumped right over him. Later a band of 15 crossed the hill within 100 feet of us, and while on the way home we came on one evidently asleep amidst the rocks. Its back was turned to us, and, although we approached within 30 feet it made no sign. Conrad had a .44 Colt pistol with him, but in his wild desire to get it off missed his aim. This was an exceptionally fine ram, and made a number of 19 we had seen on this peak in one day.

SEPT. 18TH ◆ *Kinney, Harmon and Conrad started with Curly Phillips for Laggan,*[48] *with pack outfit by trail.*

SWIFT'S. ATHABASKA RIVER. OCTOBER 16TH ◆ *On September 30th I came to Banff, where I had some business and spent a busy 30 hours. Then I started out again, first to Laggan and then to Yellowhead Pass.*

After writing my last letter we went south to Maligne Lake, where the survey ended. Mr. Wheeler went to Edmonton and the rest of us through the mountains to Banff. 180 miles. It took us 12 days. Unfortunately we had bad weather all the time. In crossing Wilcox Pass, which is between the Athabaska and Saskatchewan rivers, we had two feet of new snow, difficult for horses. For three nights we camped in snow and were every day tired from overwork.

This summer we covered almost 1000 miles. Finally we arrived safely in Banff, where I thought to rest up, but it turned out otherwise. The outfitter who brought us to Banff was from the north and had to return. He was alone and could find no one for a companion, so I went with him. We went to Laggan, where our horses were, and which could not be found for two days.

From Laggan to Swift's we took 13 days, going steadily without a day of rest. I can say that I now know the Rocky Mountains very well.

Now I am going another 70 miles to the northwest with my friend. Trapping marten and wildcat. We shall be back about the end of December or the beginning of January when the snow is deep. We hope for good luck. For this reason there is no chance of my getting home. This summer I sent my mother $100, almost 500 kronen, and I know that she will be contented. I heard from home that my grandfather was dead. I would have liked to see him once more, but it was better for him, since he had grown old and weak and life gave him no more pleasure.

Last week we snared a bear. You will see from that what good nerves I have. We found a black bear in his winter home and could not get him in any other way but by roping and pulling him out alive. Then, of course, we killed him. It was my most interesting hunting experience.

The nights are already rather cold; most of the time we sleep in the open. I am healthy as a stag in the forest and quite hardened.

The other day I had a letter from a gentleman of Washington, a naturalist, and he asked me if I would come along with him to Siberia and the Mongolian border next summer. He says we shall see Vienna too.

In this way Conrad became Phillips's trapping partner during the winter 1911–12. Of the hardships of these months he wrote the following account:

CHAPTER XI

(1911–12)

▲

A TRAPPER ON THE ATHABASKA

When I see ladies wrapped up in fine and costly fur, I sometimes wonder if they have any idea of life in the part of the world it comes from, and under what circumstances the animals are trapped. I would not be surprised to find it understood by less than 1 per cent of these ladies who are fortunate enough to secure the real, genuine furs from the animals of the wild.

I say "from the animals of the wild" because I know that so many skins from domestic fur-bearers are fixed up in fine shape, introduced and sold as genuine. But this is not what I want to criticize and describe. I wonder if people have ever given one minute's consideration to the points outlined above. Then I wonder if ladies from big cities or country towns could make for themselves a picture of a real trapper and of his primitive life in the wilds, among the fur-bearers. I ask myself, "Could they?" and I find only one answer to the question, and this is "No." It is true there are many books and stories written about wild animals and their life, from which one could learn a great deal; but on the other hand there are only a few books written about the trapper and his primitive life, the hardships he has to go through, and the many dangers which surround him in the mountains and forest in the winter.

I give here a few lines concerning one of my winter seasons as a trapper, the winter 1911–12.[49] I spent most of the time up in the north (Yellowhead), which was a newly opened-up country and promised good opportunities for trappers.

My partner and I chose the upper Moose River for one of our headquarters. Here we made a cache, and after a good look 'round we took our pack train over the Moose Pass, 7000 feet above sea level. This pass will be known in the future to mountain climbers and tourists when the Grand Trunk Pacific will be opened up for the tourist traffic. Here on Moose Pass we pitched a tent for a halfway camp between our headquarters on the Moose and the Smoky rivers. A few days later, after we had built a good comfortable cabin, we once more returned over this high pass with our pack train. But this time we travelled light, and as we found a foot of fresh snow on the summit, we shook hands with ourselves that we were just in time. A few days later and we would not have been able to return with the horses over this highway.

On the Moose River I stopped behind; my partner Curly took the pack train out to Jasper, where he wintered the horses. The sound of the cayuse bell died away in the distance, and I knew that this would be the last sound of civilization, and that I would not see or hear anything more of it till my friend returned. I got busy at once, and built a lean-to, which is a shelter with three walls and a roof, and in front of it a good fireplace. Taking traps and rifle, I went up the valley, looking for some game or tracks of game. I found all kinds of tracks of small fur-bearers like weasels, marten and beaver, and to my disgust I saw the tracks of a wolverine, the greatest enemy of the trapper. To my surprise I did not see any tracks of any kind of big game, which is the first thing the trapper is looking for; first of all for food supply, and also for bait.

The next day I started out with great hopes, as there had been some inches of fresh snow on the ground. This time I walked down the valley for some miles. From the south came a stream from a hanging valley, in which I expected some kind of a water basin and Alpland, which is always a favourite stamping ground for caribou. After a hard struggle through thick underbrush, I reached the mouth of the valley. There I found the going better, and the expected lake all right, but no signs of caribou or any other game. I kept on going, and at the end of the valley I had in front of me a wonderful alpine lake which had frozen over already. In vain I looked for signs of goats. For some miles I retraced my tracks; then I cut over a shoulder which was a shortcut back to my lean-to. Later in the evening, I got back to camp. The next morning I found marten tracks all around my lean-to. The trapper's fever came over me, and reached the highest point; that is, I must set traps. I shot some squirrels with a .22, for bait. It would take too much space if I tried to describe the feeling one has when setting the first trap in the season. There is an old saying, "Once a prospector, and always a prospector, and he lives in hopes and expectations." This applies also to the trapper, the brother of the hoping prospector.

I ran across a porcupine, which I killed, so I had more bait to set traps. Then I went back to camp and cut wood to last some days. Before daylight next morning, I went out to look at the traps round the camp, and found a marten in the second trap. Big caribou tracks took me away from the trap line. The tracks were so fresh that I was sure I would have the caribou before noon. I followed the tracks into the heavy timber, and whenever I saw an opening ahead, I saw in my mind the big fellow falling in the smoke of the first shot; but I never got a sight of him. The timber got thicker, the slope steeper and therefore progress was slow. Sometimes I could hear him, breaking through the windfall and whenever an opening was in sight I got down on my hands and knees. My heart beat, but it was all in vain. Only one hope was left to me: the timberline. At last I came there. The tracks went in the direction of an outlook, which I approached with great care and hope, and as I put my head over the ridge I saw the bull disappearing in the timber down hill. I could hear the cracking of the limbs of the trees.

A long breath, a few oaths, and I slid downhill without considering what would be ahead. My speed was great, but the bull beat me. I thought I would get a sight of him down in the valley, but it did not turn out. The bull must have known who was after him, and I am sure he knew that the heavy timber was the best protection for his life, as he went to the edge of the timber, and then turned back again and changed his course uphill. So did I. Halfway up the slope, I could see where he had rested, and my heart rose again to the highest point. Some hundred feet below the timberline we came on our old tracks, which we both followed, and it happened just as before. I saw his hindquarters disappear and that was all.

As it had already got dusk, I knew that the day's work was done. How the old fellow felt, I cannot say. I was dead tired, and breathed freely as I reached the frozen creek. A good long drink and a short rest, and I set off for the camp.

I might mention that when a man lives out in the woods, without a companion, he gets used to talking to himself. Many times I have been played out in the mountains and the woods, but never before had I such an experience as this time. When I lifted myself on my legs, they were stiff like wooden ones. To keep out of the brush, I tried to walk on the frozen creek. I could not control my feet, and felt just like a man on board ship, who had forgotten his sea legs ashore. I went down on my hands and knees. This way the rifle had been a nuisance. To make things easier, I left the rifle behind, and some hundred feet from the camp I even dropped my bag, which was almost empty, but which now felt as if it weighed half a ton.

How I got into my blankets I cannot tell. When I awoke next morning, I felt I had slept the sleep of the just. After a good solid breakfast, I went on the hunt again. I followed the Moose Pass trail up to the timberline, stalking over the Alpland, without finding any tracks. I decided to go up another valley which looked like good goat country, and I was sure I could always get a goat if there were any around on the mountains. At noon I ran on fresh tracks. "A billy" I said to myself. At about 6500 feet the snow increased very rapidly. The fresh tracks kept me going without stopping. As I came to the end of the valley I saw old billy mounting the final slope up to the ridge (or better, to the pass) but the distance was too long for a shot. I saw that he had some difficulty to reach the pass. Big cornices barred the way, but after all he got there all right. He let himself down onto an outlook and watched me struggling up the steep slope. "Struggling" is right.

If I had not seen the goat go there, I would not have thought of trying the slope in such dangerous conditions. I had only moccasins, and the rifle as a stock. I longed for my nailed Swiss boots and ice axe. There was old, hard-frozen snow underneath, with a foot of fresh snow on top, with a crust a couple of inches thick. With every step I made I thought of starting an avalanche. I was only a very short distance from the pass when the snow started to give way under my feet. A few loud reports, and the cracks opened up all over the slope. I tried for a second or two to keep my balance. I saw the cornice breaking off, and naturally I knew what had happened. For some yards the avalanche went slowly. I did not lose my head; I put myself in a sitting position, my rifle across my legs, and then the avalanche got into full speed, which cannot be described. Thoughts are quick, and can be quick as lightning. I remembered the precipice at the foot of the slope. I shut my eyes before I got there, and then I felt a stinging sharp pain in my hips and back. The next thing I saw when I opened my eyes was that the avalanche had reached its destination. For the first moment I was afraid to try to feel my legs, which were packed in the solid snow around me. I am quite convinced that such moments cannot be described.

I know that abler pens than mine have tried to do so, and they have failed. This is hard to explain in one way; on the other side, it is easy, because such experiences are, as said before, only moments, especially when one speaks of avalanches. This had been my second ride on an avalanche, and my recollections are the same. The avalanche starts to move slowly for some seconds, and after that it goes almost faster than one can think. But, when the critical moments are over, and one is in a safe position again, one thinks that he was thinking of so-and-so. There may be some people who are able to do so, but I have not met them.

I started to loosen the hard-packed snow around me with the rifle. After ten minutes or so I got free. I looked in the hole where I had been prisoner for the last fifteen minutes, and could hardly believe my eyes when I saw the colour of blood in the snow. By instinct I felt on my back, and it was wet, and by looking on my hand I saw it was blood, but did not feel any pain. I looked up the slope from where I came in such a short time, compared with the time it took me to struggle up. As I looked up the precipice, which was 20 feet high, over which I had come through the air with shut eyes, I thought myself lucky that I was still alive. By looking so, over the slope where I came from, and the masses of snow all around me, my eyes were arrested by a movement in the snow. For some seconds I looked at the spot, and did not think anything further about it. I tried to free myself from the snow, and by doing so I bent down to get the snow out of my neck and at the same time I saw the movement in the snow again.

Then I saw what seemed to me a black spot, and as I went closer I could hear a faint groan. I knew right away that it could be nothing else than the billy, and so it proved to be. The horns and the ears stuck out of the snow: the poor beast was struggling for freedom. I did not feel like a sportsman when I cut the throat of the defenceless animal, but the law of Nature in the woods is a strong one: kill or starve. I am sure the goat would have died there, as the snow was packed solid around the body. It took me quite a long time to get the carcass out. I pulled the carcass down to the timberline, and after I had finished skinning it and cutting it up into pieces, I lit a fire and boiled a small kettle I always carried along.

Then I fried some meat on the fire, and examined my wounds. There were two – one below the hips and the other just above, and heavy bruises on the hips and spine. Once more I looked back at the pass and the precipice. "A lucky escape," I said to myself again. That the goat had been in the avalanche might be a puzzle to the reader who does not know the habits and the curiosity of mountain goats. A goat will very often watch an approaching enemy without a move till the enemy disappears out of sight. Then she or he moves on to another lookout where the hunter becomes visible again, and if the hunter comes near the goat decides to get out of sight. I hope this helps the reader to understand the following.

As I struggled up the slope the billy could watch me from his outlook, till I got almost under the cornice, under which I had been hidden, and old billy naturally tried to get one more glimpse of me. This he could only do by going near to or on the cornice itself, and this he must have done when I started the avalanche, which took away the main support from the cornice, on which I suppose the goat must have stood and come down with it.

I now carried a very heavy load of meat and therefore it was late at night when I reached my shelter. After a good supper I turned in. I was too tired to wash and put a bandage on my wounds.

Next morning I felt stiff all over, especially in my hips and back. All I had along with me for accidents was a tin of Zambuk [ointment], the best thing a man can have in the woods, and as a matter of fact one does not find any trapper, prospector or lumberman without it. To protect the wounds from dirt, and from rubbing on the heavy woolen underwear, I tore a piece off the flour sack, boiled the cloth and washed it clean. Then I put the Zambuk in the centre, and to make it stick in place I melted some gum from a spruce tree and put the melted stuff all around the edge of the lining, and stuck it on the skin as hot as I could stand it. For some days I had to take it easy, but the old Zambuk proved once more its great healing power.

These are cases of accidents and dangers trappers have to face out in the woods, but that is by no means all. There are many other trying hardships and difficulties the trappers have to put up with. For instance, soft snow, one or two wolverines on his lines of traps, and running short of rations, which is almost the worst of all. I trust that every reader will have his own experience and know that the appetite increases with the temperature in the winter. Even in the cities one can feel it. That means when one is in perfect health.

I have spent all my life out of doors, and I made, every winter, the same observations. Of course, a great deal depends on the work one is doing. The greatest craving for food I experienced was when on showshoes, and I wish I could find the right words to describe this craving after 25 or 30 miles on snowshoes.

Outside of a few wolverines on the trap line, everything went fine, and as the meat supply got low I went off over a mountain range to inspect the country over there for small game. I took blankets and food to last me two days. The second day I shot a young goat. Then I went over a low pass back to the Moose River. I saw so many fresh marten and weasel tracks that I made up my mind to come back and set traps; but as I had not much food left in the lean-to on this side, I had to go to our headquarters on the

Smoky River, a distance of 25 miles. Four days later I returned to the Moose River, with provisions for over ten days. Then I went to the valley over the mountain range, which took nearly a day and a half. On the fourth day I came back again to the lean-to. Here I enjoyed a good night's rest, after three nights in the open. The next two days I went out and brought my traps in from two different valleys. With great hopes I tramped down the valley to my new trap line. On the way I picked out two fine specimens of marten. Here I also had two beaver traps. One I found upset and a claw in it. In the afternoon a snowstorm came over the mountains, which forced me to camp earlier than I intended. After having cut enough wood, I made a shelter with branches and young trees. Then I laid myself down by the fire for a night's rest.

Many people have an idea that they would lose their heads if they had to spend a week in the woods alone. I have heard of men losing their heads when alone for a considerable time in the wild, but for the man who is a lover and a student of Nature, there is no time to feel lonely. Nature is, in winter, just as generous as in summer, and supplies her students and admirers with plenty of food for thought. Winter in the mountains is more charming than the average person can imagine. There is no doubt that the fine scenery helps to overcome obstacles more easily. Many nights I spent alone by a fire in the woods, and in spite of all the hardships I had to undergo, I was happy and contented.

The following morning I started out at daybreak and the whole day was filled with disappointment. I got to the end of the line. Some traps I found upset; all kinds of tracks were visible, but nothing was in the traps. I could not understand the situation. I lit a fire and did some deep thinking on the matter. I could not find any faults with the traps and baits. What should I do? Should I take the traps out and quit the valley, or should I wait another day? I knew that by waiting a day I could meet with success; but there was another important question: the provision bag, which had been very light.

I measured the rice in a cup – three cups, three meals. A few raisins, coffee for two meals, a few bites of bread, some tea, no sugar. I saw that this was just enough to take me back to the halfway tent. I had nothing left in the lean-to, and this meant running short of food – the thought of it gave me a shiver – as I knew the meaning of being short of rations, but the fresh tracks in the snow were in my mind. So I decided to wait a day.

The next morning I went up to the timberline to try my luck for a ptarmigan, but I had to return without any success. I saw many of them, but not near enough for a pistol shot. On the way back I looked at the traps in the upper end of the valley, and found them all in order but nothing in them. A squirrel chattered down at me from a high spruce tree. I fired seven shots before I hit her, and then the body did not fall to the ground but got stuck on a big branch. To satisfy my discontented stomach I climbed the tree. I cooked the squirrel with rice. Squirrels, like other good things, are known to be good when well-prepared and cooked, but here in the woods I had nothing except salt. I can't say that it tasted very good, but a few days later I would have been glad enough to have a squirrel. The night was not very cold, and I slept quite a few hours. As I woke and found the fire extinguished, and I myself almost paralyzed with cold, I had to do different exercises to get warm before I could light the fire. As it blazed up I prepared for breakfast, and by doing so I discovered something dreadful.

I found a dead mountain rat in my food bag, which I had used for a pillow. The running rat had found a way in without disturbing me from my sleep. I must have turned over in my sleep and squeezed the ugly animal to death. The rice was all I had left, and in spite of the hunger I could not force myself to eat it. After daybreak I went to the traps up in the upper part of the valley. They were all empty. At the mouth of the valley I found a marten in one of the traps. He was still alive. By this time my hunger was so great that, when I saw the marten, the law of Nature told me "here is something to eat."

I lit a fire on the spot and took the skin off, and fried the hindquarters and the shoulders over the fire. There is an old saying that "hunger is the best sauce." I found myself a good cook and enjoyed my breakfast thoroughly. A very hungry stomach can be satisfied almost with anything. I felt very well but only for a short time. After a couple of miles of hard tramping, I felt played out. I kept my eyes open for anything I could get with the pistol, but looked in vain, and it seemed to me I never saw such a deserted valley in my life. I called this valley "The Valley of Bad Luck." I kept on moving but got so tired I had to take a rest every 10 or 15 minutes. There was only one prospect for food. That was the two beaver traps I had set in the river.

Here I had a strange experience I had never had before; that is, I hypnotized myself, and in this trance I could see myself with smiling face lighting the fire, skinning the beaver and boiling the beaver tail (beaver-tail soup is known to be one of the finest Indian dishes whenever they have a feast). These happy moments, I am sorry to say, were very short, as I soon came up to the traps and found them empty. At midnight, half dead, I reached the lean-to.

I have mentioned already that I had no food left there, but still I wanted to make sure if I could not find something eatable. Next morning I was more hungry than ever, and I congratulated myself on the idea of boiling some of the old and frozen carcasses of marten I had thrown away many weeks before. I was lucky enough to find two carcasses. I put them in the kettle and cooked them for a whole hour. The odour from the soup was fine, but the taste was unbearable. I took two spoonfuls but my stomach refused it. I think it would spoil the reader's appetite if I described the taste of that soup. I mention only that marten belongs to the cat family.

There was nothing left for me but to push on over the Moose Pass to the halfway camp, where I had some eatable things left. It was a hard task to climb up to the timberline on an empty stomach, but here I struck a piece of luck. I shot a whisky jack, known also by the name of camp robber. This is a very inquisitive bird, and there was no trouble to get near him. I never killed and tried to eat a bird of this kind, and I was very disappointed when I was finished with the cleaning. There was hardly a mouthful left. To make the best of it I roasted it over the fire to a hard crust, and then chewed it very carefully. I was played out entirely, and had to give up the idea of reaching the halfway camp the same day.

I spent a most miserable night on the timberline, and the next day, late in the evening, I reached halfway camp in an almost unconscious condition. I crossed the Moose Pass in a blizzard, and by this life and death struggle I found out how sweet life is, and how much a man can stand when he is face to face with cruel, cold Death.

I had to stop in the tent for two days to recover from the starvation. In the meantime I dried and prepared the furs. At that time it did not occur to me to think of civilization and the smiling faces wrapped in furs. But now, when I am travelling on streetcars, railways or steamships and hear ladies passing remarks about my weather-beaten face, it always brings back recollections of my life as a trapper. And I am sure that if these ladies, ever for one minute, considered the circumstances under which the furs that keep them nice and warm were obtained, and if they knew that I was one of the many trappers who bring the furs from the wilds, they would certainly give me a smile of gratitude.

BANFF. MARCH 16TH, 1912 ◆ *It is impossible to tell all of my experiences as a trapper during the past four months. But I must say that the life is at once the finest and most difficult. At times one suffers hunger and thirst, and again one lives like a lord. There are happy and sad hours, and moments of danger. But one is the free man of the forest and king of all.*

By the end of October my friend and I had reached our winter camp. In two days we built our hut on Smoky River. Then my friend left with the horses. I accompanied him over Moose Pass to Moose River. There we made a lean-to, in a protected spot under large trees, where I spent almost a month. On November 3rd I took leave of my friend and began to hunt and trap alone.

On the second day I had both fortune and misfortune. I hunted goats and followed an old billy on a steep snow slope. Suddenly it broke loose and I was in an avalanche. The snow went through my clothing down to my skin. I hurried through the forest, built a big fire and dried myself.

On the following day I began to trap. I set 35 falls on Moose River on a ten-mile line, then went back over Moose Pass to Smoky River, where I had a tent but no stove. Fire in front. On this side of the pass I had a trap line of 30 traps, and wandered back and forth across the pass watching them. On the first round I had good luck and took three marten. Then I got a big caribou, so I had lots of fresh meat.

On the second round I got to know the trapper's rival: that's the wolverine, a terrible animal that steals everything it gets a hold on and does great damage. The wolverine is hard to catch. These beasts are very keen and wise. I caught two the first week, but they went away with the traps on foot. Then I caught them with a spring pole. This time they upset the trap, but when the pole goes up in the air they are helpless and die. But the trapper likes to get them alive. The skin is not worth much, about five or six dollars.

From October 1st until the end of January I spent about 40 nights in the open, often in fearsome cold. I am hard as a beast of prey, but as soon as I got into a hotel at Edmonton I took cold and it became worse every day.

From Edmonton I went to Calgary, and then to my beloved Banff. Now I am in my old home; two Englishmen live below me and play the piano incessantly. It tires me to hear the noise all the time, although I like music and song. I am not homesick but the world at times seems so monotonous. I am getting tired of bachelor life.

Each day I work in the woods, and when I return tired and hungry the cooking annoys me and I go to the hotel for supper. There are no *white cooks there, only Chinamen and the fare is not good. Yes, my friend, it has been a long time since the last 'Wienerschnitzel!'*

I have just heard from my friend Professor Hollister that I am to go with him, and so shall have the chance to see my home once more. Hollister writes that we shall leave New York in the middle of May, travel from London to St. Petersburg, and through Siberia to the Altai mountains.

We will not climb much, but travel about. My work will be trapping and hunting, and observing little animals and flowers. I am happy to have such new experiences. Last summer I collected mice and beetles for the professor, and we became friends in the woods.

In the early part of May I am to sail from Quebec for Liverpool on the Empress of Ireland.

CHAPTER XII

(1912)

▲

TO THE ALTAI MOUNTAINS OF SIBERIA

The favourable impression made by Conrad Kain upon Ned Hollister during the course of the Robson Expedition was reciprocated, and when Hollister,[50] in the following year, was sent to the Altai Mountains of Siberia, Conrad was selected to accompany him. They left St. Petersburg on June 8, 1912, for the purpose of collecting mammals and birds. Conrad used to say he had gone all that way "to trap mice." He afterward found much amusement in showing his friends at home the Russian passport on which he was described as "Professor."

Unfortunately Conrad never wrote a full account of this journey. Two stories, however, he related to us:

> On my way to the Altai I was in St. Petersburg. In those days it was a fine city, with much gay life. Once I saw the Tsar. He rode in a carriage pulled by milk-white horses. A little man, but with a wild, cruel look in his eyes – like he could eat little children alive!

Of the Altai hunters he had this to say:

> Many years ago I went with a Smithsonian outfit to trap in the mountains of Siberia. I often was out with the native hunters. Nice fellows, und I make out good with them. I watch them how they shoot, with their comical old-fashioned rifles dot stand on two legs und fire with matchlock.
>
> Und I learned dot year dot snaring mice can be as exciting as hunting elephant if you get the point of view.

Hollister thought that even such an enthusiast as Conrad was impressed with the climbing necessary in a successful mountain collecting trip. On June 18th they began the long ride south from Biysk in a

> *basketwork buggy in which the traveller sits flat on the bottom or on top of the luggage, with legs cramped up in front.... Three horses are used for each vehicle; the centre one trots and the two side ones gallop or run, and for the first few days one constantly expects to capsize. In fact the 'carriage' in which Conrad and the interpreter were riding did overturn one evening about dark when the driver was attempting an especially brilliant grand entry into a small village.*

> ON THE OBI RIVER. BIYSK, SIBERIA. JUNE 17TH, 1912 ✦ *We went to St. Petersburg by the Nord-Express in a first-class sleeping car (fine!), stopping there for several days. Then we continued to St. Nicholaj in Siberia, four days and nights more. An indescribably huge country of splendid forests. From St. Nicholaj we went by steamer for three days on the Obi River to Biysk. Today we have been busy with purchases. Tomorrow we leave to go 325 miles by wagon, then eight days with camels or whatever we can get for pack animals. So there is a great distance before we can begin work. Then, after six weeks, we shall start for home, both men to America and I, by way of Moscow, to Austria.*
>
> *Thus far all has gone well, but now the difficulties will begin. Both of the men are kind to me; we share everything alike. I have never been spoken to or treated as a servant. One of them I already know well: Mr. Hollister. And Mr. Lyman[51] is like him, always pleasant. Naturally I am careful and try to please them. The people and the country are very poor. And extremely dirty. I am afraid we will have lice in a little while!*

Conrad was just the proper man for this expedition, possessing not only unusual ability as a trapper but also the requisite delight in natural phenomena:

> *Conrad, as ever, was tireless and was out in the mountains from morning till night, trapping and shooting mammals and birds for our collection ... Edelweiss grew in profusion about our tent, much to his delight.... Conrad's help was great. A gigantic owl, of a species*

rare in collections, visited a tall rock spire above the canyon wall two nights in succession. Conrad climbed to the tip of this pinnacle the next day and placed a wolf trap in proper position. Next morning I was awakened by his famous alpine 'yell.' I rushed out of the tent and looked almost straight above me, to see him balanced on the spire with the wings of the monstrous bird wrapped in his coat preparatory to the descent.

The work was to have required several months, but the desired ends were reached some six weeks before the date fixed.

ON THE SIBERIAN BOUNDARY. JULY 11TH ◆ *I had been thinking of you all day long, and I gathered many flowers for you. Flowers from Mongolia! They will no longer be fresh and beautiful as they now are, but I know you will take them anyhow, won't you?*

We are on the boundary between Siberia and Mongolia. I am well and so is friend Hollister. We are working hard, hunting every day and getting very tired. The region is mountainous, not heavily forested, and ever so cold. Rain, often snow, almost every day. During the day I am all alone, coming to camp at evening with my specimens and talking over experiences with my friends. We have a half-civilized Kalmuk who rides in search of fuel (wood and cow dung). My work is interesting and I like it better than guiding. Hollister is the best of men: a gentleman through and through. He teaches me many things. Mr. Lyman and the interpreter have gone away for a month. From Biysk to this place we took eight days by wagon. An awful journey! We stopped for two days in a village, and from that point have come two days with horses. From our present camp we shall travel further in Mongolia. We are collecting more than we expected, and it is possible that I shall come home about the beginning of September.

As a reward for his activity Conrad received the extra weeks as leave.

GRAND HOTEL D'EUROPE, ST. PETERSBURG. AUGUST 26TH ◆ *I have just arrived in St. Petersburg. Tomorrow, Tuesday the 27th of August, I shall take the train for Vienna, remaining in the city for a day or so. No one knows that I am coming, not even my mother.*

Conrad was at home from August 31st until November 12th. "I made a few difficult climbs," he wrote, "quenched my three-year-old thirst with beer and had a jolly time, living my youth over again."

During this vacation he paid a visit to Albert Gerngross – the "Mr. G." of his Corsican tour – telling him many interesting things about his adventures in America and Asia. But his was a wandering foot. Conrad said goodbye to his mother and never saw his home in the Alps again.

CHAPTER XIII

(1912–13)

▲

PACIFIC VOYAGE

BONN'S HOTEL, CHARING CROSS. LONDON. NOVEMBER 21ST, 1912 ◆ *I have to be a man now, but these days I sometimes feel just like a little child who has lost his mother and is alone in the world. I went by way of Innsbruck, Buchs, Zürich and Basle to Paris. I had an acquaintance there, but could not find him. Paris is a lovely city, but unfortunately the weather was bad. From Paris to London, where I was well-received by my friends.*

I am going by the Orient Line to Australia and New Zealand – a long journey! I wonder what experiences are in store for me in the distant South? I am ready for good or bad times and will fight it through. Yesterday I was invited to a dinner at the Alpine Club,[52] and met many fine people, all of them wondering at my enterprise. My address will be c/o Mr. Ross, Wellington, NZ.

I am of course going Third Class again (£21), and the vessel is completely filled. I only secured a ticket by chance, a traveller having given it up. But if New Zealand does not please me, I will go back to Banff in June.

Well, this is my last night in England. We reach Naples on November 30th. This evening Dr. Longstaff took me to the theatre. They presented The Flower Girl, *and it would have been better if I had not seen it, because the flower is just like real life. I am lying in bed and have my trunk for a table. On the dresser are some pictures from my good friends, and also the flowers I forgot to give you in Vienna. I shall send them. Now I must sleep.*

ON THE ORSOVA. NOVEMBER 22ND ◆ *We sailed at 1:10 p.m. Hundreds of people saw us off. The ship is large and clean, and pleases me better than the* Empresses. *The ship is crowded, even old people travelling, but all are English and I have heard scarcely a word in another language. The food is good – if it only stays so. A cloudy day, the sun appearing only on occasion. Now it is clear and calm. The moon shines beautifully, and I sit on deck looking in the direction of home. Perhaps our thoughts are crossing on the wide ocean.*

NOVEMBER 23RD ♦ *Today it is rather stormy and many people are seasick. I have just met an old lady of 57 who is taking the long journey to see her three children who live in Australia. We shall be six weeks on the way and I will spend Christmas at sea. Probably the Christ child cannot find one there. To be sure, he did not find me last year either on the Smoky River, and soon my name will be off his list! If only I remain on my friends' lists while I am away.*

I would like to know about poor Austria and the [Second Balkan] War. There is some crisis. I am sitting in the smoking room, reading the book you gave me (Schiller). In the music room they play very nicely.

NOVEMBER 29TH ♦ *Oh, what a lovely day! I see Corsica! Happy memories run through my head of the unforgettable journey with Mr. G. The mountains are covered with snow; I think I can see the Monte Cinto group. I hope to go there once more in my life.*

EARLY IN THE MORNING. DECEMBER 4TH ♦ *We had five hours in beautiful Naples. I was guide and had a party of two women and two men. I was pleased at how well I could make myself understood. We visited the poor quarter, then churches and museum, and the castle of St. Martino. The old church, where the bones of the royal family are kept, was most interesting. The two ladies were afraid. My party was made up of greenhorns who knew no more than what was going on in England. The dirty streets displeased them, but Naples is not the worst I have seen.*

DECEMBER 8TH ♦ *This evening I saw my first sunset off the Egyptian coast. Such a picture as I had never seen before. We were at the Port Said end of the Suez canal. The ship was moving slowly and we could see the camels pasturing – a lovely foreground. It was a long time before the magnificent colours of the sunset vanished. It is now eight o'clock and in a little while we shall stop at Suez.*

JANUARY 1ST, 1913 ✦ *Happy New Year! That is my wish for all of you, but I must write of other things lest I be homesick – which I promised not to be.*

On December 30th we landed at Melbourne, one of the largest cities in Australia. A beautiful spot. The streets are wide and clean, the harbour finely situated. My fellow passengers got out here. I went with them to their house, lovely enough, but I am sure they will be very homesick. I visited the museum and the botanical garden. There I was in the sunset, amidst the most beautiful tropical flowers and plants it is possible to imagine.

SYDNEY, AUSTRALIA. JANUARY 2ND ✦ *About two o'clock we landed in the chief city of Australia. The harbour of Sydney is incomparable, but the streets and lanes are not as fine as in Melbourne. On Saturday afternoon the other ship continues to New Zealand. I am writing this on a bench in a beautiful park. I am tired from much wandering about the streets. I shall sleep on the* Orsova *one more night; then she goes on to Brisbane. Today has been cloudy and it will surely rain. Everywhere there are gardens and parks. The harbour is the finest I have ever seen, much more so even than Naples.*

Today I visited a picture gallery, and to my astonishment found a view of the Dolomites.

JANUARY 4TH ✦ *This evening at eight the steamer leaves for Wellington. I am ready with my baggage. A fine vessel, with only two classes. I had to pay ten shillings additional and my purse is rather empty. I must weigh every penny before giving it up, but expect money from Canada at Wellington.*

WELLINGTON, NEW ZEALAND. JANUARY 8TH ✦ *Now I am at my destination in New Zealand. I write these lines in a miserable room. We arrived about one o'clock. I went to deliver a letter, but the man had gone away. Then to the post office – no money, no mail. The next post from Canada arrives in two weeks. I have only 3s. 4d. I am downcast and poor. I must think out some way for tomorrow.*

JANUARY 9TH ✦ *It is two o'clock. I am sitting in the botanical garden. My heart is broken. All night long I could not sleep. For bed and break-*

fast I paid 1s. 9d. I looked for the Canadian Consulate but there is none, and no Austrian either, for New Zealand is British.

I applied for work. There is plenty, but not in Wellington, and at the Intelligence Office one must pay 4–10 shillings. I am a total stranger and have no one to go to. I shall try to pawn my watch and my ring. I do not know what to do.

Later. I have met an acquaintance from the ship, with whom things are not going so well although he has still sufficient money. He took me to his hotel and I can sleep on the floor in his room. We lamented over our misfortunes. He is in a strange land for the first time and feels it more than I. Tomorrow I go to the German Consulate.

BOTANICAL GARDEN, WELLINGTON. JANUARY 10TH ◆ *I am sitting on a bench with birds and flowers all about me. I am out of the water, thank the Lord! At four o'clock I told my story to the consul, showed him my Führerbuch and made a good impression. Luckily his son is a climber, so he lent me 35s. I went to the Intelligence Office and took on work as a bush man. Tomorrow at four o'clock the train leaves for Featherstone, and from there it is 40 miles by wagon. The money will just get me there. I do not know how the work will be, but I can surely endure it.*

MARTINSBOROUGH. JANUARY 24TH ◆ *Now I am in the "bush," in camp. It is hard work, but I can stand it. The people are good and kind. We work nine hours per day; that makes 10s. The board is 2s. a day. We are 40 miles from the PO. My camp is far back in the forest. I am healthy and save money. The money from Canada has also arrived. There are even some blacks in camp. Think what an experience I am having!*

It would interest you to hear what the young fellows say on washday. It springs from the verse of the Bible: 'It is not well for man to be alone, so God created woman,' but sadly enough, he made none for life in the bush. It would be fine if one could rest on Sunday instead of washing and mending. But the women of New Zealand are not good housekeepers – too proud – and as long as I am well I'll do my own laundry.

Now I am more than 14,000 nautical miles from the mountains of home, and have trouble in being reasonable about it. I am alone and have no one to tell how I feel. The country is hilly; if we go up on an elevation the sea is visible. There are many birds singing beautifully, but I have seen few flowers. The land we are clearing is for a sheep farm. From now on I shall put aside 10 per cent of all my earnings against old age.

FEBRUARY 15TH ♦ *Last Sunday I went hunting and killed a young wild boar. The weather is not very good: rain and wind. The work will be finished in five or six weeks, and I must then go elsewhere, probably to America. I am expecting a letter from Mr. Hollister. There is nothing doing in the guiding line in New Zealand. I would much prefer to travel with scientists again.*

The work here is rather dangerous (felling trees), and one's thoughts must not wander. My program for the next months is to sail about May 9th from Auckland, reach Vancouver on May 27th and Banff by June 1st. I think of returning at once to the Rockies, to the green woods and the bears. By going from here to Canada I shall have been almost around the world.

Yesterday I received an unexpected letter:

SIDNEY, BC. JANUARY 27TH.

My dear Con:

I have received a letter from Mr. Hollister giving me your address. Are you coming back to Canada this summer? I can offer you a job on photo survey work along the Continental Divide for the full summer, if you care to have it. At $3.00 per day. It will be a new territory, Mt. Assiniboine and south. I need you by 1 June. We are holding two camps this summer, one at Lake O'Hara and one at Robson Pass. I should want you for Robson Camp. There will be several attempts to make the ascent of Robson from the east side. How does the prospect strike you, old boy? I expect you will know something about the New Zealand Alps before you return. We miss you in the Rockies. You know you are welcome any hour and we will do our best for you. Auf Wiedersehen!

YOURS FAITHFULLY,
A.O. WHEELER.

Now, what do you think of that? I am rather glad that they miss me there. Still, I know why. Well, I shall have to go back to Canada: $3.00 a *day and keep is not so bad, and possibly I can make something besides. Just now I am collecting beetles for friend Hollister, and have quite a number. On my way to the Rockies I shall see the islands of the Pacific, about which so much has been written.*

WELLINGTON. MAY 20TH ◆ *Often, in thinking over my youth, I say to myself what a pity it is that I had no opportunity for more education. Perhaps I should not have to struggle so. I was born poor, very poor. It might have been different had I been a scholar. It often seems to me that I ought to do something good and great for the world. I feel the little sparks in my brain, yet cannot fan them into flame. And now it is too late.*

The steamer Moana arrives this afternoon from Sydney. It is a small, old vessel of but 4000 tons, just a quarter of the size of the Orsova. I am so tired from walking on paved streets. My last night in New Zealand.

ON THE MOANA. MAY 30TH ◆ *Now I will tell you about Rarotonga. We were four hours ashore. It was lovely, although it began to rain. I had an hour's walk alone. You can imagine how it was under the palms. There were fruits of every description. The natives live mostly on them. The men are all well built, but the women are fat and did not please me. They go about almost naked, but are quite clean. It was a pleasure to wander amidst the green and to breathe the fresh air. The old ship has no proper ventilation.*

TAHITI. JUNE 1ST ◆ *I am sitting under a cocoa tree. The sun is shining and the birds are singing. We arrived last evening and all went for a walk. I was up until 11:30. The sunset was magnificent, but it made me sad. I felt so alone and forsaken.*

Tahiti is under French rule. There are not many whites, but many Chinese and natives. One sees that the people of the tropics are lazy. Among the natives there seem to be more women than men. Fruit is very cheap. For one franc one gets a whole basket of oranges and bananas – as much as one can carry.

This morning I was up early and went to the fruit market, and then along the seashore collecting shells. Next we went through gardens into a valley. It was ten o'clock by the time we returned. I bought writing paper and sat down under the cocoa tree. How good it is to be on green grass once more, especially if one has not felt well at sea. It is wonderful here: not a tree or shrub like anything at home. Everything is new and different, even the birds. Today seems to me the first spring day I have seen this year. In New Zealand it was late autumn when I left. Now I am going to lie on the grass and sleep.

AMERICAN HOTEL. 'FRISCO. JUNE 12TH ♦ *We came into harbour at eleven o'clock this morning, and after two hours' inspection were ashore at last. The steamer* Watson *sails Saturday for Vancouver. It was good to sit once more in a quiet dining room. After dinner I went for a walk. San Francisco is a beautiful city. I am glad the long voyage is over.*

JUNE 13TH ♦ *Good morning! The bed was soft and I slept well for several hours. But I have been up since four o'clock, the noise of wagons on paved streets waking me. It is a fine day. After breakfast I walked along the seashore to Golden Gate Park. In 1915 there will be an Exposition, and a large building is almost completed.*

I was in the Natural History Museum for six hours. The finest I have ever seen. The bones of prehistoric animals from Alaska were especially interesting, some as thick as my body. How I should like to go to the museum in Washington and see the animals I collected in Siberia.

CHAPTER XIV

(1913)

▲

.

1

THE MT. ROBSON ADVENTURE

My old friend Conrad Kain, a redoubtable little man
who was the first to conquer Mt. Robson.

– J.P. Farrar

The old stamping ground in the Alps sufficed no longer. "It was beautiful yet strange," wrote Conrad, "it made me feel very lonely – I longed for the solitude one finds in the Rockies, for the campfire and the carefree life."

TOPOGRAPHICAL SURVEY. GREAT DIVIDE. JULY 7, 1913 ◆ *Now I am back in the mountains again. It is spring! For the first few days in camp I was cook, but now I am climbing once more. The survey is being made to map the boundary between Alberta and British Columbia. We are old friends in the party, and I am happy to find that they are glad to have me back. They have not the eye or experience to select good routes of ascent.*

I must tell you some sad news. A friend of mine at Banff, John Wilson, was held up and shot by two robbers four miles from here. Two bullets in the chest, and his neck cut. But he is alive after lying unconscious for 30 hours. One bullet has been removed at the hospital in Banff, but he is too weak for further operation. He had been working for Mr. Wheeler and the Alpine Club. He is the son of the old packer who had the Spanish prince on a bear hunt.

Life is so short, and I think one should make a good time of it if one can. The only thing I enjoy now is Nature, especially spring in the mountains, and letters from friends. Sometimes I think I have seen too much for a poor man. There are things that make a man unhappy if he sees the wrongs and can't change them. A week ago I had a letter from Mr. Hollister. I tell you, I love this fellow! He told me he might go to South America next winter collecting, and if possible would take me along.

On July 15 the Alpine Club Camp will be opened at Hector for ten days; 150 tourists are expected. I shall not be there, but go to the Robson Camp from July 28 to August 9. I expect to have hard and possibly dangerous work there. Mt. Robson is a wicked peak. I know it very well from looking at it: I have not climbed it yet but will surely succeed. In case it is very risky I will go only with good climbers at a high price. A guide should be well paid for such expeditions, especially by those who have enough money and often throw away $100 in a day for a couple of pleasurable hours. Many friends of mine are coming from England: Mr. Mumm, Capt. Farrar and others.

From June 22nd until the 26th Kain was with Mr. Wheeler at R.D. McCaw's camp, McCaw being a BC land surveyor engaged on work in the mountain area bordering the route of the Banff–Windermere road. They then went to Stephen and spent nearly a month on the survey of the main watershed. On July 24th preparations were made at Banff and they departed next day for Edmonton.

The name of Conrad Kain will always be associated with the conquest of Mt. Robson. If his life be in any sense epic, then this was his greatest adventure. It is the highest peak of the Canadian Rockies (12,972 feet), raising its massive precipices above the Grand Fork of the Fraser in a relief rarely equalled in other mountain ranges of the world. The pioneer and the scientist had each had his turn at the mountain. Kinney and the Colemans attacked repeatedly in 1908, while Kinney and Phillips, in 1909, had victory within their grasp – a matter of yards. Amery, Hastings and Mumm, with guide Inderbinen, also tried in that season, and death had barely passed them by. So when Conrad appeared on the scene, he could play the role neither of Jacques Balmat nor of de Saussure to this Mont Blanc. But he brought the vision, tenacity of purpose and energy which at length made the mountain his.

The Indians called it *Yu-hai-has-kun*, "the mountain of the spiral road." Conrad, examining it from many viewpoints during the summer of 1911, and again during the winter of trapping that followed, knew well enough that the route would never be a direct one, but devious and stealthy. It was a gigantic mountain and a dangerous one, not to be taken lightly. It fell to him to solve the problem and to lead the way. He was not quite 30 years old at the time.

Kain, rebelling against repressed initiative in 1911, had climbed Whitehorn alone in an outburst of youthful energy. Conrad, stormer of peaks! Wheeler, possibly thinking of the danger incurred, told him it would never be counted as a first ascent.[53] "All right," said Conrad, "but I have been to the top, and have done what I liked to do."

Then, on an August day of 1913, climbers guided by Walter Schauffelberger[54] return from Mt. Whitehorn, bringing with them the metal matchbox and the paper with Conrad's signature. A.L. Mumm and G.E. Howard, with guide Inderbinen, Professor Fay and C.S. Thompson are in camp. Conrad's vindication. But Conrad thought he needed no such thing: Robson, the great mountain, rose before him – and Robson was his as well. He had led Foster and MacCarthy to the top.

Repeating his climb of Mt. Resplendent, Kain brought his party down safely on the afternoon of July 30th, Spending that night with MacCarthy and Foster at the cold bivouac of the Extinguisher, he made his successful ascent next day by the route from Robson Glacier which he had picked out two years before.

Upward on the final point of Robson,[55] like flies on a sword blade pointing toward the sky:

> *Conrad cut steps as though inspired. The flying ice combined with drifting snow blown off the higher slopes, froze upon the clothing, and the rope, which had been wet earlier in the day, became hard and difficult to handle.... A little cap of cloud covered the exact summit, and when after a short, steep piece of work Conrad turned and said, "I will take you no further," it was difficult to realize that Robson was won.*

Then the descent by way of the glacier falling toward the Fraser Valley, with Conrad's cheery "I will find a way." And when at last night traps them on a rocky shelf his remark as a heavy avalanche thunders down is, "If that goes on, it will spoil my night's rest." Conrad the irrepressible, dreaming, after a day of nerve-wracking strain, that his "friends in Austria had passed along in the night with loads of wood for a campfire," while he had forgotten to get a match!

Kain and his victorious party returned to camp on August 1st, and we find him, two days later, camping with a large party at the lower end of Berg Lake, bound for Mt. Whitehorn.[56] They rope in three groups and do not reach the summit until 4:45 p.m., but the weather is favourable and Conrad proposes a traverse.

> *Conrad's skill or instinct in avoiding the crevasses is best evidenced by the fact that for an hour or more we hastened down over this unknown glacier without mishap or appreciable delay.... "Here we sleep," said Conrad laconically.*

On August 10th two ropes set out to attempt Mt. Robson from the southwest. A.H. MacCarthy with Kain and B.S. Darling with Schauffelberger.[57] On the cliffs across the valley Conrad spies four goats, and says, "Ach, gentlemen, to perform the grand duty tomorrow we also be four white goats." They bivouac and Conrad gives out a pointed bit of his philosophy:

> *In my experience of about 500 peaks, I find mountain climbing really sport of kings; the real success and the peak comes by simply putting one foot in front of the other and always the second a little higher than the first.*

Next morning the weather is unfavourable, but the party determines to make an attempt. There is a blanket of fresh snow on the upper part of the mountain, and they encounter chimneys in such condition that Conrad observes they are a kind "to practise up, never down."

> *The mist was now very dense and snow was falling fast. The ice, however, was covered by a firm coating of snow under the fresh fall and little step cutting was required, so we made rapid progress; and at 12,000 feet Conrad cried out: "Es gehen sure!" For once he was mistaken. It did not.*

In the face of such odds they wisely desisted, gratified at having at least made contact on the ice cap with Kain's original route of descent. Conrad's vivid letter to friends in Austria has fortunately been preserved:

> *I was in camp at Lake O'Hara for one day. Then we went to Banff and on to Edmonton. On July 27th we reached the Grand Forks at the*

foot of Mt. Robson, remaining overnight at the "base camp" where we slept in the open. Next day we wandered in groups to Kinney Lake and up the cliffs past the big waterfall to Berg Lake. Needless to say that thoughts of my experiences here two years ago swept through my memory. I met my old friend Phillips again, as well as others. A storm came up at evening, and I was kept busy nailing shoes. On July 29th we had fresh snow and it was quite cold. In the afternoon I went around Berg Lake with two women and a man. We saw ice break off and fall into the lake. We caught sight of a goat on the way back. That evening we had a total of 65 persons at the campfire.

On July 30th we started for an ascent of Resplendent: two men and a lady. I took my blankets along, as I was expecting two gentlemen to meet me at timberline for the following day. It was cloudy almost all the way, and the weather was not very fine when we reached the top about one o'clock. It was the second ascent of the mountain, and I shook hands with the first lady to attain it. We made a new route of descent, a fine ridge-wandering that we had to give up because of storm.

I found my two men on the glacier. One was Deputy Minister of Public Works in the parliament of BC, the other a rich New Yorker. We had supper by the last brush, then took wood and blankets higher up. We slept on the moraine. The night was fine and not very cold. Early in the morning I wanted to take a look at the weather, but could not open my eyes for a long time. I hoped for bad weather! My eyes were swollen and as if filled with sand – just like snow blindness.

About 3:45 I lit a fire, cooked breakfast, and at 4:30 we set out, reaching the summit of Mt. Robson, "King of the Rockies," about 5:30 p.m. I was half snow-blind. I cut 500–600 steps in sheer ice, often breaking in above the knees in soft fresh snow. It was a hard day for me, but I reached the goal and made the real first ascent, for it turned out that Mr. Kinney and Phillips did not actually get to the top. The descent was very dangerous, and I would not undertake to follow the route of ascent in going down. So we descended on the southwest side. It was risky there. I knew that we must bivouac, although I said nothing of this. We went on as long as we could see, and after almost 18 hours lay down to rest on a rock band, 9000 feet above the sea. We had not much to eat, and the night passed slowly. Our feet were wet through, but still I slept several hours. In the morning the men's eyes were swollen as mine had been the day before. One of them could scarcely see. The descent over the rocks was not easy. About eleven in the morning we arrived at Kinney Lake, reaching Berg Lake about five in the afternoon, where we were greeted with hurrahs. The expedition had taken 30 hours.

On August 1st I had a day of rest. A party returned from Whitehorn, bringing the record of my first ascent in August 1911, which had been doubted! All the better for me. I had used cold compresses, and my eyes were much better. But I had pain over my entire face.

On the afternoon of August 2nd we left camp to ascend Whitehorn. Camping at the old place from which I had made the first ascent, I awakened the people at four o'clock on the morning of the 3d. We were eleven persons in all (three parties), including four women. I took two ladies and one man. It began to storm about eight o'clock, so that I gave up the ascent. But it cleared entirely in a short time and we started again. The ladies went very well, but I had to wait for the other parties. It was late when we reached the top, and I knew it would mean another bivouac. So I made a descent to the northeast over a very steep snow slope, had hard work with a bergschrund and then had to go back and fetch the others. We got down to rocks at eleven o'clock and spent the night. I made as good a bed as I could for the women, telling them how best to protect themselves from cold. I slept with the man under a rock. I slept very well for some hours, but the man was almost frozen. A mouse entertained himself with my shoe. Everyone was glad when day broke. After four hours on scree and ice we reached camp, where we had a good breakfast and rested. That evening in camp I told stories and related some of my experiences.

During the next few days I made another ascent of Lynx Mountain. On August 8th we had sick-transport: an Englishman had hurt himself slightly during a climb and developed blood poisoning. On August 9 we broke camp, and on the following day, my 30th birthday, I made an attempt to ascend Mt. Robson from the southwest side. We left camp at eight o'clock: four people – the New Yorker, a man from Vancouver, a Swiss guide and I. This guide made another attempt two days after our try, but had bad luck. We took blankets and wood along, reaching the bivouac at eight that evening. Here we had a little dispute, which I managed to settle.

A fearful storm arose. It grew better during the night, but the weather was still bad. Nevertheless we tried out the new route. It began to snow, and yet it was too fine to turn back at only 11,000 feet! Then *it began to storm in earnest, but we were at such a height that we did not want to retreat. So we went on to 12,500 feet There it became really uncomfortable and dangerous. Later on I saw that we were wise in desisting. On the way down we lost our way a little in the fog. The storm was so violent and the mists so thick that we could see only a few steps ahead. Wet from head to foot we climbed down to our things, and at 9:30 reached a cabin at Kinney Lake, where we spent the night.*

Next day we went out to the railway and on to Edmonton. I was very sleepy and tired. The Mount Robson Camp was a great success, and I had again made a name for myself in the Rockies.

Wheeler subsequently notes:

AUG. 16TH ✦ *Conrad joined my chief assistant of the Boundary Survey, A.J. Campbell, DLS, at Castle.*
AUG. 22ND ✦ *At Healy Creek, Simpson Pass and vicinity. Also at Quartz Hill near Citadel Pass. Fatigue Mtn., etc.*

Among the joys of the mountaineer is the enchanted meadow, where, peril over, one may sit and dream. For him, as with creatures of the wild, accident is the penalty for failure or mistake. The hour of victory is past, though Conrad felt it rather a partnership – knowing that only when such a peak as Robson drops its guard do men go up. But now, with that behind one, how gay the flowers, how bright the sky.

HEAD OF RED EARTH CREEK (S. FORK), BY THE SIDE OF A BEAUTIFUL LAKE. AUGUST 30TH ✦ *I am sitting here under a larch tree, on the shore of a lovely, deep-blue lake between two rocky peaks. At the end of the lake there is a waterfall, which comes from another lake farther on, above which is a third lake higher up. The background is snow and ice, an indescribable picture when one adds the fine tone of the bells worn by the horses. I see some goats on the grass slopes above timber. It is one of the most beautiful places I have ever seen. Thousands of miles lie between here and home: so near and yet so far! I must stop and hunt the horses – I can no longer hear their bells.*

Mr. P.A.W. Wallace, who was with the party, supplies the following from his diary:

SIMPSON PASS, SEPT. 4TH ✦ *Outside it has been cold, windy and wet. Rain and snow, with occasional intervals of hail, beating heavily upon our canvas covering, soaking the bushes all about our camp and covering the mountains with a white mantle. But inside it has been quite cozy. The tent that Conrad shares with me has been an editor's den. Conrad has spent most of the day on his stomach, feverishly writing up one of his trapping experiences for an Austrian paper. Now and again he would start up with, "Ah, this is good," and with one arm in the air and the other supporting himself on the ground, would read to me the thrills of excitement or tender emotions with which he had enlivened the narrative.*

Busy as he was, Kain could always find time to write home his impressions of this lovely country:

NEAR SIMPSON PASS. SEPTEMBER 18TH ✦ *The two days when we worked at Peyto's camp on Simpson Pass were most interesting. Bill is an old prospector, a trapper, a guide – a Western original! I have known him for three years. He is from Banff, the true man of the forest, and has always some new experience to relate. Fortune has not always favoured him, but most of the time he has been lucky. Eight years ago he lost his wife. He said: "If she were still alive I would be 10–15 years further from the grave." I know from other people that he was never the same old Bill afterward. His appearance is rough and coarse. He looks like a wildcat. On seeing him, without talking, one easily understands that people are afraid of him. But that is only outwardly. I think I know better: he is of the old West, quite independent, removes his hat for no one, and says whatever he thinks. But if someone comes to him in distress, he finds a soft-hearted man.*

ON THE SUMMIT OF MOUNT WONDER. SEPTEMBER 26TH ✦ *I am lying here on the summit of Mt. Wonder, Mr. Wheeler and Mr. Campbell working with instruments several yards from me. The peak was unnamed, and rightly did we christen it. It is on the Great Divide: the water on the eastern slope has a long journey to the Atlantic, while that of the southwestern side goes to the Pacific. Far below in the eastern valley are two lakes. We call the longer one Marvel Lake, the other, Lake Gloria. The latter has an indescribable blue-green colour. Marvel Lake is deep blue and has some islands, about which the water is not deep and so takes on other colours. Both lakes are surrounded by pine and fir forest. About 200 yards below the summit three wild goats lie in the grass and enjoy a sunbath. As far as the eye can reach, nothing but high mountains. On the Pacific side: meadows, below which I can count seven lakes, green forest, and Mt. Assiniboine, which so resembles the Matterhorn in outline. To the west and south I see peaks covered with snow. At the foot of Mt. Assiniboine is a lake, possibly a mile and a half in length, with glacier ending directly in it. Some little icebergs float about, without destination. Our camp is on the shore of this lake in a grove of larch, the trees all in bright autumn colouring. I think myself fortunate amidst the peace and quiet of Nature.*

Wheeler continues:

SEPT. 27TH ✦ *Conrad with Boundary Survey at Mt. Assiniboine.*
OCT. 6TH ✦ *Arrived at Banff with survey party. Season closed.*
OCT. 10TH ✦ *Working at clubhouse.*
OCT. 16TH ✦ *Conrad went with me to Crowsnest on Boundary Survey.*
OCT. 21ST ✦ *Returned to Calgary.*
OCT. 22ND ✦ *Paid off for the season.*

What a summer it had been! The loftiest summit of the Canadian Rocky Mountains had fallen, Conrad's forever. A great desire satisfied; joyous days to remember. How modestly he bore his laurels cannot be better shown than by his formal account, which follows:

2

THE FIRST ASCENT OF MT. ROBSON[58]

On reaching the Robson Glacier after the ascent of Mt. Resplendent, I went down to the timber at 6700 feet. Here I met my *Herren* for Mt. Robson. Both were busy about the fire, Mr. Foster (Deputy Minister for Public Works for British Columbia) with cooking, Mr. MacCarthy with gathering wood. After a good supper, we went up, laden with firewood, to the foot of the Extinguisher. The rock bears this name on account of its form (candle extinguisher). On the moraine we made our shelter beside a wall of stones, over which we stretched a piece of canvas and crept under it like marmots into their hole.

I awoke early next morning and felt pain in my eyes, and for a long time I could not open them. It felt as if my eyes were filled with sand. My snow glasses were no good. I saw a starry sky, which was more than we had expected. I applied cold poultices for half an hour and the pain in my eyes began to abate. I lit the fire and wakened my *Herren*. Both were delighted at the sight of a cloudless sky.

At 4:30 a.m., after an early but good breakfast, we left our bivouac. We followed the route of the previous day (ascent of Mt. Resplendent), over the glacier. Before we came to the Pass, we swerved to the right. From this point began the real climb of Mt. Robson. We climbed up an avalanche trough, then under some dangerous ice bridges to the right. The snow was in bad condition. We proceeded without any difficulties towards the steep snow slope that descends from The Dome (10,000 feet) and reached it at 7 a.m. We took a rest and deliberated over the route ahead.

Two years ago I spent hours studying this route, and did not take the bergschrund very seriously. From The Dome, one had a nearer survey of the bergschrund. We approached it over the glacier, which is here not very steep. A rib of rock comes down almost to the 'schrund. Over this rock I planned to ascend, but after every possible attempt we were forced to give it up, for at this place the glacier breaks off sheer. For about 200 feet we followed along the bergschrund to the right. Here was the only possibility at hand of overcoming it. After long chopping at the ice, I stood on its 65-degree slope. Across the 'schrund I made more steps. Then I let both *Herren* follow.

A thin layer of snow lay on the ice, and, owing to the melting of the snow, the ice was in very bad condition for step cutting. I made the steps in a zigzag. Mr. Foster counted 105 steps to a ledge of rock. The rock, when seen from below, promised good climbing and a rapid advance. But it turned out otherwise. We climbed up an icy wall, and then to our disappointment had an ice slope before us, 50 or 60 metres high. I kept as well as I could to the rocks that protruded here and there, which saved me a few steps. At the top of the slope we had another wall of rock, and above that an almost hopeless ice slope. One could see the tracks of falling stones and avalanches. On this slope I made 110 steps. It was a relief to climb on rocks again, though they were glazed with ice. But unfortunately the satisfaction was short, and for several hundred metres we had to climb again upon a slope of ice and snow. The snow here was in danger of avalanching. For safety, I lengthened the rope on the dangerous slope.

At last we reached the shoulder at twelve o'clock noon. I do not know whether my *Herren* contemplated with a keen alpine eye the dangers to which we were exposed from the bergschrund. In the year 1909 this route was attempted by Mr. Mumm and Mr. Amery with the guide Inderbinen from Zermatt. The party were in danger of their lives from an avalanche. I spoke with Inderbinen; he said, "I never before saw death so near."

On the shoulder we took a mid-day rest. There came a snowy wind that wet us to the bone. We pulled out all the clothing stowed away in our rucksacks. We found the shoulder less broad than we expected. It was a snow ridge, on the northeast side of which were overhanging cornices fringed with long icicles glittering in the sun, a glorious picture.

For a few hundred metres we had to keep to the southeast side. The snow on this side was in good condition, so that we made rapid progress. There was on each side a splendid view into the depths below [*Tiefblick*]. The more beautiful view was that of the Robson Glacier, Smoky Valley and Mt. Resplendent and the Lynx Range opposite.

From the shoulder to the peak the route was no longer so dangerous, but complicated by the loose, powdery snow. It was as if we were on an entirely different climb on the southeast side. The complications arose from walls of snow. Never before on all my climbs have I seen such snow formations. The snow walls were terraced. The ledges between the walls were of different widths, and all were covered with loose snow. I often sank in to my hips. There were forms on the walls like ostrich feathers, a truly strange and beautiful winter scene. Unfortunately we had no camera with us. Some of the walls were 15 to 20 metres high. It was difficult to find a way up from one terrace to another. At one place I worked for over half an hour without effect. We had to go back. A very narrow and steep couloir offered the only possibility. I warned my *Herren* that the piece would take considerable time to negotiate. Both had a good stand and kept moving as much as possible in order to keep warm. The wind was so bad here that I often had to stop. The steepness alone, apart from wind, made step cutting very hard work. For a number of steps I had first to make a handhold in the ice, and swing the axe with one hand. I do not think I need to describe this method any more fully, for everyone who has ever been on the ice knows that cutting steps with one hand is a frightfully slow process. I know that in such places it is not pleasant either for those behind. As soon as I was convinced that I could make it, I called to my *Herren*: "Just be patient, the bad place will soon be conquered, and the peak is ours." Mr. MacCarthy answered: "We are all right here, we are only sorry for you. I don't understand how you can still keep on cutting steps."

When we had the difficult place behind us, the reward was a fairly steep snow slope, with the snow in good condition so that we could all three go abreast. At the top of the snow slope was another wall, which, however, could be outflanked without difficulty.

The last stretch to the summit was a snowridge. I turned to my *Herren* with the words: "Gentlemen, that's as far as I can take you."

In a few seconds both stood beside me on the peak. We shook hands with one another. I added my usual alpine greeting in German, *"Bergheil."* Of course, I had to explain the word *Bergheil*, because both knew no German. There is no word in the English language which has the same meaning as *Bergheil*.

On the crest of the king of the Rockies, there was not much room to stand. We descended a few metres and stamped down a good space. It was half past five o'clock. Our barometer showed exactly 13,000 feet

The view was glorious in all directions. One could compare the sea of glaciers and mountains with a stormy ocean. Mt. Robson is about 2000 feet higher than all the other mountains in the neighbourhood. Indescribably beautiful was the vertical view toward Berg Lake and the camp below. Unfortunately only 15 minutes were allowed us on the summit, ten of pure pleasure and five of teeth chattering. The rope and our damp clothes were frozen as hard as bone. And so we had to think of the long descent – 5:45 o'clock.

As far as the steep couloir, all went well. The descent over this piece was difficult. All the steps were covered with snow. Except for this, we had no difficulties till the shoulder. As it was late, I proposed to descend by the glacier on the south side, for greater safety. Besides the question of time, it seemed to me too dangerous to make our descent over the route of ascent. As a guide with two *Herren*, one has to take such dangers more into account than do amateurs, for upon one's shoulders rests the responsibility for men's lives. Also as a guide one must consider his calling and the sharp tongues that set going on all sides like clockwork when a guide with his party gets into a dangerous situation. It was clear to me that we must spend a night on the mountain. The descent was not quite clear to me. I was convinced that on this side we could get farther down than by the way we came up. My bivouac motto is: "A night out is hardly ever agreeable, and above 3000 metres always a lottery."

After the shoulder, we had a steep snow slope to the glacier. I made about 120 steps. Once on the glacier, we went down rapidly for a few hundred metres until a sheer precipice barred the way. So far and no farther. Vain was my search for a way down. We had to go back uphill, which was naturally no pleasure. Between rocks and glacier was a very steep icy trench which offered us the only descent. I examined the icy trench for a few minutes, and the ice cliffs overhanging us. I saw the opportunity and, of course, the dangers too. Mr. Foster asked me what my opinion was, whether we could go on or not. I answered, quite truly: "We can; it is practicable but dangerous." Captain MacCarthy said: "Conrad, if it is not too dangerous for you, cutting steps, then don't worry about us. We'll trust to you and fortune."

That made matters easier for me, as I could see that both *Herren* had no fear. I lengthened the rope and left the *Herren* in a sheltered spot. I made the steps just as carefully and quickly as I could. When I had reached a good place I let both *Herren* follow. Mr. MacCarthy went last, and I was astonished at his surefootedness. This dangerous trench took a whole hour to negotiate. The rock was frozen, but the consciousness that we had such terrible danger behind us helped us over the rocks. In greater safety we rested beneath the rocks.

Below us was the glacier, which, seen from above, promised a good descent almost to timberline. I remembered that the glacier had still another break-off and knew that we must camp out. However, I said nothing of this to my *Herren*, but the opposite. I pointed with my axe to the woods with the words: "It will be a fine night down there in the woods beside a big fire." Both chimed in, for the word "fire" makes a very different impression when one is standing in soaking clothes upon ice and snow; from the word "fire" when one is aroused by it from a sound sleep.

We did not find the glacier as good as we expected. We searched our way through ice debris in an avalanche bed. Here on the glacier the sun bade us good night. The sunset was beautiful. It would have been more beautiful to us if the sun had been delayed an hour. It was a melancholy moment when the last glow of evening faded in the west. We rested and spoke on this theme. Mr. MacCarthy said: "It is as well that the law of nature cannot be changed by men. What a panic it would raise if we succeeded in delaying the sun for an hour! It is possible that somewhere some alpinists will tomorrow morning be in the same situation as we are, and will be waiting eagerly for the friendly sun."

Despite the approach of darkness we went on. About ten o'clock in the evening we reached the rocks. It was out of the question to go any farther. Our feet felt the effects of the last 17 hours on ice and rock, and so we were easily satisfied with a resting place. A ledge of rock two metres wide offered us a good place to bivouac. We made it as comfortable as we could. We built a little sheltering wall about us. Our provision bag still had plenty of sandwiches, and Mr. MacCarthy, to our surprise, brought a large packet of chocolate from his rucksack. We took our boots off. I gave Mr. Foster my dry pair of extra mitts for socks, so we all had dry feet, which is the important thing in camping out. The *Herren* had only one rucksack between them, into which they put their feet. Both *Herren* were roped up to a rock.

I gave a few hints on bivouacking, for there are some tricks in sleeping out on cold rocks that one can only learn by experience. Fortunately the night was a warm one, threatening rain. Clouds were hanging in the sky, which, however, the west wind swept away to the east. In the valley we saw flickering the campfire of the Alpine Club and of the construction camp of the Canadian Northern and Grand Trunk Railways. I was very tired and went to sleep without any trouble. A thundering avalanche woke me from a sound sleep. I heard Mr. Foster's teeth chatter as he lay beside me. I uttered no word of sympathy, but went to sleep again.

Later I was awakened by a dream. I dreamed that we were quite close to a forest. I saw wood close at hand, and dry branches ready for kindling. In the dream I reproached myself what the *Herren* would think of me, sleeping here in the forest with firewood, but without a fire and almost freezing. With these reproaches I awoke and sat up to convince myself whether the forest and firewood were really so near. But I saw only a few stars and in the east a few gray clouds lit up with the dawn. I could not get to sleep again, but lay quietly and listened to the thunder of the avalanches which broke the almost ghostly silence of Nature. At daybreak it became considerably warmer, so my *Herren*, who had spent a cold and sleepless night, now fell sound asleep.

At six o'clock the friendly beams of the sun reached us. I wakened my *Herren*. Both sat up and described the pain in their eyes, which they could not open. The eyes of both were greatly swollen. It was not a pleasant sight. I thought both were snow blind. Snow blind, at a height of 9000 feet, and in such a situation – that might have an unpleasant ending. After some cold poultices, the pain abated and both were able to keep their eyes open.

I told my dream. Both *Herren* had dreams of a similar nature, which had reference to the cold night. Mr. Foster dreamed that a number of his friends came with blankets and commiserated the barren camping ground, and no one covered him. Mr. MacCarthy, in his dream, implored his wife for more blankets, and his wife stopped him with the curt reply: "Oh no, dear, you can't have any blankets. Sleeping without any is good training if we want to go to the North Pole."

I searched for a descent over the rocks. After a quarter of an hour I came back.

"Yes, we can make it without further difficulty."

At 6:45 a.m. we left the bivouac, which will certainly remain in our memory. We did not get down so easily after all. We had to get around sheer walls. The climbing was difficult, and at some places the rock was very rotten. This was very unpleasant for my *Herren*. They could only see a few steps through their glasses and swollen eyes.

At last we had the most difficult part behind us, but not the most dangerous. We had to traverse a hanging glacier. For ten minutes we were exposed to the greatest danger. I certainly breathed freely when we lay down to rest under some overhanging rock. Our barometer showed 8,200 feet, time 10:15 a.m. That 800 feet had taken three hours to negotiate. I said to my *Herren*: "I am happy to be able to inform you that we have all dangers behind us. We shall reach the green grass in the valley safe and sound even to our swollen eyes."

We crossed loose stones to the southwest ridge. This ridge should be the easiest way up to the peak. From here we had a beautiful view of Kinney Lake below. Without further difficulty we descended through old snow. At eleven o'clock we took a long rest and devoured everything eatable we could find left in our provision bag. Then we followed the newly built trail to camp.

About five o'clock in the afternoon we came, hungry and tired, into camp, where we were hospitably received by our fellow campers with food and drink and congratulations.[59]

From what Donald Phillips himself said, our ascent was really the first ascent of Mt. Robson. Phillips's words are as follows: "We reached, on our ascent (in mist and storm), an ice dome 50 or 60 feet high, which we took for the peak. The danger was too great to ascend the dome."

Phillips and Kinney made the ascent over the west ridge. The west side is, as far as I could see, the most dangerous side that one can choose. Kinney undertook the journey from Edmonton alone with five horses. On the way he met Donald Phillips who was on a prospecting tour. Mr. Kinney persuaded Phillips to accompany him. Phillips had never before made this kind of a mountain trip and says himself that he had no suspicion of its dangers. They had between them one ice axe and a bit of ordinary rope. They deserve more credit than we, even though they did not reach the highest point, for in 1909 they had many more obstacles to overcome than we, for at that time the railway, which brought us almost to the foot of the mountain, was then no less than 200 miles from their goal, and their way had to be made over rocks and brush, and we must not forget the dangerous river crossings.

Mt. Robson is one of the most beautiful mountains in the Rockies and certainly the most difficult one. In all my mountaineering in various countries, I have climbed only a few mountains that were hemmed in with more difficulties. Mt. Robson is one of the most dangerous expeditions I have made. The dangers consist in snow and ice, stone avalanches and treacherous weather.

Ever since I came to Canada and the Rockies, it was my constant wish to climb the highest peak. My wish was fulfilled. For this ascent I could have wished for no better companions. Both *Herren* were good climbers and Nature lovers, and made me no difficulties on the way. Each had a friendly word of thanks for my guiding. In this country people are much more democratic than with us in Europe, and have less regard for titles and high officials; but still it was a great satisfaction to me to have the pleasure of climbing with a Canadian statesman.

CHAPTER XV

(1913–14)

1

FIRST NEW ZEALAND SEASON

Mystic isles of the South Seas – icy peaks soaring skyward in the land of the Southern Cross. Conrad Kain had already caught a glimpse of this during his voyage from England in 1913. Now new journeys were in store for him. He accepted an engagement to return to New Zealand[60] with Herbert Otto Frind, a young Canadian who had become enamoured of the Southern Alps during the course of a world cruise.

It would be a great experience. Until the season 1913–14, Zurbriggen was the only non-colonial guide who had stood on the summit of a Hermitage Alp. Conrad had made his reputation as a rock climber in the Dolomites. He had learned the technique of ice and snow on Swiss peaks, and had shown his proficiency on such Canadian mountains as Whitehorn and Robson. But he would need all of this knowledge on New Zealand peaks, where heavy precipitation causes the formation of extensive glaciers and snow-fields. They are treacherous, uncertain mountains, alive with avalanches.

The higher peaks had already fallen when Conrad came on the scene, but many others remained untrodden. The New Zealand Alpine Club, then lan-guishing, would revive, and the principles of guiding in vogue at the time would gradually give way to a higher alpine standard. Upon this new field Conrad's talent would be put to the test. Mt. Cook – "Aorangi," the Cloud Piercer – would be the scene of high and tragic adventure.

Mr. Frind's introduction to his journal begins in this manner:

Last October I was again standing over my luggage, labelled New Zealand once more, and wondering what alpine equipment I had to gather for my contemplated revisit to the Southern Alpine fields. I had been making overtures to a well-known and able Austrian guide, who, having had several years of invaluable experience in the Canadian Rockies, and his record of original work in the European Alps, was to all appearances all one could wish for exploring, high climbing or any of the other special hobbies a mountaineer interests himself in. I might as well say here that Conrad Kain not only fulfilled all expectations but also proved to be a very pleasant companion all the time we spent together in the mountains. . . . Conditions in New Zealand are quite different from Europe, where the supply of guides is greater than the ordinary demand, but more like the Canadian Rockies, where the railway has a staff of Swiss guides at their big hotels to take care of any climbers wishing to visit and conquer the peaks within the vicinity of the railway belt, but who could not be obtained for any lengthy exploring trips into the regions further afield. Perhaps one might be fortunate to get one of the high climbing guides for a week or two in New Zealand but during the holiday season this would be improbable.

Conrad's enthusiasm for these peaks was unbounded. From early in January until late in March he climbed with Frind or with other tourists, and if no one else was available he would take another guide or a packer or even the chambermaid from the old Hermitage and lead them up new peaks. At the close of the season he wrote to the editor of the *Alpine Journal*:

> *The mountains of New Zealand are fine. They have, like every mountain group, their own particular charm. But travelling in the mountains there means hard work in carrying. There are still hundreds of mountains to ascend. I may go out there again in October, and shall be pleased to give any information to any members of the Alpine Club. The mountains are more or less dangerous from stones and avalanches, and the weather is very changeable. The best time for expeditions is in February and March.*

The following compiled list of ascents[61] will indicate the scope of Conrad's activity during the season of 1913–14, a magnificent record:

♦ Mt. Wakefield. Jan. 7. New route. H.O. Frind, *C. Kain*.

♦ Mt. Hutton (N. and S. Pks.). Jan. 17. First ascent; traverse. H.O. Frind, *C. Kain*.

From camp up side of waterfall to hanging, moraine-filled valley W. of peaks. Up rib of rock on snow slopes to col on sw arête and over snow domes to high summit, thence traversing across snow arête to NE or second peak. Descent by NE arête into couloir running in W. direction and leading to snows of unnamed glacier. Down grass slopes to Murchison.

* Tasman Saddle. Jan. 18. First crossing from lower Murchison to Tasman. H.O. Frind, *C. Kain*.

* Mt. Thomson. Feb. 7. First ascent. H.O. Frind, *C. Kain*.
  Up face N. of Ngaroimata waterfall, traversing across avalanche snow to couloir and on to rock rib leading to junction of two unnamed glaciers of E. face and from col sw of peak, across latter onto rocks leading to col – then S. arête to top.

* Mt. Annette. Feb. 9. New traverse. H.O. Frind, *C. Kain*.
  Ascent over Sebastopol, following main ridge to summit.

* Mt. Maunga Ma. Feb. 11. First ascent. H.O. Frind, *P. Graham, C. Kain*.
  By rocks of Ngaroimata waterfall on to Ngahanohi Glacier, and up same to SE snow arête and to top. [Kain also led the next three ascents of this mountain: (2) H.F. Wright. (3) Mrs. Thomson. (4) H.C. Chambers, Miss Holdsworth.]

* The Scissors. Feb. 15. First ascent. H.O. Frind, *C. Kain*.

* Mt. Montgomery. New traverse. Same date; same party.

* The Watchtower. First ascent. Same date; same party.
  Three peaks in one day. From Barron's Saddle to col SE of Montgomery. Thence to Fyfe's Pass. Descent from Fyfe's Pass by couloir and face to Mueller névé.

* Mt. Bannie. Feb. 16. First ascent. H.O. Frind, *C. Kain*.
  By unnamed glacier sw of peak and S. arête.

* Mt. Darby. Feb. 17. Third ascent; new traverse. H.O. Frind, *C. Kain*.
  Up W. face and Williams Glacier, and couloir to sw arête. Descent by E. arête to Sladden névé.

* Mt. Sealy. Same date; same party.
  Traverse by W. arête, descending the chimney in the NE face, combining Green's and Earle's routes.

- Mt. Cook. Feb. 22. 16th ascent. H.O. Frind, *W. Brass, C. Kain.*
Traverse, connecting Earle's and Green's routes, from the Hooker side to the Tasman side.

- Tasman Saddle. Mar. 6. First crossing from Tasman to lower Murchison. H.O. Frind, *C. Kain.*

- Classen Saddle. Mar. 7. First crossing to Wataroa Pass. H.O. Frind, *C. Kain.*

- Wataroa Pass. First ascent. Same date; same party.

- Mt. Mannering. First ascent. Same date; same party.
From Murchison by Classen Saddle to Wataroa Pass and along main sw arête to W. snow face, traversing across latter to slabs and up same to summit. Descent by same route.

- Mt. Richmond. Mar. 8. First ascent. H.O. Frind, *C. Kain.*

- The Ant Hill. First ascent. Same date; same party.
Two peaks in one day. Up Harper Glacier, traversing below face of Richmond to adjacent col; thence by W. slabs to summit. From col between Richmond and Ant Hill up N. arête of latter. Descent by W. slopes to Murchison glacier.

- Godley Pass. Mar. 9. First ascent. H.O. Frind, *C. Kain.*

- Mt. Conrad. First ascent. Same date; same party.
From Murchison Glacier up Surprise Glacier to Godley Pass and main S. arête to summit. Descent by same route.

- Mt. Acland. Mar. 10. First ascent. H.O. Frind, *C. Kain.*

- Mt. Sydney King. First ascent. Same date; same party.
Two peaks in one day. Up Aida Glacier to col at E. head, and up main SE arête to summit. Descent by steep sw slabs to névé and col between Mts. Acland and King. From this col up main NW arête of Mt. King. Descent by S. snow face.

- Malte Brun Pass. Mar. 11. First crossing. H.O. Frind, *C. Kain.*
From upper Murchison to Cascade Glacier, up S. watercourse and steep slabs to Cascade Pass, traversing névé of Beetham Glacier below W. face of Malte Brun to col on W. arête and Malte Brun Hut.

- Haeckel Peak. Mar. 13. Second ascent; first traverse. H.O. Frind, *C. Kain.*
  From Darwin glacier to col between Haeckel and Hamilton, thence by
  sw arête to summit. Descent by W. face.

- Mt. Sefton. Mar. 22. 5th ascent. H.O. Frind, *R. Young, C. Kain.*
  New route, from Green Rock by route for Mt. Thomson as far as icefalls
  off E. face of latter, thence traversing to Brunner névé, Douglas Glacier
  and Karangua Saddle. Up W. snow face to summit.

- Brunner Col. Mar. 22. First E.–W. crossing. Same date; same party.

- Shark's Teeth (NE Pk.). Mar. 23. First ascent. H.O. Frind, *C. Kain.*
  From Brunner névé and col between two peaks.

- Brunner Col. First W.–E. crossing. Same date; same party.

- Lean Peak. Mar. 26. Third ascent; first traverse. Miss E. Hamlyn, E. Day, *C. Kain.*
  By main S. and N. arêtes.

- Edith Peak. First ascent. Same date; same party.

- Raureka Peak. Mar. 27. First ascent; traverse. T.C. Fyfe, *C. Kain.*

- Mt. Beatrice (E. Pk.). Second ascent; new traverse. Same date; same party.

- Dilemma Peak (W. Pk.). First ascent. Same date; same party.

- Mt. Eric. Mar. 28. Second ascent. T. Fish, *C. Kain.*

Conrad once told us he originated the building of cairns on New Zealand
summits, that previously climbers had been accustomed to carry up a section of iron pipe. It is probable that his first construction was on Mt. Hutton,
of which Frind notes:

> *Conrad had collected a few large stones and put up a small cairn –*
> *he was rather proud of this stone man on the main summit, and was*
> *speculating on the route of descent … of course, I knew Conrad's habit*
> *and fancy for traverses.*

Frind further records that they met the party of the Dennistouns and
King, with Jock Richmond at the Ball Hut. None of them knew how soon
disaster was to follow.

Maunga Ma, conquered on February 11th, was a tricky peak, and for this reason continued to hold Conrad's interest. Frind outlines a thrilling incident during the ascent:

> I was just mentioning to Conrad that we were pretty well exposed when I heard an ominous crack in the ice above. Big séracs, just about to break loose, were suspended over the precipice, and the question was where was it going to come from when it broke.
>
> Conrad alert and resourceful, however, had espied a little rock buttress, with one perpendicular side about 12–15 feet high, which was the only possible shelter in sight. A few jumps and we were there, when the loud creakings and crackings of the separating sérac above told us that we should not have to wait very long for results. We were facing the wall, and at first I crouched down, until Conrad implored me to stand up straight, as to offer less chance to blocks of ice. A breathless wait of a few seconds while the roar of the falling masses above lasted, and it was quiet again.... Suddenly I saw Conrad start, balancing himself on his ice axe as he was running along with quick short steps; he yelled to me to follow as fast as I could.
>
> We had just crossed a kind of couloir in which a lot of broken ice had collected, when we heard behind us a whiz and a whine and a big avalanche, broken off about 50 feet to the right of the other fall, descended and covered the other broken ice. We reached the névé safely and looking back congratulated ourselves on our good fortune, and increased in me that feeling of reliance on Conrad's judgment and quick action in an emergency which puts him in the forefront of his profession. It made it a good deal easier for me to follow him at times where any hesitation might have proved disastrous.

The Angel of Death was winging above Mt. Cook on February 22nd, although these mountains had waited many years before claiming victims. Two separate parties had left to traverse Mt. Cook by directly opposite routes. Mr. King, with guides Darby Thomson and J. Richmond, intended to cross the mountain by way of Linda Glacier over the highest summit and down the Hooker side, while Mr. Frind, with guides Conrad Kain and W. Brass, desired to ascend the Hooker side and descend the Linda. Both parties were to meet on the summit, taking each other's steps down.

Samuel Turner and J.R. Dennistoun were at the Ball Hut on this date and, from the bivouac, watched King's party on the final slopes. Turner[62] notes:

We rested until 1:30 a.m. on February 23rd, and were making ready to start for Mt. Cook, when Mr. Frind with guides Conrad Kain and W. Brass arrived ... they had traced Mr. King's steps from the summit, which they (Frind's party) only reached at 5:15 p.m., down an avalanche at the head of Linda Glacier, but said they could not pick them up after that.

Frind noted in his journal the events in the descent:

Our two lanterns were lit and we turned off to the right a little in amongst the heaped-up masses of an old slide. Unexpectedly after about ten minutes' going we struck a faint trail and shouted with joy. Through much broken avalanche debris it led us to the top of the big ice break and began to zigzag in amongst big crevasses. We were often puzzled as to the direction of the steps, which at times were very clear, until they took us over to the base of some steep, high rocks, when I asked Conrad if we were all right, to which he replied that they led upward but he was sure we would get down into the lower part of the icefall by following them. "You see, the ice axe marks are on our left and that proves that they ran towards us," but where are their downward tracks? ... we espied a light under the rocks some 50-odd feet ahead.

It was one o'clock or past and a loud Hulloah! from us and the tent flap opened, and we heard a voice: "Is that you, King?" I recognized Jim Dennistoun, to my amazement, believing him down country. Our anxious questions brought forth the reply that they had not seen King since noon ... The fresh steps were Dennistoun's and Turner's, who was with him – an English climber whose books on climbing are well known. But where was the other party?

Turner states that, as no entry of the missing climbers could be found in the Ball Hut book, they left for The Hermitage on the morning of February 24th, but met guides Peter Graham, Conrad Kain (who had gone down for assistance), W. Brass[63] and F. Milne.[64] Peter Graham and Conrad kicked steps over Glacier Dome, ready for the morning.

The following is from Dennistoun's account:[65]

Peter Graham suddenly caught sight of a small black object which he first thought was a stone, but which proved to be one of Richmond's boots sticking out of the upper wall of a narrow crevice ... Conrad and Peter had kicked steps up the snows of the Glacier Dome the day they had arrived at the bivouac, and considering the difficulties and hardships of the Mt. Cook climb, his trip down to and back from The Hermitage and the day of searching up the Linda, one can only describe his efforts as Herculean.

The following is an extract from the Christchurch *Press* of February 28th:

Fortunately they had with them, in Conrad Kain, a man well used to such accidents in Europe and other parts of the world, and his experience was of the greatest value. This plucky man had, with Brass, who also joined the search party, crossed the mountain from the Hooker side, and immediately on being informed of the probability of an accident, started out to help in the rescue work. Peter Graham, who is a past master in alpine work, says he could not find words to express what he thought of Conrad.

Peter Graham and Conrad agreed that in all their long alpine experience they had never seen such a huge avalanche before. Turner closes the sad story:

The three or four feet of hard snow took some considerable time to cut away off the guide's body, and Conrad Kain, having had previous experience, was an indispensable man for this work, as he was all through the whole tragic proceedings. . . . Guide W. Brass suggested carrying the body over the avalanche ice, and did his share; then guides Peter Graham and Conrad Kain took their turn, and we reached the natural blocks of the Linda Glacier, dragging the body over the snow bridges, crevasses, and up over the séracs, down ice walls, across avalanche ice.

It is unusual to have an event of this character described at length by a guide. Hence it is worthwhile to include Kain's own account, from a letter sent to Austria soon afterward:

THE HERMITAGE. MARCH 2ND, 1914 ◆ *This has been a sad week. On the afternoon of February 29th two parties left for Mt. Cook: Mr. Sydney*

King, an Englishman, with two guides to the Ball Hut; and I with Mr. Otto Frind and a guide, William Brass, for the Hooker Hut. I took a guide along so that he might learn the tour. The brothers Mahler, two young fellows from Baden, near Vienna, were at the Hooker Hut and we spent a fine evening together.

On February 21st at five a.m. we left for the bivouac, heavily laden with tent, sleeping bags etc. The Hooker Glacier is much broken. In one place we had to ascend a cliff that was not easy. About two in the afternoon we reached the bivouac, situated just opposite Harper Saddle. It was a very warm day. We made coffee and rested, then went on to the bergschrund. I crossed it alone and cut steps on a steep slope. On the way back I lost my old hat, the "Chamonix hat." It was visible in a crevasse.

As we returned to the bivouac there was a sunset, with the sort of glow that makes one melancholy. We could see the ocean. My heart stood nearly still as I watched the wonderful bright colours. I think that no one lives who would not rejoice at such a miracle of Sun and Nature! But I was chiefly sad on account of the Chamonix hat – I had had it so long.

At the bivouac we made a good supper, and talked a while about various things. I did not feel extra fine, and the bed was hard. Still we slept well, too well; in fact we overslept by an hour, until five a.m. I wanted to be at the bergschrund by that time! We started out at 6:15, following the old track. We stopped beside the crevasse where my hat was. I could not bear to lose that old hat forever, it had been with me on so many journeys. So I had myself lowered 20 metres and, with much exertion, recovered it.

About eight o'clock we were on the long ridge, likewise covered with snow. Where it was not dangerous I let Brass go ahead. It was very warm and progress was slow. I soon saw that the tour would be a long one. We had to do much cutting, and the rock was brittle. We rested at noon. The sun became hotter; avalanches from right and left of the ridge whizzed into the valleys. There was risky work for some 1200 feet, some tiny avalanches going over our heads, though fortunately the rocks protected us. Yes, it was dangerous and, if described exactly, hair raising! But, as always, I led the party quietly, without alarm. It would have been as bad to turn back as to go ahead, so I continued. About 5:15 p.m. we reached the summit of Mt. Cook, the loftiest point in New Zealand. We shook hands.

We were now on the track of Mr. King and his two guides, who were to have descended on our (Hooker) side, but decided instead to go down on their route of ascent. We left the peak at 5:50, following their trail over the ridge to Linda Glacier. I saw that we must spend the night there. We arrived at an enormous avalanche on the Linda Glacier, which could not have come down more than five or six hours before. Here the traces of our friends disappeared. After much trouble we came to the end of the avalanche. Night overtook us, and we could no longer follow the trail. Later, by lantern light, we came again upon King's tracks. Then another avalanche and, at last, the Grand Plateau. We rested and made tea, but almost froze in doing it and were glad to go on once more.

We had two lanterns and it was not difficult to follow the old footsteps. We had to ascend 500 feet to Glacier Dome, and came upon fresh tracks, making us think that our friends were at the bivouac. Bill (Brass) was a great help in descending from Glacier Dome, easily finding the way to the bivouac although it was night. Without him I doubt whether I should have found the route, the rock being broken and no path visible. About 1:40 we reached the bivouac on Haast ridge. When we saw the lighted tent and heard voices a stone fell from our hearts. Yes, it was no deception – there was light and sound!

In a few minutes we were greeted with: "Hallo, is that you, King?" My heart jumped. "No, Frind's party." "Where is King?" "We haven't seen the party, only their tracks. They must have gone down to the valley long before this."

The two men in the bivouac were Mr. Dennistoun, a friend of King, and Mr. Turner, a well-known New Zealand climber. Both had left The Hermitage on the 22nd, in hopes of joining King's party, which would only have been possible in case of bad weather. They started from the Haast bivouac about three a.m., while we lay down to rest. We still hoped that King had gone down by a new route to the Ball Hut.

At 9:15 a.m. on February 23rd we left the bivouac and descended to Ball Hut. There we found guide Thomson's barometer, but no entry of King's in the hut book. It was clear to me that our friends had been buried by the avalanche. I gave my opinion, but Brass said that he did not remember that guides ever made steps on the day preceding a climb farther than Glacier Dome. Greatly depressed we went down to The Hermitage. I had little hope that our friends would be there. We arrived at eight p.m. and there was no sign of them.

The head guide, Peter Graham, was not about, being with a party at the Hooker Hut. We dispatched a guide at once with a letter. About three a.m. on February 24th Graham, wet and agitated, came into my room. I told him everything briefly and asked how far the guides were accustomed to cut steps on the day before an ascent. He said that steps were cut as far as the place where I described the avalanche to be. So it was clear that the tracks which we had found below the avalanche were those made during the ascent on February 21st.

About five o'clock we four guides started out: Graham, Brass, Frank Milne and I. It was a dreary procession. On the way to the Ball Hut we met Mr. Dennistoun and Mr. Turner, who had no further news of the missing. Both turned around and went with us. After a short halt in the Ball Hut we continued to the Haast bivouac. We could undertake nothing further on that day. Graham and I cut steps as far as Glacier Dome and were back by 7:45.

On the 25th we left the bivouac at five a.m. and went to the terminus of the great avalanche. We searched for the place of accident, without result as we ascended. The avalanche, really an ice break, was a kilometre long and half a kilometre at its widest point. Ice blocks of all sizes lay about, the largest as big as a house. On the 23rd two more large ones had come down from Mt. Cook. During descent Graham came upon the body of guide Richmond, fearfully mutilated. We cut it out of the ice. We looked for the bodies of King and guide Thomson without success.[66] Death of the three must have been instantaneous. Transport of Richmond's body to the valley was exceedingly difficult. The disaster on Mt. Cook was the first in the New Zealand mountains and, as everywhere, the newspapers wrote much nonsense about it. I received the thanks of the Tourist Department for my part in the matter. I was pleased by their recognition, but not unduly so, for I know that I did no more than any mountaineer would in such a case. Mr. King was a member of the English Alpine Club and had spent much time in Switzerland. Mt. Cook was his 101st peak. He had ascended several mountains two or three times. Thomson was a New Zealander and one of the best guides. Richmond was also a native, and had every prospect of becoming a first-class guide. It was his first ascent of Mt. Cook. I need scarcely mention that both of them were true lovers of Nature, and took up their calling more or less from passionate love of it, for here in New Zealand there are many opportunities of reaching a higher position in life than one can hope to do as a guide.

You can imagine how it is to search for dead who have been col-leagues and mountain friends, with whom one has proposed a meeting on the highest peak of the country. Now it is over. It was a misfortune that might overtake anyone. It was hard for the native guides, for they had never before seen death in the mountains. Besides, the two guides were well liked by everybody. If the tour of Mt. Cook from the Hooker side had not been so difficult and time consuming, perhaps we our-selves would have been a sacrifice to the avalanche. Guide Thomson and Mr. King have certainly the most beautiful spot in New Zealand for their last resting place – surrounded by ice and snow, where eternal peace reigns. Every wanderer who sees Mt. Cook will think of those who are buried there.

Kain played a manly part in this unfortunate tragedy, but he and Frind were not deterred from carrying on their program. King's ascent of Mt. Cook had been the 15th, Frind's the 16th. On March 9th Conrad and Frind ascended a new peak, Frind noting:

... 3:45 saw us on top and Conrad set to build the biggest cairn he had so far attempted – and it was his masterpiece, fully seven feet high with a diameter of 4–5 feet.... I congratulated him, and suggested that his name should stand on the map for this peak, as I considered that he had more than deserved the honour to be remembered for his work in the Southern Alps.

These were the more important events of Kain's first New Zealand season. He could see no reason to alter his old motto: "You cannot put your head through a stone wall in climbing."

He wrote the two papers which follow:

2

THE SOUTHERN ALPS OF NEW ZEALAND[67]

N ew Zealand offers a unique combination of the special features of many countries, in scenery and sport, which have long appealed to the lover of outdoors. The visitor to her distant shores will find the snow-covered moun-tains and large glaciers on the South Island (named by Captain Cook the Southern Alps) have much to offer to all, from tramp to trained scientist.

The Southern Alps, roughly speaking, form the backbone of the island and run from northeast to southwest, the total length of the range approximating two hundred miles. The snow-clad peaks vary from 7000 feet to 12,349 feet above sea level, the latter elevation being the height of Mt. Cook. There are about 20 separate peaks which reach 10,000 feet. These mountains lie in the same latitude as northern Italy, but the line of perpetual snow is from 3000 to 3500 feet lower than in the European Alps, while the glaciers descend to far lower levels. The Fox and the Franz Josef glaciers descend within 700 feet of sea level, and there are many indications that they once had terminal faces washed by salt water.

The highest points of elevation and the largest glaciers are situated in the centre of the range, the best approach being from Timaru, a flourishing town where motors start for The Hermitage, a distance of 132 miles. For the first 50 miles the road runs through agricultural land, then through country resembling the foothills of the Rockies. This is known as sheep country. The road rises steadily to Burke's Pass (2300 feet), where the traveller obtains his first view of snowcapped peaks. The next scene is Lake Tekapo, fed by streams from Godley and Classen glaciers. There are no roads in these valleys and much work remains for topographers.

From Lake Tekapo the road goes over hills and coulees, which are ancient moraines, to Lake Pukaki, supplied by the rivers flowing from Tasman, Murchison, Mueller and Hooker glaciers. The view from the lake is wonderful and, although the mountains are 40 miles distant, the reflection is perfect, impressing the traveller with the clear atmosphere of the Southern Alps. Judging distance in the mountains is always guesswork until the eyes become accustomed to the surroundings. In New Zealand it is considered a good guess if a stranger estimates within half of the correct distance.

Between Tekapo and The Hermitage the road runs through the Mackenzie plains on which large flocks of sheep obtain good living in summer. I have been told that on several occasions the ranchers suffered great loss through blizzards in the winter.

The Hermitage is a comfortable, modern hotel (2350 feet), commanding a remarkable panorama, including Mt. Sefton, The Footstool, La Pérouse, St. David's Dome (Mt. Hicks), and Mt. Cook in addition to lesser peaks. Guides and porters are stationed at the hotel. If a would-be climber arrives unprepared, it is possible to rent equipment such as snow glasses, ice axe, rucksack, rope and even boots. The latter item is most important if the visitor intends to make excursions. Rented boots, as a rule, mean a blister, and there is no joy-killer more effective in the mountains. From The Hermitage the four largest glaciers east of the divide may be visited, each differing from the other in type and scenery.

The Mueller Glacier is the nearest and its terminal face (2500 feet), which joins the Hooker Valley proper, can be seen from the hotel. For nearly three miles the whole surface is covered with debris, the lateral moraines in places being more than a hundred feet high. Mt. Sefton rises in precipices and hanging glaciers from which avalanches frequently fall. About four miles up, the valley makes a slight curve and there is a fall in the glacier which may be surmounted without difficulty. Above this the valley widens out and the debris is left behind except in the medial moraine. Near its head, three glaciers from the Sealy Range join the main stream, giving rise to the central moraine.

The Mueller Hut is perched on a small shelf on the slope of the Sealy Range. Like others in the Southern Alps it is built of corrugated iron and the inside is lined with oilcloth. These huts are well stocked with provisions and blankets, and are furnished with oil stoves, since timberline is at 3000 feet and what wood occurs is not of the best.

It is said that the South is the home of all winds. I am not an authority on wind, but on many occasions I have been weatherbound in these huts and it was a great relief to know they were securely anchored with cables. In all my wanderings I have not seen better huts anywhere.

The view from the Mueller Hut is confined to nearby mountains and snowfields at the head of the glacier. Nevertheless, it is of such a nature that one can look at it for hours without tiring. The silence is occasionally broken by the roar of an avalanche or the call of the kea. The peaks in view are Footstool, Sefton, Thomson, Eagle, Maunga Ma, Bannie, Burns and McKerrow. The last six are over 8000 feet and from a mountaineering viewpoint are ideal. Space will not permit the giving of details, but it is of interest that the summit of Mt. Burns is guarded by a cornice which must be broken through – a ticklish operation, although it was the only bad cornice I ever encountered in the Southern Alps.

The return trip should be made over Sealy Range. It would not be difficult to build a mountain railway from The Hermitage to this outlook. With it would come a hotel, and a Gornergrat in the Southern Alps could be established. Thousands of people who are physically fit to climb to such an elevation would then have the opportunity to view this indescribable scenery.

The Hooker Glacier is about eight miles long, its terminal face (2880 feet) three miles from The Hermitage. Harper Saddle (8580 feet) is at its head. This is the steepest of the four large glaciers; for nearly four miles the ice is covered with debris, thus resembling the Mueller. Judging from its high, steep, lateral moraine, this glacier has depleted in height more rapidly than the others.

The Hooker Hut (4000 feet) is situated on the southern bank of the glacier, six miles from The Hermitage. One and a half miles from the hut the moraine over which the trail leads breaks up and clear ice and snow begin. A series of falls is encountered which, late in the season, are so broken that a route through the network of large crevasses and séracs can only be found with difficulty. The main attractions to these falls are the towering buttresses of Mt. Cook. La Pérouse with its hanging glacier appears at close quarters and, although in a class by itself for form and beauty, it has received less attention from climbers than other peaks which exceed 10,000 feet. Above the icefalls the glacier widens out into snowfields which sweep down from the lower and middle summits of Mt. Cook, From the high summit a buttress leads down to an isolated rock at its foot, known as the bivouac. The real climb of Mt. Cook, from the Hooker side, begins here, the campsite (7500 feet), being the highest in the Southern Alps. The view and surroundings are alpine in the full sense, but it is far from being a comfortable place. Perhaps some of the twinges of rheumatism that occasionally get into my bones may be traced to such bivouacs, and exposure in high altitudes.

The Tasman Glacier is the largest in New Zealand, 19 miles in length with an average width of one and a half miles. Its tributary streams, of which there are 16, vary from three to seven miles in length. Apart from its size it is also the most interesting. The scenery presents great variations, every corner and twist in the glacier providing magnificent views. The Tasman and its tributaries form an ideal field for the observation of glacial motion. As far as I know, only approximate test measurements on the motion of the main stream have been made, giving 18 inches for the daily maximum. This large glacier has but 190 feet of fall per mile, from névé to terminus.

The terminal face, at 2354 feet, is not of great interest, the ice caves found on nearly all large glaciers of Europe and North America being absent in the Southern Alps. For about six miles from its terminus the Tasman is totally covered with moraine, and in this stretch its width exceeds two miles. On this account the trail has been made on the southern bank, where the lateral moraine is of such tremendous size that it actually forms a valley. Trail ends at the Ball Hut (3000 feet), 14 miles from The Hermitage. This is the only hut that can be reached on horseback. A short distance from the hut, Ball Glacier, the first tributary from the south, joins the main stream. There is a large snowfield at the head, which is known as Ball Pass (7426 feet), on the southern spur of Mt. Cook. This is an alternative route for returning to The Hermitage by way of Hooker Valley. The view from the pass is fine on both sides, and chamois have made this dividing range their stamping ground.

From the lateral moraine of Ball Glacier one has a close-up view of Tasman and a further introduction into atmospheric conditions in the South. The distance from this point to the head of the Tasman is 12 miles, yet anyone with good vision can count the larger crevasses and follow the bergschrund on the most distant mountain with ease.

From Ball Glacier the descent is made over the lateral moraine, which resembles a cutbank, to the main glacier. After walking over moraine for an hour or more the newcomer will realize he has made a mistake in judging the distance. Scrambling over moraines is often very tiring, but on this glacier one finds numerous points which offer good excuse for resting. The Hochstetter icefall, 2000 feet high, with séracs of all sizes and forms, pointing in all directions, seen by the hundred, justifies a long halt. It often happens that one or more of these pinnacles will lose their balance and tumble, knocking others down in spectacular fashion. Mts. Cook (12,349 feet), and Tasman (11,475 feet), form the background of this icy scene.

On the dividing ridge between Hochstetter and Haast glaciers, at 7000 feet, is the King Memorial Hut, erected in memory of Mr. King, an English climber who with two guides climbed Mt. Cook and was killed by an avalanche while descending. The writer happened to be on Mt. Cook the day of the accident. The hut is built on the spot where the unfortunate climbers spent their last night. To erect it in tribute to a man who loved the mountains and lost his life in them is a noble deed, and in this instance would be greater if the names of the two guides were also associated with it. A visit to the hut is highly recommended, especially to those who wish to secure a close-up view of the two highest peaks in New Zealand, Mts. Cook and Tasman. The best place for this is Glacier Dome, an easy scramble from the hut. Here is probably the grandest scene of snow and ice in the Southern Alps – the sightseer is well-advised to take along an extra film.

Opposite the main range is Malte Brun, the dividing massif between Tasman and Murchison valleys. The outstanding peaks are Mts. Chudleigh,

Malte Brun (10,421 feet), Hamilton and Haeckel. Malte Brun, highest in the chain, offers the mountaineer the best rock climb in the district.

Malte Brun Hut (5700 feet) is situated on the eastern bank of Tasman Glacier, about seven miles from Ball Hut. To give the reader an idea of the vast stretch of snow to be seen, it will suffice to mention the peaks comprised in the panorama: Mts. Cook, Dampier, Silberhorn, Tasman, Lendenfeld, Haast, Haidinger, de la Bêche, Green, Elie de Beaumont and Darwin, the Minarets and Hochstetter Dome, and Douglas and Glacier peaks. The upper portion of the Tasman Glacier, about a mile in width, pure white and free of stones, is the foreground of this picture. The large snowfields at the head of Tasman Glacier form an ideal place for winter sports in summer.

Murchison Glacier was once a tributary of Tasman, but as its terminal face is now four miles from the old junction it must be considered as an individual. Hemmed in by the Malte Brun and Liebig ranges, its length is 11 miles. It has six tributaries from Malte Brun and two from the Liebig Range. The latter for miles is bare of snow, the highest point, Mt. Hutton, being crowned with three glaciers in their last stages. Mt. Acland, though a thousand feet lower, has a fairly large snowfield. At the head of the glacier are two picturesque peaks, Mt. Mannering and Brodrick Peak; there is also a pass between Hochstetter Dome and Mt. Aylmer which connects with Tasman Valley. The Murchison Valley has neither trail nor hut and is seldom visited.

Just as in other countries, the sections that receive most publicity attract the greater number of visitors. Such is the case in the Southern Alps. I believe that a fair estimate would be one visitor on the western for every 25 on the eastern slope. The difference in vegetation on the eastern and western slopes of the Southern Alps is so extreme that it would be impossible to imagine a greater contrast. On the east the country is open and stretches for miles without a single tree or bush over ten feet high. Thousands of sheep wander from the bottoms of the wide valleys to snowline. On the western side the valleys are deep and narrow; in places there are canyons of great depth, and small lakes surrounded by dense, primeval forest.

To see as much as possible of the Southern Alps, the traveller who has only a limited time is advised to make a round trip over Copland Pass (7400 feet) to the west coast and come back by way of Franz Josef Glacier and Graham Saddle (8739 feet) to Tasman Glacier and The Hermitage. Such an excursion, however, demands good physical condition and a guide. Reliable guides, in addition to those at The Hermitage, are to be obtained at Glacier Hotel, Waiho gorge.

The best way to make the trip is to start from Hooker Hut, whence a fairly good trail leads to Copland Pass. The view to the east offers an extensive panorama, including the highest peaks. To the west is a sea of lesser peaks rising out of forest-clad ranges. Trail on the west leads over rocks, shale and snow into the deep Douglas Valley, the head of the Copland River. The first stopping place is Welcome Flat Hut, in a typical western valley with high, smooth cliffs on one side and snowcapped mountains on the other. Near the hut is a hot spring with water whose temperature is just too high for bathing.

From Welcome Flat a good trail winds down through primeval forest into the Copland Valley. Ferns are a conspicuous feature, from the small maiden-hair, and lace, to the giant mamuka, or black-stemmed tree fern. In such a jungle of semi-tropical vegetation one would naturally be on the lookout for reptiles, but New Zealand is one of the few southern countries that is free of them, as well as of poisonous insects.

Where the Copland joins the Karangarua River the country widens out and road takes the place of trail. Twenty-eight miles from Welcome Flat is Cook's River Settlement. This river drains La Pérouse Glacier; its largest tributary, Balfour River, descends from St. David's Dome, Silberhorn and Tasman.

Fox Glacier is the second largest on the west coast, its terminus only 670 feet above sea level. Good trail leads for two miles from the road to the glacier, whence an interesting ice-worn pinnacle 900 feet high can be seen, as well as a hot spring near the ice.

Many who are acquainted with the glaciers of the Southern Alps claim that the Franz Josef is the most beautiful in New Zealand. No doubt the semi-tropical vegetation, a rare occurrence in glaciated regions, is the inspiration for such sentiment. In addition there is the gorge of the Callery River, which joins the Waiho a short distance from Glacier Hotel. From its source of supply, in tremendous snowfields on the divide, this glacier has a fall of more than 1000 feet to the mile, thus explaining the roughness of its surface. Measurements show a daily summer movement of 15 feet.

In this locality one has greater opportunity to study ice formation, as well as its motion and action on rock, than on slower moving streams. There are two huts, the first of which is situated on the south bank of the glacier at Cape Defiance, near the Unser Fritz waterfall, 1200 feet high. The names are often German, as Austrians were numbered among the early pioneers and played a prominent part in blazing the trails. They have also written interesting books of their travels. It was an Austrian expedition that first explored the head of the Tasman Glacier and ascended Hochstetter Dome.

The second hut is placed on the ridge by the Almer Glacier, whence the great snowfields at the head of the valley may be traversed to Graham Saddle. A fairly easy descent over rock and snow brings the traveller to Tasman Glacier and back to The Hermitage.

Instead of crossing the divide, Franz Josef Glacier may be reached with ease by rail from Christchurch, by way of Arthur's Pass tunnel (five miles long) to Hokitika, an old gold-mining town on the west coast. From railhead to Waiho gorge by motor is a distance of 90 miles, the road passing through beautiful forest with occasional glimpses of the main range.

East of the divide the flowers are limited in comparison with the luxuriant growth on the west side. The mountain lily, pure white with great, round, cup-like leaves which sometimes exceed 12 inches in diameter, grows on graceful stems and is considered the most beautiful flower in the Southern Alps. There are many mountain daisies, the largest kind sometimes having a flower three inches in diameter; it is white, with yellow centre, and has silvery leaves more than a foot in length. Among the smaller plants is found the edelweiss, not quite as large as the Swiss variety. The forests on the western slopes are filled with ferns, lichens, mosses, wild clematis and the red-flowering rata tree.

There are no native mammals of large size in New Zealand, and as Nature for some reason or other did not put them there, man has undertaken to stock the land with domesticated and wild animals from other countries. Captain Cook, to the delight of the native Maoris, introduced the pig, which to this day remains their favourite pet. In 1868 red deer were imported from Scotland, and increased so rapidly that in some districts they became a nuisance and were killed by thousands to make room for sheep. Chamois were turned out years ago and are increasing in large numbers. These were the gift of the Austrian Emperor, Franz Josef.

Moose were sent from Canada at a later period and released in the area surrounding Milford Sound, where they have done well. This section of New Zealand resembles the fjords of Norway; there are swamps, and sandflies take the place of northern mosquitoes.

None of these will ever cause so much trouble as the rabbit. This prolific animal had no enemies in the new land, with the result that they increased to such an extent that many districts became infested. Man's effort to control the pest proved of little value. Weasels were imported to combat the plague, but unfortunately played havoc with the flightless birds which are a rare treasure to the country.

Of great interest is the kea, the most impudent and fearless bird in the mountains. Belonging to the parrot tribe, he is full of mischief and amusing antics. The weka is a flightless bird and an inveterate kleptomaniac. After he has picked up everything that he can swallow around a camp he becomes quite tame and his amusing habits make him the source of much entertainment. The kiwi is a genuine flightless nightbird, a relic of past age and undoubtedly the most interesting to ornithologists. There are innumerable smaller members of the feathered tribe, of which the bellbird is considered the best singer.

There are many insects, none poisonous, some of which are found at high altitudes where vegetation has ceased to exist. How do they get there, and on what do they live? Such questions provide opportunity for testing one's intellect and adding to the sum of human knowledge.

3

MT. MAUNGA MA

In New Zealand I climbed 48 peaks, including Mt. Cook, the highest, and Mt. Sefton, the most attractive of all. These two mountains are best known in New Zealand, as they are the highest and most picturesque, but that does not mean that they must be the most interesting from a climber's point of view.

Climbing high peaks in the Southern Alps is hard and strenuous work because the timberline is much lower than in other countries and therefore the climber is compelled to carry a camp outfit on his back up the mountain to a certain height, from whence he can reach the summit next day. Carrying heavy packs and sleeping (if you can) on cold rocks takes a great deal of pleasure away. It is also known that the highest mountains do not always offer the best views, and the view is the prize and reward of the climber and Nature lover for his work.

A great number of mountaineers like a change on a climb, which means a combination of rocks, snow and ice, but such mountains are not always at hand. Mountains which offer mixed climbing and can be reached without a long weary tramp are soon known as ideal climbs, and this sort of an ideal climb I found in the Southern Alps on Mt. Maunga Ma.

This peak is on the Moorhouse Range, halfway up the eight-mile-long Mueller Glacier, and right opposite the newly built Mueller Hut, which can be reached in four or five hours from The Hermitage by two different routes. One is over the Sealy Range, the other up the Mueller Glacier. Both of them offer charming views. The hut is situated on a terrace, 400 feet above the glacier. I am quite convinced that the situation of this hut has no rival in the Southern Alps. The scenery and surroundings remind me of a picture gallery where pictures of different countries were exhibited.

Looking down the valley are steep slopes and clear outline of Footstool, and Mt. Sefton with his collar of ice, from which now and then roaring avalanches fall over the precipice nearly 2000 feet high to the glacier below. One could easily imagine that he was on the south side of the Meije, in the Dauphiné, looking up the valley to Mt. Darby, with his rugged rock ridge descending to the glacier, and Mt. Montgomery with its clear outline leading up from Barron Saddle, and the black precipice which faces the hut.

Behind is Spence Peak, with his triangular form, and still farther behind, Mt. Forster, which stands out like a roof in an Italian mountain village, bringing to one's memory scenes in the Dolomites and Pyrenees. Looking at the slope of the Sealy Range and seeing the red sandstones, green grass patches and strips of snow between, there is nothing easier than to imagine oneself to be on a *bergerie* on the beautiful island of Corsica.

From a climber's point of view this new hut is Paradise pure and simple. The following peaks can be climbed: Mt. Oliver; Kitchener Peak; Mt. Annette, an easy and grand viewpoint; Mt. Sealy with its snow and rocks; Jean and Jeanette, good and interesting rock climbs; Mt. Darby, rock and snow routes; Mts. Montgomery and Spence with mixed climbing. Mt. Burns, Mt. Bannie, Mt. Isabel, Mt. Maunga Ma, Eagle Peak, Mt. Thomson and The Shark all offer both rock and ice.

Early in the season this would be a wonderful place, offering the best opportunities in the Southern Alps for spring snowshoeing and glissading. Now let me take you up to the summit of Maunga Ma. It has been climbed four times, on each of which occasions I acted as guide. The first ascent was with H.O. Frind and Peter Graham; the second by H.F. Wright; the third by Mrs. Thomson (first lady); fourth by Miss Holdsworth and Mr. Chambers.

It takes 20–30 minutes to cross the glacier to where the real climb begins. A spur, or arête, runs up to the hanging glacier, which is marked on some old maps. A steep snow couloir leads to this arête. This place is dangerous in the afternoon on account of falling stones. To the right of this arête is a long couloir which shows tracks of stonefalls and avalanches. One can see and hear the stones whirling through the air.

It may sound ridiculous when I say I like to hear the whistling sound of falling stones and big ice crashes, but of course that means if I am in a safe and sheltered place. The rocks are very loose; one has to move with the greatest care. On such a place there is no time for daydreaming, and that makes it clear to me why so many medical men send their patients to the mountains when they are mentally run down.

On such a height and in such surroundings of bare rocks and ice, one would hardly expect any kind of life, and it is really a great surprise when one sees patches of growing plants in small cracks or crevices of the rocks. These little alpine plants are very short and tender, and yet have strength enough to fight the battle of life. They rejoice when the sun is shining on them in the rocky cranny just as much as their bigger sisters in the more sheltered valleys.

Two thirds of the way up one comes to the first difficulty of the climb: a perpendicular band 15 feet high bars the way. To overcome this obstacle one has to descend a short distance on a small ledge leading to a crack. Such cracks are known among climbers as chimneys. On top of this chimney is stuck a big boulder, so that one has to climb out on the wall, and by doing so one hangs only with his hands on the rocks. The feet are for a short time useless and they swing in the air until the climber pulls himself up or rests on his stomach.

I am used to this game, but people who do this sort of thing for the first time describe it as a very funny sensation. A couple of hundred feet higher is another hard piece. This looks like a tumbledown brick pile and appears to be a death trap, but on closer inspection it proves to be overcome without danger. But one breathes more freely when this suspicious-looking place is overcome. A short snow slope brings one to the glacier, where one can go ahead without the use of the hands.

On the glacier are several remarkable crevasses, or big ice caves. The view at this height is increasing at every step. Without any difficulties one reaches the ridge which descends from the very summit, and which can be seen from the Hooker Valley and the Mueller Hut. The first part of this ridge is easy, as far as the bergschrund. Late in the season this 'schrund has to be attacked with great care. It differs from any other I saw on my climb, forming more or less a big ice cave. Hundreds of icicles, three to six feet long, form a picture one cannot describe with words. It would sound like a far-fetched fairy story.

The slope above the 'schrund is best overcome by zigzags, until one reaches the rocks halfway up. The steepness of the slope increases very rapidly and looks by no means inviting, especially early in the season when the cornice is getting her full size. The last hundred feet of this slope I judge has an angle of 65–70 degrees. The summit is always crowned by a cornice, and that makes the final part of the climb exciting and dangerous. But when one stands on the summit and shakes the hand of his companion, and looks around to see the wonderful work of Nature, such trifles are soon forgotten.

The view from this summit proves once more that the medium mountains are the best for views. The most striking picture is looking northwest, at Mt. Sefton with his hanging glaciers, Mt. Thomson in the foreground and Mt. Cook, the king of all, in the background. Far to the north are the mountains and peaks up the Tasman and Murchison, of which Malte Brun, with his fine form, appears to be the monarch. Not to be forgotten is the view to the west – the Tasman Sea.

4

ROCKIES AND PURCELLS

K ain returned to Canada early in the spring of 1914, and Mr. Wheeler noted in his diary:

JUNE 4TH ♦ *Conrad at clubhouse, working at Boundary Survey outfits etc.*
JUNE 10TH ♦ *Conrad[68] left with Campbell's party for Morley.*
JUNE 15TH ♦ *Party started for Elk Pass.*
JULY 11TH ♦ *With me at Crowsnest Pass (Boundary Survey).*
JULY 17TH ♦ *Returned with me to Calgary.*
JULY 19TH ♦ *Left Field with Conrad for Upper Yoho camp,* ACC. *Conrad working at camp.*

It was during an ascent of Mt. Balfour that his party had a startling adventure in an electrical storm.[69] While on the summit:

The flash made directly for Conrad, but its force was divided by the ice axes of the party, several of whom were bowled over. They afterwards described the sensation as that of being hit by golf balls. Although Conrad was thrown down, he was able to shout: "Throw away

*your ice axes and run for your lives." We didn't argue the point. Down
an unknown snow arête to overhanging rocks we fled. There we cheerfully regained our composure while we waited for the storm to pass.*

One thinks, in reading an account by Rev. J. McCartney Wilson,[70] that
this must have been an unusually pleasant camp:

*I laugh again at the quaintly extravagant western humour of Jimmy
Simpson, and once again that amazing artist Conrad Kain, whom New
Zealand has taken from us, plays on my soul as on an instrument and
elicits music therefrom.*

L.C. Wilson of Calgary recalls happy days with Conrad on Mt. Marpole
and Isolated Peak, and "a joyous party over Emerald Pass to Emerald Lake."
When camp closed, Kain accompanied A.H. MacCarthy to the Purcell
Range and made the first ascent of Mt. Farnham, its loftiest summit.[71]
Thus in two seasons he had led the first ascents of the highest peaks in two
Canadian ranges. The elapsed time on the Farnham climb was more than
22 hours, with the descent made in the

*dark excepting for occasional intervals of moonlight between pass-
ing clouds. . . . The extreme care that was required in working along the
steep narrow ledges, and trying to keep the rope clear (Conrad had
declared we should treat the rope as we would treat our mother), made
progress very slow, and Conrad proposed a shift directly toward a snow
couloir, which we gained after making a 50-foot descent of the side of
a gorge wall.*

The next evening was spent by the campfire "listening to Conrad's delightful reminiscences and philosophy, which ranged all the way from snaring
mice in Siberia to the intricate problems of true government." Conrad's visits to the Purcells had sufficed to impress upon him the charm of this wild,
beautiful range of British Columbia. The railway was being built through
the Columbia Valley; no longer would one voyage from Golden on the picturesque craft piloted by Capt. Armstrong. Conrad knew then, one thinks,
that these mountains would one day become his home.

CHAPTER XVI

(1914–15)

▲

1

SECOND NEW ZEALAND SEASON

Kain's activity in searching for the bodies of S.L. King and his two guides, killed on Mt. Cook, brought him an engagement from the New Zealand Tourist Department, and he returned to The Hermitage in the autumn of 1914, as assistant to Peter Graham. This was a happy association, for Graham and Kain formed a small but genuine mutual admiration society. Graham had already made a considerable name for himself in New Zealand climbing, and had been one of Miss DuFaur's guides in the first "Grand Traverse" of Mt. Cook in 1910.

By his coaching of young native guides, Conrad undoubtedly contributed much to the improvement of technique in New Zealand, a matter which in later years would be given official attention. The list of his climbs, compiled by Peter Graham, now follows:

◆ Mt. Elie de Beaumont. Sept. 23, 1914. *F. Milne, C. Kain.*

◆ Footstool. Nov. 8. Second (?) ascent. *R. Young, C. Kain.*

◆ Unnamed (7000 ft.). Dec. 25. Sutton-Turner, *C. Kain.*

◆ Mt. Jean. Dec. 27. First ascent; traverse. D. Maughan, W. Fisher, H.N.P. Sloman, *C. Kain.*

◆ Mt. Sealy. Dec. 28. E.P. Lee, Scannell, Walton, *C. Kain.*

◆ Footstool. Jan. 1. E.P. Lee, Walton, *C. Kain.*

◆ Footstool. Jan. 2. D. Maughan, W. Fisher, H.N.P. Sloman, *C. Kain.*

◆ Mt. Mabel. Jan. 19. W. Fisher, *C. Kain.*

- Eagle Peak. Jan. 28. First ascent. H.F. Wright, *C. Kain.*

- Mt. Maunga Ma. Same date; same party.

- Mt. Low. Feb. 2. First ascent. H.C. Chambers, H.F. Wright, *C. Kain.*

- Mt. Jellicoe. First ascent. Same date; same party.

- Mt. Hicks (St. David's Dome). Feb. 3. Second ascent. H.C. Chambers, H.F. Wright, *C. Kain.*

- Mt. Sturdee. First ascent. Same date; same party.

- Mt. La Pérouse. An attempt from the east, by Chambers, Wright and *Kain*; in February.

- Unnamed (8000 ft.). Feb. 5. Mrs. J. Thomson, *C. Kain.*

- Mt. Jeanette. First ascent. Same date; same party.

- Mt. Maunga Ma. Feb. 6. Mrs. J. Thomson, *C. Kain.*

- Mt. Walter. Feb. 8. J. Robertson, H.F. Wright, *C. Kain.*

- Mt. Darwin. Same date; same party.

- Aiguille Rouge. Feb. 11. Prof. and Mrs. Robinson, *C. Kain.*

- Coronet Peak. Feb. 12. H.C. Chambers, J. Robertson, Prof. Robinson, H.F. Wright, *C. Kain.*

- Mt. Meeson. First ascent. Same date; same party.

- Mt. Maunga Ma. Feb. 16. H.C. Chambers, Miss B. Holdsworth, *C. Kain.*

- Malte Brun. Feb. 19. Mrs. J. Thomson, *C. Kain.*

- Mt. Montgomery. Feb. 28. Third (?) ascent. S. Turner, *C. Kain.*

- Spence Peak. Mar. 1. First ascent. S. Turner, *C. Kain.*

- Proud Peak. Mar. 8. Mrs. J. Thomson, *C. Kain.*

- Mt. McKerrow. Mar. 19. First ascent. S. Turner, *C. Kain.*

- Edith Peak. Mar. 27. Mrs. J. Thomson, *C. Kain.*

- Lean Peak. Same date; same party.

- Nun's Veil. Mar. 30. Mrs. J. Thomson, *C. Kain.*

♦ Mt. Edgar Thomson. Apr. 7. Mrs. J. Thomson, *C. Kain.*

Kain made a number of first ascents in company with H.F. Wright and H.C. Chambers, both members of the Alpine Club. Mr. Wright, a pioneer in New Zealand climbing, was once present when a discussion arose as to the ideal number of members for climbing party. This particular subject was a fertile matter for debate in New Zealand at that time. Conrad was asked his opinion. "Well," he said, "I think three; but if there is any difficulty, then you should leave the weakest at home."

The following is abstracted from Chambers's account[72] of the attempt on La Pérouse:

> *At the Cook bivouac, Conrad, lying dreamily on his back, gazed longingly at the great ridge of La Pérouse, which came toward us in a series of imposing curves. Presently he began to count thoughtfully to himself the number of hours it might take to get along these rocky peaks and pinnacles. On reaching five hours, he paused hopefully and turned to us an inquiring eye.*

This is very characteristic of Conrad's method of encouraging his patrons to ever greater efforts, even though

> *Looking back I have no doubt that Conrad realized more fully than any of us this attempt on La Pérouse was in the nature of a forlorn hope. In the circumstances, i.e., with the possibility of no climb the following day – it was, I think, a perfectly justifiable effort.*

In the same season Kain carried out several new expeditions with Samuel Turner,[73] that enthusiastic but self-centred climber whom Kain came to know at the time of the Mt. Cook tragedy.

> *On March 9th I had no guide, and had to spend the time at The Hermitage waiting for one. On March 16th, having arranged with Conrad Kain and R. Young for a week's expedition to climb some peaks in the Landsborough, I preceded Kain to the Mueller Hut in company with Young ... Conrad Kain and myself spent the day piling up stones and flat rocks to make the foundations of the hut stronger, as others had felt its insecurity in a gale.*

Conrad's popularity in New Zealand was not lessened by the publication in the Christchurch *Press* of his well-remembered story "The Millionaire Guide," describing his imaginary adventures on the Großglockner when, disguised as a tourist, he hired a guide to take him up.

Chamois were brought to New Zealand many years ago. In 1914 additional specimens were released, but the one surviving buck was not well-received by the older herd. He thereupon returned to seek human companionship, became something of a nuisance and met an unexpected end. Not even of Colani, the legendary hunter of the Engadine, have stranger tales been told than this, which Frank Milne related:[74]

> One day Conrad Kain was conducting a young lady to the Mueller Hut with the chamois in attendance. At a point where the path is narrow and the drop below considerable, the lady knelt down to do up a bootlace; the beast saw his chance, gleefully he stalked her from the rear, brought off his coup on her centre of gravity, and waited expectantly for her to roll down to the glacier far below. But she recovered her balance, and Kain, in a momentary access of anger, uplifted his ice axe and drove the pick into a vital portion of the unchivalrous animal. On his return he skinned it, took it to the hotel, and left it hanging out to dry, thinking it would look well stuffed. When he came back he found a dog had pulled it down and worried it, doing a serious damage to its under-jaw. But Kain was a man of resource, and replaced the injured part with the corresponding portion of a recently butchered lamb. And now that chamois, happy in his death, adorns the lobby of The Hermitage.

2

HORSETHIEF CREEK, PURCELL RANGE

K ain reached Canada once more in the spring of 1915, and went to work for A.H. MacCarthy at the latter's new ranch near Wilmer. He visited the Ptarmigan Lake Camp of the ACC in Frind's company, later guiding MacCarthy's parties in the Purcells, when the Big Salmon and Horsethief valleys were explored.

Taking part in these expeditions was Professor W.E. Stone, of Purdue University, a keen climber who became much interested in Purcell exploration.[75] The first and shorter trip took them into the south fork of the

Big Salmon, a region unknown to climbers, where the first ascent of Mt. Ethelbert was made, a striking peak named in 1886 by Capt. Armstrong for a nun who died on his vessel.

A considerable number of new ascents were then carried out from Horsethief Valley, among them Mt. Jumbo, thought at that time to be the highest summit of the range. While no climbs of outstanding difficulty were made, the pioneer work of this season added greatly to the topographical knowledge of the central uplift of the Purcells.

CHAPTER XVII

(1915–16)

▲

1

THIRD NEW ZEALAND SEASON

For a third season Conrad Kain voyaged to New Zealand, this time as private guide. He was now well-known and much in demand. The World War was at its height and, although Conrad had become a Canadian citizen, a few people, perhaps through jealousy, still looked upon him as an alien. This did not make his life easier.

The following ascents were accomplished:

◆ Mt. Bannie. Dec. 6, 1915. Mrs. J. Thomson, *C. Kain*.

◆ Mt. Burns. Dec. 11. Mrs. J. Thomson, *C. Kain*.

◆ Mt. Elie de Beaumont. Dec. 22. Mrs. J. Thomson, *C. Kain*.

◆ Mt. Darwin. Dec. 23. Mrs. J. Thomson, *C. Kain*.

◆ Aiguille Rouge. Jan. 7. D. Maughan, H.N.P. Sloman, *C. Kain*.

◆ Traverse, ascending NW arête, descending N. face.

◆ The Minarets. Jan. 8. H.N.P. Sloman, *C. Kain*.

◆ Mt. de la Bêche. Same date; same party.

◆ Mt. Maunga Ma. Jan. 16. D. Maughan, H.N.P. Sloman, *C. Kain*.
E. face from Mueller Hut.

◆ Mt. Marie. Jan. 22. First ascent. Mrs. H.N.P. Sloman, *C. Kain*.
N. face from Sladden Glacier.

◆ Mt. Darby. Same date; same party.

◆ Mt. Maunga Ma. Jan. 23. Mrs. H.N.P. Sloman, *C. Kain.*

◆ Mt. Maunga Ma. Jan. 24. Miss M. Marsden, *C. Kain.*

◆ Mt. Sealy. Jan. 25. Mrs. H.N.P. Sloman, *C. Kain.*

◆ Unnamed (8250 ft.). Same date; same party.

◆ Unnamed (8110 ft.). Same date; same party.

◆ Mt. Cook. Jan. 31. 17th ascent. Mrs. J. Thomson, *C. Kain.*
Second "Grand Traverse." Ascent from Hooker bivouac to third peak
and thence by main arête to second and on to highest summit. Descent
by Green's route.

◆ Mt. Arsinoë. Feb. 7. Second ascent. Mrs. H.N.P. Sloman, *C. Kain.*

◆ Mt. Lloyd. Mar. 14. First ascent. Mrs. H.N.P. Sloman, *C. Kain.*

This season was made pleasant by his climbing association with Canon
and Mrs. H.N.P. Sloman,[76] and by his notable achievement in traversing Mt.
Cook with Mrs. Thomson.

Mr. Arthur P. Harper, former president of the New Zealand Alpine Club,
writes:

*I never met Kain, but the Grahams and Milne, our best-known
guides, had a very great admiration for him. I think he probably
had a big influence on guides' work here. When he came out with
Frind they had a whole season to work in and could wait for their
weather.*

*I always think his most daring bit of work and, if I may say so, a
climb he should not have done, was when he took Mrs. Thomson over
the three peaks of Cook. She was an oldish lady of 59, who had gone
through a long course of lower peaks and was very keen, but personally
I do not think Conrad was quite right to do this alone with her. It is a
really big expedition and requires perfect conditions.*

*We all admit Conrad's pluck and skill in doing this particular climb
under the circumstances, but it was not safe and I think he recognized
that himself. There were several mitigating circumstances. I don't know
all the rights of the matter, but it was I believe a case of doing it alone
with her or not doing it at all. And she was so determined to give it a
go that Conrad consented.*

It should not be forgotten that Miss Freda DuFaur, who traversed the three peaks of the mountain for the first time on January 3rd, 1913, with Peter Graham and Darby Thomson, had expressed the somewhat rash doubt whether mortal being could be found bold enough to repeat the Grand Traverse. It was this challenge that Conrad accepted on January 31st, 1916, when he led Mrs. Thomson – "a marvellous feat unequalled for daring in the annals of the Southern Alps."

Mrs. Thomson recalls that Conrad was "a splendid guide, with a genius for finding new routes. He never took an established route unless it pleased him to do so. Competent judges say he was the finest mountaineer ever in New Zealand." In those days he was a handsome man with a pleasing personality and a fund of entertaining stories of his life, told in broken English.

H.N.P. Sloman has similar memories of Conrad, of whom he has recently written:

> He was a real and very dear friend of both of us, and eternal youthfulness seemed his outstanding quality. We had always regarded him as co-equal with, if not junior, to us. I find it hard to think of Conrad as a guide; we met him first the first year he came out to nz with Otto Frind, I think in January 1914, as a private guide at the old Hermitage. That year, of course, we did no formal climbs with him, but whenever he had an off day, whether owing to bad weather or other causes, he would join our party on picnics or gentle walks in the valley; he would tell his inimitable stories, sometimes in his slow, hesitating English, which, however, always found the effective, if not always the "juste" word, and sometimes in his native dialect of German, which I chanced to know pretty well. He taught us all much of birds and flowers and plants, of the way to boil our "billy" on two damp sticks in a howling wind; several of us knew mountains fairly well and loved them, but he taught us all far, far more than we had known of what love for them could be and mean to a sensitive, imaginative, yet intensely practical soul like his.
>
> I think that year I only did one actual climb with him, the quite easy Footstool ridge. But on wet days I often watched him on the problem boulders near the hotel, demonstrating his amazing skill and balance on rocks, always eager to teach and help. I learnt my climbing with Ambros Supersaxo and his son Oscar, but I had never seen such surety of foot and such perfection of balance combined with speed and judgment as

Conrad showed, and withal he had the modesty and naturalness that few experts have. We loved to compare him with Sam Turner!

We met again in January 1915 and in 1916 and I did one or two climbs with him, including *The Minarets from Malte Brun Hut*, and the *Ball Pass* and the second or third ascent of *Maunga Ma*. In one or another of these years I tried Cook with him twice, once from the Hooker side and once from the Tasman side, but on both occasions we were beaten off by weather; we spent 24 hours in a 6-foot by 4-foot Whymper tent at the Hooker bivouac in a snow blizzard on one attempt, listening to his inexhaustible fund of stories, and sometimes wishing he would smoke tobacco and drink tea instead of chewing the former and smoking the latter!

My wife did much more climbing with Conrad than I did, as I only had a month's climbing, while she had two months every year. She did at least two first ascents in NZ with him; he had taught her from scratch and she owes her love of the mountains, as well as her skill in the art, to his inspiration.

As a guide, what gave me such pleasure was the fact that Conrad never put on the rope till it was necessary in the case of the individual climber concerned, so different from most of the modern guides in the Alps. He never hurried, and loved on a fine day to dally over a fine view, even if it meant getting home late. His route finding in country quite new to him and unmapped was masterly, and his initiative in finding new routes is, I believe, largely responsible for the enthusiasm for climbing in NZ, which is now in such striking contrast to that prewar indifference, which was so surprising. Frank Milne, next to Darby Thomson and the Graham brothers, the best NZ guide, owed everything, as he told me on many occasions, to Conrad's inspiration and example.

I hope some of Conrad's stories[77] and sketches, many of which I have read in German, have survived. Some, at least, of them emphatically deserve publication. I had always hoped to get out for a season's climbing in the Rockies with Conrad, but alas! that can never be now. I owe him a very great debt, not least for saving my wife's life by getting her out of the bergschrund on Maunga Ma, into which she had gone down the full length of the rope owing to the breaking of a snow bridge, when she was alone with him on one of the very early ascents of that rather tricky mountain.

The weights that Conrad could carry without apparent fatigue were phenomenal; I well remember his back view, when he set off with Frind, I think on the Murchison trip, looking exactly like the White Knight in Alice, *with a frying pan hanging loose from the back of his rucksack with its handle below the level of his knees. Of his cooking it were superfluous to speak; no chef ever produced such succulent dishes from the most questionable ingredients, and no one ever knew the exact proportions in which tea, wood ashes and rabbits' droppings should be mixed in order to make a smokable compound when tobacco had run out in a bivouac!*

I hope Conrad's married life was as happy as it deserved to be. But somehow I don't think he could ever have given his real heart to any woman; the mountains were his life and his love.

The Grand Traverse of Mt. Cook was probably Conrad's greatest climb in New Zealand. Mrs. Thomson recalls[78] that they left the summit at 3:45 p.m. to descend by the Linda route, and that Conrad was disturbed by the bad condition of the snow. It broke away above the summit rocks:

Conrad jumping lightly from the moving mass to the stationary part adjoining, at the same time driving in his ice axe to steady himself. "I was expecting that to happen," he said, "and now I shall have to cut steps in the ice the whole way down to the rocks." It was a weary business, requiring the greatest care, the slope being so steep. "Be careful," he said to me. "If you slip here, I cannot save you."

As far as can be discovered, Conrad wrote but two papers at the time dealing with his climbs in the 1916 season. Later on he completed a third, embodying some recollections of the Mt. Cook adventure and his observations in the Southern Alps. These now follow:

2

THE FIRST ASCENT OF MOUNT MARIE[79]

In many ways during the last half century modern civilization has made life easier for thousands of people, and yet yearly there are discovered new diseases, especially mental and nervous troubles, which are easily traceable to the increased hurry and luxury in which men live. To me, a man of the wilds, there is only one explanation, that man drifting away from the life that Nature meant him to lead, has been partly against his own will forced into the struggle for existence in artificial surroundings.

Many discovered this and try to spend all the time their work will allow them in getting back close to Nature, and for this purpose there can be no place to compare with the mountains. Alpine clubs have been formed in every part of the world: these are increasing yearly, giving help and advice to out-of-doors lovers; a great progress can be seen in this direction in the Southern Alps of New Zealand. If one refers to the reports which are issued by the New Zealand Tourist Department one will appreciate the increase in numbers of climbers during the last few years, especially in the Mount Cook district. I should like to illustrate this fact by mentioning the Mueller Glacier and its mountains. There are 15 peaks, of which only three had been climbed up to the season 1912–13. The last unclimbed and unnamed peak has now been conquered by Mrs. Sloman, of Sydney.

There are many different opinions about mountaineering. Not very long ago I read the following lines: "Men strive to reach the tops of high mountains, not for anything which is to be obtained there, not for the extended and remarkable view which may possibly be enjoyed there, but simply for the satisfaction of struggling successfully with the obstacles which Nature has placed in the path."

There is a great deal of truth in these lines, but I for one, cannot agree altogether with the writer of them. For me there is an undescribable joy and charm in the mountains. I have often been asked to explain in what the charm lies, but it is impossible to describe. So I came to the conclusion that the best way to answer this question is in the following words: "Sir or Madam, I am sorry I cannot describe it to you, but if you are anxious to experience the sensation I advise you to climb a mountain yourself if your health allows. And if Nature has not forgotten to give you the sense of beauty and colour, you will see and feel that charm for yourself."

I can always find charm on any mountain, but a first ascent offers more attraction than does a mountain which has been climbed many times before. At the beginning of my mountain travels I looked back on a first ascent with a childish, almost selfish joy, but time changes man and after making over 200 first ascents[80] in different parts of the world I can feel a great change in myself. That childish pleasure has vanished, but a first ascent is still a great joy to me, though from quite another point of view. Since those early days I have learnt quite a lot about human nature, and the study has broadened my mind and taught me to read joy in my friends' and neighbours' faces and to feel joy with them.

There are two points about a first ascent which gave me pleasure as a guide. The first is to bring a Nature lover up a summit which no human foot has trod, and from which height Nature's work was never seen before. The second point, which is almost more important, is that I love to be able to have the opportunity to see the impression this grandeur makes on my companion.

I have met hundreds and hundreds of people in the mountains, among them several queer, almost unbearable characters. But the man or woman who goes to the mountains is usually more or less a Nature lover, and one can always find a good point in them; here in the heart of Nature one gets to know them as Nature really made them. One of my greatest rewards is to be able to read in my companion's face that he or she really is appreciative and shows enthusiasm for another climb, which was the case with the lady in my charge, Mrs. Sloman. I had the pleasure of meeting this lady three years ago at The Hermitage, and I discovered in her a great Nature lover with a keen sense of beauty. Unfortunately, her health prevented her from even making an attempt to scale a peak. However, I was lucky enough to meet her again in December 1915 at Mt. Cook, where she was staying with her husband and friends. This time she was in the best of health, and accompanied us to the Malte Brun Hut on the Tasman Glacier, where we made an attempt on the Hochstetter Dome, which would have been her first mountain if the weather gods had been kind to us. On this trip I saw that she would make a good climber. It did not need much diplomacy to persuade her to essay another climb, and to make it more inviting I told her I knew a nice little unclimbed peak on the Sealy Range. So on January 21 we left The Hermitage via Kea Point and the Green Rock, accompanied by Miss Crookes and Miss Campbell, and reached the Mueller Hut in time for lunch.

On the following morning, at 5 a.m. we left the hut and descended into the Glacier, which we followed up to the Sladden Glacier, where we turned off to our right up a steep snow slope, leading to what appeared from below to be forbidding green slabs. Here we roped. I was surprised that Mrs. Sloman was able to overcome this first difficulty without the aid of the rope. There is an old saying, "Some people are born mountaineers," and as I watched her scrambling over these slabs I said to myself, 'If that saying is true, she must be one of them.'

On top of the slabs we had a short rest and a good look 'round; then we scrambled over loose rocks and strips of snow to the glacier above. The sun came over Mount Sealy, and in a short time the snow was soft, which made the going more tiresome. A few 'schrunds forced us to go round, so that we could not take a straight line for the mountain. Halfway up we had to cross an old avalanche, work that is very trying, as one step may hold one perfectly and the next may drop one in a deep hole between boulders and ice hidden by snow. We took short rests all the way and admired the view. The finest sight was to look on Mount Sefton, with his sharp, knife-like south ridge, and Mount Isabel, with Mount Maunga Ma, Eagle Peak and Mount Thomson in the foreground. Roaring thunder of falling avalanches from Mount Isabel now and then broke an otherwise almost uncanny silence, and if the snow had not been soft I could not imagine a better place for daydreaming.

Occasionally I looked 'round at my new climber. In spite of the increasing heat, which made the snow softer and softer, she kept on going without showing any sign of being tired. In order to store up her energy I stopped on every rise in the glacier until we saw the point we aimed for. With every step forward the outline of our peak increased. At the foot of the peak we found a remarkably fine wind-sweep, into which we had to descend to get to the rock ridge which took us to the final part of the peak. To reach the rocks we had to cross a big, oversnowed, by no means inviting-looking bergschrund. The first part of the rock was firm; 20 feet from the bottom a cornice of snow forced us out onto a rather difficult slab. However, Mrs. Sloman overcame this difficult place without any sign of fear or excitement. In general it is not my principle to praise climbers, but on this occasion I could not help saying a few words of appreciation of her clever performance as a novice. As we had already tramped four miles over snow, we chose the rocks as our way to the summit. A ravine filled with loose shale brought us to a ragged arête, which ended in a precipice – small ledges which we followed in a zigzag fashion brought us to the top of this precipice. There was a sheer drop of a couple of hundred feet to the glacier below, but Mrs. Sloman did not mind it a bit. Over loose rocks we reached the main, or better, the east ridge. When we were 50 feet from the summit, I stopped and turned 'round with the words, "Well, Madam, that's the summit there." She replied: "It's your mountain, go ahead carefully, and lead me to the top."

In a few minutes, we stood on the summit and shook hands. There were no signs of human beings, and that the mountain had no name I knew, so I gave it the name "Marie" which is the Christian name of the lady. The ceremony was a short one; a hearty handshake, and I wished Mrs. Sloman the best of luck for mountaineering in her future. Then we rested, admired the view and took pictures. Heavy clouds came over the Main Divide: on all my travels I never have seen such magnificent cloud effects as in the Southern Alps of New Zealand. Many differ in shapes and shadows from any other clouds in mountainous countries. According to the custom of mountaineering we built a cairn on the highest point. We spent three hours on the summit and enjoyed every minute of it. I think the greatest joy of climbing is a long, long rest on the top, and three hours is certainly a luxury from a climber's point of view, as one seldom has the time to spare, even if the weather is sufficiently warm.

We descended another way, first down a steep couloir to a snow slope which brought us to the rocks and the bergschrund. The sun was still high and there was plenty of time left for another peak nearby, so we decided to climb Mount Darby. This mountain is named after guide Darby Thomson, who met his death two years ago on Mt. Cook. Mount Darby is a striking-looking peak from every side, and as we stood by the bergschrund halfway up, we had an altogether different view of our peak. We could hardly trust our eyes as we saw our own footsteps on the snow slope by which we had descended, so very steep was it. Beyond the bergschrund and over the short snow ridge up to the summit of Mount Darby, we did not find any difficulties. Here again we had a rest, this time of three-quarters of an hour. On the descent we followed our footsteps for a short distance, then made a shortcut over a steep snow slope which from below looks unclimbable. The snow was soft and therefore we started small avalanches at almost every step. It was quite fascinating to watch the snow masses falling over the berg-schrunds to the lower part of the slope, over which small avalanches wound down like big snakes through the grass. When we had the 'schrund behind us we did likewise. Three long glissades brought us back to the glacier below, over which we had ascended in the morning. A glissade is always welcome to mountain climbers, as it saves time, is a rest for the legs and a very fine sensation. It is also a great satisfaction to get down with ease that part of the mountain over which one toiled upward soaking in perspiration earlier in the day. We reached the Mueller Glacier in an hour, going down over the slabs described in the ascent.

At 6:30 p.m. we arrived back at the Mueller Hut. The lady was naturally pleased with her first climb and all she had seen, and looked back with joy on her new experience.

3

SECOND GRAND TRAVERSE OF MOUNT COOK

If Mount Cook could be spoken of as a living being one might say that he is of a mocking and an independent nature, and will only allow a man to step on his head when he is in his best temper. I could easily have believed it, as I had made four unsuccessful attempts to climb the mountain this season. Without great hopes of success I made the fifth attempt, with Mrs. Thomson of Wellington, on January 31st, 1916.

We left The Hermitage on the 29th for the Hooker Hut in fine weather. At 5:30 on January 30th we left the hut for the Hooker bivouac, accompanied by a friend as far as the Hooker icefalls. Mr. Turner, a well-known climber, with Frank Milne, his guide, were some distance ahead of us. At noon we reached the bivouac and were welcomed by these first arrivals, who had hot tea ready for us.

After a good rest we discussed the problem of climbing Mt. Cook. There are three routes to the top from this side: Green's couloir, which I personally dislike on account of falling stones from Mt. Cook and ice avalanches from Mt. Dampier, not including the bad bergschrund; Earle's route, which is known as one of the safest and easiest, had too much snow on the rocks for my liking; so there was only the route over the low and middle peak left, which had only been done once, by Miss DuFaur with guides Graham and Thomson, on January 3rd, 1913. Reading the account of this trip almost gives one cold feet. It relates that they took seven hours from the lower to the high peak; on one side were drops of 1000 feet, and the other side was steep like the roof of a house.

Seven hours step cutting at such a height is the hardest work one can imagine, and as we had no second guide I would have to do it all myself, as one could hardly ask a lady to give one a spell at such hard work. I really did not know for a while what to do, as I did not wish to return with Mrs. Thomson for the fourth time unsuccessfully, the weather being grand. After deep thinking and planning I remembered that this route had been used only once, for what is called the Grand Traverse of Mt. Cook, and it brought the really good and true saying of a world-famous mountain guide to my mind: "Never forget that almost every first ascent is difficult, and never forget that your last one was the hardest, in your own mind." This saying helped me to decide. At 2:15 p.m. I left the bivouac and tramped over the plateau of the Empress Glacier to one of the rock spurs running down from the lower peak of Mt. Cook. In two hours' time I was high up on these rocks;

no serious obstacles were in my way: only a few couloirs were dangerous, as the weather was so hot that it softened the snow right through to the ice, which caused a danger of starting an avalanche. I then cut over 200 steps on a steep ice slope to the glacier which runs down between the low and middle peaks. At 7 p.m. I was back at the bivouac. At 3:45 next morning we left for the climb, and in three hours' time had come to the end of the steps I had cut the day before. Here we found to our surprise a great change: during the night an avalanche had come down and taken the snow bridge over the bergschrund away. However, we managed to get across, but had only been on the glacier for a few minutes on which the going was good, when we heard the report of falling stones and a big rock avalanche came down from the final part of the low peak. We were fortunate enough to secure shelter behind a big ice block before the stones came to the place where we were standing. An avalanche of that kind so early in the morning is by no means a nerve tonic for the climber. As soon as it was over we hurried to a safer place, where we had a rest and painted our faces with zinc ointment.

Rounding a few crevasses and high snow walls we reached better ground where the snow was in good order and there was no delay with step cutting, except at the head of the glacier where I had to cut quite a few steps on a fairly steep ice slope in order to reach some rock slabs which brought us to the main ridge – a short distance from the low peak. Ten minutes later we stood on the summit, but without resting we went back to the place where we reached the ridge and had our second breakfast.

At exactly 11 a.m. we left for the middle peak, as the sun came over the ridge.

In exactly an hour, that is, at twelve o'clock, we arrived at the middle peak, damp with perspiration. People who have never had any experience on snow mountains can scarcely imagine such a burning heat at such a height. On this summit we stopped 20 minutes, had something to eat, refilled the water bottle with snow, and took photographs.

The view was magnificent on all sides, but the most imposing sight was the ridge up to the high summit of Mt. Cook; and it certainly does look like the roof of a Norwegian house, although when one stands on it the steepness seems to disappear.

At 12:20 we left for this most forbidding-looking ridge, the final distance to the highest point of New Zealand, on which we arrived at 3 p.m., three hours, including rests and the taking of photographs.

If I did not know from different experiences that the condition of snow and ice can change in a night, not to mention the changes during months and years, I should have wondered where the seven hours step cutting of the former climb came in on this ridge.

It was a joy to spend 45 minutes on the summit; the air was almost as warm and calm as on a sea beach on a summer day.

Many mountains were covered with clouds, and yet they were lower than we were, and from my point of view regarding the beauties of Nature I admire a sea of clouds just as much as the panorama of mountains that can be seen from Mt. Cook on a clear day.

I was glad to see that Mrs. Thomson was not overtired and that she enjoyed the view from the highest mountain of her native land.

When we started in the morning we did not intend to make the traverse; but, as the weather was fine and the snow condition good, I suggested we should descend on the Tasman side. Mrs. Thomson agreed, and we left the summit at 3:45 p.m. and descended by Green's route. In a very short time we were near the rocks which are known as the summit rocks on the Tasman side. Only a hundred feet above them we almost had a narrow shave. On the steepest part of that route where the slope is so steep that I preferred to kick steps down face to the mountain, suddenly the soft snow gave way under my feet. I clung to my ice axe like the bark to the tree, and it was for us both a good thing that Mrs. Thomson is a skilful climber and knows how to handle the rope at such critical moments.

The cutting of the steps down this clean-swept slope robbed us of a precious hour; fortunately the rocks were in good order, and hurrying down them we made up a little lost time.

From these rocks branch two routes: the Zurbriggen ridge over the rocks to the right, and Green's route over snow (Linda Glacier) to the left. We had no choice, owing to the lateness of the hour, and took the last mentioned, trusting to good luck or Providence to bring us safely through the Linda Glacier, for which most dangerous corner of Mt. Cook "The Death Trap" would in my opinion be a more suitable name.

The dangers consist of avalanches of stone and ice. It becomes worse from year to year, as the hanging glaciers lose their footing. There were crevasses to be crossed in uncountable numbers. Some of them were too wide to jump, so one is forced to go round them in all directions. Some of the bridges were so thin and frail that one had to kneel down and crawl over. After the excitement of passing through this net of crevasses we enjoyed the walk over the plateau to Glacier Dome. Here the last reflection of the sun on the clouds in the west vanished, and the stars shone out in the east and north, giving us light enough to find our way to the Haast bivouac, where we arrived at 9:40 p.m., and certainly we were not sorry to get there. A hot drink after about 18 hours tasted better than ever before.

I need hardly mention that we slept well, till late next morning, and arrived at The Hermitage safe and sound two days later.

To climb Mt. Cook is hard work for guide and tourist. I personally do not consider Mt. Cook a difficult mountain, compared with mountains in the Swiss Alps and Caucasus, that is, from a technical point of view, but where bad weather conditions are concerned there is no doubt that Mt. Cook keeps his pride of place. However, this is not the main drawback; the greatest trouble of all is that one has to bivouac, and both bivouacs are exposed to wind and weather. The only protection is a light tent which keeps the rain out only for a short time at such heights as 6500 or 8000 feet. I am sure when the new hut on the Haast ridge, which is under construction, is finished, and when a sheltered bivouac with a roof is put up on the Hooker side, and if the tourist traffic to The Hermitage keeps on increasing as it has done during the past three years, I would not be surprised in the future to hear that Mt. Cook had been climbed by 20 to 25 different parties in one season.

Many people may not believe this, but I cannot see any impossibility in it except one, but that is a very important point and must not be overlooked. It is this: "how are the climbers to get there?" They must have guides, and the less-experienced parties will require two. But the present guiding staff is small and often insufficient for existing requirements of the high climbers. Then there is the extraordinary action of the Tourist Department in warning off private guides from the Southern Alps. I have been officially informed by the Department that I shall not be allowed in these mountains again. They will not supply any explanation of their strange action. All they say is that they will not allow private guiding after this season, and, like the wise judge, refuse to give their reasons.

Now, I would like to say that, in my opinion, they have made a great mistake. I do not feel personally concerned in the matter, because I had practically made up my mind not to return to New Zealand after this season. But in the interests of high climbers all over the world, and with regard to the future prosperity of The Hermitage, I think this absurd restriction on the employment of private guides should be removed. I know some persons have come to Mt. Cook solely because they knew they could get my services as guide, and these people have spent a good deal of money there. They have been a great gain to the place.

I am therefore sure that when it becomes known that the Department will not allow private guides and that climbers will have to put up with the present insufficient staff, it will interfere with the business of The Hermitage. I am hoping, however, that the government will view the matter in a very different light. They have spent a lot of money, and as guardians of the rate-payers' interests they must naturally wish to make a profit instead of a loss as at present, and are therefore directly concerned in bringing more and more people to the mountains, and in offering them every inducement to come instead of putting obstacles in their way.

Although I may never see these mountains again I shall always love them and would like to see their wonderful beauties made known to an ever-increasing circle of people instead of the very few persons who in a season now succeed in viewing the marvellous scenes of ice-clad rocky ridges and snow-white glaciers, the wide plains and seas beyond, from the mountain-tops. There should be scores.

4

LONG AGO ON AORANGI

The climbing season in New Zealand is from November to April. Mt. Cook (12,349 feet), in the Southern Alps, has the reputation of making its own weather. In the season 1915–16 I made four attempts to climb the mountain, and on these fruitless expeditions I gathered first-hand information on this matter. There is no mystery in the evil reputation the mountain has; it is simply based on natural laws of precipitation and evaporation. Mt. Cook towers about 1000 feet above its neighbours, and is located near the main divide. The precipitation on the western slopes of the Southern Alps is extreme when compared with that on the western slopes of North America.

On January 29th, 1916, I made the fifth attempt with Mrs. J. Thomson, of Wellington.[81] We left The Hermitage at noon for the Hooker Hut (4000 feet), situated on the south bank of the glacier and six miles distant. The Hooker Glacier is about six miles long, its terminal face (2880 feet) three miles from The Hermitage. Harper Saddle (8580 feet) is at its head. This is the steepest of the four large glaciers east of the divide. For nearly four miles the ice is covered with debris, but a mile and a half from the hut the moraine, over which the trail leads, breaks up and clear ice and snow begin.

Above the icefalls the glacier widens out into snowfields which sweep down from the lower and middle summits of Mt. Cook. From the high summit a buttress leads down to an isolated rock at its foot, known as the "bivouac." The real climb of Mt. Cook begins here, the campsite (7500 feet) being the highest in the Southern Alps. The view and the surroundings are alpine in the full sense.

Next day, at noon, we arrived at the bivouac, being welcomed by Mr. Samuel Turner and his porter. The late Mr. Turner was internationally known, both as a climber and a writer on mountaineering. His literary productions were much criticized by other writers; but he and I spent many days together, and although we could not always agree on matters pertaining to climbing, I found him to be a good companion, with many fine qualities. He was, in my opinion, a fair climber and no shirker of hardships, being always willing to assist a guide by taking a turn as leader. I enjoyed his company more than reading his books. Of other authors I have met and whose works I read with great delight, some have been poor comrades when on a mountain.

There are three routes[82] from the bivouac: Green's couloir, which I believe was followed only once, in descent. This is not a practical route, because of stonefalls and avalanches. Earle's route is the second, while the third leads over the lower and middle peaks and is referred to as the "Grand Traverse."

Mr. Turner came to the bivouac with the intention of conquering Mt. Cook alone and had chosen the Earle route, while we decided on the "Grand Traverse." To lighten the work for the long climb, I tramped over the plateau of the Empress Glacier. A rock spur running down from the lower peak attracted me as the best way up, and I made good progress for about two hours before being forced to the slope between the lower and middle peaks. I had cut a number of steps and could see some distance ahead. Satisfied that I had done enough I returned to the bivouac, where I found supper waiting. Mr. Turner entertained us with balancing tricks, beginning with a sheet of notepaper on his nose and finishing by supporting a rock weighing about 50 pounds on his chin. It was a very pleasant evening.

Frost and wind were absent, a very rare occurrence at such an elevation, and it proved to be the only one of the many nights I spent here through which I slept comfortably. Next morning at 3:45 we started our day's work. The porter stayed in the bivouac, his duty being merely to keep an eye on Mr. Turner. In three hours we came to the end of the broken trail, but during the night a great change had taken place on the slopes above, an avalanche having swept away the bridge over the bergschrund, on the route I had planned, and we lost time in looking for a place to cross. Finally I managed to overcome the obstacle and cut steps on the slope above.

Then we struck better ground where the going was good, but there was danger in sight. I had just finished explaining to Mrs. Thomson that this was not a place to linger, when we heard the reports of falling stones. "There she comes, follow quick!" I shouted. We made a dash for an enormous ice block a few feet from us; it was a race with death. Fortunately our shelter withstood the impact of the avalanche and only fine snow rolled in on our feet and buried the rope. A third climber on the rope would have been disastrous on that occasion.

As the close call did not upset Mrs. Thomson's nerves, we continued the ascent by rounding a few large crevasses and snow walls, and gained safer going on a small plateau. We reached the main ridge a short distance from the lower peak, from which it appeared a long way to the middle peak, the length of snow ridges being nearly always overestimated. We left the lower summit at eleven o'clock and encountered no difficulty worth mentioning; one hour later we reached the middle peak, wet with perspiration. I have no recollection of such an intense heat wave on a mountain as we had that day.

The view was magnificent, the most striking sight being the ridge up to the highest point. Mrs. Thomson made some remarks about the steepness, but I assured her that it would not be so terrible when she got nearer. On some occasions, motherly words from the guide on a climb are a good stimulant. At 12:20 we started for the forbidding ridge. Shortly afterward I spotted Mr. Turner far down on Earle's route; he heard my yodel and waved his hat. An hour later we saw him descending on a snow slope. He told me later that conditions were not favourable for a solo climb.

We made good progress along the ridge, which we found less steep than it appeared from the middle peak, and stepped on the summit a few minutes before three o'clock. It was as warm and calm as on a tropical sea-beach. Mrs. Thomson was delighted to gain the highest point of her native land. Ladies, as a rule, do not tell their age, especially to males; therefore I was surprised when she told me that she would be 60 on her next birthday and would like to celebrate the occasion on Mt. Cook.

We climbed more than a dozen peaks together, some of them long, tiresome snow tramps and some more difficult. Our most exciting adventure was cutting the cornice on Mt. Burns, but she never played out or showed fear. It was in the early days of my career as a guide that I discovered my outstanding weakness of loafing on the summits. With this in mind I decided that three-quarters of an hour was all we could spare for the "Gipfelrast."

The snow was in fine condition, no steps were required, and in a short time we reached the rocks which are referred to as the summit rocks, on the Tasman side.

While scrambling down, my thoughts ran on Zurbriggen. From the rocks two routes branch down – Zurbriggen's to the right, and Green's (Linda Glacier) to the left. Owing to the lateness of the hour we had no choice and took the latter route. In my opinion "The Death Trap" would be a more appropriate name for this glacier, as it is the most dangerous corner of Mt. Cook. I confess that I did not feel very happy descending this glacier as it had been unusually warm and one could expect an avalanche at any moment. Added to this was the recollection that, only two years since, I had descended with a party on this route and walked over an avalanche which had killed three climbers. On the lower part of the glacier there were crevasses in uncountable numbers, and the bridges were thin and frail. After the excitement of passing through this network we enjoyed the walk over Glacier Dome, where the last reflection of the sun vanished. At 9:40 p.m. we arrived at the Haast bivouac, and half an hour later we were sipping tea, which tasted like the best ever.

On our arrival at The Hermitage, Mrs. Thomson was congratulated by the guides and climbers. Usually on the return from a climb the guides made inquiry as to what kind of a time I had had, but on this occasion no questions were asked. But, as ever, I received a hearty welcome from "Baby," the four-year-old daughter of Mr. Cook, the manager of The Hermitage. She invited me to tea and told me that she would make the "Grand Traverse" with me next year. The climb did not come off, as shortly after I was officially informed by the Tourist Department that I should not be allowed in these mountains again.

What was wrong? My explanation is as follows. In the season 1913–14 I was in New Zealand as private guide to Mr. H.O. Frind, a Canadian climber. In that season an English climber, Mr. S.L. King, with two guides, Darby Thomson and Richard Richmond, were killed on Mt. Cook. I took part in the search for their bodies and later received a letter from the Tourist Department thanking me for the assistance I had given, and offering me a place on the guiding staff. I accepted and returned to The Hermitage in September 1914.

At the end of the season I was again offered work, but I informed the department that I preferred to work as a private guide, and as no objection was made I returned to New Zealand in November 1915. I had several engagements in advance and, being well-known, had no difficulty in securing parties. Naturally, I took away some people from the government guides, which created jealousy, and, to make matters worse, this was in wartime, when race hatred was fostered by all conflicting nations. Although I was naturalized before the war broke out, in the sight of the people who did not have a mind of their own during that period, I was still an alien. The guides and their sympathizers complained to the Department and no doubt the complaints were patriotic in design, but there is another angle as to why I was not wanted there. A good friend of mine, who claimed he had inside information, told me that all would have been well if I had not broken the mountaineering record of the Southern Alps, and that with an old lady, and that I should have kept my opinion regarding Zurbriggen's climb on Mt. Cook to myself.

Before continuing, I wish to inform my readers that I was never interested in making or breaking records of any kind in connection with mountaineering. Having been reared in the mountains and having made a few minor climbs before I lost my milk teeth, the experience I gained later has convinced me that the time required to climb a mountain depends entirely on the conditions under which it is done. This is the reason I never could see any sense or merit in so-called record climbs.

What was the record climb at that time in New Zealand? I was informed that the "Grand Traverse" of Mt. Cook was considered by many climbers to be a great achievement. Having climbed 59 peaks there, of which 29 were first ascents, I agree with the sentiment and go a bit further by saying it will be looked upon as a great climb for many years to come. The first ascent by a lady was made on January 3rd, 1913, by Miss DuFaur, with guides Peter Graham and Darby Thomson. The time required was 21 hours from the bivouac on the Haast ridge. Miss DuFaur in her book relates a great deal of step cutting; it took them seven hours from the low to the high summit. I had the pleasure of meeting Miss DuFaur and the guide Thomson, but did not climb with them, although I climbed several times with Graham. At that time I had sufficient knowledge to judge a man on the mountain. Graham was a good climber and guide; not every good climber makes a good guide.

Our time from bivouac to bivouac was about 18 hours; the distance between the low and the high summit we covered in four hours including rest and time for photographs. On the day we made the ascent the snow was in good condition; there was no ice on the magnificent ridge which connects the three summits of Mt. Cook. I believe that if they had had such conditions they would have taken less time than we did; on the other hand, if we had met with the conditions they had, we would probably have been defeated, as I had no second guide.

I spent three seasons in New Zealand and came to the conclusion that where bad weather is concerned Mt. Cook keeps its pride of place. So it will not happen very often that the "Grand Traverse" is made in 18 hours or less. I sincerely hope that someone has made or will make it in less time, so that no one will point me out as the holder of a climbing record. I am well aware that no Alpine Club offers encouragement to climb for the sake of making or breaking records, but there are individuals who climb, so to speak, with watch in hand. What joy they get out of it is often a mystery to others. According to observation their careers are nearly always of short duration, but in spite of this, some climb the ladder to fame without a breathing spell.

In a few isolated cases they are referred to as authorities on mountains, but nobody knows who is responsible for the authorization. Personally, I have noticed that climbers of this type have little if any sense of beauty; therefore they find no excuse for stopping before they get to the top. Apparently they climb for climbing's sake, and in some instances to attract attention and publicity. No doubt they get a kick out of it while it lasts.

If one can remember enough on a hurry-up climb for a Pipe Dream, I have yet to find out; but I have learned that quick climbing without stops is bad for the heart and other vital organs which have to perform the extra work. I am not ignorant of the fact that there have been, and are yet, some guides who are inclined to encourage fast climbing. About 30 years ago at Dreizinnenhütte I listened to half a dozen guides discussing a record climb made by two young Viennese on the Langkofel. Amongst the guides was Sepp Innerkofler, and his remarks, roughly translated were: "Boys, don't you be foolish and encourage our Tourist to get to the top in less time than your last. I tell you if this foolish idea of running up and down the peaks gets hold of the Touristen, our mountains will be plastered with crosses and *Gedenktafeln!*"

Innerkofler's prophecy did not exactly come true, although the crosses and tablets increased every year. There is one or more on nearly every mountain in the Alps, especially in Austria. Whether those signs have any moral effect on climbers I do not know, but I know they have no effect on the local people. Neither is it exciting news to them when they hear of an accident. The following bears this out: an American climber at Hinterbärenbad, in the Kaisergebirge, asked the waitress how many accidents there had been in the last season, to which she replied calmly, "Oh, only 13 got killed, and one man broke his legs."

Glancing back to Innerkofler's remarks we can read between the lines that running up and down mountains is not only foolish, it is dangerous. Sepp Innerkofler was one of Tyrol's outstanding guides, much liked by mountaineers of many nations. Like most, he was his own philosopher. His motto on climbing was "Eile mit Weile." If every climber from the beginning would adopt this motto and stick to it religiously, many accidents might be avoided.

5

SOME RECOLLECTIONS OF MY GUIDE

BY

MRS. J. THOMSON

I t was at the old Hermitage, Mt. Cook, that I first met Conrad Kain, the young and handsome private guide of Mr. Otto Frind of Canada, but it was not until the following two years, during his second and third visits to this country that he acted as my guide, leading me to the summits of 14 peaks, including our traverse of Mt. Cook.

He was wonderful in the mountains, seeming to have an inborn instinct for finding new routes. I had absolute faith in his guidance, and never disputed it but once, with the consequence that I received one of the worst shocks of my climbing days.

It happened while descending Malte Brun, a rock peak, during our traverse of that mountain. We had arrived at a very steep rock face, which he said we must cross and descend. It looked so appalling that I suggested a more roundabout and apparently easier way.

"Very well," he said, shrugging his shoulders, while keeping a firm hold of the rope. I had only taken two or three steps downwards when a rock gave way under my foot and I found myself hanging suspended in the air by the rope round my waist. "Are you holding me?" I asked rather foolishly, while swinging about. "Yes, I am holding you very goot," was the reply, and soon I was seated on safe rock again. After a couple of minutes' rest to restore my somewhat shaken nerves, we descended by the rock face that looked so dangerous, and I never again questioned his choice of routes.

423

He was a very entertaining companion, frequently relating interesting and amusing stories about the people in the different countries he had lived in. When stormbound in a hut he was fond of writing stories for publication. One I remember was called "The Adventures of a Hobo," but I do not know if it ever appeared in print.[83]

He was very modest about his prowess as a mountaineer: "I am better as some, and not so good as others," I once heard him remark.

He considered Mr. H.F. Wright (AC) of Auckland the finest climber he had met in New Zealand. "He is fast and safe," he said. Conrad never wished to turn back. I never knew him to suggest such course except once, from illness. During our ascent of the Nun's Veil we were overtaken by a terrible storm of wind, rain and snow. How the wind roared up those crags! In describing our experience some of his friends on returning to The Hermitage they asked him why he did not turn back. "When a lady wishes to go on I never turn back," he replied.

I was ready to follow him anywhere in the mountains, whether crossing frail snow bridges, where one scarcely dared to breathe for fear of falling through, up steep rocks, as on our ascent of Mt. Darwin, where, unroped, the only view I had for what seemed quite a long time was the sight of Conrad's hobnailed boots just above me, climbing what appeared to be an interminable rock ladder leading up to the sky. Some ice traverses were rather fearsome, but his step cutting was good and safe.

But what I liked least of all was the descent of steep snow faces. I remember one such place on the Hooker side of Mt. Cook. We had been obliged to turn back when about 1000 feet below the summit by badly glazed rocks and threatening weather. As usual he was unwilling to turn back, but I insisted on doing so. During our descent we came to the top of what looked to me like an impossible precipice covered with snow, and Conrad calmly remarked, "We must go down here." I said nothing, but was prepared to do what I was told.

There were only two of us on the rope, which, under the circumstances was therefore quite useless. He went down first, face to the mountain, kicking a large step while holding on to his axe deeply plunged in the snow. I followed carefully, also face to the mountain, using his steps, my only support being, like his, my ice axe sunk in the snow.

A row of grim black rocks about 200 feet below us marked the bottom of the steep snow where it joined the glacier. I was relieved to find myself scrambling over those rocks at last, and pressing on to the inhospitable Mt. Cook bivouac, where we had passed the previous night. The adventures of the day were not yet over, however. Not relishing the idea of spending another night on those cold rocks I asked if we could go on to the Hooker Hut six or seven miles down the valley. Mt. Cook bivouac is a small island of rock rising out of a waste of snow 8000 feet above sea level, and quite unsheltered.

"Yes, we can go, but we will have to step out," Conrad replied. But, alas! the daylight had almost gone when we reached the Black Rocks, which rise above the icefall of the Hooker Glacier. There was just enough light left to see dimly the ice hundreds of feet below us, and the route lay in the shadow of the rocks.

Conrad went down first, sometimes guiding my foot to a ledge when I could find no foothold, and we at last reached the glacier safely, though without a lantern, the rope as usual being useless – as I could not have held the guide if he had fallen. We arrived at the comfortable hut at 10 p.m. after a strenuous day.

As an illustration of his skill and presence of mind in a dangerous situation I will mention an incident during our descent from the traverse of Mt. Cook.

The ice-cap near the summit was covered with loose granular snow. At first Conrad, who led the way, kicked steps in it. All went well for about a quarter of an hour, when I heard a slight exclamation. Looking down I saw him jumping lightly from the snow, which had begun to avalanche under his feet, across to a part that had not begun to move. "I was expecting that. Now I shall have to cut down the whole damned way," he said.

It took about an hour of hard, back-breaking work to cut steps downward to the rocks below. "Be careful here; if you slip I cannot save you," he said; and I knew it without being told, the rope being more a danger than a safeguard under those conditions, and those sharp rocks ready to receive us if we missed our footing.

6

MT. LOUIS AND BUGABOO SPIRE

Kain now left New Zealand, never to return to those faraway peaks that had taught him so much about ice and snow. He reached Canada for the summer of 1916, arriving at the Healy Creek Camp of the ACC with A.H. MacCarthy on July 15th.[84]

This was a summer of notable new ascents. Conrad led the way, by a difficult and complicated route, to the summit of soaring Mt. Louis,[85] the rock spire near Banff:

> *Upon reaching the edge of the timber east of Mt. Edith, we stopped and looked back at our mountain, and Conrad spoke volumes when he said, 'Ye gods, Mr. MacCarthy, just look at that; they never will believe we climbed it.'*

Returning to the Purcells, an important expedition, in which the MacCarthys, Prof. and Mrs. W.E. Stone and H.O. Frind took part, was carried out through Toby Creek and its northern tributaries.[86] Conrad regarded the descent of Monument Peak as being one of the most arduous things accomplished:

> *Clinging to smooth slabs, squeezing down narrow cracks, dodging falling stones, traversing to right and to left, using every art to defy the law of gravity, it required five hours of the most careful work before we set foot on the ice below and were able in some degree to relax the tension of our minds and muscles. Twilight was already fast merging into darkness. We were at the head of a glacier where no human foot had trod, and for an hour in the semi-darkness threaded our way among crevases.*

From the Jumbo Fork, first ascents of Truce and Cauldron were made, throwing light upon this almost unknown section of the main watershed.

Late in August, the MacCarthys, the Vincents and Frind took Conrad to the Bugaboo area.[87] Here were peaks to be compared with Conrad's best efforts in the Alps. It was pioneer work, and the loftiest mountains were the attraction; but these, unlike highest summits of many groups, were needles to test one's mettle. Howser Spire and Bugaboo Spire were conquered. Ever afterward Conrad would think of Bugaboo Spire as his most difficult Canadian ascent. At 10,000 feet:

> *Our route was completely blocked by a most formidable gendarme, whose base completely spanned the width of the ridge. Its wall on the west ran up in prolongation of the mighty cliffs that rose from the glacier below, and its top edge rose sharply like a horn ... there seemed to be no safe line of ascent, and Conrad finally decided that the face of*

the gendarme offered our only hope. Relieving himself of his rucksack, he gradually worked up this face by means of several diagonal cracks until he succeeded in getting both arms over the top edge, and here he stuck for a long time, feeling about and looking for some little thing that might afford him a hold long enough to pull himself over.... Just how he finally got into the crack is a mystery to us but, after a dozen reappearances, he smiled and said: 'I make it,' and soon began to call for rope, until about 60 feet had run out and he called from the top of the ridge above the gendarme.

Conrad had explored these spires in 1910; now he was leading the way on their heights, making mountaineering history, with the same joyous delight with which, in earlier days, he had stormed the peaks of Gesäuse and the Dolomites.

Time was passing, and adventures had followed one upon the other. Conrad was becoming reminiscent and, fortunately for us, wrote this account of his Canadian years:

7

REMINISCENCES OF SEVEN SUMMERS IN CANADA

My first two climbing seasons, 1909 and 1910, in the Rockies were spent along the main line of the Canadian Pacific Railway. In 1911 I joined Mr. A.O. Wheeler's survey, covering the territory from Jasper to Yellowhead Pass and Mt. Robson. From Maligne Lake we returned to Banff via Wilcox Pass. The most interesting ascents for me that season were Whitehorn, a first ascent which I made alone, and the first ascent of Resplendent in company with Mr. Harmon, of Banff. I enjoyed the trips through the mountains with pack train and was delighted with camp life, although on many occasions the mosquitoes made me long for other mountains where these persistent pests are unknown.

In general, I adapted myself to the New World and its ways, but at times I caught myself meditating. Visions of the Alps and the Dolomites would flash through my mind, linked up with Old World memories – of life in the inns, with music and song. I realized that these were symptoms, universally known as "Heimweh," but fortunately I was well-fortified with a prescription for this malady. It read: "Take life as it comes, and make the best of it, and always be your own adviser in small matters." But this did not help me much at the time; there was something missing, and therefore I was not quite happy.

Early in the spring of 1912 I received a letter from a man whose acquaintance I had made in the mountains. An invitation to join an expedition to the Altai. At once I decided to go, for I felt sure I would have a chance for a stiff and sporty climb. In this I discovered what was lacking in the Rockies: it was a climb with thrills and plenty of them.

For several years before I came to Canada I climbed in the Alps, and in those days made some of the sportful ascents more than once in a season. My favourites were the aiguilles of Mont Blanc and the mountains of Dauphiné. In the Dolomites I considered the following climbs ideal: the Vajolet Towers, the east face of Rosengarten, the Fünffingerspitze by the Schmittkamin, the south face of Marmolata, and the north wall of the Kleine Zinne. I was so infatuated with the Guglia di Brenta that I went many miles out of my way to climb this majestic pinnacle. In the three seasons I spent in the Rockies I had not made a single climb, and did not expect to make one, that could be compared with any of these.

After my journey to the Altai Mountains I visited my old stamping grounds in the Dolomites and the Alps and made a few difficult climbs,[88] quenched my three-year-old thirst with beer and had a jolly time, living my youth over again. It was beautiful yet strange; it made me feel very lonely – I longed for the solitude that one finds in the Rockies; for the campfire and the carefree life.

In June 1913 I landed in Canada after a long voyage from England by way of Australia and New Zealand to British Columbia. On my arrival I was told I would have an opportunity to climb Mt. Robson. This came to pass, and I traversed the mountain in August with A.H. MacCarthy and W.W. Foster. I have ascended Mt. Robson several times since; my verdict is that it is long and offers many problems to the leader. No matter from which side the ascent is made, there are dangerous sections, even under the best conditions. He who hires himself out for such a climb earns his pay, and the amateur who can lead to the summit is in my opinion a full-fledged mountaineer.

In 1914 the most interesting climbs I made were Farnham and the Farnham Tower in the Purcell Range. The tower offered rock work to my liking, and these ascents compared well with climbs in Dauphiné. In the summer of 1915 we made additional climbs in the Purcells, but nothing of outstanding interest. This was my third visit to this range, and its mountains and valleys fascinated me.

The season of 1916 turned out to be the best I had had in this land. On July 19th, with A.H. MacCarthy, I made the first ascent of Mt. Louis, near Banff, the most interesting rock climb I had made in the Rockies. Next best was the descent of the east face of Monument Peak, on the north fork of Toby Creek in the Purcells. Several years later I pointed out the route to a prospector, who remarked, "Say, you are either a fool or a doggone liar!"

The summer came to an end with a trip to the Howser and Bugaboo spires, and it was in this group that we made an ascent which I found as interesting and difficult as any I have encountered in the Alps. None of my subsequent ascents in the Rockies provided such thrills as the Bugaboo Spire. Believing that this may be of interest to mountaineers who prefer rock climbing and are looking for new ground and virgin peaks, I will give an account of this adventure.

The Howser and Bugaboo spires are reached in two days from Spillimacheen in the Columbia Valley. The group shows up prominently from Mt. Sir Donald, and from peaks at the heads of Toby and Horsethief creeks. On a clear day it is visible from the higher summits of the Rockies. I had been twice in this section, but it was not until August, 1916, when we walked around the spires in search of the highest of the group, that I had a chance to examine the pinnacles at close quarters.

These peaks are as yet unnamed on maps, although Longstaff refers to them as "The Nunataks," and MacCarthy designates them from south to north as "1, 2 and 3." The well-known guide Edward Feuz Jr. suggested "Aiguilles" for this group, as the spires resemble the aiguilles of Chamonix even more than Mt. Assiniboine duplicates the Matterhorn. Spire No. 2,[89] with sheer cliffs on all sides, is the most picturesque of all and rises some 2000 feet above the glacier. After carefully searching with powerful binoculars I came to the conclusion that this pinnacle will prove very hard to conquer. Since then I have had the opportunity to study the peak from different angles, and have not changed my opinion. I feel inclined to prophesy that this pinnacle will be the most difficult ascent in the Canadian Alps.

As our time was limited, we chose Spire No. 3[90] for our climb in this section, as it was not so forbidding. On August 29th we left camp at 4:30 a.m., the party consisting of Mr. and Mrs. A.H. MacCarthy, Mr. J. Vincent and the writer. The real climb, beginning at the saddle between No. 2 and No. 3, offered interesting but not difficult rock work in the first thousand feet. Before reaching the main ridge we encountered two chimneys about 30 feet high and several smooth slabs which required both care and technique.

On the ridge we halted and studied the route to the summit, which was in sight. Before us rose a most formidable gendarme, whose base spanned the width of the ridge. Its western wall ran up in prolongations of cliffs that rose from the glacier far below, and its upper edge lifted sharply like a horn to the point where it joined the high, smooth east wall. The western side was blocked by unsurmountable cliffs. The face of the gendarme looked anything but inviting and the only chance was to skirt around on the east side. Before reaching the base of this barrier we encountered several hard bits; in fact, on peaks of the Rockies, where the stone formation is rotten, such places would be termed difficult and dangerous; but when every hold is solid, difficulties are welcome and met with a smile.

A broken section led down for about 40 feet to a ledge, three or four feet wide, and ended in a 2000-foot drop. The wall above this was split in several places but the breaks were far apart. We returned to the gendarme and after a short rest I tackled the perpendicular 15-foot wall. Several diagonal cracks offered firm handholds but were not large enough for the toes; the old proverb "half a loaf is better than none" comes often to the climber's mind. Near the top I was stuck for a few minutes, the edge being smooth and without holds of any kind. I applied the vacuum grip and pulled myself up and over.

A few feet higher up was a dent that resembled a saucer, from which I studied the surroundings and looked for a way out. It was a tight corner; to my right the wall I had come up, and to the left a holdless slab beyond a short crack, crowned with a slight overhang. Above me a straight wall, 10 or 12 feet, led to a slab, after which nothing was visible except space filled with mist through which a streak of blue ice appeared.

The only possible way out was to the left. There was not room for two on this edge, nor was there a projecting rock or crack for anchorage, so I had to depend entirely on myself. I managed to wriggle over the holdless slab, and when I next tried to get into the crack I was stopped. Convinced that I had started wrong, and as there was no chance to change my position, I crawled back to the edge and began again. To my surprise I found myself in exactly the same position as before; but I grew bolder and stood up, balanced on the toes of my left foot and made great efforts to get into the crack, but could not find a hold.

The endurance required in balancing one's whole weight on the toes should be cultivated. Again I returned to the starting point. Searching my memory for something which resembled this bugaboo, I found the picture.

Many years ago, in Tyrol, I battled with just such an obstacle as I now had before me. I recollected that I had then overcome it with the aid of an ice axe; fortunately we had one in the party. My plan was to place the axe in a position to take the weight of the left foot, the only one I could make use of, and at the same time lift myself a few inches higher. This I thought would enable me to put my arm into the crack, which appeared just wide enough so that I could use the elbow on one wall and the palm on the other.

All went well according to this plan. Once in the crack the axe was not only useless but proved a real nuisance. I found myself in such a position that I could not dispose of the axe in any other way except by letting it drop. This I would not do, so there was nothing to do but to go back once more and make other arrangements. Finally I succeeded in pulling myself up the crack and across the overhang. To my great relief a slanting crack about two inches wide led me to a safe place. I was now only 70 feet above the others, but it had taken me an hour and a half to overcome this stretch.

To illustrate how difficulties disappear when a rope is present and the second climber knows that it will be properly handled by the man ahead, I quote from Mr. MacCarthy's account[91] of this part of the climb: "We then bent on two spare ropes and with the aid of a double rope went up, one at a time, fully realizing, as we passed over the top stretch and up the broken course above, that the real climb on a mountain is the one made by the guide." The portion between the gendarme and the summit afforded interesting climbing. The barometer registered 10,250 feet on the first peak, and, as we were not certain of the highest point, we started for the second a few hundred yards away. We encountered a break-off some 20 feet high, over which we roped off, leaving the rope for the return trip. About halfway we were forced to the edge of the east wall, the only safe method being to straddle this section. Then we met with several smooth knobs, which would have been of no consequence on a safe place; but on the edge of such a sheer wall we hugged them tight. A short, irregular chimney landed us on top, the barometer reading exactly the same as on the first summit.

The view was grand, especially of the nearest spires. No. 2 fascinated me more than any other peak in sight, though I didn't see a possible chance for a route. I made up my mind that some day I would make an assault on this dignified-looking needle. In descent, as a rule, I never worry how I am going to get off a peak; but on this occasion I did. I was not sure if I could descend the gendarme without taking too much risk. While coming up I heard Mr. MacCarthy whisper to the others that he felt confident I would not descend over such a place if any other possible place could be found. I concealed my fear carefully.

It was in the early days of my career as a guide that I learned that the leader on any climb must hold the confidence of the party. This is not always so simple. Having 30 climbing seasons to look back on, I could write columns on this subject. To mention a few of the points a guide should bear in mind will not be amiss. First, he should never show fear. Second, he should be courteous to all, and always give special attention to the weakest member in the party. Third, he should be witty, and able to make up a white lie if necessary, on short notice, and tell it in a convincing manner. Fourth, he should know when and how to show authority, and when the situation demands it, should be able to give a good scolding to whomsoever deserves it.

When we arrived at the gendarme we made a halt and looked over all sides. I decided that the safest way would be to rope off on the east wall, behind the gendarme to the ledge mentioned in the ascent. Fortunately we had three ropes along, two of 80 feet and one of a 120 feet. Having tied the two shorter ropes securely together, I threw the end down to measure the height. Luck was with us, as it just reached the ledge, about six feet from where it ended in sheer wall.

Roping off is a thrilling adventure, but not dangerous if properly carried out. The most unpleasant thing that can happen is when the rope itself gets stuck. I took all precautions to avoid such trouble, and having found a projecting rock I tied my coat in the centre of the rope to prevent it from getting pinched. Halfway down a small ledge offered a chance for a rest, but this and the narrow, sloping ledge below were not places to linger and enjoy the view. So everyone made the 80 feet down without a stop.

The rest of the descent was made without any difficulties, and so ended the most interesting climb I had in my seven seasons of Canadian mountaineering. Without hesitation I say that the ascent of Bugaboo Spire offers as many thrills and difficulties as any of the aiguilles in the Alps which I have climbed.

CHAPTER XVIII

(1917-20)

▲

THE ALPINE GUIDE AS TRAPPER AND FARMER

Conrad again felt the lure of the trapline, of the winter silences. For the time, at least, he had had enough of foreign travel, even of mountain guiding. Reaching Spillimacheen, after the Purcell climbs, he proceeded to Banff and disappeared into the wilderness.

For his destination he chose the headwaters of Simpson River, on the western slope of the divide, northwest of Mt. Assiniboine. There he would be alone with Nature, as he craved to be – in the white loneliness, with powdery snow floating down from the jackpines and only the soft thumping of snowshoes as he followed the criss-crossing tracks of forest creatures.

In the spring of 1917 he wrote to Mrs. Thomson, the only letter she received from him after he left New Zealand:

My dear Lady,

IN MY CABIN ON THE SIMPSON RIVER – ROCKIES.

Have you ever asked your spirit friends about my whereabouts, and what did they tell you? Did they tell you that I am hunderts of miles from nowhere?

Yes, I am far far away from towns and peoples. I am ones more a trapper, and I enjoy life in the wilds, and amongst the wild animals to full extense.

I have not seen or spoken anybody since 29th Sept. 1916, till today. What date it is I don't know; this man who came this morning to me thinks it is somewhere round the second week in February. He is going to civilization and he will post this letter for me. I will go with him halfway to help him to break the trail. The snow is in some places 4–5–6 feet deep, but I wont go out till late in spring.

I have enough food, and I feel so well here alone that I realy dislike to think of leaving my nice little log cabin which I have build all by myself. You will not be able to picture to yourself my life here in the wild forest. I am the King, the Master and the lover of all I have around me.

Of course I have a long beard. The face is round and brown with sunburn. I am phisically and mentally as well as I was not for a long time. I had a few little accitens, like falling in the river, etc., but nothing serious.

In Dec.–Jan. it was bitterly cold, yes too cold to go outside the cabin. Such cold spell you never get in NZ. In this cold weather I wrote a long, long story. You will probably see it in print some day, and I do hope this book will bring me a name as a writer. I gess you will enjoy reading it. There are very good and bad characters in it.

I am not quite alone. I have a most wonderful clever dog, 16 mice. They are all tame and know different tricks. Then I have a big snake, but he is most of the time asleep, but when he is awake I put him near the fire, and play music for him. He is very fond of music. His name is Satan, and he understands his name every time.

Then I have the ugliest looking toad you can imagine, but I love him for his good-natured character. Then I have a dayly visitor, a big ugly looking porkepine. He stays with me for hours. I have learnt him to shake hands.

Then I receive dayly visits from the few winter birds who stay here.

Well, it seems to me they all love me. I know that I love them all. I find them better friends as one does amongst people. No doubt some people would think me mad – crazy – but I am all right. I sometimes think that I must have been mad that I did follow up mountain guiding as long as I did. I do not say that mountain guiding is foolishness, no, by no means. I think it one of the finest healthy sports. I love the mountains, the climbing, and the view from a summit, but I think it is first class folly to try to make a living off it.

Of course we must all have our own experiences before we are wise. I wont worry much about life and future now. I know I always can make a living in the woods.

Travel I have had enough of. I have seen more of the world as the average man do. I saw and study human nature. I had good and bad time.

I once had a position which would have given me a great name, and very likely I would be well off now, but I did not like the life I had to lead. I never told you nor any body else about it. Nobody but friends in the old country know about it, but as I now have decided to give up mountain guiding I will tell you.

It will interest you to know that your simple mountain friend was once a detective, and very successful one at that. I had my training in Graz (Austria). You will know that Austria is treating her criminals more sintificly [scientifically] than any other country.

It was a hard, hard course. I was then 27 years old. I was on active service for one year, then I went to Canada, and you know, my dear Lady that I could have told you of quite a number of people we met together at Mt. Cook, what they have been and what they were.

Yes, I could have told you more about them as any fortune teller.

You can easie realize that people would not have hire me as a guide if they would have knew that I am able to read them from A–Z. And let me tell you I had been guiding quite a few men whose place should have been in the jail insted of the mountains. And so I can tell you my life as a guide was, in great many ways, a life of romance, and even now I shall keep it to myself, but it might interest you to know that from all fortune tellers there was only one who told me my past life correct. This was in Vancouver.

This winter I often thought on Spiritism, but when one lives in pure Nature – surrounded by Nature, I mean, it is hard to find any good points to hang on, for life after dead.

I also readet once more the Holy Bible, but I think just the same as before.

Very often I wonder what you are doing. I have not heard from New Zealand at all, but I guess there will be a big mail somewhere for me when I return.

If you ever should come to the Rockies I shall climb a few High Peaks with you for old times sake, that is if you let me know long before you come.

You see I had no mail since August, and will not have any till June, and this sort of life I will probably lead as long as I am able. You always will hear from me, even [if] I only get ones into town.

If you write me in future, write care of P.O. Banff. I will make Banff again my stopping place, but don't address to Alpine Club. You see I

*must forget them all, otherwise I might go climbing again, and I must
not make myself a fool again.*

I get climbing enough as a trapper.

*Now this fellow man of mine is up, so I will have to stop and cook
some supper. We shall start out early in the morning. I hope he does
not lose the letter. I would not mind to go out myself, but it is too early
for me.*

*Well my dear Lady, I must say goodbye. Accept my best wishes to all
your undertakings.*

Conrad Kain married Henriquita Ferrara in June 1917. She was then in
MacCarthy's employ, a quiet, interesting woman, the best possible partner
for Conrad. He knew it and never lost an opportunity of telling others of
his good fortune.

She was born at Georgetown [Demerara], British Guiana, June 8th, 1884,
her maiden name being Granito. Attending a convent school, she spoke
English, Portuguese and some Hindustani – coolie labour being used there
on the plantations. She first married J. Ferrara, and by him had one daughter. Ferrara died and his widow came to Canada early in 1913.

During his life in the Alps, Conrad had never been one to neglect the
ladies, and naturally he was at times lonely in the wilds. Once Mr. Wheeler
asked him why he did not take his wife with him, Conrad replying that it
was no place for a female. It was then suggested that he might get some
other woman to go with her and keep her company. Conrad said: "One
woman good, two women hell!"

After their marriage they settled down on a little farm at Wilmer in the
Columbia Valley. Conrad's wife had a talent for handling animals, and
largely to her fell the management of their small fur-farm, where they
raised mink, marten and chinchilla rabbits as long as the fur market made
it profitable.

She went on the trail with Conrad only once. As he humorously put it:
"She was too much afraid the white blankets would get dirty." On his side,
he promised to give up mountaineering, but one could scarcely imagine
either partner taking this contract seriously. At all events Conrad appeared
at the Cataract Valley Camp of the ACC on July 21st, taking Mr. and Mrs.
MacCarthy up Hungabee, the first time it was ascended by a woman.[92]

We have scarcely any record of Conrad's whereabouts in 1918. He seems to
have remained at home, working on his farm. He began to buy a few horses,

breaking them himself or with the help of local Indians, and made excursions for hunting and trapping into the adjacent Purcell valleys.

Once I see a wonderful thing. There is wild horses in the Columbia Valley. Kinda thin some of them, und not much good. But I seen a stallion lining up 30 mares. They stand in line, with their noses all even like on parade, und the stallion run up and down, shaking the head und flirting with the tail. Und if one of those mares move just a little out of line, he give her a bite, und there is an awful hollering und squealing.

Und dot is the only time I ever seen such a thing.

But, for one of Conrad's temperament, even the placid life of a farming community was not without its lighter side:

The people in the Columbia Valley are often worse off as me. Extravagant wives – dot is a funny thing. They all got to be better as the others.

Why, right in Windermere, some has got grand pianos dot they can't play on one note. Und all the time they owing a big grocery bill at the store.

In March of 1919 Kain made a solo ascent of Mt. Jumbo on snowshoes. Not only was this the first high winter ascent in the Purcells, but also one of the first recorded above 11,000 feet in the Canadian Alps.

On May 21st Mr. Wheeler received a letter from Conrad asking for work in the summer. Wheeler notes:

JUNE 18TH ◆ *Conrad arrived at Banff.*

JUNE 23RD ON ◆ *Conrad with me on Boundary Survey. Thompson Pass Castleguard meadows. Columbia Icefield. Rice Brook. Fortress Lake.*

We navigated Fortress Lake from end to end and several times by a large raft, with oars and sail. This we named the "Fortress Queen." Conrad distinguished himself amidst the party in building the raft and in navigating it.

Kain also accompanied the survey party to the head of the Athabaska, assisting with the stations opposite the mouth of Habel Creek.

He spent the winter trapping around Thompson Pass and the Castleguard and Alexandra rivers. He and Jim Simpson had planned to be together, but it did not go through and Conrad was left alone. On September 28th, as the survey party was returning home, they met Brewster's packers bringing out the supplies for the winter. Conrad was paid off, left the survey party and went back with the packers. During wet and cloudy days, when the surveyors could not photograph, Conrad had used his time building cabins and shelters along the lines of his trapping.

In February 1920, he came out on foot from the North Saskatchewan. On a tree below Mt. Patterson, on the Mistaya River, one can still read his comment pencilled on a blaze: "A Hell of a trip – soft snow."

> *Some time when you go trapping in the winter it is very cold. The snow is deep und the snowshoes sink. Pretty soon, by the end of the day, you are all in. Your foot catch in a log und you fall down.*
>
> *Und you know the cabin is only half a mile away, und you cannot make her. Und you schleep in the snow.*
>
> *You begin to have visions. You think of the fire, und you sit up. You think there is dry wood just in front of you. You make as if lighting a match. You hold out your hands to warm. But it is nothing.*
>
> *Dot is what I call my False Philosophy.*

This was indeed Conrad's own story. He was in a state of complete exhaustion when Dan McCowan found him in the Lake Louise station, having failed to get through on the night preceding and camped in the snow. He recovered on the train to Banff, telling McCowan that in the autumn he had tossed up a coin to help him decide whether to take with him a three-pound volume of Victor Hugo's *Les Misérables* or some extra and badly needed food. The book won, and Conrad thought it had saved him from going insane through loneliness.

CHAPTER XIX

(1921)

▲

TRAGEDY ON MT. EON

Kain seems to have made good his domestic promise for one more season, remaining at home during the summer of 1920. In the following year his old friends Professor and Mrs. Stone visited the Walking Tour camp run by Mr. Wheeler at Mt. Assiniboine. Stone, then president of Purdue University, had climbed Whitehorn with Conrad in 1913, as well as numerous new peaks in the Purcells during the seasons of 1915 and 1916. He was becoming an experienced guideless climber, and left camp with his wife on July 15th for a four-day trip during which he planned to ascend the virgin summit of Mt. Eon, a peak they had carefully examined while at the ACC camp the preceding year. When they did not return at the expected time, it became evident that a serious accident had occurred and search parties were organized.[93]

Dr. Stone and his wife climbed the mountain by its south side. A final steep, irregular chimney with dangerous sloping top sides opens onto the summit.

> Dr. Stone then climbed out of the chimney and disappeared for a minute or so and shortly afterwards without any warning, a large slab of rock tumbled off from above, passing over Mrs. Stone, and was closely followed by Dr. Stone, who spoke no word but held his ice axe firmly in his right hand. Horror stricken at the sight, Mrs. Stone braced herself to take the jerk of the rope, not realizing that the Doctor had taken it off to explore beyond its length ... The first fall was for about 60 feet to a narrow ledge and then the body descended....

Mrs. Stone lowered herself from ledge to ledge until trapped, and was rescued by the guide Aemmer on the 24th, eight days after the accident.

Wheeler, arriving at Banff from his survey work in the north, promptly secured additional assistance, noting:

> AUG. 1ST ♦ *Found MacCarthy and Conrad had arrived and were at the clubhouse (Banff).*
> AUG. 3RD ♦ *MacCarthy with Edward Feuz, Rudolph Aemmer and Conrad left ACC camp at Lake O'Hara meadows for Marvel Pass.*
> AUG. 4TH AND 5TH ♦ *Climbing search party out all night on Mt. Eon at 9500 feet. After six p.m. rescue party arrived at camp, having brought the body to base of the cliffs.*
> AUG. 7TH ♦ *Body brought down and packed partway to Banff.*
> AUG. 9TH ♦ *Body brought to Eau Clair camp and on to Banff. At close of recovery Conrad returned home with MacCarthy.*

The search party had ascended the mountain on August 5th, Conrad finding Stone's ice axe on the way. A cairn was built and the following statement placed in it:

> *This monument was built by the undersigned in tribute to their comrade of the mountains, Doctor Winthrop E. Stone, President of Purdue University, who, on July 16th, 1921, with his wife, virtually completed the first ascent, reaching a point not more than 50 feet from this spot. Dr. Stone's ice axe crowned this monument.*[94]

ALBERT H. MACCARTHY
LENNOX LINDSAY
EDWARD FEUZ
RUDOLPH AEMMER
CONRAD KAIN

HARLAN F. STONE TO CONRAD KAIN.
COLUMBIA UNIVERSITY, NEW YORK. OCTOBER 8TH, 1921.

I am writing this letter in behalf of Margaret Stone, my sister-in-law. She has sent me a sum of money, to which all the members of my brother's immediate family have contributed, with the request that I make distribution of it among all of those who assisted in her rescue and in the recovery of my brother's body at Mount Eon this

summer. *This I have done, dividing the money as best I could among
15 different people.*

*We quite appreciate that no sum of money could adequately express
the gratitude which we all feel for this skilful, loyal and unselfish service
of you and your associates.*

*I feel especially fortunate in having had personally the opportunity
to see you and to take you by the hand. Some day I shall hope to come
back to the Canadian Rockies. When I do come I shall not fail to see
you and to express in person the deep sense of obligation which, one
and all, we feel toward you and those who were with you on your sad
and difficult errand.*

CHAPTER XX

(1922)

▲

DYNAMITING A GLACIER

In 1922 Kain took Mrs. Best and Mrs. Shippam, of Minneapolis, with Byron Harmon on a pack train trip to the Lake of the Hanging Glaciers.[95] There were plenty of cameras and, though it was kept quiet, 36 sticks of dynamite on one of the pack horses. This was to assist Nature in an act to be called "The Birth of an Iceberg," in case it was an iceberg.

Conrad went over and dug a hole in the ice and placed his dynamite, tamped it down and lighted the fuse. When he came back he remarked that something should come loose, as there were 17 sticks about to let go. Harmon took a last anxious look into the finder.... The earth shook, the air turned purple: Mother Earth agonized, and a few pounds of ice tinkled off into the water as the smoke drifted away. But, of course, that was understood. We were waiting for the aftermath, the mighty avalanche we were sure to get.

Now, when Old Bill had been unloaded he had strolled off to browse on some tufts of green and no one had given him a second thought. When the first report of the discharge took place, Old Bill started a little charge of his own. What mattered it to him if the cameras were in his line of advance? He came down the stretch hitting on all fours, his mane flying, his nostrils dilated and flaming, his eyes holding the fire of battle. He hit Harmon first! Down went the camera and Old Bill walked up the spine of the vanquished photographer, hit the second, third and fourth cameras with sickening precision and careered off down the valley. And then it happened! The whole top of the mountains eased off a bit, toppled and crashed to the glacier below in the mightiest of mighty avalanches.

The party visited the south fork of Horsethief Creek, and then left the Purcells. Mr. Wheeler notes that on August 7th, after the Palliser Pass camp of the ACC, Conrad brought the two ladies to Mt. Assiniboine.

One would like to know the whole story of that excursion in the Purcells, for rumour will have it that Mrs. Best carried a revolver and pointed it on occasion. But the lady is no longer with us, and Conrad and Harmon would never tell.

CHAPTER XXI

(1923)

▲

COLUMBIA ICEFIELD

In the summer of 1923 W.S. Ladd and J.M. Thorington planned and carried out an expedition to the Columbia Icefield.[96] This was the beginning of an association with Conrad Kain which continued throughout the remainder of his life.

Ladd, who had ascended Mt. Fay with Conrad in 1910, wrote to him and received the following reply:

C.K. TO W.S. LADD. WILMER. MAY 17TH, 1923.

Received your letter today and hasten to answer and explain matters to you. I received a few letters from James Simpson asking me to go along on your trip to Mt. Columbia. My life as a guide in the English-speaking countries was a complete failure from a financial point of view and as I love the great hills I had to turn my hands to something else to enable me to stay in the mountains. I have now a pack train and follow up outfitting. I also climb mountains with people who hire me as guide and outfitter.

I will be leaving here tomorrow for a three-week bear hunt. I also have a fishing party for two weeks in July. The latter will bring me about 450 dollars. I could recommend another guide and outfitter for this fishing trip but no doubt it would be rather expensive for you and Dr. Thorington to pay me the above sum for 30 days. You can get one of the Swiss guides from the CPR for seven dollars per day.

In case that you do not and you don't care to make your trip to Mt. Columbia without a third climber in the party I will go, but you would have to give me your decision not later than June 15th. If I come along I will act on the trail (from Lake Louise and back) as assistant packer to Simpson, and so he would not need another man, as this would help to cut expenses down a bit.

I know the country around Mt. Columbia. I was there with Mr. Wheeler and I also spent a winter trapping in that country. I am sure you will like it. Mt. Columbia is a very long snow tramp.

Mt. Pryce [Bryce] is a first-class peak and so is Mt. Alexander [Alexandra] in the Lyell group. You can make a few first ascents. Some of these peaks you will find very interesting. Mt. Saskatchewan is another fine mountain. I am not sure if Mt. Sask. was climbed before. The best view of the Columbia Icefield you get from Castle [Castleguard] peak, don't miss this view. If I can be of any help to you in giving you information, send me a map and I will mark the high up camp where we camped on the Survey. From this camp (timber-line) you can climb Mt. Columbia, Mt. Pryce, Mt. Athabaska and Dom [Snow Dome].

I remember you and the climb of Mt. Fay with Mr. Mitchell. I believe Mr. Mitchell has not climbed a high peak since. I trust that you will get a Swiss guide from the CPR and that you will have a grand and glorious time in the great old hills.

As a result arrangements were concluded and we left Lake Louise late in June, outfitted by Jim Simpson.

In those days the Columbia region was considered wild and far away, having been visited by but few climbers (with the exception of Outram in 1902) since its discovery by Collie in 1898. Conrad was familiar with the country from his work with the Boundary Survey, but it was not at all well-known to mountaineers.

Everything went smoothly and a number of peaks were ascended, among them Castleguard, North Twin, Saskatchewan, Columbia and Athabaska, North Twin and Saskatchewan being first ascents.

On the summit of Castleguard:

Jim and Conrad are lying flat on the shale, with a map spread out; there is a great pointing of fingers toward distant valleys, and the remarks which come to my ears indicate that fur-bearing animals next trapping season had best look out for themselves.

445

Of the return from North Twin one recalls the immensity of the icefield, the brilliant sunset – the finest that Conrad could ever remember in the Rockies – and our final effort through the night.

> *While Conrad and Ladd were attempting to make tea, I walked on alone to the slopes below Castleguard. The unbroken snow was hardening a little, the air comfortably cool, and only a gentle wind stirring. I sat down to wait for the others. Beyond Athabaska dark clouds hung and lightning flashed; in another direction, above Bryce, stars appeared in all the glory of high altitudes; in the western horizon there was still a pale afterglow, and bits of mist floated about on the surface of the icefield, as if earth and sky were mingled in one.*

The highlights of other climbing were the sight of Conrad cutting through the little cornice of Mt. Columbia; and his care and concern during the descent of Mt. Saskatchewan, when our position became hazardous because of avalanching, wet snow.

A unique feature of the expedition was the taking of the pack train from Castleguard meadows to Sunwapta Pass by way of Saskatchewan Glacier. One remembers Conrad and Jim shooting ptarmigan with a pistol; and Ladd and Conrad, seated by the glacier, with pipes at full blast, searching the ice for a route for the horses.

Last of all, we traversed Mt. Gordon from Bow Lake, reaching the Yoho River during a violent storm of hail.

> *We made vain efforts to ford; even when roped together the current was too swift for us. Conrad went clear under, and came up looking like an Alpine Neptune arising from the deep – still holding his pipe between his teeth!*

Crossing the canyon lower down, leaving important sections of our garments on a spiked log, we reached the Takakkaw cabins and emptied a bottle of rum with our friend Phil Moore.

A few days later we were at Banff, Ladd and Conrad achieving the third ascent of Mt. Louis. But so much damage was done to the seats of their trousers that they waited until dark before daring to reappear in the village; and, to this moment, we can see them entering the King Edward Hotel, followed by a file of children pointing and shouting at their tattered clothing.

One evening, at Dan McCowan's house, talk turning on the things of the woods and hills, Conrad related that on a moonlight night in the spring he had seen a large group of various hares, or snowshoe rabbits, playing on a sloping sheet of glare ice by the side of a stream. They were sliding down this "slide" with apparent enjoyment, the others hopping around and watching the proceedings. A Kootenay Indian woman and her little boy had seen these creatures playing in the same fashion on a previous year in the Columbia Valley. Otters, it is well-known, resort to slippery clay banks by the sides of streams and slide for hours, but no previous observation seems to have been made of hares doing this sort of thing.

Those were good days. Conrad was continually pointing out the features of the country, helping with the packing, keeping us in an uproar with his stories and making himself generally useful. Here he had cached his traps; there he had spent a cold night in the snow, dreaming of warm fire. For those who took part, this journey stands out in memory as one of the happiest and most successful ever made in the Canadian mountains.

CHAPTER XXII

(1924)

▲

ATHABASKA PASS

In 1924 M.M. Strumia, A.J. Ostheimer and J.M. Thorington engaged Conrad for an expedition to Athabaska Pass.[97] As the following letters show, Kain had his eye on Mt. Alberta, but we, at the time, were more interested in the historic gateway of the fur traders.

C.K. TO J.M.T. WILMER. APRIL 8, 1924.

Sorry I could not answer your letter ere now as I was away from home. I have not yet made up my mind what I will do this coming summer. Next month I go grizzly hunting and will be away about four weeks. I had many letters from climbers about Mt. Robson this summer, but so far I have not made any arrangements, as I expect a party for July. Are you going climbing all by yourself this year?

I have heard that the CNR will have Swiss guides at Robson and Jasper. If this is the case it would come ever so much cheaper for you to get one of the Railway Guides. You see I am quite frank about it. I know my price is high but it wouldn't pay me to let my horses run in the pasture when there is work for them, but if you don't mind my charges I think I could come along with you, but you should take advantage of my service and make your plans to climb Mt. Alberta & Mt. King Ed. and, if you care, the South Twin.

If you get Phillips to take you out, I shall act as the second man. I will also do the cooking on the trail. You would not need many horses for this trip up the Athabaska. Then we would go up to Mt. Robson. There you would not need a pack train.

448

Besides Mt. Robson we could climb Mt. Resplendent, Mt. Longstaff or the Whitehorn. I know the mountain you mention (Mt. Hooker), and if you like to climb it, all right, but I thought I would suggest Mt. Alberta to you because it is the best looking of those yet unclimbed peaks up there, and I could find a way up. When you have made up your mind drop me a line. There is no hurry. The only thing is that I will leave home on May the 8th for about four weeks. Edward [Feuz] will be with your friends [Osgood Field and party] for the South Twin.

We started out from Jasper in June, the pack train being in the hands of Dave Moberly, one of Curly Phillips's men, but Phillips did not accompany us. Athabaska Pass was reached without incident, although the Whirlpool River was in flood. There were banks of snow about the little lakes on the pass, and a caribou went slowly up the slopes as we arrived.

Mt. Kane was traversed and Mt. Brown ascended, but our principal objective, Mt. Hooker, was not to be reached from this side. We returned down the valley and made camp below the superb Scott Glacier.

Penetrating to the upper basin, not without some strenuous ice work on Conrad's part, we ascended Mt. Oates. This was followed, two days later, by a successful attack on Mt. Hooker, a miniature Mt. Cook, during which we came into some danger through falling stones.

It was the beginning of a raking fire in which we were all struck, but luckily without damage. Conrad calmly saying "Gentlemen, we must move a little to one side" relieved the tension; we quickly got out of range, in time to avoid a heavy bombardment of larger boulders that came banging down over our intended path and would surely have done for us had we persisted. We realized afterward that in Conrad's cool leadership, in emergency, we had seen one of the finest things produced by mountaineering art.

Coming late to the summit we were obliged to bivouac and, on account of fog and snow which followed, were compelled to spend two nights in the open, high on the mountain. That we did not get into more serious difficulties was entirely due to Conrad. One never heard him utter a word of complaint.

Following this we rode back to Jasper. Arriving late in the evening, we went to the beer hall to quench our thirst after a long day on dusty trails.

We sat down and gave our order, but before it could be brought closing time arrived and we never got our drinks.

We rode our horses through the Miette Valley, and up the newly built Meadow Creek trail to Tonquin Valley. A few days later we made the first ascent of Simon Peak, highest of the Ramparts. Very few of the peaks had been climbed at that time. We made no attempt on Mt. Geikie, Mr. Cyril Wates, successful on the day of our visit to Tonquin Pass, having written requesting that a professional guide should not be taken on the mountain.

> *Conrad was in great form that evening, and treated us to tales of startling adventure: snake-collecting in Egypt, sheep-herding in Australia, gold-washing in the Northwest, wanderings in the South Seas, hunting in the Siberian Altai. The most beautiful place in the world, he believes, is the island of Madeira; there he would like to spend a little of his old age before retiring to a cottage in the Tyrol.... Slowly rose the moon; not in solemn grandeur, but rather with full face smiling, as if in sympathy with our merriment. A wind from the Tonquin Pass was gently moving the pine-tops; there was a tinkling of bells as our horses wandered across the meadows.*

Strumia then returned home, while Kain, Ostheimer and Thorington went to Mt. Robson. Meeting there the guides Hans Kohler and Alfred Streich, we made a large and lighthearted party in traversing Mt. Resplendent. Ostheimer and Thorington then took part in an ascent of Mt. Robson, the first made that season, but turned back at the upper icefall, while Conrad continued with Messrs. Pollard, Geddes and Moffat to the summit. "Gentlemen, it is risky," said Con; "I am willing to go on if you wish." But the danger from falling ice that day was greater than we cared to face, a judgment which has since had ample backing, even by Kain himself.

Conrad remained at the high camp on Mt. Robson, guiding additional parties. He told us afterward that it was always dangerous, but that the route selected was the only one by which he could have gotten the people to the top. He was keenly aware of the chances he was taking – more so, one thinks, than some of those who followed him. Yet, in the midst of it all, he could speed his lagging tourists by saying, "I will kees you if you get to the top by two o'clock."

Later in the summer he went with Messrs. Palmer and Hickson up the Athabaska.[98] Bad weather forestalled an attack on Mt. Alberta, but a successful ascent of Mt. King Edward was made.

C.K. TO J.M.T. WILMER. SEPTEMBER 15TH, 1924.

On my return (Sept. 10th) I found your letter, and by last mail I received yours of 9th inst. and book. Many thanks for all. It appears that you have already heard that I had bad weather on my trip with Dr. Hickson and Palmer; we only climbed King Edward and a little peak behind Mt. Alberta in the first 21 days. Then we made another trip up the Whirlpool, and on the way back Hickson and I climbed Mt. Edith Cavell over the east ridge. This was a real nice climb, in parts rather hard rock work; I enjoyed this climb very much. Of course we had to spend the night out as we traversed the mountain.

I got on very well with Dr. Hickson, he is OK. I believe he will go to Jasper again, he likes Mt. Alberta very much. Mt. Alberta will be an A-1 climb, nearly all rocks. There are many good-looking peaks on the Chaba Icefield (unclimbed). I guess you will have heard all about my climbs on Mt. Robson.

I am now enjoying my home for a few days, but not for very long, as I will go out again for a few weeks. I will read Mr. Palmer's book carefully and will tell you what I think about it. It was very nice of you to get the book for me.

Ed. Feuz was climbing somewhere up Toby Creek with Mr. A.A. McCoubrey, but what mountains they climbed I don't know. That's all the news I can write you from here.

CHAPTER XXIII

(1925–28)

▲

A HUNTER IN THE NORTHWEST

K ain seems to have done little or no mountaineering in the three summers that followed. He was busily engaged on his farm or with hunting and fishing parties. It was during this time that he had his adventures with motion-picture companies, looking for new locations. Conrad flew above the Purcells in an airplane, once doubling for the leading lady under such hazards, and put in a bill for an extra 25 dollars to cover the loss of his moustache!

He was amused at the vagaries of directors, telling us that, once, a cabin had to be burned as part of a scene. Conrad took them out to an old ruin on Toby Creek. The shots proved failures and had to be retaken. But the season had progressed, snow was vanishing and there were no more cabins. A shack in Windermere was purchased at a fabulous price, snow being packed in on carts to give the proper scenic effect.

In the winter Conrad trapped, and at odd times would go out alone or with his horses in the Purcell valleys. Much of his hunting was done with Mr. Randall Everett, who writes as follows:

RANDALL W. EVERETT TO J.M.T. BREVARD, N.C. MAY 22, 1934.

I was with him on five successive hunting trips, from 1926 to 1930 in-clusive and never met so thorough and fine a chap. His love of nature was remarkable and his knowledge of animal life also was astounding.

I had been wanting to make another trip with him soon, but now I have no desire to go into a country where his presence would be lacking. All our trips were in the East Kootenay country, on the head of the Palliser, on Mitchell Creek and also up Corral Creek and Cross River. Several trips we spent part of our time at the mouth of the Palliser where it flows into the Kootenay. This section was especially good for elk. I met Con on the trip I was taking to Alaska. He was special guide to Mr. Dun Waters. His personality and quiet mannerisms appealed to me and ended by my making arrangements to hunt with him.

Con and I had some very interesting experiences together. One time I killed a bear across the Kootenay. Con thought he knew a ford, but the river was higher than usual due to some warm weather that melted the glacial ice. The first thing we knew, the horses were swimming and we were immersed to our necks. The water was swift at this point and we were nearly carried down among some large boulders. After skinning out the bear, Con made the remark that we would have to attempt to swim the horses back or Siwash it in the timber all night. He thought the horses would make good, owing to their desire to reach camp.

I first went up on the high bluff to see if we could force our way through. Such a jungle met my gaze that I was willing to try the river. Con tied a rope to the saddle horn and told me if the horse turned turtle to hang on to the rope and he would pull me out. After a good deal of coaxing we got the horses started, but after being carried downstream about the same distance they had advanced they whirled around and made for the spot they had started from.

Con, seeing the uselessness of attempting it again, then started to try and hack a way through the mass of down timber. He luckily had an axe he had brought to cut up the bear. We did this until it got too dark to see and, fortunately having a waterproof matchbox, we kindled a fire and spent one of the most miserable nights it has been my misfortune to experience. A half a wet biscuit, wet clothes and not very warm in October in the Canadian Rockies. The real test of a man shows here, and Con's bright and cheerful manner assuredly helps the others.

I shot lots of game with Con – five moose, one elk, six deer, five goats, two grizzlies and four black bear. He was a great woodsman. I had made 14 trips in the Jackson Hole country in Wyoming, but he saw things that were passed up by the majority of sportsmen.

Conrad had made two hunting trips in the Purcells with J.C. Dun Waters, of Fintry, Okanagan Lake, former proprietor of the Glasgow *Herald*. Conrad and his wife once paid him a visit, giving rise to the following story:

One time my wife und me we make a visit in de Okanagan. To an old fellow I have out camping. They are Old Country people here, you understand, und live in style. Every day they go hunting wid dogs und horses und red coats und horns.

The first morning I am up early und nobody is about. So I ask a fellow, "Where is breakfast?" und he say, "Oh, you can't have dot until de Mahster come down!"

So the Mahster come down at ten o'clock, und by eleven the breakfast is finished und they are ready for the hunt.

Und a fellow blow the horn und we make ready. Then the Mahster's wife run out und say, "Mahster, Maahster, one of the servants feeling sick in the belly."

So we all wait around und soon it is dinner time. "No matter," say the Mahster, "we start a little later."

So two o'clock we make ready once more. Den a fellow come und holler, "Mahster, one of the dogs has hurt his foot."

We give it a look und tie it up, und pretty soon another gink say, "Wal, Mahster, I see your cayuse has lost a shoe."

When dot is all fixed it is near sunset. The fellow given a blow on the horn, but the Mahster say, "No, it is too late. We go hunting tomorrow."

Well, say! It is ten o'clock when we finish supper. Und next morning I say to my wife, "Py Gott, Hetta, I tink we go back to our farm in the Columbia Valley, where life is not so complicated und something is finished!"

Conrad went with Mr. Dun Waters as special guide on a hunting trip in southwestern Alaska in the autumn of 1925.

C.K. TO J.M.T. WILMER. OCTOBER 7TH, 1925.

I intended to write to you ever since my return from Alaska, and just now I learned that you are married, so I have to write at once to wish you the best of luck as a Benedick. I trust that some time I will have the pleasure to meet Mrs. T.

How did you enjoy your trip in the Alps? No doubt you climbed many peaks over 4000 m. Auch ich habe oft ein langen (sehnen) nach den Schweizer Bergen und nach Dunkles Bier. Ich hoffe dass Sie ein Mass (Stein) von den guten Saft zur Erinnerungen an unsere Bergtouren in den Rockies getrunken haben.

Now the little news I have to write. When your last letter arrived I was on my way to Alaska. We spent over six weeks in Western Alaska and yet I can't write much about the country in general. It was a wet trip, rain and snow – and talk about wind, we had one real blizzard it lasted two days. The storm drove the snow through our new tents like through cheese cloth; it was like hell frozen over and while lying there 24 hours in the blankets and covered with snow I learned the following lines:

> *Dam Alaska,*
> *Dam the Shack,*
> *Dam the journey there & back.*
> *Dam the flies,*
> *Dam the weather,*
> *Dam Alaska altogether.*

We had only a few nice days in all and on one of these fine days I climbed a mountain 7500 feet. As I started from the sea level, it was quite a good day's work; of course there was nothing difficult, the snow was frozen over, otherwise I could not have done it in a day. The view from the summit was very fine, the restless Bearing [sic] Sea was in full view. We finally got our bears, five in number (one extra large) but we had to work very hard for it. On my return home I met Mr. Fynn; he then intended to take a shot on Mt. Alberta but I believe he didn't get there in time.

Some time in August I was on a search party. Mrs. McCoubrey managed to lose herself on Toby Creek; we found her on the third day and she was OK and no doubt she knows more as she did before about mountains and trail.

The rest of the time I have been working very hard on my place; soon the Old Man Winter will be here, and to get some joy out of life I will go in the hills for a change.

The next ACC camp will be held on the South Fork of Horsethief Creek and if you intend to make a mountaineer out of your wife there is a good place to start.

Later on, Conrad told us the following story:

> *In Alahska I was bear hunting. Und it rain all the time. So while we are sitting in the tent, I tell the Indian the story of the Flood.*
> *They sit und look und make no answer.*
> *At last one say: "Ugh! It been raining here 80 days, 80 nights – no Flood!"*

In the attempt to entice us to the Purcells, Conrad wrote the account which now follows:

CHAPTER XXIV

(1928)

▲

1

THE EASTERN VALLEYS OF THE PURCELL RANGE[99]

The Purcell Range is considered to belong to the Selkirk system and is often referred to as the Southern Selkirks, but Dawson, in his 1886 report,
has adduced arguments for considering each as totally distinct from the
other. Its natural boundaries are unusually obvious, being separated from
the Rocky Mountains on the east by the valleys of the northward-flowing
upper Columbia River, and the southward-flowing upper Kootenay River,
which together constitute a part of the great Rocky Mountain Trench.

Speaking generally this mountain range has received little attention in
comparison with neighbouring ranges, though it offers much to the explorer, mountaineer and hunter.

In the west the range is separated from the Selkirks by a smaller but
equally well-defined trench. Its northern end is represented by the valley
of the northward-flowing Beaver River, whose confluence with the upper
Columbia occurs at an acute angle and defines the northern extent of the
range. Crossing the low (4600-foot) Beaver–Duncan divide, the Purcell
Trench continues southward in the course of the Duncan, through Howser
Creek, the long, fjord-like north and south arms of Kootenay Lake, and
the northward-flowing lower Kootenay River, whose acute-angled bend in
Montana forms the southern boundary of the Purcells, in a manner similar
to that in which the Big Bend of the Columbia forms the northern limit of
the Selkirk system.

The Selkirks, including the Purcell Range, are some millions of years older
than the Rocky Mountains, representing in this region and for a distance
of three hundred miles the original main axis of the North American
Cordillera. The Dogtooth Mountains and the Prairie Hills at the northern

extremity of the range have been surveyed. For the rest of the range the provincial mining maps are the best.

In the year 1910 I went with an expedition whose object was to cross the Purcell Range and make a survey of the glacier region, which would have included the south fork of the Spillimacheen, Bugaboo and Salmon rivers on the east, and Reno and Howser creeks on the west. We crossed the divide over Bugaboo Pass and occupied about a dozen stations with camera and transit.[100]

Since then I have taken part in several exploration trips and have spent winters trapping in the Purcell Range. There are many interesting and beautiful spots in this range and it would not be difficult to gather material for many volumes. But I will now touch only on the tributaries which empty into the Columbia River, beginning at the north.

The Valleys of the Spillimacheen and Bugaboo

The first and one of the largest tributary streams of the upper Columbia is the Spillimacheen. Its valley is approximately 50 miles long and has two large side-valleys, the South and North forks. Except for its forests, which shelter small fur-bearers and bears, the valley has not great scenic attractions; but its next neighbour on the south, the Bugaboo, makes up for it. In addition to the fine scenery at the head of this creek, the valley has a wagon road 27 miles long, built by a logging company in 1916.

Forest fires have destroyed most of the bridges and put the road out of commission, but it is still one of the best trails in the Purcell Range. The valley is of a different type and is not so wide as the Spillimacheen, the range dividing Bugaboo from Salmon Creek, in the next valley to the south, being a mass of jagged pinnacles. Dr. Longstaff in his account refers to this as the Septet Group. I have climbed two of the towers and can recommend them to mountaineers who make a specialty of climbing rotten-rock mountains.

The range on the north is not so steep and the formation (quartzite) is firm. The first creek from the north is known as Rocky Point Creek, which descends in torrents from a hanging valley known as the Hidden Treasure basin, named after a mining claim. An old pack trail winds up the left side of the stream, and apparently the hidden treasure has not been found. I know I cannot do justice to this alpine paradise: on my first visit to the basin I wrote in my diary, "This is one of the most beautiful and charming spots that I have seen on this continent."

From Rocky Point the main valley widens out and is nearly level; there are several waterfalls in the small creeks descending from the Septet Group. At the junction of the North Fork with the main creek the road ends, and a neat-looking cabin serves as an ideal camping place. Although the road cost $16,000, fire came before the loggers and the road was of no use to its builders.

Here the traveller gets the first real alpine view. The North Fork Glacier descends to the valley's floor, a glacier clean and flanked with timber and green shrubs, the contrast giving the finishing touch to this picture. There is a trail up the creek and horses can be taken for more than three miles, nearly to the ice. The glacier is crowned by a cluster of peaks called the Bugaboo Spires. Some day enthusiastic mountaineers will battle with these formidable-looking rock walls. For myself, I had two battles here and recorded one victory and one defeat. Spire No. 3 offered innumerable obstacles and, having climbed a number of peaks, I can say that it was my most difficult ascent in Canada.[101]

In the year 1925, while hunting bear, I made an attempt to reach the summit of No. 2, but the odds were too heavy and I had to record my first defeat. I would not say that this peak is unclimbable because it proved too much for me; someday, mountaineers who have more experience and knowledge will conquer this dignified-looking aiguille.

The highest elevation in this group is Howser Spire, 10,950 feet.[102] The first ascent was made in the year 1916. My recollection is that we had a struggle with the bergschrund which lay across the entire southeast face of the mountain. Not far below the summit we were surprised by a red squirrel running back and forth on a narrow ledge. Squirrels as a rule are home-loving creatures. On my rambles above timberline I have seen squirrels where one would not expect to find them, and on a few occasions found skeletons on glaciers, indicating that the forest-dweller breaks loose once in a while, breaks the daily routine, takes a holiday and seeks adventure away from home.

The best and quickest way to reach the snowfields and spires is to follow the left lateral moraine. Four-footed mountaineers must have used the ridge of this moraine as a promenade for many decades, and to strike a goat trail in the hills, especially after a hard day's work, is a great relief.

Returning to the main valley, the North Fork is forded near the cabin; trail leads through heavy timber for more than three miles before coming to an end where a tremendous pile of windfalls forces the traveller to the open muskegs and beaver meadows. Here is an opportunity to gather first-hand information of the force produced by an avalanche and to see the work of beavers.

The valley splits above the muskegs, a short branch containing several hanging glaciers in their last stage. There is no man-made trail up this valley, but there are enough bears to keep the game trails visible. There is good camping ground at the fork, whence the valley rises gradually to a pass, 7200 feet. On top of and to the west of the pass is an outcrop of galena. An energetic prospector once staked a claim, blazed a trail, worked hard for several seasons, finally discovering that the outcrop was not "A-1" mineral. It was a Bugaboo and the name stuck to the claim and to the valley.

The Valley of the Salmon

The next creek goes by the name of Salmon River. I have never seen salmon in this creek, but in the vicinity there are several good-sized and many small lakes, known locally as the Fish Lakes, which are well stocked. The salmon trout is the dominating fish, hence the name of the creek.

At the head of the southern fork, which is the largest, Mt. Ethelbert, 10,500 feet, towers far above all the other peaks nearby. Crowned by a snowcap it is a prominent landmark. It has been climbed once, the ascent being made from the head of the southern fork.[103] There one finds three lakes, the first being the largest and surrounded by green timber. A little beyond, a fine waterfall tumbles over a terraced wall, making a pretty picture. The other two lakes are above timberline and are not marked on the map. Beside Mt. Ethelbert there are several peaks and crags which have not yet been trodden by human foot. Except to a few prospectors and trappers this region is unknown.

The Valleys of No. 2 and No. 3 Creeks

The valley of No. 3 Creek has not much to offer in scenery, being much hemmed in. A road leads halfway, whence there is a good trail to timberline where the Steel and Lead Queen claim groups are located. These claims have attracted much attention locally on account of the mineral outcrops. Much work has been done at various times, and mining experts and geologists have been called in to help find the right key for unlocking the treasure chest.

No. 3 joins No. 2 Creek two miles from the Columbia. No. 2, or Frances Creek, has never attracted explorers and there are few local people who have any knowledge of it. The old Indian trail is nearly impassable for horses, and this is the sole reason for its neglect, as the valley has more green timber than many double in area, while at its head are several short valleys, or basins, encircled by high cliffs, the north face of Mt. Sally Serena, the highest point of the range, dividing No. 2 from Horsethief Creek.

The Valley of Horsethief Creek

The latter was once known as No. 1 Creek, but received its present romantic name from the exploits of an American and a Swede who, years ago it is said, rustled some pack ponies from a whisky peddler. They were pursued up the creek, captured and taken to Fort Steele where the episode ended in a big spree all around. Whisky, in general, is not looked upon as a peacemaker, but was in this case, as during the spree the alleged thieves were discharged.

Horsethief Creek has received more publicity than any other stream on the eastern slope of the Purcell Range. Large sums of money have been spent in operating mining claims and logging camps, and these enterprises are mainly responsible for the road, which is good for any make of car up to the 20-mile post. The road starts from Wilmer and after winding through ravines and over benches for eight miles enters the valley proper. These ravines and benches are relics of the ice time and offer a good opportunity to those who make a study of that remote period.

The first tributary to Horsethief Creek from the south is Boulder Creek, which has a side valley known as Law Creek. Both have the characteristics of hanging valleys. There is a mining road of easy grade, from which one gets glimpses through the heavy timber of the foaming stream. Two-thirds up, the valley widens out. To the south, Mt. Nelson, 10,770 feet, a prominent landmark, presents its north face, stern-looking compared with the southern side which is seen from the Columbia Valley.[104] Nearly in line to the north stands Boulder Mountain with its ever-shining coronet of snow.

A great deal of mining work has been done at different claims, but so far no great strike is recorded. This would be an ideal spot for the novelist who writes mining yarns to lay his plots; the names of the claims alone promise romance: Sitting Bull, Wild Cat, Monte Carlo, Pretty Girl, Black Prince, Marie Gee and Bald Eagle.

About ten miles from Wilmer the Horsethief Valley widens. At 13 miles there is an abandoned ranch, known as Starbird. Many years ago an attempt was made to advertise this part of the country as a tourist resort. There was then no railway through the Columbia Valley and few tourists ventured far from the Canadian Pacific. The enterprise, however, was not altogether a failure; big game hunters were attracted and, coming for grizzlies and goat, all left the valley with trophies. It is quite common to see goat on the grassy slopes of Mt. High Ball, 8000 feet. This mountain, just north of the ranch, is easy to climb, rewarding anyone who wishes to become acquainted with the lay of the land, and affording a splendid view.

McDonald Creek is the next tributary from the south, a wagon road winding up the valley, and several "tin lizzies" have made the trip to the end. The most striking feature is Mt. Farnham, 11,342 feet, highest point in the Purcell Range, and Farnham Tower. Both peaks have been climbed once.[105] The tower was considered by many as absolutely unattainable; rumour had it that Mr. Farnham offered 100 dollars for a piece of rock from the top. I packed a good-sized rock down, but have failed to locate the man with the hundred dollars. Mt. Farnham was named for a mining promoter who is said to have spent a fortune on the Ptarmigan, a claim opposite the mountain.

Another unusual peak is Delphine, with its carved glacier, the source of McDonald Creek. The North Fork is the only tributary from the north, the valley being nearly 12 miles in length, narrow and without a glacier at its end; there is a small branch coming from the west side of Mt. Sally Serena, a wild, isolated basin in which are three little lakes. There is no trail and very few people have been there.

The South Fork of this valley is especially recommended to mountaineers and to lovers of wildflowers. Mt. Jumbo, 11,217 feet, is overtopped in the Purcell Range only by Mt. Farnham, and was long thought to be loftier. The easiest and most interesting way to climb this mountain is from the south, at the junction of the short creek from Jumbo Glacier (Tiger Claw Glacier) with the South Fork, where there is good camping ground. The first ascent was made in 1915.[106] On March 5, 1919, I climbed this mountain on snowshoes; time from the foot of the glacier to the summit: four hours and a half. Mt. Jumbo on this side is a snow mountain, and an ideal average climb, with a magnificent outlook.

Other peaks that may be climbed from this camp are: Commander, Farnham, Peter, Sir Charles, Delphine, Peacock, Spearhead and several unnamed. Without going to the head of the valley a trip to the South Fork would not be complete. Trail is fairly good and goes to timberline, where the Phoenix mine and the Alpine gardens are located. In addition to the view and the flowers, there is wildlife in abundance: butterflies, hummingbirds and myriads of playful gophers. The marmot and the ever-busy cony make themselves heard; mountain goat and grizzly are not strangers to this wonderful valley.

The Lake of the Hanging Glaciers

From the junction of the South Fork with the main creek, the valley is narrower; trail leads through patches of forest alternating here and there with "slides" in which grass and herbaceous plants grow rankly, shoulder-high. As an instance, the false forget-me-not grows from two to three feet in height. There are many waterfalls, the highest and most picturesque being nearly at the head of the valley, where the entire main creek drops in three sections over the rock. The name Trinity was suggested for this fall. About a mile and a half from the end of the valley the trail for the Lake of the Hanging Glaciers turns off and winds up through a heavily wooded slope. In all there are 30 switchbacks in the trail.

The lake was first discovered by a prospector and named Lake Maye. In 1920 the trail was made and the name changed. Mr. H.W. Gleason, of Boston, was the first man to photograph the lake, the picture with a short account appearing later in the *National Geographic Magazine*. Since then the lake has had more publicity than visitors. A friend of mine who is a photographer told me that this lake is like a small gold mine – the pictures sell so fast.

It is advisable for the traveller to arrange his trip so that he may spend a whole day at the lake. The ice wall at the far end is from 90 to 100 feet high.

Starbird Glacier, the birthplace of Horsethief Creek, is also of great interest. It is possible to go on horseback to the glacier, where there is a natural ice cave nearly 20 feet high. A medial moraine makes the ascent easy, and Mt. Monica has been climbed several times. It forms a divide monument between East and West Kootenay.

Although the Purcell Range is in British Columbia, the vegetation is identical with that on the Continental Divide. The forest growth on the western slopes of the range is much denser than on the eastern side and the valleys are deeper. On my trapping trips I have crossed the range over different passes and found snow conditions similar to those on the Continental Divide – always more snow on the western slope, and much wilder country. This has a great effect on fur-bearing animals, the denser growth giving more shelter and food to the animals on which the fur-bearers live. As a rule the creatures of the western slope have better pelts.

North of the glacier is the highest peak, the third on Horsethief Creek which exceeds 11,000 feet in elevation. The mountain is unnamed but has been climbed.[107] To the west of this unnamed summit is Birthday Peak, the first ascent of which was made on August 10, 1915, the writer's birthday. Rumour has it that on top, hidden in a cairn, is a bottle of whisky and a cheque for 25 dollars. The true story is that, on this occasion, we found ourselves without paper to write a record. Mr. A.H. MacCarthy found a blank cheque in his first-aid kit, which he made out for five dollars payable to the bearer, with the request that whoever cashed the cheque should drink to Conrad's health. On the back we wrote our names, the date, and particulars of the ascent. To the present time the ascent has not been repeated. No doubt the cheque will be cashed some day and if the bearer is not a teetotaller he will surely grant the request and drink to my health!

The Valley of Toby Creek

Toby Creek, with its tributaries – North Fork and Jumbo Fork from the north; Mineral Creek, Copper Creek and South Fork from the south – offers a large area for the explorer. Most of the high peaks have been climbed, but there is any amount of detail work left for the topographer. The least-known portions of the creek are at the head of Jumbo Fork, which is about ten miles longer than the main valley. The trail over Wells Pass[108] was for many years the only highway across the Purcell Range and was used and kept up by prospectors. The trail over the pass and down Hamill Creek to Kootenay Lake has been neglected for many years and is now impassable for horses.

The Valley of Dutch Creek

Dutch Creek is the last and longest tributary to the Columbia River, emptying into upper Columbia Lake and in reality the source of the Columbia. The valley is more than 40 miles long and has three tributaries; it is narrow, and at the head are many peaks and snowfields. The peaks are all unclimbed and the glaciers unexplored. Trail is kept open by the trappers.

In the Purcell Range there is much to be seen, much exploring and topographical work to be done, much to interest the tramper, climber and hunter, much that is enticing to the man who would escape the turmoil of modern life.

2

TO THE LAKE OF THE HANGING GLACIERS

Because of climbing seasons in the Alps we did not see Kain again until the summer of 1928, when with O.E. Cromwell and J.G. Hillhouse we visited the Purcells, of which Conrad had always been talking.[109]

C.K. TO J.M.T. WILMER. NOVEMBER 15TH, 1927.

Es ist schon eine lange Zeit dass ich Ihnen nicht geschrieben habe, da ich sehr wenig Deutsch spreche und schreibe, so benütze ich die Gelegenheit Deutsch zu schreiben. Ich sehe sie gern noch in die Berge und jagen nach Erst-besteigungen – das ist ein langes Wort.

I think this is quite enough German for this time. If you should run short of first ascents let me know; I can take you in an absolutely new country that is new from a mountaineering point of view. This new ground is at the head of Dutch and Findlay creeks. I believe that some of the peaks are over 10,000 feet, mostly snow mountains, and the glaciers and snowfields are of good size. I have never heard or read that these peaks have been climbed.

I have not climbed high peaks this year. In the spring I did fairly well with beavers and in summer I had a fishing party for six weeks. The hunters got all that was coming to them; they left well satisfied. One of the men was with me last year and he says he will come again. The gentleman I had out six times bear hunting in the spring had to give it up on account of old age, so I will have to rustle up a new customer. If you should meet anyone who would like to hunt grizzlies, give them my address. I will see that they get a kick out of it, and a bear of course.

Some time ago I had a letter from S.H. Mitchell; he wrote for information re. Lake of the Hanging Glaciers. It is likely the ACC will hold their next camp here; if they do I am sure it will be a successful camp, as there are many peaks and a great variety. This winter I will be more or less at home and will spend my spare time trailing the cunning coyotes.

MAY 1ST, 1928 ✦ *I have been away up in the hills, hence the long delay. You mentioned in your letter that you could be here around July 19th. The train leaves Golden on Thursday and Friday at 2 p.m. for Lake Windermere. If there is a daily stage over the auto road it matters little, so far as time goes, which way you take, but if there is not a daily bus it is cheaper and safer to take the train from Golden and return over the highway to Banff. I would like to take you up Dutch Creek, but I am afraid that we could not accomplish very much in 10 days. So I would suggest a trip to the head of Toby; very little is known about the glacier, especially the section toward Dutch Creek. We can make camp near the glacier; the trail at the upper end of Toby is very bad for a few miles, but I might be able to clean it out a little while on the bear hunt. There are a few unclimbed peaks on the range dividing Toby and Jumbo Fork; there are three (10,000-foot) peaks unclimbed on Jumbo range, but the proper way to approach them is from the Lake of the H. Glaciers. If you intend to come, let me know what your plans are; would you go first to the ACC camp, or after? I expect I will be able to arrange things so that I can take you out. I wish you could bring Dr. Ladd along. I will hunt bears from May 15th to June 10th.*

MAY 8TH, 1928 ✦ *I just returned from the bear hunt. My lowest charges for a 10-day or a two weeks trip for three men is $40 per day. I supply tents, food, horses and make no extra charges for my services above timberline.*

The last stretch of trail on Toby Creek is in bad shape, so I will have to spend several days on the trail before you and your friends arrive, but I will get you there safely all the same.

You mentioned July 11th; this date falls on a Wednesday, apparently you intend to come over the Banff–Windermere Road. If you come by auto or by train from Golden I can save you a day by taking you the same day to the junction of Toby and Jumbo (25 miles from Wilmer) by car. You pay for the car. The cost of the car hire will be only a few dollars more as would be the hotel expense and you save a whole day.

On my last trip I sized up an unclimbed peak that I would like to climb with you.

JUNE 21ST, 1928 ✦ *Received your letter yesterday. I am sorry you cannot make connection with our Cordwood Express at Golden.*

The program for the trip is as follows: 1st day from Jumbo Fork to head of Toby Creek. Camp near timberline and close to glacier. 2nd to climb one of the highest peaks and get a bird's-eye view of the country. 3d to cross snowfield to the south, which I believe is yet unexplored. It is likely you might like the unclimbed peaks and we might have to spend another day or two in that corner; then I will show you another yet-unclimbed peak which is about 10,000 feet on the range between Toby and Jumbo. The ascent we would make from Pharaoh Creek, a short day from Glacier Camp, and if you fellows are in good trim we call moving camp a rest day.

The peak makes a very good picture from Jumbo Valley. Then if you care to climb Mt. Jumbo from the south (new route) we can do so, camp near timberline; this would mean another day move and rest.

On the ridge dividing North Fork and Jumbo is a very fine-looking yet unclimbed peak about 10,000 feet (no name). A visit to the North Fork is worthwhile; there are several unclimbed peaks.

There is a chance to go with outfit to South Fork of Horsethief Creek, but I do not know what the conditions will be, so I will not make a promise, but if it can be done I will do it, if it suits you. You will see that I have plenty of mountains to climb here, and I can keep you moving.

These letters, of course, convinced us. Conrad took us to the head of Toby Creek and into its various branches, where the first ascent of Mt. Earl Grey and the traverse of Jumbo to the Lake of the Hanging Glaciers were of his own devising. The descent to the lake was our most thrilling experience.

The rope was out at full length ... far below us, at the end of the ice, we saw a circle of larch trees and water of unbelievable blue, with tiny bergs drifted to the farther end – our first view of the Lake of the Hanging Glaciers ... During the half-hour that followed we made three crossings of a well-defined avalanche channel, it being necessary on one occasion to slide down gently from an overhanging lip to a slender slice of ice forming a bridge to the firm glacier beyond.

Kain saw many old friends at the camp in Horsethief Valley, and at the end of the trip we stopped at his little farm at Wilmer, where his wife cooked us a dinner of fried chicken and trimmings that none of us have ever forgotten. We treasure the memory of the white cottage, window-deep in sweet peas and currant bushes, with Conrad and his wife waving goodbye as we started homeward. The dusky foothills of the Rockies spread a gorgeous panorama across the Columbia Valley; Lake Windermere is almost below, and it was easy to see why Conrad had chosen it for his home.

C.K. TO J.M.T. WILMER. NOVEMBER 3RD, 1928.

You will be wondering why you have not heard from me. After you left I was at home for a few days; then I made a trip up Jumbo and over Pass to Glacier Creek. It was the first time I had made this trip in summertime and I enjoyed it. Jumbo Pass is a lovely place. Little streams and puddles and flowers everywhere. There are several interesting unclimbed peaks.

On September 14th I went on a hunting trip to the Kootenay Valley (was at Mt. Assiniboine of Sept. 25th); the hunt was again a success – two moose, two bears, two goat, four deer. On my return from the hunt I went on a lone rustling trip and just returned with a few marten and expect to stay at home with the exception of a few days of meat hunting. I will gladly save the best goat head for you and there will be no charge for same.

APRIL 15TH, 1929 ◆ *Was interested to learn that the American Alpine Club will have a journal of its own and I am sure the baby will develop to man's size in a few years. As you know 99 per cent of my patrons are Americans, so it is natural that I am interested in such movements. My rambles in the hills with men of different national types has given me the opportunity to study mankind from different angles and what I have gathered has been of great value to me as a guide.*

The years one after the other slip by and I know I will not be a leader in the hills forever, and I feel sure that some of my knowledge of mountains and men would be of interest if not of help to others. If you are able to come back to the Purcell Range next year, we will have talk on this subject. It is likely that by then I will have part written down – the title will be "Over-climbed."

Spring is here and I am busy from morning till dark; have enlarged my little fur farm, the animals are doing fine. Am breaking a few more cayuses. You remember the bucking cayuse; well I have dispatched her to the happy hunting ground and there she can buck and flirt with her kind forever.

Now about your trip to Europe. I wish I could be with you. My mother lives in Naßwald: Bahn Station Payerbach-Reichenau. As you expect to go to the Tyrol I will ask you a favour. If you see a picture of Guglia di Brenta, please buy one for me, put it in your suitcase and send it when you get home. Bon voyage.

CHAPTER XXV

(1930)

▲

THE SOURCE OF THE COLUMBIA

C.K. TO J.M.T. WILMER. OCTOBER 25TH, 1929.

Have received your card from the Tyrol. Your trip was rather short but you covered some ground all the same. Your account of the trip freshened up my memory of my old home. Apparently you did not run across our old friend "Liesl" in Mayrhofen.

Now for the little news: in August I went up the Jumbo; my intention was to look over the large snowfield at the head of Glacier Creek, but I got stuck on Jumbo Pass. The smoke from forest fires was so dense that it was useless to go on. I camped for several days on the Pass.

A few days ago I returned from the hunt, which was again a success. We got two grizzlies, two black bears, two moose, two goats and a coyote. We hunted on Mitchell Creek, Cross River. I had a good look at Mt. Aye, which is still unclimbed. On the Palliser River I met Mr. Cromwell's brother; he was travelling in comfort with 16 pack horses.

Re. Peaks on Dutch Creek. The government had a few men working on the trail. I met the man who trapped on Dutch the last three winters and he spoke of a low pass from Dutch to Findlay Creek. Apparently there is a chance to reach the peaks south of Dutch by a shortcut.

I am not certain, but it is likely I will hunt bears next spring on Dutch Creek, so I will get first-hand information about the low pass and the peaks over the Divide.

The winter is approaching and as I have not gathered the necessary fat for hibernating, I will keep moving. So you will hear again some time in the winter.

DECEMBER 2ND, 1929 ◆ *From the mouth of Cross River to Mt. Assiniboine takes three days with pack train and the return trip can be made in two days. The Cross River is shallow and has to be forded many times (no danger); the trail in general is fair. You will note that there is an auto road to Cross River, so if arrangements are made one actually can make the trip from Mt. Assiniboine to Columbia Valley in two days.*

If anyone wishes to make the trip from Columbia Valley via Palliser [River] to Banff the best way is via Tegart Pass. 1st day from Lake Windermere via Tegart Pass to Salt Lake, near mouth of Palliser. 2nd day up Palliser to Fisher Creek. 3d day to Divide. The trail on Palliser is good.

MAY 5TH, 1930 ◆ *Was glad to hear that the goat heads arrived safely. I shot them on Mt. Sally Serena, Horsethief Creek. I have been very busy at home the last two months and am still on the go. I expect to be on Dutch Creek the first week of next month.*

During winter I read The Man of the Forest *and enjoyed the book. At present we read a very interesting novel* Roper's Row, *by Warwick Deeping. It is the story of a struggling* MD *and if you have not read it already you might enjoy the yarn.*

So attractive did the Purcells prove that Cromwell and Thorington returned in 1930, bringing the guide Peter Kaufmann, of Grindelwald, with them.[110] Conrad conducted us up Dutch Creek, the source of the Columbia, a rough bit of country which required all of his woodsmanship to get us through. Kaufmann, coming from a country where timber is strictly preserved, was delighted by the freedom with which one cut down trees, and was continually calculating how much it would all be worth if piled up at his home in Switzerland.

Conrad joined us in the first ascent of Mt. Findlay, one of the highest watershed peaks of the southern Purcells, but otherwise contented himself with running the outfit. He was enchanted by the flowering basin below the little glacial source of the Columbia, which we were probably the first to see, and was as delighted as we were when a herd of blacktail deer came racing across the snowfield.

One evening Con told us the story of his fishing in Glacier Creek:

Feesh? Man alive! I tooked off da pants, made a little koorall [corral] with shticks, tied up the legs und walked down the shtream. Then

I lift up the pants und they was full of feesh, und I washed the pants at the same time!

A fortnight later Conrad brought his horses to Spillimacheen and took Cromwell and Peter to the Bugaboos. He participated in several ascents, but became ill while attempting Bugaboo Spire and was forced to desist. He was never one to take good care of himself, and took few precautions against exposure.

C.K. TO J.M.T. WILMER. AUGUST 25TH, 1930.

No doubt you will have heard from Mr. Cromwell regarding our trip on the Bugaboo. I was very sorry that I could not make the climb on the spire. I was not in trim and decided to turn back. I am now convinced that this spire was the most difficult ascent I have made in Canada. During the coming winter I will write an account of this climb – and that will mean a little extra work for you to correct it.

I wish to thank you for the sleeping bag, which will last me as long as I knock around the old hills, and can assure you that your kindness is appreciated.

OCTOBER 25TH, 1930 ♦ *A few days ago I returned from the hunt, which was again a success. We had a very warm and beautiful Fall, with the exception of one snowstorm.*

Received your map, which I consider good work. You made a mistake[111] with the south fork of Dutch: it joins the main creek several miles above cabin (Slide Creek). Al. Cochrane [game and fire warden] told me that there is a cabin near the mouth of south fork which we did not see as it is across the creek.

Al. S. Cochrane of Windermere, BC, would be pleased if you would send him your map of Dutch Creek.

I received a letter and pictures from Mr. Cromwell; his pictures are very good indeed. There was a gang of men working on the trail up Findlay last summer, in all they lost nine horses in mudholes and slides. Looks bad, don't it? But whenever you are ready for a trip up Findlay I believe I will manage to get you there all the same.

I have added a few more horses to my pack train. The horse which got a sore back on Dutch Creek trip is still on the sick list. Just at present my place is crowded with horses, as I have them all at home for a picnic.

FEBRUARY 4TH, 1931 ◆ *I was very pleased to hear that you and Mr. Cromwell intend to come out again next summer. The news I gathered regarding Findlay is that the branch we were on is known as Caribou Creek, the next branch is Granite Creek, and the main stream is supposed to pinch out Skookumchuck. And that the main creek is really degrees farther south than is given on the map, and on the other side of the divide the water flows into the St. Mary River.*

This information I received from a fellow who was on the Findlay with a timber cruiser last summer. It is said there is a fair trail up to the junction of Granite Creek, and from there I expect we will have to make our own. I think the best way to find out would be to make a trip of inspection in the spring.

My present plan is to get hold of a party of enthusiastic climbers to take a crack at the Bugaboo Spires; if I could get a party, say about a week after you and Cromwell leave me, it would fit in fine. We are having a wonderful winter; no snow to speak of, the coldest was three below zero.

MARCH 29TH, 1931 ◆ *We will start the trip with horses from a ranch six miles up Findlay. It is likely I will have a chance to look things over before you arrive. It would be to your and my advantage if you could find a third man to come along for the trip. I don't expect the peaks will be difficult. I will make the first climb with you to get acquainted with the lay of the land, and if you should need me on any other climb later I will give you a hand, but if you bring a guide it is OK with me.*

I have plans for another trip for the future. I believe that the section between Bugaboo and Horsethief creeks has not been explored by mountaineers. There are several peaks about 10,000 feet, two large snowfields, and a good size glacier descending one of the branches of Howser Creek.

CHAPTER XXVI

(1931)

▲

FINDLAY CREEK AND ST. MARY RIVER

Cromwell, his young son, Thorington and Edward Feuz visited the Purcells again with Conrad in 1931, going through the lovely tamarack forests of Findlay Creek and following the valley to its head.[112] The country was very difficult, without trails in its upper portion, and only because of recent forest fires were we able to proceed. Conrad did no climbing and the weather was generally unfavourable. Despite this, we attained the main watershed and mapped the relation of the heads of Findlay Creek and St. Mary River.

Conrad was full of an interesting experience which he described:

> Up on the slide I saw a very little black bear, und I say, "I catch you anyway und put you in the reflector!" When I got there I could not see him any more, but a drummer [blue grouse] came out of the wood, ruffed up the feathers und showed himself a bit; then lifted up about two or three feet and held, with the wings going brr, brr, and then dropped. I moved the rucksack strap to get the camera and, as I turned, there was the little bear on a rock, watching me und the bird. But when I stooped to pick up the rifle, they was both gone.

C.K. TO J.M.T. WILMER. SEPTEMBER 14TH, 1931.

> Received your paper on the 1930 trip. Thanks for the kind remarks you made about me. I feel sure that the readers who happened to believe that the "Columbia Lake is the source of the Columbia River" will read it with great interest.
>
> Well, Dr., you know I am not much of a topographer and I know it, but nevertheless I hope my criticism is of some help to you.

*Findlay Creek is now burned out right to the head, also the south
fork of Toby.*

DECEMBER 25TH, 1931 ✦ *We are having a very quiet time here. I have
heard from some of the hunters I had out, and expect I will have a
little more work next year. For the summer I have nothing in view. If I
could get a bunch of mountaineers together I would run a camp on the
Bugaboo for a few weeks. I will try to be as reasonable as possible.*

*I am writing a paper on the Grand Traverse of Mt. Cook, and will
ask you to correct it for me.*

*Whilst on a hunting trip on Toby Creek this fall, I discovered that
I was wrong in correcting your 1930 sketch map. That was a good lesson to me, and I realize that it is not wise to take other people's word
regarding the lay of the land.*

MARCH 22ND, 1932 ✦ Re. *map of the Bugaboo. On this occasion I will
play safe in correcting your work. I still believe that Vowell Creek is very
much misplaced on the map, and I believe that the summit of Howser
Spire is on the main watershed, but I have no proof to offer. I think you
must get a kick out of it when you compare the letters of your informer.*

*The robins, bluebirds, crows and geese have arrived here, and things
look a little more cheerful after the long winter. My wife was not well
for several weeks and is still sick. We are now feeling the Depression in
the Columbia Valley, but I for one look at things with hopes that all will
come right again.*

OCTOBER 11TH, 1932 ✦ *Received your cards from the Tyrol, and looking at Guglia di Brenta still brings on Ein wenig Heimweh. Although
I doubt if I could climb it now, it would make me feel happy to look at
it once more.*

*A few weeks ago I made a trip in the hills and when I stood on the
East–West Kootenay watershed I thought of you, and knowing that it
will interest you I will attempt to describe what I saw. I left the horses
at the junction of Stockdale and Horsethief creeks. I ascended the lately
burned-over valley; the going was very rough. Spent the night near timberline. Next day climbed to the Alps, lovely larch, balsam and spruce
trees. At 8:30 a.m. I stood on the Divide; the pass is about timberline,
the view was clear on all sides.*

Mt. Howser and Howser Spire stood up well. I found the lay of the land quite different from what I had expected. The valley to the west was apparently the branch of Howser Creek, above Tea Creek. It is narrow, with heavy timber and some slides.

At the head of the valley (to the right) is a peak which will be around 10,000 feet on the Divide; to the left is a large rectangular snowfield which apparently is at the head of Dunbar Creek. Farther to the left is another high peak. I expect this peak is near the south fork of the Bugaboo.

I was on my way to climb a peak west of the Divide to get a view on the Four Squatters, but it so happened that an extra-large grizzly attracted my attention, and I spent the rest of the day with the bear. The following morning I climbed again to the Divide but fog was low down so I returned to the valley (Stockdale Cr.) and went to the head and found that there was a fairly steep glacier.

CHAPTER XXVII

▲

CONRAD, HUNTER OF BEAR

BY

J.C. DUN WATERS

I have been asked to write my recollections of Conrad Kain. That is easy, because there was only one Conrad – he was individual, and there will never be another like him. One regrets that it has been so ordained that comrades and friends who have the spirit of rugged places should be asked to part, because such attachment means much more than the insipid friendships of the plains.

Conrad belonged to the timberline, but, curiously enough, he took with him to his Paradise troublesome thoughts of the incongruous world where puppet MPs move and popinjays walk and dog eats dog. Sometimes he would ramble on for hours on the demerits of some bedecked officer in Europe who had the courage to wear uniform but none to climb, or on some injustice meted out by a crude politician. He would tackle these subjects with a virulence that would have exhausted a less virile man.

Everyone who knew him in his lighter moods would laugh and laugh and laugh at his naive pictures of courting days in Tyrol, at his description of the ladder he carried around his native village as an accessory to his raids on the bowers where lived his loves.

He was vehement in denunciation of much in the Old World and the New. He hated graft, loathed meanness, and pretentiousness was anathema to him; but, all the same, he laughed long and loudly at the eccentricities of his fellows.

Conrad was practically a father to his family as well as a good son to his widowed mother. At times he went on the tramp, encountering fantastic adventures, and out of this happy, roving youth emerged possibly the best mountain man of his day, the responsibility which his profession imposed and the association with outstanding men of breeding and worth putting the hallmark on his character.

These associations bred a brave, natural gentleman, charged with integrity, a happy, buoyant lover, a good husband and a true friend. His life was spent almost entirely in the atmosphere of his beloved mountains, sometimes with men who met him on equal terms and sometimes with those who needed bolstering up to face the fickle fortunes of a climb. At other times his was the hazardous task of seeking for and bringing in injured or dead adventurers. Such experiences are bound to develop traits of character that are withheld from men who deny themselves or are denied such opportunities.

Few mountain guides confine themselves strictly to the truth regarding episodes and animals, and when their inaccuracy is detected they cease to be interesting. Conrad may have amused himself by embroidering his tales to folks who did not measure up to his standard, but once he had given you his diploma he never lied – and he always believed. That alone made him a charming companion.

My expeditions with Conrad were a combination of education, experience, adventure and mirth – and he contributed 99 per cent of the entertainment. One greeted him with delight and parted from him with regret, recognizing that he had given far more than his contract called for. He was a child of Nature and a very charming one. He didn't produce his good qualities – they fairly oozed out of him. He had something within that compelled him to do a little more after he had done his duty.

Conrad was naturally indomitable, but when I first knew him his heroism did not extend to horses. He looked on them as something to beware of. I can well remember my first experience of this rift in his otherwise impregnable armour. I had wounded a grizzly on the far side of a swollen river. Darkness compelled the crossing to be delayed till next morning, and then we decided to go over on the horses. In negotiating a gulch, Conrad's pony stumbled and they both landed on the floor together, Conrad cutting his head. If a bear or an elephant had done it, Conrad would have strangled either on the spot, but because it was a horse, and a horse was an unknown quantity, he lay there like a limp Victorian maiden while I poured water on his face and tried to reassure him. This was the untried guide with whom I proposed to look for a wounded grizzly!

When he was restored, we crossed, Conrad carrying a little "pipsqueak" Savage rifle – that proved not half so savage as the bear. I was unarmed, working a new Airedale. The bear found us on the slide where I had wounded him, and went for us bald-headed. Conrad blazed away with the only four cartridges he had and killed him with the last shot, right at our feet. The dog ran away. If it had been a horse, Conrad would have run away too, and his wonderful career would have ended on the spot. As it was, this experience forged the first link in our bond of friendship.

Two days I could have shot a grizzly in his bed, but the previous adventure had so cowed me that I funked, missed the bear (who had a mate) and had the devil's own job to stop Conrad pursuing both into the alders to see if either was wounded. If it had been a horse, I couldn't have driven him in. Horses at that time had a strange psychological effect upon him.

Since then I have read that Conrad talked to his horses like a father, and petted and spoiled them. That is true, and moreover he got more out of his horses and attempted far more with them than many a born horseman would have dared. I do not know how Austrian fathers talk to their children, but I have heard Conrad say things to his horses in a moment of stress that have kept me laughing and have since become household words in my home. And so he conquered his mistrust of the animal of which his early training in the Dolomites had probably given him the least experience.

Conrad loved bear hunting and more than once erected ingenious traps to catch them alive. He did catch them, but it was a case of Greek meeting Greek, and the bears invariably smashed his devices into the erection of which had gone a vast amount of strength and ingenuity. One snare he made in a bear's bath with a wire cable and a tree to lever the bear into the air. Another was similar but set in a cabin. The first the bear destroyed because he got leverage on an adjacent tree. On the second occasion he smashed the cabin.

I remember once trying to carry home a wet, 11-foot Kodiak bearskin and skull. We made a knapsack of it with bear's guts. I never got it off the ground. My friend staggered 50 yards and collapsed. Next day Conrad shouldered the sodden mass and marched off with it, smoking his short pipe! Our 13-stone Alaska guide looked on.

I took Conrad to Alaska with me once, because I wanted someone with me on whom I could bank. We sailed on a cannery steamer from Bellingham one evening. Next morning Conrad's temperature was 104 degrees and he was in great pain. I called the Norwegian skipper and the purser into consultation, and we prescribed castor oil – a bottle at a time. If that failed, the only alternative was to take Conrad home – if he still lived – and to abandon the trip and all that it entailed, including schooner and outfit which had been chartered and awaited us at Dutch Harbour. In the morning I found him sitting up, smoking his pipe, and when I took his temperature it was normal. I took it three times and then sent for another thermometer, as I thought mine must have boiled over and burst the night before. The new instrument proclaimed the little devil normal – as he usually was. So the trip was saved and Conrad, as ever, proved invaluable.

He never went along a trail without improving it, and always said that he could track a man through a continent by his axe marks, that they were a sure indication of individual character.

He knew to a fraction what one could do on rock or ice without help. Always in front, he would pass back the handle of his axe without a word, and if you did not take it, it was equally unobtrusively withdrawn, with a quiet smile as if to say: "Ho, ho! we are proud today, but he'll probably be asking for it soon."

I remember ragging Conrad (who always made a practice of carrying more than his share), after a long day, as to who had carried the heaviest load. Our argument became quite heated until I explained that he had only a 40-pound bear trap and I had all the other stuff which he said weighed "nuttings." He only capitulated when I reminded him of the 20 more years I had on my back!

A few years ago I was ill, and gave Conrad my dog, Jack – a sure proof of friendship. They had much in common. Both had to hunt or die. They were up to every devilment imaginable, and became the greatest friends. Jack was killed by a she-bear and cub, and Conrad collected his remains and buried him on Jumbo Creek, where Conrad should lie by his side.

Just before his death he wrote for me to come out with him on a bear hunt, offering to supply everything except the grub. He said he was lonely. Such compliments seldom come my way, but I am bound to say I felt that call the greatest I had ever had, and have regretted ever since that I could not go. I wrote him to come to me instead, but the next word was that the dear little man was dying.

Conrad always improved every trail. All who knew and appreciated him will agree that the trail through life to the Happy Hunting Grounds is all the better for his having passed over it.

CHAPTER XXVIII

▲

TALES BY THE CAMPFIRE

*It is sad to think of all that perishes with the death
of those who, for their effects, rely on the voice –
their genius can never be proved, only alleged.*

– E.V. Lucas.

C.K. TO J.M.T. WILMER. JANUARY 17TH, 1933.

Was glad to hear that you are well. The American Alpine Journal
*has not arrived yet. I just read in the paper that an American party
made the ascent of Minya Konka.*

Lately I have read the American Farmer, The Iron Hell, Austria in
Dissolution, Vienna of Yesterday and Today, The Long Rifle, *and a
few other interesting books. We too have a good winter here, so far the
lowest was 20° below and the last two weeks were especially fine, but
the winter is yet young up here.*

*I am having a hard winter, no luck at trapping or anything. There is
no money in farm products, which have to be sold at or below cost, but
we have plenty to eat.*

Kain, as will be seen from this letter, was a voluminous reader on many
subjects. His avid curiosity concerning human nature was to have been
embodied in a paper entitled "Unspoken Thoughts of a Guide." To our
everlasting regret he never found time to write this, but it would have
been revealing as is the journal of his life in the Alps. He could talk of
many things, from the history of Austrian royalty (of which he knew some

intimate details) to the domestic habits of marten and muskrat. There was always something to learn from him.

No one in the Northwest could tell a better story. With laughter and vivid expression ever at the surface, Conrad was inclined to think the world an amusing place and treated it accordingly. He styled himself a "baloney peddler," meaning that he had the "gift of gab." It was dangerous, however, especially in mixed company, to press him for a tale. A wild look of delight would come over him and he was quite apt to cut loose with a narrative bringing blushes to all within hearing distance. He did not like to be forced. But, given his own time, there was an almost oriental facility in his storytelling, and the last of a thousand and one nights would not have ended the spark of mischief in his eye, the gay mimicry in his voice and the subtle gesturing of his hand. When Conrad Kain and Jim Simpson were together, one began where Munchausen left off.

Courage

California? Sure, I have been there. Many years ago I was in Sacramento. Broke. I want a place to schleep, und as it was warm I go into a graveyard und lie between some stones.

Next day a fellow see me. "Py golly," he say, "you are a brave man." "Oh," I say, "dot is nossing. I want only a place where I am not disturbed."

"So," he reply, "I see you are not afraid. You want a job? Yes? Well, there is the shovel; you must dig the holes deep."

After dot he tooken me to a house und give me a feed. Und I digged two graves, und he given me four dollar.

Riches

One time there was a gold rush near Edmonton. I wash gold five days und make feefty cents. I say, "Poy, dot is no way to make a fortune."

The cook in the mining camp get sick, so I decide to be cook. I make a big mulligan und the fellows say, "Well, Conrad, dot is fine!" So naturally I am pleased.

I decide to make a pie. I get out the cookbook, but the page is gone. I think I use too much flour. The pie is like cement. So I walk off in the woods. Und next day I go back to gold washing. Ha, ha, ha.

Youth

Ah, the Old Country. Dot is the place to be young. Tyrol! The people there are more natural as here. Those young womans, how beautiful they are. Und in the Spring, und a rose behind the ear, you go serenading with a guitar.

Those girls, you know, are easy in a family way. You climb up to the window und talk, till it get dark. Und if they ask you in, und you go – what harm? What harm?

Horizons

The most beautiful place in the world, dot island of Madeira. Like a lovely garden, filled with colours. When I am through with the Columbia Valley, I go back there once more.

But maybe, if I make a good grubstake, I end my days in the Tyrol with a few cows and some goats, und be some kinda little squire.

Sociability

One time I was trapping on the Saskatchewan und I come in a teepee. Und there was Jeemy Seempson schmoking with a chief.

Und I want to make friendly with the chief, so I say, "Wal, chief, how many papoose you got?"

The chief he schmoke und schmoke.

Finally, he point to Jeemy. "Four," he say; "two mine, two his."

But dot was chust a leetle joke with Jeemy.

Travel

The train on the Kootenay Central run only once in the week. One time I must get to Golden und be in Lake Louise on a certain day, und there is no train. So I visit my friend, the Justice of the Peace.

I say, "Judge, do you know of any one who is in love?"

"Ja, sure," he reply, "I can think of several cases."

"Und has he got a car?"

"Ja."

"Und has he a girl in Golden?"

"Ja."

"Well, dot is fine."

So next morning I make a call on this young fellow.

"Poy," I say, "I hear you got a girl in Golden, Und you got a car. Well, we going to see her Friday afternoon, und I pay half the gas."

Und dot is how I was in Lake Louise on time.

Boots

One time in the Old Country I climbed with a woman. Some womans are very particular, you know, und this one (she given me her sack) say she have six pair boots in it.

"Py Gott," I say to myself, "dot will be a helluva load!" So I given her a bit of baloney spiel, und I persuade her to leave two pair behind. After while, when we are on the snow, I make a awful sound und roll the eyes a bit und fall down like in a faint.

"Ach," say the woman, "poor Conrad, you are so tired. We must throw away a couple pair boots." So I done dot, und when she was not looking I let go another pair in a crevasse.

So finally we are in the hut, und only the pair boots we need in the first place is in the sack.

Roundup

I am not young now, but I am still a good rider at rounding up. But when I have a bad horse to be broke I take her to Rosy, the Indian girl. I given her cayuses no other fellows can handle, und she make it fine.

But last year I hear she got killed by a bucking cayuse at Calgary. So now I do not bother with the cayuses I cannot catch myself.

Escape

Last year I was out on Jumbo Creek with my cayuses. A log bridge is rotten und the horse I am riding fallen through. I hit my head und am knocked senseless.

I do not know how long I am lying there, but when I come to, the back of my head is all blood. Und old Nelly is close beside, stuck in the logs.

Say! If dot old horse of mine had not stayed still all dot time, I would have been kicked to death.

Charm

"How is it," we ask Con, "that when you are in the Alpine Club camps the ladies all want to climb with you?" Con strikes a match, and puffs through his pipe while a smile like the expression of a harvest moon lights up his face.

"Wal," says Con, "dot is a very easy thing to explain. You see, when the ladies come into camp they are a little afraid. They want to climb a peak but they think maybe they cannot make her. So when I see one who look a little bit timid, und if she be young und a good-looker, I say, 'You want to climb a mountain? Dot is fine; I guarantee you make her.'

"So next morning we go off. Und after a little while I say, 'Now, young lady, you must excuse me a little while, but I must sit down for a schmoke.' Und so we sit down.

"After a while we go on again, und presently I stop. I pick up a rock und I look at it und turn it over, und I tell the girl all the geology I do not know. Und after a while if she is very tired, maybe I make a little bit loving to her.

"Very harmless, you understand, but dot little stimulation bring her to, und we are on the summit. Und, say, she is pleased!

"Dot is why, afterward, every day in the camp, those womans say. 'Oh, Conrad, *Connnerad*, will you not be so kind as to take me on a mountain?'"

CHAPTER XXIX

▲

THE INDIAN BRIDLE

BY

I.A. RICHARDS

The scene and the occasion for this tale were chosen by Conrad with more than usual care. For a week mysterious hints had been dropping that "one of these days" he would tell us a real story! After long reconnaissance we had returned late in a rainy night to our camp near the Bugaboo Glacier. In the morning fine rain was blurring the outlines of the hemlocks and drifting through the camp clearing. It must have been about 10:00 when Conrad came to wake us with his "Daylight in the Swamp!" As he threw open the fly of the tent the smoke of the fire was spiralling up behind him and a smell of grilling rashers came in with the damp morning air. He announced that we were to stay in our sleeping bags while he brought the breakfast and that while we ate it he would tell us that story.

Actually it lasted until lunchtime – a full three-hour composition that never slackened or hastened, but moved, chapter by appointed chapter, from its exordium to its designed, inevitable close. The v-shaped mouth of the tent was the narrator's frame. Sometimes he squatted on a log drawn just inside, but much of the time he seemed to prefer to stand half outside in the rain, stooping forward so that the folds of the canvas fell on either side of his head, his vivid hands and communicative elbows sketching incidents and making comments of their own as he proceeded. What follows cannot reproduce it. At best, it can only give a rudimentary notion of the larger and cruder characteristics of this Master's method. But it may explain how we lay spellbound without comment all through the morning.

He began with a leisurely and meditative discourse on anniversaries. This mid-September day was marked for him, again and again through the years, with events which he wouldn't find it at all easy to tell of. A girl back in Austria – among the first he ever guided – the girl who turned Conrad into a student of books among other things – here made a brief appearance; and then, with an abrupt "Well, one day...," the first chapter began.

A solitary Conrad was coming back from a long, hard trip in the fall somewhere up in the Bow River country. He'd been alone for a long time and was not expecting to see anyone. He'd just settled his camp, got his fire going, early in the afternoon, when he saw a lot of Indians coming down the valley. They were all squaws. He saw one of them, a young girl, try to cross the river at a place where some logs were jammed. He'd been looking at the place earlier, because he wanted to get across himself, and he didn't think she could make it. He thought, "If she tries she'll pretty sure get swept off in the river!" So he picked up a pole and went down to the riverbank, a little below where she was, to see what would happen. Sure enough, as he expected, a log swung loose and in she went, right under, and by the time she come to where Conrad could get to her and fish her out, "she was pretty full of water, all right!" The squaws didn't know a bit what to do, so Conrad had to turn to – just like a nurse, undo her things and give her artificial respiration. It took a long time before he got the water out of her, but in the end it was all right. The squaws put her into a warm bed, and Conrad went off "pretty tired, I tell you!"

When he opened his eyes next morning, there by his camp – waiting for him to wake – was a group of Indians with the young girl among them. When he got up they approached solemnly. The Chief signed to the girl and she came, went down on her face before Conrad and touched his foot. After that the Chief made a great speech and gave him a plaited black and white horsehair bridle – the most marvellous horsehair bridle Conrad had ever seen. It must have been a lifetime's work. Nobody he showed it to had ever seen one like it. Then the Indians said farewell and vanished.

Conrad here went off to brighten his pipe with a spill at the fire.

He used the bridle for a while – for special occasions or when he particularly hoped to have good luck. "And vairy looky I found it too; yes, vairy looky lots of times" – stray ghosts of other stories hovered near at this point but were meditatively puffed away in clouds of tobacco smoke. He then observed that a man who had to earn his own living, a man who wasn't "either a peenhead poleetician or one of these batronising pastards" needed to have some good luck at times. Especially if he had to take people of all sorts into the mountains. A man who was a guide got some funny letters at times. We'd never believe the things some people said about themselves! Or the way some of them would behave when they got into the mountains. There were some who just seemed to want to go there to make peegs of themselves! Eat everything just as nastily and dirtily as they could. Yes, the worse they pehave, the finer they took themselves to be.

Well one day he got a letter from two men who made out they were as tough as anything. They said they'd heard of him, Conrad Kain, as a man who wouldn't be afraid of a little hardship – who could show them some country where there were bears – and that would be all he need do. He wouldn't have to help them hunt the bears – leave that to them! There was nothing that had ever been heard of that they didn't know about bears – he could take that from them! As to his pay, well, though they didn't want more from him than just to show them the country and keep camp, they didn't mind what they paid. They thought there would be two of them, but they were trying to get their old friend Henry Ford (yes, Henry Ford of the automobiles) to come along with them and sometimes he figured he was coming and then again he figured he wasn't. But anyway they would be coming themselves, with him or without.

They were a father and son – the father said he'd been a timber-cruiser in Michigan and that was why he knew all about mountains and forests and bears and everything. In the end Conrad agreed to take them in for a six weeks' trip, up in the Bugaboo and Howser country. He put his charges at the usual figure – saying that if he showed them good sport and everything was all right, if Conrad Kain delivered the goods – and the Kains usually did – and they felt like showing they were satisfied, well they could and he wouldn't stop them.

They turned up in the end without Henry Ford but with a lot of talk about how much Henry was missing. Usually people like this bring such a pile of junk with them that you have to see before you believe it. Conrad wasn't feeling very happy about them from the start. They'd been asking things in their letters that he didn't somehow think an ex-timber-cruiser would want to ask. And they had a way of talking to him – a "Say, guide, who do you think you are talking to?" style that didn't please him at all. They seemed to take him for some sort of Heely Peely, that they could have a game with. A seely Heely Peely who wouldn't know how to look after himself. [Conrad never seemed quite to persuade himself that we didn't know the Hilly Billy stories or that this simpleton was not part of our native mythology.] He, Conrad, was a Heely Peely, all right, a real Heely Peely; but he thought he knew this sort of people well enough and hoped he might come out on top in the end.

Well, anyhow, the junk they brought was just fearful, though the old man, a little fat greybeard, who could look you in the eye, was not quite as bad as his son, who wore a big diamond ring, was a complete batronizer, and talked about "the guide," even when Conrad was there. Conrad had to lend them a lot of stuff to wear, and other gear, before it was safe to take them for a longish fall trip. Meanwhile he had to listen to any amount of talk about what they would shoot, and how bad it was going to be for the bears if once Conrad showed them where they were!

So they went in up the Bugaboo Creek with a big pack train and only Conrad and a packer – they wouldn't let him take a wrangler – to look after it. After a bit, where Driftwood Creek comes in, they asked him if they couldn't leave the pack train to come on at its own pace while they went ahead to look at the country. As they couldn't possibly lose the trail, Conrad said they might. They were to halt at the deserted cabins near Rockypoint. When Conrad arrived the two were nowhere to be seen. However, their tracks, on top of a lot of fresh moose tracks, showed that they had been there and had gone off up Rockypoint Creek. So he made camp and waited. Toward evening they came back much disgusted. What sort of hunting country did he think he'd brought them to? Hadn't seen a blame thing all day! – and they weren't people either that he could fool. If there had been any game in the country they would have smelt it!

It struck Conrad that they were beginning rather early, but he said nothing, winked at the packer and, after they'd had some tea, took them out and mentioned the moose tracks.

"What moose tracks?" they wanted to know. So he showed them. "Call them moose tracks? They are just ordinary cattle tracks. That's what they are! Here, guide, you get this right now! We are not as green as you think we are, see! We don't want any more of that stuff. Understand?" Conrad thought he was beginning to understand thoroughly.

Next day they went on up to the fork, where there is another cabin. Conrad could see that a bear had been around that morning. Just beside the door was a fresh sign. No one said anything and the two hunters went off while things were being unpacked. Before long they came back in bad temper. They said it was just useless, there weren't any bears in that country. It just wasn't bear country – anyone who knew anything about bears could see that!

This riled Conrad a little and so he took them and showed them the bear sign and asked them what they called that? "That, I call that a dawg sign, that's what I call that; and a pretty big dawg, too! You don't mean to say you call that a bear sign, do you?"

"You bet your life I do. I suppose your dog is looking after that cattle you saw yesterday? Here, Jack, what's that?" Jack came out of the cabin and said, "That's a bear sign." This made the two very suspicious; they went off to mutter together in their tent.

Conrad said to them at supper: "Now, gentlemen, we are well placed with this camp here at the cabin. Nothing to prevent us from going after these bears. I know you've been feeling a little impatient – but I'll be very surprised if you don't see what you want tomorrow!"

They didn't say anything to that except, "Wahl, just you show us one of these bears and it'll be a dead one!" [As he reported these speeches of his clients, Conrad's intonation and expression developed a more and more acrid strain of caricature.]

Next morning they set off and mounted to the timberline. They were just coming into a promising bit of park land, when Conrad heard a startling clamour behind him and there were his two clients running off, as though they were crazy, around a clump of bushes. Before he could follow them enough to get them in sight again, off went both their guns. When he reached them they were dancing with rage and excitement.

"Say, you never told us you had any polar bears up here! That was a polar bear, all right! You ought to have told us and then we'd have been ready!"

It turned out that they'd seen "a great big white thing as big as a polar bear" and they didn't know how they had missed it. Must have been too surprised. Conrad quieted them, stopped them from going after the old goat they must have walked into, and got them up on a shoulder where they could look over a mile or so of semi-open country. Across the Bugaboo Valley stood the jagged range of the Septet Peaks and that massive mountain whose name went on puzzling us even after Conrad had explained several times that it was "called Dorus because it was like a pool!"[113] But their eyes were on the nearer uplands. Several goats appeared, but the hunters, now satisfied that they were not polar bears, were full of contempt for them. Farther off, however, was a sizable bear, about 2000 feet away and pretty stationary and approachable. Conrad had just managed to make the old man, who was incredulous, see it, when bang! went the young man's rifle.

A hot argument about ballistics ensued, but Conrad had made up his mind not to get riled any more. The bear had made off around a corner, and one would guess that he hadn't moved far. Conrad thought they might pick up the bear again by crossing the ridge high up. So, with some trouble, he got his clients to the chosen spot. Conrad shinned up a steep, crumbling wall, put his head over and there, sure enough, was the bear only 20 feet below him. Cautioning the others to keep quiet he sent them round through a gap where they could walk in on the bear along a grassy shelf and get within a hundred feet before it would see them. Conrad stayed on the ridge to keep an eye on the bear.

Before long the hunters were again in view. They saw Conrad before they saw the bear. They got ready. The bear hadn't noticed anything. Something, though, in the way they held their guns made Conrad, just as they pulled their triggers, duck down below his ridge. "Joost in time too or they'd have spoiled my hat." Fizz went a bullet through the gap from which he had been peeking

"Well then," said Conrad, "I told them. Yes, I told them. I'd been wanting to since we left Spillimacheen, and so I told them all about it. The old man didn't seem to have anything to say. The young man had plenty still, but I didn't let him open his mouth twice. And so I took them back to camp. On the way down we walked right into another of their polar bears. Would you think it? They both started in blazing away. It was right in front of them, between them under a wall of rock. I kept well behind, I can tell you! They were right on top of it and they took 19 shots to finish that polar bear! Jack, down in camp, thought it was a bombardment! That the War had started again."

At this point Conrad went off to see about some bread he was going to bake for dinner. When he came back he filled a fresh pipe and explained that after supper they were all for having the camp moved over Bugaboo Pass into new country. They'd had enough of nearly breaking their necks up in these ridges. They knew, they said, that Conrad was pretty sore at their missing that darned bear he'd found for them, but it was only one bear. There weren't enough bears about, anyway; and they didn't see why they should almost kill themselves going after them if there really were more on the other side.

So they broke camp and made their way over – rough going in the windfalls, and heavy work cutting out the trail. But they got their horses through in the end and settled down in camp again. And then they went out after bears. This time they hadn't gone very far when, looking down, Conrad spied a fine bear busy in a slide. A steep little belt of crags intervened, so Conrad decided they must work around sideways. But the hunters wouldn't hear of this. From above they couldn't see the crags and wouldn't believe in them. They wouldn't listen. They weren't the men to get hung up on a little bit of rough ground when there was a fine bear just beneath. They were going straight down and Conrad could go where he liked if he wouldn't come with them. There was no stopping them, so Conrad shrugged his shoulders and went back to camp.

He didn't hear any shots and didn't see the hunters during the afternoon. About tea time in comes the young one, scratched and in a dreadful state. Said he'd fallen down a precipice and lost his Dad. His Dad had been killed up on the cliffs but he didn't know quite where. So Conrad and Jack went off to look for the body. Pretty soon they heard some hollering and there was Dad stuck on a ledge in the middle of a 200-foot cliff, unable to go up or down. They had brought plenty of rope, and Conrad managed to climb up to him. But when it came to lowering Dad there was a shocking fuss. Dad wasn't going to trust himself to one of those ropes, not he! Conrad had to bring Jack up and between them they tied Dad like a kicking sheep and slung him down like a sack of corn.

He was an old man, after all, and seemed fairly tired when they got him into bed at camp. They had brought up a whole stack of bottles of liquor of all sorts, and the two had already been going at them pretty heavily. Now they found out that the young one, while they were out finding his Dad, had been finishing off the last of these supplies. Dad obviously needed a pick-me-up, so Conrad gave him a dose of brandy from his own emergency reserve. Next day, Jack got the promise of a nice fat bribe from each of them independently, if he could manage somehow to steal Conrad's bottle.

The second morning, a little snow fell. Not much, the first general sprinkle of the fall, but it was not enough. First, the young man came 'round while Conrad was cooking to say that, of course, he did not want to go back; he wanted to get out after those bears; but his Dad, come to think of it, was a pretty old man and he oughtn't to risk being caught up there on the wrong side of the pass by a big snowfall. His Dad, of course, wouldn't hear of their going back, but couldn't Conrad say it was dangerous and make him go home before he got too ill to be moved?

Then there would be a lot more muttering in the tent and Dad would come out in his turn to say that, of course, neither he nor his boy wanted to go home so soon. They both wanted to go out and get some of those bears. But his boy wasn't really strong. Falling down that precipice had shaken him up and he might soon begin to start something that might be pretty nasty up there on the wrong side of the pass. He himself was an old timber-cruiser and didn't mind anything – but just before he came away, he had bought a new factory for $1,000,000 and it was worrying him. He really ought to go and see what was happening to it! Next year he would come out again, with old Henry, and they'd all have a great time.

This stuff made Conrad feel obstinate and he told them that he wasn't used to that sort of hunting trip. They had come in for six weeks and they had better make up their minds to go through with it. That made them start in on Jack – promising him $500 if he'd persuade Conrad to take them down to Spillimacheen again. In the end Conrad and Jack talked it over and agreed that there wasn't much point in going on with it. So they broke up camp and moved back over the pass again.

From the Bugaboo cabin down to Spillimacheen is a fairly long day's travel with pack animals. It is usual to break it with a night at the halfway point. But now they were on the return journey, the two seemed wonderfully full of life. Couldn't they leave the pack train to come at its own pace and ride ahead? So they did. Conrad and Jack followed after packing up. By the time they reached Rockypoint, however, something seemed to tell them that perhaps they would do well to push on themselves to Spillimacheen that evening. It was late and night had fallen before they brought the wearied animals into the corral near the Columbia River. No signs of the gentlemen or their horses. While they were getting the packs off, a man from a nearby ranch looked in:

"Say, those folks of yours were in a terrible hurry. Looked as if they'd have shot up the Depot if they hadn't made the train!"

It was a mile from camp, across the Columbia by two bridges, to the telephone. Conrad didn't lose much time in getting there. His two gentlemen hadn't paid him a cent and he had bought six weeks' provisions on their behalf. There by the station was one of the horses, hitched to a rail and looking as though it had been nearly ridden to death. Conrad then made his mistake of first calling the station at Golden: Yes, two gentlemen, an old one and a young one, had boarded the eastbound. What time did it get to the provincial boundary at Stephen? 9:19. It was then eight. The next thing was to get police headquarters. That took time, and so did the explaining. Then came a wait. At last the telephone rang.

"Sorry, the eastbound drew out before we could get word down. Five minutes sooner would have done it. It's over the Divide now. You'll have to get after your two guys with the Alberta folk now; we can't do anything here in BC about it. Guess you've lost them."

Now it was Calgary's turn. But the pair had been doing some thinking. At Lake Louise they had got off the train and hired a car. After that there was no way of intercepting them. Once across the international frontier, it was not a simple police matter any longer. So the poor Heely Peely was left helpless and defeated.

When Conrad returned to camp after a night of telephoning, Jack came out to meet him. He was looking a little rueful, Conrad thought – perhaps about his promised $500.

"Say, Conrad, have you seen anything of that Indian bridle of yours?" "Yes, it's on the pinto the old beggar was riding." "Oh, is it now! I've just brought him in and there's nothing on him."

"Was it yours?" asked the ranch hand who had watched the scene at the station. "Now that's funny! Haw, haw! ... Gaw! That is funny! I thought it was funny at the time. They had just got their baggage to the train – six trunks of it. I saw the young 'un call the old 'un out. 'Mustn't forget this, Dad! Make a good souvenir,' he said. And then they went to the horses and took it off. Lot of trouble they had with it too and nearly missed the train."

"And that," said Conrad, "was the last I heard of my lucky Indian bridle."

CHAPTER XXX

THE MILLIONAIRE GUIDE[114]

Having been a guide for a couple of years, and having travelled in different countries, and meeting many different people, I always wished that
the time would come when I could "play" the gentleman myself; meaning
by this, when I could hire a guide and act like "an elephant in the heights."
I say "elephant" because, really, some of the tourists are as helpless on the
mountainside as an elephant would be on the back stairs.

The year 1907 had been my best climbing season, and I had made plenty
of money, and so could afford to play the tourist myself. I was on my way
home from the Alps when this longing for adventure came upon me again.
The weather had been grand and the mountains looked very inviting.

In Innsbruck, the capital of Tyrol, I had some time to wait for the next
train. While walking around the streets and looking in the shop windows, I
took a great fancy to a fine Norfolk suit displayed in one of them. I may say
that it was the first decent suit I had had, and therefore I felt very happy, if
not proud, in it.

Seeing myself in this new suit, I thought here was my chance to
travel as a tourist, and I at once made up my mind that I would climb
Großglockner, which is one of the highest mountains in Tyrol, but by no
means the most difficult. It is, however, a good climb for a gentleman
whose feet are all thumbs.

I started immediately to make plans for the trip. I thought, first, I must
forget that I am a mountain guide, and secondly, I must forget the climbing
of the Matterhorn, Monte Rosa, Mont Blanc, the Meije, Les Écrins, Grépon
and many other well-known mountains in the Alps. It is very difficult for
a man who has been born, brought up and made his living by mountain
climbing to forget it all, but the spirit of adventure made this possible.

I had to change my program a great deal on account of being unable to get a new pair of boots, as my old ones were almost worn out and told tales of mountain climbing.

At Zell am See I left the train, thinking of and planning my trip. I wandered up to the high village called Heiligenblut which is the starting point for the mountain on its easiest side. I stayed at one of the best hotels and asked the hotel-keeper if he knew a guide named Schultz, and where I could find him. This hotel-keeper was a most obliging fellow and sent for the guide at once. This guide was a member of a well-known and highly-spoken-of guide family, and I found his name registered in different huts and hotels in the Alps, but I had never met him personally. However, I was sure he knew my name. After a short time a really fine specimen of a man stood before me; he was finely built, and his well-cared-for beard gave him the finishing touch necessary for a typical mountain guide. He made a respectful bow, as is the custom, and I laughed to myself when I thought of what he would say if he knew that I was a guide like himself. I asked him if his name was Schultz and he said, "Yes, that's me." I then asked him if he could take me up Großglockner, as, if so, I would like to make the trip in as comfortable a manner as possible, and I told him that this would be my first mountain-climbing expedition. When I had finished with this, he said, "I am at your service, sir."

I then asked as to the difficulties of the climb, and if there was any danger; also as to how steep the climb was, and then the weather question! This is the most difficult question to answer. Many tourists have an idea that a guide knows, or ought to know, all about the weather, and one is often forced to tell untruths in order to satisfy them. He listened to all my many questions with what I call a guide's patience, until I asked him about the handholds on the south wall over which people talk so much. I wanted to know how many handholds there were and the distance between them. That was more than any guide could stand, and he said in a loud, sharp voice that if there were none he would make some. He also said, "You will be quite safe, I will look after you. Don't be afraid, you can do it all right; an old lady 67 years of age went up the other day and had no trouble whatever."

I said, "Oh, I am not afraid with you, but I hope you will be very careful." I then explained that I had climbed quite a number of rock peaks, but had never been on a glacier or ice mountain, and that I was always a little worried when I thought of how my poor old mother would miss me if anything happened to me. My voice got quite weak with the desire to laugh, and I was very glad when the guide said, "Good night, sir."

The first act was now over, and I considered myself quite an actor. I celebrated with a few good long glasses of lager beer, and while enjoying this I had the pleasure of spinning some yarns to my neighbour at the table and the waitress. After a few glasses of beer and this boasting, I really quite forgot that I was a simple guide. During the night I completed my plans about the climb; I was really afraid I should not be able to keep from giving myself away on my holiday. After much thinking I got confidence in myself, and in the morning I could face the guide, the mountain and the wide world without any fear.

My guide was waiting for me, and I asked him to have breakfast with me. I ordered the best things I could think of, in order to make a good impression on him. I told him he could take as much wine and provisions with him as he wished, and he said it was not necessary, which showed me that he was an honest fellow.

The trail from Heiligenblut to the hut was a really good one, and as we got well on our way and out of sight of the village we began to talk about different things. I told him that I wished to go very slowly in order to enjoy the view. I knew quite well that he would not believe this, as this excuse is used by many tourists when it is necessary for them to rest, and when they are short-winded. Talking and at the same time going up hill do not agree with the lungs very well, so, as I wanted to ask many questions as to the life and living of a mountain guide, I used this excuse in order to get an opportunity to do so.

I can only give here a very small part of our conversation. I commenced by saying, "You people in the mountains certainly have a wonderful and a free life, but I suppose there are drawbacks to it as there are to everything else. However, nobody can take away the fresh air from you, and that gives you health and a good appetite." At times, I would take a deep breath as though I was storing up the fresh air in my lungs for the days in the city when I was working and where the air often feels so thick.

"What do you do in the winter?"

"Work in the woods at all kinds of work, if I can get anything to do," he replied.

"I suppose you make so much money in the summer that you can live in the winter even if you have nothing to do?"

He answered by saying, "There is a great difference in seasons, but in spite of it I did very well, and I did not come across a cross or unkind lady or gentleman the whole time. They were all most generous and kind." I stopped him here and said, "Do you mean that some of them are unkind? I do not understand this, as very often the life of a tourist depends on his guide," and he answered, "Yes, sir, you would not believe the selfish people we meet with, even among holidaymakers."

I am sorry to have to say that my guide spoke the truth in this regard. I could remember many men, and rich ones, too, who had made bargains with me and tried to get my services below the tariff prices set by the government, and had been very pleased with themselves when they had been able to do so. I did not continue asking him questions as to this, as I knew so well the characters a guide met with among the mountain climbers. My guide then told me that, generally speaking, one could make a living as a guide, but not a fortune, as even if there was a good summer, the winter was always long, and generally in the spring he was "broke," which comforted me, as it showed me that I was not the only guide in this condition in the spring.

I tried to get him to tell me some of his experiences with tourists, but with a smile on his face, he said: "I don't think it is wise to talk about the tourists," and I thought he was a very wise man, as telling tales as a guide is a dangerous game. Still I kept on asking him, and said I was sure he must have some very good tales to tell. However, I could not get him to tell me any of his yarns, so I asked him many questions, which he did his very best to answer, and thus I was able to get a great deal of information.

Just then a couple of women passed us, and I asked him what he thought of them as mountain climbers. "Well," he said, "sometimes it is surprising what some of them can stand, and I have seen some who are tougher than the average man." I then asked him whether he would sooner go on a climb with women or men, and he said he really preferred men. I then interrupted him and said, "I don't believe that," and pointed out to him that it was only natural that ladies from the city should take a fancy to the guides, as they are so fresh looking compared to the city men, and also so natural. I then added that they did not have polished manners. We mountain guides very often have to listen to this sort of nonsense, and must not kick when the tourist "pulls our legs." There is a great pleasure in "pulling someone's leg," and as this was my only day as a tourist I wanted to have that pleasure. This conversation gave me no difficulties whatever, as I was just repeating to the guide what I had heard from many tourists myself when on climbs of this kind.

"I am a married man, sir, and that is the end of it," he said.

"What difference does that make?"

"It makes all the difference in the world, as when you are acting as guide to a lady the first question she always asks is 'Are you a married man?' and if so, 'How many children have you, and do you love your wife?'"

I then said to him: "Do you think it is always necessary to tell the truth?"

"Yes, it is better; with a lie one does not get very far." This saying he then illustrated with the following story:

"Not so many years ago one of the guides from —— found out how far one could go with a lie. He had a very charming young lady to guide. I did not see her myself, but was told she was a lady no one could help liking, and of course she asked the guide the same old question, 'Are you married?' The guide was, but he said, 'Nein, Fraulein' (No, Miss). After a few days' climbing the young lady took a fancy to her guide. I might say here that the fellow was a very handsome-looking man, and besides this he was quite a humorist, and one could not blame the girl for falling in love with him. They got on very well together until the fifth day, when they met a party on a summit, and one of the members of the party, knowing this guide well, asked him how his wife was getting on. Of course, you can understand how both the guide and the young lady felt."

"Well, that was bad luck," I said, but the guide did not agree with me as to this. He thought it might have been much worse, as the young lady might have reported him and he would have then lost his guide's licence, at least for a considerable time.

We took many rests on the way, and in one of these the guide looked at my rather worn-out boots and made the remark, "It seems your boots have seen their best days, sir." Whenever he said "sir" to me an indescribable feeling came over me. I wished to speak a little more about climbing to him, so said, "You have done quite a bit of climbing in the Alps?" "Yes, sir, I have." He told me about great climbs on the Matterhorn and many other mountains around Zermatt. "I suppose you know also the Chamonix district (Mont Blanc range)?" "Oh, yes, I do; I have tramped quite a few times up that snow hill." He had the same opinion about Mont Blanc as many other guides, including myself, that it is a very tiring snow tramp.

"How do you like the Dolomites?"

"I am sorry I never had the chance to visit them," he said.

It was now time for me to tell some tales about climbing in the Dolomites, and about the gambling one does with one's neck when doing this. I think I "put it on pretty thick" like the man lecturing, and ended by pointing to my boots and saying, "This shows the effect of climbing in the Dolomites, the country of sharp stones."

"Did you climb without a guide?" he asked me.

"No, never without; I believe it is not wise to go without one and risk your neck on climbs of that sort. I made all my climbs there with Conrad Kain. Do you know that fellow?"

"Oh, yes, I know him; that is, I have heard a great deal about him. He is one of those cold-blooded lads. Personally I have never met him. He has been travelling. Last year he was down in Corsica with a gentleman I used to travel with frequently. A friend of mine met him this summer in Kaisergebirge with a lunatic."

I laughed and said, "I'm glad you did not say in the Dolomites, because I was there and I would not like anyone to take me for a lunatic." We spoke a long time about the climbs and guides there. Fortunately he spoke very well of me, Conrad Kain. He made a remark about the Dolomite guides, which is rather common among climbers: "Those fellows must be like monkeys." The conversation about guides and monkeys if continued would have caused me to laugh, so I spoke again about the beauties of Nature and the fresh air. Speaking about these I forgot that I was a tourist and not a guide, and spoke in my dialect so fluently that the guide asked me where I came from.

"You are from Vienna, are you not? What is your business, if I may ask, sir?" I stopped and looked him in the face without a smile, and said in a low voice, "My dear friend, I excuse you, but at the same time must give you warning to remember never to ask your men about their business. A man from the city comes to the mountains to get the good air to freshen up his tired brain, to get new life and strength for the rest of the year, and when he is on his holiday he tries to forget his daily life at home. He does not like to remember it. He wants to enjoy the golden freedom which he has only when he is in the mountains for a holiday."

My guide looked rather ashamed when I had said this, and answered, "Yes, it might be so, sir; I beg your pardon"; but I reassured him by saying, "Oh, never mind, don't worry, I don't mind your asking. I can tell you what I am and from where I came. I am an officer in the Post Office in a country town in Lower Austria. I have been born and brought up in the country."

"I thought so, because you speak almost the same dialect as I do," he said.

A short distance from the hut we met a party, and my guide stopped to talk with the guide with them. I went on slowly, and later was glad that I had done so. I was almost past the hut when someone called out from a window, "Conrad, what are you doing here?"

I rather feared the game was up, but I was a little ahead of my guide, and I looked around and recognized a gentleman with his wife, for whom I used to be a guide around my home. Quick as an avalanche I threw him a sign with my finger, like you throw a kiss to a lady, but to a gentleman it means "shut your mouth." Then as I came close and we shook hands, I said:

"Don't call me by name. I am travelling as a tourist like you are."

He looked queer and said, "What is the matter? Are you travelling as a tourist with a guide?"

I answered, "That is just what I am doing; for two days I am a gentleman, don't spoil the fun."

He turned away to hide a laugh.

After supper in the hut I went to the guides' room, where I talked to all the guides, and asked them how they were getting on, and how they liked being mountain guides. To get a little bit more fun in, I ordered a couple of bottles of wine for each table, and in a short time everyone in the guides' room was in good spirits, and we had a really good time until about two o'clock in the morning, when the guides raised their hats and thanked me for the wine, and very happy and satisfied I went to bed.

At six o'clock next morning the guide came to me. He made his usual bow and said good morning, and asked me how I felt.

"Oh, very well, thank you. How are you this morning? Have you a headache?"

"No, sir, I never drink in the evening before I climb. I suppose you feel a little tired from sitting up so late."

"Oh, no, I am used to it, you know. I must often sit up very late in the Post Office."

I left it to him to take what provisions were necessary for the trip, and I told him that if he liked to take a little wine or whisky along it would be all right, but he would not consider taking any, so I had to take it myself. We started out from the hut with the other party I have already mentioned. They had made the climb a couple of days before, but they went up with us for the fun of seeing me act the greenhorn.

A short distance from the hut we came to the glacier which had to be crossed. Here I asked the guide very seriously if there was any great danger of dropping into the crevasse, and he told me not to be afraid, as he would look after me, but I must step nicely and as rapidly as possible. "Just put your feet down one after the other, and they will take you safely across the ice. Don't put your whole weight on, and take your foot up as quickly as possible, in order to avoid sliding, and, above all, don't think of slipping."

I said, "Well, that is easier said than done," and I tried my first step on the ice. I think I really acted the real greenhorn. My feet went in all directions and would not stay where I had put them. If I had a good place for one foot, and wanted to bring the other up to it, I pretended I could not find it. It was very hard work. After all it is not very easy to act as a greenhorn if you are not one, and I would hate to be a "gentleman" all the time. I acted as though I wished to sit down to be more safe, and once, I really fell when I did not want to, and hit my head on the ice. I saw stars then and decided my guardian angel had fallen in love with someone else. I looked so sad that the guide said:

"If you are afraid, you had better take the rope."

And I said, "Oh, thank you," and looked as though I was thinking of my poor old mother.

He gave me a rope and put it on me. I looked at the way he was making the knots, and said:

"What do you call these knots?"

He said, "Don't you like them?"

"Oh, yes," I said, "but I should be glad to be able to make them."

He then said, "I suppose the Dolomite guides make another kind of knot for rock climbing, but the one I make is all right for snow and ice."

I asked him if he would let me try to tie the knots, so he took the rope and gave it to me. I twisted it around and around and once more around, but could not make the knot. He was very patient, and again showed me how to make it; so I took the rope again and made a knot that looked like an octopus and a big snake having a fight. It was good enough to hold an elephant, but he said it was too big, and tried to teach me once more.

"You take the rope so, and so and so!"

After that I took the rope, and tied the knot properly and the guide looked rather surprised, and said:

"You have tied this kind of knot before?"

I said: "Why, how can you ask, when I have never been on a glacier before. The only kind of knots I have ever made are those on the mail bags in the Post Office."

He was very much pleased when he heard this, and said: "Well, you pick it up very quickly."

At this point the gentleman and his wife laughed out loud, and I gave them a sign to stay behind.

This mountain is climbed almost every day in the season, and there is a good trail, so that a man really has very little trouble but as I had never been on a glacier before, I had to see and learn as much as I could, and so I asked the guide where he had to cut steps. He told me it was not necessary to cut any, as there were old ones. However, I asked him if he would show me how to cut ice steps anyway, which he did. Then I tried it myself, and handled the axe helplessly, and after I considered the steps were good enough, I told him to try them. He put his foot in and said: "That's no good. When you cut a step in the ice you must cut it so that it slopes towards the mountain, and then it must be far bigger than this."

So I made a second attempt, and let him try again, and he said: "That's far better, but you have to cut the steps more on the slope on the high side, because when you go down the steps must be big enough to put your foot on comfortably. He then showed me how to use an ice axe. "Don't keep your hands so stiff. Swing them as though you had nothing in them, and place your thumb on the handle, and then give it a twist with the other hand. Don't use all your strength, it is not necessary."

I then tried a third time, and the ice was so good that I forgot I was a "gentleman," and with a few blows I had the steps well made. He tried them, turned around, and looking sharply in my face said:

"Oh, sir, you must be fooling me; you have been cutting steps long before this."

"Why," I answered, "I have never been on a glacier before. But I am very good with an axe, because as I told you before, I come from the country."

"Well," he said, "if that is so, you are one of the best pupils I have ever had, as you pick things up so quickly."

At this point the gentleman and his wife, who had been listening, coughed, and I turned around and waved my hand to them in order to tell them not to give things away.

We then continued with the climb, with many short rests and much conversation about the beauties of Nature, until we reached the summit, where we shook hands. I thanked him for his good guiding and for the pleasure he had given me, and looked around at the many mountains, and pretended I had never seen such a sight before.

"The Post Office," I said, "is not like this. How I envy you, guide, with nothing to do in the summer but climb mountains and enjoy the beauties of Nature." I thought to myself that after this remark he would surely know I was a "gentleman," which was so, for he said:

"Yes, sir, if one could have a kind and considerate gentleman like yourself to guide, the life would be the finest in the world."

Meanwhile, the gentleman and his wife could not help laughing, as I spoke to my guide in a loud voice, in order that they might hear me. The guide wondered what was the matter, but they only laughed the more and said: "Oh, there was too much pepper in our lunch."

To make a long story short, we got back to the hotel in Heiligenblut, and as I was in a hurry to catch the train, I settled with the guide right away. I gave him what he wished, and a little more, because he had given me a good time and had believed I was a gentleman. He then gave me his book, and I wrote the very best recommendation I could think of, and signed my name, "Conrad Kain, Naßwald." Now a guide never looks in his book before a gentleman, so he put the book away and said he hoped I would not forget him when I wanted a guide for longer trips and we shook hands. I was very glad he had not found out who I was.

I then said to myself that the whole holiday was over, and that I must pack up my things and leave before he looks in his book and finds out who I am, but I was not quick enough, for in a few minutes he came back quietly, and said: "You have fooled me. Why did you fool me?"

All the people looked at us, and wondered what was the matter, so I said: "What is wrong? Did I not pay you your fee, and write a good recommendation in your book? What makes you think I am guying you?"

The hotel-keeper then came out to try and quiet the guide, but he said: "Du Himmel Sacrament, you fool me. You asked me if I knew Conrad Kain, and I told you lots about him, that he is a lunatic and a monkey, and can stretch himself. And here you are, yourself."

I really felt very bad to think that it had all come out this way, as all the ladies and gentlemen at the hotel had been talking of my big climb, and I had felt very proud of it, and now they all knew I was but a guide myself.

The gentleman and his wife I have mentioned before began to laugh, and told the whole story of how I pretended to be a greenhorn and a gentleman, and hired a guide in order to take the trip. It was impossible for me to leave at once, because they all wanted me to stay and have a good time, and all the guides crowded around and said: "What a man. When he is a mountain guide, he hires a guide to climb that easy mountain. He must be a millionaire."

I stayed there that night and told the guides many stories of my climbs in Dauphiné and Corsica. I really did boast a little that evening, like a real Dolomite guide. The guides could not forget the joke, and laughed about it a lot, and I often heard them say "The Millionaire Guide."

Next morning I went off in great style, with much waving of handkerchiefs, and everyone wished me the best of luck:

"Auf wiedersehen, millionaire guide."

Quite contented, I went home and climbed the mountain to my home. I had never returned from a trip so happy, and I told my mother all about it, and said: "Oh, mother, I am happy. I have had such a fine time."

She said: "Oh, I know the kind of time you mean; you will get into trouble if you are not careful."

"Don't worry, mother," I said. "There is nothing wrong. I only travelled as a tourist and hired a guide and was a gentleman."

To my great surprise she did not see the joke, and was very angry, and said: "Stupid, I always knew you were a fool, but I had no idea you were such a big one!"

CHAPTER XXXI

(1933)

▲

LAST CLIMBS

Kain did no climbing during the summer of 1932. Early in the following year his wife died following an operation. It was a great blow to him, and he was very lonely afterward.

C.K. TO J.M.T. WILMER. FEBRUARY 13TH, 1933.

I had the misfortune to lose my wife. She died in the hospital at Cranbrook, BC. We had been happily married for 16 years. I miss her very much, but I have the satisfaction to know that I did all I could for her while she was alive.

The death of my wife was a terrible shock to her 71-year-old mother. When she has recovered and my mind is settled I will write.

MARCH 2ND, 1933 ◆ *Many thanks to you and Mrs. T. for the sympathy in my great loss. It was a very hard blow to me. But as you and me have been together in the hills and on occasions have faced danger, you probably know that I do not lose my head very easy. You might also know that the chances for an education in my youth were rather slim, but I managed to form some philosophical views on life of my own, which have helped me along so far, and it is of interest that in your letter you touched on one of these. I refer to what you wrote regarding "the 16 years of happiness."*

Now we leave the past and look in the future. I had several letters from would-be hunters, but nothing is settled yet. It is safe to say that the Depression will not disappear overnight, and with this in mind I do not expect much work for the season. You expect to come out west; if

*you find someone to join you I will give you my lowest possible rates. If
you have to come alone, and I have nothing on hand I take you up the
Bugaboo for $5 (five dollar) per day, I supply the grub and climb with
you, you wash the dishes.*

*If Mrs. T. comes with you, she is welcome to stay on my place (no
rent) of course * * it would be better if she had a companion, and if you
should see fit to take it easy for a few days yourself I would be delighted
to have you as my guest.*

*A good friend has sent me this typwritter to keep me from the blues.
This is the very first letter I type so will excuse the many mistakes.*

*You will hear from me again, in the meantime you think over my
proposition. At present the Canadian dollar is 82¢.*

JUNE 8TH, 1933 ◆ *Your letter was delayed somewhere along the
road. We have not the best of weather here, and the chances are that
the whole month will be unsettled. The trails in the mountains all
through BC have been much neglected in the last three years; taking
this into consideration I might not be able to make the usual good
time on the trail.*

Dr. and Mrs. Thorington went with Conrad to the Bugaboos in June.[115]
He had aged (he was only 49), but was by way of regaining his old spirits
and regaled us with many a fine tale:

*The parson, a shy gink, once ask me why I do not go to church.
So I pass it off by telling him my best bear story. An Irishman from
Ireland, named Pat, was a tough kind of guy, but green. He worked in
a logging camp, und one day, when sent to the depot, was warned of
bears. He was told that if he kept his head the bears would give him
the right of way on the trail. Und so it happened the first time; but
the next time the bear did not move away. So Pat, he pray: "God, I
have not been to church, but I have not asked many favours. Now I
ask only one – that you turn this bear out of the trail." Und the bear
went away.*

*On another day the same thing happened und Pat pray once more:
"God," he say, "I promised to ask you no more favours, but this time I
ask one for the sake of the bear. Turn him back, otherwise you are going
to see the darndest fight in all Creation!"*

Our trip being chiefly for topographical purposes, we established photographic and marker stations at the glacier tongue, ascended several peaks and took bearings on known points across the Howser basin to the south.

We spent a day together hunting goat with motion-picture camera and rifle. The old poaching instinct was still in him, and we saw him bring down the last goat he ever shot. It was with the last cartridge, Conrad turning to us with the remark, "Py Gott! Doc, there is a helluva space around a goat."

A last climb was made in bad weather from the south fork of the Bugaboo:

> *In the very top of the pass there was a blue, ice-covered lakelet. A bear had come that way, neatly dodging a crevasse, and cautiously patting the ice from the shore outward until it was broken and he could slake his thirst. And, close behind, parallel, were the tracks of a wolverine. Their trails went over the hill, into the mist, soon to be blotted out by falling snow; not a sign of the animals themselves; not a sound save the plaintive chirp of a finch that followed us, and the distant rushing of water.*

It was worth a day of any man's life to watch and hear Conrad read this story from Nature's book.

We like to think that we made his last season a happy one. Late in July, H.S. Kingman joined Thorington at Lake Louise.[116] Conrad met us there and the combined party went with Simpson to Bow Lake. Placing a camp at Peyto Lake, we made several new ascents along the watershed, finally crossing the snowfields to the Yoho Valley. All the way down from Twin Falls Conrad was showing us fresh signs of marten – the little balls of mouse hair – and laying plans for a trapping foray on skis in the winter to come.

Conrad, who had not been away from the Columbia Valley since 1925, enjoyed himself hugely. He visited old friends at Banff, carrying to Bill Peyto the summit stone from Peyto Peak, which we had recently ascended. He refused George Harrison's invitation to ride by motor to Lake Louise, saying that the train was too much of a novelty to miss. He climbed such peaks as Lefroy and Louis (on his 50th birthday), and looked in on the ACC camp in Paradise Valley. How little we realized that he was saying goodbye.

At the camp he met Professor and Mrs. I.A. Richards, of Magdalene College, Cambridge, and later took them to the Bugaboos. After ascending Pigeon Spire they made a long first ascent of the highest summit[117] of the Bobbie Burns group, just to the north, descending Warren Glacier throughout its length. Conrad was delighted by the new views of his beloved Bugaboo

Spire and wrote of his plans to return there with us in another season. But his last climb was over.

My guess is that Conrad's climb on Mt. Louis on his 50th birthday was his last real hard climb. He took great satisfaction in the climb and in the fact that he was able to stand it so well. The week previous we had gotten into the final chimney when we were driven off the mountain by a terrific sleet and rain storm which encased the entire mountain with slush and verglas. The descent of Louis was quite an experience, and Conrad certainly handled himself beautifully.

After you left us at Lake Louise we went to the ACC camp and had a good time. No doubt you will have heard from Mr. Kingman. Well, we had a nice time on our climbs; Mr. Kingman enjoyed the climb on Mt. Louis, and I was very pleased with myself, as I found that I still get a kick out of climbing Louis. After Mr. Kingman left I picked up a nice girl [Miss Armington] and we spent several days in Yoho. After my return home someone wanted me for several days but I did not go. Now I am back here with the outfit, and should have started out this morning for the Bugaboos, but it is raining too hard to make a start. I have with me Old Country climbers, and if weather permits will give them their money's worth.

In Banff I saw Belmore Browne; he would like to meet you. I met Dr. and Mrs. Oastler several times. The Dr. told me he has 89,000 negatives and 300,000 feet of film. He said when I come to NY I must stay three days with him.

In general I enjoyed myself this summer, but I feel sorry to say that my little place does not look so nice as it did when my dear Old Girl looked after it in my absence.

WILMER. SEPTEMBER 20TH, 1933 ◆ *Here is the report of the trip: we climbed Pigeon Sp. over Cromwell's route & found it very interesting. Next we climbed the highest peak (No. 7) on Bobbie Burns Range, it was a long one, 12 hrs. from camp to summit; there were several inches of fresh snow. The view from the peak was good; the snowfields & gla-ciers are large & interesting. We descended Warren Glacier, spent what was left of the night in the woods near the foot of the glacier, & returned to Bugaboo via pass between the Alplands (dividing range) & North Post. On our way we visited the lake, Dr. Richards suggested the name Ice Lake. It will be from this lake that the Brenta & also the North Post will be reached? I believe both peaks will offer good rock work.*

The very best view (that is of course my fancy) of the whole trip was the Bugaboo Sp. seen from halfway down Warren Gl. If I have no other reason to go back there, I sure will go someday just to have another look at it. Had a good look for a new and better route but found noth-ing to go by; the same goes for Snowpatch.

Dr. & Mrs. Richards enjoyed the climbs, although we did not have the best of weather; they considered the Bugaboos the finest they have seen in the Rockies. I might mention that there was hardly any old snow left on the Spires. Dr. & Mrs. Richards are good on the hillside & I enjoyed the former's companionship very much.

Now I am home picking apples, harvesting the vegetables & fixing things up for the all-too-long winter. Then I will go a-hunting, & after that I might go visiting in the Okanagan Valley, as at times I get so damenable lonely. I miss my old Sweetheart more than ever.

No doubt you know the old saying "Some people if you give them a finger, they want the whole hand." Well, here it goes: I beg of you to send The Glittering Mountains of Canada *to Miss Amelia Malek. And please send her a picture of "Snowpatch from South," and write on it "The Mountain that Conrad Could* NOT *Climb."*

Sad news came unexpectedly, explaining a long silence.

F.W. GREEN, MD, CM, FACS, TO J.M.T. CRANBROOK, BC.

FEBRUARY 15TH, 1934.

I very much regret to inform you that our friend Conrad Kain passed to the great beyond on Feb. 2nd, and I am reasonably certain that the cause of death was encephalitis lethargica.

Evidently Conrad was a man well-known, not only locally, but was renowned among mountain climbers. He was buried at Cranbrook with his wife, who died here a year or so ago.

JAMES SIMPSON TO J.M.T. BANFF. MARCH 23RD, 1934.

I have nothing relative to Conrad that is other than incidentally connected with his everyday life while in Banff. When he was away I was usually absent also, but on widely separated trails. In the early days of the ACC camps Wheeler usually kept him so busy during work hours and busier during play time that one only got with him intermittently; then some member wanted a nail shifted to some other part of a climbing boot, which he would do with a smile and then remark that "it pleased them even if it didn't make a damn bit of difference; they thought it did, anyway."

His winter trapping at the Columbia Icefield was a solo affair, the winter after the Interprovincial Survey was there. Incidents cropped up that prevented me from meeting him on the Mistaya. I had packed in provisions in the fall but I did not get near them. Conrad did when he came out of the Alexandra River in March. His experiences as related to me were so much like my own at various times and like his former experiences when trapping on the Simpson River that they passed with the relating. He wrote perhaps a couple of hundred pages of a dog story while trapping on the Simpson – he read much of it to me when he came to Banff in the spring – but I do not know whether he ever added to it or destroyed it.

The village did not see much of him while in Banff. He usually made the Alpine Clubhouse his home, but he was not there often enough or long enough to be worth the mention. He gave the best years of his life to the ACC and the Dominion Govt. under A.O. Wheeler and he gave every ounce of his best at all times.

He would die for you if need be quicker than most men think of living. No matter what his creed, his colour or his nationality he was measured by a man's yardstick, no other. We shall all miss him.

AMELIA MALEK TO J.M.T. REICHENAU, AUSTRIA. MARCH 3RD, 1934.

Conrad and Hetta were such a happy couple, the more lonely he felt after her death, poor man. He couldn't have found a better woman than Hetta in the whole world. Now the Lord has joined them again. May they rest in God's peace and eternal love.

The news of Conrad's death was a great shock for me and still more for his old mother and her family. I went to Naßwald (Oh! what a lovely spot Conrad's home is! I wish you might see and admire the beautiful

*valley and mountains there!) the following day to inform poor Mrs.
Kain of the death of her dearest son. It was heartbreaking to see the
misery of a loving mother and to hear her lamenting. Holding the poor
woman in my arms, being woestricken myself, I did my best to console
her and help her over the first outburst of her sorrow.*

*Conrad's younger brother (John) and his wife were there, we were
all crying, while the children were wondering and staring at the sad
group. I shall never forget the tragedy of that day.*

*In your letter you mentioned that Conrad told you I had his guide-
book or books. No, his guidebook was lost, so he told me, but I forget
where he lost it. I only know that he was very sorry for it. But I have
his diary (1904–1909); it contains his trips and climbings in Austria,
Switzerland, Dauphiné and Corsica. It is my opinion that the reports of
his mountaineering and all his events in the mountains are written for
Austrian people, dialogues with other guides in simple Austrian dialect
(slang) and ever so many details.*

*It also contains the events of C.'s first year in the Rockies and then
there is an end of the diary: Conrad ceased to write it. He always
promised to continue to write, but he never did. Maybe he had no
leisure for it, because he had to work hard and earn money even in
winter by trapping.*

*C.'s last letter to me was written at Spillimacheen, dated August 31st.
He wrote of first ascents he had made and several new routes he had
found out; he described the merry hours of his birthday (Aug. 10th)
and how he would have liked to shake hands with me! He again spoke
of his coming home next winter, if he was lucky in his trapping and
could earn money enough.*

*Till now nobody has read Conrad's diary but Dr. Pistor, who helped
C. to get a position as official guide of the Alpine Club of Canada. C.
was very fond of him and considered him as a friend. He made his
earliest climbs with him.*

CHAPTER XXXII

▲

CONRAD THE MAN

*There is a kind of fate in this.... Every step it's you
that saves our lives; and do you suppose by any
chance that we are going to let you lose yours?*

— Treasure Island

So we come to the end. To evaluate Conrad Kain as guide alone would be as difficult as it would be rash. Remembering whence he came, his accomplishments in the Western Alps are in the best traditions of Johann Grill, and his European career is the more remarkable when one recalls that it was finished before he was 26 years old.

One met him in Canada when youthful impetuosity was no longer the main driving force, while average climb and climber were not of the calibre he had known in the Alps. On such peaks as Robson, Louis and Bugaboo Spire he showed what he could do when required; in his solitary fight with Whitehorn he evidenced his own spirit of enterprise which took no thought of consequence.

More clearly than any other, Conrad laid down the methods by which a guide might hope to maintain the confidence of a party:

• *First*, he should never show fear.

• *Second*, he should be courteous to all, and always give special attention to the weakest member in the party.

• *Third*, he should be witty, and able to make up a white lie on short notice and tell it in a convincing manner.

◆ *Fourth*, he should know when and how to show authority; and, when the situation demands it, should be able to give a good scolding to whomsoever deserves it.

On rock, in his prime, Kain was unquestionably a finished performer. On snow and ice his judgment was sound, with step cutting unfailingly conforming to the needs of his party. The latter factor determined his use or non-use of rope; he had no fixed procedure. Wide experience in various districts had taught him all the tricks. Even on new peaks he preferred to traverse and would cleverly find a way down, with almost unique ability in route finding on the mountain at hand.

With an axe in the woods Conrad was the equal of Curly Phillips or Jim Simpson – they had had an apt pupil. He was a good and a clean cook, and handled horses with gentleness, talking to them as if they were children. His great capacity for weight carrying was constantly overtaxed. He was about five feet five inches tall, stockily built, waist narrow and shoulders broad – the torso of an athlete. His hair and moustache carried a tinge of auburn; he had high colouring and a radiant, ready smile. A short, curved pipe was his constant companion.

Rarely did Conrad speak adversely of any climber. There had been more than one Rydzewski in his life, but in his narrative he has carefully suppressed their names. His "Mr. H." and his "Dr. B." are examples of what a young and struggling guide was obliged to put up with; a sense of humour was a necessity. Conrad's patrons, for the most part, were never able to satisfy their curiosity as to what he really thought of them. But it was very simple: those were always his friends who responded to the beauty of the hillside, to the sweeping panorama, to the changing effects of light and shadow. Nothing, not even technical ability, counted with him against this vision. He was only sorry for those who used peaks for personal exploitation: "mushroom mountaineers" he called them.

No desire to rush peaks or break records was to be found in Kain's makeup. He loved varying lights and colours too much for that, and would loaf on a summit if there was a chance of seeing a fine sunset, even though it meant getting in late. Light, life and joy contrasting with shadow, mystery and pathos – Conrad was keenly attuned to the drama of their interplay. His increasing proclivity for lingering near timberline may be attributed largely to his appreciation of mountain beauty as it was understood by guides in the Golden Age of mountaineering in the Alps. "Eile mit Weile" was a proverb learned from Sepp Innerkofler in the days of his youth. He knew full well that life is not compounded solely of action. He had no more important lesson to teach.

His first ascents of named peaks in the Rockies and Purcells exceed 60 in number; his new routes and ordinary climbs are countless. He held the unique distinction of having led the first ascents of the highest peaks of the Rockies and of the Purcells, and is the only one thus far to have stood on all of the three loftiest summits of the Canadian Rockies. He made first ascents in Corsica, and scaled some of the most difficult peaks of the Alps. In New Zealand, by his own count, he ascended 59 mountains, of which 29[118] were first ascents. He reckoned the number of his climbs to be in excess of a thousand.

His name is borne by a finger-like peak of the Robson area, which he himself selected. Nasswald Peak, in the Assiniboine Group, was ascended and named by him for his old home. Birthday Peak, in the Purcells, was climbed on his natal day. In the Southern Alps of New Zealand, Mt. Conrad, in the Murchison district, holds him in remembrance.

Conrad was undoubtedly the most glamorous figure in Canadian mountaineering, and those who climbed with him know that his death separates all that went before from whatever the future may bring forth, rounding out (as it almost does) the first half-century of Canadian alpinism, during which the principal peaks of the Rockies and the Interior ranges of British Columbia were conquered. Guides in days to come will scarcely have his great experience in travel, new ascents and trail breaking.

"It is good to have been once young," he said, "if only you have happy memories." He knew that the song must go on, and in his philosophy there should be no evident sadness in parting. But he was so much more than just a guide – he was your friend, playing a part in the inspiring moments of many lives and giving more to life than he asked of it. He had no routine moments on a mountain and, if you had not employed him, he would have been climbing by himself for the pure joy and beauty of it all.

"He will be much missed," wrote his neighbours in the Columbia Valley, "for he was a kind, honest man." There is probably no better epitaph.

In the rooms of the American Alpine Club an old ice axe hangs on the wall. The cutting edge is blunted, and the wooden shaft worn where the hand grips it far down in step cutting position. But it has been the silent witness of high adventure, and on a small brass plate one reads:

CONRAD KAIN (1883–1934)
GUIDE, PHILOSOPHER, FRIEND
MT. ROBSON, 1913   MT. LOUIS, 1916
BUGABOO SPIRE, 1916

A great guide has gone, and with him something that made life infinitely gay. It is no small thing to have held so much of mirth and wonder and loveliness. "Who so touches a joy as he flies, lives in Eternity's sunrise" – if this be hero worship make the most of it.

For some of us a door was opened upon a golden world, and Time has all too quickly snatched away the key.

APPENDIX

▲

Indispensable, ever-victorious Conrad Kain, whose record of new ascents must be one of the longest and most remarkable held by any guide now living.

— A.L. Mumm in
the Alpine Journal for 1917

ALPS

◆ Maritime Alps: Punta dell'Argentera.

◆ Cottian Alps: Monte Viso (4th ascent by W. ridge; traverse); Viso di Vallante.

◆ Dauphiné Alps: Barre des Écrins (traverse from sw; twice); Mont Pelvoux, Meije (traverse; twice); Grande Ruine, Aig. d'Arve Méridionale, Col du Sélé.

◆ Pennine Alps: Mont Blanc (Bosses route; also once as far as Cabane Vallot; also from Tête Rousse and down to Grands Mulets); Dôme du Goûter, Aig. de Blaitière, Aig. des Grands Charmoz, Aig. du Géant. Aig. du Grépon (three times); Weisshorn, Zinal Rothhorn (traverse); Trifthorn (traverse); Matterhorn (twice); Lyskamm, Breithorn, Riffelhorn (N. route); Monte Rosa (Dufourspitze, twice; Signalkuppe, twice; Parrotspitze, twice; Balmenhorn, Grenzgipfel, Zumsteinspitze, Ludwigshöhe); Südlenzspitze, Nadelhorn, Dom, Weissmies, Portiengrat.

◆ Silvretta Alps: Fluchthorn, Piz Buin, Gr. Litzner.

◆ Salzburg Alps:

Kaisergebirge: Totensessel, Totenkirchl (twice, including S. ridge); Predigtstuhl (twice, including Botzong Chimney).

Ennsthaler District: Planspitze (all sides, including several routes on
N. face); Hochthor (numerous routes, including N. face); Hochthor–
Ödstein; Ödstein (several routes); Reichenstein (various routes);
Gr. and Kl. Buchstein, Festkogel (N. wall); Tamischbach Tower.

Dachstein District: Gr. and Kl. Dirndl, Thorstein (all sides);
Eiskarlspitze, Gr. and Kl. Bischofsmütze, Dachstein (various routes,
including S. wall); Trisselwand (Todtes Gebirge).

Rax and Schneeberg District: All important routes, some of them
original.

♦ Ortler Alps: Cevedale, Schrötterhorn, Königsspitze, Ortler.

♦ Central Tyrolese Alps: Schwarzenstein, Zsigmondyspitze, Gr. Greiner,
Mösele.

♦ Lombard Alps: Brenta Alta, Torre di Brenta, Guglia di Brenta.

♦ Dolomites of South Tyrol: Fermeda Tower, Fünffingerspitze (including
Schmittkamin); Grasleiten Tower, Grasleitenspitze, Third Sella Tower,
Vajolet Towers (many times, including two traverses from Winkler
to Delago, and the latter twice by the Pichlriss; also Stabeler, Winkler,
Delago and the three northern towers in one day); Sasso di Stria
(Witzenmann route); Tofana di Mezzo (Via Inglese); Marmolata (S.
wall); Wundtspitze, Einser, Gr. Zinne, Kl. Zinne (E. wall).

♦ Julian Alps: Mangart, Monte Canin, Wischberg.

♦ Corsica: Monte Cinto, Punta Castelluccia (new route), Capo Tafonato
(first ascent); Paglia Orba, Capo Uccello, Punta Minuta, Cinque Frati
(four summits climbed, one of them a first ascent), Monte d'Oro.

NEW ZEALAND
(NAMED PEAKS)

♦ Mt. Acland (first ascent), Mt. Annette, The AntHill (first ascent), Mt.
Arsinoë (second ascent), Mt. Bannie (first ascent), Mt. Beatrice (E. peak;
first ascent), Mt. Conrad (first ascent), Mt. Cook (25 starts; two complete
ascents: 1. 16th ascent, connecting Earle's and Green's routes. 2. 17th
ascent, the second "Grand Traverse"), Coronet Peak, Mt. Darby (third
ascent; new traverse), Mt. Darwin, Mt. de la Bêche, Dilemma Peak (W.

peak; first ascent), Eagle Peak (first ascent), Mt. Edgar Thomson (first ascent), Edith Peak (first ascent), Mt. Elie de Beaumont, Mt. Eric (first ascent), Footstool, Haeckel Peak (second ascent), Mt. Hicks (St. David's Dome; second ascent), Mt. Hutton (first ascent), Mt. Jean (first ascent), Mt. Jeanette (first ascent), Mt. Jellicoe (first ascent), Mt. Sydney King (first ascent), Mt. La Pérouse (attempt from E.), Lean Peak, Mt. Lloyd (first ascent), Mt. Low (first ascent), Mt. Mabel, Mt. Mannering (first ascent), Mt. Marie (first ascent), Mt. Maunga Ma (first and subsequent ascents), Mt. McKerrow (first ascent), Mt. Meeson (first ascent), Mt. Montgomery (new traverse), Nun's Veil, Proud Peak, Raureka Peak (first ascent), Mt. Richmond (first ascent), Aig. Rouge, Mt. Sealy, The Scissors (first ascent), Mt. Sefton (5th ascent; new route), Shark's Teeth (NW peak; first ascent), Spence Peak (first ascent), Mt. Sturdee (first ascent), Mt. Thomson (first ascent), Mt. Wakefield (new route), The Watchtower (first ascent).

CANADA

(Based on a list written by Kain himself. As the manuscript is in pencil, it is now difficult to decipher and some peaks cannot be identified with certainty. Many of the summits were attained more than once, and some, not so indicated, may have been first ascents.)

Rockies:

♦ (International Boundary to Kicking Horse Pass.)
Pk. N. of Crowsnest (? Pt. 8500 ft.), Pk. between [blank] Creek and Oldman River, Windsor Mtn. (Middle Kootenay Pass), Pk. SE of Windsor, Pk. S. of S. Kananaskis Pass, Pk. N. of S. Kananaskis Pass, Mt. Douglas (camera sta.), Fatigue Mtn., Nasswald Peak (first ascent), Mt. Bourgeau, Pk. at head of Brewster Creek (? Brewster Cr. W.), Monarch Mtn. (first ascent), Mt. Cautley, Wonder Pk. (first ascent), Terrapin Mtn. (first ascent), Mt. Magog, Mt. Assiniboine, Wedgwood Pk., Eon (second ascent), Pk. E. of Indian Pk., Storm Mtn., Storm S., Mt. Mitchell, Mt. Whymper, Boom Mtn., Toork (*sic* – cannot identify;? Tokumm), Bident Mtn., Mt. Fay, Mt. Little, Pk. next Fay (? Quadra), Mt. Hungabee, Eiffel Pk., Mt. Temple,

Mt. Victoria, Victoria N., Mt. Huber, Lefroy, Mt. Aberdeen, Haddo Pk., Collier Pk., Popes Pk., Mt. Niblock, Mt. Whyte, Mt. Odaray, The Mitre, Mt. Stephen, Mt. Rundle.

◆ (Kicking Horse Pass to Yellowhead Pass.)
Cascade Mtn., Mt. Louis (first and two additional ascents), Mt. Edith, Pk. N. of Edith, Oyster Pk., Mt. Richardson, Unnamed near Richardson, Mt. Bosworth, Mt. Niles, Mt. Balfour, Unnamed between Hector and Bow lakes, Mt. Gordon, Mt. Collie, Mt. des Poilus (Mt. Habel), Mt. McArthur, Mt. Kerr, Mt. Pollinger, Mt. Marpole, The President, The Vice-President, Yoho Pk., Mt. Baker (second ascent), Peyto Pk. (first ascent), Mistaya Mtn. (first ascent), Trapper Pk. (first ascent), Barbette Mtn. (first ascent), Survey Pk. opposite Mt. Bryce (Bryce S.), Watchman Pk., Pk. E. of Bryce (Bryce NE), Pk. between Alexandra and Whiterose creeks (Lyell Cr. No. 2), Cathedral Mtn., Wilcox Pk., Nigel Pk., Shale (*sic* – cannot identify), Sunwapta Pk., Mt. Athabaska, Athabaska S., Terrace Mtn. (first ascent), Mt. Saskatchewan (first ascent), Castleguard Mtn. (first ascent), Mt. Columbia (second ascent), Mt. King Edward (first ascent), North Twin Peaks (first ascent), two Pks. NW of Alberta (? Pts. 9600 ft. and 9200 ft.; possibly SE – "Little Alberta"), Warwick Mtn. (first ascent), Pk. N. of Sundial (? Pt. 9200 ft.), Sundial Mtn. (first ascent), Chaba Pk. W., three Pks. E. of Fortress Lake, including Chisel (first ascent), two Pks. W. of Fortress Lake (Survey – cannot identify), Mt. Oates (first ascent), Mt. Hooker (first ascent), Mt. Kain (first ascent), Mt. Brown, Simon Pk. (first ascent), McDonell Pk., four Pks. from Jasper to Maligne Lake over Shovel Pass.

◆ (Yellowhead Pass and Northward.)
Pyramid Mtn. (Jasper; first ascent), Mt. Mowat, Pk. on Moose River (Resplendent S.), Reef Glaciers, The Colonel (first ascent), Upright Mtn. (first ascent), Pk. at head of Stone Creek (Stony River Head Sta.), Calumet Pk. (first ascent), Moose Mtn. (Moose Pass Sta.), Titkana Pk., Lynx Mtn., Mt. Resplendent (first and subsequent ascents), Mt. Robson (first and subsequent ascents), Gendarme Mtn. (first ascent), Mumm Pk., Pk. E. of Longstaff (Whitehorn E.), Mt. Whitehorn (first and subsequent ascents), Grizzly Pk. (two Pks. – Robson W.), Robson S., Red Pass Pk.

Selkirks:

♦ Mt. Afton, Mt. Sir Donald (alone), Uto Peak, Avalanche Mtn. (alone).

Purcells:

♦ Bobbie Burns Mtn. ("Mt. Conrad"; first ascent); Pk. on Bugaboo above cabin (Bugaboo Forks), Howser Spire (first ascent), Howser Pk. (first ascent), "False Howser" (two summits on E. arête of Howser Pk.), Pk. to right (N.) of Bugaboo Pass, Pk. to left (S.) of Bugaboo Pass (Quintet Group), two Pks. on range W. of Howser Spire, Pk. on range between Howser and Bugaboo creeks (Septet Group; cannot identify), Marmolata Mtn. (first ascent), Pigeon Spire (second ascent), Crescent Mtn. (first ascent), Pk. N. of Ethelbert (first ascent), Mt. Ethelbert (first ascent), Pk. S. of Ethelbert (Horeb Mtn., first ascent), Starbird Glacier (first ascent), Mt. Sally Serena, Pk. W. of Sally Serena, Birthday Pk. (first ascent), Eyebrow Pk., Mt. Monica (first ascent), The Dome (Horsethief), Jumbo (first and subsequent ascents; once alone in winter), Karnak Mtn. (first ascent), Commander Mtn. (first and subsequent ascents), Black Diamond Mtn. (first ascent), Peacock (first ascent), Spearhead Pk. (first ascent), Mt. Delphine, Mt. Farnham (first ascent), Farnham Tower (first ascent), Peter Pk. (first ascent), The Cleaver (first and subsequent ascents), Redtop Mtn. (two Pks.; first ascent), Blockhead Mtn. (three Pks.; first ascent), Truce Mtn. (first ascent), Cauldron (first ascent), Mt. Nelson, Monument Pk. (first ascent), Boulder Pk. (first ascent), Mt. Toby (traverse), three Pks. at head of Toby snowfield (first ascents), Earl Grey (first ascent), Pharaoh Pks. (first ascent), Survey Pk. E. of Earl Grey, Mt. Findlay (first ascent).

1 Conrad uses the word *Sterz*, the Naßwald dialect equivalent of *Schmarrn*, shortened from *Kaiserschmarrn* (Emperor's mishmash) a light, carmelized pancake famous in Austria.

2 Robert Kanitz, traversing unroped, fell to his death here on March 25, 1889.

3 These mountains, neither of which reaches 7,000 feet, are within 40 miles of Vienna and the points of approach are easily reached by rail in an hour. Whilst the summit of each is an undulating plateau, their sides are in many parts made up of cliffs, furrowed by ravines. There are more than 15 marked routes up the Rax.

4 The guide Daniel Innthaler, of Naßwald, Conrad's teacher, died in 1925 at the age of 77. (*AJ* 37, 388.)

5 Hofrat Erich Pistor, of Vienna, through whose influence Conrad later secured engagement in Canada.

6 "The ascent of the Planspitze by the north wall is among the most daring undertakings of modern mountaineering. The honour of conquering this wall belongs to Daniel Innthaler, native of the Reissthal (Naßwald), equal as a rock climber to the best Dolomite guides, who, after prolonged reconnaissance, led Dr. Suchanek, of Vienna, up this wall in the beginning of July 1885." —*Die Erschließung der Ostalpen.*

7 Mizzi Langer married Herr Kauba, and the famous sporting-goods house of Vienna took the name Mizzi Langer-Kauba.

8 In 1909 Liesl Lechner was in charge of the Edelhütte on the Ahornspitze, above Mayrhofen in the Zillerthal. Conrad was quite right about her good looks!

9 In later years Kain, wishing to identify himself with Tyrol and the Dolomites, would say that he was born in Tiers.

10 Giuseppe Petigax (1862–1926), Abruzzi's chief guide on the St. Elias, "Stella Polaris," Karakoram and Ruwenzori expeditions.

11 Jean-Joseph Garny (b. 1877), of La Frasse.

12 As this was written some time afterward, Kain is slightly confused as to the position of C.P. in the Grépon traverse. In reality it is on the sw arête. ["C.P." are the initials of 19th-century climbers Charlet and Payot, who painted their initials here to mark their conquest of this climb.]

13 Perren, who died at Zermatt in November 1918, had ascended the Matterhorn 89 times.

14 Karl Hermann and Karl Geldner, of Basel, August 5, 1905. (*AJ* 22, 612.)

15 Conrad was fond of relating this incident at greater length to us in Canada, contrasting the simple pleasure of the peasant woman with the jaded life of her sisters in the city.

16 Franz Zimmer, who took part in the first traverse of the Dent du Géant in 1900.

17 Franz Kostner, of Corvara, who went with Merzbacher to the Tian-Shan in 1902–03.

18 Albert Gerngross. For his account of the expedition, see "Auf Korsika's höchsten Gipfeln," *Österreichische Touristen-Zeitung* XXIX, nos. 20, 21. The chief results were first ascents of Capo Tafonato (S. summit), Punta Castelluccia (NE face) and one of the Cinque Frati (E. face).

19 Felix von Cube and L.L. Kleintjes in August 1899. See *D.Ö.A.-V.* XXII (1901).

20 This was the way it happened: While Konrad packed his rucksack I jumped across the schrund separating rock from snow, broke through on the far side, went head over heels and came into a rolling motion from the force of my jump. First I drove in the point of my axe (which I still held), but it tore out on account of my momentum. I was again lying head downward, but succeeded in forcing in the cutting edge of the axe and, holding it tightly with both hands, shot around it and was able to kick my feet in on the steep slope,

Konrad exhibited the greatest courage throughout, racing down the snowfield after me, with complete disregard for his own safety.

Konrad is wrong about the topography. The snowfield was not to be descended, but traversed to the right toward the Punta Minuta. A curve was to be made, not a descent. —Gerngross.

21 This is probably a mistake of Konrad's – who did not understand the language – for I did not introduce him as a physician. On the contrary, on our return to Calacuccia I presented him as a famous naturalist and philosopher from Vienna who was accompanying me as interpreter and servant. Through it all Konrad preserved the greatest discretion and proper demeanour in the presence of English women, Frenchmen and an old gentleman from Munich who happened to be there. —Gerngross.

22 Mattias Zurbriggen (1856–1917) of Sass Fee and Macugnaga, author of *From the Alps to the Andes.*

23 One of these was Moritz Inderbinen (1856–1926), A.L. Mumm's guide, whom Conrad met again in Canada.

24 Franz Wenter, of Tiers, whose experience embraced the Alps, Pyrenees and Tian-Shan, was 29 years of age at this time.

25 Gottlieb Lorenz, of Galtür, died March 30, 1910, in his 67th year. He had ascended the Fluchthorn more than 200 times. (*AJ* 25, 562.)

26 Sepp Innerkofler (1864–1915), killed in action on the Paternkofel July 4, 1915. He had made the first ascent of this mountain in 1896, and the Italians buried him with military honours on the summit.

27 Sigg. Bertatni and Moraschini were killed on the Meije on July 11, 1907. (*AJ* 23, 640)

28 Wessely, who went with Eckenstein, Pfannl and Jacot-Guillarmod to the Karakoram in 1902, and reached 22,000 feet on K2.

29 The same Mayer fell on New Year's Day 1907 while climbing the Kanzel ridge of the Hohe Wand with a lady. Both were killed and were buried at Grünbach.

30 Mr. (not Dr.) P., who took several of the pictures illustrating this book, had also made ascents with Kain

in the Rax and Dachstein districts. He fell to his death during a solitary climb on the Rax a few years later.

31 The Vajolet Towers are six in number, three of them being named for their first conquerors and three for their position.

32 According to Guido Rey, Tita Piaz, prior to 1914, had ascended the Vajolet Towers more than 300 times.

33 *CAJ* II, 218.

34 *Adventures of an Alpine Guide.*

35 *CAJ* II, 143. E.F.M. MacCarthy and A.M. Bartlett, "Two Englishmen in the Yoho Valley."

36 Mountain journeys are made with horses, used partly for riding, partly for carrying. For this year's camp we had 35 horses.

37 One of the three Otto brothers, famous outfitters.

38 In 1906. See note 23.

39 Possibly the remains of W.S. Green's 1888 camp at Perley Rock.

40 *CAJ* III, 193.

41 *CAJ* III, 157. B.S. Darling, "Up the Bow and Down the Yoho."

42 *CAJ* III, 26. T.G. Longstaff, "Across the Purcell Range of British Columbia."

43 This is one of the peaks of the Septet group, immediately west of Mt. Ethelbert.

44 *CAJ* IV, 1. A.O. Wheeler, "Expedition to Jasper Park, Yellowhead Pass and Mt. Robson."

45 Translated by P.A.W. Wallace for *CAJ* VI, 49.

46 Two days after Conrad gave the above extracts from his notebook (August 1913), Walter Schauffelberger's party returned from Whitehorn, bringing the Continental Oil Co. matchbox and the paper with Conrad's signature. It was found 20 or 30 feet below the summit.

47 *CAJ* IV, 64, A.O. Wheeler, "Expedition to Maligne Lake"

48 *CAJ* IV, 87. D. Phillips, "Fitzhugh to Laggan."

49 Donald Phillips, writing of this season, says: "During the winter of 1911–12, Conrad Kain and I spent several months on the headwaters of the Smoky, Moose and Beaver rivers on a trapping expedition and discovered, as we supposed, Wolverine and Bess passes, but found out later that Collie and Mumm had been ahead of us by a few months. Conrad and I worked down the Smoky as far as Short River, which we then called Chown Creek, as the big snow-covered peak back of Mt. Bess, which somehow got called by the name of Chown, stand at the head of the valley, where is located the grandest and most beautiful glacier in the whole region. Conrad also explored Twin Tree Lake, which he estimated at about eight miles in length." (*CAJ* VI, 179. "Winter Conditions North and West of Mt. Robson.")

50 *CAJ* V, 73. N. Hollister, "Camps in the Altai." The expedition was in the joint interests of the United States National Museum and the Museum of

Comparative Zoology, Harvard University. Hollister and Kain concerned themselves with collecting small vertebrates. The Trans-Siberian railroad was left at Novonikolaevsk, on the Obi River, whence they went south to the last Russian post, Kosh-Agach, near the Mongolian border in 17 days of travel. The frontier range to the south was explored for a month. (*Smithsonian Miscellaneous Collections* LX.)

51 Dr. Theodore Lyman, of Harvard, leader of the expedition.

52 Kain saw Captain Farrar again at this time, and often spoke of a day spent in Bedfordshire.

53 "Knowing him I have no doubt of its truth, but it will not count as a first ascent, as there is nothing in the way of evidence except his word and that little cairn which may never be seen again." (*CAJ* IV, 47.)

54 Schauffelberger lost his life in a ski accident on the Morteratsch Glacier in January 1915. He was 34 years old. (*AJ* 29, 199.)

55 *CAJ* VI, 11. W.W. Foster, "Mt. Robson (1913)."

56 *CAJ* VI, 55. W.E. Stone, "A Day and Night on Whitehorn."

57 *CAJ* VI, 37. A.H. MacCarthy and B.S. Darling, "An Ascent of Mt. Robson from the Southwest."

58 Translated for *CAJ* VI, 19 by P.A.W. Wallace.

59 Consult also "The Ascent of Mt. Robson" (*AJ* 28, 35), as well as the original German version, "Eine Ersteigung und Traversierung von Mount Robson, des höchsten Gipfels der Canadian Rockies" (*Österreichische Touristen-Zeitung*, 1914, vol. 1).

60 Kain sailed from Vancouver on October 29th on the ss *Makura*, noting that he stopped at Honolulu and Suva (Fiji), and read *Pioneer Work in the Alps of New Zealand* during the voyage.

61 The lists in this and following chapters are taken chiefly from Andersen's *Jubilee History of South Canterbury* and the "Reports" of the New Zealand Tourist Department. Much of this and additional information has been supplied by Mr. J.S. Shanks and other members of the NZAC.

62 *Conquest of the New Zealand Alps*. London: Unwin, 1922.

63 *NZAJ* III, 57. William Brass; b. Orkney Islands 1886; killed in action at Dardanelles during landing at Gallipoli.

64 *NZAJ* V, 273. Frank Milne (1891–1933).

65 *AJ* 28, 222. J.R. Dennistoun, "The Accident on Mt. Cook."

66 Their remains appeared below the glacier in 1928.

67 *Bull. Phila. Geogr. Soc.* XXIX, 3.

68 Kain notes at this time that he had been reading *White Fang* and *The Call of the Wild*.

69 *CAJ* VI, 241.

70 *CAJ* VI, 221. J.M. Wilson, "The Camp in the Upper Yoho Valley."

71 *CAJ* VI, 112. A.H. MacCarthy, "The First Ascents of Mt. Farnham and Farnham Tower."

72 *NZAJ* III, 67. H.C. Chambers, "La Pérouse from the East."

73 *Conquest of the New Zealand Alps.*

74 *AJ* 4, 306.

75 *CAJ* VII, 12. W.E. Stone, "Climbs and Exploration in the Purcell Range in 1915."

76 *AJ* 32, 280. H.N.P. Sloman, "Climbs in New Zealand."

77 Kain had begun to write a romance, largely autobiographical, entitled *Der Zillerthaler Sepp*. About 50 pages were completed, but the manuscript has vanished.

78 *NZAJ* III, 14. Mrs. J. Thomson, "A Traverse of Mount Cook."

79 *Lyttelton Times* (NZ), March 18, 1916.

80 Conrad, by this time, had lost count!

81 In 1933 Kain stated that, in his three seasons in New Zealand, he had started 25 times for Mount Cook, to be turned back by bad weather on 22 occasions.

82 For these routes see *AJ* 39, 277.

83 These adventures form the opening chapters of this book. That Mrs. Thomson, now in her 78th year, should have such vivid recollections of her guide is further evidence of Conrad's unusual personality.

84 *CAJ* VIII, 147.

85 *CAJ* VIII, 79. A.H. MacCarthy, "The First Ascent of Mt. Louis."

86 *CAJ* VIII, 43. W.E. Stone, "Climbs and Exploration in the Purcell Range."

87 *CAJ* VIII, 17. A.H. MacCarthy, "The Howser and Bugaboo Spires."

88 Of these there is no record save the fact that he repeated some of his routes in the Dachstein area.

89 Snowpatch Spire.

90 Bugaboo Spire.

91 *CAJ* VII, 17.

92 *CAJ* IX, 169.

93 *CAJ* XII, 14. A.H. MacCarthy, "The First Ascent of Mt. Eon and Its Fatality."

94 The axe, however, was brought down from the summit after being photographed.

95 *CAJ* XIII, 229. C.J. Best, "Horsethief Creek and the Lake of the Hanging Glaciers."

96 *The Glittering Mountains of Canada* (1925). *AJ* 35, 178. "The Mountains of the Columbia Icefield." *CAJ* XIV, 34. "A Mountaineering Journey to the Columbia Icefield."

97 *The Glittering Mountains of Canada*. *AJ* 36, 299. "The Mountains of the Whirlpool." *AJ* 37, 47, 319. "Side Valleys and Peaks of the Yellowhead Trail." *CAJ* XVI, 86. "A Mountaineering Journey through Jasper Park."

98 *AJ* 37, 306. H. Palmer, "The First Ascent of Mt. King Edward."

99 *Bull. Phila. Geogr. Soc.* XXVI, 69.

100 An account of this expedition will be found in T.G. Longstaff's paper reprinted from the *Geographical Journal* in *CAJ* III, 26.

101 *CAJ* VIII, 25.

102 *CAJ* VIII, 20.

103 *CAJ* III, 30; VII, 13.

104 *CAJ* III, 15, 28; IV, 102; VIII, 50.

105 *CAJ* VI, 104.

106 *CAJ* VI, 107, *vii*, 25.

107 This peak appears in the literature as Fyebrow Pk. or Mt. Bruce. *CAJ* III, 36; VI, 108, 240; VIII, 63. A.H. MacCarthy obtained barometric readings indicating the peak probably docs not attain 11,000 feet.

108 Earl Grey Pass.

109 *AAJ* I, 68. "Ascents in the Purcell Range."

110 *GJ* LXXVII. 455. "The Purcell Source of the Columbia River,"

111 But see letter of December 25, 1931.

112 *GJ* LXXIX, 32. "The Purcell Source of the Kootenay River." *Bull. Phila. Geogr. Soc.* XXXI, 10. "The Historical Geography of the Columbia–Kootenay Valley."

113 Taurus, named by Wheeler during the 1910 survey.

114 Conrad Kain's best-remembered story, told by him in the Altai, in New Zealand and at many Canadian campfires. It is pure invention, Kain never having ascended the Großglockner. Professor R.M. Algie, of Auckland, NZ, supplies this narrative which Conrad wrote for the Christchurch *Press* in 1915. A dialect version was published later by P.A.W. Wallace in his book *The Twist and Other Stories* (1928).

115 *AAJ* II, 184. "The Bugaboo–Howser Watershed."

116 *AAJ* II, 205. "Climbs in the Northern Waputiks."

117 For which the name "Mt. Conrad" has been proposed to the Geographic Board of Canada (*AJ* 46, 403).

118 It has since been shown that one or two of these had already been ascended.

INDEX